Reader's Digest
GREAT
BIOGRAPHIES

Reader's
Digest

GREAT
BIOGRAPHIES

selected
and
condensed by
the editors
of
Reader's
Digest

The Reader's Digest Association, Inc.
Pleasantville, New York
Cape Town, Hong Kong, London, Montreal, Sydney

READER'S DIGEST CONDENSED BOOKS

Editor-in-Chief: Barbara J. Morgan
Executive Editor: Tanis H. Erdmann
Senior Managing Editor: Marjorie Palmer
Managing Editors: Jean E. Aptakin, Anne H. Atwater,
Thomas Froncek, Herbert H. Lieberman
Senior Staff Editors: Angela H. Plowden-Wardlaw,
Virginia Rice (Rights), Ray Sipherd
Senior Editors: Dana Adkins, M. Tracy Brigden, Catherine T. Brown,
Linn Carl, Joseph P. McGrath, James J. Menick, John R. Roberson
Associate Editors: Thomas S. Clemmons, Emily Easton, Catharine L. Edmonds,
Alice Jones-Miller, Maureen A. Mackey
Senior Copy Editors: Claire A. Bedolis, Jeane Garment, Jane F. Neighbors
Senior Associate Copy Editors: Maxine Bartow, Rosalind H. Campbell, Jean S. Friedman
Associate Copy Editors: Ainslie Gilligan, Jeanette Gingold,
Tatiana Ivanow, Marilyn J. Knowlton
Editorial Administrator: Ann M. Dougher
Art Director: William Gregory
Executive Art Editors: Soren Noring, Angelo Perrone
Associate Art Editors, Research: George Calas, Jr., Katherine Kelleher

CB INTERNATIONAL EDITIONS
Senior Staff Editor: Gary Q. Arpin
Associate Editors: Eva C. Jaunzems, Antonius L. Koster

The credits and acknowledgments that appear on pages 606–608
are hereby made part of this copyright page.

FIRST EDITION

Library of Congress Cataloging-in-Publication Data
(Revised for vol. 5-12)

Reader's digest great biographies.

Contents: v. 1. The Spirit of Saint Louis/by Charles A. Lindbergh. Florence
Nightingale/by Cecil Woodham-Smith. Edison/by Matthew Josephson. Hans Christian
Andersen/by Rumer Godden—[etc.]—v. 11. Captain Bligh and Mr. Christian/by
Richard Hough. The agony and the ecstasy/by Irving Stone. The life and work of
Sigmund Freud/by Ernest Jones. Good night, sweet prince/by Gene Fowler—
v. 12. St. Francis of Assisi/by E. M. Almedingen. Napoleon/by Emil Ludwig.
Act one/by Moss Hart. My early life/by Winston S. Churchill.
1. Biography—Collected works. I. Reader's Digest Association.
II. Reader's digest. III. Great biographies.
CT101.R42   1987   920'.02   86-29816
ISBN 0-89577-259-0 (v.1)   ISBN 0-89577-298-1 (v.6)

Printed in the United States of America

Contents

A CONDENSATION OF

QUEEN VICTORIA

by
LYTTON STRACHEY

ILLUSTRATED BY ARTHUR BARBOSA

Princess Alexandrina Victoria was twelve years old when she was first informed that she would someday be Queen of England. Her immediate reply was, "I will be good."

At nineteen she did indeed become Victoria, Queen of Great Britain and Ireland, later Empress of India, and ultimately Britain's longest reigning and most beloved monarch. Her marriage to her cousin, Prince Albert of Saxe-Coburg, lasted twenty-one years and is one of the happiest of all royal love stories. By the end of her sixty-three-year reign, during which England reached the pinnacle of world power, Victoria was held in an affection and awe approaching veneration.

For many years thereafter this veil of reverence stood in the way of any attempt to view the great queen coolly as a human being. At last, in 1921, a biography appeared that did just that. Lytton Strachey's *Queen Victoria* caused a furor, and his irreverent yet strangely moving portrait has come to be regarded as a landmark in the art of biography.

CHAPTER I
Antecedents

ON NOVEMBER 6, 1817, died the Princess Charlotte, only child of the Prince Regent, and heir to the crown of England.

Her short life had hardly been a happy one. Brought up among violent family quarrels, she was by nature impulsive, capricious, and vehement; she had always longed for liberty, and never possessed it. At seventeen, she had fallen in love with Prince Augustus of Prussia, who was already married. In the end she was married, in 1816, to Prince Leopold of Saxe-Coburg.

The character of Prince Leopold contrasted strangely with that of the Princess Charlotte. The younger son of a German princeling, he was formal in manner, collected in speech, and careful in action. He was twenty-six years of age. He had served with distinction in the war against Napoleon, had shown considerable diplomatic skill at the Congress of Vienna, and was now to try his hand at the task of taming a tumultuous princess.

There was much in her, he found, of which he could not approve. She quizzed, she stamped, she roared with laughter; she had very little self-command; her manners were abominable.

There was continual friction, but he soon dominated her, and every scene ended in the same way. Standing before him like a rebellious boy in petticoats, her hands behind her back, with flaming cheeks and sparkling eyes, the Princess would say at last, "If you wish it, I will do it." "I want nothing for myself," Prince Leopold invariably answered; "when I press something on you, it is from a conviction that it is for your good."

In the household at Claremont, near Esher, where the royal pair were established, was a young German physician, Christian Friedrich Stockmar. Prince Leopold had brought him to England as his personal physician. At Claremont his position was a humble one; but the Princess took a fancy to him, called him "Stocky," and romped with him along the corridors.

Dyspeptic by constitution, melancholic by temperament, Stockmar could yet be lively on occasion, and he was known as a wit. Before long he gave proof of another quality—cautious sagacity. When, in the spring of 1817, it was known that the Princess was expecting a child, the post of one of her physicians-in-ordinary was offered to him, and he had the good sense to refuse it, perceiving that, if anything were to go wrong, it would certainly be the foreign doctor who would be blamed. Very soon, indeed, he came to the opinion that the low diet and constant bleedings to which the Princess was subjected were an error; he drew the Prince aside and told him so; but the fashionable treatment was continued for months.

On November 5, at nine p.m., after a labor of over fifty hours, the Princess was delivered of a dead boy. At midnight her exhausted strength gave way. Then, at last, Stockmar saw her; he went in, and found her obviously dying, while the doctors were plying her with wine. She seized his hand. "They have made me tipsy," she said. After a little he left, and was in the next room when he heard her call out: "Stocky! Stocky!" As he ran back the death rattle was in her throat. She tossed violently from side to side; then suddenly it was over.

The Prince, after hours of watching, had left the room for a few moments' rest; and Stockmar went now to tell him that his wife was dead. At first Leopold could not be made to realize what had happened; it was a dream; it was impossible. At last, by her bed, he knelt down and kissed the cold hands. Then rising and exclaiming, "I am desolate. Promise me never to leave me," he threw himself into Stockmar's arms.

THE TRAGEDY at Claremont was of a most upsetting kind. The succession to the throne, which had seemed so satisfactorily settled, now became a matter of urgent doubt.

King George III was still living, an aged lunatic, at Windsor Castle. Of his seven sons, the youngest was of more than middle age, and none had legitimate offspring. It seemed improbable that his oldest son, the Prince Regent, a preposterous figure of debauched obesity, could ever again become a father. The outlook for the throne, therefore, was ambiguous.

Besides the Duke of Kent, who must be noticed separately, the other sons of the King, in order of seniority, were the Dukes of York, Clarence, Cumberland, Sussex, and Cambridge; their situations and prospects require a brief description.

The Duke of York, whose escapades in times past with a Mrs. Clarke and with the army had brought him into trouble, now divided his life between London and a large, extravagantly ordered country house where he occupied himself with racing, whist, and improper stories. He had been long married to the Princess Royal of Prussia, a lady who rarely went to bed and was perpetually surrounded by vast numbers of dogs, parrots, and monkeys. They had no children.

The Duke of Clarence had lived for many years in complete obscurity with Mrs. Jordan, an actress. By her he had had a large family of sons and daughters, and had appeared, in effect, to be married to her, when he had suddenly separated from her.

The Duke of Cumberland was probably the most unpopular man in England. Hideously ugly, with a distorted eye, he was bad-tempered and vindictive, a violent reactionary in politics, and was subsequently suspected of murdering his valet and of having carried on an amorous intrigue of an extremely scandalous kind. He had lately married a German princess, but there were as yet no children by the marriage.

The Duke of Sussex had mildly literary tastes and collected books. He had married Lady Augusta Murray, by whom he had two children, but the marriage, under the Royal Marriages Act, had been declared void.

The Duke of Cambridge lived in Hanover, wore a blond wig, chattered and fidgeted a great deal, and was unmarried.

Besides his seven sons, George III had five surviving daughters. Of these, two were married and childless. The three unmarried princesses were all over forty.

THE FOURTH SON of George III was Edward, Duke of Kent. He was now fifty years of age—a tall, stout, vigorous man, highly colored, with bushy eyebrows and a bald top to his head. His dress was extremely neat, and his whole appearance was rigid. He had spent his early life in the army, and, under the influence of military training, had become at first a disciplinarian and at last a martinet. In 1802, having been sent to Gibraltar to restore order in a mutinous garrison, he was recalled for undue severity, and his active career had come to an end.

Since then he had spent his life regulating his domestic arrangements with great exactitude, and struggling to restore order to his finances, for, in spite of an income of £24,000 a year, he was hopelessly in debt. He had quarreled with most of his brothers, particularly with the Prince Regent, and it was only natural that he should have joined the political Opposition and become a pillar of the Whigs.

It has often been asserted that he was a Liberal, or even a Radical; and, if we are to believe Robert Owen, he was a Socialist. His relations with Owen—the illustrious and preposterous father of Socialism—were curious. He corresponded with him, and he even (so Owen assures us) returned, after his death, from "the sphere of spirits" to give encouragement to the Owenites on earth. Still, some uncertainty lingers over his political views. But there is no uncertainty about another circumstance: His Royal Highness borrowed from Robert Owen, on various occasions, sums of money which were never repaid and amounted in all to several hundred pounds.

After the death of the Princess Charlotte it was clearly important that the Duke of Kent should marry. From the point of view of the nation, the lack of heirs in the reigning family seemed to make the step almost obligatory. It was also likely to be expedient from the point of view of the duke. To marry as a public duty, for the sake of the royal succession, would surely deserve some recognition from a grateful country. When the Duke of York had married he had received a settlement of £25,000 a year. Why should not the Duke of Kent look forward to an equal sum? But the situation was not quite that simple; there was the Duke of Clarence; he was the elder brother, and, if *he* married, would clearly have the prior claim. On the other hand, if the Duke of Kent married, it was important to remember that he would be making a serious sacrifice: a lady was involved: namely, the duke's mistress.

The duke, reflecting upon all these matters, happened, about a month after the Princess Charlotte's death, to visit Brussels, and learned that Mr. Creevey was staying in the town. Mr. Creevey was a friend of leading Whigs and an inveterate gossip; and it occurred to the duke that there could be no better channel through which to communicate his views to political circles at home. Apparently it did not occur to him that Mr. Creevey might keep a diary. He sent for him, and a remarkable conversation ensued.

"Should the Duke of Clarence not marry," the Duke of Kent said, "the next prince in succession is myself, and although I trust I shall be at all times ready to obey any call my country may make upon me, God only knows the sacrifice it will be to make, whenever I shall think it my duty to become a married man. It is now seven-and-twenty years that Madame St. Laurent and I have lived together; we are of the same age, and have been in all climates, and in all difficulties together, and you may well imagine, Mr. Creevey, the pang it will occasion me to part with her. As for Madame St. Laurent herself, I protest I don't know what is to become of her if a marriage is to be forced upon me; her feelings are already so agitated upon the subject."

The duke then said, "My brother the Duke of Clarence is the elder brother, and has certainly the right to marry if he chooses. If he wishes to be king—to be married and have children, poor man—God help him! let him do so. For myself—I am a man of no ambition, and wish only to remain as I am. . . ." But he

QUEEN VICTORIA

went on to say that if the Duke of Clarence did nothing by
Eastertime, "it will become my duty, no doubt, to take some
measures upon the subject myself."

Two names, the duke said, had been mentioned in this connection—those of the Princess of Baden and the Princess of
Saxe-Coburg, the sister of Prince Leopold. The latter, he
thought, would perhaps be the better of the two, since Prince
Leopold was so popular with the nation; but before any other
steps were taken, he hoped and expected to see justice done to
Madame St. Laurent. "She is," he explained, "of very good
family, and has never been an actress, and I am the first and
only person who ever lived with her. If she is to return to live
amongst her friends, it must be in such a state of independence
as to command their respect."

As to his own settlement, the duke observed that he would
expect the Duke of York's marriage to be considered the precedent. "That," he said, "was a marriage for the succession, and
£25,000 for income was settled. I shall be contented with the
same arrangement. As for the payment of my debts, I don't call
them great. The nation, on the contrary, is greatly my debtor."
Here a clock struck, and seemed to remind the duke that he
had an appointment; he rose and Mr. Creevey left him.

Who could keep such a communication secret? Certainly not
Mr. Creevey. He hurried off to tell the Duke of Wellington.

As it turned out, both the brothers decided to marry. The
Duke of Kent, selecting the Princess of Saxe-Coburg, was united
to her on May 29, 1818. On June 11, the Duke of Clarence
followed suit with a daughter of the Duke of Saxe-Meiningen.
But they were disappointed in their financial expectations; for
though the government brought forward proposals to increase
their allowances, the motions were defeated in the House of
Commons. At this the Duke of Wellington was not surprised.
"By God!" he said, "there is a great deal to be said about that.
They are the damnedest millstones about the necks of any government that can be imagined." Eventually, however, Parliament increased the Duke of Kent's annuity by £6000.

The subsequent history of Madame St. Laurent has not trans-
pired.

THE NEW DUCHESS OF KENT, Victoria Mary Louisa, sister of Prince Leopold, was a daughter of Francis, Duke of Saxe-Coburg-Saalfeld. The family was an ancient one; its principality, the duchy of Saxe-Coburg, was very small, containing about sixty thousand inhabitants, but it enjoyed independent and sovereign rights. As for Victoria Mary Louisa, in 1803, when she was seventeen years of age, she had married the Prince of Leiningen, who ruled the territory of Amorbach in Lower Franconia. Three years later her father, Duke Francis, died a ruined man. The Napoleonic harrow had passed over Saxe-Coburg; the duchy was seized by the French, and the ducal family were reduced to beggary, almost to starvation. Such was the desperate plight of the family which, a generation later, was to have gained a foothold in half the reigning houses of Europe.

In 1814 Victoria's husband died, leaving her with two children. After her brother's marriage with the Princess Charlotte, it had been proposed that she should marry the Duke of Kent; but she had declined, on the ground that the guardianship of her children and the management of her domains made other ties undesirable. The Princess Charlotte's death, however, altered the case; and when the Duke of Kent renewed his offer she accepted it. She was thirty-two years old—short, stout, with brown eyes and hair, and rosy cheeks, cheerful and voluble, and gorgeously attired in rustling silks and bright velvets.

She was certainly fortunate in her contented disposition; for she was fated, all through her life, to have much to put up with. Her second marriage, with its dubious prospects, seemed at first to be chiefly a source of difficulties. The duke, declaring that he was still too poor to live in England, moved about uneasily through Belgium and Germany, attending parades and inspecting barracks in a neat military cap. The English notabilities looked askance, and the Duke of Wellington dubbed him the Corporal. One day, at Brussels, Mr. Creevey himself had an unfortunate experience. A military school was to be inspected—before breakfast. The company assembled; everything was highly satisfactory; but the Duke of Kent continued for so long examining every detail, asking meticulous questions, that Mr. Creevey at last could bear it no longer, and whispered to his neighbor that he was damned hungry. The Duke of Wellington heard him, and was delighted. "I recommend you," he said, "whenever you start with the royal family in a morning, and particularly with *the Corporal*, always to breakfast first."

Settled down at last at Amorbach, the duke found that time hung heavily on his hands. The establishment was small, and the country was impoverished. He brooded—for the duke was not without a vein of superstition—over the prophecy of a gypsy at Gibraltar who had once told him that he was to have many losses and crosses, that he was to die in happiness, and that his only child was to be a great queen.

Before long it became clear that a child was to be expected. The duke decided that it should be born in England. Funds were lacking for the journey, but a carriage was hired, and the duke himself mounted the box. Inside were the duchess and her daughter Feodora, a girl of fourteen, with maids, nurses, lapdogs, and canaries. Off they drove—through Germany, through France; bad roads, cheap inns, were nothing to the rigorous duke and the equable, abundant duchess. The Channel was crossed, London was reached. The authorities provided a set of rooms in Kensington Palace; and there, on May 24, 1819, a female infant was born.

DUCHESS OF KENT

CHAPTER 2
Childhood

THE CHILD who, in these not very impressive circumstances, appeared in the world, received but scant attention. There was small reason to foresee her destiny. The Duchess of Clarence, two months before, had given birth to a daughter; this infant, indeed, had died almost immediately; but it seemed highly probable that the duchess would again become a mother; and so it actually fell out.

More than this, the Duchess of Kent was young, and the duke was strong; there was every likelihood that before long a brother would follow, to snatch her faint chance of the succession from the little Princess.

Nevertheless, the duke had other views: there were prophecies. . . . At any rate, he would christen the child Elizabeth, a name of happy augury. In this, however, he reckoned without the Regent, who, seeing a chance of annoying his brother, announced that he himself would be present at the baptism, and signified that one of the godfathers should be the Emperor Alexander of Russia.

And so when the ceremony took place, and the Archbishop of Canterbury asked by what name he was to baptize the child, the Regent replied "Alexandrina."

At this the duke ventured to suggest that another name might be added. "Certainly," said the Regent; "Georgina?"

"Or Elizabeth?" said the duke.

There was a pause, during which the Archbishop looked with some uneasiness from one Prince to the other. "Very well, then," said the Regent at last, "call her after her mother. But Alexandrina must come first." Thus, to the disgust of her father, the child was christened Alexandrina Victoria.

The duke had other subjects of disgust. The meager grant of the Commons had by no means put an end to his financial distresses. It was to be feared that his services were not appreciated by the nation. His debts continued to grow. For many years he had lived upon £7000 a year; but now his expenses were doubled. He could make no further reductions; as it was, there was not a single servant in his establishment who was idle for a moment from morning to night.

He poured out his griefs in a letter to Robert Owen. "I now candidly state," he wrote, "that, after viewing the subject in every possible way, I am satisfied that, to continue to live in England, even in our quiet way, *without splendour*, and *without show, nothing short of doubling the seven thousand pounds will do,* REDUCTION BEING IMPOSSIBLE." It was clear that he would be obliged to sell his house; if that failed, he would go and live on the Continent. "If my services are useful to my country, it surely becomes *those who have the power* to support me in substantiating those just claims I have for the extensive losses I experienced during the period of my professional servitude in the Colonies; and if this is not attainable, *it is a clear proof to me that my services are not appreciated;* and under that impression I shall not scruple, in *due* time, to resume my retirement abroad, when the Duchess and myself shall have fulfilled our duties in establishing the *English* birth of my child."

In the meantime, he decided to spend the winter at Sidmouth, "in order," he told Owen, "that the Duchess may have the benefit of tepid sea bathing, and our infant that of sea air, on the fine coast of Devonshire, during the months of the year that are so odious in London."

In December the move was made. With the new year, the duke remembered another prophecy. In 1820, a fortune-teller had told him, two members of the royal family would die. Who would they be? He speculated on the possibilities: the King, it was plain, could not live much longer; and the Duchess of York had been attacked by a mortal disease. Probably it would be the King and the Duchess of York; or perhaps the King and the Duke of York. He himself was one of the healthiest men in England. "My brothers," he declared, "are not so strong as I am; I have lived a regular life. I shall outlive them all. The crown will come to me and my children."

He went out for a walk, and got his feet wet. On coming home, he neglected to change his stockings. He caught cold, inflammation of the lungs set in, and on January 22 he was a dying man.

By a curious chance, young Dr. Stockmar was staying in the house at the time; two years before, he had stood by the death-bed of the Princess Charlotte; and now he watched the Duke of Kent in his agony. On Stockmar's advice, a will was hastily prepared; it was important that the guardianship of the unwitting child, whose fortunes were now so strangely changing, should be assured to the duchess. The duke was just able to understand the document and to append his signature. On the following morning he breathed his last. Six days later came the fulfillment of the second half of the gypsy's prophecy. The long, unhappy, and inglorious life of King George the Third of England was ended.

THE PRINCE REGENT, as George IV, was now King of England. Meanwhile, such was the confusion of affairs at Sidmouth that the duchess found herself without the means of returning to London.

Prince Leopold hurried down, and himself conducted his sister and her family, by slow and bitter stages, to Kensington. The widowed lady, in her voluminous blacks, needed all her equanimity to support her. Her prospects were more dubious than ever. She had £6000 a year of her own; but her husband's debts loomed before her like a mountain. Soon she learned that the Duchess of Clarence was once more expecting a child. What had she to look forward to in England? Why should she remain in a foreign country, among strangers, whose language she could not speak, whose customs she could not understand?

Surely it would be best to return to Amorbach, and there, among her own people, bring up her daughters in economical obscurity. But she was an inveterate optimist, and would not be daunted. Besides, she adored her baby. "She is my happiness, my delight," she declared; the darling should be brought up as an English princess, whatever lot awaited her. Prince Leopold came forward nobly with an offer of an additional £3000 a year; and the duchess remained at Kensington.

The child herself was extremely fat, and bore a remarkable resemblance to her grandfather. "She is the image of the mad King!" exclaimed the duchess. "It's King George in petticoats!" echoed the surrounding ladies, as the little creature waddled with difficulty from one to the other.

Before long, the world began to be slightly interested in the nursery at Kensington. When, early in 1821, the Duchess of Clarence's second child, the Princess Elizabeth, died within three months of its birth, the interest increased.

Great forces and fierce antagonisms seemed to be moving, obscurely, about the royal cradle. It was a time of faction and anger, of violent repression and profound discontent. New passions, new desires, were abroad, or rather, old passions and old desires reincarnated with a new potency: love of freedom, hatred of injustice, hope for the future of man. The mighty still sat proudly in their seats, dispensing their ancient tyranny; but a storm was gathering, and already there was lightning in the sky. But the vastest forces must needs operate through frail human instruments; and it seemed for many years as if the great cause of English liberalism hung upon the life of the little girl at Kensington; for she alone stood between the country and her terrible uncle, the Duke of Cumberland, the hideous embodiment of reaction.

Inevitably, the Duchess of Kent threw in her lot with her husband's party. Whig leaders, Radical agitators, rallied round her; and she declared in public that she put her faith in "the liberties of the People." It was certain that the young Princess would be brought up in the way that she should go; yet there, close behind the throne, waiting, sinister, was the Duke of Cumberland. Dreadful possibilities were hinted at. In the seething state of public feeling, rumors constantly leaped to the surface; and, even so late as the year before her accession, the Radical newspapers were full of suggestions that the Princess Victoria was in danger from the machinations of her wicked uncle.

But no echo of these conflicts and forebodings reached the little Drina—for so she was called in the family circle—as she played with her dolls, or scampered down the passages, or rode along the avenues of Kensington Gardens on the donkey her uncle York had given her. She was to remember, from this period, a yellow rug in one particular room at Kensington, and a watch of her father's in a tortoiseshell case ticking in her mother's bedroom. A fair-haired, blue-eyed child, she was idolized by her nurses, and her mother's ladies, and her sister Feodora; and for a few years there was danger, in spite of her mother's strictness, of her being spoiled. From time to time, she would fly into a violent passion, stamp her little foot, and set everyone at defiance; whatever they might say, she would not learn her letters—no, she *would not;* afterwards, she was very sorry, and burst into tears; but her letters remained unlearned.

When she was five years old, however, a change came, with the appearance of Fräulein Lehzen. This lady, who was the daughter of a Hanoverian clergyman, had previously been the Princess Feodora's governess. She soon succeeded in instilling a new spirit into her willful charge. At first, indeed, she was appalled by the little Princess's outbursts of temper; never in her life, she declared, had she seen such a passionate and naughty child. Then she observed something else; the child was extraordinarily truthful; whatever punishment might follow, she never told a lie.

Very firm, the new governess yet had the sense to see that all the firmness in the world would be useless, unless she could win her way into little Drina's heart. She did so, and there were no more difficulties. Drina learned her letters like an angel; and she learned other things as well. The Baroness de Späth, the duchess's lady-in-waiting, taught her how to make little boxes and decorate them with tinsel and painted flowers; her mother taught her religion. Sitting in the pew every Sunday morning, the child of six was seen listening raptly to the sermon, for she was to be examined upon it in the afternoon.

The duchess was determined that her daughter, from the earliest possible moment, should be prepared for her high station in a way that would commend itself to the most respectable; her good, plain, thrifty German mind recoiled with horror and amazement from the shameless junketings at Carlton House; Drina should never be allowed to forget for a moment the virtues of simplicity, regularity, and devotion.

The little girl, however, was really in small need of such lessons, for she was naturally simple and orderly, she was pious without difficulty, and her sense of propriety was keen. She understood very well the niceties of her own position. When, a child of six, Lady Jane Ellice was taken by her grandmother to Kensington Palace, she was put to play with the Princess Victoria, who was the same age as herself. The young visitor, ignorant of etiquette, began to make free with the toys on the floor, in a way which was a little too familiar; but "You must not touch those," she was quickly told, "they are mine; and I may call you Jane, but you must not call me Victoria."

The Princess's most constant playmate was Victoire, the daughter of Sir John Conroy, the duchess's major-domo. The two girls were very fond of one another; they would walk hand in hand together in Kensington Gardens. But little Drina was perfectly aware for which of them it was that they were followed, at a respectful distance, by a gigantic scarlet flunkey.

Warmhearted, responsive, she loved her dear Lehzen, and she loved her dear sister Feodora, and her dear friend Victoire, and her dear Madame de Späth. And her dear Mamma . . . of course, she loved her too; it was her duty; and yet—she could not tell why—she was always happier when she was staying with her uncle Leopold at Claremont.

The visits to Claremont were frequent enough; but one day, on a special occasion, she paid a visit of a rarer and more exciting kind. When she was seven years old, she and her mother and sister were asked by the King to go to Windsor Castle. George IV, who had transferred his fraternal ill temper to his sister-in-law and her family, had at last grown tired of sulking, and decided to be agreeable. The old rip, bewigged and gouty, ornate and enormous, with his jeweled mistress by his side and his flaunting court about him, received the tiny creature who was one day to hold in those same halls a very different state. "Give me your little paw," he said; and two ages touched.

Next morning, driving in his phaeton, he met the Duchess of Kent and her child in the park. "Pop her in," were his orders, which, to the terror of the mother and the delight of the daughter, were immediately obeyed. Off they dashed to Virginia Water, where there was a great barge, full of lords and ladies fishing, and another barge with a band; and the King turned to his small niece. "What is your favorite tune? The band shall play it."

" 'God Save the King,' sir," was the instant answer.

The Princess's reply has been praised as an early example of a tact which was afterwards famous. But she was a very truthful child, and perhaps it was her genuine opinion.

IN 1827 the Duke of York died. Three years later George IV also disappeared, and the Duke of Clarence reigned in his stead as William IV. The new Queen, it was now clear, would in all probability never again be a mother; the Princess Victoria, therefore, was recognized by Parliament as heir presumptive; and the Duchess of Kent was given an additional £10,000 for the maintenance of the Princess, and was appointed regent, in case

of the death of the King before the majority of her daughter.

At the same time a great convulsion took place in the constitution of the state. The power of the Tories, who had dominated England for more than forty years, suddenly began to crumble. In the tremendous struggle that followed, it seemed for a moment as if the tradition of generations might be snapped, as if revolution might be the issue. But the forces of compromise triumphed: the Reform Bill was passed. The center of gravity in the constitution was shifted towards the middle classes; the Whigs came into power; and the complexion of the government assumed a Liberal tinge.

One of the results of this new state of affairs was a change in the position of the Duchess of Kent and her daughter. From being the protégées of an opposition clique, they became assets of the official majority of the nation. The Princess Victoria was henceforward the living symbol of the victory of the middle classes. The Duke of Cumberland, on the other hand, suffered a corresponding eclipse: his claws had been pared by the Reform Act, and he grew insignificant and almost harmless.

The duchess's own liberalism was not very profound. She followed naturally in the footsteps of her husband, but she did not understand very much about the Poor Law and political economy; she hoped that she did her duty; and she ardently hoped that the same might be said of Victoria. It was her supreme duty in life, she felt, to make quite sure that her daughter should grow up into a Christian queen. To this task she bent all her energies; and, when the Princess was eleven, she desired the Bishops of London and Lincoln to submit her daughter to an examination.

"I feel the time to be now come," the duchess explained, in a letter, "that what has been done should be put to some test, that if anything has been done in error of judgment it may be corrected, and that the plan for the future should be open to consideration and revision. . . . I attend almost always myself every lesson, or a part; and as the lady about the Princess is a competent person, she assists Her in preparing Her lessons, for the various masters. The general bent of Her character," added the duchess, "is strength of intellect, capable of receiving with ease, information, and with a peculiar readiness in coming to a just decision on any point."

The bishops attended at the palace, and the result of their examination was all that could be wished. "In answering a great variety of questions proposed to her," they reported, "the Princess displayed an accurate knowledge of the most important features of Scripture history and of the leading truths and precepts of the Christian religion as taught by the Church of England, as well as an acquaintance with the chronology and principal facts of English history remarkable in so young a person. To questions in geography, the use of the globes, arithmetic, and Latin grammar, the answers which the Princess returned were equally satisfactory." They did not believe that the duchess's plan of education was susceptible of any improvement; and the Archbishop of Canterbury, who was also consulted, came to the same gratifying conclusion.

One important step, however, remained to be taken. So far, as the duchess explained to the bishops, the Princess had been kept in ignorance of the station that she was likely to fill. "She is aware of its duties, and that a Sovereign should live for others; so that when Her innocent mind receives the impression of Her future fate, she will receive it with a mind formed to be sensible of what is to be expected from Her."

In the following year it was decided that she should be enlightened on this point. A scene followed which has become well known: before a history lesson, the genealogical table of the Kings of England was slipped by her governess into the history book; finding it, the Princess, surprised, made inquiries; and finally she realized the facts. When she at last understood, she was silent for a moment, and then she spoke: "I will be good," she said.

The words were something more than a conventional protestation; they were, in their limitation and their intensity, their egotism and their humility, an instinctive summary of the dominating qualities of a life. "I cried much on learning it," Her Majesty noted long afterwards. No doubt, while others were present, even her dear Lehzen, the little girl kept up her self-command; and then crept away somewhere to ease her heart of an inward, unfamiliar agitation, with a handkerchief, out of her mother's sight.

But her mother's sight was by no means an easy thing to escape. The child grew into the girl, the girl into the young woman; but still she slept in her mother's bedroom; still she had no place where she might sit or work by herself. An extraordinary watchfulness surrounded her every step: up to the day of her accession, she never went downstairs without someone beside her holding her hand.

Plainness and regularity ruled the household. The hours, the days, the years passed slowly and methodically by. The dolls—the innumerable dolls, each one so neatly dressed, each one with its name so punctiliously entered in a catalogue—were laid aside, and a little music and a little dancing took their place. Taglioni came, to give grace and dignity to the figure, and Lablache, to train the piping treble upon his own rich bass. The Dean of Chester, the official preceptor, continued his endless instruction in Scripture history, while the Duchess of Northumberland, the official governess, presided over every lesson with becoming solemnity.

Without doubt, the Princess's main achievement during her school days was linguistic. German was naturally the first language with which she was familiar; but English and French quickly followed; and she became virtually trilingual, though her mastery of English grammar remained incomplete. At the same time, she acquired a working knowledge of Italian and some smattering of Latin. Nevertheless, she did not read very much. It was not an occupation that she cared for; partly, perhaps, because the books that were given her were all either sermons, which were dull, or poetry, which was incomprehensible. Novels were strictly forbidden.

It was her misfortune that the mental atmosphere which surrounded her during these years of adolescence was almost entirely feminine. No father, no brother, was there to break impetuously in upon the gentle monotony of the daily round. The Princess was never called by a voice that was loud and growling; never felt, as a matter of course, a hard rough cheek on her own soft one; never climbed a wall with a boy. The

visits to Claremont—delicious little escapes into male society—
came to an end when she was eleven years old and Prince Leopold left England to be King of the Belgians. She loved him
still; he was still *"il mio secondo padre"*—"my second father"—
but his fatherliness now came to her dimly, through the cold
channel of correspondence.

Henceforward female duty, female elegance, hemmed her in;
and her spirit was hardly reached by those two great influences
without which no growing life can truly prosper—humor and
imagination. The Baroness Lehzen—for she had been raised to
that rank in the Hanoverian nobility by George IV before he
died—was the real center of the Princess's world. When Feodora
married, when Uncle Leopold went to Belgium, the baroness
was left without a competitor. The Princess gave her mother
her dutiful regards; but Lehzen had her heart. The girl would
have gone through fire for her *"precious* Lehzen," her "best and
truest friend." Her daily journal, begun when she was thirteen,
bears on every page the traces of the baroness's influence. The
young creature that one sees there, ingenuously self-depicted,
with her sincerity, her quick affections and pious resolutions,
might almost have been the daughter of a German pastor herself. Her enjoyments and admirations clothed themselves naturally in underlinings and exclamation marks. "It was a *delightful*
ride. We cantered a good deal. SWEET LITTLE ROSY WENT
beautifully!! We came home at a 1/4 past 1. . . . At 20 minutes
to 7 we went out to the Opera. . . . Rubini sang *quite beautifully*.
We came home at 1/2 past 11."

In Victoria's comments on her readings, the mind of the
baroness is clearly revealed. One day, by some mistake, she was
allowed to take up a volume of memoirs by Fanny Kemble.
"One would imagine by the style that the authoress must be
very pert. . . . It is a great pity that a person endowed with so
much talent should publish a book which is so full of trash and
nonsense." Madame de Sévigné's letters, which the baroness read
aloud, met with more approval. "How truly elegant and natural her style is!" But her highest admiration was reserved for
the Bishop of Chester's *Exposition of the Gospel of St. Matthew*.
"It is a very fine book indeed. Just the sort of one I like; which

is just plain and comprehensible and full of truth and good feeling. Lehzen gave it me on the Sunday that I took the Sacrament."

A few weeks previously she had been confirmed, and she described the event as follows: "I felt that my confirmation was one of the most solemn and important events and acts in my life. I felt deeply repentant for all what I had done which was wrong and trusted in God Almighty to strengthen my heart and mind; and to forsake all that is bad and follow all that is virtuous and right. I went with the firm determination to become a true Christian, to try and comfort my dear Mamma in all her griefs, and to become a dutiful and affectionate daughter to her. Also to be obedient to *dear* Lehzen, who has done so much for me. I was dressed in a white lace dress, with a white crape bonnet with a wreath of white roses round it. I went in the chariot with my dear Mamma and the others followed in another carriage."

In that conventional existence visits were exciting events; and when the Princess was fourteen she was delighted by the arrival of a couple of boys from Würtemberg, the Princes Alexander and Ernst, sons of her mother's sister. "They are both *extremely tall,*" she noted; "Alexander is *very handsome,* and Ernst has a *very kind expression.* They are both extremely *amiable.*" And their departure filled her with corresponding regrets. "We saw them get into the barge, and watched them sail away from the beach. They were so amiable and so pleasant to have in the house; *always good-humored.* Alexander took such care of me in getting out of the boat, and rode next to me; so did Ernst."

Two years later, two other cousins arrived, the Princes Ferdinand and Augustus. "Dear Ferdinand," the Princess wrote, "has elicited universal admiration from all parties. . . . He is so very unaffected, and has such a very distinguished appearance. Augustus is very amiable, too, and, when known, shows much good sense." On another occasion, "Dear Ferdinand came and sat near me and talked so dearly and sensibly. I do *so* love him. Augustus is also a dear good young man, and is very handsome." She could not quite decide which was the handsomer of the two. On the whole, she concluded, "I think Ferdinand handsomer than Augustus, his eyes are so beautiful, and he has such a lively clever expression; *both* have such a sweet expression."

Shortly afterwards, however, two more cousins arrived, who threw all the rest into the shade. These were the Princes Ernest and Albert, sons of her mother's eldest brother, the Duke of Saxe-Coburg.

This time the Princess was more particular in her observations. "Ernest," she remarked, "is as tall as Ferdinand and Augustus; he has dark hair, and fine dark eyes and eyebrows, but the nose and mouth are not good; he has a most kind, honest expression, and a very good figure. Albert, who is just as tall as Ernest but stouter, is extremely handsome; his hair is about the same color as mine; his eyes are large and blue, and he has a beautiful nose and a very sweet mouth with fine teeth; but the charm of his countenance is his expression, which is most delightful; it is full of goodness and sweetness, and very clever and intelligent."

"Both my cousins," she added, "are so kind and good; they are much more *formés* and men of the world than Augustus; they speak English well, and I speak it with them. Ernest will be 18 years old on the 21st of June, and Albert 17 on the 26th of August." A little later, "I sat between my dear cousins on the sofa and we looked at drawings. They both draw very well, particularly Albert, and are both exceedingly fond of music; they play very nicely on the piano. The more I see them the more I am delighted with them, and the more I love them."

When, after a stay of three weeks, the time came for the young men and their father to return to Germany, the moment of parting was a melancholy one. "It was our last HAPPY HAPPY breakfast, with this dear Uncle and those *dearest* beloved cousins, whom I *do* love so VERY VERY dearly. Dearly as I love Ferdinand, and also good Augustus, I love Ernest and Albert MUCH *more*. ... They have both learnt a good deal, and are very clever, particularly Albert, who is the most reflecting of the two, and they like very much talking about serious and instructive things and yet are so *very very* gay and happy, like young people ought to be; Albert always used to have some fun and some clever witty answer at breakfast and everywhere; he used to play and fondle Dash [Victoria's spaniel] so funnily too. ... Dearest

Albert was playing on the piano when I came down. At 11 dear Uncle, and my *dearest beloved* cousins, left us. I embraced both my cousins most warmly, as well as my Uncle. I cried bitterly, very bitterly."

The Princes shared her ecstasies and her italics between them; but it is clear enough where her secret preference lay. "Particularly Albert!" She was just seventeen; and deep was the impression left upon that budding organism by the young man's charm and goodness and accomplishments, and his large blue eyes and beautiful nose, and his sweet mouth and fine teeth.

KING WILLIAM could not abide his sister-in-law, and the duchess fully returned his antipathy. A bursting, bubbling old gentleman, with quarterdeck gestures, round rolling eyes, and a head like a pineapple, His Majesty's sudden elevation to the throne after fifty-six years of utter insignificance had almost sent him crazy. He rushed about doing preposterous things, spreading amusement and terror in every direction, and talking all the time. His speeches, made repeatedly at the most inopportune junctures, were the consternation of ministers. He was one part blackguard, people said, and three parts buffoon; but those who knew him better could not help liking him—he meant well; and he was really kindhearted, if you took him the right way.

If you took him the wrong way, however, you must look out for squalls, as the Duchess of Kent discovered.

She had no notion of how to deal with him. Occupied with her own responsibilities, she had no attention to spare for his susceptibilities. She was the mother of the heiress of England; and it was for him to recognize the fact—to put her upon a proper footing—to give her the precedence of a dowager Princess of Wales. It did not occur to her that such pretensions might be galling to a king who had no legitimate child of his own, and who yet had not altogether abandoned the hope of having one.

She pressed on, with bulky vigor; and Sir John Conroy, an Irishman with no great judgment who was her intimate counselor, egged her on. It was advisable that Victoria should become acquainted with the various districts of England, and through several summers a succession of tours—in the West, in the Midlands, in Wales—were arranged for her. The journeys, attracting enthusiastic crowds, took on the air of royal progresses. Addresses were presented by loyal citizens; the delighted Duchess of Kent, swelling in sweeping feathers and almost obliterating the diminutive Princess, read aloud, in her German accent, gracious replies prepared beforehand by Sir John Conroy; and Sir John, bustling and ridiculous, seemed to be mingling the roles of major-domo and prime minister. Naturally the King fumed over his newspaper at Windsor. "That woman is a nuisance!" he exclaimed.

Poor amiable Queen Adelaide did her best to smooth things down; but it was useless. News arrived that the Duchess of Kent, sailing in the Solent, had insisted that whenever her yacht appeared it should be received by royal salutes from all the men-of-war and the forts. The King declared that these continual poppings must cease; and the Premier and the First Lord of the Admiralty wrote privately to the duchess, begging her to waive her rights. But she would not hear of it; Sir John Conroy was adamant. "As Her Royal Highness's *confidential adviser*," he said, "I cannot recommend her to give way on this point." Eventually the King, in a great state of excitement, issued a special order-in-council, prohibiting the firing of royal salutes to any ships except those which carried the reigning sovereign or his consort on board.

When King William quarreled with his Whig ministers the situation grew still more embittered, for now the duchess, in addition to her other shortcomings, was the political partisan of his enemies. In 1836 he made an attempt to prepare the ground for a match between the Princess Victoria and one of the sons of the Prince of Orange, and at the same time did his best to prevent the visit of the young Coburg princes to Kensington. He failed in both these objects; and the only result of his efforts was to raise the anger of the King of the Belgians, who, forgetting for a moment his royal reserve, addressed an indignant letter to his niece.

"I am really *astonished*," he wrote, "at the conduct of your old Uncle the King; this invitation of the Prince of Orange and

his sons, this forcing him on others, is very extraordinary. . . .
Not later than yesterday I got a half-official communication
from England, insinuating that it would be *highly* desirable that
the visit of *your* relatives *should not take place this year—qu'en
dites vous?*—What do you say to *that?*"

Shortly afterwards King Leopold came to England, and his
reception was as cold at Windsor as it was warm at Kensington.
"To hear dear Uncle speak on any subject," the Princess wrote
in her diary, "is like reading a highly instructive book; his
conversation is so enlightened, so clear. He is universally admitted to be one of the first politicians now extant." But her
other uncle by no means shared her sentiments. He could not,
he said, put up with a water drinker; and King Leopold would
touch no wine. "What's that you're drinking, sir?" King William asked him one day at dinner. "Water, sir." "God damn it,
sir!" was the rejoinder. "Why don't you drink wine? I never
allow anybody to drink water at my table."

It was clear that there would soon be a great explosion; and in
August it came. The duchess and the Princess had gone down
to Windsor for the King's birthday party, and the King himself,
who was in London for the day to adjourn Parliament, paid a
visit at Kensington Palace in their absence. There he found that
the duchess had just appropriated, against his express orders, a
suite of seventeen apartments for her own use.

He was extremely angry, and when he returned to Windsor,
after greeting the Princess with affection, he publicly rebuked
the duchess for what she had done. But this was little to what
followed. Next day was the birthday banquet; there were a
hundred guests; the Duchess of Kent sat on the King's right
hand, and the Princess Victoria opposite. At the end of the
dinner the King rose, and, in a long, passionate speech, poured
out the vials of his wrath upon the duchess. She had, he declared,
insulted him—grossly and continually; she had kept the Princess
away from him in the most improper manner; she was incompetent to act with propriety in the high station which she
filled; and he hoped to God that his life might be spared for
six months longer, so that the calamity of a regency might be
avoided, and the functions of the Crown pass directly to the

heiress presumptive instead of into the hands of the "person now near him."

The flood of vituperation rushed on, while the Queen blushed scarlet, the Princess burst into tears, and guests sat aghast. When the tirade was over the duchess in a tornado of rage called for her carriage. It was only with the utmost difficulty that some show of a reconciliation was patched up, and the outraged lady was prevailed upon to put off her departure till the morrow.

Her troubles, however, were not over when she had shaken the dust of Windsor from her feet. In her own household she was pursued by bitterness and vexation, for the apartments at Kensington seethed with subdued disaffection.

There was a deadly feud between her major-domo, Sir John Conroy, and Baroness Lehzen. But that was not all.

The duchess had grown too fond of Sir John Conroy. There were familiarities, and one day the Princess Victoria discovered the fact. She confided what she had seen to the baroness, and to the baroness's beloved ally, Madame de Späth. Unfortunately, Madame de Späth could not hold her tongue, and was foolish enough to reprove the duchess; whereupon she was instantly dismissed.

It was not so easy to get rid of the baroness. That lady, prudent and reserved, maintained an irreproachable demeanor. Her position was strongly entrenched; she had managed to secure the support of the King; and Sir John found that he could do nothing against her. But henceforward the household was divided. The duchess supported Sir John; but the baroness, too, had an adherent who could not be neglected. The Princess Victoria said nothing; but she adored her Lehzen.

The duchess knew only too well that in this horrid embroilment her daughter was against her. Chagrin, annoyance, tossed her to and fro. She did her best to console herself with Sir John's affectionate loquacity, or with the sharp remarks of Lady Flora Hastings. Lady Flora, one of her maids of honor, had no love for the baroness. The subject lent itself to satire; for Baroness Lehzen, the pastor's daughter, with all her airs of stiff superiority, had habits which betrayed her origin. Her passion for caraway seeds, for instance: little bags of them came to her from

Hanover, and she sprinkled them on her bread and butter, her cabbage, and even her roast beef. Lady Flora could not resist a caustic observation; it was repeated to the baroness, who pursed her lips in fury; and so the mischief grew.

THE KING had prayed that he might live till his niece was of age; and a few days before her eighteenth birthday—the date of her legal majority—a sudden attack of illness nearly carried him off. He recovered, however, and the Princess was able to go through her birthday festivities—a state ball and a drawing room—with unperturbed enjoyment.

"Count Zichy," she noted in her diary, "is very good-looking in uniform, but not in plain clothes. Count Waldstein looks remarkably well in his pretty Hungarian uniform." With the latter young gentleman she wished to dance, but there was an insurmountable difficulty. "He could not dance quadrilles, and, as in my station I unfortunately cannot valse and gallop, I could not dance with him."

Her birthday present from the King was of a pleasing nature, but it led to a painful domestic scene. In spite of the anger of her Belgian uncle, she had remained upon good terms with her English one. He had always been very kind to her, and the fact that he had quarreled with her mother did not appear to be a reason for disliking him. He was, she said, "odd, very odd," but "his intentions were often ill interpreted."

He now wrote her a letter, offering her an allowance of £10,000 a year, to be at her own disposal and independent of her mother. Lord Conyngham, the lord chamberlain, was instructed to deliver the letter into the Princess's own hands. When he arrived at Kensington, he was ushered into the presence of the duchess and the Princess, and the duchess put out her hand to take the letter. Lord Conyngham begged her pardon and repeated the King's command. Thereupon the Princess took the letter. She immediately wrote to her uncle, accepting his kind proposal. The duchess was much displeased; £4000 a year, she said, would be quite enough for Victoria; as for the remaining £6000, it would be only proper that she should have that herself.

King William had thrown off his illness, and returned to his normal life. Once more the royal circle at Windsor—Their Majesties, the elder Princesses—might be seen ranged for hours round a mahogany table, while the Queen netted a purse, and the King slept, occasionally waking to observe "Exactly so, ma'am, exactly so!" But this recovery was of short duration. The old man suddenly collapsed; he showed no power of rallying; and it was clear to everyone that his death was now close at hand.

All eyes, all thoughts, turned towards the Princess Victoria; but she still remained, shut away in the seclusion of Kensington, a small, unknown figure, lost in the shadow of her mother. The preceding year had in fact been an important one in her development. The soft tendrils of her mind had for the first time begun to stretch out towards unchildish things. In this King Leopold encouraged her. After his return to Brussels, he had resumed his correspondence in a more serious strain; he discussed details of foreign politics; he laid down the duties of kingship. "The business of the highest in a State," he wrote, "is, in my opinion, to act with great impartiality and a spirit of justice for the good of all." At the same time the Princess's tastes had been opening out. Though she was still passionately devoted to riding and dancing, she had now begun to have a genuine love of music as well, and to drink in the roulades and arias of Italian opera with high enthusiasm. She even enjoyed reading poetry—at any rate, the poetry of Sir Walter Scott.

When King Leopold learned that King William's death was approaching, he wrote several long letters of advice to his niece. In the crisis that was approaching, he said, she was not to be alarmed, but to trust in her "good natural sense and the *truth*" of her character; she was to do nothing in a hurry, and to continue her confidence in the Whig administration. Not content with letters, however, King Leopold determined that the Princess should not lack personal guidance, and sent over to her aid the trusted friend, whom, twenty years before, he had taken to his heart at Claremont. Thus, once again, as if in accordance with some preordained destiny, the figure of Stockmar is discernible—present at a momentous hour.

On June 18, the King was visibly sinking. The Archbishop of

Canterbury was by his side, with all the comforts of the church. It was the anniversary of the Battle of Waterloo, and the dying man remembered it. He should be glad to live, he said, over that day; he would never see another sunset.

"I hope Your Majesty may live to see many," said Dr. Chambers. "Oh! that's quite another thing," was the answer. One other sunset he did live to see; and he died early the following morning. It was on June 20, 1837.

When all was over, the Archbishop and the Lord Chamberlain ordered a carriage, and drove posthaste from Windsor to Kensington. They arrived at the palace at five o'clock, and it was only with difficulty that they gained admittance. At six the duchess woke up her daughter, and told her that the Archbishop of Canterbury and Lord Conyngham wished to see her. She got out of bed, put on her dressing gown, and went, alone, into the room where the messengers were standing.

Lord Conyngham and the Archbishop fell on their knees, and Lord Conyngham officially announced the death of the King; the Archbishop added some personal details. Looking at the bending, murmuring dignitaries before her, she knew that she was Queen of England. "Since it has pleased Providence," she wrote that day in her journal, "to place me in this station, I shall do my utmost to fulfill my duty; I am very young, and inexperienced, but I am sure, that very few have more real good will and more real desire to do what is fit and right than I have."

But there was scant time for resolutions and reflections. At once, affairs were thick upon her. Stockmar came to breakfast, and gave some good advice. She wrote a letter to her uncle Leopold. The Prime Minister, Lord Melbourne, came at nine and kissed her hand. She saw him alone, and repeated to him the lesson which, no doubt, the faithful Stockmar had taught her at breakfast. "It has long been my intention to retain your Lordship and the rest of the present Ministry at the head of affairs"; whereupon Lord Melbourne again kissed her hand and shortly after left her.

At eleven, Lord Melbourne came again; and at half past eleven she went downstairs into the red saloon to hold her first Council. The great assembly of lords and notables, bishops, generals, and Ministers of State saw the doors thrown open and a very short, slim girl in deep plain mourning come into the room alone and move forward to her seat with extraordinary dignity and grace; they saw a countenance not beautiful but prepossessing—fair hair, blue prominent eyes, a small curved nose, a tiny chin, a clear complexion and, over all, the strangely mingled signs of innocence, of gravity, of youth, and of composure; they heard a high unwavering voice reading aloud with perfect clarity; and then the ceremony was over. They saw the small figure rise and, with the same consummate grace, pass out from among them, as she had come in, alone.

BARONESS LEHZEN

CHAPTER 3
Lord Melbourne

THE NEW QUEEN was almost entirely unknown to her subjects. In her public appearances her mother had invariably dominated the scene. Her private life had been that of a novice in a convent; and no human being at all, except her mother and the Baroness Lehzen, had ever been alone with her in a room. Thus it was not only the public at large that was in ignorance of everything concerning her; the inner circles of statesmen and officials and highborn ladies were equally in the dark.

When she suddenly emerged from this deep obscurity, the impression that she created was profound. Her bearing at her first Council filled the whole gathering with astonishment and admiration; the Duke of Wellington, Sir Robert Peel, even the cold and caustic Charles Greville, Clerk of the Privy Council—all were completely carried away. Everything that was reported of her subsequent proceedings seemed to be of no less happy augury. Her perceptions were quick, her decisions sensible; she performed her royal duties with extraordinary facility.

Among the outside public there was a great wave of enthusiasm. Sentiment and romance were coming into fashion; and the spectacle of the little girl-queen, innocent, modest, with

37

fair hair and pink cheeks, driving through her capital, filled the hearts of the beholders with raptures of affection. What, above all, struck everybody with overwhelming force was the contrast between Queen Victoria and her uncles. The nasty old men, debauched and pigheaded—they had vanished like the snows of winter, and here at last, crowned and radiant, was the spring. Lord John Russell, in an elaborate oration, gave voice to the general sentiment. He asked England to pray that the illustrious Princess who had just ascended the throne might see slavery abolished, crime diminished, and education improved. He trusted that her people would henceforward derive their strength from enlightened religious and moral principles, and that, so fortified, the reign of Victoria might prove celebrated to posterity and to all the nations of the earth.

Very soon, however, there were signs that the future might turn out to be not quite so simple and roseate as a delighted public dreamed. The "illustrious Princess" might perhaps, after all, have something within her which squared ill with the easy vision of a well-conducted heroine in a storybook. When, after her first Council, she had crossed the anteroom and had found her mother waiting for her, she had said, "And now, Mamma, am I really and truly Queen?"

"You see, my dear, that it is so."

"Then, dear Mamma, I hope you will grant me the first request I make to you, as Queen. Let me be by myself for an hour." For an hour she had remained in solitude. Then she had reappeared, and had given a significant order: her bed was to be moved out of her mother's room.

It was the doom of the Duchess of Kent. The long years of waiting were over at last; the moment of a lifetime had come; her daughter was Queen of England; and that very moment brought her own annihilation. She found herself, absolutely and irretrievably, shut off from every vestige of influence, of power. She was surrounded, indeed, by all the outward signs of respect; but that only made the inward truth of her position the more intolerable. Through the mingled formalities of court etiquette and filial duty, she could never penetrate to Victoria. She was unable to conceal her disappointment and her rage.

"There is no more future for me," she exclaimed to Madame de Lieven; "I have become a nothing." For eighteen years, she said, this child had been the sole object of her existence, her hopes, and now—! Sailing so gallantly through the buffeting storms of life, the stately vessel, with sails still swelling and pennons flying, had put into harbor at last; to find there nothing—a land of desolation.

Within a month of the accession, the whole royal household moved from Kensington to Buckingham Palace, and, in the new abode, the Duchess of Kent was given a suite of apartments entirely separate from the Queen's. By Victoria herself the change was welcomed, though, at the moment of departure from Kensington, she could afford to be sentimental. "Though I rejoice to *go* into Buckingham Palace for many reasons," she wrote in her diary, "it is not without feelings of regret that I shall bid adieu *for ever* to this my birthplace! I have gone through painful and disagreeable scenes here, 'tis true," she concluded, "but still I am fond of the poor old palace."

At the same time she took another decided step. She had determined that she would see no more of Sir John Conroy. She rewarded his past services with a baronetcy and a pension of £3000 a year; he remained a member of the duchess's household, but his personal intercourse with the Queen came to an abrupt conclusion.

IT WAS CLEAR that these interior changes—whatever else they might betoken—marked the triumph of one person—the Baroness Lehzen.

Discreet and victorious, she observed the ruin of her enemies, and remained in possession of the field. More closely than ever did she cleave to the side of her mistress, her pupil, and her friend; and in the recesses of the palace her mysterious figure was at once invisible and omnipresent. When the Queen's ministers came in at one door, the baroness went out by another; when they retired, she immediately returned.

Nobody knew—nobody will ever know—the precise extent and nature of her influence. She herself declared that she never discussed public affairs with the Queen, that she was concerned with private matters only—with private letters and the details of private life. Certainly her hand is everywhere discernible in Victoria's early correspondence. The journal is written in the style of a child; but the letters are not so simple; they are the work of a child, rearranged—perceptibly—by a governess.

The governess was no fool: narrow, jealous, provincial, she might be; but she was an acute and vigorous woman who had gained a peculiar ascendancy. That ascendancy she meant to keep. No doubt it was true that technically she took no part in public business; but the distinction between what is public and what is private is always subtle; and in the case of a reigning sovereign it is often imaginary. Considering all things, it was something more than a mere matter of private interest that the bedroom of Baroness Lehzen at Buckingham Palace should have been next door to the bedroom of the Queen.

But the influence wielded by the baroness, supreme as it seemed within its own sphere, was not unlimited; there were other forces at work. For one thing, the faithful Stockmar had taken up his residence in the palace. During the twenty years which had elapsed since the death of the Princess Charlotte, the unknown counselor of a princeling had gradually risen to a position of European importance. His devotion to his master had been not only wholehearted but cautious and wise. It was Stockmar's advice that had kept Prince Leopold in England during the critical years which followed his wife's death, and had thus secured to him the essential requisite of a *point d'appui* [focal point] in the country of his adoption. It was Stockmar who had induced the Prince to become the constitutional sovereign of Belgium. It was Stockmar's diplomatic skill which, through a long series of complicated negotiations, had led to the guarantee of Belgian neutrality by the great powers.

His labors had been rewarded by a German barony and by the complete confidence of King Leopold. Nor was it only in Brussels that he was listened to with respect. The statesmen who governed England—Lord Grey, Sir Robert Peel, Lord Palmerston, Lord Melbourne—had learned to put a high value upon his probity and his intelligence.

"He is one of the cleverest fellows I ever saw," said Lord

Melbourne, "the most discreet man, the most well-judging, and most cool man."

King Leopold and his counselor provide in their careers an example of the curious diversity of human ambitions. The correct mind of Leopold craved for the whole apparatus of royalty. Mere power would have held no attractions for him; he must be an actual king—crowned—recognized. The ambition of Stockmar took a form exactly complementary to his own. The sovereignty that the baron sought for was by no means obvious. The satisfaction of his being lay in obscurity, in invisibility—in passing, unobserved, through a hidden entrance, into the very central chamber of power, and in sitting there, quietly, pulling the subtle strings that set the wheels of the whole world in motion. A very few people, in very high places, knew that Baron Stockmar was a most important person: that was enough. The fortunes of the master and the servant, intimately interacting, rose together. The baron's secret skill had given Leopold his kingdom; and Leopold, in his turn, as time went on, furnished the baron with more and more keys to more and more back doors.

Stockmar took up his abode in Buckingham Palace partly as the emissary of King Leopold, but more particularly as the friend and adviser of a queen who was almost a child. For it would be a mistake to suppose that either of these two men was actuated by a vulgar selfishness. King Leopold, indeed, was well aware on which side his bread was buttered; but then, he was a constitutional monarch; and it would be highly indecorous in a constitutional monarch to have any aims that were low or personal. As for Stockmar, disinterestedness was undoubtedly a basic element in his character. The ordinary schemer is always an optimist; and Stockmar, racked by dyspepsia, was constitutionally a melancholy man. A schemer, no doubt, he was; but he schemed distrustfully, splenetically, to do good.

With Lehzen to supervise every detail of her conduct, with Stockmar in the next room, so full of wisdom, with her uncle Leopold's letters, too, pouring out so constantly their stream of encouragements, Victoria, even had she been without other guidance, would have stood in no lack of private counselors.

But these influences paled before a new star, of the first magnitude, which, rising suddenly upon her horizon, immediately dominated her life.

WILLIAM LAMB, Viscount Melbourne, was fifty-eight years of age, and had been for the last three years Prime Minister of England. In every outward respect he was one of the most fortunate of mankind. He had been born into the midst of riches, brilliance, and power. Nature had given him beauty and brains; the unexpected death of an elder brother had brought him wealth, a peerage, and the possibility of high advancement.

With little effort, he attained political eminence, and on the triumph of the Whigs he became a leading member of the government. His mind was at once supple and copious; his temperament, calm and sensitive. In society he was a notable talker, a captivating companion, a charming man. If one looked deeper, one saw at once that he was not ordinary, that the piquancies of his conversation and his manner—his free-and-easy vaguenesses, his abrupt questions, his lollings and loungings—were the outward manifestation of an individuality that was fundamental.

The precise nature of this individuality was difficult to gauge: it was complex, perhaps self-contradictory. Certainly there was an ironical discordance between the inner history of the man and his apparent fortunes. His marriage, which had seemed to be the crown of his youthful ardors, was a long, miserable, desperate failure: the incredible Lady Caroline was very nearly the destruction of his life.

When at last he emerged from the anguish and confusion of Lady Caroline's folly, he was left alone with endless memories of farce and tragedy, and an only son, who was an imbecile. But there was something else that he owed to Lady Caroline. While she had whirled with Byron in a hectic frenzy, he had stayed at home and occupied his solitude with reading. It was thus that he had acquired those habits of study which formed so unexpected a part of his mental equipment. His passion for reading never deserted him; even when he was Prime Minister he found time to master every new important book. With an incongruousness that was characteristic, his favorite study was theology; and at any odd moment he might be found turning over the pages of the Bible.

The paradox of his political career was no less curious. By temperament an aristocrat, by conviction a conservative, he came to power as the leader of the popular party, the party of change. He had profoundly disliked the Reform Bill, which he had only accepted at last as a necessary evil; and the Reform Bill lay at the root of the very existence of his government. He was far too skeptical to believe in progress of any kind. "You'd better try to do no good," was one of his dictums, "and then you'll get into no scrapes." Education at best was futile; education of the poor was positively dangerous. The ballot was nonsense; and there was no such thing as a democracy. Nevertheless, he was not a reactionary; he was simply an opportunist. The whole duty of government, he said, was "to prevent crime and to preserve contracts." All one could really hope to do was to carry on.

He himself carried on in a remarkable manner—with compromises and contradictions, and yet with shrewdness. He conducted transactions with extraordinary nonchalance. Important persons, ushered up for some grave interview, found him in a touseled bed, littered with books and papers, or vaguely shaving in a dressing room; but, when they went downstairs again, they would realize that somehow or other they had been pumped. When he had to receive a deputation, the worthy delegates of the tallow chandlers, or the Society for the Abolition of Capital Punishment, were mortified when, in the midst of their speeches, the Prime Minister became absorbed in blowing a feather, or suddenly cracked an unseemly joke. How could they have guessed that he had spent the night before diligently getting up the details of their case?

Probably, if he had been born a little earlier, he would have been a simpler and a happier man. As it was, he was a child of the eighteenth century whose lot was cast in a new, unsympathetic age. He was an autumn rose. With all his humor, his happy-go-lucky ways, a deep disquietude possessed him. He was restless and melancholy at heart. Above all, he could never harden himself; those sensitive petals shivered in every wind. Whatever else he might be, one thing was certain: Lord Melbourne was always human, supremely human—too human, perhaps.

And now, with old age upon him, his life took a sudden, extraordinary turn. He became the intimate adviser and companion of a young girl who had stepped all at once from a nursery to a throne.

His relations with women had been, like everything else about him, ambiguous. Lady Caroline had vanished; but female society of some kind or other was necessary to him, and a great part of every day was invariably spent in it. There were rumors and combustions. Lord Melbourne was twice a corespondent in a divorce action. On each occasion he won his suit. But it was clear that, with such a record, the Prime Minister's position in Buckingham Palace must be a highly delicate one.

He met the situation with consummate success. His behavior was from the first moment impeccable. His manner towards the young Queen mingled, with perfect facility, the respect of a statesman and a courtier with the tender solicitude of a parent. At the same time the habits of his life underwent a surprising change. His comfortable, unpunctual days became subject to the unaltering routine of a palace; no longer did he sprawl on sofas; not a single "damn" escaped his lips. The man of the world who had been the friend of Byron, the talker whose paradoxes had held Holland House enthralled, the lover whose soft words had captivated so much beauty, might now be seen, evening after evening, talking with infinite politeness to a schoolgirl, bolt upright, amid the silence and the rigidity of court etiquette.

ON HER SIDE, Victoria was instantly fascinated by Lord Melbourne. The good report of Stockmar had no doubt prepared the way; and the first highly favorable impression was never afterwards belied. She found him perfect; and perfect in her sight he remained.

Her absolute adoration was very natural; what innocent young creature could have resisted the charm of such a man? But, in her situation, there was a special influence which gave a peculiar glow to all she felt. After years of emptiness and dullness, she had come suddenly, in the heyday of youth, into freedom and power. She was mistress of herself, of great domains and palaces; she was Queen of England. Responsibilities and difficulties she might have; but one feeling dominated all others—the feeling of joy.

Everything pleased her. She was in high spirits from morning till night. Mr. Creevey, grown old now, catching a glimpse of her at Brighton, was much amused. "A more homely little being you never beheld, *when she is at her ease*," he wrote. "She laughs in real earnest, opening her mouth as wide as it can go, showing not very pretty gums. . . . She eats quite as heartily as she laughs, I think I may say she gobbles. . . . She blushes and laughs every instant in so natural a way as to disarm anybody."

But it was not merely when she was laughing or gobbling that she enjoyed herself; the performance of her official duties gave her intense satisfaction. "I really have immensely to do," she wrote in her journal a few days after her accession; "I receive so many communications from my Ministers, but I like it very much." And, a week later, "I *delight* in this work." Through the girl's immaturity the vigorous predestined tastes of the woman were eagerly pushing themselves into existence.

One detail of her happy situation deserves particular mention. Apart from the momentousness of her political position, she was a person of great wealth. As soon as Parliament met, an annuity of £385,000 was settled upon her. When the expenses of her household had been discharged, she was left with £68,000 a year of her own. She enjoyed besides the revenues of the duchy of Lancaster, an annual £27,000. The first use to which she put her money was characteristic: she paid off her father's debts. She had the instincts of a man of business; and she never could have borne to be in a financially unsound position.

With youth and happiness gilding every hour, the days passed merrily enough. And each day hinged upon Lord Melbourne. Her diary shows us, with clarity, the life of the young sovereign during the early months of her reign—a life full of delightful business, a life of simple pleasures, riding, eating, dancing—an easy, unsophisticated life.

If she is the heroine of the story, Lord Melbourne is the hero. Lehzen, the baron, Uncle Leopold, are unsubstantial shadows— the incidental characters of the piece. Her paradise was peopled by two persons. One sees them together still, in the artless pages of her diary, under the magical illumination of that long-ago dawn: the polished gentleman with the whitening hair and whiskers and the dark eyebrows and the mobile lips and the big expressive eyes; and beside him the tiny Queen—slim, active, in her plain girl's dress and little tippet, looking up at him earnestly, adoringly, with eyes blue and projecting, and half-open mouth. So they appear upon every page of the journal.

Their long conversations touched upon a multitude of topics. Lord M. would criticize books, throw out a remark or two on the British constitution, tell some story or make some passing reflections on human life. Then there would be business—a dispatch perhaps from Lord Durham in Canada, which Lord M. would read. But first he must explain a little.

"He said that I must know that Canada originally belonged to the French, and was only ceded to the English in 1760, when it was taken in an expedition under Wolfe: 'a very daring enterprise,' he said. Canada was then entirely French. . . . Lord M. explained this very clearly and said a good deal more about it. He then read me Durham's despatch, which took him more than 1/2 an hour to read. Lord M. read it beautifully with that fine soft voice of his, and with so much expression, so that, needless to say, I was much interested by it."

Then the talk would take a more personal turn. Lord M. would describe his boyhood, and she would learn that "he wore his hair long, as all boys then did, till he was 17 (*how* handsome he must have looked!)." Or she would find out about his queer tastes and habits—how he never carried a watch. " 'I always ask the servant what o'clock it is, and then he tells me what he likes,' said Lord M."

The day's routine, whether in London or at Windsor, was almost invariable. The morning was devoted to business and Lord M. In the afternoon the whole court went out riding. The Queen, in her velvet riding habit and a top hat with a veil about the brim, headed the cavalcade; and Lord M. rode beside her.

The lively troupe went fast and far, to the exhilaration of Her Majesty. Back in the palace again, there was still time for a little more fun before dinner—a game of battledore and shuttlecock perhaps, or a romp along the galleries with some children.

Dinner came, and the ceremonial tightened. The gentleman of highest rank sat on the right hand of the Queen; on her left—it soon became an established rule—sat Lord Melbourne. After the ladies had left the dining room, the gentlemen were not permitted to remain behind for very long; indeed, the short time allowed them for their wine drinking formed the subject— so it was rumored—of one of the very few disputes between the Queen and her Prime Minister; but her determination carried the day, and from that moment after-dinner drunkenness began to go out of fashion.

When the company was reassembled in the drawing room the etiquette was stiff. The Queen spoke in turn to each of her guests; and during these short uneasy colloquies the aridity of royalty was apt to become painfully evident. One night Mr. Greville was present; his turn soon came; the middle-aged, hard-faced *viveur* was addressed by his young hostess. "Have you been riding today, Mr. Greville?" asked the Queen.

"No, Madam, I have not," replied Mr. Greville.

"It was a fine day," continued the Queen.

"Yes, Madam, a very fine day," said Mr. Greville.

"It was rather cold, though," said the Queen.

"It *was* rather cold, Madam," said Mr. Greville. There was a pause, after which Mr. Greville ventured to take the lead, though he did not venture to change the subject. "Has Your Majesty been riding today?" asked Mr. Greville.

"Oh yes, a very long ride," answered the Queen animatedly.

"Has Your Majesty got a nice horse?" said Mr. Greville.

"Oh, a very nice horse," said the Queen.

It was over. Her Majesty gave a smile and an inclination of the head, Mr. Greville bowed, and the next conversation began with the next gentleman. When all the guests had been disposed of, the Duchess of Kent sat down to her whist, while everybody else was ranged about the round table—perhaps to discuss the contents of one of the large albums of engravings with which the round table was covered—until it was half past eleven and time to go to bed.

Occasionally, there were little diversions: the evening might be spent at the opera or at a play. Next morning the royal critic would note down her impressions. "It was Shakespeare's tragedy of *Hamlet.* . . . Mr. Charles Kean (son of old Kean) acted the part of Hamlet, and I must say beautifully." But, undoubtedly, the evenings which the young Queen most enjoyed were those on which there was dancing. She was always ready enough to seize any excuse—the arrival of cousins—a birthday—to give the command for that. Then, when the figures of the dancers swayed to the music, and she felt her own figure swaying too—then her happiness reached its height, her eyes sparkled, she must go on and on into the small hours of the morning. For a moment Lord M. himself was forgotten.

THE MONTHS flew past. The summer was over: "the pleasantest summer I EVER passed in *my life,* and I shall never forget this first summer of my reign."

With surprising rapidity, another summer was upon her. The coronation came and went—a curious dream. The antique, intricate ceremonial worked itself out like some machine of gigantic complexity which was a little out of order. The small central figure went through her gyrations. She sat; she walked; she prayed; she carried about an orb that was almost too heavy to hold; the Archbishop of Canterbury came and crushed a ring upon the wrong finger, so that she was ready to cry out with the pain; old Lord Rolle tripped in his mantle and fell down the steps as he was doing homage; she perceived Lehzen in an upper box and smiled at her as she sat, robed and crowned, on the Confessor's throne. "I shall ever remember this day as the *proudest* of my life," she noted. But the pride was soon merged once more in youth and simplicity. When she returned to Buckingham Palace at last she was not tired; she ran up to her private rooms, doffed her splendors, and gave her spaniel Dash its evening bath.

Life flowed on again with its accustomed smoothness—though, of course, the smoothness was occasionally disturbed.

For one thing, there was the distressing behavior of Uncle Leopold. The King of the Belgians had not been able to resist attempting to make use of his family position to further his diplomatic ends—to test the opportunity of bending to his wishes, by means of personal influence, the foreign policy of England. He set about the task with becoming precautions, continuing to write his usual letters of admirable advice. Within a few days of her accession, he recommended the young Queen to lay emphasis, on every possible occasion, upon her English birth; to praise the English nation and "the Established Church." And then—"before you decide on anything important I should be glad if you would consult me; this would also have the advantage of giving you time"; nothing was more injurious than to be hurried into wrong decisions unawares.

His niece replied at once with all her accustomed affection; but she wrote hurriedly—and, perhaps, a trifle vaguely. "*Your advice is always of the greatest importance* to me," she said.

Had he, possibly, gone too far? Well, he would be careful; he would draw back—*pour mieux sauter*—in order to jump the better—he added to himself with a smile. In his next letters he made no reference to his suggestion of consultations with himself; he merely pointed out the wisdom, in general, of refusing to decide upon important questions offhand. So far, his advice was taken; and it was noticed that the Queen, when applications were made to her, rarely gave an immediate answer.

King Leopold's counsels continued. The Princess de Lieven, he said, was a dangerous woman; there was reason to think that she would pry into what did not concern her; let Victoria beware. "A rule which I cannot sufficiently recommend is *never to permit* people to speak on subjects concerning yourself or your affairs, without you having yourself desired them to do so." Should such a thing occur, "change the conversation, and make the individual feel that he has made a mistake."

This piece of advice was also taken; for it fell out as the King had predicted. Madame de Lieven sought an audience, and appeared to be verging towards confidential topics; whereupon the Queen, becoming slightly embarrassed, talked of commonplaces. The individual felt that she had made a mistake.

The King's next warning was remarkable. Letters, he pointed out, are almost invariably read in the post. This was inconvenient, no doubt; but the fact, once grasped, was not without its advantages.

"I will give you an example: we are still plagued by Prussia concerning those fortresses; now to tell the Prussian Government many things, which we *should not like* to tell them officially, the Minister is going to write a despatch to our man at Berlin, sending it *by post;* the Prussians *are sure* to read it, and to learn in this way what we wish them to hear." Analogous circumstances might very probably occur in England. "I tell you the *trick,*" wrote His Majesty, "that you should be able to guard against it."

It seemed that the time had come for another step. The King's next letter was full of foreign politics—the situation in Spain and Portugal, the character of Louis Philippe; and he received a favorable answer. It appeared that Victoria was not unwilling to exchange observations on such matters with her uncle. So far so good. King Leopold, with a crisis impending in his diplomacy, hung back no longer. It was of the utmost importance to him that, in his maneuverings with France and Holland, he should have, or appear to have, English support. But the English government was adopting a neutral attitude; it was too bad; not to be for him was to be against him—could they not see that? Yet, perhaps, they were only wavering, and a little pressure upon them from Victoria might still save all.

"All I want from your kind Majesty," he wrote, "is, that you will *occasionally* express to your Ministers that, as far as it is *compatible* with England's interests, you do *not* wish that your government should take the lead in such measures as might bring on the *destruction* of this country, as well as that of your uncle and his family."

The result of this appeal was unexpected; there was dead silence for more than a week. When Victoria at last wrote, she was prodigal of her affection—"it would, indeed, my dearest Uncle, be *very wrong* of you, if you thought my feelings of devoted attachment to you could ever be changed—" but her references to foreign politics, though they were elaborate, were noncommittal in the extreme; they were almost cast in an official form. Her ministers, she said, entirely shared her views; she understood and sympathized with the difficulties of her beloved uncle's position; and he might rest assured "that both Lord Melbourne and Lord Palmerston are most anxious at all times for the prosperity and welfare of Belgium."

That was all. The King in his reply declared himself delighted, and reechoed the affectionate protestations of his niece. "My dearest and most beloved Victoria," he said, "you have written me a *very dear* and long letter, which has given me *great satisfaction*." He would not admit that he had had a rebuff.

A few months later the crisis came. King Leopold determined to make a bold push, and to carry Victoria with him, this time, by a display of royal vigor and avuncular authority. In an abrupt, almost peremptory letter, he laid his case, once more, before his niece. "You know from experience," he wrote, "that I *never ask anything of you*. . . . But, as I said before, if we are not careful we may see serious consequences. . . . I remain, my dear Victoria, your affectionate uncle, Leopold R."

The Queen immediately dispatched this letter to Lord Melbourne, who replied with a carefully thought-out form of words, signifying nothing whatever, which, he suggested, she should send to her uncle. She did so, copying out the formula, with a liberal scattering of "dear Uncles" interspersed; and she concluded her letter with a message of "affectionate love to Aunt Louise and the children."

Then at last King Leopold was obliged to recognize the facts. His next letter contained no reference at all to politics. "I am glad," he wrote, "to find that you like Brighton better than last year. I think Brighton very agreeable at this time of the year, till the east winds set in. Before my marriage, it was there that I met the Regent." Like poor Madame de Lieven, His Majesty felt that he had made a mistake.

THE CORRESPONDENCE with King Leopold was significant of much that still lay partly hidden in the character of Victoria. Her attitude towards her uncle never wavered for a moment. To all his advances she had presented an unyielding front. The foreign policy of England was not his province; it was hers and her ministers'; his insinuations, his entreaties, were quite useless.

The rigidity of her position was the more striking owing to the respectfulness and the affection with which it was accompanied. From start to finish the unmoved Queen remained the devoted niece. Leopold himself must have envied such correctitude; but what may be admirable in an elderly statesman is alarming in a maiden of nineteen. And observers were not without their fears. The strange mixture of ingenuous lightheartedness and fixed determination, of frankness and reticence, of childishness and pride, augured a future full of dangers.

As time passed the less pleasant qualities in this curious composition revealed themselves more often. There were signs of an imperious temper, an egotism that was strong and hard. It was noticed that the palace etiquette, far from relaxing, grew ever more inflexible. The slightest infringements of the freezing rules of deference were invariably visited by sharp and haughty glances from the Queen. Yet Her Majesty's eyes, crushing as they could be, were less crushing than her mouth. The self-will depicted in those small projecting teeth and that small receding chin was of a more dismaying kind than that which a powerful jaw betokens; it was a self-will imperturbable, unintelligent; a self-will dangerously akin to obstinacy. And the obstinacy of monarchs is not as that of other men.

Within two years of her accession, the storm clouds which, from the first, had been dimly visible on the horizon, gathered and burst. Victoria's relations with her mother had not improved. The Duchess of Kent still remained in Buckingham Palace, a discarded figure, powerless and inconsolable. Sir John Conroy, banished from the presence of the Queen, still presided over the duchess's household, and the hostilities of Kensington continued unabated in the new surroundings. Lady Flora Hastings still cracked her malicious jokes; the animosity of the Baroness Lehzen was still unappeased.

One day, Lady Flora found the joke was turned against her. Early in 1839, traveling in the suite of the duchess, she had returned from Scotland in the same carriage with Sir John Conroy. A change in her figure became the subject of jest; tongues wagged; and the jest grew serious. It was whispered that Lady Flora [an unmarried lady of thirty-two] was with child.

The state of her health seemed to confirm the suspicion; she consulted Sir James Clark, the royal physician, and after the consultation, Sir James let his tongue wag, too. On this, the scandal flared up sky-high. Everyone was talking; the baroness was not surprised; the duchess rallied to the support of her lady; the Queen was informed. At last the extraordinary expedient of a medical examination was resorted to, during which Sir James, according to Lady Flora, behaved with brutal rudeness, while a second doctor was extremely polite.

Finally, both physicians signed a certificate entirely exculpating the lady. But this was by no means the end of the business. The Hastings family, socially a powerful one, threw itself into the fray with all the fury of outraged pride. Lord Hastings insisted upon an audience of the Queen, wrote to the papers, and demanded the dismissal of Sir James Clark. The Queen expressed her regret to Lady Flora, but Sir James Clark was not dismissed. The tide of opinion turned violently against the Queen and her advisers; and by the end of March, the popularity, so radiant and abundant, with which the young sovereign had begun her reign, had entirely disappeared.

There can be no doubt that a great lack of discretion had been shown by the court. Ill-natured tittle-tattle, which should have been instantly nipped in the bud, had been allowed to assume disgraceful proportions; and the Throne itself had become involved. A particularly awkward question had been raised by the position of Sir James Clark. The Duke of Wellington, upon whom it was customary to fall back, in cases of difficulty in high places, had been consulted, and he had given it as his opinion that, as it would be impossible to remove Sir James without a public inquiry, Sir James must certainly stay where he was. Probably the duke was right; but the fact that the peccant doctor continued in the Queen's service made the Hastings family irreconcilable and produced an unpleasant impression of unrepentant error upon the public mind.

As for Victoria, she was very young and inexperienced; and she can hardly be blamed for having failed to control an extremely difficult situation. That was clearly Lord Melbourne's task; he was a man of the world, and, with vigilance, he might have quietly put out the ugly flames while they were still smoldering. But he did not do so; he let things slide; he was lazy and easygoing; the baroness was persistent; and Victoria herself was very headstrong. Did he possess the magic bridle which would curb that fiery steed? He could not be certain. And then, suddenly, another violent crisis revealed more unmistakably than ever the nature of the mind with which he had to deal.

THE QUEEN had for long been haunted by a terror that the day might come when she would be obliged to part with her minister. The power of the Whig government was steadily declining; the general election of 1837 had left them with a very small majority in the House of Commons, and since then, they had been in constant difficulties—abroad, at home, in Ireland. The Queen watched the development of events in great anxiety. She was a Whig by upbringing, by every association; and, even if those ties had never existed, the mere fact that Lord M. was the head of the Whigs would have determined her politics. The fall of the Whigs would mean a sad upset for Lord M. But it would have a still more terrible consequence: Lord M. would have to leave her; and the daily, the hourly, presence of Lord M. had become an integral part of her life.

Of the wider significance of political questions she knew nothing; all she saw was that her friends were in office and about her, and that it would be dreadful if they ceased to be so. "I cannot say," she wrote when a critical division was impending, "(though I feel *confident* of *our success*) HOW low, HOW *sad* I feel, when I think of the POSSIBILITY of this excellent and truly kind man not *remaining* my Minister! Yet I trust fervently that *He* who has so wonderfully protected me through such manifold difficulties will not *now* desert me!"

Lord Melbourne realized clearly enough how undesirable was such a state of mind in a constitutional sovereign who might be called upon at any moment to receive as her ministers the leaders of the opposite party; he did what he could to cool her ardor; but in vain. With considerable lack of foresight, too, he had himself helped to bring about this unfortunate condition of affairs. From the moment of her accession, he had surrounded the Queen with ladies of his own party; the mistress of the robes and all the ladies of the bedchamber were Whigs. In the ordinary course, the Queen never saw a Tory. She disliked the whole tribe; and she particularly disliked Sir Robert Peel, who would almost certainly be the next Prime Minister. His manners were detestable, and he wanted to turn out Lord M.

But the dreaded hour was now fast approaching. Early in May the ministers were visibly tottering; on a vital point of policy they could only secure a majority of five in the House of Commons; they determined to resign. When Victoria heard the news she burst into tears. Was it possible, then, that she was about to see Lord M. for the last time?

Lord M. came; the conversation was touching and prolonged; but it could only end in one way—the Queen must send for the Duke of Wellington. When, next morning, the duke came, he advised Her Majesty to send for Sir Robert Peel. She was in "a state of dreadful grief," but she swallowed down her tears, and braced herself, with royal resolution, for the odious interview.

Peel was by nature reserved, proud, and shy. He was easily embarrassed, and, at such moments, he grew stiff and formal, while his feet mechanically performed upon the carpet a dancing master's measure. Anxious as he now was to win the Queen's good graces, his very anxiety to do so made the attainment of his object the more difficult. He made no headway whatever with the hostile girl before him. She coldly noted that he appeared to be unhappy and "put out," and, while he stood in painful fixity, with an occasional uneasy pointing of the toe, her heart sank within her at the sight of that manner —"Oh! how different, how dreadfully different, to the frank, open, most kind warm manner of Lord Melbourne."

Nevertheless, the audience passed with only one slight hint of disagreement. Peel had decided that a change would be necessary in the composition of the royal household. The Queen must no longer be entirely surrounded by Whigs, by the wives and sisters of his opponents; some, at any rate, of the ladies of the bedchamber should be friendly to his government. When this matter was touched upon, the Queen intimated that she wished her household to remain unchanged; to which Sir Robert replied that the question could be settled later, and shortly afterwards withdrew to arrange the details of his cabinet.

While he was present, Victoria had remained, as she herself said, "very collected, and betrayed no agitation"; but as soon as she was alone she broke down. Then she wrote Lord Melbourne an account of her wretchedness. Lord Melbourne replied with a very wise letter. He attempted to calm the Queen; and he had nothing but good words for the Tory leaders. As for the question of the ladies of the household, the Queen, he said, should strongly urge what she desired, as it concerned her personally, "but," he added, "if Sir Robert is unable to concede it, it will not do to refuse and to put off the negotiation upon it."

On this point there can be little doubt that Lord Melbourne was right. The question was a complicated one, and it had never arisen before; but subsequent constitutional practice has determined that a queen regnant must accede to the wishes of her prime minister as to the *personnel* of the female part of her household. Lord Melbourne's wisdom, however, was wasted. The Queen would not be soothed. It was outrageous of the Tories to want to deprive her of her ladies. She made up her mind that, whatever Sir Robert might say, she would refuse to consent to the removal of a single one of them.

Accordingly, when, next morning, Peel appeared again, she was ready for action. When he had detailed the cabinet appointments, he added "Now, Ma'am, about the ladies."

"I cannot give up *any* of my ladies," she said.

"What, Ma'am!" said Sir Robert, "does Your Majesty mean to retain them *all?*"

"*All,*" said the Queen.

Sir Robert could not conceal his agitation. In vain he pleaded and argued; in vain he spoke of the constitution, and the public interest. Victoria was adamant; but he, too, through all his embarrassment, showed no sign of yielding; and when at last he left her nothing had been decided—the whole formation of the government was hanging in the wind.

A frenzy of excitement now seized upon Victoria. Sir Robert, she believed, had tried to outwit her, to take her friends from her; but that was not all: she had suddenly perceived the one thing that she was desperately longing for—a loophole of escape. She seized a pen and dashed off a note to Lord Melbourne.

"Sir Robert has behaved very ill," she wrote, "he insisted on my giving up my Ladies, to which I replied that I *never* would consent, and I never saw a man so frightened. . . . I think you would have been pleased to see my composure and firmness; the Queen of England will not submit to such trickery. Keep yourself in readiness, for you may soon be wanted."

Hardly had she finished when the Duke of Wellington was announced. "Well, Ma'am," he said as he entered, "I am very sorry to find there is a difficulty."

"Oh!" she replied, "*he* began it, not me." The venerable conqueror of Napoleon was outfaced by the equanimity of a girl in her teens. At last she even ventured to rally him. "Is Sir Robert so weak," she asked, "that even the Ladies must be of his opinion?" On which the duke made a brief expostulation, bowed low, and departed.

Had she won? Time would show; and in the meantime she scribbled another letter. "Lord Melbourne must not think the Queen rash in her conduct. . . . The Queen felt this was an attempt to see whether she could be led and managed like a child." The Tories were not only wicked but ridiculous.

The end of the crisis was now fast approaching. Sir Robert returned, and told her that if she insisted upon retaining all her ladies he could not form a government. She replied that she would send him her final decision in writing. Next morning the late Whig cabinet met. Lord Melbourne read to them the Queen's letters, and the group of elderly politicians were overcome by an extraordinary wave of enthusiasm. They knew very well it was doubtful whether the Queen had acted in strict accordance with the constitution; but such considerations vanished before Victoria's passionate urgency. The intensity of her determination swept them headlong down the stream of her desire. They unanimously felt that "it was impossible to abandon such a Queen and such a woman."

Forgetting that they were no longer Her Majesty's ministers, they took the unprecedented course of advising the Queen by letter to put an end to her negotiation with Sir Robert Peel. She did so; all was over; she had triumphed. That evening there was a ball at the palace. Everyone was present. "Peel and the Duke of Wellington came by looking very much put out." She was perfectly happy; Lord M. was Prime Minister once more, and he was by her side.

HAPPINESS HAD RETURNED with Lord M., but it was happiness in the midst of agitation. The domestic imbroglio continued unabated, until at last the Duke of Wellington, rejected as a minister, was called in once again in his old capacity as moral physician to the family. Something was accomplished when, at last, he induced Sir John Conroy to resign his place about the Duchess of Kent and leave the palace forever; something more when he persuaded the Queen to write an affectionate letter to her mother.

The way seemed open for a reconciliation, but the duchess was stormy still. She didn't believe that Victoria had written that letter; it was not in her handwriting; and she sent for the duke to tell him so. The duke, assuring her that the letter was genuine, begged her to forget the past.

"But what am I to do if Victoria asks me to shake hands with Lehzen?" the duchess asked.

"Do, ma'am? Why, take her in your arms and kiss her."

"What!" The duchess bristled in every feather.

"No, ma'am, no," said the duke, laughing. "I don't mean you are to take *Lehzen* in your arms and kiss *her*, but the Queen."

The duke might perhaps have succeeded, had not all attempts at conciliation been rendered hopeless by a tragical event. Lady Flora, it was discovered, had been suffering from a terrible internal malady, which now grew rapidly worse. There could be little doubt that she was dying.

The Queen's unpopularity reached an extraordinary height. More than once she was publicly insulted. "Mrs. Melbourne," was shouted at her when she appeared at her balcony; and, at Ascot, she was hissed. Lady Flora died. The whole scandal burst out again with redoubled vehemence; while, in the palace, the two parties were henceforth divided by an impassable, a Stygian, gulf.

Nevertheless, Lord M. was back, and every trouble faded under the enchantment of his presence. He, on his side, was very happy. In spite of the dullness of the court, his relationship with the Queen had come to be the dominating interest in his life; to have been deprived of it had been heartrending; he was installed once more, in a kind of triumph; let him enjoy the fleeting hours to the full! And so, cherished by the favor of a sovereign and warmed by the adoration of a girl, his life, like the autumn rose, came to a wondrous blooming. To watch, to teach, to encourage the royal young creature beside him— that was much; to feel with such a constant intimacy the impact of her quick affection, her radiant vitality—that was more. The springs of his sensibility, hidden deep within him, were overflowing. Often, as he bent over her hand and kissed it, he found himself in tears.

Upon Victoria, with all her impermeability, it was inevitable that such a companionship should have produced, eventually, an effect. She was no longer the simple schoolgirl of two years since. The change was visible even in her public demeanor. Her expression, once "ingenuous and serene," now appeared to a shrewd observer to be "bold and discontented." She had learned something of the pleasures of power and the pains of it. Lord Melbourne with his gentle instruction had sought to lead her into the paths of wisdom and moderation, but the whole unconscious movement of his character had swayed her in a very different direction. Was it possible that the secret impulses of self-expression, of self-indulgence even, were mastering her life? For a moment the child of a new age looked back, and wavered towards the eighteenth century. It was the most critical moment of her career. Had those influences lasted, the development of her character would have been completely changed.

And why should they not last? She, for one, was very anxious that they should. Let them last forever! She was surrounded by Whigs, she had Lord M. Any change would be for the worse;

and the worst change of all . . . no, she would not hear of it; it would be quite intolerable, it would upset everything, if she were to marry.

Everyone seemed to want her to—the general public, the ministers, her Saxe-Coburg relations—it was always the same story. Of course, she knew very well that there were excellent reasons for it. For one thing, if she remained childless, and were to die, her uncle Cumberland, who was now the King of Hanover, would succeed to the throne of England. That, no doubt, would be a most unpleasant event; and she entirely sympathized with everybody who wished to avoid it. But there was no hurry; naturally, she would marry in the end— but not just yet—not for three or four years. What was tiresome was that her uncle Leopold had apparently determined, not only that she ought to marry, but that her cousin Albert ought to be her husband. It was true that long ago, before her accession, she had told him that Albert possessed "every quality that could be desired to render her perfectly happy." But that had been years ago, when she was a mere child; her feelings, and all the circumstances, had now entirely changed; and Albert hardly interested her at all.

In later life the Queen declared that she had never for a moment dreamed of marrying anyone but her cousin; but her letters and diaries tell a different story. On August 26, 1837, she wrote in her journal: "Today is my *dearest* cousin Albert's 18th birthday, and I pray Heaven to pour its choicest blessings on his beloved head!" In subsequent years, however, the date passes unnoticed.

It had been arranged that Stockmar should accompany the Prince to Italy, and the baron left her side for that purpose. He wrote to her with sympathetic descriptions of his young companion; but her mind was by this time made up. She admired Albert very much, but she did not want to marry him. "At present," she told Lord Melbourne in April 1839, "*my* feeling is quite against ever marrying."

When her cousin's Italian tour came to an end, she grew nervous; she knew that, according to a long-standing engagement, his next journey would be to England. He would prob-

ably arrive in the autumn, and by July her uneasiness was intense. She wrote to her uncle to make her position clear; it must be understood, she said, that "there is *no engagement* between us." If she should like Albert, she could "make *no final promise this year*, for, at the *very earliest*, any such event could not take place till *two or three years hence*." To Lord Melbourne she was more explicit. She told him that she "had no great wish to see Albert, as the whole subject was an odious one"; she hated to have to decide about it; and she repeated once again that seeing Albert would be "a disagreeable thing."

But there was no escaping the horrid business; the visit must be made. The summer slipped by and was over; and on the evening of October 10 Albert, accompanied by his brother Ernest, arrived at Windsor.

Albert arrived; and the whole structure of her existence crumbled into nothingness like a house of cards. He was beautiful—she gasped—she knew no more. In a flash, a thousand mysteries were revealed to her; the past, the present, rushed upon her with a new significance; and an extraordinary certitude leaped into being in the light of those blue eyes, the smile of that lovely mouth.

The succeeding hours passed in a rapture. She was able to observe a few more details—the "exquisite nose," the "delicate mustachios and slight whiskers," the "beautiful figure, broad in the shoulder and a fine waist." She rode with him, danced with him, talked with him, and it was all perfection. She had no shadow of a doubt. He had come on a Thursday evening, and on the following Sunday morning she told Lord Melbourne that she had "a good deal changed her opinion as to marrying."

Next morning, she told him that she had made up her mind to marry Albert. The morning after that, she sent for her cousin. "After a few minutes I said to him that I thought he must be aware *why* I wished them to come here—and that it would make me *too happy* if he would consent to what I wished (to marry me)." Then "we embraced each other, and he was *so* kind, *so* affectionate." She said that she was quite unworthy of him, while he murmured that he would be very happy *"Das Leben mit dir zu zubringen,"*—"to spend my life with you."

They parted, and she felt "the happiest of human beings," when Lord M. came in. At first she talked of the weather and indifferent subjects. Somehow or other she felt a little nervous with her old friend. At last, summoning up her courage, she said, "I have got well through this with Albert."

"Oh! you have," said Lord M.

SIR ROBERT PEEL

CHAPTER 4
Marriage

IT WAS DECIDEDLY a family match. Prince Francis Charles Augustus Albert Emmanuel of Saxe-Coburg-Gotha—for such was his full title—had been born just three months after his cousin Victoria, and the same midwife had assisted at the two births. The children's grandmother, the Dowager Duchess of Coburg, had from the first looked forward to their marriage; as they grew up, the Duke of Saxe-Coburg, the Duchess of Kent, and King Leopold came equally to desire it. The Prince, ever since the time when, as a child of three, his nurse had told him that someday "the little English May flower" would be his wife, had never thought of marrying anyone else.

The Duke of Saxe-Coburg had one other child—Prince Ernest, Albert's senior by one year, and heir to the principality. The duchess, Ernest's and Albert's mother, was a sprightly and beautiful woman, with fair hair and blue eyes; Albert was very like her and was her declared favorite. But in his fifth year he was parted from her forever. The ducal court was not noted for the strictness of its morals; the duke was a man of gallantry, and it was rumored that the duchess followed her husband's example. There were scandals; at last there was a separation, followed by a divorce. The duchess retired to Paris, and died unhappily in 1831. Her memory was always very dear to Albert.

He grew up a pretty, clever, and high-spirited boy. Usually well-behaved, he was, however, sometimes violent. He had a will of his own; his elder brother was less passionate, less purposeful, and, in their wrangles, it was Albert who came out top. The two boys lived for the most part in one or another of the duke's country houses, among pretty hills and woods and streams. At a very early age they were put under a tutor, in whose charge they remained until they went to the university. They were brought up in a simple manner, for the duke was poor and the duchy small and insignificant.

Before long it became evident that Albert was a model lad. At the age of eleven he surprised his father by telling him that he hoped to make himself "a good and useful man." And yet he was not overserious, but full of fun—of practical jokes and mimicry. He was no milksop; he rode, shot, and fenced; above all he delighted in being out of doors. Never was he happier than in his long rambles with his brother through the wild country round his beloved Rosenau—stalking the deer, admiring the scenery, and returning laden with specimens for his natural history collection.

He was, besides, passionately fond of music. In one particular it was observed that he did not take after his father: owing either to his peculiar upbringing or to a more fundamental idiosyncrasy he had a marked distaste for the opposite sex. At the age of five, at a children's dance, he screamed with disgust when a little girl was led up to him for a partner; and though, later on, he grew more successful in disguising such feelings, the feelings remained.

The brothers were very popular in Coburg, and when the time came for them to be confirmed, the preliminary examination which, according to ancient custom, was held in public in the "Giants' Hall" of the castle, was attended by an enthusiastic crowd. "The dignified and decorous bearing of the Princes," we are told, "their strict attention to the questions, the frankness, decision, and correctness of their answers, produced a deep impression on the numerous assembly."

Albert's mental development now proceeded apace. In his seventeenth year he began a careful study of German literature and philosophy. Placed for some months under the care of King Leopold at Brussels, he came under the influence of Adolphe Quetelet, a mathematical professor, who was particularly interested in the application of the laws of probability to political and moral phenomena; this line of inquiry attracted the Prince, and the friendship thus begun continued till the end of his life.

From Brussels he went to the University of Bonn, where his energies were absorbed in metaphysics, law, political economy, music, fencing, and amateur theatricals. Thirty years later his fellow students recalled with delight the fits of laughter into which they had been sent by Prince Albert's mimicry.

After a year at Bonn, the time had come for a foreign tour, and Baron Stockmar arrived from England to accompany the Prince on the expedition to Italy. Two years previously, the baron had already been consulted by King Leopold as to his views upon the proposed marriage of Albert and Victoria. With a characteristic foresight, Stockmar had pointed out what were, in his opinion, the conditions essential to make the marriage a success. Albert, he wrote, was a fine young fellow, well grown for his age, with agreeable qualities; and it was probable that in a few years he would turn out a strong, handsome man, kindly, simple, yet dignified. "Thus, externally, he possesses all that pleases the sex." Supposing, therefore, that Victoria herself was in favor of the marriage, the further question arose as to whether Albert's mental qualities were such as to fit him for the position of husband of the Queen of England. On this point the baron preferred to reserve his opinion until he could observe Albert further. He added: "The young man ought to have not merely great ability, but a *right* ambition, and great force of will as well. To pursue for a lifetime a political career so arduous demands more than energy and inclination—it demands also that earnest frame of mind which is ready of its own accord to sacrifice mere pleasure to real usefulness."

Such were the views of Stockmar on the qualifications necessary for Victoria's husband; and he hoped, during the tour in Italy, to come to some conclusion as to how far the Prince possessed them. Albert on his side was much impressed by the baron, whom he had previously seen but rarely; he also became acquainted with a young Englishman, Lieutenant Francis Seymour, who had been engaged to accompany him, and with whom he struck up a warm friendship. He delighted in the galleries and scenery of Florence, though with Rome he was less impressed. "But for some beautiful palaces," he said, "it might just as well be any town in Germany."

On his return to Germany, Stockmar's observations, imparted to King Leopold, were still critical. Albert, he said, was intelligent, amiable, and full of the best intentions. But great exertion was repugnant to him; his good resolutions too often came to nothing. It was particularly unfortunate that he took not the slightest interest in politics, and never read a newspaper. In his manners, too, there was still room for improvement. "He will always," said the baron, "have more success with men than with women, in whose society he is too indifferent and retiring." One other feature of the case was noted by the keen eye of the old physician: the Prince's constitution was not a strong one.

On the whole, however, Stockmar was favorable to the projected marriage. But by now the chief obstacle seemed to lie in another quarter. Victoria was apparently determined to commit herself to nothing. And so it happened that when Albert went to England he himself had made up his mind to withdraw from the affair. Nothing would induce him, he confessed to a friend, to be kept vaguely waiting; he would break it all off at once. His reception at Windsor threw an entirely new light upon the situation. The wheel of fortune turned with a sudden rapidity; and he found, in the arms of Victoria, the irrevocable assurance of his overwhelming fate.

HE WAS NOT in love with her. Affection, gratitude, the natural reactions to the unqualified devotion of a lively young cousin who was also a queen—such feelings possessed him, but the ardors of passion were not his. Though he found that he liked Victoria very much, what immediately interested him in his curious position was less her than himself.

Dazzled and delighted, riding, dancing, laughing, amid the splendors of Windsor, he was aware of a new sensation—the stirrings of ambition in his breast. His place would indeed be a high, an enviable one! And then, on the instant, came another thought. The teaching of religion, the admonitions of Stockmar, his own inmost convictions, all spoke with the same utterance. He would not be there to please himself, but for a very different purpose—to do good. He must be "noble, manly, and princely in all things," he would have "to live and to sacrifice himself for the benefit of his new country."

One serious thought led on to another; after all, it was Coburg that had his heart. "While I shall be untiring," he wrote to his grandmother, "in my efforts and labors for the country to which I shall in future belong, I shall never cease *ein treuer Deutscher, Coburger, zu sein"*—"to be a true Coburg German." And now he must part from Coburg forever! Sobered and sad, he sought his brother Ernest's company; and the two young men, sitting down at the piano, would escape from the present and the future into the sweet gaiety of a Haydn duet.

They returned to Germany; and while Albert, for a few fare-well months, enjoyed the happiness of home, Victoria, for the last time, resumed her old life in London and Windsor. She corresponded daily with her future husband in a mingled flow of German and English; but the accustomed routine reasserted itself; Lord M. was once more constantly beside her; and the Tories were as intolerable as ever. Indeed, they were more so. For now, in these final moments, the old feud burst out with redoubled fury.

The impetuous sovereign found, to her chagrin, that there might be disadvantages in being the enemy of one of the great parties in the state. On two occasions the Tories directly thwarted her. She wished her husband's rank to be fixed by statute, and their opposition prevented it. She wished her hus-band to receive a settlement from the nation of £50,000 a year; and, again owing to the Tories, who pointed out that the bulk of the population was suffering from great poverty, he was only allowed £30,000. Angrily she determined to revenge herself by omitting to invite a single Tory to her wedding. Even the Duke of Wellington she nearly refused to ask. "That old rebel! I won't have him," she was reported to have said; but eventually she was induced to send him an invitation.

Nor was it only against the Tories that her irritation rose. As the time for her wedding approached, her temper grew steadily sharper. Queen Adelaide annoyed her. King Leopold, too, was "ungracious" in his correspondence. Even Albert himself was not impeccable; he failed to appreciate the complexity of English affairs; he wanted to appoint his own private secretary. But obviously Lord M. was best qualified to make the appointment; and Lord M. had decided that the Prince should have George Anson. Albert protested, but Victoria simply announced that Anson was appointed.

And on one other matter she was insistent. Since the affair of Lady Flora Hastings, a sad fate had overtaken Sir James Clark; his practice had quite collapsed. But the Queen remained faithful, and she desired Albert to make "poor Clark" his physician in ordinary. He did as he was told; but, as it turned out, the appointment was not a happy one.

The wedding day was fixed, and it was time for Albert to tear himself away from the scenes of his childhood. With an aching heart, he revisited his beloved woods and valleys; in deep depression, he sat through farewell banquets; and then it was time to go. The streets were packed as he drove through them; for a short space his eyes were gladdened by a sea of friendly German faces. At Calais a steamboat awaited him, and, together with his father and his brother, he stepped, dejected, on board. A little later, he was more dejected still. The crossing was very rough; the duke went hurriedly below; while the two princes, we are told, lay on either side of the cabin staircase "in an almost helpless state." At Dover a large crowd was collected on the pier, and "it was by no common effort that Prince Albert, who had continued to suffer up to the last moment, got up to bow to the people." His sense of duty triumphed. It was a curious omen: his whole life in England was foreshadowed as he landed on English ground.

Meanwhile Victoria, in growing agitation, was a prey to temper and to nerves. She grew feverish, and Sir James Clark pronounced that she was going to have the measles. But, once again, Sir James's diagnosis was incorrect. Not measles but a different malady was attacking her; she was suddenly prostrated by alarm and doubt. For two years she had been her own mistress—the two happiest years of her life. And now it was all to end! She was to come under an alien domination—she would have to promise that she would honor and obey . . . someone, who might, after all, oppose her! Why had she embarked on this experiment? No doubt, she loved Albert; but she loved power too.

He reappeared, in an exquisite uniform, and her hesitations melted in his presence like mist before the sun. On February 10, 1840, the marriage took place, and the wedded pair drove down to Windsor, but they were not, of course, entirely alone. They were accompanied by their suites, and, in particular, by two persons—the Baron Stockmar and the Baroness Lehzen.

ALBERT HAD FORESEEN that his married life would not be all plain sailing; but he had by no means realized the gravity and the complication of the difficulties which he would have to face. Politically, he was a cipher. Lord Melbourne was not only Prime Minister, he was in effect the private secretary of the Queen, and thus controlled the whole of the political existence of the sovereign. A queen's husband was an entity unknown to the British constitution. In state affairs there seemed to be no place for him; nor was Victoria herself at all unwilling that this should be so. He would, she hoped, make a perfect husband; but, as for governing the country, he would see that she and Lord Melbourne could manage that very well, without his help.

But it was not only in politics that the Prince discovered that the part cut out for him was a negligible one. Even as a husband, he found, his functions were to be extremely limited. Over the whole of Victoria's private life the Baroness Lehzen reigned supreme; and she had not the slightest intention of allowing that supremacy to be diminished by one iota.

Since the accession, her power had greatly increased. Besides the enormous influence which she exercised through her management of the Queen's private correspondence, she was now the superintendent of the royal establishment and controlled the important office of Privy Purse. Albert very soon perceived that he was not master in his own house. Every detail of his own and his wife's existence was supervised by a third person: nothing could be done until the consent of Lehzen had first been obtained. And Victoria, who adored Lehzen, saw nothing in all this that was wrong.

Nor was the Prince happier in his social surroundings. A shy young foreigner, awkward in ladies' company, it was improbable that, in any circumstances, he would have been a society success. His appearance, too, was against him. Though in the eyes of Victoria he was the mirror of manly beauty, her subjects, whose eyes were of a less Teutonic cast, did not agree with her. To them what was distressingly striking in Albert's face and whole demeanor was his un-English look. His features were regular, no doubt, but there was something smooth and smug about them; he was tall, but he was clumsily put together. Really, they thought, this youth was more like some kind of foreign tenor than anything else.

These were serious disadvantages; but the line of conduct which the Prince adopted from the moment of his arrival was far from calculated to dispel them. Owing partly to a natural awkwardness, and partly to a desire to be absolutely correct, his manners were infused with an extraordinary stiffness and formality. Whenever he appeared in company, he seemed to be surrounded by a thick hedge of prickly etiquette. He never went out into ordinary society; he never walked in the streets of London; he was invariably accompanied by an equerry when he rode or drove. He wanted to be irreproachable and, if that involved friendlessness, it could not be helped. Besides, he had no very high opinion of the English; so far as he could see, they cared for nothing but fox hunting and Sunday observances. Since it was clear that with such people he could have very little in common, there was no reason whatever for relaxing in their favor the rules of etiquette. In strict privacy, he could be natural and charming; but from the support and solace of true companionship he was utterly cut off.

A friend, indeed, he had—or rather, a mentor. The baron, established once more in the royal residence, was determined to work with as wholehearted a detachment for the Prince's benefit as, more than twenty years before, he had worked for his uncle's. Albert of course was no Leopold. He had none of his uncle's ambition to be personally great; he took no interest in politics, and there were no signs that he possessed any force of character. Left to himself, he would almost certainly have subsided into a high-minded nonentity, a dilettante busy over culture, a palace appendage without influence or power. But he was not left to himself. Forever at his pupil's elbow, Stockmar pushed him forward, with tireless pressure, along the path which had been trod by Leopold so many years ago. But, this time, the goal at the end of it was something more than the mediocre royalty that Leopold had reached. The prize which Stockmar, with his disinterested devotion, had determined should be Albert's was a tremendous prize indeed.

The beginning of the undertaking proved to be the most arduous part. Albert was easily dispirited: what was the use of struggling to perform in a role which bored him and which, it was clear, nobody but the good baron had any desire that he should take up? It was simpler to let things slide. But Stockmar would not have it. Incessantly, he harped upon two strings—Albert's sense of duty and his personal pride. Had the Prince forgotten the noble aims to which his life was to be devoted? And was he going to allow himself, his wife, his family, his whole existence, to be governed by Baroness Lehzen?

The latter consideration was a potent one. Albert was constantly exasperated by the position of the baroness in the royal household. He was, he knew very well, his wife's intellectual superior, and yet he found, to his intense annoyance, that there were parts of her mind over which he exercised no influence. When, urged on by the baron, he attempted to discuss politics with Victoria, she drifted into generalities, and then began to talk of something else. When at last he protested, she replied that her conduct was merely the result of indolence; that when she was with *him* she could not bear to bother her head with anything so dull as politics. The excuse was worse than the fault: was he the wife and she the husband? The baron declared that the root of the mischief was Lehzen: that it was she who encouraged the Queen to have secrets; who did worse—induced her to give false reasons to explain away her conduct.

Minor disagreements made matters worse. The royal couple differed in their tastes. Albert, brought up in a regime of Spartan simplicity and early hours, found court functions intolerably wearisome, and was invariably observed to be nodding on the sofa at half past ten; while the Queen's favorite form of enjoyment was to dance through the night and then to watch the sun rise behind Saint Paul's. She loved London and he detested it. Only in Windsor did he feel he could really breathe; but Windsor too had its terrors: though during the day there he could paint and walk and play on the piano, after dinner black tedium descended like a pall. He would have liked to summon distinguished scientific and literary men to his presence; but unfortunately Victoria "had no fancy to encourage such people"; knowing that she was unequal to taking a part in their conversation, she insisted that the evening routine should remain unaltered; the regulation interchange of platitudes with official persons was followed as usual by the round table and the books of engravings, while the Prince, with one of his attendants, played game after game of double chess.

It was only natural that in such a situation there should have been occasionally something more than mere irritation—a struggle of angry wills. No more than Albert was Victoria in the habit of playing second fiddle. But she fought at a disadvantage; she was, in truth, no longer her own mistress; a profound preoccupation dominated her, seizing upon her inmost purposes for its own extraordinary ends. She was madly in love.

The details of their battles are unknown to us; but Prince Ernest, who remained in England with his brother for some months, noted them with a friendly and startled eye. One story, indeed, survives, ill authenticated, yet summing up, as such stories often do, the central facts of the case. When, in wrath, the Prince one day had locked himself into his room, Victoria, no less furious, knocked on the door to be admitted. "Who is there?" he asked. "The Queen of England" was the answer.

He did not move, and again there was a hail of knocks. The question and the answer were repeated many times; but at last there was a pause, and then a gentler knocking. "Who is there?" came once more the relentless question. But this time the reply was different. "Your wife, Albert." And the door was immediately opened.

Very gradually the Prince's position changed. He began to find the study of politics more interesting than he had supposed; he read Blackstone, and took lessons in English law; he was occasionally present when the Queen interviewed her ministers; and he was shown dispatches relating to foreign affairs. Sometimes he would commit his views to paper, and read them aloud to the Prime Minister. An important step was taken when, before the birth of the Princess Royal, the Prince, without any opposition in Parliament, was appointed Regent in case of the death of the Queen.

Stockmar had intervened with the Tories to bring about this happy result; now he felt himself at liberty to take a holiday with his family in Coburg; but through innumerable letters he still watched over his pupil. "Dear Prince," he wrote, "I am satisfied with the news you have sent me. Mistakes, misunderstandings, obstructions, coming in vexatious opposition to one's views, are always to be taken for just what they are— namely, natural phenomena of life, which represent one of its sides, and that the shady one. In overcoming them with dignity, your mind has to exercise, to train, to enlighten itself." The Prince had done well so far; but he must continue in the right path; above all, he was "never to relax."—"Never to relax in keeping yourself up to a high standard—in the determination, daily renewed, to be consistent, patient, courageous." It was a hard program, perhaps, for a young man of twenty-one; and yet something in it touched the depths of Albert's soul; he sighed, but he listened.

Before long, the decisive moment came. There was a general election, and it became certain that the Tories, at last, must come into power. The Queen disliked them as much as ever; but they now had a large majority in the House of Commons. They would now be in a position to insist upon their wishes being attended to. Lord Melbourne himself was the first to realize the importance of carrying out the inevitable transition with as little friction as possible; and with his consent, the Prince opened a negotiation with Sir Robert Peel. In a series of secret interviews, a complete understanding was reached upon the difficult and complex question of the bedchamber; and it was agreed that, on the formation of the Tory government, the principal Whig ladies should retire, and their places be filled by others appointed by Sir Robert. Thus, in effect, though not in form, the Crown abandoned the claims of 1839, and they have never been subsequently put forward.

The transaction was a turning point in the Prince's career. He had conducted an important negotiation with skill and tact; he had been brought into friendly relations with the new Prime Minister; it was obvious that a political future lay before him. Victoria was impressed and grateful. "My dearest Angel," she told King Leopold, "is indeed a great comfort to me." She was in need of all the comfort he could give her. Lord M. was going; and she could hardly bring herself to speak to Peel. Yes; she would discuss everything with Albert now!

Stockmar, who had returned to England, watched the departure of Lord Melbourne with satisfaction. If all went well, the Prince should now wield a supreme political influence over Victoria. But would all go well? An unexpected development frightened the baron. When the dreadful moment finally came, and the Queen, in anguish, bade adieu to her beloved minister, it was settled between them that, though it would be inadvisable to meet very often, they could continue to correspond.

Never were the inconsistencies of Lord Melbourne's character shown more clearly than in what followed. So long as he was in office, his attitude towards Peel had been irreproachable; he had done all he could to facilitate the change of government. Yet no sooner was he in opposition than his heart failed him. He could not bear the thought of surrendering altogether the privilege and the pleasure of giving counsel to Victoria. Though he had declared that he would be perfectly discreet in his letters, he could not resist taking advantage of the opening they afforded. He discussed various public questions, and, in particular, gave the Queen a great deal of advice about appointments. This advice was followed.

Stockmar was much alarmed. He wrote a memorandum, pointing out the unconstitutional nature of Lord Melbourne's proceedings and the unpleasant position in which the Queen might find herself if they were discovered by Peel; and he instructed Anson, the Prince's secretary, to take this memorandum to the ex-minister. Lord Melbourne, lounging on a sofa, read it through with compressed lips. "This is quite an apple-pie opinion," he said. When Anson ventured to expostulate further, he lost his temper. "God eternally damn it!" he exclaimed, leaping up from his sofa. "Flesh and blood cannot stand this!" And two more violent bombardments from the baron were needed before he was brought to reason. Then, gradually, his letters grew less frequent, with fewer references to public concerns; at last, they were entirely innocuous. The baron smiled; Lord M. had accepted the inevitable.

The Whig ministry resigned in September 1841; but more than a year was to elapse before another momentous change was effected—the removal of Lehzen. For, in the end, the mysterious governess was conquered.

The steps are unknown by which Victoria was at last led to accept her withdrawal with composure; but it is clear that Albert's domestic position must have been greatly strengthened by the appearance of children. The birth of the Princess Royal had been followed in November 1841 by that of the Prince of Wales; and before very long another baby was expected. The baroness, with all her affection, could have but a remote share in such family delights. She lost ground perceptibly. It was noticed as a phenomenon that, once or twice, when the court traveled, she was left behind at Windsor.

Still the Prince was cautious; but time was for him; every day his predominance grew; and at length he perceived that he need hesitate no longer—that every wish of his had only to be expressed to be at once Victoria's. He spoke, and Lehzen vanished forever. Returning to her native Hanover she established herself in a small but comfortable house, the walls of which were entirely covered by portraits of Her Majesty. The baron, in spite of his dyspepsia, smiled again: Albert was supreme.

THE EARLY DISCORDS had passed away completely—resolved into the absolute harmony of married life. Victoria had surrendered her whole soul to her husband. The beauty and the charm which so suddenly had made her his at first were, she now saw, no more than the outward manifestation of the true Albert. There was an inward beauty, an inward glory which, blind that she was, she had then but dimly apprehended, of which now she was aware in every fiber of her being—he was good—he was great!

How could she ever have dreamed of setting up her will against his wisdom, her fancies against his perfect taste? Had she really loved London and late hours and dissipation? She who now was only happy in the country, she who jumped out of bed every morning—oh, so early!—with Albert, to take a walk, before breakfast, with Albert alone! How wonderful it was to be taught by him! To be told by him which trees were which; and to learn all about the bees! And then to sit doing cross-stitch while he read aloud to her Hallam's *Constitutional History of England*! Or to listen to him playing on his new organ! And, after dinner, too—oh, how good of him! He had given up his double chess! And so there could be round games at the round table, or everyone could spend the evening in the most amusing way imaginable—spinning counters and rings.

When the babies came it was still more wonderful. Pussy was such a clever little girl ("I am not Pussy! I am the Princess Royal!" she had angrily exclaimed on one occasion); and Bertie —well, she could only pray *most* fervently that the little Prince of Wales would grow up to "resemble his angelic dearest Father in *every*, *every* respect, both in body and mind." Her dear Mamma, too, had been drawn once more into the family circle, for Albert had brought about a reconciliation. In Victoria's eyes, life had become an idyll of happiness, love and simplicity. "Albert brought in dearest little Pussy," wrote Her Majesty in her journal, "in such a smart white merino dress trimmed with blue, which Mamma had given her, and a pretty cap, and placed her on my bed, seating himself next to her, and she was very dear and good. And, as my precious, invaluable Albert sat there, and our little Love between us, I felt quite moved with happiness and gratitude to God."

Happy as she was, she wanted everyone to know it. Her letters to King Leopold are sprinkled thick with raptures. "Oh! my dearest uncle, I am sure if you knew *how* happy, how blessed I feel, and how *proud* I feel in possessing *such* a perfect being as my husband. . . ." Such ecstasies gushed from her pen unceasingly.

But this new happiness was no lotus dream. On the contrary, it was bracing, rather than relaxing. She worked more methodically than ever at the business of state; she watched over her children with untiring vigilance. She carried on a large correspondence; she was occupied with her farm—her dairy—a multitude of household avocations—from morning till night. Her active, eager little body hurrying with quick steps after the long strides of Albert down the corridors of Windsor seemed the very expression of her spirit. But amid all the softness, the deliciousness of unmixed joy, her native rigidity remained. "A vein of iron," said Lady Lyttelton, who, as royal governess, had good means of observation, "runs through her most extraordinary character."

Sometimes the delightful routine of domestic existence had to be interrupted. It was necessary to exchange Windsor for Buckingham Palace, to open Parliament, to interview official personages, or, occasionally, to entertain foreign visitors. Then the quiet court put on a sudden magnificence, and sovereigns from over the seas—Louis Philippe, or the King of Prussia, or the King of Saxony—found at Windsor an entertainment that was indeed a royal one. Few spectacles in Europe, it was agreed, produced an effect so imposing as the great Waterloo banqueting hall, crowded with guests in sparkling diamonds and blazing uniforms. But, in that wealth of splendor, the most imposing spectacle of all was the Queen. The little *hausfrau*, who had spent the day walking with her children and inspecting the livestock, suddenly shone forth, by a spontaneous transition, the very culmination of majesty. The Tsar of Russia himself was deeply impressed. Victoria on her side viewed with secret awe the tremendous Nicholas. "A great event and a great compliment *his* visit certainly is," she told her uncle. "He is certainly a *very striking* man; still very handsome. But the expression of the *eyes* is *formidable*, and unlike anything I ever saw before."

When the time came for returning some of these visits, the royal pair set forth in their yacht. "I do love a ship!" Victoria exclaimed, running up and down ladders and cracking jokes with the sailors. She and Prince Albert visited Louis Philippe at the Château d'Eu and they visited King Leopold in Brussels.

Another year, Germany was visited, and Albert displayed the beauties of his home. When Victoria crossed the frontier, she was much excited—and astonished as well. "To hear the people speak German," she noted in her diary, "and to see the German soldiers, etc., seemed to me so singular." Having recovered from this slight shock, she found the country charming. She was feted everywhere, and pretty groups of peasant children presented her with bunches of flowers. The principality of Coburg with its romantic scenery particularly delighted her; and when she woke up one morning to find herself in "dear Rosenau, my Albert's birthplace," it was "like a beautiful dream."

THE HUSBAND was not so happy as the wife. In spite of the great improvement in his situation, in spite of a growing family and the adoration of Victoria, Albert was still a stranger in a strange land, and the serenity of spiritual satisfaction was denied him.

It was something, no doubt, to have dominated his immediate environment; but it was not enough. Victoria idolized him; but it was understanding that he craved for, not idolatry; and how much did Victoria, filled to the brim though she was with him, understand him? How much does the bucket understand the well? He was lonely. He went to his organ and improvised with modulations until the sounds, swelling and subsiding, brought some solace to his heart. Then, with the elasticity of youth, he hurried off to play with the babies, or to design a new pigsty, or to read aloud the *Church History of Scotland* to Victoria, or to pirouette before her on one toe, like a ballet dancer, with a fixed smile, to show her how she ought to behave when she appeared in public places. Thus did he amuse himself; but there was one distraction in which he did not indulge. He never flirted—no, not with the prettiest ladies of the court. Throughout their married life no rival female charms ever had cause to give Victoria one moment's pang of jealousy.

What more and more absorbed him—bringing with it a comfort of its own—was his work. With the advent of Peel, he began to intervene actively in the affairs of the state. In more ways than one—in the cast of their intelligence, in their moral earnestness—the two men resembled each other; there was a sympathy between them; and thus Peel was ready enough to urge the Prince forward into public life.

A royal commission was about to be formed to inquire whether advantage might not be taken of the rebuilding of the Houses of Parliament to encourage the fine arts in the United Kingdom; and Peel, with great perspicacity, asked the Prince to preside over it. The work was of a kind which precisely suited Albert: his love of art, his love of method—it satisfied them both; and he threw himself into it *con amore*. Some of the members of the commission were somewhat alarmed when, in his opening speech, he pointed out the necessity of dividing the subjects to be considered into "categories"—the word, they thought, smacked dangerously of German metaphysics; but their confidence returned when they observed His Royal Highness's extraordinary technical acquaintance with the processes of fresco painting. When the question arose as to whether the decorations upon the walls of the new buildings should, or should not, have a moral purpose, the Prince spoke strongly for the affirmative, and the commission was convinced. The frescoes were carried out, but unfortunately before very long they became totally invisible. It seems that His Royal Highness's technical acquaintance with the processes of fresco painting was incomplete.

The next task upon which the Prince embarked was a more arduous one: he determined to reform the organization of the royal household. This reform had been long overdue. For years past the confusion and extravagance in the royal residences, and in Buckingham Palace particularly, had been scandalous; no reform had been practicable under the rule of the baroness; but her functions had now devolved upon the Prince, and in 1844, he boldly attacked the problem.

Three years earlier, Stockmar, after careful inquiry, had revealed in a memorandum an extraordinary state of affairs. The control of the household, it appeared, was divided in the strangest manner between a number of authorities, each independent of the other. Of these authorities, the most prominent

were the lord steward and the lord chamberlain—noblemen of political importance, who changed office with every administration. The distribution of their respective functions was uncertain and peculiar. In Buckingham Palace, it was believed that the lord chamberlain had charge of the whole of the rooms, with the exception of the kitchen, sculleries, and pantries, which were claimed by the lord steward. At the same time, the outside of the palace was under the control of neither of these functionaries—but of the Office of Woods and Forests; and thus, while the insides of the windows were cleaned by the department of the lord chamberlain—or possibly, in certain cases, by the department of the lord steward—the Office of Woods and Forests cleaned their outsides.

Of the servants, the housekeepers, pages, and housemaids were under the authority of the lord chamberlain; the cooks and porters were under that of the lord steward; but the footmen and underbutlers took their orders from yet another official—the master of the horse. Naturally, in these circumstances the service was extremely defective. The Queen once observed that there was never a fire in the dining room. She inquired why. The answer was, "The lord steward lays the fire, and the lord chamberlain lights it"; the underlings of those two great noblemen having failed to come to an accommodation, there was no help for it—the Queen must eat in the cold. As for Her Majesty's guests, there was nobody to show them to their rooms, and they were often left to wander helpless by the hour in the palace's complicated passages.

A surprising incident opened everyone's eyes to the confusion and negligence that reigned in the palace. A fortnight after the birth of the Princess Royal the nurse heard a suspicious noise in the room next to the Queen's bedroom. She called to one of the pages, who, looking under a large sofa, perceived there a crouching figure "with a most repulsive appearance." It was "the boy Jones." This enigmatical personage, whose escapades dominated the newspapers for several ensuing months, was an undersized lad of seventeen, the son of a tailor, who had apparently gained admittance to the palace by climbing over the garden wall. He declared that he had spent three days in the palace, hiding under various beds, that he had "helped himself to soup and other eatables," and that he had "sat upon the throne, seen the Queen, and heard the Princess Royal squall." His motives remained ambiguous, and he was sent for three months to the House of Correction. When he emerged, he immediately returned to Buckingham Palace. He was discovered, and sent back to the House of Correction for another three months. When he was found yet once again loitering round the palace, the authorities shipped him off to sea. So he passes at last out of history.

But discomfort and alarm were not the only results of the mismanagement of the household; the waste and extravagance that also flowed from it were immeasurable. There were preposterous malpractices of every kind. It was, for instance, an ancient rule that a candle that had once been lighted should never be lighted again; what happened to the old candles, nobody knew. Again, the Prince, examining accounts, was puzzled by a weekly expenditure of thirty-five shillings on "Red Room Wine."

Inquiring into the matter, he discovered that in the time of George III a room in Windsor Castle with red hangings had been used as a guardroom, and that five shillings a day had been allowed to provide wine for the officers. The guard had long since been moved elsewhere, but the payment for wine continued, the money being received by a half-pay officer who held the position of underbutler.

After much laborious investigation, and a stiff struggle with a multitude of vested interests, the Prince succeeded in effecting a complete reform. The various conflicting authorities were induced to resign their powers into the hands of a single official, the master of the household; great economies were made, and the whole crowd of venerable abuses was swept away. There were outcries and complaints; but the Prince held on his course, and before long the admirable administration of the royal household was recognized as a convincing proof of his perseverance and capacity.

At the same time his activity was increasing enormously in a more important sphere. He had become the Queen's private secretary, her confidential adviser, her second self. He was now always present at her interviews with ministers. He took, like the Queen, a special interest in foreign policy; but there was no public question in which his influence was not felt. Nobody anymore could call him a dilettante; he was a worker, a public personage. Stockmar noted the change with exultation. "The Prince," he wrote, "has improved very much lately. His mental activity is constantly on the increase, and he gives the greater part of his time to business, without complaining. . . . The relations between husband and wife," he added, "are all one could desire."

Long before Peel's ministry came to an end, there had been a complete change in Victoria's attitude towards him. Peel's appreciation of the Prince had softened her heart; she spoke now of "our worthy Peel," for whom, she said, she had "an *extreme* admiration"; and she dreaded his removal from office almost as frantically as she had once dreaded that of Lord M. It would be, she declared, a *great calamity*.

Six years before, what would she have said if a prophet had told her that the day would come when she would be horrified by the triumph of the Whigs? Yet there was no escaping it; she had to face the return of her old friends. In the ministerial crises of 1845 and 1846, the Prince played a dominating part. Everybody recognized that he was the real center of the negotiations —the actual controller of the forces and the functions of the Crown. The process by which this result was reached had been so gradual as to be almost imperceptible; but it may be said with certainty that, by the close of Peel's administration, Albert had become, in effect, the King of England.

WITH THE FINAL emergence of the Prince came the final extinction of Lord Melbourne. A year after his loss of office, he had been struck down by a paralytic seizure; he had apparently recovered, but his old elasticity had gone forever. Moody, restless, and unhappy, he wandered like a ghost about the town, bursting into soliloquies in public places, or suddenly asking odd questions. "I'll be hanged if I'll do it for you, my lord," he was heard to say in the hall at Brooks's, standing by himself, and addressing the air. Sitting at home, brooding in miserable solitude, he turned to his books—his classics and his Testaments—but they brought him no comfort. He longed for the past, for the impossible, for he knew not what; his friends had left him, and no wonder, he said in bitterness—the fire was out. His correspondence with the Queen continued, and he appeared from time to time at court; but he was a mere simulacrum of his former self; "the dream," wrote Victoria, "is *past*." She was kind to him, writing him long letters, and always remembering his birthday; but it was kindness at a distance, and he knew it. He had become "poor Lord Melbourne." The Whigs ignored him now and the leadership of the party passed to Lord John Russell. When Lord John became Prime Minister, there was much politeness, but Lord Melbourne was not asked to join the cabinet; and he understood, at last, that that was the end.

For two years or more he lingered, sinking slowly into unconsciousness and imbecility. A few days before his death, Victoria, learning that there was no hope of his recovery, turned her mind for a little towards him. "You will grieve to hear," she told King Leopold, "that our good, dear, old friend Melbourne is dying. . . . One cannot forget how good and kind he was, and it brings back so many recollections to my mind, though God knows! I never wish that time back again."

She was in little danger. The tide of circumstance was flowing now with irresistible fullness towards a very different consummation. The seriousness of Albert, the claims of her children, the movement of the whole surrounding world, combined to urge her forward along the way of public and domestic duty. Her family steadily increased. Within eighteen months of the birth of the Prince of Wales the Princess Alice appeared, and a year later the Prince Alfred, and then the Princess Helena, and, two years afterwards, the Princess Louise; and still there were signs that the pretty row of royal infants was not complete.

The parents, more and more involved in family cares and family happiness, found the pomp of Windsor galling, and longing for some more intimate retreat, they purchased the estate of Osborne, in the Isle of Wight. Their skill and economy in financial matters had enabled them to lay aside a substantial sum of money; and they could afford not merely to buy the property but to build a new house for themselves and to furnish it at a cost of £200,000.

At Osborne, by the seashore, and among the woods which Albert had carefully planted, the royal family now spent every hour that could be snatched from Windsor and London. The public looked on with approval. A few aristocrats might sniff or titter; but with the nation at large the Queen was once more extremely popular. The middle classes in particular were pleased. They liked a love match; they liked a household which combined royalty and virtue, and in which they seemed to see, reflected as in some resplendent looking glass, the ideal image of the very lives they led themselves.

It was indeed a model court. Not only were its central personages the patterns of propriety, but no breath of scandal, no shadow of indecorum, might approach it. For Victoria, with all the zeal of a convert, upheld now the standard of moral purity with an inflexibility surpassing, if that were possible, Albert's own. She had become the embodiment, the living apex of a new era in the generations of mankind. The last vestige of the eighteenth century had disappeared; cynicism and subtlety were shriveled into powder; and duty, industry, morality, and domesticity triumphed. The Victorian Age was in full swing.

ONLY ONE THING more was needed: material expression must be given to the new ideals and the new forces so that they might stand revealed, in visible glory, before the eyes of an astonished world. It was for Albert to supply this want. He mused, and was inspired: the Great Exhibition came into his head.

He thought out the details of his conception with care. There had been exhibitions before in the world, but this should surpass them all. It should contain specimens of what every country could produce in raw materials, in machinery and mechanical inventions, and in the applied and plastic arts. It should not be merely useful and ornamental; it should also be an international monument to peace, progress, and prosperity. Having matured his plans, the Prince summoned a small committee and laid an outline of his scheme before it. The committee approved, and the great undertaking was set on foot without delay.

Two years, however, passed before it was completed. The Prince labored with extraordinary energy, and at first all went smoothly. The leading manufacturers warmly took up the idea; the colonies were sympathetic; the great foreign nations were eager to send in their contributions; the support of Sir Robert Peel was obtained, and the use of a site in Hyde Park was sanctioned by the government. Out of 234 plans for the exhibition building, the Prince chose that of Joseph Paxton, famous as a designer of conservatories; and the work was on the point of being put in hand when suddenly opposition to the scheme, which had long been smoldering, burst forth.

There was an outcry, headed by *The Times*, against the use of the park for the exhibition; but, after a fierce debate in the House, the supporters of the site in the park won the day. Then it appeared that the project lacked sufficient financial backing; but this obstacle, too, was surmounted, and eventually £200,000 was subscribed as a guarantee fund. The enormous glass edifice rose higher and higher, covering acres and enclosing towering elm trees beneath its roof: and then the fury of its enemies reached a climax. It was pointed out that the exhibition would serve as a rallying point for all the ruffians in England; and that on the day of its opening there would certainly be a riot and probably a revolution. It was asserted that the glass roof was porous, and the droppings of fifty million sparrows would utterly destroy every object beneath it. Agitated nonconformists declared that the exhibition was an arrogant enterprise which would infallibly bring down God's punishment.

The Prince, with unyielding perseverance and infinite patience, pressed on to his goal. His health was seriously affected; he suffered from sleeplessness but he never relaxed. He toiled at committees, presided over meetings, and made speeches—and his efforts were rewarded. On May 1, 1851, the Great Exhibition was opened by the Queen before an enormous concourse of persons, amid scenes of dazzling brilliancy and triumphant enthusiasm.

Victoria herself was in a state of excitement which bordered on delirium. She performed her duties in a trance of joy, and, when it was all over, her feelings poured themselves out into her journal. The day had been an endless succession of glories—or rather one vast glory—one vast radiation of Albert. Her remembering pen rushed on from splendor to splendor—the huge crowds, so well behaved and loyal—flags of all the nations floating—the inside of the building, so immense, with myriads of people and the sun shining through the roof—a little side room, where we left our shawls—palm trees and machinery—dear Albert—the place so big that we could hardly hear the organ—a curious assemblage of distinguished men—God bless my dearest Albert, God bless my dearest country!—a glass fountain—Mr. Paxton, who might be justly proud, and rose from being a common gardener's boy—Sir George Grey in tears, and everybody astonished and delighted.

A striking incident occurred when, after a short prayer by the Archbishop of Canterbury, the choir of six hundred voices burst into the Hallelujah Chorus. At that moment a Chinaman, dressed in full national costume, stepped out into the nave and did obeisance to Her Majesty. The Queen, much impressed, had no doubt that he was an eminent mandarin; and, when the final procession was formed, orders were given that, as no representative of the Celestial Empire was present, he should be included in the diplomatic cortege. He subsequently disappeared, and it was rumored, among ill-natured people, that, far from being a mandarin, the fellow was a mere impostor. But nobody ever really discovered the nature of the comments that had been lurking behind that impassive yellow face.

A few days later Victoria poured out her heart to her uncle. The first of May, she said, was "the *greatest* day in our history, the most *beautiful* and *imposing* spectacle ever seen, and the triumph of my beloved Albert. . . . The triumph is *immense*."

It was. The enthusiasm was universal; even the bitterest scoffers were converted, and joined in the chorus of praise. The financial results were equally remarkable. The total profit made by the exhibition amounted to £165,000, which was employed in the purchase of land for the erection of a permanent national museum in South Kensington. During the six months of its existence in Hyde Park over six million persons visited it.

But there is an end to all things; and the time came for the

Crystal Palace to be removed to the seclusion of Sydenham. Victoria sadly paid her final visit. "It looked so beautiful," she said. "I could not believe it was the last time I was to see it. An organ, accompanied by a fine wind instrument called the sommerophone, was being played, and it nearly upset me."

When all was over, she expressed her boundless satisfaction in a dithyrambic letter to the Prime Minister. Her beloved husband's name, she said, was forever immortalized, and this to her was a source of immense happiness and gratitude. "She feels grateful to Providence," Her Majesty concluded, "to have permitted her to be united to so great, so noble, so excellent a Prince, and this year will ever remain the proudest and happiest in her life."

CHAPTER 5
Lord Palmerston

IN 1851 THE PRINCE'S fortunes reached their high-water mark. The success of the Great Exhibition enormously increased his reputation. But meanwhile his unpopularity in high society had not diminished. For a moment, LORD PALMERSTON   indeed, it had appeared as if the dislike of the upper classes was about to be converted into cordiality; for they had learned with amazement that the Prince, during a country visit, had ridden to hounds and acquitted himself remarkably well. They had always taken it for granted that his horsemanship was of some second-rate foreign quality, and here he was jumping five-barred gates and tearing after the fox as if he had been born and bred in Leicestershire. They could hardly believe it; was it possible that Albert was a good fellow after all?

Had he wished to be thought so he would certainly have seized this opportunity, purchased several hunters and used them. But hunting bored him. He continued, as before, to ride, as he himself put it, for exercise or convenience, not for amusement; and it was agreed that though the Prince, no doubt, could keep in his saddle well enough, he was no sportsman.

This was a serious matter. It was not merely that Albert was laughed at and thought unfashionable by fine ladies and gentlemen. The Prince, in a word, was un-English. What that word precisely meant it was difficult to say; but the fact was patent to every eye. Lord Palmerston, also, was not fashionable; the Whig aristocrats looked askance at him, and only tolerated him as an unpleasant necessity. But Lord Palmerston was English through and through—the very antithesis of the Prince.

By a curious chance it was to happen that this typical Englishman was to be brought into closer contact than any other of his countrymen with the alien from over the sea. Differences which, in more fortunate circumstances, might have been smoothed away, became accentuated to the highest pitch. All the mysterious forces in Albert's soul leaped out to do battle with this adversary, and, in the long violent conflict that followed, it almost seemed as if he was struggling with England herself.

Palmerston's whole life had been spent in the government of the country. His reputation had steadily grown, and when, in 1846, he became Foreign Secretary for the third time, his position in the country was almost, if not quite, on an equality with that of the Prime Minister, Lord John Russell. He was a tall man of sixty-two, with a jaunty air, a large face, dyed whiskers, and a long sardonic upper lip. Powerful, experienced, and supremely self-confident, he naturally paid very little attention to Albert. Why should he? The Prince was interested in foreign affairs? Very well, then, let the Prince pay attention to *him*, who had been a cabinet minister when Albert was in the cradle. Not that he wanted the Prince's attention—far from it: so far as he could see, Albert was merely a young foreigner whose only claim to distinction was that he had married the Queen of England.

This estimate, as he found out to his cost, was a mistaken one. Albert was by no means insignificant, and, behind Albert, there was another figure by no means insignificant either—there was Stockmar.

But Palmerston, busy, brushed all such considerations on one side; it was his favorite method of action. He lived by instinct— by a quick eye and a strong hand, a dexterous management of every crisis as it arose. He was very bold; and nothing gave him more exhilaration than to steer the ship of state in a high wind, on a rough sea, with every stitch of canvas on her that she could carry. When he saw that the case demanded it, he could go slow—very slow; but when he decided to go quick, nobody went quicker.

His immense popularity was the result partly of his diplomatic successes, partly of his extraordinary affability, but chiefly of the genuine intensity with which he responded to the feelings and supported the interests of his countrymen. The public knew that it had in Lord Palmerston not only a high-mettled master, but also a devoted servant. When he was Prime Minister, he noticed that iron hurdles had been put up on the grass in the Green Park; he immediately wrote to the minister responsible, ordering their instant removal, declaring that the purpose of the grass was "to be walked upon freely and without restraint by the people, old and young, for whose enjoyment the parks are maintained." It was in this spirit that, as Foreign Secretary, he watched over the interests of Englishmen abroad.

Nothing could be more agreeable for Englishmen; but foreign governments were less pleased. They found Lord Palmerston interfering and exasperating. In Paris they spoke of *ce terrible milord Palmerston;* and in Germany they made a little song—

> *Hat der Teufel einen Sohn,*
> *So ist er sicher Palmerston.*

> [If the Devil had a son
> Surely he'd be Palmerston.]

But their complaints were in vain; Palmerston, with his upper lip sardonically curving, braved consequences, and held on his course.

In 1848, in that year of revolutions, when, in all directions and with alarming frequency, crowns kept rolling off royal heads, Albert and Victoria were appalled to find that the policy of England was persistently directed—in Germany, in Switzerland, in Austria, in Italy, in Sicily—so as to favor the insurgent forces. The situation, indeed, was just such a one as the soul of Palmerston loved. There was danger and excitement, the oppor-

tunity for action, on every hand. He had an English gentleman's
deep contempt for foreign potentates, and the spectacle of the
popular uprisings, and of the oppressors bundled ignominiously
out of their palaces, gave him unbounded pleasure. He was
determined that there should be no doubt whatever, all over the
Continent, on which side in the great struggle England stood.
It was not that he had the slightest tincture in him of radicalism;
he was quite content to be inconsistent—to be a Conservative
at home and a Liberal abroad. There were very good reasons for
keeping the Irish in their places; but when he read an account
of the political prisons in Naples his gorge rose. He did not want
war; but he saw that without war a skillful and determined use
of England's power might do much to further the cause of the
Liberals in Europe. It was a difficult and a hazardous game to
play, but he set about playing it with delighted alacrity.

And then, to his intense annoyance, just as he needed all his
nerve and all possible freedom of action, he found himself being
hampered and distracted at every turn by . . . those people at
Osborne.

He saw what it was; the opposition was systematic, and the
Queen alone would have been incapable of it; the Prince was at
the bottom of it. It was exceedingly vexatious; but Palmerston
was in a hurry; the Prince, if he insisted upon interfering, must
be brushed on one side.

Albert was very angry. He highly disapproved of Palmerston's
policy. He was opposed to absolutism; but in his opinion Palmerston's proceedings were simply calculated to substitute for
absolutism, all over Europe, something worse—mob violence.
The dangers of this revolutionary ferment were grave; even in
England Chartism* was rampant—a sinister movement, which
might at any moment upset the constitution and abolish the
monarchy. Surely, with such dangers at home, this was a very
bad time to choose for encouraging lawlessness abroad. He
naturally took a particular interest in Germany. Having considered the question of Germany's future from every point of

* A workingmen's reform movement (1838–1848) which advocated universal
manhood suffrage and other political reforms. (Editors' note.)

92

view, he came to the conclusion, under Stockmar's guidance, that the great aim for every lover of Germany should be her unification under Prussia. The intricacy of the situation was extreme; yet he saw with horror that Palmerston neither understood nor cared to understand the niceties of the problem, but rushed on blindly, dealing blows to right and left, quite—so far as he could see—without system or motive—except, indeed, a totally unreasonable distrust of the Prussian state.

But his disagreement with the details of Palmerston's policy was in reality merely a symptom of the fundamental differences between the characters of the two men. In Albert's eyes Palmerston was a coarse, reckless egotist, whose combined arrogance and ignorance must inevitably have their issue in folly and disaster. Nothing could be more antipathetic to him than a mind so strangely lacking in patience, in reflection, and in the habits of ratiocination. To him it was intolerable to think in a hurry, to act on instincts; everything must be done in due order, with careful premeditation; the premises of the position must first be established, and actions must be made in strict accordance with some well-defined principle. What did Palmerston know of economics, of science, of history? How much consideration had he devoted in his life to the general amelioration of the human race? Yet it is easy to imagine what might have been Palmerston's jaunty comment. "Ah! Your Royal Highness is busy with fine schemes and beneficent calculations. Well, as for me, I must say I'm quite satisfied with my morning's work—I've had the iron hurdles taken out of the Green Park."

The exasperating man, however, preferred to make no comment, and to proceed in smiling silence on his way. The process of "brushing on one side" very soon came into operation. Important Foreign Office dispatches were either submitted to the Queen so late that there was no time to correct them, or they were not submitted to her at all; or, having been submitted, and some passage in them being objected to, they were after all sent off in their original form.

The Queen complained; the Prince complained; both complained together. It was quite useless. Palmerston was most apologetic—could not understand how it had occurred—must give the clerks a wigging, and such a thing should never happen again. But, of course, it very soon happened again.

The royal remonstrances redoubled. Victoria, thoroughly aroused, imported into her protests a personal vehemence which those of Albert lacked. Did Lord Palmerston forget that she was Queen of England? How could she tolerate a state of affairs in which dispatches written in her name were sent abroad without her approval or even her knowledge? What could be more derogatory to her position than to be obliged to receive indignant letters from the crowned heads to whom those dispatches were addressed—letters which she did not know how to answer, since she so thoroughly agreed with them?

Summoning the Prime Minister, Lord John Russell, to her presence, she poured out her indignation, and afterwards, on the advice of Albert, noted down what had passed in a memorandum: "I said that I thought that Lord Palmerston often endangered the honour of England by taking a very prejudiced and one-sided view of a question; that his writings were as bitter as gall and did great harm, which Lord John entirely assented to, and that I often felt quite ill from anxiety."

Then she turned to her uncle. "The state of Germany," she wrote in a comprehensive review of the European situation, "is dreadful, and one does feel quite ashamed about that once so peaceful and happy country. In France a crisis also seems at hand. *What* a very bad figure we are cutting! Really it is quite immoral, with Ireland quivering in our grasp and ready to throw off her allegiance at any moment, for us to force Austria to give up her lawful possessions. What shall we say if Canada, Malta, etc., begin to trouble us? It hurts me terribly."

Lord John Russell's position grew more and more irksome. He did not approve of his colleague's treatment of the Queen. When he begged him to be more careful, he was met with the reply that 28,000 dispatches passed through the Foreign Office in a year; that, if every one of these were to be subjected to the royal criticism, the delay would be most serious; that, as it was, the time involved in submitting drafts to the meticulous examination of Prince Albert was almost too much for an overworked minister. These excuses would have impressed Lord John more favorably if he had not himself had to suffer from a similar neglect. As often as not Palmerston failed to communicate even to him the most important dispatches. The Foreign Secretary was becoming an almost independent power, swaying the policy of England on his own responsibility. On one occasion, in 1847, he had actually been upon the point of threatening to break off diplomatic relations with France without consulting either the cabinet or the Prime Minister.

Such incidents were constantly recurring. When this became known to the Prince, he saw that his opportunity had come. If he could only drive in to the utmost the wedge between the two statesmen, if he could only secure the alliance of Lord John Russell, then the suppression or the removal of Lord Palmerston would be almost certain to follow.

He set about the business with all the pertinacity of his nature. Both he and the Queen put every kind of pressure upon the Prime Minister. Lord John, attacked by his sovereign and ignored by his Foreign Secretary, led a miserable life. With the advent of the dreadful Schleswig-Holstein question—the most complex in the whole diplomatic history of Europe—his position, crushed between the upper and the nether millstones, grew positively unbearable. He became anxious above all things to get Palmerston out of the Foreign Office.

But then—supposing Palmerston refused to go?

In a memorandum made by the Prince, at about this time, of an interview between himself, the Queen, and the Prime Minister, we catch a curious glimpse of the states of mind of those three high personages—the anxiety and irritation of Lord John, the vehement acrimony of Victoria, and the reasonable animosity of Albert. At one point in the conversation Lord John observed that he believed the Foreign Secretary would consent to a change of offices; Lord Palmerston, he said, realized that he had lost the Queen's confidence—though only on public, and not on personal, grounds. But on that, the Prince noted, "The Queen interrupted Lord John by remarking that she distrusted him on *personal* grounds also, but I remarked that Lord Palmerston had seen rightly; that he had become disagreeable to the Queen, not on account of his person, but of his political doings—to which the Queen assented." Then the Prince suggested that there was a danger of the cabinet breaking up, and of Lord Palmerston returning to office as Prime Minister. But on that point Lord John was reassuring: he "thought Lord Palmerston too old to do much in the future (having passed his sixty-fifth year)." Eventually it was decided that nothing could be done for the present; but that the *utmost secrecy* must be observed; and so the conclave ended.

At last, in 1850, deliverance seemed to be at hand. There were signs that the public were growing weary of the alarums and excursions of Palmerston's diplomacy; and when his support of Don Pacifico, a British subject, in a quarrel with the Greek government, seemed to be about to involve the country in a war, a heavy cloud of distrust appeared to be gathering over his head. A motion directed against him in the House of Lords was passed. The question was next to be discussed in the House of Commons, where another adverse vote was not improbable, and would seal the doom of the minister.

Palmerston received the attack with complete nonchalance, and then, at the last possible moment, he struck. In a speech lasting over four hours, a speech of consummate art, he annihilated his enemies. The hostile motion was defeated, and Palmerston was once more the hero of the hour. Simultaneously, fate itself conspired to favor him. Sir Robert Peel was thrown from his horse and killed.

By this tragic chance, Palmerston saw the one rival great enough to cope with him removed from his path. He judged—and rightly—that he was the most popular man in England; and when Lord John revived the project of his exchanging the Foreign Office for some other position in the cabinet, he absolutely refused to stir.

Great was the disappointment of Albert; great was the indignation of Victoria. The Prince, perceiving that Palmerston was more firmly fixed in the saddle than ever, decided that something drastic must be done. Five months before, the prescient baron had drawn up, in case of emergency, a memorandum, which had been carefully placed in a pigeonhole. The emergency had now arisen, and the memorandum must be used. The Queen copied out the words of Stockmar, and sent them to the Prime Minister, requesting him to show her letter to Palmerston.

"She thinks it right," she wrote, "in order *to prevent any mistake* for the *future*, to explain *what it is she expects from her Foreign Secretary*. She requires: (1) That he will distinctly state what he proposed in a given case, in order that the Queen may know as distinctly to *what* she has given her Royal sanction; (2) Having *once given* her sanction to a measure, that it be not arbitrarily altered or modified by the Minister; such an act she must consider as failing in sincerity towards the Crown, and justly to be visited by the exercise of her Constitutional right of dismissing that Minister." Lord John Russell forwarded the Queen's letter to Palmerston. This transaction, of grave constitutional significance, was entirely unknown to the outside world.

If Palmerston had been a sensitive man, he would probably have resigned on the receipt of the Queen's missive. But he was far from sensitive; he loved power, and his power was greater than ever. Nevertheless, he was seriously perturbed. He understood at last that he was struggling with a formidable adversary, whose skill and strength might do irreparable injury to his career. He therefore wrote to Lord John, acquiescing in the Queen's requirements—"I have taken a copy of this memorandum of the Queen and will not fail to attend to the directions which it contains"—and he asked for an interview with the Prince.

Albert at once summoned him to the palace, and was astonished to observe, as he noted in a memorandum, that when Palmerston entered the room "he was very much agitated, shook, and had tears in his eyes, so as quite to move me, who never under any circumstances had known him otherwise than with a bland smile on his face."

The old statesman was profuse in excuses; the young one was coldly polite. At last, after a long and inconclusive conversation, the Prince, drawing himself up, said that, in order to give Lord Palmerston "an example of what the Queen wanted," he would "ask him a question point-blank." Lord Palmerston waited in respectful silence, while the Prince proceeded to ask him what he would do if Holstein were to be attacked, as Schleswig had already been attacked by Denmark. "What will you do, if this emergency arises (provoking most likely an European war), and which will arise very probably when we shall be at Balmoral and Lord John in another part of Scotland?"

Strangely enough, to this point-blank question the Foreign Secretary appeared to be unable to reply; the whole matter, he said, was extremely complicated. For a full hour the Prince struggled to extract a categorical answer, until at length Palmerston bowed himself out of the room. Albert threw up his hands: what could one do with such a man?

What indeed? For, in spite of all his apologies, within weeks the incorrigible reprobate was at his tricks again.

The Austrian general, Baron Julius von Haynau, notorious as a suppressor of rebellion in Hungary and Italy, and in particular as a flogger of women, came to England and took it into his head to pay a visit to Messrs. Barclay and Perkins's brewery. The features of "General Hyena," as he was everywhere called —his grim thin face, his enormous pepper-and-salt mustaches— had gained a horrid celebrity; and it so happened that among the clerks at the brewery there was a refugee from Vienna, who had given his fellow workers a firsthand account of the general's characteristics. The Austrian ambassador, scenting danger, begged Haynau not to appear in public. But the general would take no advice. He went to the brewery, was recognized, surrounded by angry draymen, pushed about, shouted at, and pulled by the mustaches until, bolting down an alley with the mob at his heels, he managed to take refuge in a public house, whence he was removed, protected by several policemen.

The Austrian government was angry and demanded explanations. Palmerston, privately delighted by the incident, replied, regretting what had occurred, but adding that in his opinion the general had "evinced a want of propriety in coming to England at the present moment"; and he delivered his note to the ambassador without having previously submitted it to the Queen or to the Prime Minister. Naturally, when this was discovered, there was a serious storm. The Prince was especially indignant; the conduct of the draymen he regarded, with alarm, as "a foretaste of what an unregulated mass of illiterate people is capable"; and Palmerston was requested by Lord John to withdraw his note, and to substitute for it another omitting all censure of the general. The Foreign Secretary threatened resignation, but the Prime Minister was firm. For a moment the royal hopes rose high that Palmerston would actually resign, but they rose only to be dashed to the ground again. Palmerston, suddenly lamblike, agreed to everything; the note was withdrawn and altered, and peace was patched up once more.

It lasted for a year, and then, in October 1851, the arrival of Lajos Kossuth in England brought on another crisis. Palmerston's desire to receive the Hungarian patriot at his house in London was vetoed by Lord John; once more there was a sharp struggle; once more Palmerston yielded. But still the insubordinate man could not keep quiet. A few weeks later at the Foreign Office a deputation of Radicals from Finsbury and Islington presented him with an address, in which the emperors of Austria and Russia were stigmatized as "odious and detestable assassins." The Foreign Secretary in his reply, while mildly deprecating these words, allowed his real sentiments to appear with a most undiplomatic insouciance. There was an immediate scandal, and Victoria, in an agitated letter, urged Lord John to assert his authority. But Lord John perceived that on this matter the Foreign Secretary had the support of public opinion, and he judged it wiser to bide his time.

He had not long to wait. The culmination of the long series of conflicts came before the year was out. On December 2, Louis Napoleon's coup d'etat took place in Paris; and on the following day Palmerston, without consulting anybody, expressed in a conversation with the French ambassador his approval of Napoleon's act. Two days later, he was instructed by the Prime Minister, in accordance with a letter from the Queen, that it was the policy of the English government to maintain an attitude of strict neutrality towards the affairs of France. Nevertheless, in an official dispatch to the British ambassador in Paris, he repeated his approval of the coup d'etat. This dispatch was submitted neither to the Queen nor to the Prime Minister. Lord John's patience, as he himself said, "was drained to the last drop." He dismissed Lord Palmerston.

Victoria was in ecstasies; and Albert knew that the triumph

was his even more than Lord John's. It was his wish that Lord Granville, a young man whom he believed to be pliant to his influence, should be Palmerston's successor; and Lord Granville was appointed.

Henceforward, it seemed that the Prince would have his way in foreign affairs. After years of struggle and mortification, success greeted him on every hand. In his family, he was an adored master; in the country, the Great Exhibition had brought him respect and glory; and now in the secret seats of power he had gained a new supremacy. He had wrestled with the terrible Lord Palmerston and his redoubtable opponent had been overthrown. Was England herself at his feet? It might be so; and yet . . . it is said that the sons of England have a certain tiresome quality: they never know when they are beaten. It was odd, but Palmerston was positively still jaunty. Was it possible? Could he believe, in his arrogance, that even his ignominious dismissal from office was something that could be brushed aside?

THE PRINCE'S TRIUMPH was short-lived. A few weeks later, owing to Palmerston's influence, the government was defeated in the House, and Lord John resigned.

A coalition between the Whigs and the followers of Peel came into power, under the premiership of Lord Aberdeen. Once more, Palmerston was in the cabinet. It was true that he did not return to the Foreign Office; that was something to the good; in the Home Department it might be hoped that his activities would be less dangerous. But the Foreign Secretary was no longer the complacent Granville; and in Lord Clarendon the Prince knew that he had a minister who had a mind of his own.

These changes, however, were merely the preliminaries of a far more serious development. Events, on every side, were moving towards a catastrophe. Suddenly the nation found itself under the shadow of imminent war. For several months, amid the shifting mysteries of diplomacy, the issue grew more doubtful and more dark, while the national temper was strained to the breaking point. At the very crisis of the long and ominous negotiations, it was announced that Lord Palmerston had resigned.

The pent-up fury of the people burst forth. They had felt

that in the terrible complexity of events they were being guided by weak and embarrassed counsels; but they had been reassured by the knowledge that at the center of power there was one man with strength, with courage, whom they could trust. They now learned that that man was no longer among their leaders. The moment that Palmerston's resignation was known, there was a universal outcry, and an extraordinary tempest of anger burst, with unparalleled violence, upon the head of the Prince.

It was everywhere asserted that the Queen's husband was a traitor to the country, that he was a tool of the Russian court, that in obedience to Russian influences he had forced Palmerston out of the government, and that he was directing the foreign policy of England in the interests of England's enemies. For many weeks these accusations filled the press; repeated at public meetings, elaborated in private talk, they flew over the country, growing every moment more extreme and more improbable. The wildest rumors spread. In January it was even whispered that the Prince had been seized, that he had been found guilty of high treason, that he was to be committed to the Tower; and the Queen herself, some declared, had been arrested.

These fantastic hallucinations, the result of the fevered atmosphere of approaching war, were devoid of any basis in fact. Palmerston's resignation had been in all probability totally disconnected with foreign policy; it had been entirely spontaneous, and had surprised the Court as much as the nation. Nor had Albert's influence been used in any way to favor the interests of Russia. As often happens in such cases, the government had been swinging backwards and forwards between two incompatible policies—that of noninterference and that of threats supported by force—either of which, if consistently followed, might well have had a successful and peaceful issue, but which, mingled together, could only lead to war. Albert, with characteristic scrupulosity, attempted to thread his way through the complicated labyrinth of European diplomacy, and eventually was lost in the maze. But so was the whole of the cabinet; and, when war came, his anti-Russian feelings were quite as vehement as those of the most bellicose of Englishmen.

Nevertheless, though the charges leveled against the Prince

were without foundation, there were underlying elements in the situation which explained, if they did not justify, the popular state of mind. It was true that the Queen's husband was a foreigner, with foreign ideas and closely related to a multitude of foreign princes. The Prince's German proclivities were perpetually lamented by English ministers. But this was not all. A constitutional question of the most profound importance was raised by the position of the Prince in England. His presence gave a new prominence to an old problem—the precise definition of the functions and powers of the Crown. Those functions and powers had become, in effect, his; and what sort of use was he making of them?

His views as to the place of the Crown in the constitution are easily ascertainable, for they were Stockmar's; and it happens that we possess a detailed account of Stockmar's opinions upon the subject in a long letter addressed by him to the Prince at the time of this very crisis, just before the outbreak of the Crimean War. Constitutional monarchy, according to the baron, had suffered an eclipse since the passing of the Reform Bill. It was now "constantly in danger of becoming a pure Ministerial Government." To prevent this from happening, it was of extreme importance, said the baron, "that no opportunity should be let slip of vindicating the legitimate position of the Crown." In his opinion, the very lowest claim of the royal prerogative should include "a right on the part of the King to be the permanent President of his Ministerial Council." The sovereign ought to be "in the position of a permanent Premier, who takes rank above the temporary head of the Cabinet, and in matters of discipline exercises supreme authority."

Now it may be that this reading of the constitution is a possible one. But it is also clear that such a reading invests the Crown with more power than it possessed even under George III; it runs counter to the whole development of English public life since the Revolution. The fact that it was held by Stockmar, and instilled by him into Albert, was of serious importance. For there was good reason to believe not only that these doctrines were held by Albert in theory, but that he was making a deliberate, sustained attempt to give them practical validity. The history of the struggle between the Crown and Palmerston provided startling evidence that this was the case. That struggle reached its culmination when, in Stockmar's memorandum of 1850, the Queen asserted her "constitutional right" to dismiss the Foreign Secretary if he altered a dispatch which had received her sanction. The memorandum was, in fact, a plain declaration that the Crown intended to act independently of the Prime Minister; and Lord John Russell, anxious to strengthen himself against Palmerston, in accepting the memorandum, had implicitly allowed the claim of the Crown.

This new development in the position of the Crown, grave as it was in itself, was rendered peculiarly disquieting by the unusual circumstances which surrounded it. For the functions of the Crown were now, in effect, being exercised by a person unknown to the constitution, who wielded over the sovereign an undefined and unbounded influence. The fact that this person was the sovereign's husband, while it explained his influence, by no means diminished its strange and momentous import. An ambiguous, prepotent figure had come to disturb the ancient, subtle, and jealously guarded balance of the English constitution.

Such had been the unexpected outcome of the tentative and fainthearted opening of Albert's political life. Stockmar's pupil had assuredly gone far. Stockmar's pupil!—precisely; the public, painfully aware of Albert's predominance, had grown, too, uneasily conscious that Victoria's master had a master of his own. Deep in the darkness the baron loomed. Another foreigner! A foreign baron controlled a foreign Prince, and the foreign Prince controlled the Crown of England. And the Crown itself was creeping forward ominously; and when, from under its shadow, the baron and the Prince had frowned, a great minister, beloved of the people, had fallen. Where was all this to end?

Within a few weeks Palmerston withdrew his resignation, and the public frenzy subsided. When Parliament met, leaders in both the Houses made speeches in favor of the Prince. Immediately afterwards, the country finally plunged into the Crimean War. In the struggle that followed, Albert's patriotism was put beyond a doubt, and the animosities of the past were forgotten. But the war had another consequence, less gratifying to the royal couple: it crowned the ambition of Lord Palmerston. In 1855, the man who five years before had been pronounced by Lord John Russell to be "too old to do much in the future," became Prime Minister of England, and, with one short interval, remained in that position for ten years.

SIR JAMES CLARK

CHAPTER 6
Last Years of Prince Consort

THE WEAK-WILLED YOUTH who took no interest in politics and never read a newspaper had grown into a man of unbending determination whose energies were incessantly concentrated upon the business of government. He was busy now from morning till night. In the winter, before the dawn, he was to be seen, seated at his writing table, working by the light of the green reading lamp which he had brought over with him from Germany. Victoria was early too, but not so early as Albert; and when, in the chill darkness, she took her seat at her own writing table, placed side by side with his, she invariably found upon it a neat pile of papers arranged for her inspection and signature.

The day, thus begun, continued in unremitting industry. At breakfast, the newspapers—the once hated newspapers—appeared and the Prince would peruse them. After that there were ministers and secretaries to interview; there was correspondence to be carried on; there were memoranda to be made. Victoria, preserving every letter, was all breathless attention and eager obedience. Sometimes Albert would actually ask her advice, or consult her about his English: *"Lese recht aufmerksam, und sage wenn irgend ein Fehler ist."*—"Read this carefully and tell me if there is any mistake in it." Thus the absorbing hours passed by. Fewer and fewer grew the moments of recreation and exercise. The demands of society were narrowed down to the smallest limits. It was no longer a mere pleasure, it was a positive necessity, to go to bed early in order to be up and at work on the morrow betimes.

The exacting business of government, which became at last the dominating preoccupation for Albert, still left unimpaired his old tastes and interests; he remained devoted to art, to science, to philosophy; and a multitude of subsidiary activities showed how his energies increased as the demands upon them grew. For whenever duty called, the Prince was all alertness. With indefatigable perseverance he opened museums, laid the foundation stones of hospitals, or made speeches to the Royal Agricultural Society. The National Gallery particularly interested him; he drew up careful regulations for the arrangement of the pictures according to schools; and he attempted—though in vain—to have the whole collection transported to South Kensington.

As she watched him, her beloved Albert, Victoria, from the depth of her heart, felt certain that no other wife had ever had such a husband. His mind was apparently capable of everything, and she was hardly surprised to learn that he had made an important discovery for the conversion of sewage into agricultural manure. Filtration from below upwards, he explained, was the principle of the scheme. "All previous plans," he said, "would have cost millions; mine costs next to nothing." Unfortunately, owing to a slight miscalculation, the invention proved to be impracticable; but Albert's intelligence was unrebuffed, and he passed on, to plunge with his accustomed ardor into a prolonged study of lithography.

But naturally it was upon his children that his private interests and those of Victoria were concentrated most vigorously. The royal nurseries showed no sign of emptying. The birth of the Prince Arthur in 1850 was followed, three years later, by that of the Prince Leopold; and in 1857 the Princess Beatrice was born. A family of nine must be, in any circumstances, a grave responsibility; and the Prince realized to the full how much the high destinies of his offspring intensified the need of parental care. It was inevitable that he should believe profoundly in the importance of education; he himself had been the product of education; Stockmar had made him what he was; it was for him, in his turn, to be a Stockmar to the young creatures he had brought into the world. Victoria would assist him; a Stockmar,

no doubt, she could hardly be; but she could be perpetually vigilant, mingling strictness with her affection, and she could always set a good example.

These considerations, of course, applied preeminently to the education of the Prince of Wales, the future King of England. Albert set to work with a will. But, watching with Victoria the minutest details of the training of his children, he soon perceived, to his distress, that there was something unsatisfactory in the development of his eldest son. The Princess Royal was an extremely intelligent child; but Bertie, though he was good-humored and gentle, seemed to display a deep-seated repugnance to every form of mental exertion.

This was most regrettable, but the remedy was obvious: the parental efforts must be redoubled; instruction must be multiplied. More tutors were selected, the curriculum was revised, elaborate memoranda were drawn up. It was above all essential that there should be no slackness: "Work," said the Prince, "must be work." And work indeed it was. The boy grew up amid a ceaseless round of paradigms, syntactical exercises, dates, and genealogical tables. Constant notes flew backwards and forwards between the Prince, the Queen, and the tutors, with inquiries, reports of progress, and recommendations. It was, besides, vital that the heir to the throne should be protected from the slightest possibility of contamination from the outside world. The Prince of Wales might, occasionally, be allowed to invite sons of the nobility, boys of good character, to play with him in the garden of Buckingham Palace; but his father presided, with alarming precision, over their sports.

In short, every conceivable effort was made; yet, strange to say, the object of all this solicitude continued to be unsatisfactory—appeared, in fact, to be positively growing worse. It was certainly odd; the more lessons that Bertie had to do, the less he did them; and the more carefully he was guarded against frivolities, the more desirous of mere amusement he seemed to become. Albert was deeply grieved and Victoria was sometimes very angry; but grief and anger produced no more effect than supervision and timetables. The Prince of Wales, in spite of everything, grew up into manhood without the faintest sign of "adherence to and perseverance in the plan both of studies and life"—as one of the royal memoranda put it—which had been laid down with such extraordinary forethought by his father.

AGAINST THE INSIDIOUS worries of politics, and the boredom of society functions, Osborne had afforded a welcome refuge; but it soon appeared that even Osborne was too little removed from the world.

Ever since Victoria, together with Albert, had visited Scotland in the early years of her marriage, her heart was in the Highlands. She had returned to them a few years later, and her passion had grown. And how Albert enjoyed them too! His spirits rose quite wonderfully as soon as he found himself among the hills and conifers. "It is a happiness to see him," she wrote. "Oh! What can equal the beauties of nature!"

The Highlanders, too, were such astonishing people. "They never make difficulties," she noted, "but are cheerful, and happy, and merry, and ready to walk, and run, and do anything." She loved everything about them—their customs, their dress, even their musical instruments. "There were nine pipers at the castle," she wrote, after staying with Lord Breadalbane; "sometimes one and sometimes three played. They always played about breakfast time, again during the morning, at luncheon, and whenever we went in and out; again before dinner, and during most of dinner time. We both have become quite fond of the bagpipes."

It was quite impossible not to wish to return to such pleasures again and again; and in 1848 the Queen had taken a lease of Balmoral House, a small residence in the wilds of Aberdeenshire. Four years later she bought the place outright. Now she could be really happy every summer; now she could be simple and at ease; now she could be romantic every evening, and dote upon Albert, without a single distraction, all day long.

The diminutive scale of the house was in itself a charm. Nothing was more amusing than to find oneself living in two or three little sitting rooms, with the children crammed away upstairs, and the minister in attendance with only a tiny bedroom to do all his work in. And then to be able to run in and out of doors as one liked, and to sketch, and to walk, and to watch the red deer coming so surprisingly close!

Occasionally one could be more adventurous—one could go and stay for a night or two at the bothy at Alt-na-giuthasach—a mere couple of huts with "a wooden addition"—and only eleven people in the whole party! And there were mountains to be climbed and a cairn to be built in solemn pomp. "At last, when the cairn . . . was nearly completed, Albert climbed up to the top of it, and placed the last stone; after which three cheers were given. It was a gay, pretty, and touching sight." And in the evening there were sword dances and reels.

But Albert had determined to pull down the little old house, and to build in its place a castle of his own designing. With great ceremony a foundation stone for the new edifice was laid, and by 1855 it was habitable. Spacious, built of granite in the Scotch baronial style, with turrets, gables, and a tower a hundred feet high, the castle was skillfully arranged to command the finest views of the surrounding mountains and of the River Dee. Upon the interior decorations Albert and Victoria lavished all their care. The Balmoral tartan, in red and gray, designed by the Prince, and the Victoria tartan, with a white stripe, designed by the Queen, were to be seen in every room. Watercolor sketches by Victoria hung upon the walls, together with innumerable stags' antlers, and the head of a boar, which had been shot by Albert in Germany. In an alcove in the hall stood a life-sized statue of Albert in Highland dress.

Victoria declared that it was perfection. "Every year," she wrote, "my heart becomes more fixed in this dear paradise, and so much more so now, that *all* has become my dear Albert's *own* creation . . . and his great taste, and the impress of his dear hand, have been stamped everywhere."

And here, in very truth, her happiest days were passed. In afteryears, when she looked back upon them, a kind of glory, a radiance, seemed to glow about these golden hours. Each hallowed moment stood out clear, beautiful, eternally significant. Albert's stalkings—an evening walk when she lost her way—Vicky sitting down on a wasps' nest—with what intensity such things, and ten thousand like them, impressed themselves upon her! And how she flew to her journal to note them down! The news of the Duke of Wellington's death! What a moment—when, as she sat sketching by a loch in the hills, Lord Derby's letter had been brought to her, and she had learned that *"England's* pride, her glory, her hero, the greatest man she had ever produced, was no more!" And she filled a whole page of her diary with panegyrical regrets. "To *us* his loss is *irreparable....* To Albert he showed the greatest kindness.... Not an eye will be dry in the whole country."

These were serious thoughts; but they were soon succeeded by others hardly less moving—by events as impossible to forget. Without doubt, the most memorable, most delightful of all the moments were the expeditions—the rare, exciting expeditions up mountains, across rivers, through strange country, and lasting several days. With only two attendants—Grant and Brown—for servants, and with assumed names . . . it was more like something in a story than real life. "We had decided to call ourselves *Lord and Lady Churchill and party!* Brown once forgot this and called me 'Your Majesty' as I was getting into the carriage, and Grant on the box once called Albert 'Your Royal Highness,' which set us off laughing, but no one observed it."

Strong, vigorous, enthusiastic, bringing, so it seemed, good fortune with her—the Highlanders declared she had "a lucky foot"—she relished everything—the scrambles and the views and the rough inns with Brown and Grant waiting at table. She could have gone on for ever and ever, absolutely happy with Albert beside her and Brown at her pony's head. But the time came for turning homewards; alas! the time came for going back to England. She could hardly bear it; she sat disconsolate in her room and watched the snow falling. The last day! Oh! If only she could be snowed up!

THE CRIMEAN WAR brought new experiences, and most of them were pleasant ones. It was pleasant to be patriotic and pugnacious, to seek out appropriate prayers to be read in the churches, to have news of glorious victories, and to know oneself, more proudly than ever, the representative of England.

With that spontaneity of feeling which was so peculiarly her own, Victoria poured out her admiration, her pity, her love, upon her "dear soldiers." When she gave them their medals her exultation knew no bounds. "Noble fellows!" she wrote to the King of the Belgians. "I feel as if these were *my own children;* my heart beats for *them* as for my *nearest and dearest.* They were so touched, so pleased; many, I hear, cried—and they won't hear of giving up their medals to have their names engraved upon them for fear they should *not* receive the *identical one* put into *their hands by me,* which is quite touching. Several came by in a sadly mutilated state." She and they were at one. They felt that she had done them a splendid honor, and she, with perfect genuineness, shared their feeling.

Albert's attitude towards such things was different; there was an austerity in him which quite prohibited such expansions of emotion. And he had other things to occupy him. He was ceaselessly at work on the tremendous task of concluding the war. State papers, dispatches, memoranda, poured from him in an overwhelming stream. Between 1853 and 1857 fifty folio volumes were filled with the comments of his pen upon the Eastern question. Weary ministers staggered under the load of his advice; nor was it advice to be ignored. Again and again the Prince's suggestions, unheeded at first, were adopted under the stress of circumstances and found to be full of value. The enrollment of a foreign legion, the establishment of a depot for troops at Malta, the institution of periodical reports as to the condition of the army at Sevastopol—such were his achievements. He went further: in a lengthy memorandum he laid down the lines for a radical reform in the entire administration of the army. This was premature, but his proposal for "a camp of evolution" for troops proved to be the germ of Aldershot.*

Meanwhile Victoria had made a new friend: she had suddenly been captivated by Napoleon III. Her dislike of him had been strong at first; she considered that he was a disreputable adventurer who had usurped the throne of poor old Louis Philippe. For a long time, although he was her ally, she was unwilling to

---

* The largest and most complete military training center in the United Kingdom. (Editors' note.)

meet him; but at last a visit of the Emperor and Empress to England was arranged.

Directly he appeared at Windsor her heart began to soften. She was charmed by his quiet manners, his low, soft voice. There was something deep within her which responded vehemently to natures that offered a romantic contrast with her own. From behind the vast solidity of her conventionality, she peered out with a strange delicious pleasure at that unfamiliar, darkly glittering foreign object, moving so meteorically before her. And, to her surprise, where she had dreaded antagonisms, she discovered only sympathies. He was, she said, "so quiet, so simple, *naïf* even, so gentle, so full of tact. . . . There is something fascinating, melancholy, and engaging, which draws you to him." She observed that he rode "extremely well"; he danced "with great dignity and spirit." Above all, he listened to Albert with the most respectful attention; and afterwards was heard to declare that he had never met the Prince's equal. On one occasion, indeed—but only on one—he had seemed to grow slightly restive. In a diplomatic conversation, "I expatiated a little on the Holstein question," wrote the Prince in a memorandum, "which appeared to bore the Emperor as *'très compliquée.'* "

Victoria, too, became much attached to the Empress, whose looks she admired without a touch of jealousy. Eugénie, indeed, in the plenitude of her beauty, exquisitely dressed in Parisian crinolines which set off her tall and willowy figure, might well have caused some heartburning in the breast of her short, stout hostess, in her garish middle-class garments. But to Victoria it mattered nothing that her face turned red in the heat and that her purple porkpie hat was of last year's fashion, while Eugénie, cool and modish, floated in flounces by her side. Was she not Queen of England? True majesty was hers, and she knew it. More than once, when the two were together in public, it was the woman to whom, as it seemed, nature and art had given so little, who, by the sheer force of an inherent grandeur, threw her adorned and beautiful companion into the shade.

There were tears when the moment came for the guests to leave; but before long Victoria and Albert paid a return visit to France. There everything was very delightful, and Victoria

drove incognito through the streets of Paris in a "common bonnet," saw a play at Saint-Cloud, and, one evening, at a great party given in her honor at Versailles, talked to a distinguished-looking Prussian gentleman, whose name was Bismarck. Her rooms were furnished so much to her taste that she declared they gave her quite a home feeling—that, if her little dog were there, she should really imagine herself at home. Three days later her little dog barked a welcome to her as she entered the apartments. The Emperor himself had personally arranged the charming surprise. She returned to England more enchanted than ever.

The alliance prospered, and the war drew towards a conclusion. Queen Victoria rode about on horseback reviewing the troops. At last Sevastopol was captured. The news reached Balmoral late at night, and "in a few minutes Albert and all the gentlemen in every species of attire sallied forth, followed by all the servants, and gradually by all the population of the village, up to the top of the cairn." A bonfire was lighted, pipes were played, and guns were shot off. "About three-quarters of an hour after, Albert came down and said the scene had been wild and exciting beyond everything. The people had been drinking healths in whisky and were in great ecstasy." The "great ecstasy," perhaps, would be replaced by other feelings next morning; but at any rate the war was over.

AN UNEXPECTED CONSEQUENCE of the war was a complete change in the relations between the royal pair and Palmerston. The Prince and the minister drew together over their hostility to Russia, and thus it came about that when Victoria found it necessary to summon her old enemy to form an administration she did so without reluctance. The premiership, too, had a sobering effect upon Palmerston; he grew less impatient and dictatorial; considered with attention the suggestions of the Crown, and was, besides, genuinely impressed by the Prince's ability and knowledge. Friction, no doubt, there still occasionally was—especially with regard to Italy. Albert, theoretically the friend of constitutional government, distrusted Cavour, and was horrified by Garibaldi. Palmerston, on the other hand, was eager for Italian independence. The struggle was fierce;

nevertheless Palmerston's policy was carried through, and the vigorous sympathy of England became one of the decisive factors in the final achievement of Italian unity.

Towards the other European storm center, also, the Prince's attitude continued to be very different to that of Palmerston. Albert's great wish was for a united Germany under the leadership of a constitutional and virtuous Prussia; Palmerston did not think that there was much to be said for the scheme. But he took no particular interest in German politics, and was ready enough to agree to a proposal which was warmly supported by both the Prince and the Queen—that the royal houses of England and Prussia should be united by the marriage of the Princess Royal with the Prussian Crown Prince.

Accordingly, when the Princess was not yet fifteen, the Prince, a young man of twenty-four, came over on a visit to Balmoral, and the betrothal took place. Two years later, in 1857, the marriage was celebrated. At the last moment, however, it seemed that there might be a hitch. It was pointed out in Prussia that it was customary for princes of the blood royal to be married in Berlin, and it was suggested that there was no reason why the present case should be treated as an exception. When this reached the ears of Victoria, she was speechless with indignation. In a note, emphatic even for Her Majesty, she instructed the Foreign Secretary to tell the Prussian ambassador "not to *entertain* the possibility of such a question. . . . Whatever may be the usual practice of Prussian princes, it is not *every* day that one marries the eldest daughter of the Queen of England. The question must therefore be considered as settled."

It was, and the wedding took place in St. James's Chapel. There were great festivities—illuminations, state concerts, immense crowds. At Windsor a magnificent banquet was given to the bride and bridegroom in the Waterloo room. Victoria's feelings had been growing more and more emotional, and when the time came for the young couple to depart she very nearly broke down. "Poor dear child!" she wrote afterwards. "I clasped her in my arms and blessed her, and knew not what to say. I kissed good Fritz and pressed his hand again and again. He was unable to speak and the tears were in his eyes. I embraced them both again at the carriage door . . . The band struck up. General Schreckenstein was much affected."

Albert, as well as General Schreckenstein, was much affected. He was losing his favorite child, whose opening intelligence had already begun to display a marked resemblance to his own. An ironic fate had determined that the daughter who was taken from him should be sympathetic, clever, and interested in the arts and sciences, while not a single one of these qualities could be discovered in the son who remained.

Certainly the Prince of Wales did not take after his father. Victoria's prayer had been unanswered, and with each succeeding year this became more obvious. But Bertie's parents only redoubled their efforts: it still might not be too late to incline the young branch, by careful fastenings, to grow in the proper direction.

Everything was tried. The boy was sent on a continental tour with a picked body of tutors, but the results were unsatisfactory. At his father's request he kept a diary; on his return it was found to be distressingly meager. On his seventeenth birthday a memorandum was drawn up over the names of the Queen and the Prince informing their eldest son that he was now entering manhood, and directing him henceforward to perform the duties of a Christian gentleman.

"Life is composed of duties," said the memorandum, "and in the due, punctual and cheerful performance of them the true Christian, true soldier, and true gentleman is recognised. . . . A new sphere of life will open for you in which you will have to be taught what to do and what not to do, a subject requiring study more important than any in which you have hitherto been engaged." On receipt of the memorandum Bertie burst into tears. A year later he was sent to Oxford, where the greatest care was taken that he should not mix with the undergraduates. Yes, everything had been tried—everything . . . with one single exception. The experiment had never been made of letting Bertie enjoy himself. But why should it have been? "Life is composed of duties." What possible place could there be for enjoyment in the existence of a Prince of Wales?

The same year which deprived Albert of the Princess Royal

brought him another and a still more serious loss. The Baron Stockmar had paid his last visit to England. For twenty years, as he himself said in a letter to the King of the Belgians, he had performed "the laborious office of a paternal friend and trusted adviser" to the Prince and the Queen. He was seventy; he was tired; it was time to go.

The baron returned to his home in Coburg, exchanging, once for all, the momentous secrecies of European statecraft for the tittle-tattle of a provincial capital. In his chair by the fire he nodded now over old stories—not of emperors and generals—but of neighbors and relatives and the domestic adventures of long ago. Dyspepsia and depression still attacked him; but, looking back over his life, he was not dissatisfied. He had created the Prince—an indefatigable toiler, presiding, for the highest ends, over a great nation. But had the baron no misgivings? Did he never wonder whether, perhaps, he might have accomplished not too little but too much? Albert, certainly, seemed to be everything that Stockmar could have wished—virtuous, industrious, intelligent. And yet—why was it?—all was not well with the Prince. He was sick at heart.

For in spite of everything Albert had never reached happiness. His work, which at last he came to crave with an almost morbid appetite, was a solace and not a cure; the dragon of his dissatisfaction devoured with dark relish that ever growing tribute of laborious days and nights; but it was hungry still.

The causes of his melancholy were hidden, mysterious, unanalyzable perhaps. There were contradictions in his nature, which to some made him seem an inexplicable enigma: he was severe and gentle; he longed for affection and he was cold. He was lonely, not merely with the loneliness of exile but with the loneliness of conscious and unrecognized superiority. There was something that he wanted and that he could never get. What was it? Some absolute sympathy? Some extraordinary success?

Possibly he wanted a mixture of both. To dominate and to be understood! But he could see only too clearly how faint were the responses of his actual environment. Who could appreciate him in England? The gentle virtue of an inward excellence availed all too little. Doubtless he had made some slight impression: but how very far it was from the goal of his ambitions!

How feeble and futile his efforts seemed against the enormous coagulation of dullness, of folly, that confused him! England lumbered on, impervious and self-satisfied, in her old intolerable course. He threw himself across the path of the monster with rigid purpose and set teeth, but he was brushed aside. Yes! even Palmerston was still unconquered—was still there to afflict him with his jauntiness, his muddleheadedness, his utter lack of principle.

It was too much. Neither nature nor the baron had given him a sanguine spirit; the seeds of pessimism lodged within him and flourished. He

> *questioned things, and did not find*
> *One that would answer to his mind;*
> *And all the world appeared unkind.*

He believed that he was a failure and he began to despair.

Yet Stockmar had told him that he must "never relax," and he never would. He would go on, working and striving to the bitter end. His industry grew almost maniacal. Earlier and earlier was the green lamp lighted; more vast grew the correspondence. His very recreations became duties. He enjoyed himself by timetable and went deer-stalking with meticulous gusto—it was the right thing to do. The mechanism worked with astonishing efficiency, but it never rested and it was never oiled. The Prince would not relax; he had absorbed the doctrines of Stockmar too thoroughly.

Victoria noticed that her husband sometimes seemed to be depressed and overworked. She tried to cheer him up. Realizing uneasily that he was still regarded as a foreigner, she hoped that by conferring upon him the title of Prince Consort (1857) she would improve his position in the country. But unfortunately Albert remained as foreign as before; and as the years passed his dejection deepened.

She worked with him, she watched over him, she walked with him through the woods at Osborne. When his birthday came round, she took the greatest pains to choose him presents that he would really like. In 1858, when he was thirty-nine, she gave him "a picture of Beatrice, life-size in oil, by Horsley, a complete collection of photographic views of Gotha and the country round, and a paperweight of Balmoral granite and deers' teeth, designed by Vicky." Albert was of course delighted, and his merriment at the family gathering was more pronounced than ever; and yet . . . what was there that was wrong?

No doubt it was his health. He was wearing himself out; and his constitution, as Stockmar had perceived from the first, was ill adapted to meet serious strain. He constantly suffered from minor ailments, and his appearance in itself indicated infirmity. The handsome youth of twenty years since had grown into a sallow, tired-looking man, whose body, in its stoop and its loose fleshiness, betrayed the sedentary laborer, and whose head was quite bald on top. Unkind critics, who had once compared Albert to an operatic tenor, might have remarked that there was something of the butler about him now. Beside Victoria, he presented a painful contrast. She, too, was stout, but it was with the plumpness of a vigorous matron; and an eager vitality was everywhere visible in her bearing.

Suddenly, however, Victoria was reminded that there were other perils besides those of ill health. During a visit to Coburg in 1860, the Prince was nearly killed in a carriage accident. He escaped with cuts and bruises; but Victoria's alarm was extreme, though she concealed it. "It is when the Queen feels most deeply," she wrote afterwards, "that she always appears calmest, and she dared not allow herself to speak of what might have been, or even to admit to herself (and she dare not now) the entire danger, for her head would turn!"

Shortly afterwards the Queen underwent, for the first time in her life, the actual experience of close personal loss. Early in 1861, her mother, the Duchess of Kent, was taken ill, and in March she died. The event overwhelmed Victoria. With a morbid intensity, she filled her diary for pages with minute descriptions of her mother's last hours. The horror and the mystery of death—death, present and actual—seized upon her imagination. She tried to forget, but she could not. Her lamentations continued with a strange persistency. It was almost as if, by some mysterious and unconscious precognition, she realized that for her, in an especial manner, that grisly majesty had a dreadful dart in store.

For indeed, before the year was out, a far more terrible blow was to fall upon her. Albert, who had long been suffering from sleeplessness, went, on a cold and drenching day towards the end of November, to inspect the buildings for the new Military Academy at Sandhurst. On his return it was clear that exposure had seriously affected his health. He was attacked by rheumatism, his sleeplessness continued, and he complained that he felt thoroughly unwell.

Three days later a painful duty obliged him to visit Cambridge. The Prince of Wales, who had been placed at that university in the previous year, was behaving in such a manner that a parental visit and a parental admonition had become necessary. His father, suffering in mind and body, carried through his task; but on his return journey to Windsor he caught a serious chill.

During the next week he gradually grew more miserable; yet he continued to work. It so happened that at that very moment a grave diplomatic crisis had arisen. The Civil War had broken out in America, and it seemed as if England, owing to a violent quarrel with the northern states, was upon the point of being drawn into the conflict. A severe dispatch by Lord John Russell was submitted to the Queen; and the Prince perceived that, if it was sent off unaltered, war would be the almost inevitable consequence.

At seven o'clock on the morning of December 1, he rose from his bed, and with a quavering hand wrote a series of suggestions for altering the draft, by which its language might be softened, and a way left open for a peaceful solution of the question. These changes were accepted by the government, and war was averted. It was the Prince's last memorandum.

He had always declared that he viewed the prospect of death with equanimity. "I do not cling to life," he had once said to Victoria. "You do; but I set no store by it." And he had added: "I am sure, if I had a severe illness, I should give up at once. I have no tenacity of life."

He had judged correctly. Before he had been ill many days he told a friend that he was convinced he would not recover.

He sank and sank. Nevertheless, if his case had been properly treated from the first, he might conceivably have been saved; but the doctors failed to diagnose his symptoms; and it is noteworthy that his principal physician was Sir James Clark. When it was suggested that other advice should be taken, Sir James pooh-poohed the idea. But the illness grew worse. At last, after a fierce letter from Palmerston, Dr. Watson was sent for. Dr. Watson saw at once that he had come too late. The Prince was in the grip of typhoid fever. "I think that everything so far is satisfactory," said Sir James Clark.

The restlessness and the acute suffering of the earlier days gave place to a settled torpor and a deepening gloom. Once the patient asked for music—"a fine chorale at a distance"; and, a piano having been placed in the adjoining room, Princess Alice played on it some of Luther's hymns, after which the Prince repeated "Rock of Ages." Sometimes his mind wandered; sometimes the distant past came rushing upon him; he heard the birds in the early morning, and was at Rosenau again, a boy. Or Victoria would come and read to him, and then she would bend over him, and he would murmur *"liebes Frauchen"* and *"gutes Weibchen,"* stroking her cheek.

Her distress was great, but she was not seriously frightened. Buoyed up by her own abundant energies, she would not believe that Albert's might prove unequal to the strain. Only two days before the end, which was seen now to be almost inevitable by everyone about her, she wrote, full of confidence, to the King of the Belgians: "There is nothing to cause alarm." The Princess Alice tried to tell her the truth, but her hopefulness would not be daunted.

On the morning of December 14, Albert, just as she had expected, seemed to be better; perhaps the crisis was over. But in the course of the day there was a serious relapse. Then at last she allowed herself to see that she was standing on the edge of an appalling gulf. The whole family was summoned, and, one after another, the children took a silent farewell of their father. "It was a terrible moment," Victoria wrote in her diary, "but, thank God! I was able to command myself, and remained sitting by his side."

He murmured something, but she could not hear what it was; she thought he was speaking in French. Then all at once he began to arrange his hair, "just as he used to do when well and he was dressing." *"Es ist kleines Frauchen"*—"It is your dear little wife," she whispered to him; and he seemed to understand.

For a moment, towards evening, she went into another room, but was immediately called back. She saw at a glance that a ghastly change had taken place. As she knelt by the bed, he breathed deeply, breathed gently, breathed at last no more. His features became perfectly rigid; she shrieked one long wild shriek that rang through the terror-stricken castle—and understood that she had lost him forever.

BARON STOCKMAR

CHAPTER 7
Widowhood

THE DEATH of the Prince Consort was the central turning point in the history of Queen Victoria. She herself felt that her true life had ceased with her husband's, and that the remainder of her days upon earth was of a twilight nature—an epilogue. With Albert's death a veil descends. The sudden removal of the Prince was not merely a matter of overwhelming personal concern to Victoria; it was an event of national, of European importance. He was only forty-two, and ordinarily he might have been expected to live at least thirty years longer. Had he done so it can hardly be doubted that the whole development of the English polity would have been changed. Already at the time of his death he filled a unique place in English public life; and, as time went on, his influence would certainly have enormously increased. He was permanent; while politicians came and went, he would have been perpetually installed at the center of affairs. Who can doubt that by the end of the century, such a man, grown gray in the service of the nation, would have acquired an extraordinary prestige and power? If, in his youth, he had been able to pit the Crown against the mighty Palmerston and to come off with equal honors, of what might he not have been capable in his old age? What minister, however able, could have withstood the wisdom, the authority, of the venerable Prince?

One human being alone felt the full force of what had happened. The Baron Stockmar, by his fireside at Coburg, suddenly saw the tremendous fabric of his creation crash into ruin. Albert was gone, and he had lived in vain. Even in his blackest hypochondria he had never envisioned quite so miserable a catastrophe. He looked into the fire; he murmured that he was going where Albert was—that he would not be long. He shrank into himself. His children clustered round him and did their best to comfort him, but it was useless; the baron's heart was broken. He lingered for eighteen months, and then, with his pupil, explored the shadow and the dust.

WITH APPALLING SUDDENNESS Victoria had exchanged the serene radiance of happiness for the utter darkness of woe. In the first dreadful moments those about her feared that she might lose her reason, but the iron strain within her held firm, and in the intervals between the intense paroxysms of grief it was observed that the Queen was calm.

Yet there were moments when her anguish would brook no restraints. One day she sent for the Duchess of Sutherland, and, leading her to the Prince's room, fell prostrate before his clothes, weeping, while she adjured the duchess to tell her whether the beauty of Albert's character had ever been surpassed. At other times a feeling akin to indignation swept over her. "My *life* as a *happy* one is *ended!*" she wrote to the King of the Belgians. "The world is gone for *me!* . . . Oh! to be cut off in the prime of life—to see our pure, happy life CUT OFF at forty-two— when I *had* hoped with such instinctive certainty that God never *would* part us, and would let us grow old together—is *too awful,* too cruel!" The tone of outraged majesty seems to be discernible. Did she wonder in her heart of hearts how the Diety could have dared?

But all other emotions gave way before her overmastering determination to continue, absolutely unchanged, and for the rest of her life on earth, her reverence, her obedience, her idolatry. "I am anxious to repeat *one* thing," she told her uncle, "and *that one* is *my firm* resolve, my *irrevocable decision*, viz., that *his* wishes—*his* plans—about everything, *his* views about *every* thing are to be *my law!*"

At first, in the tumult of her distresses, she declared that she could not see her ministers. The Princess Alice, assisted by the keeper of the privy purse, Sir Charles Phipps, performed, to the best of her ability, the functions of an intermediary. After a few weeks, however, the cabinet, through Lord John Russell, ventured to warn the Queen that this could not continue.

She realized that they were right: Albert would have agreed with them; and so she sent for the Prime Minister. But when Lord Palmerston arrived at Osborne, in the pink of health, brisk, with his whiskers freshly dyed, and dressed in a brown overcoat, light gray trousers, and green gloves, he did not create a very good impression.

Nevertheless, she had grown attached to her old enemy, and the thought of a political change filled her with apprehension. The government, she knew, might fall at any moment; and therefore, six months after the death of the Prince, she took the unprecedented step of sending a private message to Lord Derby, the leader of the Opposition, to tell him that she was not in a fit state to undergo the anxiety of a change of government. If he turned the present ministers out of office, she said, it would be at the risk of sacrificing her life—or her reason. When this message reached Lord Derby he was considerably surprised. "Dear me!" was his cynical comment. "I didn't think she was so fond of them as *that*."

Though the violence of her perturbations gradually subsided, her cheerfulness did not return. For years, she continued in settled gloom. Her life became one of almost complete seclusion. Arrayed in thickest crepe, she passed dolefully from Windsor to Osborne, from Osborne to Balmoral. Refusing to take any part in the ceremonies of state, shutting herself off from the slightest intercourse with society, she became almost as unknown to her subjects as some potentate of the East. They might murmur, but she ignored them.

She was the devoted guardian of a sacred trust. Her place was in the inmost shrine of the house of mourning—where she alone had the right to enter. That, and that only was her glorious, her terrible duty.

So the years passed. Above all else, what she had to do was to make her own the master impulse of Albert's life—she must work, as he had worked, in the service of the country. That vast burden of toil which he had taken upon his shoulders it was now for her to bear.

She assumed the gigantic load; and naturally she staggered under it. While he had lived, she had worked, indeed, with conscientiousness; but it was work made easy by his care, his forethought, and his advice. The mere sound of his voice, asking her to sign a paper, had thrilled her. But now there was a hideous change.

Now there were no neat piles and docketings under the green lamp; now there were no simple explanations of difficult matters. She had her secretaries, no doubt: there were Sir Charles Phipps, and General Grey, and Sir Thomas Biddulph; and they did their best. But they were mere subordinates: the whole weight of responsibility rested upon her alone. For so it had to be. She would follow the Prince in all things. He had refused to delegate authority; he had examined into every detail with his own eyes; he had never signed a paper without having first, not merely read it, but made notes on it too. She would do the same. She sat from morning till night surrounded by huge heaps of dispatch boxes, reading and writing at her desk—at her desk, alas! which stood alone now in the room.

Within two years of Albert's death a violent disturbance in foreign politics put Victoria's faithfulness to a crucial test. The fearful Schleswig-Holstein dispute, which had been smoldering for more than a decade, showed signs of bursting out into conflagration. The complexity of the questions at issue was indescribable. "Only three people," said Palmerston, "have ever really understood the Schleswig-Holstein business—the Prince Consort, who is dead—a German professor, who has gone mad —and I, who have forgotten all about it."

But, though the Prince might be dead, had he not left a vice-regent behind him? Victoria threw herself into the seething embroilment, devoting hours daily to the study of the affair. But she had a clue through the labyrinth: whenever the question had been discussed, Albert, she recollected, had always taken the side of Prussia. Her course was clear. She became an ardent champion of the Prussian point of view.

She did not realize that the Prussia of the Prince's day was dead. A new Prussia, the Prussia of Bismarck, had been born; and Palmerston and Lord John wished to support Denmark against Prussia's claims. But opinion was sharply divided, not only in the country but in the cabinet. For eighteen months the controversy raged; while the Queen, with persistent vehemence, opposed the Prime Minister and the Foreign Secretary.

When at last the final crisis arose—when it seemed possible that England would join forces with Denmark in a war against Prussia—Victoria's agitation grew febrile in its intensity. She poured out upon her ministers a flood of appeals and protests. "The only chance of preserving peace for Europe," she wrote, "is by not assisting Denmark, who has brought this entirely upon herself. . . . The Queen suffers much, and her nerves are more and more totally shattered." In the end England did not go to war, and Denmark was left to her fate; but how far the attitude of the Queen contributed to this result it is impossible, with our present knowledge, to say. On the whole, however, it seems probable that the determining factor in the situation was the powerful peace party in the cabinet rather than the imperious pressure of Victoria.

It is, at any rate, certain that the Queen's enthusiasm for the sacred cause of peace was short-lived. Within a few months her eyes were opened to the true nature of Prussia, whose designs upon Austria were about to culminate in the Seven Weeks' War. Veering from one extreme to the other, she now urged her ministers to interfere by force of arms in support of Austria. But she urged in vain.

Her political activity, just as much as her social seclusion, was disapproved by the public. As the years passed, and the royal mourning remained as unrelieved as ever, the disapproval grew more severe. It was observed that the Queen's protracted privacy not only cast a gloom over society, and deprived the populace of its pageantry, but also exercised a highly deleterious effect upon the dressmaking, millinery, and hosiery trades. This latter consideration carried great weight.

At last, early in 1864, the rumor spread that Her Majesty was about to go out of mourning, and there was rejoicing in the newspapers; but unfortunately it turned out that the rumor was without foundation. Victoria, with her own hand, wrote a letter to *The Times* to say so. "This idea," she declared, "cannot be too explicitly contradicted. The Queen," the letter continued, "heartily appreciates the desire of her subjects to see her. . . . But there are other and higher duties than those of mere representation which are now thrown upon the Queen, alone and unassisted—duties which she cannot neglect without injury to the public service."

The justification might have been considered more cogent had it not been known that those "other and higher duties" emphasized by the Queen consisted for the most part of an attempt to counteract the foreign policy of Lord Palmerston and Lord John Russell. A large section—perhaps a majority—of the nation were violent partisans of Denmark in the Schleswig-Holstein quarrel; and Victoria's support of Prussia was widely denounced.

A wave of unpopularity, which reminded old observers of the period preceding the Queen's marriage more than twenty-five years before, was beginning to rise. The press was rude; Lord Ellenborough attacked the Queen in the House of Lords; there were curious whispers in high quarters that she had had thoughts of abdicating—whispers followed by regrets that she had not done so. Victoria, outraged and injured, felt that she was misunderstood. "Oh, how fearful it is," she herself wrote to Lord Granville, "to be suspected—uncheered—unguided and unadvised—and how alone the poor Queen feels!"

Nevertheless, suffer as she might, she was as resolute as ever. And so, when Schleswig-Holstein was forgotten, and even the image of the Prince had begun to grow dim in the fickle memories of men, as solitary watcher she remained immutably concentrated at her peculiar task. The world's hostility, steadily increasing, was confronted and outfaced by the impenetrable weeds of Victoria. It was not mere sorrow that kept her so strangely sequestered; it was devotion, self-immolation; it was the laborious legacy of love. Unceasingly the pen moved over the black-edged paper. The flesh might be weak, but that vast burden must be borne.

TO CARRY ON Albert's work—that was her first duty; but there was another, second only to that, yet nearer, if possible, to her heart—to impress the true nature of his genius and character upon the minds of her subjects. She realized that during his life he had not been properly appreciated; the full extent of his goodness had been necessarily concealed; but death had removed the need of barriers, and now her husband, in his magnificent entirety, should stand revealed to all.

She set to work methodically. She directed Sir Arthur Helps to bring out a collection of the Prince's speeches, and the weighty tome appeared in 1862. She commanded General Grey to write an account of the Prince's early years—from his birth to his marriage; General Grey obeyed, and the work was completed in 1866. But the principal part of the story was still untold, and Mr. Theodore Martin was forthwith instructed to write a complete biography of the Prince Consort. Mr. Martin labored for fourteen years. The first bulky volume was published in 1874; four others followed; and in 1880 the monumental work was finished.

Mr. Martin was rewarded by a knighthood; and yet it was sadly evident that neither Sir Theodore nor his predecessors had achieved the purpose which the Queen had in view. Sir Theodore and the others faithfully carried out the task which she had set them—faithfully put before the public the very image of Albert that filled her own mind. The fatal drawback was that the public did not find that image attractive.

Victoria's people refused, in spite of all her efforts, to rate her husband at his true worth; and Victoria herself, disappointed and chagrined, bore a grudge against them for this. She did not understand that the picture of an embodied perfection is distasteful to the majority of mankind. The cause of this is not so much an envy of the perfect being as a suspicion that he must be inhuman; and thus it happened that the public, when it saw

displayed for its admiration a figure resembling the sugary hero of a moral storybook rather than a fellow man of flesh and blood, turned away with a shrug and a flippant smile. But in this the public was the loser as well as Victoria. For in truth Albert was a far more interesting personage than the public dreamed. By a curious irony an impeccable waxwork was fixed by the Queen's love in the popular imagination, while the creature whom it represented—the real creature, so full of stress and torment, so mysterious, so unhappy and so very human—altogether disappeared.

WORDS AND BOOKS may be ambiguous memorials; but who can misinterpret the visible solidity of bronze and stone? At Frogmore, near Windsor, Victoria constructed, at the cost of £200,000, a vast mausoleum for herself and her husband. But that was a private and domestic monument, and the Queen desired that wherever her subjects might be gathered together they should be reminded of the Prince.

Her desire was gratified; all over the country—at Aberdeen, at Perth, and at Wolverhampton—statues of the Prince were erected. Nor did London lag behind. A month after the Prince's death a meeting was called together at the Mansion House to discuss schemes for honoring his memory. Opinions, however, were divided; was a statue or an institution to be preferred? Meanwhile a subscription was opened; a committee was appointed, and the Queen was consulted as to her wishes in the matter.

In the end it was agreed that a memorial hall should be erected, together with a statue of the Prince; and eminent architects were asked to prepare designs. The architect whose design was selected was Mr. George Gilbert Scott, whose industry had brought him to the head of his profession, and whose lifelong zeal for the Gothic style had given him a special prominence. "My idea in designing the memorial," he wrote, "was to erect a kind of ciborium to protect a statue of the Prince; and its special characteristic was that the ciborium was designed in some degree on the principles of the ancient shrines." At the Queen's request a site was chosen in Kensington Gardens as near as possible to that of the Great Exhibition; and in May 1864 the first sod was turned.

The work was long and complicated; a great number of workmen were employed, besides subsidiary sculptors, while at every stage sketches and models were submitted to Her Majesty, who criticized all the details with minute care and constantly suggested improvements.

After three years of toil the memorial was still far from completion, and Mr. Scott thought it advisable to give a dinner to the workmen to show "his appreciation of their skill and energy." "Two long tables," we are told, "constructed of scaffold planks, were arranged in the workshops, and covered with newspapers, for want of tablecloths. Upwards of eighty men sat down. Beef and mutton, plum pudding and cheese, and beer and gingerbeer were supplied in abundance."

Gradually the edifice approached completion. The one hundred and seventieth life-size figure in a frieze which encircled the base of the monument was chiseled, the granite pillars arose, four colossal statues representing the greater Christian virtues, and four other colossal statues representing the greater moral virtues, were hoisted into their positions; the eight bronzes representing the greater sciences—astronomy, chemistry, geology, geometry, rhetoric, medicine, philosophy, and physiology —were fixed on their glittering pinnacles, high in air; and, eight years after its inception, in July 1872, the monument was thrown open to the public.

But four more years were to elapse before the central figure was ready to be placed under its starry canopy. It was designed by Mr. John Henry Foley, though in one particular the sculptor's freedom was restricted by Mr. Scott. "I have chosen the sitting posture," Mr. Scott said, "as best conveying the idea of dignity befitting a royal personage." To identify the figure with one of the most memorable undertakings of the Prince's life—the International Exhibition of 1851—a catalogue of the works collected in that exhibition was placed in the right hand. The statue was of bronze gilt and weighed nearly ten tons. It was rightly supposed that the simple word "Albert," cast on the base, would be a sufficient means of identification.

CHAPTER 8
Mr. Gladstone and Lord Beaconsfield

LORD PALMERSTON'S LAUGH—a queer me-
tallic "Ha! ha! ha!" with reverberations in
it—was heard no more in Piccadilly; Lord
John Russell dwindled into senility; old
Lord Derby tottered from the stage. A new
scene opened; and new protagonists—Mr.

MR. GLADSTONE

Gladstone and Mr. Disraeli—struggled together in the limelight.

Victoria watched these developments with passionate and personal interest. Mr. Gladstone had been the disciple of Sir Robert
Peel and had won the approval of Albert; Mr. Disraeli had
hounded Sir Robert to his fall with hideous virulence, and the
Prince had pronounced that Mr. Disraeli "had not one single
element of a gentleman in his composition." Yet she regarded
Mr. Gladstone with distrust, while upon his rival, Mr. Disraeli,
she lavished confidence, esteem, and affection.

Her attitude towards Mr. Disraeli had changed when she had
found that he alone among public men had divined her feelings
at Albert's death. Of the others she might have said, "They pity
me and not my grief"; but Mr. Disraeli's condolences had
taken the form of eulogies of the departed. The Queen declared
that he was "the only person who appreciated the Prince." She
began to show him special favor; gave him and his wife two of
the coveted seats in St. George's Chapel at the Prince of
Wales's wedding, and invited him to stay a night at Windsor.

When the grant for the Albert Memorial came before the
House of Commons, Disraeli, as leader of the Opposition, elo-
quently supported the project. He was rewarded by a copy of
the Prince's speeches, bound in white morocco, with an inscription in the royal hand. In his letter of thanks he "ventured to
touch upon a sacred theme," and dwelled at length upon the
absolute perfection of Albert. "The Prince," he said, "is the
only person whom Mr. Disraeli has ever known who realized
the Ideal." As for his own acquaintance with the Prince, it had
been, he said, "one of the most satisfactory incidents of his life:
full of refined and beautiful memories, and exercising over his

132

existence a soothing and exalting influence." Victoria was much affected by "the depth and delicacy of these touches," and henceforward Disraeli's place in her affections was assured.

When, in 1866, the Conservatives came into office, Disraeli's position as Chancellor of the Exchequer and leader of the House necessarily brought him into a closer relation with the sovereign. Two years later Lord Derby resigned, and Victoria, with intense delight, welcomed Disraeli as her Prime Minister.

Only for nine agitated months did he remain in power. The ministry, in a minority in the Commons, was swept out of existence by a general election. Yet by the end of that short period the ties which bound together the Queen and her Premier had grown far stronger than ever before; the relationship between them was now no longer merely that between a grateful mistress and a devoted servant: they were friends.

His official letters developed into racy records of political news and social gossip, written, as Lord Clarendon said, "in his best novel style." Victoria was delighted; she had never, she declared, had such letters in her life. In return, she sent him bunches of flowers picked by her own hands. He dispatched to her a set of his novels, for which, she said, she was "most grateful." She herself had lately published her *Leaves from the Journal of our Life in the Highlands*, and it was observed that the Prime Minister, in conversing with Her Majesty at this period, constantly used the words "we authors, Ma'am." Upon political questions, she was his staunch supporter. And when the government was defeated in the House she was "really shocked." She again dreaded the prospect of a change; a change there had to be, and Victoria tried to console herself for the loss of her favorite minister by bestowing a peerage upon Mrs. Disraeli.

Mr. Gladstone was in his shirt sleeves at Hawarden, cutting down a tree, when the royal message was brought to him. "Very significant," he remarked, when he had read the letter, and went on cutting down his tree. His secret thoughts were more explicit. "The Almighty," he wrote in his diary, "seems to sustain and spare me for some purpose of His own, deeply unworthy as I know myself to be. Glory be to His name."

The Queen, however, did not share her new minister's view of the Almighty's intentions. She could not believe that there was any divine purpose to be detected in the program of sweeping changes which Mr. Gladstone was determined to carry out. But what could she do? Mr. Gladstone, with his powerful majority in the House of Commons, was irresistible; and for five years (1869–1874) Victoria found herself condemned to live in an atmosphere of reform—reform in the Irish Church and the Irish land system, reform in education, reform in elections, reform in the organization of the army and the navy.

She disapproved, she struggled; but her protests were unavailing. The mere effort of grappling with the mass of documents which poured in upon her was terribly exhausting. When the draft of the lengthy Irish Church Bill came before her, accompanied by an explanatory letter from Mr. Gladstone covering a dozen closely written pages, she almost despaired. At last she handed the papers to Mr. Theodore Martin, who happened to be staying at Osborne, and requested him to make a précis of them. When he had done so, her disapproval of the measure was marked; but, such was the strength of the government, she actually found herself obliged to urge moderation upon the Opposition, lest worse should ensue.

In the midst of this crisis, when the future of the Irish Church was hanging in the balance, Victoria's attention was drawn to another proposed reform. It was suggested that the sailors in the navy should henceforward be allowed to wear beards. "Has Mr. Childers ascertained anything on the subject of the beards?" the Queen wrote anxiously to the First Lord of the Admiralty. On the whole, Her Majesty was in favor of the change. "Her own personal feeling," she wrote, "would be for the beards without the moustaches." After thinking over the question for another week, she wrote a final letter. She wished, she said, "to make one additional observation, viz., that on no account should moustaches be allowed without beards. That must be clearly understood."

Changes in the navy might be tolerated; to lay hands upon the army was a more serious matter. From time immemorial there had been a particularly close connection between the army and the Crown. But now Mr. Gladstone's fiat went forth, and the commander in chief was to be removed from his direct dependence upon the sovereign, and made subordinate to Parliament. Of all the liberal reforms this was the one which aroused the bitterest resentment in Victoria. But she was helpless, and the Prime Minister had his way. When she heard that the dreadful man had yet another reform in contemplation— that he was about to abolish the purchase of military commissions—she could only feel that it was just what might have been expected.

Unacceptable as were Mr. Gladstone's policies, there was something else about him which was even more displeasing to Victoria. She disliked his personal demeanor towards herself. It was not that Mr. Gladstone, in his manner towards her, was in any degree lacking in respect. On the contrary, an extraordinary reverence impregnated his manner with the sovereign. Indeed, Mr. Gladstone viewed Victoria through a haze of awe which was almost religious—as a sacrosanct embodiment of venerable traditions—a vital element in the British constitution —a Queen by Act of Parliament. But unfortunately the lady did not appreciate the compliment. The well-known complaint which Victoria is supposed to have made—"He speaks to me as if I were a public meeting"—whether authentic or no, undoubtedly expresses the essential element of her antipathy. She had no objection to being considered as an institution; she was one, and she knew it. But she was a woman too, and to be considered *only* as an institution—that was unbearable.

Thus all Mr. Gladstone's zeal and devotion, his ceremonious phrases, his low bows, were utterly wasted; and when, in the excess of his loyalty, he went further, and imputed to the object of his veneration the subtlety of intellect, the wide reading, the grave enthusiasm, which he himself possessed, the misunderstanding became complete. The discordance between the actual Victoria and this strange divinity made in Mr. Gladstone's image produced disastrous results. Her discomfort turned at last into positive animosity, and, though her manners continued to be perfect, she never for a moment unbent; while he on his side was overcome with disappointment and perplexity.

Yet his fidelity remained unshaken. When the cabinet met,

the Prime Minister would open the proceedings by reading aloud the letters which he had received from the Queen upon the questions of the hour. The assembly sat in absolute silence while, one after another, the royal missives boomed forth in all the deep solemnity of Mr. Gladstone's utterance. Not a single comment was ever hazarded; and, after a fitting pause, the cabinet proceeded with the business of the day.

LITTLE AS Victoria appreciated her Prime Minister's attitude towards her, she found that it had its uses.

The popular discontent at her uninterrupted seclusion had been gathering force for many years, and now burst out in a new and alarming shape. Republicanism was in the air. Radical opinion in England, stimulated by the fall of Napoleon III, suddenly grew more extreme than it ever had been since 1848. The monarchy was attacked. And it was attacked at a vital point: it was declared to be too expensive.

What benefits, it was asked, did the nation reap to counterbalance the enormous sums which were expended upon the sovereign? Victoria's retirement gave an unpleasant handle to the argument. It was pointed out that the ceremonial functions of the Crown had virtually lapsed; and the awkward question remained whether any of the other functions which it did perform were really worth £385,000 per annum. The royal balance sheet was examined. An anonymous pamphlet entitled *What does she do with it?* appeared, setting forth the financial position with malicious clarity. The Queen, it stated, was granted by the Civil List £60,000 a year for her private use; but the rest of her vast annuity was given, as the Act declared, to enable her "to defray the expenses of her royal household and to support the honor and dignity of the Crown." Now it was obvious that, since the death of the Prince, the expenditures for both these purposes must have been considerably diminished, and it was difficult to resist the conclusion that a large sum of money was diverted annually to swell the private fortune of Victoria.

Though it is certain that estimates of Victoria's riches were much exaggerated, it is equally certain that she was an exceedingly wealthy woman. She probably saved £20,000 a year from the Civil List, she had inherited a considerable property from the Prince Consort, and she had been left, in 1852, an estate of half a million by Mr. John Neild, an eccentric miser. In these circumstances it was not surprising that when, in 1871, Parliament was asked to vote a dowry of £30,000 to the Princess Louise on her marriage with the son of the Duke of Argyle, together with an annuity of £6000, there should have been a serious outcry.

In order to conciliate public opinion, the Queen opened Parliament in person, and the vote was passed. But a few months later another demand was made: Prince Arthur had come of age, and the nation was asked to grant him an annuity of £15,000. The outcry was redoubled.

Towards every aspect of this distasteful question, Mr. Gladstone presented an iron front. He absolutely discountenanced the extreme section of his followers. He declared that the whole of the Queen's income was justly at her personal disposal, argued that to complain of royal savings was merely to encourage royal extravagance, and successfully convoyed through Parliament the unpopular annuities, which, he pointed out, were strictly in accordance with precedent. Victoria was relieved; but she grew no fonder of Mr. Gladstone.

It was perhaps the most miserable moment of her life. The ministers, the press, the public, all conspired to vex her, to blame her, to misinterpret her actions. She was "a cruelly misunderstood woman," she told Mr. Martin, declaring to him that "the great worry and anxiety and hard work for ten years, alone, unaided, with increasing age and never very strong health" were breaking her down.

The situation was indeed deplorable. It seemed as if her whole existence had gone awry; as if an irremediable antagonism had grown up between the Queen and the nation. If Victoria had died in the early seventies, there can be little doubt that the voice of the world would have pronounced her a failure.

BUT SHE WAS RESERVED for a very different fate. The outburst of republicanism had been in fact the last flicker of an expiring cause. The liberal tide, which had been flowing steadily ever since the 1830's, had reached its height; and the inevitable ebb began. In the general election of 1874, Mr. Gladstone and the Liberals were routed; and the Tory party, for the first time in over forty years, attained an unquestioned supremacy. Their triumph was preeminently due to Disraeli. He returned to office, no longer the dubious commander of an insufficient host, but with drums beating and flags flying, a conquering hero. And as a conquering hero Victoria welcomed her new Prime Minister.

There followed six years of excitement, of enchantment, of glory, of romance. The amazing being, who now at last, at the age of seventy, after a lifetime of extraordinary struggles, had turned into reality the absurdest of his boyhood's dreams, knew well enough how to make his own, with absolute completeness, the heart of the Sovereign Lady. In women's hearts he had always read as in an open book; the more curious they were, the more intimately at home with them he seemed to be.

He surveyed Queen Victoria with the eye of a past master; and he was not for a moment at a loss. He realized everything— the interacting complexities of circumstance and character, the personal arrogance, the emotionalism, the laborious respectability shot through so incongruously by cravings for the colored and the strange, the singular intellectual limitations, and the mysteriously essential female elements impregnating every particle of the whole. A smile hovered over his impassive features, and he dubbed Victoria "the Faery." The allusion to Edmund Spenser's great poem *Faerie Queene* was very pleasant— the elegant evocations of Gloriana, Queen of Fairyland; but there was more in it than that: there was the suggestion of a diminutive creature, endowed with magical—and mythical—properties.

The Faery, he determined, should henceforward wave her wand for him alone. Bowing low with Oriental gravity, he set himself to his task. He had understood from the first that in dealing with the Faery the appropriate method of approach was the very antithesis of the Gladstonian; and such a method was naturally his. It was not his habit to harangue and exhort in official conscientiousness; he liked to scatter flowers along the path of business; to compress a weighty argument into a happy phrase, to insinuate what was in his mind with an air of friendship. He was nothing if not personal; and he had perceived that personality was the key that opened the Faery's heart.

Accordingly, he never for a moment allowed his intercourse with her to lose the personal tone; he invested all the transactions of state with the charms of familiar conversation; she was always the royal lady, the adored and revered mistress, he the devoted and respectful friend. When once the personal relation was firmly established, every difficulty disappeared. But to maintain that relation uninterruptedly in a smooth and even course a particular care was necessary: the bearings had to be most assiduously oiled. Nor was Disraeli in any doubt as to the nature of the lubricant. "You have heard me called a flatterer," he said to Matthew Arnold, "and it is true. Everyone likes flattery; and when you come to royalty you should lay it on with a trowel."

He practiced what he preached; his adulation was incessant, and he applied it in the very thickest slabs. "There is no honor and no reward," he declared, "that with him can ever equal the possession of your Majesty's kind thoughts." "In life," he told her, "one must have for one's thoughts a sacred depository, and Lord Beaconsfield* ever presumes to seek that in his Sovereign Mistress." She was not only his own solitary support; she was the one prop of the state. "If your Majesty is ill," he wrote during a grave political crisis, "he is sure he will himself break down. All, really, depends upon your Majesty." "He lives only for Her," he asseverated, "and works only for Her, and without Her all is lost."

Such tributes were delightful, but they remained in the nebulous region of words, and Disraeli had determined to give his blandishments a more significant solidity. He deliberately encouraged Victoria to hold high views of her own position. He professed to a belief that the constitution gave the sovereign a leading place in the councils of government, and he emphatically declared that there ought to be "a real Throne." His pronouncements upon the subject were indistinct; but the vagueness of his language was in itself an added stimulant to Victoria.

---

* Disraeli took the name Beaconsfield when he was granted a peerage in 1876. (Editors' note.)

Skillfully confusing the woman and the Queen, he threw, with a grandiose gesture, the government of England at her feet. In his first audience after returning to power, he assured her that "whatever she wished should be done." When the Public Worship Regulation Bill was being discussed by the cabinet, he told the Faery that his "only object" was "to further your Majesty's wishes in this matter." When he brought off his great coup of buying the controlling share of the Suez Canal for England, he used expressions which implied that the only gainer by the transaction was Victoria. "It is just settled," he wrote in triumph; "you have it, Madam!"

Nor did he limit himself to highly spiced insinuations. Writing with all the authority of his office, he advised the Queen that she had the constitutional right to dismiss a ministry which was supported by a large majority in the House of Commons. To the horror of Mr. Gladstone, he not only kept the Queen informed as to the general course of business in the cabinet, but revealed to her the part taken in its discussions by individual members of it. Lord Derby, the son of the late Prime Minister and Disraeli's Foreign Secretary, viewed these developments with grave mistrust. "Is there not," he ventured to write to his chief, "just a risk of encouraging her in too large ideas of her personal power? I only ask; it is for you to judge."

As for Victoria, she accepted everything—compliments, flatteries, prerogatives—without a single qualm. After the long gloom of her bereavement, after the chill of the Gladstonian discipline, she expanded to the rays of Disraeli's devotion like a flower in the sun. The change in her situation was indeed miraculous. No longer was she obliged to puzzle for hours over the complicated details of business, for now she had only to ask Mr. Disraeli for an explanation and he would give it her in the most concise, amusing way. He was surely the most fascinating of men. The strain of charlatanism, which had unconsciously captivated her in Napoleon III, exercised the same enchanting effect in the case of Disraeli. She became intoxicated, entranced. Believing all that he told her of herself, she completely regained the self-confidence which had been slipping away from her throughout the dark period that followed Albert's death.

Under the compelling influence, her very demeanor altered. Her short, stout figure, with its folds of black velvet, its muslin streamers, its heavy pearls at the heavy neck, assumed an almost menacing air. In her countenance, from which the charm of youth had long since vanished, and which had not yet been softened by age, the traces of grief and of displeasure were still visible, but they were overlaid by looks of arrogance and sharp lines of hauteur. But, when Mr. Disraeli appeared, the expression changed in an instant, and the forbidding visage became charged with smiles.

For him she would do anything. Yielding to his encouragements, she began to emerge from her seclusion; she appeared at hospitals and concerts; she opened Parliament; she reviewed troops. But such public signs of favor were trivial in comparison with her private attentions. During his hours of audience, she could hardly restrain her delight. "I can only describe my reception," he wrote to a friend on one occasion, "by telling you that I really thought she was going to embrace me. She was wreathed with smiles, and, as she tattled, glided about the room like a bird."

In his absence, she talked of him perpetually, and there was a note of unusual vehemence in her solicitude for his health. She often sent him presents; an illustrated album arrived for him regularly from Windsor on Christmas Day. But her most valued gifts were the bunches of spring flowers which were gathered by herself and her ladies in the woods at Osborne. Among these it was, he declared, the primroses that he loved best. "They show," he told her, "that your Majesty's sceptre has touched the enchanted Isle." He sat at dinner with heaped-up bowls of them on every side and told his guests that "they were all sent to me this morning by the Queen from Osborne, as she knows it is my favorite flower."

As time went on, and as it became clearer and clearer that the Faery's thralldom was complete, his protestations grew steadily more highly colored and more unabashed. At last he ventured to import into his blandishments a strain of adoration that was almost romantic. He addressed her as "the most loved and illustrous being," as the "Sovereign whom he adores."

Did he smile as he uttered such words? Perhaps; and yet it would be rash to conclude that his declarations were altogether without sincerity. Detachment he possessed in a supreme degree. Nonetheless, actor and spectator both, the two characters were so intimately blended together in him that they formed an inseparable unity, and it was impossible to say that one of them was less genuine than the other. When he wrote to a lady about the court, "I love the Queen—perhaps the only person in this world left to me that I do love," was he not creating for himself an enchanted palace out of the Arabian Nights, in which he actually believed? Victoria's state of mind was far more simple; untroubled by imaginative yearnings, she never confused feeling and fancy. Her emotions, with all their exaggeration, retained the prosaic texture of everyday life. She was, she told her Prime Minister, at the end of an official letter, "yours aff'ly V.R. and I." In such a phrase the deep reality of her feeling is instantly manifest. The Faery's feet were on the solid earth; it was the artful cynic who was in the air.

He had taught her, however, a lesson, which she had learned with alarming rapidity. In May 1874 the Tsar was in London following the marriage of his daughter to Victoria's second son. By an unfortunate error, it had been arranged that his departure should not take place until two days after the date on which his royal hostess had previously decided to go to Balmoral. Her Majesty refused to modify her plans. It was pointed out to her that the Tsar would certainly be offended, that the most serious consequences might follow, but the Faery was unconcerned; she had settled to go to Balmoral on the 18th, and on the 18th she would go.

At last Disraeli, exercising all his influence, induced her to agree to stay in London for two days more. "My head is still on my shoulders," he told Lady Bradford. "The great lady has postponed her departure! Everybody had failed, even the Prince of Wales; . . . Salisbury says I have saved an Afghan War."

But before very long, on another issue, the triumph was the Faery's. Disraeli, who had suddenly veered towards a new imperialism, had thrown out the suggestion that the Queen of England ought to become the Empress of India. Victoria seized upon the idea with avidity, and pressed it upon her Prime Minister. He demurred; but she was not to be balked; and in 1876, in spite of his unwillingness, he found himself obliged to add to the troubles of a stormy session by introducing a bill for the alteration of the royal title. His compliance, however, finally conquered the Faery's heart. The measure was angrily attacked in both Houses, and Victoria was deeply touched by the untiring energy with which Disraeli defended it.

At last the affair was successfully concluded, Victoria was proclaimed Empress of India, and the triumph was celebrated in a suitable manner. On the day of the Delhi proclamation, the Prime Minister went to Windsor to dine with the new Empress of India. That night the Faery, usually so homely in her attire, appeared in a glittering panoply of enormous uncut jewels, which had been presented to her by the reigning Princes of her *raj*. At the end of the meal Disraeli, breaking through the rules of etiquette, arose, and in a flowery oration proposed the health of the Queen-Empress. His audacity was well received, and his speech was rewarded by a smiling curtsy.

These were significant episodes; but a still more serious manifestation of Victoria's temper occurred in the following year during the crowning crisis of Disraeli's life. His growing imperialism, his desire to magnify the power and prestige of England, had brought him into collision with Russia. The terrible Eastern Question loomed up, and when war broke out between Russia and Turkey, the gravity of the situation became extreme.

The Prime Minister's policy was fraught with difficulty. Realizing perfectly the appalling implications of an Anglo-Russian war, he was yet prepared to face even that eventuality if he could obtain his ends; but he believed that Russia in reality was still less desirous of a rupture, and that, if he played his game with sufficient adroitness, she would yield all that he required without a blow.

It was clear that the course he had marked out for himself was full of hazard, and demanded an extraordinary nerve. But nerve he had never lacked. He began his diplomatic egg dance with high assurance. And then he discovered that, besides the

Russian government, besides the Liberals and Mr. Gladstone, there were two additional sources of perilous embarrassment with which he would have to reckon. In the first place there was a strong party in the cabinet, headed by Lord Derby, the Foreign Secretary, which was unwilling to take the risk of war; but his culminating anxiety was the Faery.

From the first, her attitude was uncompromising. The old hatred of Russia surged up within her; she remembered Albert's prolonged animosity; she felt the prickings of her own greatness; and she flung herself into the turmoil with passionate heat.

Her indignation with the Opposition—with anyone who ventured to sympathize with the Russians in their quarrel with the Turks—was unbounded. When anti-Turkish meetings were held in London, she considered that "the Attorney General ought to be set at these men. . . . It can't," she exclaimed, "be constitutional." Never in her life, not even in the crisis over the ladies of the bedchamber, did she show herself a more furious partisan. But her displeasure was not reserved for the Radicals; the backsliding Conservatives equally felt its force. She was even discontented with Disraeli himself. Failing entirely to appreciate the delicate complexity of his policy, she constantly assailed him with demands for vigorous action, interpreted each finesse as a sign of weakness, and was ready at every juncture to let slip the dogs of war.

As the situation developed, her anxiety grew feverish. "The Faery," Disraeli told Lady Bradford, "writes every day and telegraphs every hour; this is almost literally the case."

"The Queen," Victoria wrote, "is feeling terribly anxious lest delay should cause us to be too late and lose our prestige for ever!" She raged loudly against the Russians. "The language," she cried, "the insulting language—used by the Russians against us! It makes the Queen's blood boil!" "Oh," she wrote later, "if the Queen were a man, she would like to go and give those Russians, whose word one cannot believe, such a beating!"

The unfortunate Prime Minister, urged on to violence by Victoria on one side, had to deal, on the other, with a Foreign Secretary who was fundamentally opposed to any policy of interference at all. Between the Queen and Lord Derby he held

a harassed course. He gained, indeed, some slight satisfaction in playing off the one against the other—in stimulating each to attack the other. But this only gave a temporary relief; and it soon became evident that Victoria's martial ardor was not to be sidetracked by hostilities against Lord Derby; hostilities against Russia were what she wanted. Casting aside the last relics of moderation, she began to attack her friend with a series of extraordinary threats. Not once but many times she held over his head the formidable menace of her abdication. "If England," she wrote to Disraeli, "is to kiss Russia's feet, she will not be a party to the humiliation of England and would lay down her crown." When the Russians advanced to the outskirts of Constantinople she fired off three letters in a day demanding war; and when she learned that the cabinet had only decided to send the fleet to Gallipoli she declared that "her first impulse" was "to lay down the thorny crown, which she feels little satisfaction in retaining if the position of this country is to remain as it is now."

It is easy to imagine the agitating effect of such a correspondence upon Disraeli. This was no longer the Faery; it was a genie whom he had rashly called out of her bottle, and who was now intent upon showing her supernal power. More than once, dispirited, shattered by illness, he had thoughts of withdrawing altogether from the game.

He held on, however, to emerge victorious at last. The Queen was pacified; Lord Derby was replaced by Lord Salisbury; and at the Congress of Berlin he carried all before him. But soon there was an unexpected reverse. At the general election of 1880 the country, mistrustful of the forward policy of the Conservatives, returned the Liberals to power.

Victoria was horrified, but within a year she was to be yet more nearly hit. The grand romance had come to its conclusion. Disraeli, worn out with age and maladies, but moving still, an assiduous mummy, from dinner party to dinner party, suddenly moved no longer.

When she knew that the end was inevitable, she seemed, by a pathetic instinct, to divest herself of her royalty, and to shrink, with hushed gentleness, beside him, a woman and nothing more. "I send some Osborne primroses," she wrote to him with touching simplicity, "and I meant to pay you a little visit this week, but I thought it better you should be quite quiet. And I beg you will be very good and obey the doctors." She would see him, she said, "when we come back from Osborne, which won't be long." "Everyone is so distressed at your not being well," she added; and she was, "Ever yours very aff'ly, V.R.I."

When the royal letter was given him, the strange old comedian, stretched on his bed of death, poised it in his hand, appeared to consider deeply, and then whispered to those about him, "This ought to be read to me by a privy councillor."

JOHN BROWN

CHAPTER 9
Old Age

MEANWHILE IN Victoria's private life many changes had taken place. With the marriages of her elder children her family circle widened; grandchildren appeared; and a multitude of new interests sprang up.

The death of King Leopold in 1865 had removed the predominant figure of the older generation, and the functions he had performed as the center of a large group of relatives in Germany and in England devolved upon Victoria. These functions she discharged with industry, carrying on an enormous correspondence and following every detail in the lives of the ever-ramifying cousinhood. She also took a particular delight in her grandchildren, though she could be, when the occasion demanded it, severe. The eldest of them, little Prince Wilhelm of Prussia, was a remarkably headstrong child. Once, when she told him to bow to a visitor, he disobeyed her outright. The order was repeated, and the naughty boy, noticing that his grandmama had suddenly turned into a most terrifying lady, submitted, and bowed very low indeed.

It would have been well if all the Queen's domestic troubles could have been got over as easily. Among her more serious distresses was the conduct of the Prince of Wales, who was now independent and married; and beginning to do as he liked.

Victoria's worst fears seemed to be justified when in 1870 he appeared as a witness in a society divorce case. Clearly the heir to the throne had been mixing with people of whom she did not approve. What was to be done? She saw that it was not only her son that was to blame—that it was the whole system of society; and so she dispatched a letter to Mr. Delane, the editor of *The Times*, asking him if he would "frequently *write* articles pointing out the *immense* danger and evil of the wretched frivolity and levity of the views and lives of the Higher Classes."

More and more did she find refreshment in her Highland domain; and twice yearly, in spring and in autumn, she set her face northwards, in spite of the protests of ministers, who murmured vainly in the royal ears that to transact the affairs of state over an interval of six hundred miles added considerably to the cares of government. Her ladies, too, felt occasionally a slight reluctance to set out, for the pilgrimage was not without its drawbacks. The royal railway train remained for long immune from modern conveniences, and when it drew up, on some moorland, far from any platform, the high-bred dames were obliged to descend to earth by the perilous footboard.

But Victoria cared for none of these things. She was only intent upon regaining, with the utmost swiftness, her enchanted castle. And it was not only the place that she loved; she was equally attached to "the simple mountaineers," from whom, she said, "she learned many a lesson of resignation and faith." Smith and Grant and Ross and Thompson—she was devoted to them all; but, beyond the rest, she was devoted to John Brown.

Brown, the Prince's attendant, had now become the Queen's personal attendant—a body servant from whom she was never parted, who accompanied her on her drives, waited on her during the day, and slept in a neighboring chamber at night. She liked his strength, his solidity, the sense he gave her of physical security; she even liked his rugged manners and speech. She allowed him to take liberties with her which would have been unthinkable from anybody else. To bully the Queen, to order her about, to reprimand her—who could dream of venturing upon such audacities? And yet, when she received such treatment from John Brown, she positively seemed to enjoy it.

The eccentricity appeared to be extraordinary; but, after all, it is no uncommon thing for an autocratic dowager to allow some trusted servant to adopt towards her an attitude of authority. When Victoria meekly obeyed the abrupt commands of her henchman to get off her pony or put on her shawl, people might wonder. She could not help that; this was the manner in which it pleased her to act.

John Brown had, too, in her mind, a special connection with Albert. In their expeditions the Prince had always trusted him more than anyone; the gruff, kind, hairy Scotsman was, she felt, in some mysterious way, a legacy from the dead. She came to believe at last—or so it appeared—that the spirit of Albert was nearer when Brown was near. Often, when seeking inspiration over some complicated political question, she would gaze with deep concentration at her late husband's bust. But it was also noticed that sometimes in such moments of doubt Her Majesty's looks would fix themselves upon John Brown.

Eventually, the "simple mountaineer" became almost a state personage. The influence which he wielded was not to be overlooked. Disraeli himself was careful, from time to time, to send courteous messages to "Mr. Brown" in his letters to the Queen, and the French government took particular pains to provide for his comfort during the visits of the English sovereign to France. It was only natural that among the elder members of the royal family he should not have been popular, and that his failings—for failings he had, including too acute an appreciation of Scotch whisky—should have been the subject of comment at court. But he served his mistress faithfully, and to ignore him would be a sign of disrespect in her biographer.

The Queen herself, far from making a secret of her affectionate friendship, took care to publish it to the world. By her orders two gold medals were struck in Brown's honor; and on his death, in 1883, a long and eulogistic obituary notice of him appeared in the *Court Circular*. In the second series of extracts from the Queen's *Highland Journal*, published in 1884, her "devoted personal attendant and faithful friend" appears upon almost every page, and is in effect the hero of the book. With a remarkable absence of reticence, Victoria seemed to demand, in this private matter, the sympathy of the whole nation; and yet—such is the world!—there were those who actually treated the relations between their sovereign and her servant as a theme for ribald jests.

THE BUSY YEARS hastened away; and old age, approaching, laid a gentle hold upon Victoria. The gray hair whitened; the mature features mellowed; the short firm figure amplified and moved more slowly, supported by a stick. And, simultaneously, in the whole tenor of the Queen's existence an extraordinary transformation came to pass. The nation's attitude towards her, critical and even hostile as it had been for so many years, altogether changed; and there was a corresponding alteration in the temper of Victoria's own mind.

Many causes led to this result. Among them were the repeated strokes of personal misfortune which befell the Queen during a cruelly short space of years. In 1878 her daughter Alice, who had married in 1862 the Prince Louis of Hesse-Darmstadt, died [of diphtheria]. In the following year the Prince Imperial, the only son of the Empress Eugénie, to whom Victoria had become devotedly attached, was killed in the Zulu War. Two years later, in 1881, she lost Disraeli, and, in 1883, John Brown. In 1884 her son Leopold, who had been an invalid from birth, also died. Victoria's cup of sorrows was indeed overflowing; and the public, as it watched the widowed mother weeping for her children and her friends, displayed a constantly increasing sympathy.

An event which occurred in 1882 revealed and accentuated the feelings of the nation. As the Queen, at Windsor, was walking from the train to her carriage, a youth named Roderick Maclean fired a pistol at her from a few yards away. An Eton boy struck up Maclean's arm before the pistol went off; no damage was done, and the culprit was at once arrested.

This was the last of a series of seven attempts upon the Queen —attempts which, taking place over a period of forty years, resembled one another in a curious manner. All, with a single exception, were perpetrated by adolescents, none of whose pistols was loaded. In 1842 an Act had been passed making any attempt to hurt the Queen a misdemeanor, punishable by transportation for seven years, or imprisonment for three years. Subsequent attempts were all dealt with under this new law; but Roderick Maclean's attempt in 1882 was treated differently. On this occasion the pistol was found to have been loaded; public indignation, emphasized as it was by Victoria's growing popularity, was great.

But it was not only through the feelings—commiserating or indignant—of personal sympathy that the Queen and her people were being drawn more nearly together; they were beginning, at last, to come to a close agreement upon the conduct of public affairs. Mr. Gladstone's second administration (1880–1885) was a succession of failures, ending in disaster and disgrace; liberalism fell into discredit, and Victoria perceived with joy that her distrust of her ministers was shared by an ever-increasing number of her subjects.

During the crisis in the Sudan, the popular temper was her own. She had been among the first to urge the necessity of an expedition to Khartoum, and, when the news came of the catastrophic death of General Gordon, her voice led the chorus of denunciation against the government. It was even rumored that she had sent for Lord Hartington, the Secretary of State for War, and vehemently upbraided him. "She rated me," he was reported to have told a friend, "as if I'd been a footman." "Why didn't she send for the butler?" asked his friend. "Oh," was the reply, "the butler generally manages to keep out of the way on such occasions."

But the day came when it was impossible for the butler to keep out of the way any longer. Mr. Gladstone was defeated, and resigned. Victoria, at a final interview, received him with her usual amenity, but, besides the formalities demanded by the occasion, the only remark she made to him was to the effect that she supposed he would now require some rest.

Such was Mr. Gladstone's exit; and then, in the general election of 1886, the majority of the nation showed decisively that Victoria's politics were now identical with theirs. Casting the contrivers of Home Rule into outer darkness, they placed Lord Salisbury in power. Victoria's satisfaction was profound.

A flood of new hopefulness swept over her, stimulating her vital spirits with a surprising force, and she threw herself vigorously into a multitude of public activities. She appeared at drawing rooms, at concerts, at reviews; she laid foundation stones; she went to Liverpool to open an exhibition, driving in her open carriage in heavy rain amid vast applauding crowds. Delighted by the welcome which met her everywhere, she warmed to her work; she visited Edinburgh, where the ovation of Liverpool was repeated and surpassed; and in London, seated on a gorgeous throne of hammered gold, she opened in high state the Colonial and Indian Exhibition.

Next year was the fiftieth of her reign, and in June the anniversary was celebrated in solemn pomp. Victoria, surrounded by the highest dignitaries of her realm, escorted by a glittering galaxy of kings and princes, drove through the crowded enthusiasm of the capital to render thanks to God in Westminster Abbey. In that triumphant hour the last remaining traces of past antipathies and disagreements were altogether swept away. The Queen was hailed at once as the mother of her people and as the embodied symbol of their imperial greatness; and she responded to the double sentiment with all the ardor of her spirit. At last, after so long, happiness had returned to her. The unaccustomed feeling filled and warmed her consciousness. When, at Buckingham Palace again, the long ceremony over, she was asked how she was, "I am very tired, but very happy," she said.

AND SO, after the toils and tempests of the day, a long evening followed—mild, serene, and lighted with a golden glory. For an atmosphere of success and adoration invested the last period of Victoria's life. The solid splendor of the decade between Victoria's two jubilees can hardly be paralleled in the annals of England; the country seemed to settle down, with calm assurance, to the enjoyment of an established grandeur. And—it was only natural—Victoria settled down too.

Her own existence came to harmonize more and more with what was around her. Gradually, the image of Albert receded. It was not that he was forgotten—that would have been impossible—but that the void created by his absence grew less agonizing, and even, at last, less obvious. And, as Albert's figure slowly faded, its place was taken, inevitably, by Victoria's own. Her egotism proclaimed its rights; and her force of character, emerging at length in all its plenitude, imposed itself absolutely upon its environment by conscious effort.

It was in her family that Victoria's ascendency reached its highest point. All her offspring were married; the number of her descendants rapidly increased; there were many marriages in the third generation; and no fewer than thirty-seven of her great-grandchildren were living at the time of her death. Over all of this family she ruled with a most potent sway. The small concerns of the youngest aroused her passionate interest; and the oldest she treated as if they were children still. The Prince of Wales, in particular, stood in tremendous awe of his mother. It could not be denied that he enjoyed himself—out of her sight; but, in that redoubtable presence, his abounding manhood suffered a miserable eclipse. Once, at Osborne, when he was late for a dinner party, he was observed standing behind a pillar, wiping the sweat from his forehead, trying to nerve himself to go up to the Queen. When at last he did so, she gave him a stiff nod, whereupon he vanished immediately behind another pillar, and remained there until the party broke up. At the time of this incident the Prince of Wales was over fifty years of age.

With no Albert to guide her, with no Disraeli to inflame her, Victoria at last grew willing to abandon the dangerous questions of diplomacy to the wisdom of her Prime Minister, Lord Salisbury. She concentrated her energies upon objects which touched her more nearly. Her home—her court—the monuments at Balmoral—the livestock at Windsor—such matters played now an even greater part in her existence than before. Every moment of her day was mapped out beforehand; the dates of her journeys —to Osborne, to Balmoral, to the South of France—were hardly altered from year to year. She demanded from those who surrounded her a rigid precision in details. Unpunctuality was one of the most heinous of sins. But sometimes somebody was unpunctual; then her dreadful displeasure became all too visible. At such moments there seemed nothing surprising in her having been the daughter of a martinet.

But these storms, unnerving as they were while they lasted, were quickly over, and they grew more and more exceptional. With the return of happiness a gentle benignity flowed from the aged Queen. Her smile, once so rare, flitted over her features with an easy alacrity; the blue eyes beamed; the whole face brightened and softened and cast an unforgettable charm over those who watched it. For in her last years there was a fascination in Victoria's amiability which had been lacking even from the vivid impulse of her youth. Over all who approached her—or nearly all—she threw a peculiar spell. Her grandchildren adored her; her ladies waited upon her with a reverential love. The honor of serving her obliterated a thousand inconveniences.

What, above all, seemed to make such service delightful was the detailed interest which the Queen took in those around her. She became the confidante of the household affairs of her ladies; her sympathies reached out to the palace domestics; even the housemaids and scullions—so it appeared—were the objects of her searching inquiries, and of her heartfelt solicitude when their lovers were ordered to a foreign station, or their aunts suffered from an attack of rheumatism.

Nevertheless the due distinctions of rank were preserved. Every evening after dinner the Queen's guests were still led up to her one after the other, and, while duologue followed duologue, the rest of the assembly stood still, without a word. Only in one particular was the severity of the etiquette allowed to lapse. Throughout the greater part of the reign the rule had been absolute that ministers must stand during their audiences with the Queen. When Lord Derby, as Prime Minister, had had an audience with Her Majesty after a serious illness, he mentioned afterwards, as a proof of the royal favor, that the Queen had remarked "How sorry she was she could not ask him to be seated." Once Disraeli, after an attack of gout, had been offered a chair; but he had thought it wise humbly to decline the privilege. In her later years, however, the Queen invariably asked Mr. Gladstone and Lord Salisbury to sit down.

Sometimes the solemnity of the evening was diversified by a concert, an opera, or even a play, for now Victoria resumed—after an interval of thirty years—her old custom of commanding dramatic companies from London to perform before the court at Windsor. On such occasions her spirits rose high. She loved acting; she loved a good plot; above all, she loved a farce. Engrossed by everything that passed upon the stage she would follow, with childlike innocence, the unwinding of the story. Her sense of humor was of a vigorous though primitive kind. She could roar with laughter, in the privacy of her household, over some small piece of fun—some oddity of an ambassador, or some ignorant minister's faux pas. When the jest grew subtle she was less pleased; but, if it approached the confines of the indecorous, the danger was serious. To say something improper called down at once Her Majesty's most crushing disapprobation. Then the royal lips sank down at the corners, the royal eyes stared in astonished protrusion. The transgressor shuddered into silence, while the awful "We are not amused" annihilated the dinner table.

In general, her aesthetic tastes had remained unchanged since the days of Mendelssohn and Sir Edwin Landseer. She still delighted in the roulades of Italian opera; she still demanded a high standard in the execution of a pianoforte duet. Her views on painting were decided; Sir Edwin, she declared, was perfect. As for literature, she was devoted to Lord Tennyson.

But as a rule the leisure hours of that active life were occupied with recreations more tangible than the study of literature or art. Victoria was a woman not only of vast property but of innumerable possessions. She had inherited an immense quantity of furniture, of ornaments, of china; her purchases, throughout a long life, made a formidable addition to these stores; and there flowed in upon her, besides, from every quarter of the globe, a constant stream of gifts. Over this enormous mass she exercised an unceasing supervision, and the contemplation of it, in all its details, filled her with an intimate satisfaction.

When she considered the multitudinous objects which belonged to her, she saw herself reflected from a million facets, and was well pleased. But then came the dismaying thought—everything slips away, crumbles, vanishes; Sèvres dinner services get broken; golden basins go unaccountably astray; even one's self, with all the recollections and experiences that make up one's being, fluctuates, perishes, dissolves. . . . But no! It could not, should not be so! There should be no changes, no losses! Nothing should ever move—neither the past nor the present—and she herself least of all! And so the tenacious woman, hoarding her valuables, decreed their immortality. She would not lose one memory or one pin.

She gave orders that nothing should be thrown away—and nothing was. There, in drawer after drawer, in wardrobe after wardrobe, reposed the dresses of seventy years. But not only the dresses—the furs, the muffs, the parasols, and the bonnets—all were ranged in chronological order, dated and complete. A great cupboard was devoted to the dolls; in the china room at Windsor a special table held the mugs of her childhood, and her children's mugs as well. Mementos of the past surrounded her in serried accumulations. In every room the tables were powdered thick with the photographs of relatives; their figures, in solid marble, rose up from pedestals, or gleamed from brackets in the form of statuettes. The dead, in every shape—in miniatures, in porcelain, in oil paintings—were perpetually about her. John Brown stood upon her writing table in solid gold. Her favorite horses and dogs, endowed with a new durability, crowded round her in silver and in bronze. And it was not enough that each particle of the past should be given the stability of metal or of marble: the whole collection, in its arrangement, was immutably fixed. There might be additions, but there might never be alterations. To ensure this, every article in the Queen's possession was photographed from several points of view. These photographs were placed in a series of albums. Then, opposite each photograph, an entry was made, indicating the number of the article, the room in which it was kept, and its exact position in the room. The fate of every object which had undergone this process was henceforth irrevocably sealed. And Victoria, with a gigantic volume or two of the endless catalogue always beside her, to look through, to ponder upon, could feel, with contentment, that the transitoriness of this world had been arrested by the amplitude of her might.

Thus the collection, ever multiplying, became one of the dominating influences of her existence. And it was a collection not merely of things but also of thoughts, of states of mind. The celebration of anniversaries grew to be an important branch of it—of birthdays and marriage days and death days. Especially around the circumstance of death commemorative cravings clustered thickly. On a certain day, for instance, flowers must be strewn on John Brown's monument at Balmoral.

Every bed in which Victoria slept had attached to it, at the back, on the right-hand side, above the pillow, a photograph of the head and shoulders of Albert as he lay dead, surmounted by a wreath of immortelles. And the suite of rooms which Albert had occupied in Windsor Castle was kept for ever shut away. Within those precincts everything remained as it had been at the Prince's death. Victoria had also commanded that her husband's clothing should be laid afresh, each evening, upon the bed, and that, each evening, the water should be set ready in the basin, as if he were still alive; and this incredible rite was performed with scrupulous regularity for nearly forty years.

Such was the inner worship; and still the daily hours of labor proclaimed Victoria's consecration to duty and to the ideal of the dead. Yet, with the years, the sense of self-sacrifice faded; the natural energies of that ardent being discharged themselves with satisfaction into the channel of public work. In her old age, to have been cut off from her papers would have been, not a relief, but an agony to Victoria.

Thus the whole process of government continued, till the very end, to pass before her. Nor was that all; ancient precedent had made the validity of an enormous number of official transactions dependent upon the application of the royal signature; and a great proportion of the Queen's working hours was spent in this mechanical task. At last, when the increasing pressure of business made the delays of the antiquated system intolerable, she consented that, for certain documents, her oral sanction should be sufficient. Each paper was read aloud to her, and she said at the end, "Approved." Often, for hours at a time, she would sit, with Albert's bust in front of her, while the word "Approved" issued at intervals from her lips. The word came forth with a majestic sonority; for her voice now—how changed from the silvery treble of her girlhood!—was a contralto, full and strong.

THE FINAL YEARS WERE YEARS OF apotheosis. Criticism fell dumb; deficiencies were ignored; and in the dazzled imagination of her subjects Victoria soared aloft towards the regions of divinity through a nimbus of purest glory.

That the nation's idol was a very incomplete representative of the nation was hardly noticed, and yet it was conspicuously true. For the vast changes which, out of the England of 1837, had produced the England of 1897, seemed scarcely to have touched the Queen. The immense industrial and scientific development of the period, the significance of which had been so thoroughly understood by Albert, meant little indeed to Victoria. Her conception of the universe, and of man's place in it remained, throughout her life, entirely unchanged. Her religion was the religion which she had learned from the Baroness Lehzen and the Duchess of Kent. She seemed to feel most at home in the simple faith of the Presbyterian Church of Scotland. For many years Dr. Norman Macleod, an innocent Scotch minister, was her principal spiritual adviser; and, when he was taken from her, she drew much comfort from quiet chats about life and death with the cottagers at Balmoral.

From the social movements of her time Victoria was equally remote. Towards the smallest no less than towards the greatest changes she remained inflexible. During her youth and middle age smoking had been forbidden in polite society, and so long as she lived she would not withdraw her anathema against it. Kings might protest; bishops and ambassadors, invited to Windsor, might be reduced, in the privacy of their bedrooms, to lie full-length upon the floor and smoke up the chimney— the interdict continued.

It might have been supposed that a female sovereign would have lent her countenance to one of the most vital of all the reforms to which her epoch gave birth—the emancipation of women—but, on the contrary, the mere mention of such a proposal sent the blood rushing to her head. In 1870, her eye having fallen upon the report of a meeting in favor of Women's Suffrage, she wrote to Mr. Theodore Martin in royal rage— "The Queen is most anxious to enlist everyone who can speak or write to join in checking this mad, wicked folly of 'Woman's

Rights.' Lady——ought to get a *good whipping*. It is a subject which makes the Queen so furious that she cannot contain herself. . . . The Queen is sure that Mrs. Martin agrees with her." The argument was irrefutable; Mrs. Martin agreed; and yet the canker spread.

In another direction Victoria's comprehension of the spirit of her age has been constantly asserted. It was for long the custom for polite historians to compliment the Queen upon the correctness of her attitude towards the constitution. But such praises seem hardly justified by the facts. In her later years Victoria alluded with regret to her conduct during the bedchamber crisis and let it be understood that she had grown wiser since. Yet in truth it is difficult to trace any fundamental change either in her theory or her practice in constitutional matters throughout her life.

The same despotic spirit which led her to break off the negotiations with Peel is equally visible in her animosity towards Palmerston and in her threats of abdication to Disraeli. The complex and delicate principles of the constitution cannot be said to have come within the compass of her mental faculties; and in the actual developments which it underwent during her reign she played a passive part. From 1840 to 1861 the power of the Crown steadily increased in England; from 1861 to 1901 it steadily declined. The first process was due to the influence of Prince Albert, the second to that of a series of great ministers. Perhaps, difficult as Victoria found it to distinguish clearly between the trivial and the essential, she was only dimly aware of what was happening. At the end of her reign, the Crown was weaker than at any other time in English history. Paradoxically enough, Victoria received the highest eulogies for assenting to this political evolution; yet, had she completely realized its import, the evolution would have filled her with supreme displeasure.

But if, in all these ways, the Queen and her epoch were profoundly separated, the points of contact between them also were not few. Victoria understood very well the meaning and the attraction of power and property, and in such learning the English nation, too, had grown to be more and more proficient.

During the last fifteen years of the reign imperialism was the dominant creed of the country. It was Victoria's as well.

Under Disraeli's tutelage the British dominions over the seas had come to mean much more to her, and, in particular, she had grown enamored of the East. India fascinated her; she learned a little Hindustani; she engaged some Indian servants who became her inseparable attendants, and one—Munshi Abdul Karim—eventually almost succeeded to the position which had once been John Brown's.

At the same time, the imperialist temper of the nation invested her office with a new significance. For imperialism is a faith as well as a business; as it grew, the mysticism in English public life grew with it; and simultaneously a new importance began to attach to the Crown. The need for a symbol—a symbol of England's might, of England's extraordinary destiny—became felt more urgently. The Crown was that symbol: and the Crown rested upon the head of Victoria. Thus it happened that while by the end of the reign the power of the sovereign had appreciably diminished, the prestige of the sovereign had enormously grown.

Yet this prestige was not merely the outcome of public changes; it was an intensely personal matter, too. Victoria was the Queen of England, the Empress of India—but how much more besides! For one thing, she was of a great age—an almost indispensable qualification for popularity in England. She had given proof of persistent vitality—she had reigned for sixty years, and she was not out. And then, she was a character. The outlines of her nature were firmly drawn. The great majority of the nation prized goodness above every other human quality; and Victoria, who had said that she would be good at the age of twelve, had kept her word.

Such qualities were obvious and important; but, in the impact of a personality, it is something deeper, something fundamental and common to all its qualities, that really tells. In Victoria, it is easy to discern the nature of this underlying element: it was a peculiar sincerity. Her truthfulness, her single-mindedness, the vividness of her emotions and her unrestrained expression of them, were the varied forms which this central characteristic assumed. "She talks all out," Lady Lyttelton, the royal governess, once said, "just as it is, no more and no less." She talked all out, without reserve; and she wrote all out, too. Undoubtedly it was through this kind of writing that she touched the heart of the public. Not only in her *Highland Journals*, where the mild chronicle of her private proceedings was laid bare without a trace of affectation or of embarrassment, but also in those remarkable messages to the nation which, from time to time, she published in the newspapers, her people found her very close to them indeed. They felt instinctively Victoria's irresistible sincerity, and they responded.

The little old lady, with her white hair and her plain mourning clothes, in her wheeled chair or her donkey carriage—one saw her so; and then—close behind—with their immediate suggestion of mystery, and of power—the Indian servants.

That was the familiar vision, and it was admirable; but, at chosen moments, it was right that the widow of Windsor should step forth apparent Queen. The last and the most glorious of such occasions was the Jubilee of 1897. Then, as the splendid procession escorted Victoria through the thronged reechoing streets of London, the greatness of her realm and the adoration of her subjects blazed out together. The tears welled to her eyes, and, while the multitude roared round her, "How kind they are to me! How kind they are!" she repeated over and over again. That night her message flew over the Empire: "From my heart I thank my beloved people. May God bless them!"

The long journey was nearly done. But the traveler, who had come so far, and through such strange experiences, moved on with the old unfaltering step. The girl, the wife, the aged woman, were the same: vitality, conscientiousness, pride, and simplicity were hers to the latest hour.

THE EVENING had been golden; but, after all, the day was to close in cloud and tempest. Imperial needs, imperial ambitions, involved the country in the South African War. There were checks, reverses, bloody disasters; for a moment the nation was shaken. But the Queen's spirit was high, and neither her courage nor her confidence wavered for a moment. Throwing herself heart and soul into the struggle, she interested herself in every detail of the hostilities, and sought by every means in her power to render service to the national cause.

In April 1900, when she was in her eighty-first year, she made the extraordinary decision to abandon her annual visit to the South of France, and to go instead to Ireland, which had provided a large number of recruits to the armies in the field. She stayed for three weeks in Dublin, driving through the streets, in spite of the warnings of her advisers, without an armed escort; and the visit was a complete success. But, in the course of it, she began, for the first time, to show signs of the fatigue of age.

Though in periods of depression she had sometimes supposed herself an invalid, Victoria had in reality throughout her life enjoyed remarkably good health. In her old age, she had suffered from a rheumatic stiffness of the joints, which had necessitated the use of a stick, and, eventually, a wheeled chair; but no other ailments attacked her, until, in 1898, her eyesight began to be affected by incipient cataract. In the summer of 1900, however, more serious symptoms appeared. Her memory now sometimes deserted her; there was a tendency towards aphasia.

While no specific disease declared itself, by the autumn there were signs of a general physical decay. Yet, even in these last months, the strain of iron held firm; the daily work continued. By midwinter, however, the last remains of her ebbing strength had almost deserted her. On January 14, she had at Osborne an hour's interview with Lord Roberts, the victorious general who had just returned from South Africa. She inquired into all the details of the war; she appeared to sustain the exertion successfully; but, when the audience was over, there was a collapse.

On the following day her medical attendants recognized that her state was hopeless; and yet, for two days more, the indomitable spirit fought on; for two days more she discharged the duties of a Queen of England. But after that there was an end of working. The brain was failing, and life was gently slipping away. Her family gathered round her; for a little more she lingered, speechless and apparently insensible; and, on January 22, 1901, she died.

When, two days previously, the news of the approaching end had been made public, astonished grief had swept over the country. The vast majority of her subjects had never known a time when Queen Victoria had not reigned over them. She had become an indissoluble part of their whole scheme of things, and that they were about to lose her appeared a scarcely possible thought.

She herself, as she lay blind and silent, seemed to those who watched her to be divested of all thinking—to have glided already, unawares, into oblivion. Yet, perhaps, in the secret chambers of consciousness, she had her thoughts, too. Perhaps her fading mind called up once more the shadows of the past to float before it, and retraced, for the last time, the vanished visions of that long history—passing back and back, through the cloud of years, to older and ever older memories—to the spring woods at Osborne, so full of primroses for Mr. Disraeli—to Lord Palmerston's queer clothes and high demeanor, and Albert's face under the green lamp, and Albert's first stag at Balmoral, and Albert in his blue and silver uniform, and the baron coming in through a doorway, and Lord Melbourne dreaming at Windsor with the rooks cawing in the elm trees, and the Archbishop of Canterbury on his knees in the dawn, and Uncle Leopold's soft voice at Claremont, and Lehzen with the globes, and her mother's feathers sweeping down towards her, and a great old repeater watch of her father's in its tortoiseshell case, and a yellow rug, and some friendly flounces of sprigged muslin, and the trees and the grass at Kensington.

YANKEE
FROM
OLYMPUS

YANKEE
FROM
OLYMPUS

Justice Holmes
and
His Family

by
CATHERINE
DRINKER
BOWEN

ILLUSTRATED
BY HOWARD SANDEN

"Life is action and passion," wrote Justice Oliver Wendell Holmes, and during the ninety-four tumultuous years of his country's history through which he lived he shared mightily in the action and passion of his time. For this scholarly Boston aristocrat was a revolutionary of the law, "The Great Dissenter" whose eloquence and logic were to play a crucial part in reshaping the laws under which we live.

But it was "to bring Justice Holmes out of legal terms into human terms" that Catherine Drinker Bowen set out to write about him; for this is one of the most attractive human beings America has produced—warm, cultivated, witty, acute. And his life was full of drama and conflict: the arduous, deadly years as a soldier in the Civil War; the bitter, silent struggle for his own identity in the shadow of his famous father; the judicial career risked time and again when principle dictated an unpopular opinion.

Of this biography, *The New York Times* said, "Justice Holmes lives in these pages in all his genuine nobility of mind, in all his fierce integrity of spirit, in all his salty, practical, tolerant wisdom."

Chapter 1

ON AN AUTUMN MORNING of the year 1800, the Reverend Abiel
Holmes, aged thirty-six, handsome, widowed and lonely, sat
down in his study near Harvard Square in Cambridge, Massachusetts, to begin the writing of his new book. It was his fourth
book; it was to be called *American Annals*, and the very contemplation of it caused its author's blood to run faster.

Since that day when, a boy of fifteen, as poor as he was eager,
he had traveled down from Woodstock, Connecticut, to enter
Yale College, there had run in the veins of Abiel Holmes this
unremitting sense of adventure where things of the mind were
concerned. So would it run in the veins of his son Oliver Wendell Holmes and his son's son of the same name. Minister of the
First Parish Church in Cambridge, Autocrat of the Breakfast-
Table, Justice of the Supreme Court—none made literature his
calling. But all three lived hard and wrote what they lived, and
for all three, the utterance was as important as the living.

ABIEL HOLMES, lifting his eyes from the notes on his desk, looked
out the window across the parsonage yard to where bare maple
branches swept low over a board fence. In the middle of the yard

the free end of the long pump arm slanted skyward. Old Liza had left it up again, Abiel noted. Why didn't she wait and let him carry in the water as he had told her to? Liza was getting too old to keep this big ramshackle house. Even Mary Holmes had hated it. The image of his young wife, dead five years, rose dimly before Abiel. Mary had been too gentle, too meek to hate anything. When chimneys would not draw, when wells went dry or roofs leaked; when life, in short, became too difficult—Mary had sighed and had taken to her bed. Without complaint, smiling gently, she had left chimneys and house and a hard world forever.

What this parsonage needed, Mary's widower reflected now, was a wife. Frowning, Abiel turned back to his desk. This was no time to be thinking of wives. There was a task at hand. He would begin these *Annals* at the beginning, with Columbus, and he would keep on with them, God willing, until his hand was too palsied to hold a pen.

Abiel Holmes loved challenge and looked as if he loved it. Under the clerical gown and bib his shoulders were broad; his thick dark hair hung to his shoulders, curling crisply at the ends; his level deep eyes sparkled with health, his color was high. A passionate antiquarian and scholar, he had read histories of states and of towns, military accounts and the records of travelers. And as he read, there had formed in Abiel's mind a picture into which these several parts fell into place, so that it seemed to him extraordinary that no one, among all these makers of particular histories, had taken the broad view and written of the country as a whole.

Abiel had a warm pride in his country. His father, Captain David Holmes, had fought in two American wars, and Abiel remembered well his father's stories of fighting Indians in the old French War of 1758. And of the war that began at Lexington he had told tales of hardship and heroism to be forgotten by no man's son.

There was so much of history that Abiel knew by word of mouth! It was in his blood. And for years he had collected facts. Military facts, economic facts, facts of American church history, jumbled together, set down any old way:

1791 . . . Samuel Slater sets up his cotton gin.
1792 . . . Connecticut raises mulberry trees and silkworms and
the Rev. Jason Atwater at Branford has a silk gown
from his own worms.

And now the facts were gathered, they lay on Abiel's desk, overflowing the shelves of his study, ready to be "written." He could not put off any longer the shaping of his first page.

He dipped his quill and wrote on the title page:

AMERICAN ANNALS;

OR

A CHRONOLOGICAL

HISTORY OF AMERICA

The first sentence was already formed in his head; the words burned in their author's mind. Moved by the panorama of his country's history, his prose swung out with a bold cadence:

A NEW WORLD has been discovered, which has been receiving inhabitants from the old, more than three hundred years. A new empire has arisen, which has been a theatre of great actions and stupendous events. . . .

Abiel's quill went on and on. The wind rose, windows rattled. Squinting down at his manuscript, Abiel was conscious suddenly that it was dusk. He stood up, his head light with fatigue. There was no sound in the house; outside was a great clamor of November wind. Downstairs he found his dinner, cold hours ago, on the dining-room table: stewed rabbit in cold yellow gravy, cold boiled potatoes. The fires had gone out, the house was like a tomb. . . . Tonight was Monday, there was no prayer meeting. He would not stay alone in this cold house, Abiel decided suddenly. He would go over to Boston and call on his old friend Judge Wendell and tell him the *Annals* was actually begun.

Abiel went into the hall for his wide black hat and greatcoat and, coming back to the dining room, seized an apple from the table. He hurried out the parsonage door. On the steps he

171

paused. It would not do for the Reverend Dr. Holmes to be seen crossing West Boston Bridge eating an apple. Throwing it away, Abiel walked out the gate and turned left. As he crossed the bridge, the full force of the wind caught him; he held his hat with both hands. It was good to lean against the wind, good to feel it buffet him, after all those hours of sitting still. With every step his spirits rose.

Accustomed, like his Puritan forebears, to intense self-analysis, Abiel Holmes, stepping off the bridge to the cobblestones of Boston, wondered why he felt so elated. Sally Wendell would be at home. She was always at home on Monday nights. Perhaps she would open the door to him, dressed in the blue India silk he thought so pretty. Sally Wendell . . . Suddenly, and with the force of something long felt and never confessed, Abiel knew it was not the judge he was walking this distance to see. It was Sally. But Sally was not a girl, she was thirty-one; Boston thought of her as a spinster, long past marriageable age. Sally was a tiny little thing, and so slim with her quick movements like a bird, she did not seem any age at all. When a man was with Sally he did not think about age and suitability.

The Holmeses, Abiel's mother had told him once, were slow at courting. Deacon Holmes, his grandfather, would never have married at all if the young lady had not suddenly, one evening, suggested it herself. Abiel smiled to himself. Turning east toward Oliver Street, he was aware only of his exhilaration, aware that in a moment he would be with Sally Wendell.

Against a narrow, dark street the tall windows of the Wendell mansion shone with candlelight between drawn curtains. Walking up the brick path to the door, Abiel heard the pleasant tinkle of a piano. Sally must be playing. Her voice rose, high and sweet:

> *"Behold, my love, how green the groves,*
> *The primrose banks, how fair."*

Abiel Holmes, taking three steps in a highly unministerial bound, reached for the brass door knocker that shone under the lantern, and felt his heart pound pleasantly in his breast.

IN MARCH, 1801, Thomas Jefferson was inaugurated third President of the United States, bringing with him a new era and a new philosophy. In that same month of March, in the First Parish Church of Cambridge, Sally Wendell became Mrs. Abiel Holmes and, without benefit of wedding journey, walked down the meetinghouse steps and across to take charge of the parsonage. Already the old house wore a different aspect. Its new mistress had had it swept and garnished from top to toe and had brought roomfuls of handsome furniture —cabinets and tables and lowboys and highboys of dark satiny wood.

SALLY WENDELL HOLMES

Abiel Holmes found life suddenly extraordinarily pleasant. He was deeply in love with his wife. In his study, writing the *Annals*, preparing his sermons, he thought of Sally, listened for her high clear voice down the steep stairway. It troubled him, this passionate connubiality. Was it quite in keeping with God's representative—and a man of nearly forty at that? But Sally, cutting straight through his tortured introspection, said, "People don't have to be dreary to be good."

Within a year after they were married, Sally presented her husband with a daughter. Two years later, she presented him with another daughter; and still another year later, she presented him with a third. In that same year, 1805, Abiel's *American Annals* appeared, two stout volumes published in England and the United States. They were received everywhere with acclaim, and Abiel began to prepare for a new edition. On a clean sheet he wrote the date 1805, and under it:

Thomas Jefferson was chosen President, and George Clinton Vice President, of the United States. . . . A Professorship of Natural History, with a botanic garden, was founded in Cambridge. . . .

And in 1806 . . .

The President sent captains Lewis and Clarke to explore the river Missouri, and the best communication from that river to the Pacific ocean. . . .

Life was good, Abiel thought, happy in his work, in his meetinghouse. From the doorsill of his parsonage he looked out on Cambridge Common where a seventeen-starred flag hung now from the staff and the revolutionary cannon sat fat and cocky, not yet rusted through. It was good to see the Common green with summer. The months passed, and in his almanac Abiel made occasional notes of meetings and appointments, adding little that was personal. But on August 29, 1809, Abiel broke his rule. Alongside the date and the printed prediction that the day would be "pleasant," he added a little mark:

> = August 29   Pleasant
>   August 30   Commencement, Cambridge College
> = *son b.*

Thus modestly was announced the advent of Oliver Wendell Holmes, doctor, professor, Autocrat of the Breakfast-Table— and poet laureate to Boston for half a century.

Chapter 2

AUGUST, 1809, a boy born into a quiet college town. Not even a town—a village of tree-lined lanes, of open fields where raspberries grew wild, of salt marshes where the heron built his nest. A courthouse on the square, a markethouse nearby with the big hay scales outside.

Abraham Lincoln was born that year too, far westward in Kentucky, one among thousands of sons born to the new settlers beyond the western ridge of mountains. Josiah Quincy, down in Washington representing Massachusetts in Congress, heard with alarm about these potential voters appearing in log huts. What would become of New England's commercial interests if these farmer-woodsmen brought votes to Washington? When Oliver Holmes was two years old, it was proposed to bring Louisiana in as a state. Josiah Quincy rose to his feet and thundered. The bonds of the Union, said he, must be dissolved rather than admit these Westerners!

Keep the West out! roared New England—and Abiel Holmes wrote quietly in his *Annals:*

> 1812 . . . An act of congress was passed for the admission of Louisiana into the Union . . .

Meanwhile young Oliver, Abiel's son, throve and grew; and presently John, a fat, fair-haired little creature born in 1812, tagged after him. Oliver was an active child, fond of whistling and singing; John was more silent, slower moving.

To Abiel, Oliver sometimes seemed appallingly frivolous; but Oliver was so like his mother it was hard to rebuke him. If he had had his way Oliver would never have stopped talking. At the table he was forever being shushed and forever breaking out again. And how busy he was! Always deep in some project, making wooden skates to use on Craigie's Pond, or out with his gun looking for squirrels. His small hands were surprisingly dexterous. But would the boy never grow? He was small and slight and homely, with a long upper lip, blue eyes and heavy straight brown hair that fell down continually over his forehead. He was voluble and mischievous too. By the time he was fourteen he had been caught twice smoking cigars behind the barn and had been punished for taking John to the public hanging over north by Jones Hill. Abiel Holmes was troubled; neither punishment nor prayer made this boy look sternly on solemn things. His most frequent sin seemed to be laughing at the wrong time. The long faces of visiting Calvinist ministers in particular sent him, for no sound reason, into gales of mirth.

"Be prudent," Abiel advised Oliver. "Be diligent. Be punctual. Avoid bad company." How, wondered Oliver Holmes, did fathers think sons could grow up at all, with ten hundred admonitions weighing them down? He was away at Phillips Academy in Andover now, and on the study-hall clock was written in large letters: YOUTH IS THE SEED-TIME OF LIFE.

The more Oliver read this handy motto the more he resented it; he was far too alive to accept any dreary Calvinist notion that the present was a mere time of preparation for the future. Now was now, and Oliver was prepared to enjoy it as such. He had a delightful friend named Phineas Barnes; the two laughed over everything that happened, whether grave or comic.

Once Oliver was feruled severely at school. But the episode left no scar; the boy was too busy to cherish yesterday's malice. He liked the Latin versifying he was required to do. Translating the *Aeneid* into couplets, he made a phrase one morning that pleased him: *The boiling ocean trembled into calm.* When his Latin master praised it Oliver was thrilled, and put the line away to show his father when he went home.

Next autumn he was a schoolboy no longer. October, 1825 ... Oliver Holmes was a Harvard scholar and proud of it. He was sixteen—quite sure he was a man. Every morning he rose in the dark at the clanging of the college bell and ran across a brown, grassy field to chapel.

He had a splendid time. Lessons were not hard. Oliver played cricket, rowed on the river, skated with his friends and regaled himself afterward with beer. But when he became a senior he had no idea what he was going to do after he had received his diploma. Everyone else in his class, it seemed, had settled upon a career. He was class poet and he would have liked to be an author, but how could a man keep alive on a few poems and stories? Perhaps the law was a good starting point for a career. So Oliver Holmes enrolled as a law student under Judge Story.

Soon he felt a slight uneasiness. The books seemed boring and quite impossible to understand. The suspicion assailed him that if he ever did understand them, they would still be dull. This, he told himself, would wear off; ignorance always makes a man timid. But it did not wear off. For four months, Oliver pursued the law, becoming each month more dismayed. What awful stuff it was! Sawdust and more sawdust ... equity, agency, carrier, procedure ...

Spring came, and instead of writing law Oliver sat by the window looking out on a green world, and wrote poetry. How easily the verses came, pouring out upon the paper! He spent his time, he wrote Barnes, "writing poetry like a madman, and talking sentiment like a turtle dove." Cambridge had the most delightful girls, and lately Oliver had made excursions into Boston too. There was one girl in particular who seemed quite perfect, Miss Amelia Jackson of Bedford Place. She was almost as small as he—a prerequisite for any man of five feet five—and she loved to listen to him talk. Her father was Judge Jackson and her uncle was Dr. James Jackson who taught physic in the medical school, and whose stories of patients fascinated Oliver. And Miss Jackson liked poetry, Oliver discovered. Especially the poetry of O. W. Holmes. Oliver wrote more verses than ever, covering the backs of his old law papers with lines evenly matched.

In September of 1830 he conceived a poem that had nothing to do with love or Miss Amelia Jackson. It had to do with an old, worn-out ship, but it came from the heart all the same and was written furiously, in anger and indignation.

The frigate *Constitution*—"*Old Ironsides*"—whose victorious return to harbor Boston had once greeted with such wild joy, lay now rotting at the wharf. The government announced suddenly that the vessel was to be scrapped. The whole country protested, but with no result. Abiel was almost ill over it; Oliver, bursting in one afternoon, found him sitting moodily at his desk, trying to compose a letter to the Boston *Daily Advertiser*. What weapon, said Abiel Holmes, had he against such outrage?

Oliver went upstairs and, sitting down, got out pen and paper. The lines poured from him, swept from him in a tide.

> *Ay, pull* her tattered ensign down!*
> *Long has it waved on high,*
> *And many an eye has danced to see*
> *That banner in the sky. . . .*
> *Oh better that her shattered hulk*
> *Should sink beneath the wave;*
> *Her thunders shook the mighty deep,*
> *And there should be her grave;*
> *Nail to the mast her holy flag,*
> *Set every threadbare sail,*
> *And give her to the god of storms,*
> *The lightning and the gale!*

---

*Oliver later changed *pull* to *tear*.

177

There were three stanzas. Oliver took them downstairs. His father was still at his desk. Silently, he laid his poem on the desk and left the room. A moment later his father called him. When Oliver came in, Abiel Holmes was standing, the poem in his hand. He began to speak, and his voice choked. With enormous surprise and a great lift of the heart, Oliver saw tears in his father's eyes, saw that the hand holding his verses was trembling.

The poem, published next day in the *Advertiser*, swept Boston like wildfire, then reached beyond Boston all over the country. Printed in broadsides, the verses were sold on the streets of Washington. The government, overwhelmed, gave orders that the frigate *Constitution* be preserved. And in Boston, Cambridge, and far beyond the river Charles, Oliver Wendell Holmes, son of the Reverend Dr. Abiel Holmes, was famous.

SUDDEN FAME did not determine Oliver Holmes to be a poet by profession. The conditions of being an American gentleman of letters were as baffling as ever; *Old Ironsides* brought fame but not money. What success did for Oliver Holmes was to give him courage to abandon the law and study medicine, in which he had become increasingly interested.

In the study of medicine he found himself. Once he had recovered from the initial shock of the operating theater and the dissecting room, he began to love his new profession. By 1833 he had completed his studies under Amelia's uncle, Dr. Jackson, and the next step was a foregone conclusion—he must go abroad and become familiar with the great European hospitals. For thirty months he sat at the feet of the great doctors of La Pitié and the Hôtel Dieu in Paris, and it was December, 1835, before he saw Cambridge again. He found his mother looking well and as brisk as ever, but when he saw his father, Oliver was shocked. Why, he was an old man, white-haired, frail. Oliver, watching from a window, saw him stop outside the gate to speak to a child, reach into his greatcoat pocket and give the child something. He had always carried candy to give to children. But this time it was an old man's gesture. Tears scalded Oliver's eyes.

His brother John was working away at law, and Oliver himself now sought his medical degree from Harvard. In 1836 he won not only his degree but the Boylston Prize as well, the latter for a dissertation on "Intermittent Fever in New England."

He had moved across the river to Boston, rented a room, and set himself up as a physician when, late in May of 1837, his father had a stroke. It left Abiel helpless; he could speak only with difficulty. Sally Holmes, still strong and competent at sixty-eight, tended him, her sons helping. Sitting by her husband's side, she waited through the long hours. When Abiel roused, she seemed to know by a touch of the hand what he wanted. Once Oliver, coming in the door, stood while she finished singing, softly, Abiel's own hymn that he had written long ago about his meetinghouse:

> *"Thy flock, Immanuel, here was fed,*
> *In pastures green and fair,*
> *Beside still waters gently led,*
> *And thine the shepherd's care. . . ."*

Abiel had lost his cherished meetinghouse some years before in a parish controversy, when he had refused to accept the new Unitarian doctrines which had become popular. Sixty of his congregation had gone with him to build a new church. But no new church, Sally knew, had ever taken the place in Abiel's heart of the old wooden meetinghouse where he had worshipped for so long.

On Sunday morning, June 4, the watchers round the bedside noticed a change. Abiel was restless, his lips moved. Oliver, leaning over, caught the words his father was trying to articulate: "If any have injured me, let the injuries—let the injuries—"

Oliver repeated the words aloud, looking at his mother with a puzzled face. Sally did not hesitate. She spoke clearly to her husband: "If any have injured me, let their injuries be written in sand."

Abiel's eyes opened, his lips moved in acquiescence. On the dark plank floor the sun made a pattern by the window; outside, maple leaves stirred in the breeze. A church bell sounded, then another, and Sally Holmes, her eyes on her husband's face, waited for the bell from his own meetinghouse. Among many voices she would know it and so, she was aware, would her husband.

The bell spoke. Abiel turned his face toward the sound, and died.

AFTER HIS FATHER'S FUNERAL, Oliver Holmes returned to Boston. John stayed on in the old house with his mother.

Little by little Oliver became established in his profession. Within three years he was teaching anatomy in addition to practicing medicine, and he had also seen a volume of his verse in print. At last he felt secure about his prospects and, walking over of an evening to call on Amelia Jackson, Oliver eyed the smaller houses along the side streets. Here would be a pleasant, economical place to live. There was no longer any doubt which of the young women in his eye held first place—Amelia of the warm heart and quick tongue. He had not even hinted of love to her. Amelia gave him no chance; she was always talking and asking questions. He was at his best with her.

One day he entered the Jackson residence and found Amelia in the library. On the table there was a small blue volume called *Poems* by Oliver Wendell Holmes. She was standing by the table; her long full skirts swept the floor. She picked up his poems.

"This," she said, "is a very small book, and already I know it by heart. When are you going to write more poetry?"

Oliver laughed. With Milton and Horace and Coleridge on the shelves, surely she did not need more volumes by O.W.H.?

"But I like my poets better alive than dead," Amelia said. She moved a little forward, his book in her hand, her bright brown eyes looking sidewise at him.

For once, his tongue failed. He stood there, silent, and now there rang in his ears something his brother had said to him in a moment of exasperation: "If you can find a girl who can shut you up, marry her, Oliver, and marry her quick."

He knew now what John had meant. Amelia Jackson could make him stop talking and feel life itself, warm and urgent. It was a sensation exhilarating and irresistibly impelling. Oliver took a step forward.

"Amelia," he began. "My *dear* Amelia . . ."

THEY WERE MARRIED on the fifteenth of June, 1840, and Oliver and his bride drove gaily off in Judge Jackson's carriage. It was autumn when they returned to Boston, and they went straight to their new three-story brick house on Montgomery Place, just off the Common.

Amelia plunged happily into housekeeping. She had a talent for domesticity, for making a man comfortable. In all her duties, in fact, Amelia Holmes displayed exemplary promptness. Eight months and twenty-two days after her marriage—the date was March 8, 1841—she gave birth to a son. There was no hesitancy over his name; what could it be but Oliver Wendell Holmes? They would call him Wendell, his father decided; he himself had always preferred it to Oliver.

Looking into the cradle upon his son, young Dr. Holmes was content. He wrote his friend Phineas Barnes that there was "a second edition of your old acquaintance, an o.w.h."

In his cradle o.w.h. lay quiet and noisy by turns, as a healthy baby should. "o.w.h., a second edition." There was none to prophesy that the letters might grow large and larger until the whole country might see them, and countries beyond the water:

OLIVER WENDELL HOLMES, Chief Justice of Massachusetts, author of *The Common Law*, Associate Justice of the United States Supreme Court.

Chapter 3

o.w.h. was born into a Union of twenty-seven states, presided over by President William Henry Harrison. In a month Harrison was dead of pneumonia, and John Tyler took his place. Daniel Webster was Secretary of State and Boston's hero. Shipowners and millowners could count on his shrewd, eloquent support. The China trade flourished; Boston aristocracy lived comfortably, worked hard and prospered. In Lawrence and Lowell, spindles whirled. Every sound businessman knew the twelve-hour day was an excellent thing for workers, whose morals must necessarily suffer from the leisure of a shorter workday. Hard, continuous labor was a Puritan principle, a Calvinistic inheritance. If the labor resulted in money, so much the better.

181

And yet—voices rose in protest. In New England, in Boston, the very center of the creed, voices cried nay. Combat this new materialism with good works! Reform the prisons, the insane asylums! Reform! And if reform moves too slowly for the winged spirit, withdraw from wickedness to Brook Farm,* that ideal community, and dig the soil.

It was all mad, foolish, inspired—and to Dr. Holmes it held no appeal. Of all the literary group about to burst into flower—Emerson, Lowell, Longfellow and the rest—Dr. Holmes was the only one with a scientific training. In the hospital, the sight of people dying left him no heart to reform the living; first of all a way must be found to make men stay alive. In particular, the numerous deaths from puerperal fever distressed Holmes, who suspected the fever was contagious. But Lister was still a boy, the germ theory was unknown, contagiousness could be proved only by the observations of common sense.

Common sense happened to be the quality Dr. Holmes possessed perhaps beyond all other qualities. Slowly, painstakingly, he collected his evidence. Puerperal fever was carried from bed to bed by doctors, nurses, midwives. Case by case Dr. Holmes put it all down. He called his paper "The Contagiousness of Puerperal Fever." In April, 1843, he published it.

The profession rose up in arms, hurling angry refutation. Dr. Holmes had trod on too many toes. Now and again Holmes answered his critics. "I am too much in earnest for either humility or vanity, but I do entreat those who hold the keys of life and death to listen to me also for this once. I beg to be heard in behalf of those women whose lives are at stake."

Holmes's own wife was safely delivered again that autumn. They named the baby after her mother: Amelia Jackson Holmes. The household on Montgomery Place was very busy. Holmes lectured and wrote medical essays. He also wrote humorous verses. Wit bubbled from him and he hated solemnity; he had seen too much of it in his youth.

In the spring of 1847, Dr. Holmes was named professor of

---

*An experiment in group living, begun by transcendentalists, which flourished between 1841 and 1847. Nathaniel Hawthorne and Charles A. Dana were among the members.

anatomy and physiology in the Harvard Medical School. It was an enormous satisfaction. His life path stretched ahead now, broad and brisk, filled with honorable business.

OLIVER WENDELL HOLMES, SR.

Looking at his family, Dr. Holmes felt content. Wendell, now six years old, was a sturdy boy with alert, blue-gray eyes, a high color, and dark shiny hair that fell over his high forehead. And Wendell had a new brother: Edward Jackson Holmes, born October 17, 1846, and called Neddy.

Two boys and a girl; the family was complete. The household prospered. Along the Oregon Trail, prairie schooners crawled westward, a dusty, never-ending line. Two by two the states came into the Union: Arkansas and Michigan, Iowa and Florida, slave and free, free and slave, always one to balance the other. And as the country expanded the towns raised their standards of living, contrived ways to be comfortable, ways to be clean. On an autumn day of 1848, Boston's great new aqueduct from Cochituate was finished, and the town held a grand celebration. Wendell Holmes, holding his small fat sister Amelia by the hand, stood on Tremont Street to watch his father pass in the long parade with the president of Harvard and all the professors.

The year Wendell was ten, he was sent to Epes Dixwell's school for older boys. Dixwell, a brilliant scholar who loved Latin and Greek, was just starting his school that year. Every morning, Wendell waited in the yard with the other boys till Mr. Dixwell appeared, a tall man, walking briskly, dressed in a costume that caused the boys to marvel: purple frock coat, a green velvet waistcoat and black-and-white checked trousers.

Wendell made no particular record as a scholar at Epes Dixwell's school. He was healthy, red-cheeked, strong, and while he cared little for football and cricket, he loved to do things outdoors.

In winter he skated or, on days when the snow was good, dragged his sled to school, and afterward hurried with his friends to the "Long Coast." This ran right through Boston Common. It was exciting business. Nobody merely coasted— they raced. The fastest sleds had names: spectators bet on them. Wendell's sled was long, it curved upward in front and was painted yellow, adorned with a bright red flying horse.

At thirteen, he was as tall as his father. His face was too thin for beauty, his chin too long. He was growing like a weed; his hands and feet were hard to manage. But there was something arresting in his face; and his eyes were startlingly clear and intelligent.

He was an entirely normal boy; healthy, strong, active. But he was not like the rest of the family. And already, the beholder felt it. The doctor, Amelia, Neddy—even Mrs. Holmes—were chatterers, quick, voluble, always moving about the room, jumping up, sitting down, interrupting each other. They were like a nest of wrens, a visitor said, leaving the house one after-noon. Among them Wendell stood apart. He could be noisy; his laugh was a great shout, coming from deep within. But often, when his father held forth at the tea table, he closed his mind automatically, retreating to a world of his own. There was about him a quality of reserve, something romantic, something that beckoned, giving promise of depths to be explored.

Two months of each summer the Holmes family spent in the Berkshire Hills, near Pittsfield, where Dr. Holmes had built a house. Longfellow lived nearby, and Mr. Nathaniel Hawthorne. From the wide front porch you could see Greylock Mountain and the swift-tumbling Housatonic River. The hillsides were wild with scrub and pine, high pastures where the granite rocks showed rough and gray, warm under a boy's bare foot at noon-tide. Wendell, starting off for an afternoon's fishing or going out with his pail to gather blueberries, would meet his mother and Amelia trundling the red wheelbarrow with soil for their little garden. Dr. Holmes was always busy about the place, fixing and mending, making small contraptions. There was a smell of clover in the south meadow. And at night the stars looked down on a wide, quiet countryside.

Amelia Holmes, saying good-night to her children in their

rooms, carried the lamp to the hall bracket above the stairs. How good it was here, she thought, with a little sigh of thankfulness, and how safe! God grant the children's lives would stay this way always—peaceful and content, free from harm and those dark evil winds that blow across the world.

THE TRANSITION from Dixwell's school to Harvard College was for Wendell, at sixteen, no revolution. He was doing what his father and uncle had done, what his cousins were doing.

The Cambridge scene was little changed since Dr. Holmes's day: it was still very rural and neighborly. There was no choice of subjects at the college; and teaching was the same old system of grammar-school recitation. You got through by memorizing the textbooks. A student was not expected to question either textbook or lecturer. The students were treated like boys at boarding school—forbidden to shout from the windows of their dormitory, forbidden to "collect in groups." Their days were regulated, nearly every hour accounted for. In the College Yard the penalty for swearing was high; you could not throw snowballs or get into a good fistfight with your friends.

Being a boarder at the house of a Mr. Danforth, Wendell was not subject to quite as strict rules as the boys in the dormitory—but he was subject to almost the same discomforts. His room, bleak and uncarpeted, was nearly filled with a large featherbed and warmed only by the open fire. In the dormitory, boys heated a cannonball on extra cold days and placed it over the fire in a skillet. It gave out a pleasant round red glow. A large part of every student's time was spent trying to keep warm. One boy used to pour water round his window frames; ice makes excellent insulation.

It upset Dr. Holmes that the boys did not show more interest in athletics, and he said so in *The Autocrat of the Breakfast-Table*, the title he had given to his column in a new magazine, *The Atlantic Monthly*. "Such a set of black-coated, stiff-jointed soft-muscled, paste-complexioned youth," he wrote, "as we can boast in our Atlantic cities never before sprang from loins of Anglo-Saxon lineage. . . . We have a few good boatmen—no good horsemen that I hear of . . ."

But what Wendell liked in the way of exercise was an hour's skating on the Fresh Pond, with plenty of beer and oysters afterward with his friends. Or a stroll up to Garden Street for tea with Fanny Dixwell, Epes Dixwell's attractive eldest daughter.

Most certainly he did not embrace exercise because the Autocrat recommended it. The *Autocrat* was out in book form now; even the Germans were going to publish it under the grandiose title of *Der Tisch-Despot.* But the more famous the Autocrat became, the more Wendell distrusted his father in this new guise of town prophet and interpreter. There was no telling what he would expose next. Wendell was afraid to talk at home, to tell about the class dinner or club elections. Everything was grist to the Autocrat's mill. Wendell suffered agonies concerning this indecent lack of privacy. He went gloomily across the Square to talk to his uncle John, who had given up his law practice to look after his mother.

"Don't take it so hard, Wendell," he said. "You will get used to your father. I did, long ago."

BY THE END of his sophomore year, Wendell had fallen from twenty-second in his class to thirtieth. Dr. Holmes grumbled to his wife. "Thirtieth! What kind of position in the class is that?"

Amelia Holmes shook her head. "The boy is just eighteen, thin as a fence rail, and six feet three. I don't believe he has his growth even yet. It takes *energy* to grow."

Dr. Holmes, observing his own five feet five in the mirror over the bureau, remarked that that was something he didn't know much about. But the boy seemed so lazy. Spent hours mooning on the window seat in the library, a book in his hand.

Amelia, sitting in the bedroom rocker darning a sock, remarked to her husband that he was growing more like his own father every day. The things he expected from the boys! Neddy was half dead trying to be first in his class at Dixwell's. One night long ago, when she and Oliver Holmes were engaged, Oliver's father had given him a long lecture about something. Oliver, furious, had burst into Amelia's house complaining that fathers ought not to become too steeped in virtue. . . . When she reminded him, Dr. Holmes laughed. "Did I say that, 'Melia?"

He looked pleased. " 'Too steeped in virtue!' Graphic kind of phrase." Amelia Holmes went on with her darning. A sigh escaped her. One quoted phrase of his own, and already her husband had forgotten everything she had said about her sons. It would be useless now to pursue the subject. Something was wrong between father and son, and nothing she said could right it.

THE FOLLOWING CHRISTMAS, Wendell received Plato's *Works* as a present. All through his six weeks' winter vacation, Wendell read the *Republic*, searching its pages with curiosity. He found it not wholly to his taste. After a month's study, he wrote out fifteen pages of conclusions; he might offer them to the *University Quarterly;* there was a yearly prize for the best undergraduate essay. But someone not connected with Harvard should read it first. He thought of Ralph Waldo Emerson, an old family friend. When you asked Emerson a question he looked you straight in the eye and answered you as man to man.

Wendell gave his essay to Emerson, and Emerson read it through. When he was done he held it out to Wendell and shook his head. "When you shoot at a king, you must kill him."

That was all. Wendell took his fifteen pages to his room and flung them in the wastebasket. A month later he saw Emerson again. "Have you given Plato another chance?" Emerson asked, the deep eyes kind under the bushy gray brows. "Say to yourself, 'Plato, you have pleased the world for two thousand years. Now let's see if you can please *me.*' "

For the first time in his life, Wendell Holmes began to work his mind. He studied deeply, painstakingly, hour after hour in his room, forgetful of time, surprised when the gong rang for supper or when, on the landing below, the clock struck deep, slow midnight. When the yearly marks were computed, he stood thirteenth in his class. All the following summer he worked over a new essay on Plato. The *University Quarterly* published it in October, and it won the undergraduate prize.

It was becoming a habit with Wendell to drop in at the Dixwells'. When the prize was announced, Fanny asked him to bring the essay and read it to her. Wendell looked at her suspiciously. "Are you going to laugh at me, Fanny?"

YANKEE FROM OLYMPUS

She liked the Plato article—but wasn't there room for a trifle more investigation on the subject? At the Athenaeum the Holmes library card grew thick with titles. He even bought a six-volume German edition of Plato.

"Can you read it?" Fanny Dixwell asked suspiciously.

Wendell laughed. "No—but I can spell it out . . . Fanny, you attack a man's vanity like a—like a she-wolf. You are a witch." She was twenty now. Her mind was quick and so was her tongue.

This was not the first time Fanny had been accused of being slightly fey. She smiled, looking slantwise at Wendell, her strong fine hands clasped in her lap. "You are cleverer than I, Wendell Holmes," she said softly. "But sometimes I think it is going to take you a long time to grow up."

FAR MORE SERIOUS MATTERS were soon to occupy Wendell and his classmates. In the fall of 1860, he started his senior year at Harvard; it was an election year. Wendell lacked sixteen months of voting age and regretted it. Lincoln did not need his vote, that was becoming pretty certain. But Wendell would have liked to give testimony as to where he stood.

Election Day fell on the sixth of November—a morning of pale blue, cloudless sky. Men stood in groups on the street corners, talking. They did not ask, "Will Lincoln win?" They asked, "Will the cotton states secede when they see a black Republican in the White House?"

The black Republicans won. Through the winter and into the spring the sense of crisis deepened. On Friday the twelfth of April, Confederate forces bombarded Fort Sumter. On Monday, April fifteenth, Lincoln sent out the call for 75,000 militia.

On the twenty-fourth of April, Wendell Holmes joined the Fourth Battalion, New England Guard. At the armory the next day, he signed his name and climbed into his Zouave trousers—light blue and baggy, tucked into gaiters. His tunic was dark blue, his red cap highly becoming. Dr. Holmes thought so anyway; he came to the armory to see the boys off. He busied about, talking ten to the dozen, greeting the new recruits by name. Everyone was glad to see him. Everyone, that is, but his son. Catching his father's eye upon him, Wendell recognized only

188

too well that eager, abstracted stare. Surely, some things were sacred, exempt from the rapacious literary eye? Surely, his father would not take advantage of war itself to make word pictures?

(In a few months, the first word picture would flaunt itself in the *Atlantic:* "If the young Zouave of the family looks smart in his new uniform, its respectable head is content. . . . He will cheerfully calm the perturbed nap of his old beaver by patient brushing in place of buying a new one, if only the Lieutenant's jaunty cap is what it should be.")

But in April, 1861, Wendell Holmes was a simple private and

RALPH WALDO EMERSON

he wished his father would mind his own business. Out at Fort Independence Wendell drilled six hours a day, but the Harvard boys with the battalion were to take their final examinations in June with the rest of the class. Holmes and his friend Norwood Hallowell had been elected class poet and class orator; their respective creations would have to be hammered out in barracks.

On a fine June twenty-first, the class of '61, in gowns and high beaver hats, met in front of Holworthy Hall for class day. Under his gown Wendell Holmes clutched his poem. The band played a march; the procession started. Hallowell and Holmes walked together. They had both sworn to burn their pieces when the day was over.

Marching into the meetinghouse, the seniors took their seats on the platform. Holmes, looking down at the audience, saw his family right out front—his father and mother, Amelia and Neddy. Hallowell delivered his oration, Holmes his poem; the class ode was sung; the audience applauded wildly, and audience and performers poured out of the meetinghouse and went visiting round. Later, the band, under the trees, struck up dance music. The lancers . . . quadrilles.

Girls in light summer dresses, seniors in black gowns. A sprinkling of uniforms, white gloves, shiny new swords. Wendell's sister Amelia looked pretty as a picture in her pink bonnet and white silk dress. Fanny Dixwell wore gray, with a touch of red at her throat. She was surrounded by beaux; Wendell could hardly get a word with her. How handsome she looked, he thought suddenly. Today, everything stood out in sharp relief; something in the air made every face, every sound, etch itself deeply, terribly in the mind. It was not only that Wendell Holmes was leaving college. He would come back from this war, he told himself. . . . But when he returned he would be a boy no longer. His heart ached strangely within him.

They were singing the class song: *"Classmates as the hasting moments . . ."* Rings of students formed round the tree. Hand in hand, freshmen outside, seniors inside close to the tree. Round and round the tree they danced, swinging their clasped hands in the ancient ceremony. Faster and faster until the rings broke and the boys leaped scrambling for the wreath of flowers that encircled the tree above their heads.

Wendell got a rose and flung it across the crowd to Fanny. His breath came hard; he stood stock-still in the scrambling, shouting crowd and was amazed to find himself weeping.

Chapter 4

JULY, 1861 . . . Eight miles south of Boston the railroad cars jerked to a stop at Readville Station. Lieutenant Holmes, holding a commission now in the Twentieth Massachusetts Volunteer Infantry, got down and walked across a grassy plain to a line of white tents. There were shouts of welcome; Hallowell and other Harvard friends ran out to meet him.

Holmes found his company small. But if Company A was small, it was more than large enough for Lieutenant Holmes to handle. He was green as grass and very nervous—far more used to taking suggestions from his elders than to giving out commands himself. Each time a new batch of Nantucket men came in, Holmes prayed he would not get them in his company. All these boys were Yankee-independent. "Why shouldn't a man go where he pleased when his day's work was done without asking leave of any goddam officer?" When drill was over the men simply departed—without leave—across the plain to Mill Village and got thoroughly drunk.

Marching orders came on the second of September, and the regiment moved to Maryland. Camp was laid in a wheatfield about two miles from Edwards Ferry on the Potomac. September, October. . . . The regiment still camped on its hillside, golden now with autumn. A mile away across the river the rebels moved soft-footed among the trees. Their aim was good; now and then a man did not return from guard duty.

Sunday, October twentieth, was warm and clear, the camp very quiet. After dinner, Lieutenant Holmes sat in the door of his tent, looking downhill toward the river. On the riverbank the maples flamed yellow. Above the river a hawk wheeled slowly. At home they were just sitting down to Sunday dinner. . . . The quiet was broken by a bugle. It was the call to arms. From everywhere, men ran to position, grabbing up equipment.

It was more than the call to arms. It was the call to battle. By the following morning, in a field on Ball's Bluff on the Virginia side of the river, the Twentieth lay in high grass and waited. Across the field the enemy waited too, hidden by thick trees. It had taken the men half the night to cross the river in four leaky old scows. . . . The lines were formed, and now, at command, Holmes's company cocked their rifles, fired straight into the woods.

After that things happened fast. Charging out of the woods the rebels yelled, high and savage, like Indians. Up from the river came the Tammany Regiment, and the California, single file in the smoke. Holmes had not fired twice when a spent ball hit him in the stomach. When he got his wind he struggled up.

Over by the grove, they were fighting hand to hand. Going down on one knee, Holmes aimed. . . . The blow came again, in the chest this time. He fell, vomited, lay with his eyes shut. The pain in his chest was terrible. In his tunic pocket was a bottle of laudanum. He lifted a hand to see if he could reach it. . . . Why, he had no shirt on! His breast was wet and slippery. Wendell fainted. Around him the battle went on and on. . . .

BOSTON, HALF CRAZY WITH ANXIETY, waited for news. There had been an engagement in Virginia, the *Post* said, but gave no word as to defeat or victory, named no casualties. Mrs. Holmes went dumbly about the house, her face blank, stricken. On Friday—five days after the battle—word came at last by telegram from a friend. Wendell had been hit in the chest. He was in the field hospital, and doing well. He would travel to Philadelphia with Hallowell when able. They were not to worry.

That same day, the *Post* carried a full account of the battle. Reading it, Dr. Holmes turned white. The whole thing had been a horrible defeat for the North. WORSE THAN A CRIME—A BLUNDER! said the headlines. The boys had fought all day. Toward dusk they had been driven back into the river, trying to swim, calling for help in the swift current. The river ran blood; there had been no plan apparently for rescue.

Three weeks later, when Wendell could travel, Dr. Holmes went to fetch him in Philadelphia. He found his son white as a sheet, barely able to walk, but very glad to see his father. Wendell had been incredibly lucky; the ball had passed right through his chest, missing heart and lungs by a fraction. Dr. Holmes engaged six seats on the cars to Boston and had a mattress spread across them. Leaning on his father's arm, Wendell climbed into the train. . . . How tractable he was! Dr. Holmes marveled, looking down at the face on the bed, the eyes closed, the lashes dark against the pallor. . . . But the boy would not talk. Dr. Holmes itched to know all. What was it like when those minié balls whined by your ear? Was it true that the rebels yelled when they went into battle? Was it true that Will Putnam had died? Will—the golden-haired, the handsomest man in Harvard College? It was true, Wendell replied wearily.

Back home, Wendell was carried upstairs and put to bed. The reticence of the first weeks presently left him. He was still very white, but the haunted look left his eyes and returned only at night or when he was tired. By the New Year, his wound was healed. He was ordered to stay home on recruiting duty for a while. Then, on the twenty-third of March, his next orders came. He was to rejoin the regiment at Hampton, Virginia, with the rank of captain. He was just twenty-one.

CAPTAIN HOLMES FOUND HIS REGIMENT on the Virginia Peninsula. This time he would learn what war really meant to soldiers in the field, for now began the march up the peninsula to find Stonewall Jackson and fight him down to Richmond. Through swamp and tangled thicket the men struggled, their blue uniforms coated with mud. The rains began; the men stood in water by day and lay in it by night. The enemy was always near; at dawn the sharpshooters got to work. Scurvy broke out, and dysentery; the men lay in misery on the ground. May, June, July. . . . To Wendell Holmes, marching endlessly under the steaming sun, all faculties of the soul seemed to depart, leaving only a dumb animal power to set the teeth and persist. By the time they met the enemy face-to-face, a third of the regiment was sick, and many were sent back by ambulance to the James River, moaning, half delirious.

Wendell Holmes was sick too, but he managed to keep on his feet, numb with misery and fatigue . . . *Fair Oaks, Gaines' Mills, Garnett's, Golding's, Glendale, Malvern Hill.* . . . Battle after battle across plowed fields, cornfields, thicket and wood. With rifle, bayonet and pistol, they fought the enemy, hand to hand sometimes, rolling on the ground together.

Back at Harrison's Landing on the James River, after four months of fighting, Captain Holmes lay under the stars, too tired to sleep. . . . What a mess the regiment was now! Hallowell wounded. Sixteen thousand Federal troops killed or missing on the peninsula since June. War was not gallantry, heroism, adventure. War was terrible and dull.

The Army of the Potomac moved northwest, out of the wilderness of the peninsula, on to Antietam. For Wendell Holmes, Antietam looked as if it would be just one more battle—horrible, exhausting, leading nowhither—but to be gone through to the topmost level of a man's ability. The Twentieth moved across country by the Hagerstown Pike. Firing began; Holmes's company was ordered forward, at double-quick, into the West Wood. Holmes got them through the wood and out to a cornfield beyond. The morning was misty; smoke from the guns lay heavy. Holmes lost his bearings completely, and then the enemy poured in on their rear. In rows, men fell among the corn, but the ranks of the Twentieth did not break. What was left of them "retired to the right"—the official account says laconically—"at ordinary step, with arms at the shoulder."

Captain Holmes did not retire. He lay on the ground where he had fallen, shot through the neck. Blackness closed on him. Later a captain from Ohio named Leduc helped him to a farmhouse, its floor covered with wounded men. Holmes lay on the floor and waited with the rest. Flies buzzed and settled and buzzed again. Like thunder the guns roared, over by Sharpsburg. . . . It was turning dusk when Holmes was called, tried to stand, felt sick, felt an ambulance sway and jolt beneath him.

IT WAS MIDNIGHT when the messenger knocked at the Holmes's door in Boston. Dr. Holmes reached for the telegram.

HAGERSTOWN 17TH [Dr. Holmes read aloud] CAPTAIN HOLMES WOUNDED SHOT THROUGH THE NECK THOUGHT NOT MORTAL AT KEEDYSVILLE

WILLIAM G LEDUC

"If I start tomorrow," Dr. Holmes said to Amelia, "I can reach Philadelphia by Friday, and plan from there."

And now began for Dr. Holmes a crazy journey that was to last six days, a bewildered search after his son that led him by rail, hack and hired team through Baltimore, Frederick, Middletown, Keedysville. The things he saw on his journey, the things he heard, were etched by anxiety upon his memory. The ruined bridge over the Monocacy, the girders lying crushed on the bank. A shallow grave nearby, with two hands sticking up—belonging to the boy who fired the explosion. And on the far side of Frederick the terrible procession of wounded, a never-ending stream. Leaning from his wagon, Dr. Holmes scanned the faces. That tall boy ahead? . . . No, his hair was too light. That long figure lying by the roadside? . . . No, not Wendell. . . . At last, in Harrisburg, a message reached him. Captain Holmes, cared for in Hagerstown at the house of a Union sympathizer, was leaving immediately by train for Harrisburg.

Dr. Holmes was able to meet Wendell and to escort him

homeward. But it was not easy, he found on the train, to talk to his son. In his faded blue uniform, the bandage round his neck, Wendell sat opposite his father and responded in monosyllables.

They reached Boston at last, and to Dr. Holmes the sight of his own doorplate had never been so welcome. Mrs. Holmes and Amelia took Wendell upstairs and put him to bed. After supper the doctor went to his study, closed the door, poked up the fire, sat down at his desk and reached for his pen. "My Hunt after the Captain" would make a good title. He could finish a piece for the *Atlantic* in three days if he kept at it. . . .

Rest and sleep did not alter Wendell's silence. While he had been in Virginia, Sally Holmes had died. She was ninety-three; it was time for her to go. But for Wendell it was one less thing to come home to, one less thing to be certain of.

Visitors who asked about the war were offended by what he said. "War?" he repeated coldly, his blue-gray eyes remote. "War is an organized bore." To Wendell it seemed incredible that people would ask for stories of the battlefields as for tales of a circus or a boat race. What he knew now of battlefields was better forgotten. But he could not forget, and his flesh crawled when he read his father's piece for the *Atlantic*, "My Hunt after the Captain." He tried to skip, tried to stop reading, but continued in horrid fascination to the end . . . *In the first car, on the fourth seat to the right, I saw my Captain; there I saw him, even my first-born, whom I had sought through many cities.*

"How are you, Boy?"

"How are you, Dad?"

Oh my God! thought Captain Holmes, blushing to the roots of his hair, "Boy?" . . . His father had never called him Boy in his life. What if Company A should get hold of this? There was no need for Wendell Holmes to tell his father what he thought of this latest performance of the literary mind. Dr. Holmes knew what his son thought—and ignored it cheerfully. The young were ridiculously sensitive; why should not a man desire to share his experiences with a waiting world?

After six weeks Wendell's wound was healed, and he returned to his regiment. Snow had fallen; winter quarters on the Rappahannock were bleak, and the Army of the Potomac was

demoralized. The arrival of spring at last meant but one thing—
renewal of battle. And in early May came Chancellorsville.
Captain Holmes's company advanced up the river road to
Chancellorsville in the early mist. Firing had not begun, but at
the canal, knowing he was in full view of the enemy's guns from
the hills beyond, Holmes ordered his men sharply to lie down.
He had not finished speaking when the first shell came over—
and tore the cape from his overcoat. He threw himself down full
length, grabbed a rifle from one of his men and sighted it at
the enemy.

When the next volley came, Holmes buried his face in the
grass. His long legs were crossed, one ankle over the other.
Shrapnel that missed his head caught the heel of the foot that
was uppermost. A terrific blow, tearing ligament and tendons.
My leg is gone, he thought, and fainted.

IT WAS HOLMES's third and last wound. It would keep him out
of the war for nine months, it would trouble him for years to
come. Recuperating back in Boston, he watched the casualty
lists grimly. Gettysburg . . . Vicksburg . . . Day after day the
bodies of his friends returned to the city—"Packed in ice," the
newspapers announced, proud of the new arrangement. Waiting
here in the city, seeing one by one the bodies of his friends
come home, standing while the muffled drums beat farewell,
with no tear permitted, no relaxing of the soldier's brow—how
awful it was! By the time Holmes returned to the front in
January, 1864, there was almost nothing left of the old Twentieth Regiment. The number of casualties to date almost equaled
the roster of the regiment when Holmes had joined it.

This time Wendell was put on staff duty. His part in the war
was nearly done. But there was one memorable moment in a
fortification outside Washington. Jubal Early was burning and
looting his way through Maryland, and Grant, busy before
Petersburg, ordered General Wright to take three brigades
north to defend the capital. As they took up positions in Fort
Stevens, Lincoln himself came out to see them. Below the para-
pets, Early's troops lay waiting.

The President climbed a parapet. The firing began. "You had

better get out of the fire," General Wright said. The President
did not move. On the parapet five feet from him a man was shot.
Just three feet away an officer fell dead.

"Get down, you fool!" a young voice shouted. The President
stepped back. It was Wendell Holmes, angry and terrified.

Lincoln looked down at the white face, streaked with dirt.
"Captain," he said, "I am glad you know how to talk to a
civilian."

It was the only time Holmes spoke to his President—and it
was the last fighting he would ever see.

On the first of August, 1864, Holmes, with the other three-
year men, was mustered out of the Twentieth Regiment on
Boston Common. Holmes carried the title of lieutenant colonel,
brevetted for "gallant and meritorious service at the battle of
Chancellorsville."

"Don't call me hero," Holmes said long after the war was
over. "I trust I did my duty as a soldier respectably, but I was
not born for it and did nothing remarkable in that way."

It was true. But it is true also that to do one's duty as a soldier
respectably has its own peculiar definition. During those years
the soldier's creed became part of Holmes, part of his blood
and bone, engendering its own philosophy. Again and again, he
gave testimony to what he had learned in the war:

> To ride boldly at what is in front of you, be it fence or
> enemy; to pray, not for comfort, but for combat; . . . to love
> glory more than the temptations of wallowing ease, but to know
> that one's final judge and only rival is oneself. . . .

War can make cynics; it can make a "lost generation." Or
perhaps like life itself, war merely makes cynics of cynics—and
saints of saints.

Chapter 5

SEPTEMBER, 1864 . . . A young man walks up the steps of Dane
Hall on Harvard Square and takes his seat in the lecture room of
Judge Joel Parker.

"Law student," Holmes had written three years ago in his

army identification papers. On his return from the war he would have liked to enroll in the law school immediately. But he hesitated. Was the law really his objective in life? There was one other possibility: philosophy, with the eventual goal a professorship at Harvard. Since the prize essay on Plato, Holmes's passion for philosophy had grown steadily deeper. The question was: Should such knowledge be pursued with only itself as goal, or was it better to have a focus, some clinical application outside the classroom such as a moneymaking law practice that brought a man up against the world and its living problems?

Holmes now recognized clearly that his powers were intellectual, that he was an "internal" man, to whom ideas were more interesting than things. But if he embraced pure scholarship, if he followed in the footsteps of such a man as Emerson, might he not, at forty, find himself dwelling in a cloud land of pure speculation, his vital force diluted in this rarefied region?

He examined himself, he discussed his problem with Emerson. Then one morning he knocked on the door of his father's study. "I am going to the law school," he said without preamble.

Dr. Holmes looked up from his desk. "What is the use of that, Wendell?" he said. "A lawyer can't be a great man."

If he had tried, Dr. Holmes could not have devised a statement more provocative to his son. The words struck home, pointed, steel-shafted. If there had been doubts, they were resolved now. "A lawyer can't be a great man." When he was ninety, Wendell Holmes would quote that phrase.

Still, Wendell knew in all fairness, there was tradition behind Dr. Holmes's remark. Not so very long ago, America had looked upon lawyers as tradesmen who earned a questionable living by cleverness and chicanery. The Harvard Law School in 1864 was not yet fifty years old. It had three lecturers, all elderly men. There were no requirements for admission. The student could enter at any time during the winter, sit down with the others and try to catch up. At the end of eighteen months he would receive, without examination, a certificate called LL.B. which would not, of course, admit him to the bar.

Wendell Holmes had no complaint to make concerning this system. How could he, when nothing existed with which to compare it? To him the law was a door opening out on all mankind, and he was soon immersed in his studies. While he had been gone, his family had moved to a house on Charles Street. Wendell now lived there, going back and forth in the horsecars over the West Bridge, carrying his large brown books. Austin's *Jurisprudence*. Walker's *Introduction to American Law*. Walker advised the student to shun delights and live laborious days. "Genius, without toil," Holmes read on page nineteen, "may, to some extent, distinguish a man elsewhere; but here he must labor, or he cannot succeed. No quickness of invention can supply the place of patient investigation."

Wendell reveled in this investigation. In the Marshall Club, the students' law club, he argued cases with fellow law students. And it was not only the law he talked about; it was all the problems of the universe. He brought home many young men, drew them upstairs to his room under the flaring gas lamp. William James and Henry Bowditch, both medical students. Charles Pierce, the ferocious young philosopher. Men who were not embarrassed by the largest, angriest topic. Whiskey would be on the table, the air would be blue with pipe smoke.

Talk also turned on the war. In February, 1865, Charleston fell. Two weeks later, Lincoln was inaugurated. And on Monday, April 10, the news came for which the people had waited. PRAISE GOD! the headlines said. SURRENDER OF LEE AND HIS WHOLE ARMY. In Boston that day, nobody did anything but shout, dance, pray and make speeches. By night the city was crazy with fireworks. The Holmes family walked downtown. In the streets beyond the Common there was singing, the refrain came over the hill. *"The Union forever, Hurrah, boys, hurrah!"*

Mrs. Holmes pressed her husband's arm; Dr. Holmes became aware that she was talking to herself, saying something over and over, quietly. Tears streamed down her face. "The war is over," she was saying. "Thank God, thank God, the war is over."

IN THE AUTUMN of 1865, Holmes resumed his studies at the law school. Now in his second year, he looked at his courses with a dispassionate eye and found them wanting. His teachers were admirable men, but when you had mastered the subjects they presented, where did it lead? Holmes had thought to make all knowledge his province, walking from ignorance to light through a door labeled THE LAW. Now he found himself wandering in a maze of technicalities, with no progress made, no path revealed.

The trouble was that in 1865 the tools of legal education were dishearteningly inadequate. Year after year the same ancient books were given the student, the same rules to learn by rote.

And yet, observing Holmes at twenty-four as he pursues his way through the law, one has the impression that the lack of compass and chart was for him a not unfavorable circumstance. Lack of tools may cause the weak to abandon their project. But to the strong it is a constant, irksome challenge. What pioneer ever had chart and a lighthouse to steer by?

Wendell Holmes could not know that in the field of historical jurisprudence he was to be a pioneer. He sought a perspective based on that ordered precedent which is history. No wonder he could not find it. He was himself to be its spokesman.

"THE ONLY FELLOW here I care anything about is Holmes," wrote William James in 1866 to a friend. "He is on the whole a first-rate article, and one which improves by wear. He is perhaps too exclusively intellectual, but sees things so easily and clearly and talks so admirably that it's a treat to be with him." Young James, later to become famous as a philosopher, was studying medicine at Harvard. Not only was the attraction mutual between him and Wendell, but Dr. Holmes also was charmed with James.

Dr. Holmes would have agreed with him that Wendell was too exclusively intellectual. But the doctor would not have used such flattering terms. He would have said that Wendell took himself too seriously. Once he seized upon a subject, Wendell could not let it go. There was fire in his eye when he talked; he shouted, waving his arms, striding up and down, banging out his pipe against the mantel as if his pipe were the common enemy and he must smash it. But his words were cold, logical. "*Feeling* counts," James said one night. The doctor applauded. Wendell's reply was quick. "To know is not less than to feel," he said.

But it was not to his father that Wendell Holmes expounded

his views on the universe. Upstairs under the gas lamp that smelled and sputtered, he and James and their friends argued passionately about everything in creation. It was a time of extraordinary intellectual and spiritual ferment. Darwin's *Origin of Species* was six years old. The English-speaking world was going through a complete rebirth in science, theology, economics, sociology, and last of all, law. Wendell sat up all night practicing new terminologies upon his friends. Very soon, his ideas were to have but one focus, the law. But now he was trying his wings, was exercising tongue and brain upon every subject, every person available—including Fanny Dixwell.

William James wrote to a friend: "I made the acquaintance the other day of Miss Fanny Dixwell. Do you know her? She is decidedly A1, and (so far) the best girl I have known." And to his brother: "Miss Dixwell is about as fine as they make 'em. That villain Wendell Holmes has been keeping her all to himself out at Cambridge for the last eight years; but I hope I may enjoy her acquaintance now. She is A1, if anyone ever was."

That villain Wendell Holmes would have been astonished at this description of his relationship with Fanny. She was perhaps his most intimate friend, and he had known her since they were children; but Holmes saw plenty of girls. Fanny was twenty-five now. She was the girl a fellow could take his troubles to, talk to by the hour, and Wendell felt as much at home at the Dixwells' house as he did on Charles Street.

This spring he talked much to Fanny about the trip to England he was to make when his course at the law school was over. After the manner of women listening to masculine plans they may not share, Fanny's words were enthusiastic. It would be splendid, she said, the clear color high in her cheeks. "But your father tells me you will have entrée to some very big houses. Do you think you will be able to hold your own?"

At home that evening, Wendell repeated Fanny's words, and a queer little silence fell. It was Neddy, now a junior at Harvard, who broke it. "You are not very discerning about Fanny Dixwell, Brother," he said.

Dr. and Mrs. Holmes smiled, their eyes meeting down the length of the table. But as the family rose from supper, Mrs.

Holmes told herself that Neddy was right. Wendell was *not* very discerning about Fanny.

Toward the middle of May, Holmes sailed. Before he left Boston, George Shattuck, a superb trial lawyer, asked him to come into his office next winter and read for his bar examination. Holmes accepted gladly. The firm of Chandler, Shattuck and Thayer was famous as a training ground.

His trip abroad was a great success; he made important friends in England, he went climbing in Switzerland. Returning to Boston in September, 1866, he went to work in Shattuck's office and was presently admitted to the bar.

WHAT NOW BEGAN TO HAPPEN to Holmes did not happen in a day or a year. It would be absurd to dramatize it, to see him suddenly entering the lonely, bitter solitude of the scholar. On the contrary, his life for the next few years pursued a normal, even humdrum outward course. But he was embarking on a path of thought that left no room for friendship, perhaps no room for love. As he was to say later, "A man of high ambitions . . . must leave . . . his fellow-adventurers and go forth into a deeper solitude and greater trials. He must start for the Pole. In plain words he must face the loneliness of original work. No one can cut new paths in company. He does that alone."

Meanwhile, he went down each morning to Shattuck's office, each evening returned. Around him the town, recovering from battle and heroism, pursued also its daily course, desiring nothing so much as business as usual. Business! Holmes himself was a businessman now, committed to business and the making of money. And this, he told himself gloomily, was an idea he must learn to live with even though he was beginning to find that, to him, the practice of law was quite horrifyingly dull.

On Court Street, Wendell observed George Shattuck receiving his clients, and marveled. Shattuck actually seemed to like to shoulder the troubles of his fellowmen. But Wendell had little desire for personal influence over the lives of his fellows. It was a far different power he craved. The man of action has the present, but "the thinker commands the future from his study." He again took dozens of books from the Athenaeum, and studied them.

In the fall of 1868 he seized eagerly upon a fresh task. A new edition of Kent's *Commentaries on American Law* was due; the editor, James Bradley Thayer, asked Holmes to help him. To make the new edition would be a long, exhaustive study. Holmes would have to do his part in his spare time; but, as the weeks passed, Thayer turned the job over to his assistant entirely.

Holmes was pleased, but the magnitude of the undertaking affected him visibly. He searched, wrestled with footnotes, was obsessed with the work, pursued by it. What he was doing was to look upon the common law analytically, in the light of history. Why were laws made? How and when did they lose their force? For America it was pioneering work, and the further he went, the more absorbed he became. Talking with his friends, he became curt and opinionated, and they regarded him as insufferably arrogant. Soon for him the whole of creation lay in the green lawyer's bag that contained his work. Each night it was carried up two long flights of stairs to his bedroom, carried down in the morning and set, at mealtimes, carefully by the front door. From kitchen to attic the household knew its place and had instructions to save it in case of fire.

In the autumn of 1870, Holmes left Chandler, Shattuck and Thayer and opened a law office with his brother Ned, who had done amazingly well in the law school. Ned looked taller and thinner than ever, he wheezed with asthma when he ran upstairs. But in the firm of Holmes and Holmes, he was by far the more interested partner. For Wendell the office business only retarded the real business of life, which was to work on Kent. Moreover, he was by now lecturing at Harvard on constitutional law, and serving as editor of the *American Law Review*.

"Wendell Holmes," William James reported to his brother Henry, the novelist, "spent an evening here last week. He grows more and more concentrated upon his law. His mind resembles a stiff spring, which has to be abducted violently from it, and which every instant it is left to itself flies tight back."

THE HOLMES FAMILY had by now moved into a tall brownstone house on Beacon Street. In the autumn of 1871, the house became suddenly very empty. Amelia Holmes had married in the spring; and in October, Ned married Henrietta Wigglesworth. Wendell's law practice with Ned was negligible. It brought in next to nothing, but Wendell was busy by day and by night on his other projects, and the only people who could make him stop were his uncle John Holmes and his friend Fanny Dixwell.

When Amelia had lived at home, Fanny had stopped in often for tea or lunch. Now she did not come at all. Wendell was vaguely irritated. "Fanny," he complained, "was Amelia the only person in our house worth seeing? I haven't seen you for a week."

"A week?" Fanny said. Her voice was quiet, a little tired. She had not seen Wendell since Christmas afternoon, more than three weeks ago.

"By the way," Wendell was saying, "Uncle John is driving over for tea Sunday. Will you come with him? Mother said to tell you she was very lonely now, without a daughter."

Fanny looked at Wendell strangely and looked away. She was pale, thin. Her natural high color had left her cheeks. Yes, she told Wendell. She would come to tea Sunday with Uncle John.

Next Sunday John Holmes asked his nephew to go with him to the third story after tea, under pretext of looking for some special tobacco. Wendell, following him, was puzzled. He watched his uncle let himself down in the worn leather chair.

John Holmes grunted. "Wendell, I didn't climb these penitential stairs for nothing," he said. "I came about you—and Fanny Dixwell. The best girl in Cambridge. She is in love with you . . . and pining away. Fanny, of all people! I am not the only one to notice it." He frowned. "What is the matter with you, man? Haven't you *looked* at Fanny lately? She is thirty-one. You are thirty, Wendell, and you have loved that girl for years. We've all waited patiently for you to find it out. But there is an end to patience. We don't like it. *I* don't like it."

John Holmes paused. Wendell's back was turned, he stood by the window. At the first words he had whipped round, crossed the room. The back of his neck was scarlet. He could not have spoken if his life depended on it. Fanny, in love with him? Fanny, *pining?* Why, Fanny was the one who had always told him off, pricked his bubble, brought him back to earth. There had never been need to tell Fanny what he was thinking. She knew it before he spoke. And she was warm, generous. Her voice reached him as no music had ever reached him.

Wendell turned from the window. When he stepped forward he almost stumbled. Whatever he said to Uncle John, he could not remember a word of it afterward.

Chapter 6

ON THE SEVENTEENTH OF JUNE Fanny Bowditch Dixwell married Oliver Wendell Holmes, Junior. There was no time for a long honeymoon. Chancellor Kent, Fanny observed, was no respecter of romance.

By September the two were settled with the senior Holmeses. Lack of money left them no choice of where they would live; but they had the whole third floor to themselves.

Fanny Holmes was happy, that winter. How splendid to be of use to Wendell, to make things smoother for him at home, to ease the tension between father and son. For Dr. Holmes asked his son the most tactless questions, prodding him as one prods a lazy man; when Fanny's instinct, knowing better the depth of his ambition, was to hold him back.

As the months went by she told herself again and again that there was no *harm* in Dr. Holmes. She was even sure he loved his son. And yet, and yet . . . They must get out of this house. Even one room, anywhere, would be better than this.

The move at last became financially possible when George Shattuck, reorganizing his law firm, offered Holmes a partnership. Holmes accepted, and he and Fanny found living space for themselves at Number 10 Beacon Street. The rooms were upstairs, over a drugstore, but they were pleasant and sunny. Here, thought Fanny, would be paradise, and she the mistress of it.

FANNY AND WENDELL now lived frugally—but to neither of them did it seem frugality. It seemed adventure. They were both over thirty, yet for the first time in their lives they were free of the parental nest, independent financially, domestically. They could come and go as they pleased, with no questions asked. Even after a year, two years, it still seemed a miracle to Wendell Holmes that he could start down the stairs without his father's voice following him: "Wendy—where are you going?"

FANNY DIXWELL HOLMES

Almost every night the two walked to the Parker House for supper; often they met friends who dined with them. Fanny wore her new gray cloak, edged with brown fur, and carried her little round muff. There was a flash of scarlet in her bonnet. Wendell thought he had never seen a woman who held herself so well. They lived quietly; they were a young couple making their way, laying the groundwork for what was to come.

The work on Kent was finished by now; as Shattuck said, it was a work to be proud of. At the office, Holmes again found that he was bored. Cases related to questions in equity, contracts, torts, mortgages, bankruptcy and the like—"the small change of legal thought," Holmes had begun to call them. Was this, he asked himself, to be his life, forever, year after year?

Slowly, painstakingly—and withal passionately—Holmes began to make his escape. And he did not escape out of the law but into it. He wrote articles for the *American Law Review*. The work was a godsend. The moment he walked out of his office, fatigue dropped from him; he strode quickly, eagerly, up the hill like a man whose day is not ended but just beginning.

Fanny Holmes, watching this double life, wondered how long a man could stand it, even a man as invincibly healthy as Wendell Holmes. At thirty-five he was as lean as ever, his color high and fresh. He had let his mustache grow to cavalry proportions; he held himself magnificently, he had never lost his army bearing. And the look of a man was more becoming to him than the look of a boy that he had worn for so long. The blue-gray eyes shone with purpose, with a hard masculine ambition.

William James recorded this change in Holmes—less a change than a development. Fanny had rented a small cottage for the summer at a remote, unfashionable spot on Buzzards Bay. Holmes brought his friends sometimes for weekends. In a letter to his brother after a July weekend with the Holmses, William James wrote: "I fell quite in love with she; and he . . . he is a powerful battery, formed like a planing machine to gouge a deep self-beneficial groove through life. . . ."

To the discerning eye then, "she" was adorable—"he" a powerful machine, gouging his groove through life. . . . Slowly, the plane made deeper cuts, slowly its gains were consolidated. The actual events, the landmarks of success, were in no way spectacular—but they were significant. In 1876, Holmes was made an overseer at Harvard. Two years later, when a seat on the district bench fell vacant, Holmes's friends of the Boston bar recommended him for the place. An older man got the judgeship, but for Holmes the incident was encouraging; his name was becoming known.

Shortly afterward, Holmes was invited to give twelve lectures at the Lowell Institute in Boston. He had nearly a year to prepare them; and it was the focus he needed. Twelve lectures—there would be material enough here for a book on the common law. Now at last he had a definite program. "No man can go far," he had come to say, ". . . until he has learned to lay his course by a star which he has never seen. . . . " The lectures and the book would embody all Holmes had learned in fifteen years of study. He was thirty-nine. And he had a conviction—or superstition—that if a man was to make his mark in life, he must do it before forty. By then a man has found his dominant, leading conceptions; the rest of life is working out details.

The Common Law, he would call both book and lectures. And by the time the twelve lectures were delivered, Holmes would have passed his fortieth birthday—March 8, 1881. His book must be out by then or it would never be out. The thought drove him day and night.

"The law," he would say, "embodies the story of a nation's development through many centuries, and it cannot be dealt with as if it contained only the axioms and corollaries of a book of mathematics. . . . The life of the law has not been logic: it has been experience. The felt necessities of the time . . . even the prejudices . . . have had a good deal more to do than the syllogism in determining the rules by which men should be governed."

So Wendell Holmes wrote; and what he wrote was new. He was looking at the law pragmatically; he was saying that a good judge unconsciously interprets law according to the effect it will have on the community, that judicial decision does not derive wholly from precedent.

Someday, as a judge, Holmes would act out his beliefs. Now he merely struggled to present them. And the work crawled. Days and nights disappeared without leaving more than one new page written, two new pages. Wendell became more and more abstracted, lost weight, looked white, drawn. Wendell Holmes, his friends said, was heading for a nervous breakdown.

Fanny was frightened. She had seen Wendell look this way before, when he was working on Kent. But Wendell had been a young bachelor then. Now he was nearly forty. This was in a sense his last chance. If he failed now— To Fanny it was unthinkable that he should fail. What she feared was not failure but illness, some nameless, sudden collapse.

There was only one way Fanny could help her husband. She could divert him, make him laugh. Wendell had always loved her stories; now she thought them up deliberately, saved them for when she knew he was nearing his limit of strength. Did he realize, she demanded one evening, that her sister Mary was actually going to marry George Wigglesworth? Ned Holmes's son was seven years old. Did Wendell realize he was the uncle of a half-grown Wigglesworth? The tribe was alarmingly prolific. "Look out on the Common any time of day and what do you see? A squirrel and a Wigglesworth." Wendell threw back his head, laughed aloud and felt the better for it.

October. Wendell Holmes sat at his desk. The publishers must have the book in their hands by January at the latest. On March 8 he would be forty. . . . Forty! Holmes shook his head. Would his capacity measure up to the task he had set himself? Looking up, he fastened haggard eyes on his wife and waited for her answer. He had not asked the question aloud, but he thought he had. He did not know he had asked it every night now for a month.

Fanny did not seem disturbed. She pulled bright silk through the tapestry work on her knee. "It took Adam Smith ten years to write the *Wealth of Nations*," she said. She smiled at her husband. And there was in her smile something of reassurance, of love—perhaps something merely of dailiness—that caused her husband to smile back at her, the strain to leave his face. Drawing a long, comfortable sigh, he bent once more over his desk. In the room there was no sound but the scratching of a pen until in Park Church belfry the clock struck midnight.

ON A NOVEMBER AFTERNOON of 1880, at the Lowell Institute, Holmes gave the first of his lectures on the common law. And by January, 1881, his book was in the printer's hands.

On the third of March—in the nick of time, five days before his fortieth birthday—Wendell and Fanny walked down Beacon Street to the parental mansion. Under Holmes's arm was a new, brown-covered book: *The Common Law*. He handed it to his father. On the flyleaf was written:

> *O. W. Holmes,*
> *from his affectionate son, O. W. Holmes, Jr.*
> *March 3, 1881.*

How many books on Wendell Holmes's shelves bore a like inscription! They went all the way back to 1848, when Wendell was seven. Each of his father's works as they came out. *Oliver Wendell Holmes, Jr., from his loving father, Oliver Wendell Holmes.* Now at last the inscription was reversed, now the son could pay the father in his own coin.

On the evening of her husband's birthday, Fanny Holmes brought out a bottle of champagne. She and Holmes drank it, toasting *The Common Law*. At last, draining his glass, Holmes picked up the empty bottle, carried it to the sink. Forty years old, and he had arrived at a viewpoint and expressed it in print. It was a day to remember. With a quick motion, a half smile, Holmes put the champagne cork in his pocket.

RECOGNITION, HOWEVER, WAS SLOW in coming. Not even scholars accepted the book unanimously; one famous library committee refused it shelf room. But among the initiated Holmes had made his mark. The *London Spectator* called the book a "most original work of legal speculation." And suddenly, one year later, Holmes received recognition in another form; he was offered a professorship at the Harvard Law School.

When Holmes was notified of the appointment he went to his old law partner. Shattuck was in no way surprised. "Take the job," he said instantly. "It is your kind of job. But don't let Harvard tie you to more than a year's contract. Have it in writing that if you are offered a judgeship you can resign."

Holmes followed Shattuck's advice. Charles Eliot, president of Harvard College, agreed to the proviso: after all, a Harvard professorship was a thing seldom relinquished. Holmes would surely desire to continue a career so distinguished, so secure.

Holmes found teaching exhilarating; he enjoyed his classes. Yet among the cautious, indifferent faces how many, when he flung out a challenge, showed an answering light? Two, perhaps three . . .

Going back and forth to Cambridge in the horsecars, that autumn of 1882, thinking about the law school, about his students, Professor Wendell Holmes wondered if this was to be his life henceforth. There was something in the very familiarity of the scene that made the months seem like years. How little time it seemed since he had been a student himself! And now these boys who called themselves *college men* touched their hats to *him*, made a place for him in the cars.

Any judgeship seemed remote. . . . Shattuck and his resignation clauses! Most likely, it had all been unnecessary. He would be at Harvard Law School, thought Professor Holmes—forever.

Chapter 7

ON THE MORNING of December 8, 1882, Professor Holmes was called out of his classroom. In the foyer stood George Shattuck, his eye alight with news. "Otis Lord has resigned from the state supreme court," he said. "Governor Long wants you for the judgeship. He has to submit your name to the council by twelve o'clock, and he has to have your consent first." Shattuck took out his watch. "It's eleven now," he said.

Outside, a bell sounded; students poured from the classrooms. The Massachusetts Supreme Court! In his heart, Holmes had hoped—but he had never really expected it. It left him stunned, speechless. It was a stroke of lightning that in one second wiped out the past, changed his whole future. . . .

"Why are you standing there?" Shattuck asked. He was almost as excited as Holmes. "We have an hour to get to President Eliot's office and then across the river to the courthouse."

Holmes got his hat and coat. The two walked toward Eliot's house. "How do you think he will take this?" Holmes asked.

"Badly," Shattuck replied, his voice cheerful with the prospect of imminent battle.

Holmes looked at him gratefully. In every crisis of his life, Shattuck had stood behind him. Now in the clear air Shattuck's breath emerged in steamy blasts. "Holmes, you have a stride like an antelope. . . . Here we are now." He shook Holmes's hand. "Good-by, my boy. I'll meet you in the car shed on the Square." He paused. His face was suddenly serious. "You have a philosophy, Holmes, about the judicial function and the common law. Until now you've talked about it." He looked sharply at Holmes. "Now you must live it through."

ONE WEEK LATER, on December 15, Holmes was formally appointed to the court. On the third of January, 1883, he took his seat in the supreme court, the youngest of seven judges. He was forty-one. Justice Walbridge Field was fifty. The other five were white-haired, white-bearded. They had no special reason to trust Holmes. For a judge, Holmes was young, and he was known as a theoretical fellow. The other six judges had arrived on the bench through years of law practice, an appointment to the superior court or a place in the state legislature. *Experience* was what made a judge—not scholarship or theoretical conceptions of the judicial function.

In 1883 the supreme court badly needed men of vision. These were times of vast social change. A pioneer economic individualism was giving way to corporate trade. A country that in Holmes's youth had been rural in tone now rushed to build cities. Men lived piled upon one another, struggling for survival under smoking factory chimneys.

It was more than a change; it was a revolution, and Holmes recognized it. He had studied the formation of great states and the causes of their dissolution. When the pattern of society changes, legislation meets the change—or the state perishes.

When Holmes came to the bench, the burning issues of the day were labor's grievance against the employer, and the people's grievance against the corporations: two manifestations of the individual's battle for survival in an industrial economy. The battle would rage all during Holmes's lifetime and beyond. Desperately, America needed judges who possessed historical awareness, whose social prejudices were leveled by the long view of the scholar. Holmes was such a man. "A constitution is not intended to embody a particular economic theory, . . ." he said. "Constitutional law, like other mortal contrivances, has to take some chances. . . . The Constitution is an experiment, as all life is an experiment."

THAT FIRST SUMMER of the judgeship, Wendell and Fanny Holmes left their second-floor rooms and took a house at 9 Chestnut Street. It was in a pleasant neighborhood of white doorways, brass knockers and brick steps. Fanny loved the house. There was room at last for all her things—old silver, furniture she had acquired in ten years of married life. Holmes's salary was $6000 a year, and Fanny was able to engage a cook, a housemaid. The Holmeses at last lived well. Fanny hung the parlor windows with red damask, bought a white fur rug for their bedroom. The house was bright, filled with color and sunshine.

Fanny knew by now that she was to be childless forever. She did not mourn, or if she did, it was not her nature to show it. From Beacon Street she brought her two caged finches, talkative small brown birds that she addressed always by name. One day she brought home two nightingales, then a mockingbird. Every morning after breakfast she fed them, talked to them. Wendell loved to watch her. "Aren't you going to court?" Fanny would ask. "What are you waiting for, Wendell? Aren't you ever going about your business so that I can go about mine?"

"I am waiting for you," Holmes would reply. "Fanny, isn't it time for you to feed your birds?"

He was too busy now to go often to the doctor's house. But when he did go, he became silent once more, watchful, ironic, restless. Fanny marveled. Forty-odd, and a judge of the supreme court! Did a son never grow up, in the presence of such a father?

Elsewhere, Wendell Holmes was most certainly a confident, mature man. The work at court was hard and exacting, though an enormous amount of it was routine. Besides the cases in the big courtroom with the other judges, Holmes held equity court by himself downstairs, handled probate jury cases, divorces, contests over wills. From time to time he went off to hold equity court all over the state. But he loved the work, every minute of it. The dull spots were not dull to him.

On Memorial Day, 1884, Holmes went up to the village of Keene, New Hampshire, to make a speech. Fanny drove up with her husband. The afternoon was sunny, not too warm. In the center of Keene Common between square white houses, the soldiers' monument was garlanded with flowers—roses, iris and columbine. Judge—once Captain—Holmes spoke:

"Not long ago I heard a young man ask why people still kept up Memorial Day, and it set me thinking of the answer. . . ."

The answer Wendell Holmes gave, remembering his friends who had died in battle, was simple and brief: "Through our great good fortune, in our youth our hearts were touched with fire. It was given us to learn at the outset that life is a profound and passionate thing. While we . . . do not pretend to undervalue the worldly rewards of ambition, we have seen with our own eyes, beyond and above the gold fields, the snowy heights of honor, and it is for us to bear the report to those who come after us. But, above all, we have learned that whether a man accepts from Fortune her spade and will look downward and dig, or from Aspiration her axe and cord and will scale the ice, the one and only success which it is his to command is to bring to his work a mighty heart."

Presently Wendell Holmes was called upon often to speak in public. He found he liked to speak; he did it well. He took great pains with his talks that sounded, on delivery, so spontaneous, rehearsing them to Fanny. One evening, a lawyer,

AMELIA JACKSON HOLMES

young Arthur Hill, and his wife stopped in to call, interrupting a rehearsal. At their insistence, Holmes kept on. What he said was so solemn, so real, that both the Hills were on the verge of tears. Suddenly, Holmes broke off, turned to his wife. "Well, Fanny!" he said briskly. "How about it? Too much *tremolo?*"

The summer after Holmes's Memorial Day speech in New Hampshire, his brother Ned died. Holmes missed him greatly. And within another two years there was to be another sorrow.

Wendell's mother fell ill; her mind was affected. It soon became patent she was not going to improve. She did not leave her bedroom, but moved about all day from bed to sofa, tranquil, contented, her white hair soft about her face.

For two winters, Mrs. Holmes lingered. In February of 1888, she died, making her departure painlessly. Dr. Oliver Wendell Holmes, now seventy-eight years old, had lost the thing he loved most. He was deeply grief-stricken. She had been part of himself, the kind part, the warm part, for nearly fifty years.

Wendell and Fanny were more than thankful for Wendell's sister Amelia: but for her, they would have to give up their house and move in with the doctor. Amelia, widowed now, came home to live, and the doctor began, miraculously, to rally. But barely a year later, Amelia herself fell suddenly ill. Watching by the bedside, Fanny Holmes took charge and ran the house. One thought was uppermost. If Amelia went, the doctor could not be left alone.

In April of 1889, Amelia died. Fanny did not hesitate. "I

will tend to the moving," she told Wendell promptly. "You can forget all of it." But he knew that this move was one of the bitterest things life had ever held out to her.

It was bitter also to Wendell Holmes. Yet in matters of duty they both belonged to a generation and a group that neither hesitated nor questioned. "Fanny!" Wendell said when the decision was made, his voice troubled out of all proportion to his words. "Fanny—you will take your birds with you, of course? And your needlepoint pictures. The one of the apple orchard will look very fine, hanging at the head of the stairs."

"Why, yes, Wendell," Fanny said. "The head of the stairs! That is just the place for the apple orchard. I was wondering where there was a bare space that would hold it."

DR. HOLMES WROTE to an old friend: ". . . the loss of my daughter is a heavy blow . . . [but] I am not left alone. My daughter-in-law, a very helpful, hopeful, powerful as well as brilliant woman, is with me, and my household goes on smoothly . . ."

That summer, Wendell went to England on a previously scheduled trip and Fanny took her father-in-law down to Beverly on the North Shore, to a little house where he had spent many summers. In August, Dr. Holmes had his eightieth birthday. The schoolchildren of Beverly, dressed in white and carrying flowers, trooped up to the front porch to wish him a happy birthday. From all over the world, telegrams poured in, and eleven ladies of Boston brought a huge silver loving cup.

A few days later, Fanny took the household back to Beacon Street, and Wendell returned from Europe. How old his father looked, Wendell thought with a shock, following him to the dining room. The tiny figure was still erect, but the thick hair was snow-white, the face lined with wrinkles.

Dr. Holmes caught his son's eye upon him. "I'm getting old, Wendell," he said cheerfully. "I'm beginning to dissolve."

Fanny watched her husband. For how many years Wendell had looked upon his father as his enemy! Now the battle was taken out of Wendell's hands. Now time itself was granting him a final victory. Yet here was no victory at all. . . .

Fanny was glad that her husband was especially busy now,

away from home. In 1890, Walbridge Field, now chief justice of Massachusetts, entered upon a long illness. The fact that Holmes wrote his opinions with extraordinary quickness made it natural for him to be assigned a large share of work; the judges had long ago discovered that this quickness did not mean any carelessness. Holmes had always possessed a talent for seeing to the heart of an intellectual situation. Lawyers were allowed two hours for oral argument. After the English fashion, Holmes liked to decide from the oral argument, not wait for the brief. He went at it zestfully, as a man goes after game. The moment the lawyer started to speak, Holmes leaned forward, listening raptly, making penciled notes. Sometimes, five minutes were not gone when he threw himself back, closed his eyes. Counsel hasn't stated the point yet—but Holmes has somehow got it, the other judges told themselves.

Holmes's opinions, when he handed them in, did not read like other judicial opinions. They were pithy, filled with both learning and common sense. . . . "If it is a bad rule, that is no reason for making a bad exception to it." "A boy who is dull at fifteen probably was dull at fourteen." And when the philosopher peered out from behind Holmes's briefs, it came with a flash: "All values are anticipations of the future."

This was straight pragmatism—and brand-new. None of the other judges could have conceived it, and they were aware of this. To have such a mind on the bench was highly stimulating, whether or not you agreed with its premises. "Holmes is like rum to the other judges," a lawyer said, and the phrase went round.

In 1891, Holmes, at fifty, was still the youngest man on the bench. In seven years, he had dissented only twice from his brethren. Now a labor case came up that impelled him to utter the first of the dissenting opinions that were to mark him—to his rather ironic amusement—as a friend of labor.

An employer was indicted for withholding part of an employee's wages. A Massachusetts statute made it unlawful to "impose or exact a fine" or withhold part of the wages of a worker for imperfect work. The court declared this statute unconstitutional, on the grounds that it violated fundamental rights by impairing the obligation of contracts. Holmes dissented. "I have the misfortune to disagree with my brethren," he wrote. ". . . I do not see that [the statute] interferes with the right of acquiring, possessing, and protecting property any more than the laws against usury or gaming. . . ."

The public read Holmes's statement in the *Daily Advertiser* in the columns allotted to the court records. It reached the laboring men whom it affected, reached also those employers whose interests would have been injured had it not been a minority report. But even these might have forgotten the case had it not been followed by others of equal importance.

A year later, the Massachusetts House of Representatives asked the justices' opinion as to the constitutionality of a bill to enable cities to purchase, sell and distribute coal and wood as fuel. Five justices said no, that cities could not sell these articles. Holmes disagreed. If the government could take land for railroads, why, he asked, couldn't it sell coal? "I see no ground for denying the power of the Legislature to enact the laws mentioned. . . . The need or expediency of such legislation is not for us to consider."

So wrote Oliver Wendell Holmes, Junior. And from State Street and Beacon Street a roar went up—radical! Fanny Holmes was enormously entertained by this suspicion of her husband in respectable quarters. One evening in the library, Dr. Holmes, dozing in his chair, looked up when he heard laughter, and asked what the joke was. Wendell shook his head. "Fanny just told me that George Wigglesworth thinks I'm an anarchist," he told his father. "I think I can endure the charge."

The old doctor still kept up a valiant daily routine, rising early in the morning, spending the forenoon answering letters, taking a walk at noontime down Beacon Street and around the Common. But in 1894, he failed visibly. Something within him seemed to break and crumble. He had had a long bout of grippe; he was up and about now, but frail. Did his father know, Wendell Holmes wondered, that the end was near? Autumn came; and on these October afternoons his father sat in his chair, gazing into the fire, his tiny wrinkled hands crossed on his knee.

One day Fanny, reading to her father-in-law at teatime, rose to draw the curtains and saw across the river, beyond the spires of Cambridge, the sky alight with the setting sun. How Dr. Holmes loved that view! "I seem to look out on all creation," he had once said.

Fanny moved back to her place by the lamp. Wendell came in, and the three talked quietly of the day's events. The white head sank a little lower. Father is going to sleep, Wendell Holmes thought, and saw his wife get up and move swiftly to the old man's side. Wendell got up himself. Leaning over the chair the two waited, motionless.

The frail shoulders moved with an even breathing. The white head sank a little lower. Wendell Holmes, putting out his hand, knew suddenly that the shoulders had ceased to move.

FANNY AND WENDELL HOLMES did not leave 296 Beacon Street; they simply stayed on, settling the doctor's affairs, tending to the mail that poured in. Oliver Wendell Holmes, Junior, was now the head of his house. It contained many of his father's possessions, constant reminders of the Autocrat, but these things were oppressive to Holmes no longer. He was in his father's house from choice now, not compulsion. Fanny watched him with amusement as he settled down, gradually assuming the privileges of the manor.

A year or so later—in 1896—Fanny had a long, severe illness. Rheumatic fever, the doctors called it. Her recovery was slow; week after week she remained upstairs. And when finally she emerged from the bedroom to sit by the fire, she looked extraordinarily thin and white. A kind of listlessness wrapped her round. The physician said it was the natural effects of the disease, but to Wendell Holmes it seemed anything but natural. She who had been so busy, so gay, sat idly now, her long, fine hands in her lap. As spring came on she would not go out, except sometimes into the backyard to throw crumbs to the birds or tend to her flower borders.

"You must see more people," Wendell told her, puzzled, dismayed. "I saw Nina Gray today after court. She and John want us for dinner. So does Mrs. Whitman."

"Go and dine without me," Fanny said. "I am tired, Wendell.

An evening alone will suit me beautifully. And besides, my hair looks odd."

During the fever they had cropped Fanny's hair all round like a boy's. The result was indeed odd. What remained, brown on top, gray round the face, bristled or lay in discouraged streaks. Fanny had always been shy; now she was implacable about being seen. Little by little, Boston got used to Mrs. Holmes's nonappearance at dinner parties, and the judge also got used to it. Nobody, least of all her husband, knew whether she minded staying home alone. She had always avoided fashionable Boston; hostesses who to Wendell seemed beautiful and witty Fanny disposed of in words brief and pungent. And when she did venture out, Fanny did not make it particularly easy for her hostess. Her tongue was quick and she used it. The plain fact was that Fanny was tired, she wanted to be left alone.

In the same year, 1896, the case of *Vegelahn* v. *Guntner and Others* reached the Massachusetts Supreme Court. Vegelahn was a shop owner; Guntner an employee, who with his friends patrolled the pavement outside, informing the public that Vegelahn was unfair. There was no violence, but this was 1896, and the violence and horror of Homestead and the Haymarket riots were fresh in mind. Vegelahn succeeded in getting an injunction against the pickets.

It was a natural decision for the court to make; but Justice Holmes dissented. The picketing outside Vegelahn's shop was legal, he said. There had been no force used, no threats to physical property. His dissent contained a powerful plea for labor unions as the necessary counterpart to combination by capital.

> One of the eternal conflicts out of which life is made up is that between the effort of every man to get the most he can for his services, and that of society, disguised under the name of capital, to get his services for the least possible return. Combination on the one side is patent and powerful. Combination on the other is the necessary and desirable counterpart, if the battle is to be carried on in a fair and equal way. . . .

It was straight speaking and strong speaking. Holmes was well aware that he had thrown himself bodily against the vested interests; the fact that he had done it from intellectual conviction rather than from sympathy with labor would make no difference to the men at the top. Restlessly, the night of the Vegelahn dissent, he went out and walked up Beacon Street to the Arthur Hills'. "Arthur!" he said in the hallway of his friend's house. "I have just handed down an opinion that shuts me off forever from judicial promotion."

What Holmes did not realize was the respect and even affection with which the court had come to look upon him. In thirteen years, he had moved up, on the bench, from the end of the line to the seat on the right of Chief Justice Field. The other judges no longer suspected him of being a theoretical fellow. However mistaken, however dangerous Holmes's judicial opinions—still, they were indubitably bolstered by the legal thinking that is a judge's first business. Better than any one of the six, this man knew the common law. Moreover, neither in the Vegelahn dissent nor in the others had he defied the court; he had been at pains to explain his stand in language that was deferential to his brethren. And he had done it with perfect sincerity. These men who saw him every day, who knew him well, recognized this sincerity.

In August of 1898, the Holmeses were vacationing, as they often did, in Beverly. Judge Holmes, aged fifty-seven, got out his new bicycle and rode proudly down to the village. He had progressed far enough to be able to take one hand off the bars and wave to his friends—a matter that had bothered him greatly at first. Once, crossing the milldam on Beacon Street, he had met his old friend Robert Grant, the probate judge, also on a bicycle. Grant had waved gayly. Holmes, his hands glued to the bars, had cursed long and loud. "Damn that fellow! He was just showing off. Next chance I get in court I'll overrule him."

Fanny went driving every day with her husband, her long starched white skirts flowing in the victoria, a veil on her sailor hat, her parasol up. Since her illness she had become very susceptible to bright light, kept the shades drawn at home. Her husband did not mind, Fanny's arrangements always seemed to him perfection. One week they drove to New Hampshire to their nephew Ned Holmes's wedding. It was a wonderful trip,

Holmes wrote to a friend. The bobolinks sang in the meadows, and all the way there and back Fanny talked as she had not talked in two years. "I was more than happy," Holmes wrote. "My wife who hasn't by any means got back to where she was before her rheumatic fever, was wonderful in her resources of imaginative humor and forethought and seemed to awaken to a life and joy which she has not known for a good while."

IN JULY OF 1899, Chief Justice Field died. The governor immediately appointed Holmes as his successor. Holmes's dissents had not "shut him off" from judicial promotion.

From the first he filled his new place with ease, and was happy in it. Chief Justice Holmes was soon a legend in Boston. Reporters, notebooks in hand, followed him up the hill to the courthouse. "His long frame is singularly youthful. He does not mind Beacon Hill, and breasts it with a long, quick step."

Holmes was fifty-nine when the century turned. It was extraordinary how young he looked. His face with its high color was lined and showed all the marks of living. But the blue-gray eyes were more searching than ever and there was a quickness about him that seemed to stem from far within, from a wellspring unending and joyful. Young Judge Caleb Loring, in particular looked upon his chief with amazement. One day, worried over an opinion Holmes had assigned him to write, Loring took it to Beacon Street, carrying along all the papers of the case.

Holmes glanced through the material, turning the pages. Then he got up and went to the high old desk in the corner. Standing, he wrote ten lines, handed them to Loring. The younger man was appalled. Surely the chief justice was not going to let this cursory examination suffice?

But when Loring submitted the report it was accepted by the other judges without question. In ten minutes, Holmes had seen to the heart of the matter.

Fanny Holmes gave her husband a little birthday party that year, as she always did. If Wendell at fifty-nine looked forty, his wife, at sixty, looked every inch her age. And she knew it. She made no effort to conceal it, to keep pace with a husband so handsome, so cavalier. She still wore always a dash of color—a red bow on the shoulder, or turquoise beads. But her gray hair swept grimly up from her forehead, netted, pulled back so tightly that her eyebrows went up with it. She wore at all times a high collar of white net, boned. But when she walked out to her carriage with Wendell, there was something invincibly distinguished about her. She had got her strength back; she walked swiftly, held herself well. She not only dressed as she pleased, but now that she was sixty, Fanny Holmes did as she pleased. Twice, that winter, she and Wendell were seen running to fires along Beacon Street . . . the chief justice of Massachusetts and his wife!

The Boston subway was finished now, and downtown the buildings soared high, steel-girdered. A few enterprising souls came to the Harvard football games in gasoline carriages. In the November election the Republican party won again, hands down, and business held its head high; the watchword was expansion. Under the leadership of J. P. Morgan, seven great steel companies planned a merger—"the billion-dollar trust." The country was not yet aware of the man who would wield the "big stick." Colonel Theodore Roosevelt, late of the Rough Riders, was simply McKinley's vice-president, and the reforms he had fought for in New York were of small moment.

But early in September, President McKinley went to Buffalo to greet holiday throngs at the exposition. He put out his hand to greet a citizen; the man raised his hand, a shot was fired.

McKinley lived for eight days. The country as a whole was ready for Roosevelt—though the conservative Republicans were not. After Roosevelt's first message to Congress, there was no mistaking the fact that the government was going to assume a new relation to business. The "square deal" for all parties would include labor and the public as well as capital.

Roosevelt and Holmes were poles apart in temperament and in their approach to social problems. Yet it was natural, reading the Vegelahn dissent, that Roosevelt should see here a justice who would support the policies he believed in. Huge issues could depend—as Roosevelt himself said—on "whether a judge of the Supreme Court came down heads or tails."

In June, 1902, one of the justices was ill: Horace Gray of Boston. Newspapers speculated, and in their prophecies the name of the chief justice of Massachusetts loomed large.

Holmes soon knew that the appointment was coming his way. He had by no means made up his mind to accept; he was happy as chief justice of Massachusetts. The question of money did not enter: Holmes had his father's inheritance now. But if Holmes hesitated, his wife did not. From the first, she made her position clear. Holmes must accept the appointment. "Wendell, you have gone as far in Massachusetts as you can go. Your family lives forever, and so will you. Are you going to *stop*, just because the calendar says 'sixty'?"

When Justice Gray resigned, Holmes followed Fanny round the house, watched her feed her birds in their cages. "Fanny, what do *you* want to do?" he asked. "Won't you mind it, up-rooting your whole life?" He caught her by the shoulders. "We shall have to dine with the President, Fanny. In tails, Fanny, and white satin. You will sit next to ambassadors and ministers of state."

Fanny's expression did not change. She freed herself, turned and poked her finger through the bars at a Japanese robin, chirruping at him. "The judge is frightened, Koko," she said.

ON THE ELEVENTH of August, Holmes's appointment was an-nounced. All New England, it seemed, was pleased. In Boston, Holmes's colleagues of the bar and bench gave a dinner for him. "It is a good deal of a wrench to leave old friends," Holmes said at the dinner. "But, gentleman, it is a great adventure, and that thought brings with it a mighty joy. . . ."

Fanny Holmes had no opportunity to rise and speak before the crowd. Her role was now one of silence—and she did not find it easy. The thought of Washington terrified her. Her mir-ror showed a woman old and gaunt. Twice, during the autumn, people had mistaken her for Wendell's mother. For the past few winters, Wendell had gone out in Boston by himself. The situation had been of Fanny's own making. She did not like fashionable Boston, and she had made her own life here at home. But in Washington, there would be no chance for this kind of easy independence. As wife of a justice of the Supreme Court her presence at social functions would be required. Fanny was scared. It was not the important men of Washington she feared. It was their fashionable wives. If she could have told her husband it would have been easier, but she could not tell him.

Fanny had few close friends. One of these was a younger woman, not Boston born, in whom she could confide. One afternoon, this friend, coming in, found Fanny alone. With a kind of desperate humor Fanny put up both hands to her hair. "Mary," she said. "Look at me. How can I go to Washington—I, who look like an abandoned farm in Maine?"

Chapter 8

ON MONDAY, December eighth, 1902, Holmes, dressed in his long black gown, stood in the old courtroom in the Capitol building and laid his hand on the Bible before him. On this Bible, the great justices had been sworn in: John Marshall, Roger Taney, Joseph Story. Around him in niches on the wall, justices in marble looked down; overhead the red, white and blue shield of the United States gleamed. . . .

Holmes felt himself profoundly moved. Here in this ancient room, heavy and quiet with tradition, he was to be part of the highest court in the land, the court of last resort.

Chief Justice Fuller made a sign; Holmes's voice rose clearly in the quiet room:

"I, Oliver Wendell Holmes, do solemnly swear that I will administer justice without respect to persons, and do equal right to the poor and to the rich, and that I will faithfully and impartially discharge and perform all the duties incumbent on me as Associate Justice of the Supreme Court of the United States according to the best of my abilities and understanding, agreeably to the Constitution and laws of the United States, So help me God."

Fanny was not yet in Washington. When she did arrive, three days later, she found their new house at 10 Lafayette Square in hideous disorder. Doherty, Holmes's old court messenger whom he had brought with him, was upstairs in the study unpacking the last crate of books. Coming quietly up the long stairs, Mrs. Holmes heard her husband's voice, roaring at Doherty. "Doherty—no! Damn it—not on that shelf. What the hell did you put those books on that shelf for? I told you I wanted them here, where I can reach them from the desk."

Standing in the doorway, Fanny surveyed the scene. Always, when these thousands of books were in order, her husband considered the household settled. "Well," she said. "Well, Wendell!"

When he saw her, Wendell began immediately to talk. Fanny must come to Court. Right away. Tomorrow, if she could. It was amazing. The old Senate chamber where they sat was beautiful, with its light gray walls, the bright shield of the Union, the eagle snarling over the chief justice's chair. The whole scene was extraordinary, the feeling of tradition behind it. The whole thing was *big*. A man had no need to search within himself, to find his sense of the infinite. The infinite was right there, in that old courtroom. . . .

On the following morning, in the chamber of the Supreme Court, Fanny found that it was all just as Wendell had described. She felt the spell of the old room settle upon her. Light came benignly from the domed ceiling. On a raised dais, nine tall black leather chairs faced the chamber. In one of those great chairs, Wendell Holmes would sit, his gray hair outlined against the cushions. . . .

There was a stir to the left; in a long black line the justices came in. Slowly the nine walked to their places.

"Oyez! Oyez! Oyez! . . . God Save the United States and This Honorable Court!"

Fanny Holmes looked up at her husband, standing there straight and tall in his robes. She was swept with sudden, deep emotion. They had done right to come to Washington, to break away from the associations of a lifetime. Fanny knew it and rejoiced. Gazing up at her husband from under her prim dotted veil, she felt tears surge to her eyes, hot and overflowing.

WASHINGTON IN 1903 was the most exuberant place on earth. And in the center of it was Theodore Roosevelt with his big stick, shaking his fist, grinning from newspaper cartoons. The captains of industry, railroads and Wall Street looked with anger and apprehension upon the dude cowboy. But the country liked him, glad of a leader who was not afraid of Wall Street. The public conscience was aroused; in the big new magazines, *McClure's*, *Collier's*, *Everybody's*, the muckrakers were out to expose "big business." Ida Tarbell was preparing her indictment of the Standard Oil trust. Now in the White House was a man who would do something about things. What the country desired just now was neither legality nor reason, but revenge. Let T.R. smash somebody *big*—a meat-packer, the sugar trust, anybody or anything so long as there was action.

The country had not long to wait. Looking round, Roosevelt seized upon the biggest, newest railroad merger of them all—the Northern Securities Company—and asked his attorney general to investigate its legality under the Sherman act. In February, 1902, suit against the Northern Securities Company burst upon the captains of industry like a declaration of war.

The new justice from Massachusetts watched a trifle sardonically. The Sherman Anti-Trust Act, obviously, was going to be Roosevelt's favorite weapon . . . and Holmes had always disliked the act. "The Sherman act isn't fair," he said often. "It won't let the strong man win the race." Besides, mere bigness didn't make a merger illegal. How it behaved, what it did, determined its legality. Well, possibly this case would never reach the Supreme Court. Suit was brought in Saint Paul; as weeks passed, the public forgot it and turned to other matters.

Meanwhile, in Washington, Justice and Mrs. Holmes took their place in society. Their first function at the White House was to be a big formal dinner, to introduce the new justice from Massachusetts. Fanny approached it with secret horror. She dressed in silence and stepped into the cab. How magnificent Wendell looked in tails and white tie, his silk hat under his arm.

Fanny was wearing gray silk; at her bosom were her favorite flowers, violets from Wendell, and from under her décolletage rose her usual white net guimpe, well boned to the ears. In the Green Room, filled with chattering, laughing people, the President himself came forward, greeting her. He spoke to her kindly, making conversation. Had she seen much of Washington since her arrival? Had she met many people? Quite a number of congressmen's wives had called on her, Fanny replied politely.

There was a veiled note in her voice that caused the President to look up. "You found the ladies pleasant?"

"Washington," Mrs. Holmes replied blandly, "is full of famous men and the women they married when they were young."

THEODORE ROOSEVELT

The President roared with laughter. Around them people turned inquiring heads. Dinner was announced. Supreme Court justices, of course, took precedence over everyone but ambassadors, and there were no ambassadors present. The President bowed to Fanny. Moving across long carpets, Fanny Dixwell Holmes of Garden Street, Cambridge, laid her hand on the arm of the President of the United States and led the company in to dinner. She was seated at the President's right. Wendell was a mile away, at the other end of the table. Roosevelt turned to Mrs. Holmes, asked a question. Fanny's reply was quick. The President laughed. From across the table Fanny was aware once more of heads turned in her direction. She felt suddenly light, as free as air. Why, this was not difficult at all! She could say anything, or just sit and listen to the President. In this company she was first by order of ceremony. Among all these women, so beautifully dressed, so charming, she need wait for no one to speak, for no one but her hostess to make a move.

All evening, Holmes watched his wife. But Fanny was marvelous! This sparkling creature, easy, quick—for the first time in company he saw her be herself, the self that never failed to fascinate. Later that evening, in the cab going home, he spoke. "Fanny," he said, "you were magnificent." He reached out, laid his hand over hers. "Are you happy? Fanny—tell me."

Fanny turned to her husband. "I think we shall be very much at home here, Wendell," she said. "I—find it somehow easier to go in to dinner at the head of all the company."

As the months passed, cordial relations with the White House deepened, officially as well as unofficially and, rather to their surprise, Justice and Mrs. Holmes took their place among the inmost circle of Roosevelt familiars—Harvard men, many of them, whom Holmes had known in Boston.

But in December, 1903, the case of the *Northern Securities Company* v. *The United States* reached the Supreme Court.

The country turned its eyes eastward; this, obviously, was a test case. Would the Court dissolve the huge railroad merger, or would the merger slip through? Never mind legalities and technicalities. The question was whether the government of the United States lay in Wall Street or Washington.

On March 14, 1904, the Court's decision was ready. When the nine justices walked to their seats, they found the courtroom jammed with spectators. Justice Harlan began to read the majority opinion: "The Northern Securities Company was in restraint of trade. No scheme came more certainly within the words of the Sherman Anti-Trust Law."

There was a stir in the courtroom. The government had won! The vote was five–four—in itself a surprise. But to those who considered themselves especially knowing, the greatest surprise of all was Justice Holmes's dissent. Not merely the fact that he had voted against the government, against dissolution of the company, but his words, which were outspoken and very strong:

> "Great cases like hard cases make bad law. For great cases are called great not by reason of their real importance in shaping the law of the future but because of some accident of immediate overwhelming interest which appeals to the feelings and distorts the judgment. These immediate interests exercise a kind of hydraulic pressure ... before which even well-settled principles of law will bend.... We must read the words before us as if the question were whether two small exporting grocers shall go to jail....
>
> "I am authorized to say that the Chief Justice, Mr. Justice White and Mr. Justice Peckham concur in this dissent."

Theodore Roosevelt heard the decision of the Court and was

jubilant. The suit, he said, was one of the greatest achievements of his administration. But it was a crime that the decision had not been more nearly unanimous. Justice Holmes's dissent in particular was outrageous. What did the man mean, turning against him that way? Obviously, Holmes had simply lost his nerve. "I could carve out of a banana," shouted T.R., "a judge with more backbone than that!"

It was the end of the incipient friendship between Roosevelt and Holmes. Holmes himself cared nothing whatever about the President's, or anyone else's, reactions. He was, in fact, as angry as the President.

In the Northern Securities dissent Holmes had upheld the side of capital—although he would have disliked to hear it called a "side." But to him, combination on one side was as lawful, within limits, as on the other. A year later, in the Lochner case, he was to uphold the other "side"—the right of a state to regulate the hours of labor.

Holmes's dissent in the Lochner case was among his most significant utterances in Court. It heralded a long and noble list of such dissents, opinions which were to prove him at once prophetic in vision and tough-minded in the law.

The fact that Holmes's most famous opinions were dissenting ones by no means sets him down as a rebel or a no-sayer: he always believed that too many dissents detract from the prestige of the Court. But the blunt fact remained that in a period of vast and almost revolutionary social change, Holmes found himself on the Supreme Court with a majority so conservative as to be not merely stubborn but blind. He had to voice his dissent— to remain silent would have been to shirk his duty.

Moreover, it was not the number of his dissents that won for Holmes the title of the Great Dissenter. Some of his brethren dissented more often than he did. It was the *quality* of Holmes's dissents that made them famous. When a justice writes a majority opinion, he is speaking for the Court. But when he dissents he has a chance to say what he thinks personally, and these individual expressions play a significant part in the function of the Supreme Court. "A dissent in a court of last resort," wrote Charles Evans Hughes, "is an appeal to the brooding spirit of

the law, to the intelligence of a future day, when a later decision may possibly correct the error into which the dissenting
judge believes the court to have been betrayed."

The Lochner dissent was most certainly such an appeal—and
it became, years later, the majority opinion and therefore the
law of the land. The Lochner case concerned moreover a conviction that Holmes held very deeply: the conviction that under
the Constitution, the states have a right to make their own social
experiments. When these experiments—these state laws—seem
to conflict with federal authority, then let the case be decided
not on the basis of whether the Supreme Court believes the law
concerned to be a good law or a bad law. Let it be decided solely
on the basis of whether the Constitution forbids it.

In the Lochner case, New York State had passed a law prohibiting more than ten hours work per day in bakeries. A man
named Lochner who owned a bakery broke the law twice and
was fined for it. Lochner appealed on the grounds that the ten-
hour law was class legislation, favoring the workers. It denied,
said his counsel, "equal protection of the laws." The justices
voted five–four in favor of Lochner. Justice Peckham wrote the
majority opinion and announced it in Court. The ten-hour law,
he declared, was a "meddlesome interference"; the spread of
such laws in the various states was deplorable.

When Peckham had finished, Holmes leaned forward and
began to read his dissent:

> "This case is decided upon an economic theory which a large
> part of the country does not entertain. . . . But a constitution
> is not intended to embody a particular economic theory. . . .
> It is made for people of fundamentally differing views. . . ."

These were fighting words, and on the Court there was no
other man equipped to say them. "The people have a right to
make their own mistakes," William Jennings Bryan had once
said. Holmes too believed that freedom means, above all, the
right to experiment. This was his stand. It was calm, it was
consistent. The nation could count on him to sustain it for
twenty-six years.

Chapter 9

MARCH 8, 1911 . . . Oliver Wendell Holmes is seventy. Taft is President now. On the Supreme Court are four new justices; White of Louisiana has moved up to the chief justice's seat. Holmes says he doesn't care who is chief justice; he himself is too old to be appointed. . . . To Holmes, his brethren seem possessed of a very demon of long-windedness. They take from two weeks to six months to write an opinion he can turn off between Saturday and Monday. Washington knows him as the only justice who can sum up a case while the lawyer is still arguing. But the lawyers themselves, if they lose a case, protest loudly: this haste must mean inadequate consideration; Holmes, they complain, should deliver longer opinions. "May God twist my tripes," roars Oliver Wendell Holmes, "if I string out the obvious for the delectation of fools!"

Each justice was entitled to a secretary, paid by the government. Holmes had a new one every year, sent from the Harvard Law School, the pick of the graduating class. Filled with zeal they sat down at the big desk beyond the open doors from Holmes's study, expecting to read important briefs for the justice, to examine papers. It did not take a day to discover that the justice did not need a secretary. He wrote out his opinions, looked up his citations.

The young men, recovering from this shock, made their own job—which was to learn from the justice whatever he chose to teach about life, law and the nature of man. They were like sons to Holmes. "Sonny," he called them. "Young feller— Idiot boy." He showed them his opinions, talked to them about the cases. There were in the end thirty of them. Holmes's Annuals, they were called. They became, later on, attorney generals of the United States, chairmen of the board of U.S. Steel, presidents of banks, professors at Harvard. . . . But when they arrived in Washington, autumn after autumn, they were young, eager, and some were shy. Mrs. Holmes took charge, saw that they met everyone, took them to parties.

The household was settled now on I Street [which Washingtonians call Eye Street], in a comfortable, four-story brick house.

The Holmes family had become old inhabitants of Washington. Yet New England was in their bones, it was the tradition of their house and the visitor felt it the moment he entered the front door. To the left of a narrow hallway the white staircase rose, mahogany-railed; there was a gleam of dark furniture: Chippendale, Queen Anne.

And there was also in this quite elderly household an extraordinary air of life and movement. Young people came in often—to tea and dinner; and late at night passersby would see lights blazing from cellar to attic.

Toward his work also, Justice Holmes had the attitude of a young man—a young man's eagerness, a young man's stage fright if a big case came his way. Each Saturday afternoon his messenger brought the portfolio from Court. "I am frightened weekly," Holmes confessed to Sir Frederick Pollock, an English friend to whom he wrote many letters. "But always when you walk up to the lion and lay hold the hide comes off and the same old donkey of a question of law is underneath."

NINETEEN FOURTEEN CAME, and Europe was at war. . . . President Wilson urged neutrality. At the French Embassy in Washington, the British Embassy, men talked of strategy, diplomacy, propaganda. But there was a new group of young men in Washington who talked far differently, who passionately desired this to be the last war of all wars. Felix Frankfurter, Francis Hackett, Walter Lippmann, Herbert Croly, Philip Littell. They came and went—Frankfurter was already teaching at the Harvard Law School—but when they were in town they were to be found in bachelor quarters on Nineteenth Street. They were the fastest talkers, the quickest thinkers, Holmes had met in many a year. They used a new word—"internationalism." They brought their books round to I Street hot off the press. They were starting a weekly, *The New Republic*. Holmes subscribed to it "with hope," he said. He teased them a little about their solemn intensity. "You young men seem to think that if you sit on the world long enough you will hatch something out."

Returning from Court in the afternoon, Holmes would find the young men at his house, talking about the war, arguing passionately. "What is it?" he would ask. "Tell me, I'll take the opposite side."

In January of 1916, President Wilson named the liberal Louis Brandeis to the Supreme Court. It was totally unexpected and it pushed the war temporarily off the front page. Newspapers took sides. Businessmen protested, declaring Brandeis was a socialist, a labor sympathizer—next door to an anarchist. A Senate investigation was started; forty-three witnesses were heard, thirteen hundred pages of testimony taken.

Throughout the battle, Holmes kept his mouth discreetly shut. No one knew better than he that the Court needed a Brandeis— a judge who knew economics, with a mind rapier sharp. Holmes had known Brandeis since his own teaching days at Harvard, when Brandeis had been a young Boston lawyer, and he liked and respected him profoundly.

Brandeis had gone through the law school in two years instead of three, earning his living while he did it—an extraordinary record. He was deeply stirred by social injustice; the slums of the industrial towns near Boston had made him restless for reform. Like Holmes, he came from a long line of liberty-loving ancestors, and his parents had come from Bohemia in 1848 to escape the political troubles.

Holmes had been enormously drawn to this young man. There was a sympathetic quality to their minds. Both were brilliant, incisive, thoroughly independent, with an extraordinary faith in the future.

And Brandeis in his turn was drawn to the scholar with the soldier's bearing who carried three historic names, who did not know what poverty meant, what persecution meant, yet who understood intuitively things that he, Brandeis, had had to learn through suffering, learn by the feel and bitter taste of life.

The Senate finally voted forty-seven to twenty-two in favor of Brandeis, and it wasn't long before the country had forgotten him.

For soon American soldiers were sailing for France: America was at war. But within an ancient, shabby chamber of the Capitol, the business of the Supreme Court moved forward as usual. It was the concern of nine men to make it move, war or no war. Fighting abroad must not interfere with the administration of justice at home.

Justice! Holmes thought of it, walking from Court of an afternoon. Right now, in the very middle of the war—June, 1918—a case had come up that outraged every conception of justice. By a five–four vote the Supreme Court was going to declare the Child Labor Law of 1916 unconstitutional.

Fifteen years of struggle had been required to get the Child Labor Law through Congress. Almost immediately a farmer named Dagenhart, desiring to keep his young sons in a cotton mill, brought suit. Millowners backed him, making it a test case. Sitting in Court, Holmes listened, cold with contempt, to the old Lochner argument over again. . . . "Abuse of the police power, invasion of States' rights . . ." If Congress can thus regulate matters, said Justice Day in the majority opinion, "our system of government will be practically destroyed."

It was flagrant, outrageous. Even old Justice McKenna dissented. So did Clarke and so of course did Brandeis.

Holmes wrote the dissent, which was brief and undramatic. "If there is any matter upon which civilized countries have agreed . . . it is the evil of premature and excessive child labor. . . ." Afterward in the robing room, Holmes and Brandeis eyed each other. It was too late for talk, the thing was done. . . . God only knew for how many years this decision would hold.

Time and again in years to come these two, Holmes and Brandeis, would find themselves alone, or at least in the minority, in taking a stand for the flouted rights of individuals and minorities. The 1920's were to be for America fat years, intolerant years. Oliver Wendell Holmes could stand the sight of his country suffering and heroic better than the sight of it sleek and intolerant. "I have had to deal," he wrote Pollock, "with cases that made my blood boil and yet seemed to create no feeling in the public or even in most of my brethren."

There was for instance the Abrams case. Abrams, a Russian-born American, had protested against the sending of American troops into Russia after the revolution of 1917. He and his friends, meeting in a basement in New York, put their protest in print, then went up on the roof and scattered their leaflets. The

238

Department of Justice picked them up; a week later the pack was in full cry, to be supported, eventually, by seven justices of the Supreme Court.

Privately, Holmes felt that the whole thing should have been ignored, but the seven justices thought differently. After the majority opinion had been delivered, Holmes said in dissent:

> "Congress certainly cannot forbid all effort to change the mind of the country. . . . Sentences of twenty years' imprisonment have been imposed for the publishing of two leaflets that I believe the defendants had as much right to publish as the Government has to publish the Constitution of the United States now vainly invoked by them. . . . The best test of truth is the power of the thought to get itself accepted in the competition of the market. . . . I think we should be eternally vigilant against attempts to check the expression of opinions that we loathe and believe to be fraught with death. . . ."

MARCH, 1921 . . . Oliver Wendell Holmes watched with curiosity the approach of his eightieth birthday. He felt well, filled with vigor. How could a man tell if his mental powers were diminishing? On the afternoon of his birthday he walked home from Court, but at home there was no sign of the usual birthday party. The cook was sick, Mrs. Holmes said. They would have to go round to the Hotel Arlington for supper. Wendell must put on a white tie; they would try to make a celebration of it—although Prohibition would prevent her drinking his health in public.

Grumbling, Holmes went upstairs and struggled into his dress suit. Grumbling he came down, roared at the houseboy. "Child of hell! Son of Satan, where are my cigars?"

Grinning, the houseboy Jones pointed to the drawing room. Holmes walked in. Before the fireplace stood Fanny in her best gray satin. At eighty-one, she seemed somehow smaller, thin almost to transparency. But as he looked at her, an enormous pride filled Holmes. This woman, so frail and old, with her ridiculous net guimpes under her décolletage, the prim violets at her bosom—this woman still had fire enough for ten.

The dining-room doors flung open. In a blaze of light—white damask, silver, flowers—stood a crowd of young men. Holmes saw in amazement that it was his secretaries, at least a dozen of them. Fanny had got them here from all over the country. "We came up through the cellar!" someone shouted. "Mrs. Holmes made us hide in the coal bin almost an hour."

Holmes stood in the doorway. "I knew that she-devil was up to something." He walked over and picked up a long-stemmed glass at his place. "What are these for?"

"Champagne," Fanny said.

"Close the shutters." Holmes grinned. "I wish my daddy could see me now. He always said I'd die a drunkard."

AFTER THE DEATH of Chief Justice White, the President appointed Taft as chief justice. Holmes knew he was too old to be appointed, yet knew also that if he were younger the place would be his. "I *really* don't care," he wrote to Pollock.

It was true; Holmes had never been motivated by ambition for office. If at the end he could tell himself that in the law somehow, somewhere, he had touched the superlative, he would die content. No office, no title, could give him that.

It was now, in his eighties, that the nation became aware of Justice Holmes. People liked his brief opinions and most of all they liked his dissents. "The Great Dissenter," they called him.

The older he got, the more Holmes admired economy of expression. Old age, it would seem, reduced a man to the ultimate simplicities; at eighty a man had neither time nor spirit for complicated self-deceptions—he was too near the abyss. Was there perhaps actual qualitative difference in the mode of thinking of the young? Holmes watched his secretaries and their friends. Just now, in the 1920's, intellectual youth flaunted a bright and brittle cynicism. Holmes listened and was not alarmed. The boys, he said, were merely experimenting in negation.

In 1928, Holmes was eighty-seven and proud of it. If he could live until November he would be the oldest justice on record, beating even Taney. Legal scholars wrote articles about him. "The old gentleman," Chief Justice Taft called him. But strange, how the old gentleman's words struck home to the nation, how deeply they had begun to bite! Even men who would not have dreamed of reading a legal opinion had become somehow aware of him. One day a newspaperman, seeking copy, decided to walk round Capitol Square and ask passersby if they had heard of Justice Holmes.

A mechanic in overalls was sitting on a bench reading the sports page. The reporter strolled up. "Holmes?" the mechanic said. "Oh, sure! He's the young judge on the Supreme Court that's always disagreeing with the old guys."

FANNY HOLMES was eighty-eight. For some time it had been obvious that she was failing. At eighty-eight, her back was straight as ever, her eye as bright. But at Beverly Farms this summer, when the Holmeses came for vacation, people noticed a change. What would the judge do without her? The two had been together fifty-six years. Reminiscently the town talked it over. At the livery stable, Larcum told about a time when he had driven Mrs. Holmes to the depot to meet the judge. The horse had run away. Mrs. Holmes hadn't acted scared. She just leaned out and called, waving her parasol. "Larcum! If you kill me, tell him I loved him."

Back in Washington, a few months later, Mary, Mrs. Holmes's maid, went into the bedroom and found her mistress lying on the bed, her face distorted. She had fallen, managed somehow to reach the bed. She had not called out. "It's nothing," she said. "Mary, tell the judge it is nothing." The doctor came. Mrs. Holmes had broken her hip. He spoke gravely. They would put it in a cast, do all they could. But the patient was old.

The days passed. The doctors said that Fanny did not suffer. She had no actual illness, no fever. But sitting near her, Holmes saw her face drawn as though with suffering. Her head turned toward him slowly. "I am tired, Wendell," she said. "That's all. Perhaps you had better go now, and I will take a little nap."

One afternoon, Walter Howe, the young lawyer from next door, rang the bell. "I won't come in," he said to the servant, Jones—"I just wanted to ask—"

"Please come in, sir," Jones said. "I know the judge would like to see you. He is lonely."

Holmes came down the long stairs.

"Come in, Walter," he said. "Fanny is asleep. . . . She was

very tired." He paused. "We don't think she will wake up, ever."

That evening—it was the last day of April, 1929—Mary brought Mrs. Holmes's supper tray as usual. She found her mistress dozing, the judge in his chair by the window. Gently, Mary roused her mistress and turned to the tray.

Before she could turn back—without a sigh or sound—Fanny Holmes leaned her head against the pillows and died.

Fanny was buried in the soldiers' burying ground at Arlington. It was Chief Justice Taft who made arrangements for this. Holmes had always wanted to be buried there, but he had been too shy to ask for the favor. Now he and Fanny would lie there together.

In the following weeks there was no one in the house with the judge but the servants and John Lockwood, Holmes's secretary. In those weeks, alone with the judge, young Lockwood saw philosophy tested in a hard hour. Often, Holmes had talked of life and death, saying gravely that life was action, the use of one's powers. And now, with half of his life snatched from him, the judge went on, doing his work hour by hour. It was like the routine of a soldier, inexorable, accomplished in the face of death itself. Simply, the judge was living out his philosophy.

A case had come up in Court concerning freedom of speech. *The United States* v. *Schwimmer*. Rosika Schwimmer had been denied citizenship because she had testified that in case of war she would not bear arms. She was a pacifist . . . fifty years old.

Holmes reached for his pen to write his dissent.

> . . . If there is any principle of the Constitution that more imperatively calls for attachment than any other it is the principle of free thought—not free thought for those who agree with us but freedom for the thought that we hate. . . . I would suggest that the Quakers have done their share to make the country what it is. . . . I had not supposed hitherto that we regretted our inability to expel them because they believe more than some of us do in the teachings of the Sermon on the Mount.

It was the last week of May before the Court rendered decision. Holmes read his dissent. When it was over he drove to Arlington, up the winding hill to Fanny's grave. There he got out of the car. Buckley, the driver, followed across the grass. Standing a little aside, Buckley watched his master—as he would watch again and again for six long years.

The ritual would be always the same. Walking to the stone, Holmes laid his flower on it—a rose, a poppy, a spray of honeysuckle—then stood silently. Silently still, his hand touching the stone, he moved round it with a little patting motion of the fingers. Then he turned, and walked downhill through the trees.

HOLMES'S NINETIETH BIRTHDAY—March 8, 1931—fell on a Sunday. The newspapers greeted him warmly, and there were birthday messages from the great of two continents. Sitting in his library, Holmes read his birthday messages. That evening there was a microphone on his library desk. The president of the bar association and Dean Clark of the Yale Law School were to speak from New York, Chief Justice Hughes from Washington. Holmes was to answer them briefly.

Up in Cambridge, five hundred people gathered in Langdell Hall. There were speeches about Holmes, until at last the room was silent, all faces turned to the loudspeaker. The familiar voice came through at last, speaking slowly—a little tired but clear and articulate, rhythmic as always:

"... The riders in a race do not stop short when they reach the goal. There is a little finishing canter before coming to a standstill. There is time to hear the kind voices of friends and to say to one's self: 'The work is done.' But just as one says that, the answer comes: 'The race is over, but the work never is done while the power to work remains.' The canter that brings you to a standstill need not be only coming to rest. It cannot be while you still live. For to live is to function. That is all there is in living. ..."

Next day—Monday—the nation noted with pride that Justice Holmes was at his place on the Bench and delivered a majority opinion. All that spring he did not miss a day. But the people near him, the household, knew that his strength was very limited now—that he tired quickly.

On January 11, 1932, Holmes had a majority opinion to deliver. When his time came, he leaned forward, picked up his papers. But when he began to read, his voice faltered, thickened. He shook his head impatiently and went on. But what he said was barely audible beyond the front row of benches.

That night, he wrote his resignation to the President . . . "The time has come and I bow to the inevitable. I have nothing but kindness to remember from you and from my brethren. My last word should be one of grateful thanks."

Next day, at noon, the justices wrote to Holmes and sent the note around by messenger. Holmes sent back his reply:

> My Dear Brethren:
>   You must let me call you so once more. Your more than kind, your generous, letter, touches me to the bottom of my heart. The long and intimate association with men who so command my respect and admiration could not but fix my affection as well. For such little time as may be left for me I shall treasure it as adding gold to the sunset.
>
> Affectionately yours,
Oliver Wendell Holmes.

Silence, resignation. To sit in one's library in the morning and read eulogies of oneself, receive admiring visitors. . . . In all his life, Holmes had never been without a job to do. Anxiously the household watched him. For the past ten years Dr. Adams, the family physician, had said the judge would die if he stopped work. Holmes, indeed, had said it himself. Now the prophecy seemed in danger of fulfillment.

But it was not fulfilled. For Holmes, fate had not reserved this particular defeat—to die of heartbreak because he was no longer useful. Three years of life remained, and they were not to be unhappy years. Once more Holmes rallied, once more his spirit reasserted itself. There was so much to learn! His secretary read aloud to him by the hour. Often he seemed to doze, but if the secretary stopped reading, Holmes sat forward instantly. "What?" he would say. "What, Sonny?" And he would begin instantly to discuss the book. His secretary at one point calculated they had read 4,500,000 words—mostly philosophy—but "sweetened," Holmes said, by rereading all of Sherlock Holmes.

OLIVER WENDELL HOLMES
CAPTAIN AND BREVET COLONEL
20TH MASS. VOL. INF. CIVIL WAR
JUSTICE SUPREME COURT OF THE UNITED S
MARCH 1841

HIS WIFE
FANNY BOWDITCH HOLMES
DECEMBER 1840   APRIL 1929

There was now a singular and striking beauty to Holmes's face, a quality almost luminous. Sitting on the porch at Beverly that summer he discussed life with Betsy Warder, aged sixteen. "I won't refrain from talking about anything because you're too young," Holmes told her, "if you won't because I'm too old."

In the fall, as usual, Frankfurter sent down a new secretary from Harvard. It would do the young men good, he said, to be with Holmes even if he was no longer on the Court. Holmes protested, but he was very glad to have a man in the house to talk to. The secretary, arriving in October, watched the judge with amazement. Why, the old man attacked his breakfast like a cavalry officer in the field! Porridge—with thick cream—fruit, broiled fish, muffins, marmalade, coffee. After breakfast the judge announced he was going to loaf. Half an hour later he was calling for the secretary to read to him. "Let's have a little self-improvement, Sonny."

Beyond all other traits, this perpetual thirst to learn surprised both young and old. Franklin D. Roosevelt, a few days after his inauguration in 1933, came round to call. He found Holmes reading Plato. The question rose irresistibly. "Why do you read Plato, Mr. Justice?"

"To improve my mind, Mr. President," Holmes replied.

Three days earlier—March 5—Roosevelt had closed the banks. Tomorrow the President, before Congress, would present his plan for dealing with the worst financial panic in the nation's history. Rising when his visit was ended, Roosevelt turned earnestly to Holmes and addressed him. "You have lived through half our country's history; you have seen its great men. This is a dark hour. Justice Holmes, what is your advice to me?"

Holmes looked at him. "You are in a war, Mr. President," he said. "I was in a war too. And in a war there is only one rule: Form your battalions and fight."

LATE IN FEBRUARY, 1935, Holmes went out with his secretary for a drive. It was a bitter afternoon, windy, with a threat of snow. Next morning Holmes had a cold. He went to bed, sneezing, and the sneeze turned to a cough, to something worse. Holmes was ninety-three, and he had pneumonia.

By the first of March, the city knew that he was mortally ill. Holmes knew it too, and was not dismayed. "Why should I fear death?" he had remarked to his secretary a few weeks earlier. "I have seen him often. When he comes he will seem like an old friend." Holmes had loved life, and he had believed in it. "If I were dying my last words would be: Have faith and pursue the unknown end."

Now he was dying. He lay quietly, joking with the nurses. What was the use of all this—coaxing an old man to eat, giving him stimulants? On the fifth of March, late in the afternoon, newspapermen saw an ambulance stop outside the door. An oxygen tent was carried in. Holmes opened his eyes. "Lot of damn foolery," he said clearly.

At two in the morning the doctors knew the end was near. They took the oxygen tubes away. Holmes lay with his eyes closed, breathing quietly. Outside, in the March garden, wet branches creaked. As the doctors watched, Holmes died, taking his departure so quietly it was hard to tell when he was gone.

Mark Howe, the secretary at that time, the signs of grief plain on his face, went downstairs, opened the front door. From across the street a dozen newsmen rushed at him, notebooks in hand. They listened, then raced for the telephone. Justice Oliver Wendell Holmes was dead.

THE FUNERAL was held at All Souls' Church—the old, white-pillared Unitarian Church that stands at the head of Sixteenth and Harvard streets. A wet wind blew across the square. People stood on the curb, watching the justices go in. The bell tolled. . . . Inside the minister was reading from Holmes's own words: "At the grave of a hero we end, not with sorrow at the inevitable loss, but with the contagion of his courage; and with a kind of desperate joy we go back to the fight."

At Arlington, the President and justices waited beside Holmes's grave. Soldiers bore the coffin, covered with the American flag, across wet turf. Eight infantrymen raised their rifles and fired . . . a volley for each wound. . . .

Ball's Bluff . . . Antietam . . . Fredericksburg.

A soldier, standing a little apart, raised his bugle and blew taps.

OLIVER WENDELL HOLMES
CAPTAIN AND BREVET COLONEL
20th Mass. Vol. Inf. Civil War
JUSTICE SUPREME COURT OF THE UNITED STATES
March 1841   *March 1935*

From the floor of Congress, from the White House, from the Inns of Court in London, scholars and statesmen gave tribute, and for a few days the people mourned. But Holmes's real fame was to come slowly; the growth of his influence was to be as measured, as deep and sure, as the forces that had shaped him. History itself would prove his dissents. One by one they became law.

There had indeed been a great contagion in Holmes's courage —a courage not born with Holmes but handed down with all the accumulated force, the deep spiritual persuasion, of the generations behind him. Abiel Holmes and Abiel's father, Captain David. Sally Wendell and Sally's father the judge. Abiel's eldest son, the Autocrat, small and light-minded but as fierce, when his heart was roused, as any patriot of them all. "I am too much in earnest for either humility or vanity, but I do entreat those who hold the keys of life and death to listen. . . ."

Men called the doctor's son the Great Dissenter. The title was misleading. To want something fiercely and want it all the time —this is not dissent but affirmation. The things Holmes wanted were great things, never to be realized. How can man realize the infinite? Have faith and pursue the unknown end.

"Whether a man accepts from Fortune her spade and will look downward and dig, or from Aspiration her axe and cord and will scale the ice, the one and only success which it is his to command is to bring to his work a mighty heart."

RvR
THE LIFE &
TIMES OF
REMBRANDT
VAN RIJN

A CONDENSATION OF

RvR
THE LIFE & TIMES OF REMBRANDT VAN RIJN

BY
HENDRIK WILLEM
VAN LOON

RvR

An account of the last years and the death of one
Rembrandt Harmenszoon van Rijn
a painter and etcher of some renown who lived
and worked (which in his case was the same)
in the town of Amsterdam (which is in
Holland) and died of general neglect and divers
other unfortunate circumstances on the fourth
of October of the year of Grace 1669 (God have
mercy upon his soul) and who was attended
in his afflictions by one
Joannis van Loon
Doctor Medicinae and Chirurgeon who
during a most busy life yet found time to write
down these personal recollections of the
greatest of his fellow citizens and which are
now for the first time presented (with as few
notes and emendations as possible) by his
great-great-grandson, nine times removed
Hendrik Willem van Loon
in the year of Grace 1930 and in the town
of Veere, which is in Zeeland.

Amsterdam, October 9, 1669.

Explaining How I Came to Write This Book

WE BURIED HIM YESTERDAY and I shall never forget that terrible morning. The rain had ceased and a cold, gloomy fog had thrown a dark and chilling pall over the whole city. In the empty street the small group of mourners stood silently outside the church door waiting for the coffin to arrive.

Last Friday, a few hours before he died and during a moment of semiconsciousness, he had whispered to me that he wanted to rest next to Saskia. He must have forgotten that he had sold her grave long ago, when Hendrickje passed away; caught without a penny, he had been forced to sell the family lot in the Old Church to buy a grave for his second wife. I promised him I would do my best, though of course it was out of the question, and he went to his last sleep fully convinced that soon his dust would mingle with that of the woman he had loved in the days of his youth.

And then three days ago Magdalena van Loo called. I had always found her mean and jealous and apt to whine, but I had tried to like her on account of her father-in-law and of the poor boy she had married. She told me a long rambling story about some gold pieces which apparently had belonged to Cornelia and to her. She felt convinced that the old man had appropriated some of them. For weeks and weeks he had sold nothing. He had just sat and stared or he had scratched meaningless lines on the backs of some old copperplates. He had been without a cent when Titus died, for Uncle Uijlenburgh had paid for the funeral. That she knew for a fact. All the same, the old man had been able to buy himself food and drink, especially drink. He must have stolen some of Cornelia's gold, and "half of it was to come to me!"

To change the subject, I asked her if the sexton had been around to see her about the funeral. She broke into tears once more. The sexton had not come. He had merely sent one of the gravediggers, a rude man, quite drunk, who had laughed out loud when she said she could not afford to pay more than five guilders. People from the poorhouse were given a better burial, he said, but what could one expect of a fine gentleman who never did a stroke of work, who merely sat before an easel all day and gave himself airs! Finally she had called for the shoemaker who lived on the ground floor to come and help her. He had thrown the ruffian out into the street.

She then told me that no woman had ever been treated as she had been treated since she had married into that irresponsible family of painter people, and much more to the same effect, until in sheer despair I had ordered a hackney coach and had driven her to the Rozengracht to see the sexton and had asked him to explain. At once the miserable creature became most obsequious, and apologized for the behavior of his gravedigger. "If only you knew, Doctor," he said, "how hard it is to get good workmen these days!"

I bade him hold his tongue and after some preliminaries we settled on a "full funeral"—sixteen men to carry the coffin and the usual length of broadcloth to cover the remains. I paid him fifteen guilders and he promised everything would be done quietly and with dignity.

When I got to the church yesterday morning, the men were there, but they gave evidence of having already visited the alehouse. I mentioned this to Abraham Francen, one of the master's old friends, who was leaning against a tree in the yard.

"This is an outrage," I said.

But one drunken scoundrel heard me and gave me an evil look. "And why not?" he leered. "Our friend here didn't mind a drop himself at the right time, did he?"

When I called the sexton to task, he merely repeated that it was terribly difficult to get respectable men for his sort of work. Now that the war with England had ended, everybody had plenty of money and nobody wanted to be a gravedigger.

Finally we came to the spot that had been chosen and without further ceremony the coffin was lowered into the grave. I had meant to say a few words to bid my old friend a last farewell, but as soon as the ropes had been pulled out from under the coffin the sexton said loudly: "Come men, don't just stand there! We have four other customers this morning." Whereupon we all turned around (there were only a handful of us) and I walked to the part of the church reserved for divine service. I knelt down and I prayed to whatever God there might be that He deal mercifully with the soul of this poor, suffering mortal, who had given so much to the world and received so little in return.

Then I slowly walked home, but while crossing the Dam, I ran across old Joost van den Vondel, the poet. I hardly recognized him, shivering beneath his shabby, threadbare coat. It hurt me to see such a person in such a condition.

I asked how he was getting along. Vondel, with an eager face, informed me that things could not be better. Poor devil! Here was the greatest genius that ever handled our language—a shabby, broken-down clerk—explaining that he had every reason to feel grateful for the way fate had treated him.

"Of course, the pawnshop can't afford to pay me much," he explained, "but my needs are small, I have a lot of time for myself. I rarely work more than ten hours a day. Next year I hope to get my pension. I want to finish my last play, *Noah*, and I must get at it before I am too old to handle a pen."

I told him that I rarely visited this part of Amsterdam, but that I was going home from the funeral of a friend.

"And who might that be?" the old poet asked, "for I am not aware that anyone of importance has died."

"No," I answered, "I suppose not. He died quite suddenly. Yet you knew the man. It was Rembrandt van Rijn."

"Of course I knew him," he said. "A very great artist. Of course, he thought very differently from me upon many subjects. For one thing, I don't believe that he was ever truly a Christian. But a great painter, nevertheless."

Vondel paused. "Strange, very strange!" he murmured. "Rembrandt died right here in this town, and I did not even know he was still alive!"

Hofwyck, Voorburg, October 23, 1669.

TWO WEEKS HAVE GONE BY and many things have happened.

The evening of the funeral I dropped in to prescribe a sedative for poor Magdalena who was still worrying about that little bag of gold that had belonged to Cornelia and her. A few days later, Cornelia was to find it behind a pile of clean sheets, but just then Rembrandt was still suspected of having stolen his daughter's money and so Magdalena wept and whined until at last she dropped off to sleep.

I went back to the hospital and composed a letter to My Lord Constantijn Huygens in The Hague, who had had some dealings with the dead painter and had been ever full of admiration for his genius. Three days later I received an answer from the famous old diplomat, who must have been well past seventy.

> I was deeply shocked, my dear Doctor [he wrote], to hear your news. I knew him well, this extraordinary miller's son upon whom the gods had bestowed such exceeding gifts. What a most sad ending! But such seems to be the fate of those among us who dare to storm the tops of high Olympus. In any other country he would have been deemed worthy of a national funeral; kings would have felt honored to march behind his bier.
>
> I am an old man now, my friend, and I live far from the noise of the turbulent world. You must be in need of a change after these distressing events. Why not visit me here for a few days? Tell me the hour of your arrival and a carriage will await you at Veur, and it is only a short ride to the humble roof of your faithful and obedient servant, C.H.

I had no reason to refuse. Young Willem was away at his studies in Leiden. The excellent Jantje, my housekeeper, could look after the household and my cousin Fijbo (one of the Frisian van Loons, come to settle in Amsterdam three years ago) could take care of my practice. I answered that I would accept with pleasure and three days later I took the boat for the south.

The voyage was pleasant and dull (as a pleasant voyage should be) and at Veur I found Pieter, the old coachman, waiting for me. An hour later I was here at Hofwyck, sitting in front of a bright open fire in that corner room that I knew so well.

I can't say that I ever enjoyed a holiday quite so much. For a holiday it has been so far—a holiday enlivened by good talk, good fare and the constant consideration of a courteous host.

I breakfast and spend the morning in my own room, which overlooks the old marshes of Schieland, now turned into fertile pastures. There is an excellent library on the ground floor and I am urged to take as many books to my own quarters as suits my fancy. At one o'clock I take a walk in the garden. At two o'clock My Lord Constantijn and I take a drive and the evening we spend together. And of course the conversation almost invariably turns to the loss of our friend of the Rozengracht.

I am a physician and familiar with death. I am not much of a churchman and I accept the wisdom of people of ancient times who knew that there is no light unless there be darkness, no joy unless there be sorrow, no life unless there be death. So it is not so much the fact that Rembrandt has ceased to exist that worries me (God knows, life held little of pleasure for him) as the realization of the utter futility of all effort.

I sometimes am afraid of the conclusions to which this sort of reasoning may lead and yesterday My Lord Constantijn read me a serious lecture upon the dangers of such speculation.

"Have a care," he said, "or I shall have to send your doubts to my neighbor, the learned Jew Spinoza, and he will wash them in a mixture of Cartesian and Baconian philosophies and then bleach them in the light of his own merciless logic."

"No," I answered, "that would not solve the difficulty. I knew Baruch Spinoza in the old days, before his own people so kindly tried to murder him. A charming man. A learned man.

An honest man. But I am a little wary of philosophers who try to weave their spiritual garments out of their own inner consciousness. And my worries are not theological. What worries me is not the fate of poor old Rembrandt. He is either entirely out of it or he is trying hard to solve the problem of reducing the Light Everlasting to a few smears of chrome yellow and flake white. No, it is something else."

"The living, rather than the dead?"

"Exactly. Since we got our freedom, our land has been greatly blessed. We have turned a swamp into another Rome. We rule black people and yellow people and red people— millions of them in every part of the world. We probably have a larger navy than any other country and we seem always to have enough funds. We supply the whole world with grain and fish and whalebone and linen and hides and our storehouses fairly burst with bales of nutmeg and pepper. In between we fight a couple of wars and the people at home go to church and pray for victory and then go back and make a little more money and speculate in tulips and in Spitsbergen sperm oil and in Amsterdam real estate.

"Still, it is not the fact that we are rich that fills me with such anxiety for the future. It is what we are going to do with all our wealth. As long as our merchants can make one hundred percent on their money, by buying something for a guilder and selling it for two, we ask no questions. We are content to be rich and smug. Yet we let our greatest poet handle a goose quill in a dirty pawnshop ten hours a day to keep from starving; we drag our greatest painter through every court in the bailiwick and a couple of rice peddlers swindle him out of his last pennies and even your fine old prince has to be dunned eight or nine times before he will pay him.

"And what happens to Rembrandt and Vondel has happened to all the others. The King of Spain and the King of Denmark and the Emperor and the King of England and even that wild potentate of Muscovy keep agents in Amsterdam to supply them with the work of our great men. And we quietly let them die in the poorhouse as if they were so many tramps."

I talked in that vein for some time and My Lord Constantijn

Self-portrait, 1656–

listened with great patience, but I do not think that he answered me very fully. Perhaps he did, but I am a bit hazy about it. . . .

I am tired and have a pain at the back of my head. I shall go to bed and finish this tomorrow.

Hofwyck, December 20, 1669.

FOR A WHILE, it looked as if there were to be no tomorrow.

I must have caught a cold on the day of Rembrandt's funeral, for I remember that I had one or two chills on the canalboat to Voorburg and that my teeth were chattering when I reached Hofwyck. I hear that my kind host consulted with three doctors from The Hague and when they were unable to break the fever, he sent to Leiden for a young professor who was experimenting with cinchona bark and who gave me of his tincture. From that day on I am told that I began to improve. The cinchona bark was quite effective (I shall try it on my own patients when I return to practice) or perhaps it was the excellent care which I received at the hands of my good host which kept me from join-ing the Great Majority.

As soon as I was allowed to sit up and once more began to take an interest in my surroundings, I noticed (what had so often worried me with my own patients) that I seemed mentally exhausted and could not rid myself of a few simple thoughts which kept repeating and repeating themselves in my mind until I was ready to shriek.

The death of Rembrandt, I confess, had made more of an impression upon me than almost anything else that had ever happened to me. I had come to Hofwyck full of his sad fate and until I was taken ill I had thought and talked of practically nothing else. All during the fever, whenever I wandered in my delirium (so My Lord Constantijn told me last week) I had been fighting Rembrandt's battles. No doubt he had deserved a better fate, but I used to be possessed of a certain philosophic calm and could accept the iniquities of this world with great equanimity.

"Once you begin to take the human race too seriously," our grandfather used to warn us, "you will either lose your sense of humor or turn pious, and in either case, you had much better be dead."

I had always been able to stick to this wise and tolerant outlook. But now I could not rid myself of the obsession that in some way I was responsible for the death of my friend and I could not purge my poor, tired brain of the vision of that last terrible morning with the grinning pallbearers and the drinking, cursing gravediggers who handled that sacred coffin as if it had held the carcass of some indifferent lout, killed in a street brawl. And yet, if life, if my life at least, had to go on, I must forget all this. I knew it and at the same time I could not do it. Hell itself held no such terrors as I experienced during those weeks I was trying to regain my physical health and mental equilibrium.

I know not what the end would have been, had not My Lord Constantijn called on me one day in the company of the learned Jew of whom we had been talking a short time before I was taken ill. I had almost forgotten what a charming fellow he was. Spinoza proved a godsend to a man recovering from a long illness and I bade him (with my host's gracious permission) to come again, as often as he could.

He was living in very modest quarters in the village of Voorburg, only a few minutes away, and frequently, after he got through with his day's work, he used to drop in for a short talk. I admired the liberality of mind of my host, for soon the people of The Hague must have heard that Hofwyck was being patronized by the most dangerous heretic then alive. But as My Lord Constantijn merely shrugged his shoulders, I did not let it worry me and continued to enjoy the visits of this keen-eyed young Jew with the soft Portuguese accent, who actually seemed to believe that all the eternal verities could be reduced to mathematical equations.

I do not know whether or not my host had mentioned my strange mental affliction to this amiable and kindly prophet, but in the most tactful way Spinoza one day brought the conversation upon the subject of Rembrandt and how shocked he had been to hear of his untimely death and how much he had admired his work—and then he asked me to tell him about the last days of the great master and about his funeral. Of course,

I was only too delighted and he repeated this performance three days in succession, and then quite suddenly one day he said:

"You know, Doctor, you are bound for the lunatic asylum, and they tell me it is not pleasant in there."

With unusual calm and clearness of vision, I answered: "Yes, my friend, I know that, but what can I do about it?"

To which he gave me the totally unexpected answer: "Write it all down and get rid of it that way, before you go insane."

Amsterdam, April 3, 1670.

THE CURE HAS WORKED.

And I, in my old age, discover that I have most unexpectedly become the father of a book. I did not mean to write one, for I am a physician and not an author, but what of it? These pages will be carefully packed away among my other belongings. They have no literary value. My son is not interested in such things and they will never be published. And Rembrandt, if he knows, will understand.

And so I bid farewell to this labor of love which has well served me during my days of convalescence. I must go back to the business of living. From now on, my hand shall only touch the scalpel. May it be as true and honest in all things as the brush that lies on my desk, the only tangible memory of the dearest of my friends and the greatest of my race.

Jan van Loon.

CHAPTER I

THE FALL OF THE YEAR 1641 was a period of endless rainstorms and the month of November was by far the worst. There were floods, cattle were drowned, cities lay drenched, and walls were covered with mildew, for the available fuel was all waterlogged and either refused to burn at all, or filled the room with such clouds of smoke that most people preferred to shiver rather than choke.

There was a great deal of sickness and when Jantje, who was

then my housemaid, entered late one rainy evening and told me that someone had come to ask me to visit a sick woman, I thought: Oh, well, another case of a bad cold! I wish that they would leave me in peace.

For by this time, thanks to a sizable inheritance from my uncle in Veere, I had practically discontinued general practice. I could now give all my time and strength to the work of my choice— the study of those pain-alleviating drugs which eventually (so I hoped) would elevate the chi- rurgeon from a mere butcher (which he now only too often was) to a merciful healer. I still went often to the hospital be- cause I wanted to learn as much of surgery as I could, but I spent most of my time in a small laboratory I had fixed up in the basement of my house.

I went into the hall and found a middle-aged woman, whose face did not in the least appeal to me. I was about to bid her go to someone else, when she said in a scolding tone: "If it were not most urgent, my master would have sent for a well-

No. 4 Jodenbreestraat, Rembrandt's home from 1639 to 1658

known physician, but my mistress seems to be dying and he told me to get the nearest leech I could find—anyone would do."

Somehow, the utter lack of graciousness, the painful direct- ness of this person who had come to ask a favor and who offered an insult, appealed to my sense of humor. So I did not answer as I should have done, but took my cloak and followed her.

We did not have far to go before we turned into the Bree- straat, where we stopped before a handsome two-story brick house. The door was opened almost before we had knocked and an anxious voice asked, "Is that the doctor?" To which my unpleasant companion answered, "Well, it is some sort of a leech. He was the nearest one I could find." The voice replied,

"Keep a civil tongue in your head, my good woman, and ask the master to step in while I get a candle."

The hall was very dark and was filled with a sharp odor. For a moment I thought I had come to the house of a person who occupied himself with experiments in alchemy. But when the candle was lit, I saw that this was not a laboratory, for a small table and all the chairs were covered with drawings and sketches, and against the walls stood canvases, painted in such somber colors that I could not make out their subjects.

Rembrandt in working dress

Nor could I place the man who had apparently made them. He was a stock-ily built fellow with the shoulders and arms of a mason or carpenter. Indeed, the first impression I got when he opened the door was that of a workingman. Such a fellow would hardly have lived in a house of his own on one of the best streets in town, but in that strange city of ours, with new blocks of houses going up like mushrooms and new fortunes being made overnight, all things were possible.

So I quietly accepted the situation and asked: "Where is the patient?"

"In the big room," he answered. And his voice was very gentle, not in the least in keeping with his rough exterior. While I removed my coat, I introduced myself: "I am Doctor van Loon."

He extended his hand, gave me a slight bow and said: "I am glad you came, Doctor. My name is van Rijn and it is my wife who needs your services." He led me across the hall into a room where a small oil lamp was burning and there was a fire and so it was not quite dark. The feeling of discomfort which had come over me when I first entered the house increased.

It is always very difficult to define such emotions and a doctor lives so closely with his patients that he often loses track of the sequence of events. Because this particular patient eventually died, it would be easy to argue that those initial presentiments of doom had been invented by me long after as unconscious consolation for the complete failure of my ministrations.

But in this instance at least that was not true. As I have explained, I am not a religious man in the conventional sense. I am, alas, a true descendant of my gloriously blasphemous grandfather, who composed his own faith by rejecting everything except that famous law of Christ which bids us be amiable to our neighbors; that rule of K'ung Fu-tse [Confucius], the great Chinese philosopher, which states that the truly wise man minds his own business; and one single line borrowed from a famous Latin poet, who fifteen hundred years before had discovered that there really was no reason why we should not speak the truth with a smile.

In this homemade system of theology there was no room for spooks and miracles. And when I speak of certain chill premonitions which gripped me when I entered this house, I do not refer to anything supernatural. But when the time has come to surrender that spark of energy which one has been allowed (for a shorter or a longer period) to borrow from the great storehouse of the eternal force, there are certain unmistakable evidences of the impending change, such as occur in nature just before a thunderstorm or just before the eruption of a volcano. I have never been able to classify them as I am able to classify the flowers in my garden or to describe them as I can describe the symptoms of a throat affliction. But I have met people in the street and suddenly I have known that "that man" or "that woman" would not live much longer and very shortly afterwards I have heard that he or she had died before the end of a month or a week.

And the moment I entered this house on the Anthonie Breestraat, I knew: Here the eternal process of change is about to take place and there will be crape on the door before the passing of another year.

This whole meditation had flashed through my mind in less than two seconds and then I assumed that air of grave concern which sick people expect in their physicians and which often proves more beneficial than powders or pills.

The patient was lying in a big bed that had been built within the wall. By her side was a cradle and I had to move it before I could come near enough to examine her. I asked the husband to let me have his candle and whispered to him to ask if his wife were asleep. But the woman opened her eyes and in a very low and listless tone of voice, she said, "No. I am not asleep. But I am so tired—so dreadfully tired."

I sat down by the bed, went through the customary examination and asked a number of questions. These seemed to exhaust the patient so terribly that I made the ordeal as short as possible, and told her to try and go to sleep. Then I turned to her husband (and suddenly it came over me that I had seen him before—but where?) and beckoned to him that I wanted to speak to him alone. He picked up his candle, went to the door and said to the woman who had waited all this time in the hall:

Saskia in childbed

"Geertje, you watch over your mistress and take care of the child, while I go upstairs a moment with the doctor."

We climbed the stairs and went into a big room which was so full of vases and plates and pewter tankards and old globes and bits of statuary and strange swords and helmets and pictures . . . pictures everywhere . . . on the walls, leaning against chairs, leaning against the table, leaning against each other, that I thought, This man must be a dealer in antiquities.

But a moment later he bade me be seated (on a chair from which he had first removed a heavy book, a dozen or so etchings or sketches, and a small Roman bust), and he did this with so much grace and ease of manners that I came back to my first impression that he must be a painter or an engraver. And all the while I knew positively that this was not our first meeting.

He then picked up a large lacquered box and two small porcelain figures which had been balancing perilously on the seat of another chair, placed them on a table, sat down, folded his hands, threw back his head with a curious gesture (which is so common among shortsighted people) and said in an even tone: "You need not lie to me. Her illness is very dangerous, isn't it?"

To gain time, I said, "It may be dangerous or not. But before I draw any definite conclusions, you had better answer a few questions." I asked about his wife's previous history and he told me they had been married seven years. His wife came from Friesland, across the Zuider Zee. He himself was born in Leiden. His father had been a miller and had died eleven years before at the age of sixty-two and his mother had died only a year ago at the age of fifty-one and there had been six children, two girls and three other boys besides himself. They had all been well enough as far as he knew.

"Of course," he said, "that had really nothing at all to do with the case of poor Saskia, but I am thinking of my Titus, for the baby does not look very strong to me and I want you to know that from my side at least he comes of fairly healthy stock."

But from his wife's side the report was not so favorable. "You see," he explained, "she is really of much better family than I and I have noticed that such children don't seem to get along as well in the world as we who slept three in a bed when we were very young and who were left to shift for ourselves."

Her father, Rombertus van Uijlenburgh, had been burgomaster of Leeuwarden. He, van Rijn, had never known his father-in-law, for the old man had died in '24 when Saskia was just twelve. There had been eight other children in the family but after the death of the parents (the mother had died a year or so before the husband) the home had been broken up and Saskia had come to Amsterdam with her cousin Hendrick, who had a curiosity shop and occasionally dealt in pictures, and there he had met her and then she had sat for him for her portrait a couple of times.

"Hendrick, who was not much of a businessman, borrowed

some money from me and he probably felt that I would not dun him quite so easily if his young relative posed for me," the painter told me. "Besides, the poor girl knew few people in Amsterdam and was rather bored and coming to my studio with her sister was quite an adventure, for you know what the respectable world thinks about us painters."

The end had been that they had become engaged and then they had been married. "And now," he continued, "I am afraid

Rembrandt's father . . .

that I shall lose her, for ten months ago, a short time before our boy was born, she had a hemorrhage and she hardly lived through the confinement and this evening she had another one. The surgeon who usually tends her has himself fallen sick and I would like to have a doctor who lives nearby."

This was not the most fortunate of grounds for the choice of a physician, but the man interested me (where had I seen that face before?) and he was such a strange mixture of a rather arrogant grand seigneur and a helpless child that I accepted the case.

"Thank you," he said, though without any great show of gratitude. He apparently wanted to go back downstairs, but I had to ask him a few more questions before I could express an opinion upon the chances of recovery.

"Have there been any children besides the boy downstairs?"

"Yes, several. A boy who was born a year after our marriage and who died while quite small, and two girls who died soon after they were born. They just did not seem to have strength enough to live. They never cried. They just lay very still and then they died."

"And the present child was strong when it was born?"

"No! For several hours the boy looked as if he too were going to die right away." Then the midwife had given him a cold bath and he began to cry and that apparently had saved him. But his mother had never been able to nurse him. They had a nurse now, the woman who had fetched me. But the child did not gain. It cried a good deal and looked terribly pale.

Then I asked: "Have you another room where you could put the child up for the time being?"

"Yes, several. There is one downstairs and there is this room and my studio and also the room with the etching press."

"Which has most sun and air?"

"The one in which my wife is."

"Is there no other?"

"A small one where my press stands."

"Let the child sleep there."

"But then it will be impossible to work there. I have four boys who do my printing for me. They have just started on a new plate of Dominie Anslo. I have had orders for twenty-five copies. It will be a great nuisance if I have to turn that room into a nursery."

"Nevertheless, the child had better not be in the same room with the mother for some time. The nurse had better take him to your

. . . and his mother

printing room. She can probably fix herself some sort of a bed in there."

"And you will come again tomorrow?"

"I certainly will. Meanwhile, she ought to sleep as much as possible. I will pass by the apothecary on my way home and order a sleeping potion. If she is restless you can give her two small spoonfuls in some water every other hour. But not more than three times. I don't want to tax her heart. And now I had better be going."

The painter got up and opened the door for me. Once more I noticed the powerful shoulders underneath the blue linen smock and the broad forehead and the sad, troubled eyes, together with the common nose and the broad chin that was almost a challenge to the world to come and be damned. A strange mixture of the gentleman and the hod carrier and where had I seen it before?

On my way out I passed through the sickroom but the poor woman seemed asleep. I put my hand upon her forehead, which was cold and clammy. She no longer had fever, but her color had grown worse. When I had first seen her, she had been very pale with a brilliant red spot on each cheek. Now the red spots were gone and her skin was an unhealthy gray. Her pulse had grown so weak that I could hardly notice it. I put my hand upon her heart. It was beating, but faintly. She seemed to have reached that point of exhaustion when the slightest shock might be fatal. If she could sleep through the night, we had a thin chance to bring her back to life in the morning, but I was not hopeful.

Just then I heard the angry voice of the nurse, talking to the painter in the hall. "I won't do it! I just won't do it!"

And when he answered, "Sh-sh! Not so loud. My wife will wake up," she continued, "Sh-sh yourself! I just won't do it."

"But the doctor says you must."

"Bah! Doctors don't know anything. I have taken care of children all my life. I never heard such nonsense. It is just a little cold your wife has caught. But of course, doctors must give you their fool advice so they can ask you for more money."

At that moment, the sick woman whimpered softly. I tiptoed to the door and spoke sharply to the nurse. "You will do what I say," I told her, "or tomorrow I shall report you to the medical guild. You may not care for my opinion, but you will care if you never get another case."

She looked at me arrogantly. "All right, Doctor," she said sweetly, and she went into the room to get the child.

Van Rijn saw me out. "I am sorry," he apologized, "but it is so terribly hard to get a good nurse just now."

"Yes," I answered, "but if I were you, I would get rid of this woman as soon as I could. I don't like her eyes. She looks as if she might go crazy any moment."

"I will try and find another one tomorrow," he promised me, and then I bade him farewell.

I went to an apothecary who kept late hours. While he was preparing the dose for my new patient, I asked him if he had a boy who could deliver the medicine to the big house in the Breestraat, the second one from the Saint Anthonie Lock.

"You mean the new house of Rembrandt?"

"I thought his name was van Rijn?"

"So it is. But he is usually known by his first name."

"Then he is well known?"

The apothecary looked at me in wonder. "They say he is painting quite a number of pictures for the Prince of Orange. He must be pretty good."

On my way home I passed by the Breestraat. There still was a light in the upstairs room.

A strange man, I said to myself. And soon he will be a very unhappy man. But where did I ever see that face before?

CHAPTER 2

I WAS SOAKING WET when I came home and so I put my clothes to dry in front of the fire in my bedroom. I took the kettle that hung over the fire, made myself a hot rum punch and crept between the sheets.

I slept soundly for a couple of hours.

Then my cat Cocaine (I had called the animal after a new American plant which seemed to bear pain-killing qualities and which had recently been brought to Europe by a Spanish friar) wanted to get into the house and then she insisted upon having some milk, and then of course wanted to get out again. I was so thoroughly awake that I lay rolling over in bed, thinking of a million things—and suddenly it struck me where I had seen that man's face before and I remembered the whole episode.

And so I continue my story by going a few years back. It must have been in 1626. I had been in Amsterdam a little over a year and I had just opened my first office on the Bloemgracht, which then was in a comparatively new part of town. For a young, unmarried physician—this was before my short-lived marriage to the woman who died following the birth of our son—the Bloemgracht seemed to offer better opportunities than one of the older neighborhoods, where the rents were so much higher. And the days I spent there were the happiest of my life. It is true that I was very poor, but my God, what glorious friends I had!

I am grateful that I was born in a time so active, so full of color, so rich as the present. And most of all I give thanks that I was able to start my career in a city which happened to be the center of the whole civilized world. For where else on this planet but in this incredible town of Amsterdam would it have been possible to bring together such a strange group of human beings as my three dear friends of yesteryear?

There was Jean-Louys de la Tremouille, the son of a French duke, a young man who through ancient precedent was allowed to remain covered and seated in the presence of his sovereign and was now a quiet student of mathematics and philosophy. "I moved to Amsterdam, took those tower rooms in the old mill," he once told me, "and have never left the town; nor do I mean to leave it until I finish my tables of logarithms, and that, according to my best knowledge, will take me between two and three hundred years." Jean-Louys was the perfect French gentleman, ever courteous, ever agreeable, ever ready to laugh at himself or at fate. He had a brilliant mind and an inexhaustible curiosity about everything and everybody.

Then there was Bernardo Mendoza Soeyro, that strangely romantic creature, one of the few people who had ever been in a prison of the Inquisition and lived to tell the tale. A Sephardic Jew, descendant of kings of Israel, a wanderer, no wife, no children, no home, poor as a church mouse and proud as a peacock, Bernardo had been one of the richest students of the University of Salamanca, but was now content to make a bare living as bookkeeper in the fish shop of old Isaac Ashalem.

And then there was Selim, whose real name we could never discover, whose father had been grand vizier to Murad IV, who at the age of ten had had forty servants of his own and who had quarreled with his father, had then been obliged to leave the country and was living in Amsterdam in amiable splendor. Selim explained his presence in these northern climes by his desire to translate Homer into Arabic, "in order," as he said, "that my compatriots may learn of the glorious deeds of their ancestors, for what after all were the Trojans but the earliest keepers of the holy road to Stamboul?"

How did four such utterly different characters as we ever happen to meet? It was one of those mysteries one accepts and does not question. Of course we were rather outside the pale of polite society. A Jew was pretty bad. A Turk was a little worse. A Papist was beyond the limit. A combination of the three, plus a Dutchman who was suspected of being a libertine (the word then did not mean a rake, as it does today, but a liberal in questions of theology), was something even Amsterdam had never seen before and hoped never to see again.

THANK GOD, I am not trying to write a book, for here I have wasted several goose quills describing my dear friends, while I ought to have been busy with my patient. But poor Saskia was such a colorless person that she could not make herself interesting even on her deathbed, while her husband came to play such a role in my life that every detail connected with our first meeting had become important to me. When I tell under what circumstances this happened it will be seen that my strangely assorted companions had something to do with it. Besides, they were such wonderful people, it does me good to write about them.

It is April of the year 1626 and the sun is shining. It is Easter morning and the good people of Amsterdam have all gone to church, but the bad people, Selim and Jean-Louys and Bernardo and myself, have decided to start forth upon a new venture. During the winter we only saw each other for chess on Saturday evenings, but when spring came the four of us often used to meet on Sundays for a walk into the country and afterwards we had dinner either at a tavern in town or in the rooms of Jean-Louys' tower.

On this Easter Sunday we had decided to hire a small yacht and sail to the island of Marken. This was quite an undertaking, for the people there enjoyed a reputation as amateur pirates and highway robbers. But Selim declared that he had experience along that line having once, as captain, taken a Turkish man-of-war to the northern shores of the Black Sea, a desolate region inhabited by wandering tribes of a strange race, called the Slavs. Furthermore we were accompanied by Jean-Louys, who had an extraordinary ability to win the goodwill of almost any creature on either two or four legs.

Anyway, we had arranged to meet at ten o'clock at the old tower near the harbor. I arrived a little earlier than the others and immediately felt there was something unusual in the air. Excited men and women were standing in small groups along the side of the canal, and all had their eyes fixed on one perfectly commonplace house. Occasionally someone would shout, "I saw one of them!" or "The whole place is full of them!" or again, "There is one now! He is trying to get across the roof!" followed by a cry of "Look out! They are going to shoot!" Whereupon everyone would run to safety behind a tree or the bales of merchandise that were lying beneath tarpaulin covers.

The whole thing seemed absurd. Our town was famous for its orderliness. The militia was a heavy-fisted organization and Their Lordships, who might be persuaded to overlook certain misdemeanors of a private nature, knew no mercy when it came to rioting. If a rioter was caught, he was hung from a window of the Town Hall and that was all there was to it.

I turned to a tight-lipped individual with mean yellow eyes, who was standing by my side. "Pray tell me," I asked, "what is going on?"

He at once grew suspicious. "Oh, don't you know?"

I assured him that I had only just come.

"Well," he said, "the house is full of Arminians. They are holding a service there and they just tried to kill a child and use its blood for their ceremonies."

Of course, I should not have continued this conversation. No one short of a lunatic would have started an argument with that type of religious zealot and under such circumstances. But I was not very bright in those days and still believed in the efficacy of orderly argumentation so I answered:

"But surely, my dear sir, the people have not revived that silly old lie about the Jews and applied it to the Arminians?"

Good Lord, how the fellow bristled! But he was the typical

coward. He turned to a group of men and boys stationed behind a dozen big wooden boxes. "Hey, boys!" he shouted. "This fellow here is a black Arminian. Come and get him."

Whereupon the crowd left its shelter and swooped down on me and no doubt would have attacked me, when suddenly the door of the house opened and a dozen men and women, like frightened rabbits, made a dash towards the left of the street, which did not seem so well guarded. The mob rushed after

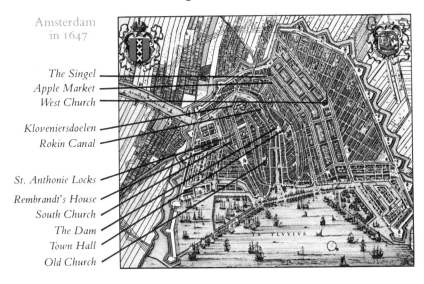

Amsterdam
in 1647

The Singel
Apple Market
West Church

Kloveniersdoelen
Rokin Canal

St. Anthonie Locks
Rembrandt's House
South Church
The Dam
Town Hall
Old Church

its victims and I was left standing alone, looking sheepish.

A pleasant voice behind me spoke: "Trying to solve the problems of this world by the usual appeal to reason?" And there were Jean-Louys and Bernardo and they said: "Selim was here a moment ago but he left, as he said it always hurt his tender Moslem heart to see Christians murder each other. He is waiting for us in the Ridderstraat. You had better come along."

But ere we could turn into the next side street, we heard drums and a company of militia came marching from the north. Caught between the rioters and the soldiers (and the mob looked as if it wanted to fight), we stood aimlessly for a moment. Then Bernardo said, "Look! There is a tavern!"

We made for the door of the inn just as someone from the other side was trying to lock it. By a stroke of good luck, however, I recognized the innkeeper as an old patient of the city hospital. He recognized me too, for he said: "Come in as fast as you can, for there is going to be trouble and I don't want them to plunder my house."

For the moment we were safe. We ordered three glasses of gin and asked our host what had caused all the trouble. He said

Self-portrait, 1629

the house in question belonged to a member of the Arminian community. Since the followers of Jacobus Arminius had been read out of the Church by act of the General Synod some years before, they had been meeting at this house to listen to one of their ministers. These clandestine meetings were of course against the law and the clergy of Amsterdam had protested violently. But the Arminians, or Remonstrants, were industrious and respectable citizens and Their Lordships of the Town Hall refused to proceed against them, even if those black-souled sinners publicly confessed that they had serious doubts about predestination and infant damnation. As long as they paid their taxes and were discreet about their gatherings, they could pray and preach as they liked.

Well, this morning some boys who had stayed away from Sunday school had used the stoop of this house for a noisy game of knucklebones. Someone had come out and told them to go play somewhere else. But no other stoop would do. Half a dozen times they had been told to go away and half a dozen times they had used vile language, until the poor Arminian, forgetting all the precepts of his creed, had lost his temper and had boxed the ears of a young lout who had called him a name which I shall not here repeat. The youthful mucker had then shrieked that he had been murdered. A few passersby had taken his side. Someone had raised the cry of "The Arminians and the Papists are in that house!" and the fat had been in the fire.

By the time our host had finished his story, the angry horde outside had been augmented by those returning from early service and they were in no mood to obey the orders of the officer of the guard who bade them disperse. I was looking through a peephole in one of the tavern blinds and I saw the crowd direct a fresh volley of stones and sticks and mud against the offending house. A stone hit one of the soldiers who were waiting at some distance. I saw him level his musket. At the same moment an evil-looking ruffian, with a cobblestone in each hand and a long knife held between his lips, made for the officer who was still alone, with his sword undrawn, and undoubtedly he would have killed him, had not the soldier fired his gun and caught the assailant right between the eyes.

This precipitated a general melee and, since the tavern was now in considerably less danger, we persuaded our host to let us open the

Sketch of two crippled beggars

blind. Such outbreaks of popular fury are very interesting to people with a philosophical turn of mind and we did not want to miss the opportunity of studying our neighbors in the act of breaking skulls and windows for the greater glory of their mysterious God.

Then suddenly I saw something extraordinary. Leaning unconcernedly against a tree, a young man was making a sketch of one of the beggars who had hastened to be present when the plundering should begin and who now was debating with his colleagues whether to go on or whether to retreat, as the game had been spoiled anyway by the arrival of the guards.

While they were still debating, the battle between the rioters

and the soldiers took a fresh impetus from the arrival of a number of sailors from some nearby East Indiamen, who armed with
cutlasses were all for showing the damned heretics that they
could not preach their stinking doctrines in *their* city. Many
heads were broken and stones flew. But through it all that
strange young man kept working away at his sketches as if
unaware that at any moment he might be killed. All three of us
were fascinated by him. He was simply dressed, like a student or
a better-class artisan, and he wore his hair long as was then the
fashion. But all three of us remarked on his eyes.

"We must speak to him," Jean-Louys cried, delighted with
so much sangfroid. "We must invite him to come on our boat
trip. He will be very useful in our negotiations with the natives."

But when the soldiers had swept away the rabble and we
could go out, the young man was gone. We looked for him
everywhere, but could not find him. And so we thanked our
host and gave him a handsome tip (for maybe he had saved our
lives) and went to the Ridderstraat and at the appointed tavern
found Selim busily engaged in explaining the mysteries of a
ring he wore to the serving girl, who was so fascinated that
she had let him put an arm around her—"So that she should be
closer to the subject," as he told us when we entered.

Of course, our sailing party had been spoiled, for that whole
part of the town remained smoldering with anger. At the suggestion of Jean-Louys we went to his tower and he made us an
omelet in the true French style. Selim made us a strange dish of
little bits of meat which he called *ish-kebab*. Bernardo mixed us
a Portuguese salad, which was not unpleasant though a little too
oily and garlicky. And I sat wondering who this strange young
man might have been who could lose himself so completely
in the task of drawing pictures while all around him people
were killing each other.

For a long time his face continued to haunt me. But I never
saw him again. Until that rainy evening in the month of November of the year 1641 when suddenly it dawned upon me, as
I lay tossing in my bed. The strange young man of the riot of
fifteen years before was none other than the husband of my new
patient. It was Rembrandt van Rijn.

278

WHEN I CALLED AGAIN at the house in the Breestraat, I mentioned the riot as we sat in the studio after I had visited my patient. I had been right. Rembrandt had been there. Just by chance. For at that time he was living in Leiden and he had only been in Amsterdam for a fortnight to try and sell some of his pictures. The trip had not been very successful and he had returned to Leiden, as he explained, "because the meals at home cost nothing and I could send my laundry to the family wash."

As for the riot, yes, he remembered vaguely that there had been a lot of shouting while he was drawing. "But all I really remember," he added, "is that I found myself face-to-face with one of the most picturesque hoodlums I had ever seen, one of those wandering vagabonds who obey neither God nor man. They lie and steal and cheat and loaf and gamble and get hung or die miserably by the roadside, but they make no pretense; when they are dirty, they are dirty, and when they are drunk, they are drunk, and one knows what one is painting. I will show you the one I saw that day. I have done him in an etching. Some other time—when Saskia is better."

Better! I thought. You poor devil, I ought to tell you now. But no! You might as well hope until the end. And so we talked of this and that. But the subjects that were important to most of my patients—how it would affect our trade if there should be war between the King of England and his Parliament, and how a book had been written to prove that somewhere in the southern part of the Pacific there must be a large piece of land, and how certain local merchants wanted to send out an expedition to take possession of this mysterious land, which would mean a new source of revenue—these ideas did not interest my new friend. Invariably after a few minutes of such talk our minds went back to the sick woman and the baby and whether the child had inherited her weak constitution.

The child looked strong enough but it was restless and wept a great deal and this tired the mother. For as soon as I was out of the house, the nurse would find a pretext to move the child from the etching room upstairs back to the living room downstairs. If I happened to come in upon such an occasion, there always was a vague excuse. The master had to use his press that morning, or the room smelled so badly of ink that it had to be aired and the child might catch cold or she had to tend to the baby's laundry and could not leave him alone while she was in the garden.

There are undoubtedly a number of nurses who are faithful, efficient and competent. But there are all too many who are

The nurse, Geertje Dircx

lazy and indifferent and whose superstitious methods go straight back to the Middle Ages. Geertje Dircx belonged to this latter category. She had large, coarse features and an arrogant voice with a whine in it. She was (as I afterwards discovered) the widow of an army trumpeter and often talked of the days when she had had her own place and had not been obliged to eat other people's bread. Her game was so simple that any other man would have seen through it right away. She knew enough about sick people to understand that the man for whom she worked would soon be a widower. She meant to fill the empty place. She probably felt that I, as an outsider, might not be so easily deceived and would try to upset her plan of becoming the second Mrs. van Rijn.

It may seem that I pay more attention to this woman than she deserves. But soon after the death of Saskia it appeared that I had been right in my diagnosis of Geertje's hidden intentions and for years the poor painter's life was made miserable by this former servant and her lamentations and complaints.

From all this Rembrandt might have saved himself if he had done what I bade him do and had sent her packing. But this man, who was without mercy for himself when it came to his work, who would actually live and sleep and sit and paint and walk in his clothes for weeks at a time if he got interested in a problem of light and dark, who would content himself with a slice of bread and a couple of herrings as his only meal for months at a time because he was too busy with an etching to think of anything else, this man was weak as butter when it came to women.

He did not understand them and in his heart of hearts I think he rather disliked them. He was a vigorous fellow with the strength of a bull and he was sometimes in dire need of a woman, just a woman, any woman would do. He was by nature exceedingly kindhearted and, of course, the other sex was quick to recognize and to use his vulnerability. As a result Rembrandt was forever in some sort of trouble about his domestic relations.

Such a man should never have married. For the moment he promised to love and cherish a certain female for the rest of his days, he was uttering a lie. He had already given his word years ago to a most jealous mistress who would never let go of him.

Once shortly after Saskia's death I tried to explain this to one of her relatives, a respectable Frisian dominie. He was horrified. "Then you mean to say," he stammered, "that my poor niece was married to an adulterer?"

"Yes," I answered, "just as much as any other woman who undertakes to become the life companion of a man who is more in love with his work than with anything else."

For that, alas, was the truth. And it caused a vast amount of misery to a few human beings and brought inconceivable beauty into the lives of millions of others.

SASKIA WAS TOTALLY UNAWARE of the seriousness of her condition. She was losing weight rapidly, but she felt no pain, and except for an occasional fit of coughing, she would hardly have known anything was the matter. Perhaps the gods, not always renowned for their mercy, recognized that phthisis was an affliction most people would be unable to bear if it were not mitigated by some spiritual anesthetic, consisting in this instance of an irrepressible gaiety and a steadfast optimism.

Every time I visited her, Saskia was doing "just a little better than the last time you saw me, dear Doctor." She was so lovely, so pathetic, so patient and so totally ineffectual, that my heart was full of pity for her and sometimes I bought her a few flowers from the flower woman just around the corner.

Upon such occasions Saskia was as happy as a child and one day I remember I had brought her a bunch of country violets and she made a little wreath and put it on the head of the baby, for of course, no matter what I might say, the child continued to live in the room where the mother lay dying. She even tried to make little Titus dance on her knees while she was sitting

Saskia

propped up in her chair in front of the fire. But the effort was too much for her and she had a coughing spell. When I tried to make her lie down, she refused and said she would be all right as soon as she had taken some of her medicine.

This puzzled me, for I had given her no medicine except a sleeping potion, knowing only too well that there was no drug that could prevail against the onslaughts of this dreadful disease. I then discovered to my horror that that unspeakable nurse had prevailed upon her to try the mixture of a well-known mountebank, who pretended he was a Babylonian prince who had discovered

the secret formula of King Solomon's elixir of life, hidden among the ruins of the temple of Jerusalem, and who sold this Elixir Vitae for a florin a bottle. As soon as we had put Saskia back to bed and she was resting quietly, I was careful to remove the bottle. At home I examined the contents and found that it consisted of licorice, camomile and water with a dash of sugar. No wonder this quack could afford a handsomer carriage than any member of our Surgeons' Guild.

I spoke to the husband the next day about this and told him that this licorice water might not be harmful to his wife, but neither would it do her any good. She needed plenty of milk and eggs and must avoid things that would upset her stomach or spoil her appetite. He was very angry and promised to dismiss the nurse at once. When I returned the next day, I found her gone. I expressed my joy and asked where the child was.

"Oh," the painter answered with a somewhat sheepish look, "the nurse is taking the child out for a little walk. She said that she thought it needed some air and it was such a lovely day!"

A lovely day indeed! A sharp east wind was rattling the blinds. The streets were full of dust. When I came into the sickroom I found it filled with smoke. And the mother lay gasping in her bed.

Teaching a child to walk

"The nurse said it would be all right," she whispered to me hoarsely, "but there is such a storm and it is blowing down the chimney and I could not get up and I called, but no one heard me."

And she wept bitterly for this was one of the rare days when her customary cheerfulness had left her.

I was now thoroughly angry with van Rijn. He had remained upstairs in his studio working, for he felt so helpless in the midst of these domestic upheavals that he tried to persuade himself they did not exist. I told him in no uncertain tones that something had to be done or I would no longer be responsible. And suddenly I realized that he had never understood the seriousness of his wife's illness. His thoughts had been so concentrated upon his paintings that only a brutal point-blank announcement of imminent disaster could break through his unawareness.

Now he went to the other extreme. He accused himself bitterly of neglect, called himself his wife's murderer, carefully washed his brushes in a jar of turpentine, wiped them on a rag, took off his painter's blouse, turned his easel away from the light, went out, locking the door behind him, and went downstairs, sat down by the side of his wife's bed, took her hand and said: "Saskia sweet, now I shall be thy nurse."

As far as I know he never returned to his work until she died.

After this there was some sort of order in the big house on the Breestraat. Van Rijn put a cot up in a corner of the big room. A cleaning woman was called in and the bottles of acid and the pans with rosin were removed and one or two paintings which smelled too strongly of fresh varnish were relegated to the studio. The peat fire was changed for one of wood. It cost a good deal more, but the man seemed to be making plenty of money. Geertje Dircx was still on the premises, but she usually kept out of my sight. Three times a day she brought the child to see its mother and on those occasions, if mere looks could have killed, I would have died miserably. But as long as she obeyed my instructions I did not care how much she hated me. My patient needed rest and regular hours and she now had both, for van Rijn guarded her day and night with a patience and care which were as touching as they were ineffectual.

For once he had escaped from the dreadful mistress who heretofore had given him no respite. And although I had heard that he had been ordered to do a large piece for the new clubhouse of the town guards, I never saw him busy with sketches. I asked him if it had been finished and he said no, it had been begun, but it could wait. And he sat by his wife's side for hours and spoke to her softly, which seemed to be the best way to make her go to sleep. She would close her eyes and lie very still with a smile upon her lovely face and she looked so young that it seemed incredible that she was dying. So the winter passed and the new year came and I knew that it would be Saskia's last.

NOW IT WAS CUSTOMARY in those days for each member of the Surgeons' Guild in town to give a course in anatomy for the benefit of the students of medicine and those leeches and barbers who wanted to prepare themselves more thoroughly for their daily tasks. I had last given this course of lectures and demonstrations in 1636, and now I was asked by the dean of our guild to prepare to teach elementary anatomy once more. As I had devoted myself almost entirely to the study of drugs during the last decade, I felt the need of refreshing my memory and so I went to Anatomical Hall of the Surgeons' Guild.

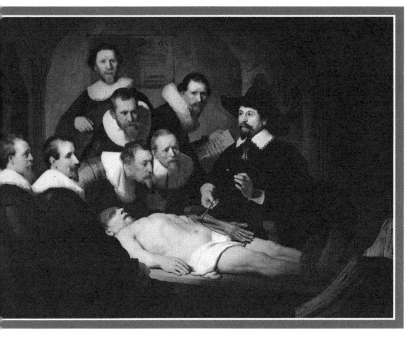

THE ANATOMY LESSON OF DR. TULP (1632)

I had not been near the place since my last lectureship and I was surprised to find one wall entirely filled with a large picture, showing Doctor Nicolaes Tulp in the midst of his students. Tulp had been high sheriff of our town since he posed for this portrait and had been elected burgomaster several times.

The picture struck me forcibly for in it I found something which I had rarely discovered in any other painting—though I must confess I had never known much about this form of art until I met Rembrandt. Of course there always had been certain pictures I liked and others I did not like quite so well. I had taken them more or less for granted. Now I suddenly made the discovery that such things could have a soul.

I don't like the word soul. It smacks too much of theological discussions. But I can't think of any other expression that describes equally well what I mean—this animate quality of supposedly inanimate substances. The revelation came to me that morning as I stood in front of the portrait of Nicolaes Tulp and half a dozen of my colleagues, busy with some anatomical demonstration.

During my student days I had attended hundreds of dissections. I knew it had become fashionable among my better-known colleagues to have themselves painted carving up some unfortunate victim of the gallows or the poor ward. Together with the whole town I had laughed when one rather vain old physician, who had engaged in a bitter professional quarrel with a younger man, had ordered such a portrait and had bribed the artist to make one of the students look like his hated rival, thereby drawing attention to his own superior position in life. And together with the whole town I had roared when the younger man, not to be outdone, had favored the Surgeons' Guild with a large canvas in which he himself was shown demonstrating the entrails of a very unappetizing corpse which bore a striking if somewhat greenish resemblance to the learned professor who had humiliated him in picture No. 1.

But all those paintings were mere records of events. They told the spectator that "on such and such a day, in such and such a room, Doctor A, surrounded by Doctors B, C, D and E, had dissected the mortal remains of the late F and had found that the precentral gyrus was still situated (as it ought to be) between the postcentral gyrus and the superior frontal gyrus."

I don't know how to explain it, but Rembrandt's picture of Nicolaes Tulp was different. It did not merely tell a story. It gave tangible expression to an abstract idea. Nicolaes Tulp ceased to be a fashionable practitioner in an opulent town—a clever politician, a distinguished anatomist and a talented executive who had reorganized the entire pharmaceutical system of his time. Instead, he became the living symbol of that divine curiosity which, prying into the secrets of nature, may some-day set the human race free from most of its manifold ills and miseries.

And the faces of the men around him were no longer those of humdrum hardworking leeches, come hither to learn a few things and perhaps improve their standing in the medical world and charge a little higher fees. Those eyes looked beyond the corpse stretched out before them and saw more than the tendons of a single arm. They were gazing into the mystery that underlies all existence: What was it that made those muscles move?

Later, when Rembrandt and I were sitting together one night in the etching room (Saskia had had a bad attack of coughing but at last she had fallen asleep), I told him what had happened to me and I grew rather rhetorical as I spoke of art and the mission of art.

He was not particularly impressed. "You seem to be an intelligent person, Doctor," he said. "And yet, here you are, forty years old, or more, and you have only now discovered what all truly intelligent people have known since the beginning of time. Which is that nothing counts in this world except the inner spirit of things."

"Meaning the immortal soul of man?"

"Meaning the immortal soul of everything ever created."

"The immortal soul of tables and chairs and cats and dogs and houses and ships?"

"Just so."

"And of books and scissors and flowers and clouds?"

"Exactly."

I was silent for a while. Then I looked at this strange man with the tired eyes and the tired droop of the strong unwieldy shoulders. "How many people in all the world will be able to understand that?" I asked.

He smiled and lifted up both hands in a gesture of resignation. "Well, perhaps three or four in every hundred. At the most, four. The others will never know what we are talking about, but they will have their revenge."

"In what way?"

"They will let us starve to death."

The conversation was rapidly getting beyond my depth.

"Good night," I said, and held out my hand. He took it.

"Good night, Doctor, and thank you. If you have a few moments after dinner tomorrow, say about three, I wish you would come here. There is something I want to take you to see." And with that he showed me through the hall and bade me good night.

CHAPTER 4

THE NEXT AFTERNOON I called at the Breestraat. The patient was having one of her bad days. Nevertheless she was sitting in a chair, propped up with many pillows. The child was on her lap. The nurse was hanging some clothes to dry near the fire. I had told her not to do the washing in the same room with the sick woman, but of course she had not obeyed my instructions. She grumbled something when I entered, picked up the baby's things, threw them into a wicker basket, slammed the door behind her and left.

"I can do nothing with her," Saskia complained. "Sometimes I almost think she is mad."

"I am sorry," I replied. "Your husband ought to have discharged her long ago."

"I know it. But he hates to be bothered with such things. He is a good man and he tries to interest himself in the household. But his heart is in his work. And Geertje is devoted to the baby."

Just then Rembrandt came in. He was in great anger and was swearing heartily. "The idiot!" he shouted. "The clumsy idiot! I thought I had at last shown him how to use that press. Last time he soaked the paper until it turned to pulp. Now he has put the plate underneath the roller without using any felt. The copper is bent like a hoop. I shall have to do the whole thing over."

Saskia held out her hand, very white and thin, but lovely of shape. "Come sit down for a moment, my dear," she said. "Why don't you tell the boy to go home if he is just a nuisance?"

At once her husband's anger vanished. "I had thought of it," he answered, "but the next one would probably be worse. And this one pays me a hundred florins a year for the privilege of being one of my pupils. But I know what I will do. I'll turn him out into the yard to cut wood. I'll tell him that the exercise is good for his biceps and that a painter needs strong muscles. A brilliant idea. And I owe it to you. If I had been left to my own devices, I would have fired him. And now, my good Doctor, you and I will take a walk and I will show you something —that is, if my wife will let you go for a few minutes?"

Poor Saskia made a faint effort to smile, but she looked wasted and coughed terribly while we carried her back to bed.

"She ought not to be doing so much," I warned as we left.

Rembrandt shook his head. "I know it," he said, "but she insists upon getting up."

Well, we all are as we are and what we are and there is no use trying to change the human race. And with this wise reflection I followed my host into the street.

A synagogue in the Jewish quarter

REMBRANDT LED ME THEN to the Jewish quarter, a world that was as different from the rest of the city as the moon from the sun. Forty years ago this suburb had been a swamp. Later on it had been drained after a fashion, but the houses were still very damp and so they could be rented to no one but the poorest among the poor. Of these there were vast quantities, for ever since we had declared ourselves independent from Spain, our town had been a refuge to people from every part of the world. Some had come because they had heard that we were rich and therefore it was easier to make a living in Holland than anywhere else. Others belonged to one of the innumerable sects that had sprung up after the Reformation. These had hastened to the great and free republic because they hoped to escape persecution in a country where the magistrates were reported to be very lenient.

Then, during the eighties of the last century, Portugal had been annexed by Spain and the first thing King Philip II had done was to pass an edict by which he had deprived his newly acquired territory of the only people who ever thought it worth their while to do a little work. My grandmother used to tell me how the Portuguese Jewish immigrants arrived. She described the terrible conditions on board those vessels—men and women and children all huddled together with their few belongings (they never were given more than twenty-four hours' warning before they were expelled and were obliged to sell their houses and real estate and their merchandise during those hours besides doing their packing) and how quite often when the hatches were opened it was found that half of them had died from lack of food, drink and fresh air, and how the survivors were taken to the houses of private citizens to recuperate.

That was long ago and the former immigrants have grown rich and moved to a more fashionable neighborhood. But every year some new recruits arrive from foreign lands and, in the part of the town through which Rembrandt took me, one still hears more Spanish and Portuguese and German dialects than Dutch; the shops still look like bazaars and the food continues to smell like the devil.

Rembrandt seemed to know this part of the town by heart and was apparently on speaking terms with half the population. Wherever we went he was greeted as if he were a burgomaster or some great official instead of being merely a painter.

But he explained it to me at once. "Don't think for a moment that they are so civil because they understand my work. I am a good customer. I pay cash whenever I can and I don't bargain more than is necessary. That is all." And then he told me that this ghetto was a veritable treasure-house and contained more color than all the rest of Amsterdam put together.

"Our civilization is drab and gray," he said. "We seem to regard color as an expression of the sinful flesh. Our men and women are dressed in black, our children are dressed in black, our churches look like whitewashed sepulchers. When we give a party, we sit around with sour faces until we get drunk. Then we behave as Jan Steen shows us in his pictures, and a clever boy he is, too, even if he came from Leiden, as I do. I wish I knew more about my own family. I don't mean my brothers and sisters. They are good, but commonplace. My grandparents were dull, small tradespeople. But how about my great-grandparents or further back? Was there ever an Italian in our family? I sometimes wonder if I would have been happier if I had been born in Italy."

"Did you ever think of going there?"

"Of course I did. Every youngster who paints thinks of going to Italy at some time in his career. I even talked it over with Jan Lievens when we were studying together in Leiden in '31. We could have got the money too. That mill of my father's was not doing badly and there were some rich people—My Lord Constantijn Huygens,

Two Jewish strollers

for one—who were taking an interest in us. I wanted to use every hour of daylight and could not afford to waste a couple of months trying to get to a place where the daylight probably was not so different from what it is here. Of course there have been some great masters in Italy. But I can see their work in Amsterdam. I have made copies of a number of them and they are being sold as genuine, but then, our art dealers would sell pictures by Saint Luke himself if they saw a chance for a profit."

By now we had almost reached the outskirts of the Jewish quarter and I asked Rembrandt whether he hadn't forgotten what he was going to show me.

"That is in another part of the town," he answered. "I am

after something else here. I think that I have got hold of a genuine bit by Michelangelo. It is a small thing, the head of a child. If they will let me have it for fifteen hundred guilders, I shall take it."

He mentioned the sum as casually as if it had been a couple of shillings. I had heard that he got much more for his portraits than anyone else and of course everybody knew he had married a rich wife, but I was not prepared for such nonchalance. I asked if that was not a great deal of money for one picture.

He seemed surprised. "I suppose so. But Michelangelo was a wonderful painter. No, I don't think fifteen hundred guilders is too much. I am getting more than that myself."

"For a single picture?"

"Yes, and if you will have patience for a few minutes longer, I will show it to you. But first I must go down the cellar."

The cellar, when we came to it, proved to be an antique shop in the dark basement of a tavern. It was run by a black-bearded Jew in a long cloak, who spoke a jargon compounded of two-thirds Portuguese, one-sixth German and one-sixth Dutch with a liberal sprinkling of what I took to be the original language of King David's psalms.

I discovered to my amazement that Rembrandt not only understood this homemade dialect, but spoke it with great fluency. Once the product of Michelangelo's brush had been produced from a corner, he addressed himself to the hirsute dealer in such an eloquent and vituperative mixture of the tongues just enumerated that I was sure the two men must come to blows. But nothing happened. On the contrary, after half an hour's animated conversation they separated in the best of spirits. Rembrandt had succeeded in forcing the price down by one hundred florins. The art dealer had persuaded him to buy the frame, which he swore was worth two hundred guilders, but which he would let him have for half the amount.

In the fresh air outside I awaited some explanation of the mysterious proceedings, and I got one.

"I wanted that picture badly," Rembrandt confessed. "The old Jew asked too much. I got it for a hundred guilders less."

"But the frame! He charged you a hundred guilders for it."

Rembrandt looked puzzled, like a child that has been caught in some foolish expenditure. But he quickly recovered. "After all," he asked, "what is money for except to spend? Fifteen hundred guilders is rather a large sum. But next week, next month at least, I shall have eighteen hundred florins coming in for some work I have just finished. And I did want that painting!"

With which irrefutable logic we retraced our steps, crossed the Rokin Canal and then turned right towards the Amstel.

A view of the Amstel River

WE WERE WALKING in the general direction of the Kloveniers-doelen, an old stone dungeon that was now used as a meeting place by some of the smartest militia regiments.

During the great war of independence, it was those town companies that enabled us to gain our freedom. For the German, Swiss and English mercenaries hired to fight for us had nothing much to gain and everything to lose and they usually disappeared when the fighting began and did not return until the signal had been given to start looting. But many of the militia regiments were now degenerating into mere social organizations. Each company was trying hard to attract desirable recruits and all the social and economic advantages of associating one's self with this or that captain were carefully enumerated and discussed in the better-class taverns.

When he stood in front of the Kloveniersdoelen, Rembrandt said: "Let us go in here a moment." These buildings had been added to so often and were composed of so many remnants of walls and towers that one almost needed a guide to find one's way. But he opened the door of the taproom and said: "It has been quite a walk. You will like some beer. I am not a member, but I have worked here so often that they let me use their common room."

We sat down and Rembrandt ordered two mugs of beer. Then he said: "You must be hungry! You are not? Do you mind if I eat something? The meals at home have become a little sketchy since Saskia was taken sick." He asked that they bring him a plate of fried eggs and one of fresh herring and between the beer and the fish he told me why he had brought me there.

"I don't want to talk about myself, but these last four years have been rather lonely. I have had a hard struggle, what with an ailing wife, a difficult family-in-law, and a new house which is really too big and expensive for me. Are you sure you don't want any herring? It is exceedingly good. Well, here is my story.

"You know that in Flanders they think so much of Rubens that they made him an ambassador. They tell me there is a man in Spain by the name of Velazquez who is the greatest painter that ever lived. I hear that he can make an empty room look really like an empty room. It will take me another twenty years of practice to learn to do that. And I hear that this Don Diego Valazquez is held in such esteem that he is allowed to sit in the presence of the King.

"Well, in this republic people look upon an artist as a laboring man. Some of us make fairly good wages, but not any better than those which a dike worker or a bookkeeper or a baker's assistant makes with much less trouble. Our parents always fear that in the end we will share the fate of old Hercules Seghers and die in the almshouse or in a grogshop.

"That this poor fellow came to such an end because his neighbors were too dull to appreciate him never seems to dawn upon most people. They think it a joke that Hercules finally had to paint his pictures on his old shirts and the back of his old breeches and had to sell his etchings to the butchers of the Rokin for wrapping paper.

"I loved old Seghers. I was a youngster and he was quite an old man when I first came to Amsterdam and I did not see him often. But one night I went to his place with a few friends. A bare room with a horrible-looking woman in one corner doing something to a large stone jar filled with vegetables. She seemed to be his wife. Half a dozen dirty children on the floor and the old man with a pleasant bun on, completely oblivious of the mess around him, working at a storm, as fine a piece of painting as I have ever seen. He had fastened it against the wall with two nails and he stood in front of it. That afternoon, it seemed, while his wife had gone out to pawn his easel, he had stolen the last sheet out of the children's bed and had cut it up to be used as canvas. He was crazy with work. He worked morning, noon and night. They say he was a drunkard. Well, drunken people don't paint the sort of pictures he did. But sometimes he would take a glass or two, just enough not to hear the bawling wife and the howling infants.

"I was not very rich then and, anyway, he had nothing for sale as everything had been pawned or bartered away for butter, eggs and milk for the children. Afterwards, with a great deal of trouble, I got hold of six of his pictures. You may have seen them in my house. I like them immensely and also they are a constant reminder. They take me back to the day when I stood in Seghers' stable (it really wasn't a house he was living in) and said to myself: Rembrandt, my boy, you are a good deal of a dreamer and you are apt to do foolish things. Well, do all the foolish things you want, but see that you get paid well in the meantime.

"I need a lot of money. And I need color around me. I would have died in a place like that of Hercules in less than a week. I want to buy things. And when I want something, I want it then and there and not next week or a year later. I must be able to experiment if I am to do good work. Saskia is a lovely woman. You ought to have seen her before she got so sick. But I must try her out, see what is in her, dress her up in silks and satins and hang pearls on her and rubies, paint her a hundred different ways. Poor child, I don't think she always enjoyed it. But she was very good-natured about it. And I needed that sort of foolishness to find out what I could do. All that is, however, beside the point. Want to smoke?"

Rembrandt ordered two fresh mugs and two pipes of tobacco and then, leaning his elbows on the table, he went on:

"You know that I have been doing a great deal of portrait

Saskia

work. People paid me four, five, even six hundred guilders. I don't know why. Even Bartholomeus van der Helst never got more than that amount for a picture as big as a house with a dozen or twenty figures and each one of those twenty fools thinking he was the handsomest of the crowd and insisting upon being done in great detail. So you see I had no kick coming. It became the fashion for rich people to have themselves painted by me. I was even asked to do some pictures for the Prince.

"Very well, I used to say to myself, I shall paint those who are rich and sometimes I shall even paint them as they want to be painted. For I needed

the money. Our first child was coming. There was the new house I wanted (I had to mortgage it rather heavily). People used to say that I was a lucky devil because I had married a rich wife. But Saskia was not rich. There were nine children and old Uijlenburgh had been too busy with politics to pay much attention to his estate.

"When he died, some eight years before I met my wife, each of the children was supposed to get about forty thousand guilders. Quite a sum, I grant you, and my neighbors added a couple of zeros and made it four hundred thousand. They might have made it forty million florins, for all the cash we ever saw. For everything was invested in farms and houses and as soon as we wanted to divide the estate the farms could not be rented and the houses could not be sold. And of course I am living here in Amsterdam and the other heirs are in Friesland, a couple of days away.

"The Frisians are surely the most pigheaded people in the world. And stingy! My God! They kiss every stiver a dozen times before they spend it and when I made a lot of money painting portraits and bought a few pictures and statues and things (and after all, it was my money) they jabbered to all the neighbors about the scandalous way in which I was squandering Saskia's patrimony. I had to go to law and sue them for libel.

"Squandering, indeed! When I needed thirteen thousand guilders to buy my house, I gave notes that will keep me busy for the rest of my days. Would I have done that if I could have laid hands on a little cash? No, that story of the poor painter and the rich wife is so much moonshine.

"Only I get interested in a subject. I see or rather I feel a lot of things others don't see or don't feel. I put them into my picture and the man who sat for his portrait gets angry, says the likeness is not there or I have given him a look that will prove to his neighbors he is a miser or mean to his wife. In the end he refuses the picture or pays half what he promised.

"This won't do, for just now I want to make all the money I can. I have to pay for that house and Saskia will probably be sick for a long time and the boy will have to go to a good school and to the university afterwards. Besides, there exists a fashion in portrait painters. I have been the fashion for several years and people will soon say: 'Oh, yes, that van Rijn! He has lost something of his old pep and stamina.' What they mean of course is that I am beginning to paint them as they are.

"Hey there, Hendrick, bring me the bill. Thank you! And now I shall take you upstairs, and I shall show you."

WE WALKED UP two flights of broad stairs and came into a large assembly hall. It was quite dark. The high windows were covered with green baize curtains. On the walls I vaguely noticed one or two large pictures—the kind of company portraits by van der Helst and Govaert Flinck that one finds in all such places.

Then, when my eyes got accustomed to the dim light I saw that at the other end of the hall there was a vast wooden structure supporting an enormous canvas, but what it was meant to represent I could not make out.

Suddenly Rembrandt pulled the curtains aside and the room was flooded with sunlight and I suffered a physical shock, as if I had been struck in the face by a palette full of the richest colors ever devised by the hand of man. Dante might have been able to put an impression like that into poetic words. But I, being only a humble leech, could only say: "Damnation!"

Whereupon Rembrandt, who was not given much to outward manifestations of affection, threw both arms around me and shouted: "Splendid! Now I know that at least one person has understood what I meant to do."

He pulled a bench in front of the picture, once more closed the curtains that were furthest away from it (thereby causing the figure in white in the center of the painting to march right out of the frame), made me sit down, himself sat down and said:

"Now you know why I dragged you here. This is my great chance! It came to me by accident. The company of Captain Frans Banning Cocq was going to have its portrait done. First they talked of van der Helst doing it and then someone wanted Flinck, but one day the captain, My Lord of Pumerlandt, came to me and said he had seen the portrait I had done of Dominie Anslo and his wife and he liked the way in which I had arranged the subjects, with books on the table and the man talking to the woman—not two people just sitting, but a husband and wife really talking to each other—and he had had an idea. Most of the men in his company wanted the usual painting—soldiers and officers grouped around a table with a couple of pewter plates filled with dead oysters and a lot of wine bottles—everybody looking very proud, very brave and slightly the worse for having eaten so much. But wasn't there some other way such a picture could be painted?

"Well, at first I was a little frightened by the idea. I had never tried my hand at large groups. But then I said I'd like a few days to think it over. He answered that he would be delighted and would I come and see him when I was ready.

"So I set to work, but most of the sketches I did not like at all and I threw them away. And then it came to me that those regiments of volunteers don't mean much today. Just an excuse for pleasant social gatherings. But that is because we are living in times of peace. If there were another war they would once more amount to something. And there is a very definite ideal hidden somewhere in the idea of an armed citizenry.

"It is easy to poke fun at those pompous house painters and gin distillers and fishmongers marching forth in plumes and feathers, toting heavy swords and carrying gigantic arquebuses and powder horns as if they were going to drive the Turks out of Europe when all of us know that they are going to spend the greater part of the night throwing dice in the guardhouse and drinking small beer. But those men are sons and grandsons of just such house painters and gin distillers and fish dealers who got hanged and burned and broken on the wheel, fighting for something that had nothing to do with selling gin or codfish. There was something in them somewhere, that made them rather fine and noble. Well, if it was there, I was going to find it and paint it.

"And so I went to see My Lord of Pumerlandt one evening. We sat in his office and I took some paper (I can't talk without drawing at the same time) and I explained to him what I wanted to do—paint him and his men just as they were leaving the arsenal for a turn of duty—everything still in great disorder, one old fellow beating the alarm and some of the soldiers taking down their pikes and others getting their guns ready and little boys and little girls getting out from underneath the feet of the men and the inevitable dog that is present at every parade and one man who is the leader—one man who has himself in hand and knows what he is doing, who is quietly going ahead because he realizes that the others will follow no matter what he does.

"I am not sure I am making myself clear. But you told me that you had liked my picture of Nicolaes Tulp. Well, in that case I did not paint a learned doctor giving a lesson in anatomy. I tried to paint science, rather than a group of scientists. Just as here I have done my best to give an impression of civic duty rather than merely show a number of inconsequential citizens doing their own little particular duties. Do you follow me?"

I followed him so well I could say nothing in reply. It is strange that whenever I find myself face-to-face with something really beautiful, I grow absolutely dumb. Only after hours of silent wandering along the back streets or sitting alone in a darkened room am I able to regain my composure.

But Rembrandt, who was not always the most tactful of men and apt to be rather brusque, seemed to understand what had happened to me, for he found an excuse to bid me farewell.

"It is getting late," he said. "I shall run back home and see how Saskia is faring. I am sorry that I have taken so much of your time, but now you will understand why I brought you here. I had to do something really tremendous, to make the people see what I can accomplish when they give me free rein. And this picture will do it. The world will hear. I shall have more customers than ever and greater freedom to experiment. Mark my words, this picture will make people talk."

CHAPTER 5

REMBRANDT WAS RIGHT.

People talked about his picture.

As a matter of fact, they have not stopped talking yet.

The first result of this attempt to put an idea into colors and translate an emotion into lights and shades was a roar of laughter. The members of Captain Cocq's company started it, and soon the whole town laughed. Then suddenly the victims of this "unseemly hoax" ceased to be quite as hilarious. For a joke could be carried too far and they were the ones who would have to pay, weren't they? And pay for what?

Pay a hundred or two hundred guilders apiece for the privilege of having the back of their heads shown or their feet or one hand or one shoulder? For the honor of being a dim, unrecognizable figure in the dark recesses of an enormous gate, while others who had not paid a penny more had been placed right in the center of the stage and in the full light of day? What had that poor fool been thinking of while he was painting?

There had been pictures of boards of regents and military companies in Amsterdam long before this smart young man had left his mill in the distant town of Leiden to come tell the benighted people of the metropolis how the thing ought to be done. If he would visit the Town Hall or any of the guild houses, he would see what customers had a right to expect from the artist they employed. There was a lot of talk of going to the law about it and downright refusals to pay.

Even men and women who ought to have known better joined in the chorus of abuse. Vondel, our great poet, composed a ditty in which Rembrandt's work was found wanting on account of its "artificial gloom." He wound up by dubbing Rembrandt one of the "sons of darkness," a witticism that stuck to him for the rest of his days. The art dealers with whom Rembrandt had refused to do business were gleeful. "Another bubble has burst!" they announced.

Why go on with this sad recital of human stupidity?

Here was a man who had dared to think a new thought and tell a new truth. Proudly he had turned to his fellowmen saying these noble words: "Behold! A little yellow and a little black and a little green and ocher and red and presto, I change them into an idea." And the philistines had guffawed and shouted: "The clown! He wants to show us! As if we were not bright enough to know what we want for ourselves!"

And from that moment on, Rembrandt was doomed.

OF COURSE THERE WERE a few people who felt convinced that something very fine and extraordinary had been added to the sum total of the world's beauty.

I discussed the matter with my friends during one of our Sunday outings. We had walked to a mill about half an hour beyond the city's bulwarks and the miller, glad for amusement on a rather dreary Sabbath, had invited us to come in and drink a glass of beer. Even in this remote spot the story had become known, for it seemed that Rembrandt had often sketched the mill and had promised the people that he would someday make an etching of it. They all liked him, for he always had a pleasant word for the children and often brought them a bit of candy and once even a toy house which he had carried all the way from town. The miller therefore was a partisan of the painter and cursed the soldiers, who, he said, were no good anyway and much more proficient at the business of drinking than that of fighting. His eyes shone with honest indignation. "If their foolish talk makes it impossible for this man to gain his livelihood in the city, all he needs to do is to come out here. We will see to it that he does not starve. If he can paint animals too, I have a job for him right away. We have a pet hog. We are so fond of it, we have never been able to kill it. If he will paint it for us, I will gladly give him five guilders."

We reassured him that Rembrandt still had a few friends and was in no immediate danger of starvation, whereupon the excellent fellow said, "That is good," breathed deeply a few times, and dozed off, to spend the Sabbath afternoon in his usual fashion.

It was then that Jean-Louys, who knew a good picture from a bad one and had expressed admiration for one or two small sketches which Rembrandt had given me, made me a suggestion.

"Why not invite us all to your house sometime and let us meet this painting prodigy from Leiden? Then we will tell you what we think of him."

THE MEETING BETWEEN Rembrandt and my friends took place sooner than I had expected and this is the way it came about.

A couple of times a week I would go to the painter's house to spend the evening. Saskia, by now, could no longer leave her bed and Rembrandt used to sit by her side and read to her from the Bible. For she no longer expected to get better. She did not complain. She was almost too weak to care very much. She just wanted to go to sleep, but she was too tired to come to rest. The poor girl would lie tossing in her bed, her cheeks flushed and her lovely eyes wide open—a picture of abject misery.

After an hour or so, even listening to the quiet voice of her husband as he read aloud would exhaust her and she would whisper to him to cease. But she would beg not to be left alone. Then Rembrandt would occupy himself quietly with his own business. He would sharpen a steel needle for his drypoints,

THE NIGHT WATCH (1642)

correct a plate that had not come out as he wished, or sign the pictures his pupils had printed that day. But he had suffered slightly from nearsightedness since early childhood and drawing or etching by candlelight was painful to him. So often he and I would play backgammon.

After a short time, even the clicking of the dice as we threw them got to be too exhausting for Saskia, who complained that the noise sent shivers all through her. As we could not talk either, and neither of us had the slightest liking for cards, we were hard put to it to find some way of passing the evening.

Then one day I mentioned to Rembrandt that I had just learned an interesting game from Jean-Louys. It was called chess and was so old that some said it had been played by the heroes outside of Troy. Originally it had been a war game, devised for the amusement of the shahs of Persia.

The very name, *schaak*, calling forth visions of Oriental tyrants with beautiful diamond-studded turbans, lying in tapestried tents in the heart of some windswept desert, appealed to Rembrandt's imagination and he at once asked me to introduce him to my friend and let him learn the game too. I waited until Saskia was feeling a little better and then one evening I invited Rembrandt to my house for supper and to meet my friends.

Jean-Louys, who held that cooking, after mathematics, was the greatest contribution towards human progress, had promised to prepare for us his famous omelet.

We really had a very pleasant evening. Selim at first held himself slightly aloof. "The graphic arts," he offered as an excuse, "are not quite in my line. The Koran does not allow me to take an interest in them."

"And in which chapter, my friend, does the Koran mention the graphic arts?" asked Bernardo, who knew that this excellent follower of the Prophet (not unlike a good many Christians) never gave a thought to these holy works except when he needed their authority to get out of doing something. But it was not Rembrandt or talk of the arts which he was avoiding this evening. Selim, a brilliant but inconsequential chess player who would overpower his opponents with his openings and then lose all interest in the game, was avoiding chess. True to his custom, he had no sooner relieved himself of his noble sentiment about the Koran and the art of painting, than he asked for a pencil and paper and spent the rest of the evening entertaining my small son, Willem, with accounts of the glorious deeds of Harun al-Rashid and illuminating his talk with amusing little pictures.

As for the rest of us, immediately after dinner we went to my workroom and spent the evening playing chess. We got the board (a homemade affair, for in the whole of Amsterdam I had not been able to buy one) and Jean-Louys got out his instruction book which he had ordered all the way from Spain. He carefully followed all instructions from opening to attack and in eighteen moves he had been checkmated by Bernardo, who had learned the game only the week before and who now beat us all with regularity.

But what interested me most of all was Rembrandt's reaction to this game. I had already taught him the moves and he had learned it in an astoundingly short time. One or two evenings had been enough to give him a general idea of the game. But he played chess as he painted, as he himself realized.

He rarely talked about the theory of his art, but a few nights after our dinner party he brought up the subject himself. "I like your Frenchman," he said in connection with some remark of mine upon the excellence of Jean-Louys' virtuosity as a cook, "even though these fancy dishes are not very much to my taste. I am accustomed to simpler fare. But I like him for the line he follows in playing that strange new game and it is upon line that everything in this world depends.

"You know that I have a number of pupils. Some of them have been rather successful. Flinck has already made his mark and you will hear of Ferdinand Bol and Gerard Dou. Of course I have not the slightest inclination to play the schoolmaster. But I can't make a living merely painting portraits. I need pupils. And I can at least be careful that I don't waste my time on hopeless material. So I have made it a rule that they must bring me their drawings.

"Their drawings, mind you, not their paintings. For almost anybody, if he is not absolutely color-blind, can be taught to paint some sort of picture. But a line never lies. Give me a scrap of a man's drawings and in five seconds I will tell you whether he has any talent or whether he had better become a brewer. Besides, an artist must have temperament, character, personality.

"Perhaps I don't make myself quite clear. But mark my words, a man has a line or he has not. And that Frenchman has a line. He has it in his manner and in his manners. He has it in his cooking, in his chess, in everything. While I . . ."

I looked at him in surprise; this was a new note I had not heard before. "While you?"

"While I have got too much of it in my drawing and too little in my life. But give me a few more years of experience, and I too may learn."

REMBRANDT DID LEARN CERTAIN things about life and he learned them much sooner than he had expected. It was a fortnight after our dinner party and I had brought two of my medical colleagues to see Saskia. They had studied her disease in Grenoble and in London, but I introduced them to her as art dealers from Antwerp who wanted to inspect Rembrandt's etchings. She felt quite flattered that two such distinguished-looking gentlemen should have come all the way from Flanders to pay homage to her husband's genius. But the short interview soon exhausted her.

Then we bade Rembrandt leave the room and the three of us examined the drowsy woman. I had shown them my record of the case and they both had looked solemn and had shaken their heads. The elder of the doctors said: "One month more, at the most." And the younger, to show his superior experience, said: "It seems to me that she might live another six weeks."

But I had seen her lose weight steadily for the last two months and I knew it was a question of days rather than weeks. I took them upstairs and we uttered some platitudes to Rembrandt, who had used that half hour to pull two proofs of a little etching of the three Magi, which he now offered to my two doctor friends, who were rather touched. Then they bade him farewell and he and I went down to the big room and made ready for our evening's game.

Saskia was asleep. Her right hand, dreadfully white and thin, was resting on the counterpane. She had always been fond of flowers and now that summer had come at last, Rembrandt brought her fresh roses every morning. One of these she had stuck in her hair to give herself a more festive appearance, before the arrival of the "Antwerp art dealers." It lay on her pillow. It was a red rose and her cheeks by contrast looked even more pallid than usual. But she was breathing easily and there was a smile on her lips. I softly pulled the curtains of the bed together and tiptoed back to the table.

"She seems to be doing very well," I said. "What will you play, backgammon or chess?"

"Chess," Rembrandt answered. "Last time I lost my queen almost at the beginning. I will do better tonight."

We began in the usual way, but after only five or six moves

he brought his queen out and was using her to force me into a defensive position. What he was doing had a certain quality of brilliancy. It might make him win the game in about ten or fifteen moves, but only on condition that I overlooked a fatal counterattack which I could make with my knights. He was so engrossed in his own calculations that he seemed completely unaware of the danger and I warned him of it.

"I know that I am running a few risks," he answered, "but I shall beat you after the next move if I can extricate my queen."

"But can you?" I asked him, taking his bishop's pawn and thereby opening an avenue of attack.

"I think I can— Why, it would be absurd if I couldn't! I had the position so well in hand only a moment ago and now—"

"And now," I answered, "I have your queen and you are mate in three moves."

He pushed back his chair. "Too bad," he consoled himself. "Too bad. I thought that I had you this time. Let me try again. Just a moment till I make sure that Saskia is all right."

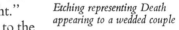

Etching representing Death appearing to a wedded couple

He picked up a candle, went to the bed and pushed aside the curtains. Then he turned to me and whispered: "Look how quiet she is tonight! I never saw her sleep so soundly. She must be really getting better."

I stood by his side and put my hand upon her heart.

Saskia was dead.

I AM WRITING THIS in the year 1669 and Saskia died in '42. That is twenty-seven years ago and twenty-seven years are a long time in a man's life. I can't complain about my memory. It is causing me very little trouble, and as I shall be seventy next year, I have no right to expect too much. But dates and hours mean very little to me, and as I have never kept a diary until now,

I find it difficult to state when exactly Saskia departed this life.

I do remember that it was during the same year in which Abel Janszoon Tasman discovered that mysterious island in the Pacific Ocean which was called Nieuw Zeeland, after my beloved Zeeland, and sailed around the great southland about which we had had so many strange reports during the last forty years. And I was interested in any reports he might bring home about the narcotics in use among the natives. I am con-

Tower of the West Church

vinced that someday we shall find a plant which will enable us to perform surgery without that dreadful agony which now turns the operating room into a torture chamber.

Well, that famous voyage happened in 1642 (though I only heard about it two years later) and the date stuck in my memory, so I can remember that poor Saskia died in 1642 also. It was in June, for the pushcart vendors were selling their first cherries and there were flowers everywhere, and the trees along the Burgwal looked fresh and green as we slowly carried Saskia to her last resting place in the Old Church.

The ceremony took only a few minutes. The heavy black cloth which had covered the casket was carefully folded up by two of the professional pallbearers. Then the coffin was placed upon two heavy ropes. Eight men, four on each side, took hold of the ropes. The minister stepped forward with an enormous Bible which he opened and placed on a small wooden stand which had been put there for the occasion and while he read the one hundred and third psalm, Saskia was slowly and silently lowered into the cavernous darkness of her open grave.

I have gone to many funerals and every time I have been struck by the inability of the creed of Calvin and Luther to express its emotions in anything beyond mere words. Take that funeral of Saskia. Surely if there was a tragedy it was the death of this lovely creature. She was young and, until a few months before her death, very lovely. She was married to one of the most remarkable men of her time, who was devoted to her and could have given her a life full of beauty and interest. She had a child. She had many friends. She was not very bright, perhaps, but no one asked of her that she be able to translate Auveer into Latin hexameters. And then she died. Died before she was fully thirty years old. Died and left everything she loved behind, to become a mere number in a row of hideous graves.

A ghastly negation of everything that men and women are supposed to live for. But a marvelous opportunity for the Church to stand forth as the prophet of hope, to maintain boldly and in the face of all this incriminating evidence that life is good and that death is but another form of living, to surround these assertions with beautiful gestures and honest music, with symbols that speak of the eternal verities.

Instead of which a young farmhand turned minister read some very fine verses, the meaning of which he did not seem to understand in the least. Then a group of men who during the rest of the day were drivers of beer wagons and eel fishers took the large wooden box containing all this loveliness, hurriedly lowered it into its stone cage, and hastened to the door to gather in the tips of the mourners. There were those among us who wanted to linger a moment longer—to say something for the last time to the shadow that lay at our feet. But we were given no time. The minister left. The sexton was rattling his keys. There was nothing for us to do but to go.

And so we returned to the house in the Breestraat. The nurse with the help of some of the neighbors had prepared a meal and the table was set in the same room from which they had carried the corpse away only an hour before (a dreadful and barbarous custom which we have undoubtedly inherited from our savage ancestors) and we were all of us bade to enter and regale ourselves.

I remained a few minutes, for not to have done so would have attracted too much attention. Then I looked for Rembrandt. He was not there. Softly I tiptoed upstairs to the studio.

Rembrandt, still in his mourning clothes, a long veil of black crape hanging down from his hat and black gloves on his hands, but completely oblivious of the world around him, was busy painting. I went up to him and put my hand on his shoulder, but he never turned his head and I don't think he noticed me.

For he was working once more at a portrait of Saskia, a portrait of Saskia as she had looked the day he had married her.

I LEFT THE STUDIO without saying a word, went home, changed my clothes and walked to the hospital, where I spent the rest of the day. I had just finished my supper that evening when the maid told me that Mr. van Rijn had come to see me. I bade him come in. Then I noticed that he was still in the same black clothes he had worn at the funeral and that there was something wild about the way in which he stared around the room.

In the case of anyone else, I would have thought: This man has been drinking. But he was dead sober and indeed it was not until much later, when anxiety about losing his eyesight was added to all his other worries, that he occasionally tried to find a few moments of oblivion by such means.

There was but one other explanation for his disheveled looks; he was utterly exhausted.

I asked him when he had last dined. He tried to remember. "Two or three days ago," he answered. I went into the kitchen and with my own hands prepared a meal of soft-boiled eggs and toasted bread and I sent the maid out for some milk, which I slightly heated. He ate everything and then said: "I am dreadfully tired," and I took him upstairs and practically had to undress him (for he could hardly lift a finger). I put him into my own bed, went downstairs again and made myself a sort of couch out of chairs and cushions.

It seemed to me that I had hardly slept an hour when I was awakened by a banging on the front door, and I thought it was a patient. But when I opened the door I noticed that the sun was shining so brightly that it must be between eight and nine o'clock in the morning, and there stood Geertje Dircx, her hair hanging down her forehead and her bare feet in leather slippers.

Saskia, 1643 (posthumous portr

"This is a fine thing to happen!" she began, but I shushed her and said sharply: "What is it you want?"

"Is Rembrandt here?" she asked.

"And since when do you call your master by his first name?"

"Oh, well, he isn't so much, and for a widower to spend the night after his wife's funeral outside of the house! It is disgraceful! The neighbors will talk. And here I am, slaving myself to death to keep everything going nicely, and I cooked the finest meal ever served in our street after a funeral, and he forgets to give me money to buy beer and I have to pay for it out of my own pocket and then he does not even come down to the meal!" and so on and so forth, an hysterical woman feeling very sorry for herself.

There was no use arguing. I told her that her master had been sadly negligent in his duties and that I would speak to him as soon as he had rested from the terrible exhaustion of the last few days, and having quieted her somewhat, I prevailed upon her to go back home and take care of the baby.

I returned to the dining room to dress and to make up my mind what to say to Rembrandt, for although his household no longer needed my professional assistance, I felt that it was in even greater need of my services as a fairly sober-minded and not entirely unpractical human being. When Rembrandt came downstairs, a little after eleven, and after he had eaten three ordinary breakfasts, I said: "Listen, my good friend, I have told you ten dozen times, that Dircx woman is no good. She is irresponsible. Pay her her wages and let her go right away, for she is rapidly losing her mind and she may end by murdering you or your child."

This startled him considerably, but he answered that that was not as easy as it seemed. Just as he was taking his leave, however, he made a remark which puzzled me. "You are right," he said. "I will try to raise the money today."

"Raise the money today . . ." A question of twenty or thirty guilders, when one lived in the biggest house on the Breestraat, bought pictures by Rubens and Raphael as if they had been ten-cent prints and was known to have married one of the richest girls of Friesland—something was wrong there.

I decided to have a serious talk with him as soon as he should have recovered from the emotions of the last few days. But one can't very well ask questions of that sort. I therefore made up my mind that I would not call at the Breestraat, but would make the usual rounds of my professional duties. For I knew that troubled people must sooner or later relieve themselves or go mad. The days grew into weeks, however, and Rembrandt never came near my house.

And then late one afternoon when I returned from the hospital I found him in my working room. He must have been waiting a long time, for he had amused himself copying a bust of Hippocrates that stood on my bookcase, and the drawing was almost finished.

"I have come to ask you something," he said, without offering me the usual salutation. "I am in a difficult position. Can you let me have fifty guilders?" And then he told me his story.

"I AM JUST BACK from the Old Church," he began. "I have bought the grave in which Saskia is buried and she will never have to lie there with strangers. I had to sell two of my pictures to raise the amount. I don't know what has happened. I had thought that they would bring me six hundred florins. I only got half. But the grave is mine. The papers are in my pocket. Now could you let me have fifty guilders? I owe the nurse thirty for past wages and twenty for letting her go without the usual notice."

I decided not to be too delicate. The tenderhearted surgeons who try to save the feelings of their patients are the ones who do the most harm. And so I said: "Of course I will gladly give you the money, but why do you need it? There is the house. You once told me that you had paid thirteen thousand guilders for it. And one day when you were pulling a proof and I was talking to you in the little room upstairs, you remarked that you made more than two thousand florins a year from your etchings alone. Then there are your pupils. I don't know how much they pay you, but it must be a fairly decent sum. There are also your portraits. There is the picture of Banning Cocq's company. The other day young Hendrick Uijlenburgh, Saskia's

cousin, told me that you had got five thousand florins for it.
And then there is Saskia's inhéritance. She must have had a good
deal. Her father was a man of importance. I suppose you got
some of it."

"I got everything."

"Well, you ought to be able to realize on it." (I hated to talk
like a schoolmaster, but in many ways the man to whom I was
speaking was still a child.)

"I can," he answered. "It is merely a question of time. You
see, Saskia made a will about two weeks before she died. I did
not know about it until it was all finished. But the thing had
been on her mind for quite a time and one afternoon, when I
had gone out to talk about a new portrait, she sent the nurse to
get her a notary. He came to her and drew up everything in true
legal form. She signed the documents nine days before she died
and she left everything to me. It is understood that I will look
after the boy and see that he gets a first-rate education and if I
ever marry again, which I doubt, all the money goes to Titus.
But the most wonderful thing—and I never thought that the
poor girl had cared quite so much for me—came at the end.
She stipulated that I should never be asked to give any sort of an
accounting. It is all mine to do with as I please. Of course, I
shall merely regard it as a trust fund for little Titus. I may use
some of it to pay for the house. I still owe some seven thousand
florins on it and a few years' interest. In the end it will go to
Titus anyway so that means nothing.

"I am really much better fixed than ever before. But I have
no head for business. I would rather paint three pictures than add
one single sum of figures. And things have been slow coming in
these last six months. I know that people say that I got five
thousand guilders for that big militia piece. Well, sixteen hundred is nearer to the truth, and even of that I am not quite sure;
some of the soldiers threaten that they won't give me a cent
unless they show up as well as the rest of the company. And
then there are four or five of that crowd who claim that I have
not done them justice. One of them, a sergeant, stopped me
the other day on the street. What did I mean hiding his face behind the arm of another fellow who was only a corporal?

"You are right, I used to have a number of pupils, but those who have talent are usually too poor to pay me anything and those who can pay have no talent and are just a nuisance. So you see how it goes. I have several thousand guilders still coming to me for portraits I have done. But it seems that it is harder to collect nowadays than formerly. If I had ever kept books I could tell you where all the money has gone, for I must have made a great deal these last ten years. Anyway, it is only a question of a few months—until the formalities connected with the inheritance are completed. I don't understand such legal complications. They worry me and keep me from working and so I try to forget them. But everything will soon be all right.

"Meanwhile, it will be better for everybody concerned if that damned Dircx woman goes before the end of another day. I could sell something out of my collection, but then the whole town would say that those Frisian relations who said I was wasting my wife's money had been right. I need fifty guilders right away and I need them very quietly. I can pay you back in September or October and I shall give you six percent, which seems fair."

I went to the little safe in my bedroom in which I kept the United East Indian Company shares I had inherited from my uncle. I took out five golden rijders, gave them to Rembrandt, and bade him forget about the interest—it was just a small loan between friends.

THAT EVENING I wrote to a friend in Leeuwarden, a young man with whom I had studied in Leiden, but who had given up medicine and had gone in for the law. I asked him to find out for me whether Saskia van Uijlenburgh had really been as rich as people said and to give me the particulars—that I had a friend who was greatly interested.

Three weeks later I had his answer and his letter showed that he had not changed a bit from the carefree days of old:

Ornatissime!

Magno cum gaudio accepi letteras tuas atque maximo cum—now what in thunder was "haste" in Latin? But anyway, I got your letter and your friend can be only one person, the great Maestro

Rembrandtus van Rijn, painter-in-extraordinary to the rabbis of Amsterdam, who not long ago, if I am to believe my correspondents, gave up the use of colors altogether and now distills himself a new sort of picture out of a mixture of soot, lampblack and coal ashes.

For who else could be interested in the affairs of that poor Uijlenburgh girl, who left here so long ago that few people remember her? Be reassured, however. I have done a little investigating and here is my impression of the case.

Most of the renowned Uijlenburgh millions exist only on paper, or are so hopelessly mortgaged, hypothesized, debentured and generally tied up, that in case of a sudden sale, I doubt whether they would realize one-twentieth of their normal value. I am on agreeable terms with the notary who has handled the affairs of the family. He threw up his hands in despair and said: "Solomon in all his wisdom could not unravel that estate." And then he explained that there never has been a division of the funds, and although the father has now been dead for almost twenty years, the estate has not yet been settled. It is furthermore doubtful a settlement would be possible at the present time, when money is so tight that one is glad to pay twenty or even twenty-five percent for a loan of a few thousand guilders. In short, there was once a considerable fortune which belonged to the Uijlenburgh children and of which they received so much per annum in the form of rents. But if any one of them should get into trouble and ask for an immediate accounting, I am doubtful whether the matter could be arranged without a dreadful sacrifice on the part of all concerned.

Wherefore, if your friend should be hard up for ready cash, I would advise him to go to the moneylenders. They will give him better terms and be more charitable than his beloved relations on this side of the Zuider Zee. From all I have been able to gather, they are none too friendly towards this "foreign" connection whose father ran a mill, who paints rabbis and associates openly with Turks and Frenchmen and other immoral races and who once paid 424 guilders for a picture by a certain Rubens, an out-and-out Papist.

I put the document aside and did some fast thinking. My old friend had told me everything I needed to know and my heart was filled with forebodings. For by this time I had come to know

Rembrandt quite well. He lived in a world of his own making and thus far life had been fairly easy to him. Now he had reached a crisis. His wife was dead. He had a small boy to bring up. It would cost a great deal to maintain the house in the Breestraat and people no longer looked with favor upon what they had begun to call his fantastic experiments. The fact that he had asked me for a loan of fifty guilders showed that he was very hard up for ready cash. True, he was a hard worker and never spent a penny upon his own comforts. But there was this strange streak of the grand seigneur in him. He must play fairy godfather to his poor colleagues and at auctions he must outbid the professional art dealers, just to show them that he was the great Rembrandt who need not bother about trifles.

If only he could have faced the fact that he did not have a cent! But he had fallen heir to Saskia's "fortune"! There was that pathetic will, leaving everything to her "beloved man" without restrictions. If only she had insisted upon a guardian for her son, then there would have been a public appraisal and Rembrandt might have discovered what I now knew and could not tell him without running the risk of being called a meddler and a busybody.

My hands were tied and I was forced to watch the poor fellow play the millionaire on the strength of a worthless paper promise. Nevertheless, I might have done something. I am not thinking of the financial end of things. I could have helped him out of a few of his difficulties there. But Rembrandt was indeed blind upon most subjects related to the business of living a quiet and respectable existence.

He was a man possessed of a single idea. Within the realm of color and form, his ambition assumed almost divine proportions. He wanted to capture the entire world around him and hold it his prisoner on canvas or paper. Life, alas, was so short and there was so much to be done. He had to work and work and work. He was sick. Never mind, he must work. His wife (one of the few persons who ever assumed the shape of a definite human being in his preoccupied mind) died. He must rush through the funeral and go back to work. He was acclaimed the fashionable painter of the hour and made twenty or thirty thousand guilders a year. Go to the Jew around the corner and buy out his whole stock of curiosities or give the money to some poor devil of a fellow painter who lies starving in a garret. A letter has just arrived from the sheriff saying that a number of outstanding notes are overdue and should be paid right then or there would be difficulties. Visits from the Honorable Masters in Bankruptcy. Forced sales—fines—imprisonment, even.

Fiddlesticks! It is winter and at three o'clock in the afternoon it is too dark to paint. One has to save every minute in times like these. The sheriff is a fool. Tell him so. Bid him come or stay away, for it is all the same as long as one can only work and work and work.

No, such a man could not be helped with an occasional check—with the loan of a few thousand guilders. All one could give to an unfortunate fellow like this, mad with the beauty of the outer world, crazy with joy at the myriad manifestations of the inner spirit, was understanding and then some more understanding and still more understanding and ask for nothing in return. Amen.

And that is what I might have done for Rembrandt. But just then something occurred that upset my own life completely and I became an exile from my own country for almost eight years. I can never quite get over the feeling that things might have gone differently with Rembrandt if only I had been in Amsterdam.

CHAPTER 6

FROM THE VERY BEGINNING I had meant to keep myself and my own affairs as much as possible out of these recollections. But when two lives are as entwined and interwoven as those of Rembrandt and my own, it is difficult to accomplish this completely. The next few pages therefore will be mainly about myself. But I shall be very short and I shall try to be honest.

When I was a small boy I was taught that all of life was tragedy, and when I grew a little older I sometimes tried to convince myself that all of life was comedy. But now I know that life is melodrama and melodrama so primitive that any playwright daring to put it on the stage would be publicly derided.

I learned this in the fall of that fatal year of 1642, when my only brother was found murdered. My brother, the most peaceful and lovable of men—a hardworking, intelligent silversmith returning from a trip to London—had been stabbed, beaten, robbed and left for dead on the doorstep of a mean alehouse near the Amsterdam waterfront.

I objected as mankind has objected since the beginning of time. I fought back. I cursed. I insisted upon an answer. And the gods remained aloof. I did my work and went to the hospital at the usual hours and made my rounds and saw my patients, but I resembled one of those automatic machines they make in Nürnberg—one that had been wound up and the key of which had been mislaid.

Like most people of these northern climes, I had a very decided tendency towards melancholia. Thus far I had always rather despised the infamous "black humor" as a confession of moral weakness. And now, so help me God, I too was fast becoming one of its victims.

Plainly it was impossible for me to continue in a town where every stick and stone reminded me of the calamity that had overtaken me. My friends urged me to take a trip, to visit some of the universities of Italy where I would be able to learn much that would be of interest to my own investigations. But I lacked the courage and the energy. Then the hand of fate intervened. It picked me up, threw me bodily across the ocean and left me stranded amidst such strange surroundings that I was soon forced to forget all about my own woes.

My adventures began with a note which was delivered early one morning a few months after my brother's murder. My Lord Andries Bicker requested the pleasure of my company at his house on such and such a date for dinner and a private talk afterwards.

This in itself was rather mysterious, for although I had visited the burgomaster's house once or twice in my professional capacity, that was hardly a social introduction. And most of my neighbors regarded me as a better-class barber. Today the study of medicine is beginning to be elevated to the dignity of a science. But thirty years ago no mayor of the sovereign city of Amsterdam would break bread with a humble disciple of Aesculapius unless there was something he wanted very much to get from him. Not that I expected anything unusual. His Lordship probably contemplated some change in the conduct of the city's hospitals and wanted to consult a physician before he introduced the subject in the meeting of the burgomasters.

Man with a golden helmet

But it came quite different. Our dinner was more elaborate than I had anticipated. The whole family was present and I was introduced to the ladies of the household, which was a signal honor to a member of my humble profession.

Immediately the feast had been served, the women bade us good-day and my host and his brother Cornelis suggested that I follow them upstairs. They took me to a large room in the front of the house, the walls of which were entirely covered with bookcases and maps, and bade me sit down in a low chair beside a large globe. Then the maid came in with a tray on which were bottles of French wines and of Malaga and Madeira and glasses.

My Lord Andries filled me a glass and said, "Try this wine." And then both brothers, lifting their glasses, said, "Here is to ourselves. God knows, we are coming on hard times."

My looks must have showed that I was slightly bewildered by this strange performance. The four Bicker brothers, on the death of their father, had inherited his vast fortune and then quietly divided the entire world among themselves as if it had been a parcel of real estate in one of the suburbs. There were even those who said that the republic ought not to be called the Seven United Netherlands but the Four United Bickerlands, and they were right.

320

"Fear not, dear Doctor," Cornelis said. "This is just our little joke. Now let us come to business."

"Doctor," My Lord Andries began, "we want your help. Only one thing I must beg of you. All this must remain strictly between ourselves. What we are about to propose can only serve the weal of our own fatherland. But if our plans are to succeed, we must keep them a secret. At least for quite a number of years." I nodded my assent and he continued.

"I don't want to give you a lecture on current politics, but you are no fool. Otherwise we would never have sent for you. And you know as well as I what is actually happening and that someday very soon the war with Spain will come to an end. We are practically independent now, but when peace is signed, the whole world will have to recognize us as a sovereign commonwealth. What is going to happen then? And what will the House of Orange try to do?

"We merchants have always appeared to be on good terms with those German princes. The people believe that the stadtholders of the republic and the burgomasters of

A mounted officer

Amsterdam are bosom friends, cooperating for the benefit of our common country. And in truth, if we are to continue to be prosperous, such a balance should be maintained. We merchants have no objection to a strong central government. We are too busy with our own affairs to look after a lot of executive details. These can be better attended to by the stadtholder, who is trained for that sort of work and whose family has made a specialty of it for centuries.

"We need such a man in the republic and we really don't care whether the Prince of Orange wants to call himself a stadtholder or a king or anything else, as long as he remembers he is an employe of the people, does not interfere with us and leaves us free to make the money which brings prosperity to the entire commonwealth.

"But the present stadtholder has a weak chest. By the time he gets the last Spaniard out of our last city, he will be dead. Mark my words, we will sign our peace over his coffin. And then, what will become of all those German Junkers who are now making a fine living as officers in our armies? They will all be out of jobs and they won't like it. They will want to remain here. And how will they accomplish this? By making themselves indispensable to the only man who has any need of their services, to the young Prince of Orange.

"The young prince is only sixteen, but he is old enough to give us some inkling about his character and I don't trust him. If he merely aspired to his father's place as stadtholder, the highest paid official in the republic, why was he in such a hurry to marry the English princess, the daughter of King Charles?

"Well, what will he do next? He has the army officers, but we still have credit with the banks. We could send to Switzerland for a dozen regiments of infantry. And the navy is on our side. But the church party has mighty little love for us.

"I am a good Christian myself, as my father was before me. But I'd rather flood the land and die in the last ditch than give in to the dominies—those narrow-minded, vainglorious plowboys who spend four years in some theological seminary and then come to town and frighten the rabble with their stories about hell and tell us—us!—how we should run our own country! And that, I think, is the way all of us feel in the Town Hall. Well, of course the dominies know it and the Prince knows it. So, as soon as the war with Spain is over, the war at home will begin. On the one hand, we the merchants who have made this country what it is, and on the other hand the Prince who wants to become a king and the rabble that believe he will lead them out of what they are pleased to call the wilderness of paganism into the promised land of that terrible man, Calvin.

"This commonwealth was built upon the principle of live and let live, believe and let believe. If we cannot maintain ourselves upon that basis, we shall fight. Meanwhile, like good merchants, we should provide for the future and that is why we asked you to come here. We are delighted to see you as our guest. But we also want to make you a business proposition."

I looked at him in bewilderment. "My Lord, how in Heaven's name do I come to figure in your plans and calculations?"

"Very simply. We want you to go and find a little monopoly for us." His Lordship picked up his pen and began to do some figuring. "In order to hold our own against the political combination we anticipate and fear," he said, "we need a great deal of added revenue. The best way to acquire it is to get exclusive control of one of the necessities of life. Most of these are already in other hands. The East India Company has got all the spices. The West India Company has got the slave trade. Besides, that is a nasty sort of business. Then, in the north, there is whale oil and whalebone. But all this is in the hands of a single company.

"Of course, my brother and I are stockholders in those companies, and we get our share of the dividends. But the partisans of the Prince are stockholders too and occasionally they are able to outvote us. That is what we don't want to happen. We want a monopoly of our own that shall be entirely in the hands of our relatives. And we think that we have found one: grain.

"Let me explain. Man has to eat in order to live. Granted! The staple food article of daily consumption in most households is bread. Also granted! Bread is made out of grain. Where does that grain come from? Most assuredly not from the territory of the republic.

"Of course our country, with its hundreds of ships, has practically a monopoly of the carrying trade of all grain. But we must no longer content ourselves merely with transporting and selling other people's grain. We must grow it ourselves. . . .

"Come over here a moment please, Doctor." His Lordship picked up a candle, went to a map on the wall, pointed to the central part of the North American continent and said: "All this belongs to the West India Company. It was given to them by the charter of 1621. But that company has never done well, I suppose because the East India Company has absorbed all our surplus capital. Now what we want to do is to get hold of vast tracts of land in America where grain can be grown at a very small cost. According to the best of our information the coastal regions are too rocky and too densely covered with woods to be suitable. But a few hundred miles inland there are enormous plains where grain will grow almost overnight. All that land belongs to the West India Company, and since that organization is hard up for money, the directors would listen with both ears if we offered to buy a few hundred thousand square miles and pay cash. But first we must know if the land is really right. And that is where you come in.

"You are a man of tact and we shall give you a shipload of gimcracks—little mirrors, beads and bangles—that seem to delight the American natives. Then, at your leisure, we want you to sail across the ocean to Nieuw Amsterdam. We have collected a great deal of information about you and we know you are deeply interested in the problem of reducing the pain connected with surgical operations. Very well. Let it be known that you are taking a trip to America because you want to investigate those stories that are coming to us continuously about certain plants which the natives of the New World use to alleviate pain.

"My bookseller sends me every account of American exploration that appears. He has standing offers for such books in London and Seville and Lisbon. I can't read those printed in Portuguese, but I have them translated by a bright young Jew, a curious fellow who seems to be the only man who ever got away from the Inquisition and lived to tell the tale."

"I know him," I said. "He is one of my best friends."

"Really? Well, he is a bright fellow and ought to have a better job than he has now. We have offered to employ him ourselves, but he seems content to jog along. Anyhow, I have learned from my reading that the Indians seem to be able to deaden their bodies against pain. So you won't be wasting your time if you consent to spend a few years collecting shrubs and weeds and interviewing medicine men."

I agreed that it would be a wonderful opportunity, and My Lord Andries hurried on.

"If when you come back you tell us that the soil is suitable for our purpose, we shall proceed with our plans. We shall depend greatly upon your report. If you say that the land will grow grain, we shall buy vast tracts. We are already at work upon a system of colonization. We want permanency. We want to turn our possessions over there (if ever we get them) really and truly into some sort of a New Netherlands. Then, if things go wrong over here in the old Netherlands, we shall have another home in another world upon which we can fall back." He stopped abruptly and turned to his brother. "All this seems clear to you?"

"Perfectly," My Lord Cornelis answered.

"Then," turning to me, "have you any questions to ask?"

"Yes," I replied. "Why all this secrecy? Why can't I let everybody know the true purpose of my voyage?"

"For a variety of reasons. First, if the Prince and the church people are conspiring to deprive us of our power and turn the republic into a monarchy, they will take measures to spoil our ideas. Second, if the directors of the West India Company hear of this, they would ask such extortionate prices for their land that the plan would come to nothing. Third . . ."

But I did not have to hear any further reasons. It was a chance for me to escape for a while from a city where everything reminded me of the tragedy that had befallen our family. Furthermore I would be given the opportunity to make serious experiments in a field of science that seemed to me enormously worthwhile. And finally, my personal sympathies were entirely on the side of those two brothers who saw the ideals for which our fathers had fought going to ruin on the cliffs of selfishness, partisanship and religious bigotry. Of course they were businessmen and figured things out in terms of florins and daalders. But I did not doubt the integrity of their motives.

I told them, however, that I would need a little time to think things over. They agreed most cordially, and we bade our adieus.

ON MY WALK HOME, I crossed the bridge of the Saint Anthonie Locks, near the Breestraat. I noticed that there was still light burning in the upstairs windows of Rembrandt's house. I had not seen anything of him since the funeral of my brother and thought that I would drop in for a minute. I needed someone with whom to talk things over before I went to bed, for I was much too excited to sleep.

I knocked on the door but got no answer.

I knocked again and a little louder.

I heard people stumbling about in the back part of the house.

Finally the door was opened a few inches. Geertje Dircx was standing there. She was holding a candle in her hand and looked at me as if she were ready to kill me.

"The master has gone to bed and can't be disturbed," she snapped. "Please go away." And she locked the door in my face.

I went home.

I didn't quite like what I had just seen.

CHAPTER 7

THE NEXT SUNDAY, during our walk in the country, I told my friends of my future plans. I needed their reassurance that I was doing the right thing. They agreed that I was. They were sorry to lose me for so long a time, but it was a rare chance. I absolutely must accept. They would write me about all that happened of any importance and would call on my small son to see that he fared well. (Good God! I had completely forgotten little Willem, but I supposed I could safely leave him with the old nurse who took care of him anyway whether I was there or not.) And then, suddenly, everyone in Amsterdam seemed to know my plans.

When I was having breakfast, my housekeeper said, "And so I hear, Master, that you are going to America, and what will become of me? And the child when I am gone?" And when I went to the hospital, the old gatekeeper said, "Good morning, Doctor, and so I hear you are going to America." And when I visited the barber, he said, "Ah, my sly friend, I hear that you are going to leave us and are going to America." So it went all week and then one evening when I returned home I found a note from Rembrandt. It really was not a note, but an old sketch, underneath which he had scribbled these words:

"I hear that you are going to America and I want to ask you and your friends to drop in next Thursday evening, for I have finished a picture I want to show you."

This message I received with a certain amount of irritation.

My reception when I had recently knocked at his door had hardly been of a sort to make me want to call again. Indeed, I was so annoyed by the recollection of that occasion that I threw the letter into the fire, but it landed upside down and I saw that there was writing on the back of the sheet. I fished it out of the flames and read:

"I am terribly sorry I missed you the other night. I was pulling a few proofs of a new landscape I had just started (most unsatis-

A Dutch countryside

factorily, so far) and the miserable woman never even let me know it was you who had called. I want to see you badly." And then three times underlined, "The woman is hopeless. I hope to God I shall be able to get rid of her positively before the end of next week."

I understood. The terrible nurse had had one of her attacks of ill temper. And to Rembrandt's wish to be rid of her positively I could say Amen with all my heart.

When the appointed evening came, I was detained at the hospital, and it was past nine o'clock before I reached the house on the Breestraat. My friends were there and the famous rabbi, Samuel Manasseh ben Israel, of whom Rembrandt had made an etching some years before and which had had a very favorable sale among the members of his congregation. Like Bernardo, he had been born in Lisbon. As a boy he and his family had fled to the republic when Portugal had been occupied by the Hapsburgs and the Inquisition had been reestablished in that unfortunate country. After their arrival in Amsterdam the boy had been apprenticed to a painter, but he had wanted to study theology. His father, a well-known man of great common sense, suggested that he could practice both professions at the same time.

Manasseh ben Israel

Manasseh was so broad-minded, so learned, so full of the true spirit of tolerant brotherhood that many Christians, exasperated by the sectorial hairsplitting of their own clergy, had fallen into the habit of going to his synagogue to hear this pleasant-voiced man hold forth upon the affairs of the day with irrepressible good humor.

That evening I found Rembrandt's guests sitting around the table examining a heavy volume bound beautifully in leather and Rembrandt said, "Look at this—I wish that I could draw the way our friend here paints." And he showed me a page of something I could not read. It was a Hebrew edition of the Psalms printed in the basement of the house diagonally across from that of Rembrandt where Manasseh lived and had his workshop.

Quite naturally the talk then drifted to my future plans. "They tell me that you are going to America soon," said the rabbi.

I said yes, and added in a spirit of fun, "Wouldn't Your Reverence care to come with me?"

The good man suddenly became very serious. "There is nothing I would like to do better. But the time has not yet come for God's people to come out of the wilderness."

I showed, I am afraid, some surprise at this remark, and he continued, "Most honored Doctor, you are a cultured man. Do you not know that the Indians of America are the lost tribes of the people of Israel? They moved across the Pacific Ocean when it was still dry land and today they dwell in America." He made this extraordinary announcement so solemnly that all of us looked at each other in mute astonishment.

He then delivered quite a lecture and told us how ten of the long-suffering tribes (I have forgotten their names, and anyway, that is a detail) after the destruction of Jerusalem had wandered across Turkestan and China and had finally crossed over into the vast and uninhabited land that stretched from pole to pole and that had been given unto them as their eternal heritage.

It was an interesting story, but it did not sound convincing to me. I did not say so, however, and as the nurse just then entered and announced that supper was ready, we turned our attention to the excellent herring salad and boiled barley with sugar which awaited us in the front room.

After supper Rembrandt took us up to his studio and showed us a number of sketches he had recently acquired. And the good rabbi again endeavored to prove his theory about the ten lost tribes. There was no point in arguing with him. Every one of us is entitled to at least one pet delusion.

MY LORD ANDRIES PROVED a man of his word. No sooner had I accepted his offer than wheels within wheels began to move with that silence and efficiency one expects from a competent engine. Within less than a week I was informed that the Amsterdam chamber of the West India Company had appointed me one of its doctors, with orders to proceed at once to the New Netherlands. And on the seventh of February, 1643, I received my patent as ship's surgeon.

I was to sail in April.

A week before I left, Bernardo called on me. One could never tell whether he was sad or happy, but this time the animation of his voice told me that something extraordinary had occurred. I asked him what the good news was.

"I am going with you," he answered.

"Coming with me? Why—how—what are you going to do over there? Keep books for a fish dealer?"

"I am through with fish and through with bookkeeping," he replied. "I am an explorer now, and an investigator."

"Investigator of what?"

"Of the lost tribes of Israel." And then he told me that Rabbi Manasseh ben Israel had so convinced a number of Jews in Amsterdam of the truth of his hypothesis about the American Indians being the ten lost tribes that they had subscribed enough money to send someone across the ocean to investigate.

"You know," Bernardo remarked dryly, "ever since my little trouble with the Inquisition, I have been regarded by my fellow countrymen as a kind of phenomenon, a survivor of a great natural cataclysm. I am deemed the ideal messenger to send to the other end of the world. And I accepted almost humbly. I have done enough figuring to last me for all eternity. I have sold enough fish to stock a dozen planets. You never guessed it, but I was born to be the hero of strange adventures. So if you care to have me, I shall be your faithful traveling companion."

I answered him (and with absolute sincerity) that no one could have been more welcome to share my cabin and my loneliness.

I HAD BADE FAREWELL to all my other friends but I had kept Rembrandt for the last moment. I had grown very fond of this lonely soul and vaguely sensed a disaster in the household on the Breestraat. Under the pretext that little Titus had developed a cold and needed her care more than ever lest he die of the same disease as his mother, the Dircx woman was making herself more indispensable every day. She undoubtedly loved the child, but in a strange and violent fashion, not pleasant to behold and decidedly dangerous for the object of her affection. One moment she would be kissing and petting the poor infant and the next she would scold him or cuff him for some trifling mistake.

The woman was really not responsible for her actions. She suffered from hysteria, a mysterious affliction not uncommon in females of her age. For days she would be perfectly normal. Then without any provocation she would have a fit of frenzied anger, would smash dishes, would pull the clothes off her back, while Rembrandt stood hopelessly by and tried to pacify her by extravagant promises. Finally, she would burst into tears and that, for the moment, would be the last of the seizure and she would be quite all right for a fortnight or so.

Once or twice, when the attacks were very severe, Rembrandt had sent for me. There was nothing I could do, but every time I would warn him that he ought to get rid of the woman. She was too dangerous. People who suffer from hysteria are not only absolutely untrustworthy but malicious and they are very clever liars.

I tried to make the painter see the sort of trouble the woman might cause him. In a small religious community like ours every artist was held to be a rake and a spendthrift, even though he lived the most straitlaced life possible, loving, yea, even supporting his wife and children in decent comfort. When such a man was living alone in the same house with the widow of a soldier, every good Christian would be convinced that she was his

Drawing of two women holding babies

mistress and they would shun this house of sin as they would avoid doing a kind deed for someone who belonged to a different creed.

But when I told Rembrandt so, he would only get irritated. "Nonsense," he would reply. "Of course I shall let her go eventually, but not just now. It would be unfair, after all she has done for the child."

Of course that was not the real reason. It was the old story. He wanted to paint or etch, morning, noon and night. Nothing must interfere with the routine of studio and printing room. A new nurse would mean a slight loss of time. He would have to break her in, show her what was needed in that happy-go-lucky household of his. Out of devotion to his palette and his brushes, he neglected his own interests and those of Titus. Geertje Dircx, with all her failings, her tantrums, her everlasting complaining, at least allowed him to work in peace, and that was what he wanted.

"Listen," I continued in a final attempt, "you are a portrait painter. A landscape painter can be a drunkard and a scoundrel, but those who buy his pictures don't see him personally and so they don't care. But people have to come to your studio. The moment they hear talk about Geertje and you, you are lost."

He just could not see it that way. "If people care so little for my work that they won't come to my house because they think I sleep with the nurse, they had better stay away," was his impatient reply.

It was my last evening with him, but something had come between us. Try as we might, we could not remove this miserable woman from our consciousness.

In the end, I made a fatal mistake. Rembrandt was a great painter, probably the greatest we ever had, but he was also of very simple origin. More than once his rich patrons had made him feel what they thought of the social status of an artist whose father had been a miller and whose brother was a cobbler. Because Rembrandt was sensitive about such slights (foolishly sensitive I thought) and because at heart he was exceedingly shy, he could on occasion be most abrupt and ill-mannered.

On this particular evening he was at his worst. He was fond of me, as I was of him, and he hated to see me go. I too was unhappy and therefore terribly ill at ease. Otherwise I would never have been so foolish as to say what I did. It was about eleven o'clock and I still had a great many things to do at home. I got up and lightly remarked, "Au revoir, and if ever you are in need of anything, write me and I will come right back."

He jumped from his chair. "I am not in need of anything," he almost snarled. "I can take care of myself, thank you."

I held out my hand. "Good-by then," I said.

"Good-by," he answered, but he did not take the hand I offered him, and he (on other occasions the most punctiliously polite of all my friends) let me find my way to the door alone.

All the next day I tried to find an excuse to call on my poor friend again, to tell him I was sorry, to show him in what friendship and affection I held him. But my house was filled with people and I had no opportunity to rush to the Breestraat before they came for the trunks and I had to go.

Such, then, was the manner of our farewell.

And on the eighth of April of the year of grace 1643 I left Amsterdam with the recollection of that terribly unhappy moment uppermost in my mind.

CHAPTER 8

I WAS TO HAVE SPENT two years in America. I stayed seven. My many strange experiences and my many voyages through the interior of the New Netherlands that kept me so much longer than I had planned have been all set down with great care in the diary I kept. This, together with my final report, I surrendered to My Lord Andries and his brother Cornelis upon my return to Holland. Since they asked me to keep my detailed observations secret, I shall not mention them here. Nor shall I say much about the interesting subject which had been my special hobby. The meager results of my investigations about the so-called narcotics used in the New World have all been set down in my little book, *The Art of Medicine Among the American Indians.* Suffice it to say that the Indians, although possessing fair skill in the use of certain herbs, were just as ignorant about anesthetics as we are.

No, from a purely practical point of view, this voyage was not a success. The only person who benefited from it was myself. When I returned home, many of my friends pitied me. "Seven years in a howling wilderness among painted savages. Good God! What a waste of time!" was a remark I frequently heard. But that was hardly true.

What the New World did for me was this: it made me accept humanity as God had made it, not as I thought that He ought to have made it or as I would have made it if I had been given the chance. This new attitude came to me as I traveled through the endless forests and plains of our American possessions.

I came to know naked and painted savages whose manners were so exquisite that they could have been presented at the court of King Louis himself and would have been examples of good behavior and innate charm to polished courtiers. And I ran across others that were fat, cruel and lazy. I met simple farmers in the remotest corner of the colony who by thrift and industry and incredibly hard work had cleared wide acres of forest land, built themselves splendid homes and educated their children to be fine men and women.

And I have also been obliged at times to spend the night underneath the roof of some worthless, lazy younger son of a good Amsterdam family whose parents gave him a thousand acres of fertile grassland and who had been too shiftless to raise a single crop. These experiences in the New World convinced me that human nature is the same in every clime, for there are no nations and no races and no classes of men—only individuals good or bad, interesting or dull, wise or foolish, according to their natural inclinations.

Rembrandt at work in his studio

Bernardo, too, found a new certainty in the wilderness. Once, during my early years in America, I heard that somewhere in the West there lived the Five Nations who were vastly superior in civilization and political organization to the natives along the seaboard.

I decided to pay a visit to these regions and see what opportunities they offered to those future wheat growers whom My Lord Andries and his brother hoped to settle in the New World. As there was a certain degree of danger connected with such a trip, I tried to persuade Bernardo not to accompany me, but he stubbornly refused.

"I came on this voyage to find the ten lost tribes of Israel," he reasoned. "I believe just as little in those lost tribes as you do. All the same, I am here as the emissary of a few pious Jews in Amsterdam who entrusted me with their hard-earned florins to perform a certain, well-defined task. The very name, the Five Nations, attracts me and intrigues me. I would never forgive

JACOB TRIP

PHILIPS LUCASZ

NICOLAES RUTS

Three Dutch merchants typical of the many who commissioned portraits painted by Rembrandt

myself if I did not use this opportunity to visit those long-lost brethren."

So Bernardo went with me, and the famous Five Nations proved to be no myth, but a reality. And he decided to remain behind in a Mohawk village and watch over our luggage while I and two guides moved farther west.

Much later, when I was safely back in Nieuw Amsterdam, I sent word to Bernardo asking him to rejoin me but he favored me with a rather cryptic reply. It was a small piece of parchment with a rough drawing of an Indian on it, an Indian who bore a slight outer resemblance to Bernardo himself, and underneath it the cryptic words:

335

"The ten lost tribes have been joined by one more."

I therefore gave up hope of seeing him until I should be able to travel again to the land of the Mohawks. When, months later, I made the journey, I found Bernardo in a village ten miles to the north, so changed, so bronzed and healthy-looking, that at first I took him for an Indian brave.

Bernardo threw both arms around me and kissed me and took me into the house where a young and very handsome Indian woman was nursing a baby and he said, "Behold the additional lost tribe! And now go back to the good Rabbi Manasseh and give him my love and admiration and tell him that I am never, never coming back.

"I have not discovered a trace of the other ten tribes. But I have found myself. I am happy. This woman is a joy. This child is the handsomest ever born. I shall miss you and my other friends at home, but in losing all that I have gained more than I ever thought possible. For the first time in my life I am not a Jew but a man. Nobody here knows or cares whence I came. And I ask for nothing but that I be allowed to stay. Now come in and I will cook you a steak. Not just an ordinary steak— a steak I shot and killed myself."

And that is how Bernardo Mendoza Soeyro, who had the blood of the kings of Israel in his veins, who had spent two years in a dungeon of the Portuguese Inquisition, and who for more than ten years had kept books for Isaac Ashalem, a fish dealer of Amsterdam, came to die as an Indian chieftain and now lies buried underneath a small mound of stones and earth in the forests that are the hereditary hunting grounds of the famous tribe of the Mohawks.

But I am running ahead of my story.

WHENEVER I RETURNED to Nieuw Amsterdam after a western journey, I would spend many hours catching up with news from the other side of the ocean. Most of the letters, especially the bulky ones, were from Jean-Louys, but occasionally one proved to be from Selim. It was usually short and rather sad.

"This big city has grown very lonely," he wrote, "since you and Bernardo have left. Jean-Louys is a charming person, but he is mixing more and more mathematics into his omelets and I do not like to sit down to a meal and draw the cubic root from the soup and find decimal points in the pudding. And so I sit by myself much of the time.

"Of late I have been greatly diverted by the visits of the Reverend Simon Gallinovius, who hopes to convert the diplomatic representative of the grand Padishah. Can't you see me going up for baptism in an enormous green turban? He has actually taken the trouble to read the Koran in a Spanish translation. He tells me that he has concluded that Mohammedanism and Calvinism are the same, as both creeds believe in the preordination of every fact connected with human existence. This, I suppose, is interesting to the sort of people who care for that sort of thing.

"But I am bored and the banks of the Bosporus begin to look more and more attractive to this peace-loving exile. Three more visits from the long-winded Gallinovius and I shall set sail for the land of my fathers. What am I doing here anyway?

"I embrace you and the excellent *A Turk* Bernardo. Mark my word, that boy will turn native if you do not look out. He is as much of a wanderer as I am. He is almost as lonely. Allah have mercy upon the likes of us. Farewell!"

Followed by a postscript: "Your good friend Rembrandt has been to see me once or twice. That man has a veritable passion for Turks. He wants me to pose for him. I asked him whether he was running short of models and he said, 'No, but my models are mostly Dutch vagabonds. I can dress them up in silks and satins and put a turban on their heads, but that does not make them Turks. They remain Dutch vagabonds who happen to be dressed up in Moslem finery.' Perhaps I shall oblige him one of these days."

337

In contrast to Selim's brevity, Jean-Louys offered a complete history of the years I was absent from Amsterdam. His letters—sometimes there would be forty or fifty pages covered with his precise handwriting—were, in their way, as perfect as the meals he sometimes had prepared and which left one with a feeling of utter contentment.

I liked these epistles so much that I gave them to Governor Peter Stuyvesant to read and he told me that they had given

him more and better information about conditions at home than all the reports from his directors. He forgot to return them when I unexpectedly had to sail for home, so I must rely upon memory to reconstruct the most important items that they contained.

Every letter began with the news that Jean-Louys had just visited my house and had found my son to be in perfect health.

Sketch: "The Concord of the State" (never finished)

The child had completely forgotten me (as was of course to be expected), he was growing up to be a fine boy, had nice manners and went to see Master Rembrandt twice a week to be instructed in drawing. He seemed to have a decided gift for that form of art and Rembrandt was devoting a great deal of his time to helping the boy along.

Then he talked of political matters. Peace had been declared at last between Spain and the republic and the latter had been officially recognized as an independent and sovereign nation. The old Prince had not lived to see this final victory of the cause for which he had fought so long and so bravely.

His son, the one who had married the Englishwoman, had

succeeded him as commander in chief of the army and might cause considerable trouble, for he was a very ambitious young man. Their Lordships of the Town Hall and His Highness the Prince now openly regarded each other as enemies and friction between the two had caused a general feeling of uneasiness.

Business conditions were very uncertain now that the republic was no longer at war. And of course, as Jean-Louys remarked several times, the poor artists were the first to notice the scarcity of ready money. Rembrandt had told him that he had not had an order for a new portrait for over six months. During the first moment of triumph there had been a slight demand for allegorical pictures to celebrate the manifold victories of the Dutch nation. But the two most important orders had gone to Flinck, a pupil of Rembrandt's, and to van der Helst. The master himself had made a number of sketches for an imaginary historical picture representing the pacification of Holland, but no one wanted it and it was still standing in his studio at the time of writing. Nothing he touched seemed to be a success nowadays.

Indeed, throughout those letters there ran an undercurrent of worry about the house in the Breestraat.

True, Rembrandt was working harder than ever, turning out a number of beautiful and interesting etchings, but he had retired so completely from the company of his former friends that no one knew exactly how he stood in regard to funds. Some people thought he had borrowed money from Geertje which he was unable to pay back. The inheritance of Saskia had never yet been settled. Any lawsuit involving money would cause the court to examine the affairs of both parties and the general opinion was that Rembrandt could not afford to have the magistrates pry closely into his muddled business arrangements.

A few good friends had offered to put some order into this chaos, but he had thanked them most kindly but also most determinedly. He himself would attend to this matter as soon as he had finished a new etching on which he had set great hope. It was a picture of Christ healing the sick and he meant to sell it for a hundred guilders, a record price for etchings. That print would once more bring him into the public eye. Then he would be able to enjoy a little leisure from the potboilers he had been obliged to make the last few years and he would call on some reliable notary to help him with his accounts.

The terrible nurse was still there, growing more and more unbearable as the years went on. Often she would buttonhole visitors who came to see her master and would tell them all her woes—how she slaved keeping the household going because "he," pointing to the door of the master's workroom, was too lazy and indifferent to attend to anything, but she was not going to stand for it much longer. She could tell a great many things about herself and the famous Rembrandt van Rijn that would astonish the world, a great many things, and had they ever seen the pearls he had given her and the golden ring?

Several friends had at last combined to go directly to Rembrandt and suggest that he have the woman examined by some medical man familiar with lunacy. Rembrandt had listened patiently, but he had hinted at several difficulties which made it impossible for him to be as drastic as he wanted to be.

This made Jean-Louys fear that there was some pressing reason for Rembrandt's unwillingness or inability to send the nurse packing. He had lived a very solitary life since Saskia's death. He might have promised Geertje that he would marry her, or she might be in the family way, or she might pretend to be in the family way and blame the master. It was difficult to get at the truth. Meanwhile his friends hoped and prayed that the situation would not develop into a public scandal. Already there had been a few veiled references from the pulpit about people who had better heal themselves before they made pictures of the Saviour healing others.

The problem was to get the woman safely out of the house before this whispering campaign got a little too outspoken, but Rembrandt in all things, both good and bad, was known to be almost as obstinate as the gallant warrior who was then reported to be at the head of the government of the New Netherlands and with this charming compliment to My Lord Stuyvesant, the excellent Jean-Louys, who knew that letters were sometimes opened and read by the authorities, closed his account of affairs in the Breestraat.

CHRIST HEALING THE SICK, *known as The Hundred–Guilder Print*

He then told me a lot of gossip about European affairs: that the English were on the point of executing their king; that the government probably would fall into the hands of someone called Cromwell, who was known to be strongly in favor of a drastic policy of protection for all British interests; that an Italian who called himself Mazarin, having been a henchman of the infamous Cardinal Richelieu, had now got hold of the French government by making himself indispensable to the old king's wife, a Spanish lady with whiskers.

"A strange experience!" I once told a friend in Nieuw Amsterdam after reading one of these letters for the third time. "The Old World suddenly making its presence felt in the New. It is as if someone were making music in a room in another part of the house. I try to listen, but it means nothing to me, except a little, vague noise. What has happened to me?"

"It is the horizon. That strange horizon that means the beginning of something new and unknown. Unless those old fools in Amsterdam who rule us without ever having seen us force me to go away, I shall never return to the mother country. Send for your boy and set up as a surgeon right here. The others are all quacks. Settle down here and be happy!"

And I might have followed his advice if it had not been for the scrap of paper that reached me with some other letters exactly two months later. It said nothing but: "I wish you would come home. I need your help and your friendship very badly," and it was signed with a large capital letter *R*.

CHAPTER 9

THAT NOTE ARRIVED just as I was to start on a new voyage to the south. Rembrandt had treated me with abominable rudeness just before I left, but I could bear him no ill will on account of that outburst. He needed me.

I had no idea if he was in love with Geertje. I did not think so. He had been devoted to Saskia, but he was a man of terrific physical energy. In short, what I feared and what Jean-Louys seemed to fear (unless I had misread his last letters) was that the woman had seduced Rembrandt, or to speak a little less harshly, that circumstances had induced the two to forget the strict rules of morality prevalent in our country.

It was a terrible thing to leave a man alone at a moment like that, but I considered myself in the service of the Bicker family until I should have accomplished everything they had asked me to do. Besides, a contract was a contract.

Wherefore I sat me down and wrote to Rembrandt that I hoped to be back in Amsterdam early the next fall, and meanwhile if he had any troubles, to talk them over with Jean-Louys, who was a most trustworthy friend and of good, sound, common sense. And I told him that when I sailed into the harbor of Amsterdam I expected to find him standing near the Montelbaanstoren with little Titus, to whom I sent my best love. I purposely omitted all reference to Geertje. That seemed the better policy to me, though God knows I may have been wrong.

The next day I left for the south. During this trip I made the only discoveries which could possibly have been of any practical use to My Lord Andries and I therefore do not think it proper for me to give an account of this expedition in a book that deals with my personal adventures and reflections.

When I finally returned to Nieuw Amsterdam, I found waiting for me, among a number of letters from home, one from my boy, the first I had ever received from him. It showed me that young Willem was growing up rapidly, for not only did he write an excellent hand (in sad contrast to the illegible pot-

View of Amsterdam Harbor

hooks of his father) but he had interspersed his epistle with diverse quotations from Ovid, all correct. He expressed a polite regret at not having seen me for such a long time and suggested that I might soon return, but all this sounded very formal and I realized with a painful shock that I had neglected the only person in the world to whom I was bound by something more enduring than the ties of friendship. I felt grateful that my years of wandering were about to end.

As for Jean-Louys, he had outdone himself this time. Not less than nine letters and all brimful of information. Most of them have been lost, but one that I managed to save I shall copy here as it seems worth preserving.

A week ago today I ran across your old bookseller on the Rokin who also handles some of Rembrandt's etchings. He asked for news of you and then inquired whether I had heard of the latest troubles of Rembrandt. I said no, I had not been near the house on the Breestraat for months. So the bookseller told me there had been an open break between the nurse Geertje and her employer and then began a series of petty persecutions of Rembrandt—which still continue.

For example, she went before a judge and swore that her former master had borrowed money from her and had never repaid her, and another time she complained that he had promised to marry her and had not kept his word, and still a third time she stated definitely that she and her old employer had had carnal intercourse and that he had turned her out as soon as he had done his will upon her. It had finally become clear to all concerned that she was stark raving mad and thereupon she had been taken away to the town of Gouda, whence she came originally, and had been committed to the local lunatic asylum.

But that was only half of the story. For it appears that the lady in question has certain relatives who are not above a bit of blackmail, whenever it can be practiced without too much risk. And the risk in this case was very small, for Rembrandt, who is the world's most muddleheaded financier, has undoubtedly borrowed small sums of money from his son's nurse whenever he was in momentary need. Very foolish, no doubt, but when he is working and does not want to be disturbed he would take cash from the Devil himself. The whole thing is a mess.

About a week ago I desired a fish for dinner and behold! whom should I meet in the fish market but the good painter from the Breestraat. I thought that he would try to avoid me, for our last meeting had not been pleasant, but he came right up, shook me by the hand, and said, "You have heard of course what has happened?" I answered yes, and he smiled rather sheepishly and said, "Phew!" I replied, "Yes, indeed, phew!" and then we both roared with laughter.

Then he turned to a woman who was standing behind him and casually remarked, "You had better buy another turbot, for if I am not mistaken our friend here will share our dinner tonight." And it was said so pleasantly that I forgot all my previous feelings of irritation.

That night I dined with him and I never saw such a change

before. The house was scrupulously clean. Little Titus, now quite a handsome boy with long blond curls like his mother, was allowed to stand at the table and he had lost that look of a hunted creature which he had had ever since I first knew him. The meal was well cooked and the food was not thrown at us as in the olden days. I asked Rembrandt where he had found this jewel, and he told me that she was a peasant girl from a small village near the German border, but she had come to Amsterdam to find employment as a general maid, and that a friend had sent her to him when he was looking for someone after the Dircx woman had been sent to the madhouse.

"I know nothing about her," he confessed, "except that she seems to have no other relatives than a sister who lives in a village called Breevoort, some distance from here, something that suits me exceedingly well, as I have had enough of servants with brothers and sisters just around the corner, ready to perjure themselves at a moment's notice. For the rest, she is an excellent cook, keeps our rooms in order, is as nice to little Titus as if she were his own mother, and has a pleasant shrewdness when it comes to spending money, a quality which is perhaps not out of place in this particular household."

"She is also a very handsome woman," I ventured to remark.

"Yes," he answered, "she will suit me wonderfully well as a model. I was thinking of using her for quite a large picture I mean to make some time—a picture of Bathsheba."

I looked at Rembrandt and I looked at the maid who had then turned nurse and was telling little Titus that it was time for him to say good-night and go to bed.

"Remember David!" I warned him.

"There is very little danger of such a thing," he answered. And he got up to kiss his son good-night and went to the door to open it for the servant. I noticed that he bade her farewell as if she were a grand lady. And it suddenly struck me: She *is* a grand lady, even if she cannot read and write.

Rembrandt then took me upstairs and we looked at his etchings and when I went home, it was as if nothing had ever happened between us.

When you return, you will witness a miracle—the man is showing signs of becoming a normal and civilized human being. He also seems very hard up. But he is doing beautiful work, so who cares? Fare ye well and come back to us soon. We miss you.

This letter further convinced me that I ought to return. I paid an official call on My Lord Stuyvesant and was touched by the emotion he showed in bidding me Godspeed.

"It will be the last time we see each other," he said, and stamping the floor impatiently with his wooden leg he repeated words I had heard him use before: "A century hence this land will be of infinitely greater value than Java and all the Moluccas put together."

ONE AFTERNOON, some two months later, I found myself on the docks of Amsterdam. And in half an hour I was knocking at the door of my house. It took some time before I heard footsteps in the hall. First the little peephole in the upper part of the door was opened, then the door itself opened and the honest Jantje rushed out to tell me how happy she was to see me once more and then I went into the house for the great moment when I should see my son again—the moment about which I had dreamed for so many years—for which I had prepared so many fine speeches.

The boy was in the garden, picking radishes which he put into a little basket. He looked up when he heard my footsteps, and he wiped his muddy hands on his trousers.

Now it was going to happen!

I would open both arms wide and whisper, "My son!" and he, dumbfounded, would shriek, "Father!" and throw himself at my breast.

Instead the child held one large, red radish up for inspection and said: "Look, isn't this a big one?" I answered: "Yes, quite a big one." It was not a very brilliant retort, but one had to say something. Then I asked him: "Do you know who I am?" And he wiped his nose with the back of his muddy little hand and said: "No, unless you are the man who has come to fix the chimney."

And I said: "I am your father." And he answered: "Oh?" and went on picking radishes and so I stammered a bit helplessly: "Isn't there something you want to say to me?"

Suddenly he smiled brightly and came up to me and put his hand on my arm and asked: "Father dear, do you always wear that funny-looking cap?" And he pointed to it with a great deal of embarrassment.

"Why, yes, of course," I said. "That is a beaver-skin cap. Everybody wears them in Nieuw Amsterdam."

"Perhaps so," he said, "but nobody does in Amsterdam."

And then I said: "Now come in with me and I will go upstairs and wash and comb my hair and then we will go out together and buy a new hat."

View of a lake with sailboat

In that way I took my first walk with young Willem and I felt very proud as I listened to him tell how the old bridge, just off the Verwersgracht, had come down one day under the weight of a heavy piece of basalt which they were moving to the Dam to be used in the construction of the new Town Hall, how the horses that pulled the cart had been dragged into the water and had stood there for hours with their noses just above the surface until a boy had dived into the canal and cut them loose. And when we came to the bridge, I saw that it had been recently rebuilt and right in the middle of it there stood a familiar figure holding a pad of paper in one hand and a pencil in the other.

It was Rembrandt, not a day older than when I had last seen him, making a sketch of some boats. He was so engrossed in his work that he did not notice me until I was right beside him.

Whereupon he turned around and threw both arms around my neck and kissed me on both cheeks (to the terrible confusion and shame of my small child, who hastily looked the other way) and then he said: "Well, you have spoiled my sketch for me. I hate to tell you how I have missed you. What are you going to do now? Whither are you bound?"

I told him. And he took my son by the other hand and led the way to the hat store.

Half an hour later, once more provided with a respectable headgear, black of color, and of a most conservative pattern, we returned to the Houtgracht. But just as I was about to turn the corner, Rembrandt shouted: "Oh, no, my dear friend, that will never do! Today you belong to me." And he took me and my boy to the house on the Breestraat, pushed the door open and shouted: "Hendrickje, go out and kill the fatted calf. The prodigal has returned."

And a moment later I was looking into as handsome a pair of brown eyes as I had ever seen and a pleasant-looking girl was curtsying to me and was saying: "Oh, I suppose you are the doctor of whom the master has so often spoken. I am very glad, sir, that you are back. I have known your son for some time. He sometimes visits and plays with Titus."

And that is how I first met Hendrickje Stoeffels, the kind, simple, understanding peasant girl who lost herself in order to save the man she loved.

CHAPTER 10

THE NEXT FEW YEARS of my life were busy and interesting. My personal participation in the great American adventure had ended. The struggle between the burgomasters and the young Prince of Orange (which the Bickers had foreseen) ended, too. Soon after my return to Holland, the Prince died of small-pox. A week later his widow was delivered of a son, called Willem after his father, and for convenience' sake numbered

Willem III. We all prayed that the boy might take after his great-grandfather, who had led our people during the rebellion.

As for myself, I never regretted the humble role I had been allowed to play during those years. I received all my trunks and my collection of American plants and shrubs in perfect order. All but two or three specimens had survived the hardships of the voyage. I gave them to the Botanical Garden in Leiden, where they proved of great value to the students of botany.

My papers, too, which I had entrusted to the ship's captain, I received without losing a single letter, and after copying them and rewriting parts, I offered my report to Their Lordships Andries and Cornelis Bicker. They expressed themselves as being highly appreciative of my efforts. However, the changing political situation made it impossible for them to act immediately upon my suggestions. They would carefully consider all I had told them and would take the necessary steps as soon as possible. Then, in '52, My Lord Andries died. His brother followed him to the grave two years later. What became of my report I was never able to find out.

During my last interview with My Lord Andries, however, he had asked me what I expected in way of reward. I told him that I expected nothing. I had already been generously paid and was content.

"But isn't there some office you would like? Our colleagues still listen to us when we offer a little suggestion."

I assured His Lordship that this was out of the question. But perhaps he could render me one great service, the nature of which I then explained. Two trips across the ocean and a long residence in the New World had shown me once more how terribly neglected surgery was. I wanted to continue my researches in the field of anesthetics. And if Their Lordships would talk to their friend and colleague, Doctor Tulp, and ask him to bring about some sort of arrangement which would allow me to continue my studies along that line in the hospitals of the city, I would be deeply grateful.

My Lord Andries was as good as his word. Within less than two weeks after our last interview, Doctor Tulp sent for me, declared himself to be in hearty sympathy with my plans, and gave me practically carte blanche to do whatever I wanted to do within my particular field of investigation.

Of course, many of my colleagues accused me of being a meddler, and even a quack. But they gradually relented when they saw I charged nothing for my labors and that both the surgeon and his victims benefited greatly from my efforts.

I was often asked the secret of the vapors which I used. These vapors are very dangerous in the hands of an unskilled amateur. I therefore decided not to put the result of my studies into print until I should have made the method absolutely foolproof. I have not reached that point even today.

THOUGH MY PERSONAL LIFE continued to run its placid course, such was not the case with the republic. Our first war with England broke out in the year 1652. The cause was mutual jealousy. We were jealous of England's success in Asia and America, and England was jealous of our shipping trade.

The war lasted two years and it affected our lives in many ways. The quarrel between the Prince and Their Lordships of Amsterdam had slowed the development of adequate means of defense for the country as a whole, and as a result we suffered one defeat after another. Within less than ten months we had lost more than sixteen hundred merchant vessels. Our trade was temporarily ruined. In Amsterdam, vast fortunes were lost and some two thousand houses were for sale without anyone wishing to buy them.

And while the Lord Protector Cromwell across the North Sea and Their Lordships, our own protectors, fought to decide who should get the greater part of spoils that belonged to neither of them, I withdrew almost completely from public gatherings and came to depend more and more upon the companionship of my friends.

Selim had by now departed for the hospitable shores of the Bosporus and had become a man of importance in the land of his birth. (Returning sea captains told wonderful stories about the luxury displayed at his palace and of the two hundred women, said to be guarded by no less than three hundred eunuchs.) Bernardo, as I have told, had disappeared into the

American wilderness to become a Mohawk chieftain. So, of the four who had gone on frequent Sunday outings together, only Jean-Louys and I remained. And we drifted into the habit of spending at least part of the day at the house in the Breestraat, where we were welcomed by both Rembrandt and by the handsome Hendrickje with the utmost cordiality.

A little after eleven, about the time when other people went to church, Jean-Louys would drop in on me. After dinner, during which we would be joined by my son Willem who had a seat and a knife and a spoon of his own (I never approved of the prevailing habit of keeping children standing at the table and letting them eat only with their fingers), we would smoke a pipe of tobacco, then we would take our hats and capes and walk around the corner to the house on the Breestraat which by this time had acquired a look of pleasant familiarity.

Inside, the ground floor still looked like the storeroom of a dealer in antiques. On top of a large cupboard were two globes and a foreign-looking helmet which had

Hendrickje Stoeffels

recently adorned the head of Rembrandt's brother Adriaen when he had served as a model for the painter. The staircase to the second story was half hidden by a bit of old Flemish tapestry. On the table in the center of the hall were a marble wine cooler and a couple of Italian daggers. Over the door to the side room was a Venetian mirror in an ebony frame. But the old disorder had undergone a change. Now everything was neat and clean. People were living in this house, not just camping out.

The big living room in the back still served as sitting room, dining room and reception room to the whole family, and Rembrandt continued to sleep in the large bed built in the wall in which Saskia had died. Someday I suppose people will learn not to sleep in beds in which patients with pulmonary trouble have died. From my own experience I would say that it is a very bad thing to do. But I have never been able to convince anyone else. Even Rembrandt, by nature a man of sound common sense, would not hear of it when I told him that he must never let Titus come near anything his mother had worn. He laughed and said that we doctors were always trying to scare the poor laity merely to show the world how learned we were, and

The young Saskia . . .

he pointed to Titus and asked me whether I had ever seen a boy that looked so strong and healthy.

I was thinking of that when I first met Titus again after seven years of absence. He must have been almost eleven years old then. A handsome and pleasant-looking youngster with his mother's fine profile and that same agreeable smile that Saskia must have had in the days Rembrandt drew the little picture of her in a large straw hat. But the child did not seem robust. His cheeks were a little too thin for his age and his large, wondering eyes shone with a strange brilliancy.

My first impulse was to tell Rembrandt my suspicions— suggest that the boy be kept outdoors more and not be allowed to spend much time in the etching room where the acid vapors caused even a healthy man to gasp for breath. But I felt hesitant on account of Doctor Bueno, who had taken care of Rembrandt's household after I left for America.

Bueno was a Jew. His full name was Ephraim Bueno after his father from whom he had learned his profession. He was pleasant and modest and from all I had ever heard an excellent physician. But his position in the community had always been a little difficult. In the first place, it had not been until just before the war with Cromwell (I think it was in the year 1652) that the Portuguese immigrants of Jewish extraction had been given full civil rights. Up to that time, from a legal point of view, they had been merely tolerated. And this had made it impossible for them to join one of the guilds. Even when they opened a shop or started a business, they had been technically guilty of a breach of law.

Quite frequently the guilds had sent delegations to the Town Hall to ask the magistrates to forbid these unwelcome competitors from exercising their trade. But Their Lordships had refused to take any such steps. Our town, first, last and always, was a business establishment. Since the average Portuguese Jew had proved himself a most industrious citizen, he was considered a good business asset and all attempts to oust him failed.

... *and her son Titus*

But the situation for Jews was often awkward. I therefore was very careful how I treated Ephraim Bueno. I had a great respect for his learning and did not want to hurt his feelings. Sometimes if I happened to be within hailing distance and some slight accident took place (once, one of the pupils burned himself heating a copper plate and once Titus had an attack of coughing which frightened Rembrandt almost out of his wits), I would be called in and then I did whatever was necessary (in the case of Titus it was only necessary to tell him not to eat so many green nuts), but as soon as the emergency was over I invariably sent a hasty note to Doctor Bueno asking him to proceed to the Breestraat as soon as would be convenient. It was Bueno himself who put a stop to my somewhat exaggerated civility.

"My dear colleague," he said one day, as we were returning from the hospital together, "we Jews are said to be thin-skinned, and perhaps we are a little too suspicious about the intentions

353

of our neighbors. But my people have lived here now for half a century. We shall probably live here as long as this town lasts. Suppose we cease insulting each other by being so frightfully polite and become friends." And he added as an afterthought, "I am a Jew and that is pretty bad. But we are both leeches, and that is infinitely worse."

In this he was right. On my return to Amsterdam I had been struck once more by the anomaly of our position. In the New Netherlands there had been so few physicians that the people, depending upon our goodwill, had treated us with respect. But the republic was overrun by charlatans and people seemed unable or unwilling to differentiate between serious practitioners who had studied at half a dozen universities and spent seven or eight years walking the hospitals, and those jugglers and bone-setters and ointment vendors who frequented the country fairs. It was pretty bad. But as Bueno said to me on another day, it might have been worse still. We might have been artists!

I am not exaggerating. There is a man by the name of Mein-dert Hobbema living in an attic on the Rozengracht not far from the house where Rembrandt died. I am told that he is the best landscape painter we have ever had, but the other day, in the boat to Haarlem, I overheard two young businessmen cursing him roundly because one of them had bought a land-scape from the poor devil for two hundred guilders and had been told by his father that he could have had the thing for one quarter the price if he had only bargained harder.

Not to mention poor Frans Hals of Haarlem, who died only a few years ago, who was undoubtedly as great a man as Rembrandt, who was forced into bankruptcy by his baker (can one man eat so much bread?), and whose belongings at the time, amounting to three mattresses, one cupboard and a table, were sold at public auction.

Indeed in our country the artist is thought of as an amiable loafer and not as a respectable member of society.

I DOUBT IF ANY MAN ever had such thoroughgoing aversion to exercise as Rembrandt did. I used to scold him and Doctor Bueno used to back me up whenever I told him that he was digging his own grave with his easel and his chair. I delivered endless lectures on elementary physiology. Rembrandt never lost his temper and I admired his patience until I discovered one evening that he did not even listen. He just went on painting and let me talk.

Only the week before he had complained to me that he would wake up in the middle of the night with his heart beating like fury and a severe pain in the side of his head. I told him to ask Doctor Bueno to examine his heart and then I said: "When do you notice this trouble most?" He could not quite remember but he thought that it came when he had spent the whole day at his etching press.

Dr. Ephraim Bueno

"You see," he remarked casually, "those boys of mine mean well, and they do their best, but if I want a really good copy I have to do it myself. I have not had many orders for portraits of late—you know how it is when there is a war. Everybody is scared. Everybody saves all the money he can. And portraits, after all, are a luxury. But people will buy etchings. They are good investments and I had orders for several hundred. So in the evening when those children go to bed, I strike off a few copies."

"At what time do you begin?"

"About seven."

"And when do you stop?"

"Oh, sometimes quite early. Other evenings I work until four or five, though I sometimes stop for a quarter of an hour or so and have a glass of beer. One gets thirsty. It is hard work."

Seven until four or five—that meant nine hours of standing on his feet in a small room that was suffocatingly hot, pulling the wheel of a press that was almost too heavy for a cart horse.

"How long have you been doing this?" I asked.

355

"Since January last year when orders came in for those plates."

January of last year—that meant fifteen months of a sort of labor that would have killed a hod carrier in less than six.

"But of course," I said, "when you do that sort of thing, you don't paint?"

"Yes, I paint most of the day in my studio, as long as there is light. Then I take a candle and go to the pressroom. Sometimes when my eyes bother me, I light a second one."

"Do your eyes bother you much?"

"Not much. I have good eyes. I still can do a drypoint without using glasses. But after five or six hours I find myself weeping big tears and after ten hours I get funny pains. As if someone were sticking pins into my eyeballs. Not the pain in my head which I just mentioned—that only comes when my heart does its funny tricks—but irritating little pinpricks and I have to stop for a few minutes until they disappear."

Truly, the man was hopeless.

"Has it ever dawned upon you," I asked him, "that if you go on working that way you may lose your eyesight completely? A fine painter you would be then!" And I made ready to leave.

At once he changed his tone. "Don't be angry, Doctor," he begged me, "you are probably right, but I have to go on—"

"Why?" I interrupted him.

Rembrandt wiped both his hands on his blue painter's smock, a habit which made some of his enemies of the popular Italian school say that he carried his best works on his belly. "I will be good for this once and obey orders," he said. "My whole head aches and I might as well call it a day. You ask me why I work like a madman? Very well. I will tell you. Because I am really a little crazy."

"Professionally speaking," I said, "I never noticed it."

"Of course not. I am not crazy in the sense the Dircx woman was crazy. You need not lock me up. But I know that I am not an ordinary, well-balanced, respectable member of society and I never shall be. That is what is the matter with my work. So far I have kept out of the poorhouse. But only because I happen to have inherited all that money from Saskia. The inheritance is a little slow in collecting, but anyway it gives me credit, which is almost as good as having money. Without that, I don't know what would have happened to me. My work does not sell.

"For the first ten years after I came here from Leiden, I was a sort of curiosity. I was the fashion. That older generation liked my work. But the younger generation is afraid of me. I can paint, if I say so myself, and they know it. But I can't paint the way they want me to and they know that too.

"You will say that I ought to be practical and paint the way they want me to paint. Well, I have tried, but I just can't do it! And that is why I am a little crazy. An ordinary person who sells raisins or herrings or cheese or who makes pictures for a living carefully studies his market, which after all is his bread and butter. When the taste of his customers changes, he changes the nature of the goods he is trying to sell them. If they want their herring dried instead of pickled, he buys a couple of acres of land and hangs his fish in the sun. If they want their cheeses colored red instead of yellow, he colors them red instead of yellow. If the fashion of the moment prescribes Italian landscapes, he will paint Italian landscapes.

"Personally I don't blame those people. Sometimes I am accused of being too proud or too haughty to paint differently from the way I paint. But it isn't so. I just can't do differently. And so I stick to my own line and I suppose I shall stick to it until I go to the poorhouse or the cemetery and you may put a stone on my grave, saying: 'Here lies a fool.' "

CHAPTER II

NOTWITHSTANDING THE WAR, there was a good deal of money abroad at that time. Thousands of people were losing all they had; but a few hundred, who had been shrewd enough to speculate in grain and wood and gunpowder and other supplies of which the fleet was in great need, made vast sums of money. And they were buying luxuries right and left.

One day pictures would be all the rage. The next day it would be china; the little Japanese cups that had sold for three florins apiece had gone up to three thousand. Almost overnight the

Nürnberg watchmakers reaped a fortune with extraordinary timepieces that showed not only the minutes but also the seconds. And as the newly rich had heard that there lived a painter in the Jewish quarter whose house was a museum of everything one could hope to collect, many of them found their way to the Breestraat.

In the beginning, Rembrandt was flattered, thinking this meant a renewed interest in his work. But soon he discovered that those noisy visitors with their even more noisy wives did not care in the least for his art. They would ask how much he would take for an enameled Turkish sword or an ivory carving from the Indies. Then he would grow angry (for he well knew the value of his own work) and, instead of making these miserable war profiteers pay an outrageous sum for some article which he had bought in a moment of weakness and for which his visitors were willing to pay ten times the original price, he would abruptly show them the door. They would depart to spread it among their friends that this so-called artist, who gave himself such airs, was a sullen fellow whose swinish ill temper had turned him into an involuntary recluse. For our newly rich did not like people of an independent character.

I do not mean to imply that Rembrandt was a saint. Nothing could have been less true. He was of this earth earthy. But like most other artists he was too busy with his own problems to enjoy that leisure which is the breeding ground of gossip and spite.

It was this devotion to a single ideal that also manifested itself in Rembrandt's sublime unconcern with the value of money. The smiling excuse, "I wanted it," justified any extravagance from a painting by Giorgione to an ebony chest for Titus.

At one moment he got greatly interested in a certain Adriaen Brouwer, a pupil of Frans Hals. This young man, of phenomenal ability, had died at the age of thirty-two. His works therefore were rare and in the decade after his death they had greatly increased in price.

One evening I found Rembrandt's front room filled with Brouwers, a most heterogeneous collection, a woman, a child, a pastry cook, a couple of gamblers, and a cook busy with a very greasy dish, all done with beautiful economy of line and color.

Self-portrait, 1643

"Aren't they wonderful?" asked Rembrandt.

I said yes, they were very interesting but they must have cost a small fortune and I pointed to one which probably represented my household expenses for half a year. Then I congratulated him and said I was glad he had done so well recently.

"Done well? Good God! I haven't sold a thing for two years."

"Then your Indian venture must have turned out prosperously." (For I knew that he had been speculating in the shares

of a rather doubtful Indian company.)

"Oh, you mean those three ships. You heard of those?" (Who had not heard of them?) "No, there was some trouble with the crews and the scurvy; they only got as far as the Cape. That money is lost, I am afraid."

"But I suppose they wanted cash for these Brouwers?"

"They did. I borrowed it. Aren't they marvelous?"

Then he took me in the side room, lit a fire, got me a bottle of ale and spent at least two hours explaining his conception of the uses of money and the duties of artists towards themselves.

A slaughtered ox

"You are a man of tact," he began, "and rather than tell me outright not to buy pictures and helmets and such things, you have encouraged me to buy books—and read. If he is kept busy reading, you probably said to yourself, he won't spend so much on antiques. But what good has the reading of other people's books ever done to an artist?

"You remind me of those people who say, 'This is all very pretty but you can't learn your trade here. We in the north are barbarians when it comes to arts. Italy, the south, that is the country for you.' And they recite long lists of names of artists who go to Rome and Florence and Venice to learn painting.

"Painting is nothing but seeing. You see something that impresses you and then you paint it, or you draw it or hack it out of a piece of marble, as the Greeks used to do. A good artist could get more inspiration out of a dead bullock hanging in some village butcher shop, than a bad one out of half a dozen beautiful churches in the village where Raphael himself was born. Italians living in Italy should get their emotion (the word inspiration is good enough for theologians and for amateur artists) from Italian subjects, but we in Holland should get our emotions from the subjects with which we are familiar and not from something a thousand miles away.

"Even such a broad-minded man as My Lord Constantijn, who has been a friend to me all my life, could not see it that way. He scolded me because I refused to take the opportunities that were offered me to go to Italy and told me of the wonderful landscapes he had seen on his way to Venice and that landscapes were only possible in a region where the sun was a brilliant ball of golden fire and not a greasy speck made by the nose of an inquisitive child on a pane of window glass as it is in our own muddy country.

"But I answered him that a rainstorm, if seen and felt by someone with the ability to see and feel rainstorms as intensely as some of the Italians were able to see and feel sunsets, would make just as good a subject for a picture as his dearly beloved Forum by moonlight. And a dozen years later (it was in '43 if I remember rightly) I sent him a copy of my etching of those three trees with the rainstorms in the distance, and I wrote him:

" 'My Lord, do you remember a talk we had when I was twenty-five years old? And will you graciously accept this poor etching as a token of my extreme gratitude and tell me whether I was right when I said that rainstorms could be made just as interesting as sunsets?'

"And he answered me with his usual courtesy that he was beginning to understand. Then in '50, when he was here in Amsterdam a few days, I showed him that picture of a windmill that was afterwards sold to someone in England and I asked him: 'My Lord, isn't that mill as good in its own way as the little house that Giorgione painted in the background of his *Concert Champêtre* (a picture which is in Paris but of which I have seen some very fine copies)?'

"He looked at it for quite a long while. Then he said yes, that I might be right after all. And then, abruptly changing the subject, he said: 'I want to ask you something. It has always puzzled me. What are you really trying to do?'

"I told him as best I could. And I shall try to tell you. It began one day long ago when I was working in my father's mill. I don't mean that I was painting in my father's mill. In those days I was not encouraged to become an artist. My people were simple folk and very pious, and when I first told them that I wanted to be a great painter, like Lucas van Leyden, who was the first man whose works I had ever seen, they shook their heads and said no, they wanted me to be a good Christian and get ahead in the world.

"I seemed to be much cleverer than my brothers. One of them could succeed Father in the mill and the others would be taught a trade. I was to get a degree so that my parents could proudly say, 'Our son, the Doctor of Laws.' Well, I went to the university. I got a piece of paper informing me most solemnly that Rembrandus Hermanius Leydensis or some such thing was now, at the age of fourteen, if you please, a duly enrolled *stud-litt*—whatever that meant—in the glorious university of Leiden.

"But it was no use, I came home after one year at the university. (I cared as little about books then as I do now.) And I went to Jacob Isaacsz van Swanenburgh, who was a famous man in our town. He was one of those artists who had learned their trade in Italy—and when he came one day and told my parents that I had it in me to become a successful and fashionable portrait painter, they forgave me for not wanting to be a scholar. And as van Swanenburgh's charges were less than the tuition fee of the university, they decided to let me stay where I was and work out my salvation according to my own abilities. But before that time, I could only draw when no one was looking, and every afternoon after school, my brother Cornelis and I used to go to the mill and help Father with his work.

"Have you ever been in a windmill on a sunshiny sort of a day? No. Well, then you have missed something. The windows of a mill are usually very small, but when the sun is shining brightly, especially in the spring when the air has just been cleaned by three weeks of wind or rain, the whole inside of the mill is flooded with a curious and brilliant light—a strange light that is like nothing else I have ever seen. I have not traveled far, but I suspect this light may only be found here on this floating pancake of ours, where sun and fog do queer things to the light, both inside our houses and out of them.

"Well, it was just such a day in April and Cornelis and I had been told to count a number of sacks that lay on the first floor and carry them up to the second floor where the grinding was done and stack them up neatly in a corner. We did so and then my father inspected the sacks and found that one or two needed repairing and told me to get a needle and thread and attend to the job, while Cornelis was sent away on an errand. I sat down in a corner to do the task and it did not take me long. But I was afraid that if I told my father that I was through,

Etching of three trees

he would give me something else to do and so I said nothing, but stayed quietly where I was and pretended to be busy. There was a brisk east wind blowing outside and the wings of the windmill went past the window, *g'chuck—g'chuck—g'chuck*, a sort of guttural sound like the snapping of a musket and then the sudden swish of those enormous wooden arms cleaving the air. And every time a wing passed by one of the windows, the light was cut off for perhaps a hundredth part of a second—just a flash—but visible, just the same—for every time it happened, the room became pitch-dark.

"Now you may remember that when we were young—perhaps as a result of the siege and the large number of people who had died—our houses and our cellars were full of rats. And there were people who made a business of catching the rats.

"Earlier that morning one of these professional ratcatchers had been at work in our mill. He had left for a while but one enormous wire cage full of rats was hanging by a strong chain from a rafter. Those rats—great big fellows—all seemed to be sitting on their hindsides, trying to gnaw through the steel chain that held their cage. They hadn't a chance. But through the

Rembrandt's mill

scurrying and pattering of all these excited bodies, with their bright beady eyes and their long, disgusting tails, the cage was slowly beginning to swing from left to right and it was making a curious shadow upon the wall. And all the time, the wings of the mill kept swishing past the window and every time they swished past, the room would be pitchdark and then for just one, two, three seconds, it would be filled once more with brilliant sunlight.

"I had seen that sort of thing hundreds of times before and it had never struck me as remarkable. Now suddenly it came to me that that cage was not merely hanging in the light or in the air, as I had always taken for granted, but that it was an object surrounded by a whole lot of different sorts of air—all of different texture.

"I can't expect to tell you what I mean in two words, but you know that there are a number of colors, like yellow and blue and red and combinations of colors and we painters are supposed to know all about those colors and their combinations. We tell stories in daubs of color, just as others tell stories in words. At least, that is what I had always taken for granted.

"But that morning in the mill there weren't any colors, at

least none with which I had been familiar from earliest child-hood, when someone gave me my first box of paints. The light in front of that rat cage was different from the light behind it, which was different again from the light on the left of it, and all these different sorts of light changed every moment.

"And then the idea suddenly struck me: Does all this space—this air—really have a color in our sense of the word and is it possible to translate that color into terms of paint? I have now spent the greater part of every day during the last forty years trying to find the answer and I know just as little about it as I did when I first saw those excited rats in their wire cage, hanging from the rafter of my father's mill. Sometimes I think that in at least a few of my pictures I have solved the problem pretty well. But I confess that I have been working backwards, paint-ing the picture first and trying to discover afterwards why I had done what I had done and how I had happened to get those effects.

Self-portrait, 1630

"What I want to know is this: Why are people able to say, when they look at one of my pictures, 'That man is actually sitting on a chair in a room, not leaning up against a mere background of chair and room.' Or, 'That angel is really floating through space, not falling or resting on a cloud.'

"Of course, the public has no notion of what I am trying to do. Perhaps four hundred years from now, if any of my pictures are left, they will say to each other: 'This fellow van Rijn at least was going in the right direction.' But my neighbors—they sneer, 'This man is a mere amateur. He does not paint things the way we ourselves see them.'

"Heaven forbid that I should ever see things as they do!

365

Anyone can learn to paint things that are there. But to paint things that one merely suspects to be there while one can't possibly prove that they are there—that, my good Doctor, that sort of task makes life interesting. And that is what makes people afraid of me. Now let us go to the back room."

"For a game of chess?" I asked.

"No, no more chess. Life is too short. At least for me. But if you will come with me, I will show you something. You remember the etching I made of a scholar in his study, one or two years ago? Well, it didn't entirely please me. I have worked a lot of drypoint into it since then and now at last I think it is right. I will let you see it and you will understand how it is possible (even in black and white) to make different sorts of light that flow into each other like wine that is poured into a glass of water. Speaking of which, Hendrickje shall make us a kettle of *bisschop*, but please don't scold me anymore if I continue to buy pictures. There is always a chance that they will teach me something new. I am almost fifty. More than two-thirds of my days are gone and there is still so terribly much to do. So terribly much."

We went to the back room. Rembrandt lit two candles and got the plate of the scholar. Titus was fast asleep in one of the two beds built in the wall. Hendrickje went to get the wine and the spices that were necessary for our drink. The kettle was standing on the floor in front of the fire. She leaned over to pick it up just as I looked her way. And suddenly my professional eye registered an unmistakable professional fact. She was pregnant and she was well along.

That too was a problem in space but one which Rembrandt seemed to have overlooked.

CHAPTER 12

IT IS VERY STRANGE, but there are certain things which one man just can't possibly tell another. He may, under certain circumstances, draw his friend's polite attention to the fact that he is a scoundrel or a thief, but he can never inform him that his shirt cuffs are badly in need of the laundry. Nor can he go up to him and say, "Pardon me, but isn't that housekeeper of yours about to give birth to twins?"

But for once fate intervened in a very welcome and discreet fashion. Hendrickje suffered an accident, and as Rembrandt's regular doctor was out of town for the day to attend a funeral, they sent for me.

I found Rembrandt painting in the large back room while Hendrickje was lying panting and gasping for breath in the same bed in which, almost a dozen years before, Saskia had died. I thought of course that Hendrickje lacked air because of her physical condition, but Rembrandt at once told me what had happened. Then I understood her ailment to be much simpler.

Hendrickje had gone upstairs to clean the studio as usual that morning. The evening before, two of the pupils had been biting a plate in a new mixture that consisted of aquafortis and blue vitriol and a few other ingredients. Those bright boys had become so engrossed in their task that they had forgotten to close the jar containing the mixture.

The faithful Hendrickje had paid no attention to the strange odors in the room—had carefully swept and cleaned and brushed—had breathed the poisoned air—had felt her chest gradually beginning to ache and her eyes beginning to smart and to tear. In great panic she finally had left the room and gone to tell Rembrandt that she was going to faint and would he please send at once for the surgeon.

It was not a very difficult case. I asked to be shown the room in which she had worked, and as soon as we entered, we saw what had happened. Rembrandt pushed open the windows, looked for the jar containing the aquafortis mixture, closed it and then called for the two pupils, whose ears he boxed in such a way that these young men probably remembered until the end of their days that etching compounds should be treated as circumspectly as a loaded gun.

We then took Hendrickje out of the badly ventilated back room and put her down on a couch in the garden and immediately she began to feel better. In a few minutes she fell asleep but I decided to stay and reassure Rembrandt who was greatly perturbed.

"I have lost one wife in this house through what was more or less my own carelessness," he said when we had returned to the studio, where the mild hurricane that was blowing in through the open windows had not only driven away the fumes but had upset a picture on which Rembrandt was working. It showed Hendrickje wearing the big pearl earrings which he had bought for Saskia about fifteen years before and when Rembrandt had dusted it off with a soft cloth I noticed that it was a fine piece of work. Perhaps he had made Hendrickje a little more of a lady than she actually was, but all the kindness and goodness of her beautiful eyes were there. I liked it and I told him so and he sat down in front of his easel and mixed some white with ocher to touch up the earrings (slightly damaged by the fall), and said, "I am glad you like it. I have worked on this very hard. She has been so good to Titus and me. I would like to do something for her."

This was more or less my opportunity.

"I was obliged to examine her when I came in," I said, "for to tell you the truth, my first impression was that she was pregnant. And I discovered that she was. That isn't what you mean when you say that you wanted to do something for her?"

No sooner had I spoken these words than I knew I had committed a blunder. I regretted them, for I was sure that they would anger my touchy friend.

Rembrandt, however, lightly touched the background with some raw umber, stepped back to look at what he had done and then remarked in a most casual tone: "No, that is not what I meant. I was thinking of this picture. It is one of the best things I have ever done and people will admire it—and her—long after we shall be dead. As for the other little item you just mentioned, that I am sorry to say was an error on our part. We are both of us glad it happened, now that it did, but it was a mistake. It happened once before, but you weren't in town at that time and the child died. Pity, for it was a girl and it would have been nice to have a girl. Perhaps we shall have better luck this time."

He made this announcement as if he were telling me of some new picture he was planning to paint and I really don't believe that it meant very much more to him than that. The picture was merely an incident in life, an interesting episode in which one pitted one's intelligence against the unwilling forces of nature. The child was an incident in life in which nature pitted its unreasoning forces against the intelligence of man. Sometimes man won. As a rule nature won. It made no difference.

"But," said I, who after all had been brought up in an atmosphere of profound middle-class righteousness, "surely, now that Saskia is gone, you can marry Hendrickje and you ought to."

"I ought to, all right." Rembrandt smeared some more ocher on his palette knife. "I know it, but I can't."

"Why? You are a free man."

"I am absolutely free. We have talked about it. But I can't afford it. I think I have found a new way to handle a lighted candle in a picture I may be asked to do for the new Town Hall. And then I bought an old piece of armor—rather expensive, but I am going to use that for all sorts of things, for I have never done brass the way it really

The rat killer

looks when the sun shines on it, and I want to try my hand at some more landscapes and I have got at least two dozen etchings to do. You see, work enough for ten years! If I live that long. If I tried to get my money problems straightened out too, I could never do it."

"Are they as bad as all that?" I interrupted him.

"Much worse. The only way I can go on is by forgetting that they exist. One of these days the public will understand what I am trying to do. I am a fast worker. In less than a year I will be able to paint myself out of this financial hole. Then I can pay my creditors and marry Hendrickje. She is a good girl. She gives me everything I want. I would be a scoundrel not to marry her,

369

but she will have to wait until then. And she does not mind. She says it makes very little difference to her and meanwhile it keeps this household out of trouble."

"But meanwhile will you be able to prevent gossip? Surely the neighbors will notice her condition and will talk."

Rembrandt dropped his palette knife and looked at me with anger blazing in his eyes. "What of it?" he asked brusquely. "They talk anyway. They always have talked. They always will

Etching of Faust in his study

talk. The neighbors, indeed! Damn the neighbors! I am not thinking of them. Neither is Hendrickje. Let them go on—how does the Bible say it?—hewing wood and drawing water. That is all they are good for. But this house is worth saving. Hendrickje likes it. Titus loves it. I have been happy in it. Some mighty fine pieces of work have been done in this house."

I did not see the connection and told him so.

"Do you remember the will, Saskia's will?" he asked me.

I told him that I did so only in a very vague way.

"Well," Rembrandt said, "Saskia left everything to me to handle, but on certain conditions. I was to give Titus a first-rate education and establish him in some profession of his own as soon as he should become of age. In case, however, I died or married again, her fortune was to pass directly to Titus.

"Do you get the meaning of that? If I married Hendrickje, then according to the terms of the will I would have to go before the courts and fill out endless papers and swear a dozen oaths and turn everything over to Titus. And how am I to turn over everything when there isn't anything—when there never was any cash, only promises and lawsuits and family feuds.

"Meanwhile the whole world has taken for granted that I am a rich man. It has been, 'Rembrandt, buy this!' or 'Rembrandt, my little ones have not had a square meal for a fortnight. Let me have ten guilders.' And I am a weak man where it comes to money. We never had any when we were children. It was fun to be considered a Croesus. Anyway, what did it matter? Someday that inheritance would be paid out in full and I would have almost fifty thousand guilders to pay all my creditors.

"I went on painting, but since the Banning Cocq picture, the public does not seem to like my work anymore. What could I do? Move away? Give up this house? The moment I whisper a word about wanting to sell, I shall have all my creditors on my back. I have got to keep up appearances if I want to keep up my credit. And the moment my credit is gone, we shall all be in the poorhouse. Titus—Hendrickje—I. The kind friends who encouraged me to borrow when they thought everything was fine will fall upon me like a pack of wolves. And so," (with a final dab at the foreground of Hendrickje) "don't ask me, 'Why don't you marry the girl?' for I can't and she knows it and she is very wonderful about it. We had better let matters stand where they are."

I agreed with him in the main yet I could not help saying: "But, Rembrandt, my friend, you must know approximately where you stand!" He smeared his hands on his smock, smiled pleasantly at me and answered:

"I have not the faintest idea and that is the truth."

Then I tried to reason with him. I explained that he never could get out of debt without first knowing approximately how much debt he had—that fighting unknown debts was like fighting an invisible enemy in a dark cellar. But he tried to distract my attention by conducting me into the pressroom where three pupils were busy with a large etching of the Crucifixion. Presently he discovered a flaw in the shading of the figure of the bearded Pharisee in the foreground and ordered one of the boys to sharpen the steel needle he had bought that afternoon, for he would make his correction by drypoint. I stayed and watched him working by the light of a single candle for about an hour and then, realizing that I might sit there until four in the morning without being noticed, I went downstairs, found Hendrickje asleep and little the worse for her accident, and went home.

The next morning I got up early.

During the night I had evolved a plan. It was impossible to let Rembrandt go on the way he was going. Someone must do something and I meant to be that someone. I took my hat and coat and went to see Jean-Louys.

Now Jean-Louys, at one time in his career, had been obliged to handle large sums of money. He had even tried to discover the theoretical mathematical formula that must underlie the highly practical system of double-entry bookkeeping which had been introduced into the republic. He was an ideal person to act as one's financial counselor. But when I had explained my predicament to him, I found him deliberately aloof.

"What does it matter?" he asked me, with tantalizing calm.

"Everything," I answered, slightly upset by his indifference.

"But why? The man paints better than ever. In a hundred years, no one will care whether he died in the poorhouse or in the guest room of his illustrious friend, My Lord Jan Six."

"I know that. But meanwhile he has to support a son and a wife, or at least a woman who will soon be the mother of one of his children. They need three meals a day and he himself would die if he ever had to give up that museum he calls his home."

"It might be good for his work."

"Or it might kill him—not to speak of Hendrickje and Titus."

Jean-Louys confessed that he had never thought of it in that light. Then he asked me what I meant to do.

"I don't know," I answered. "If I did, I would not bother you with my questions. Every time I mention it to Rembrandt, he gets fidgety, takes me to his studio to show me a picture he has just started, explains an idea for some large allegorical figure for the new Town Hall (as if they'd give him a chance to work there!) or tells Hendrickje to bring something to drink."

"Yes," Jean-Louys said, "it probably makes him feel uncomfortable. He is a man of but one single obsession. He wants to paint. All the rest of him is detail. You will never find out anything from him directly."

"And yet I must know a few things if I am to avert a disaster."

"You never will. It is not in your line. How about your friend Lodewijk?"

"But he is my banker and not Rembrandt's, if Rembrandt allows himself such a sensible luxury, which I doubt."

"Of course he is not Rembrandt's banker, but Lodewijk makes a living handling other people's money. It is his business to know the financial condition of everybody in town. Go see him tomorrow and you will be surprised to find out how much he can tell you. If he puts his mind to it, he can give you a complete balance sheet before the end of next week, but I don't think that balance sheet will make you any happier. And if I were you, I would leave the matter alone and come sailing tomorrow with me and my new manservant, Francois, whose onion soup you will taste one day soon. He can sail as well as he cooks, having run away to sea as a boy. Last week I bought a boat of my own. I have a new idea about rigging the sails to cause more of a vacuum. If you come, you may witness the birth of a new era in navigation."

But my one determination now was to visit Lodewijk. And at ten o'clock next morning I was knocking at the well-known door on the Singel.

The night before, little Titus had come to my house to ask whether Mother could perhaps have half a dozen eggs for there was nothing to eat in the house and Father had not yet had his dinner.

Surely it was high time that something be done!

CHAPTER 13

WHEN I ENTERED HIS OFFICE, I found Lodewijk busy cutting himself a new pen. "What a day!" he shouted as soon as he saw me. "Was there ever such a climate? My sixth pen this morning. They melt in your hand—like fresh butter." Then, when he had fashioned the nib according to his desire: "Well, what can I do for you today?"

I told him.

He listened patiently, but did not seem surprised. "I know all about that," he answered. "We all do. That man owes everybody. He will end in the bankruptcy courts."

"That is what I feared," I told him. "Exactly how bad is it?"

"Ah, there now! When I said I knew all about the case, I meant that I knew enough never to give the man a single penny if he came here to ask me for a loan. Further than that my interest did not go. But if you want a balance sheet with all the details, come back in a week's time and you shall have it." And then Lodewijk dropped the subject and we talked for a time about certain of my own affairs.

I had encountered, among certain fellow physicians during the past year, some bitter and increasingly threatening criticism of my "childish experiments with the fumes of a pagan and nauseating drug" which, they said, polluted the delicate atmosphere of the city hospital. And I had recently set in motion a plan to safeguard my search for pain-relieving anesthetics against my colleagues' interference. I had decided to build and run my own hospital.

In order to finance this project, I had asked my banker to convert into cash the bulk of the East India Company shares I had inherited from my uncle in Veere. And Lodewijk, whose kindness of heart was tempered by a dry sort of common sense, had been bemused but not disapproving when I first asked his advice about the plan.

"Blessed are the fools," Lodewijk had said, "for they shall see the shadow of God. When do you want the money?"

The hospital was now a reality—a large remodeled house on the Groene Burgwal, with my office, study, examining room and operating room on the first floor; twenty small rooms for patients on the second floor; and, on the third floor, living quarters for the dozen young Moravian women who were being trained as nurses by two deaconesses who followed me from the city hospital despite religious scruples. (I was, after all, trying to make people escape the pain which the Almighty had meant them to suffer as punishment for their sins.)

I reported on the progress of these matters to Lodewijk, and then I left him and went to the hospital.

A week later I called again at the Singel and received a short report, writ by Lodewijk himself and containing facts which confirmed my worst fears about Rembrandt's position.

"Hopeless, I tell you!" Lodewijk warned, as he handed it to

me. "The man is one of those chain borrowers. He seems to keep no accounts and his affairs are in a hopeless muddle. To make matters still worse, he occasionally borrows money on pictures that have not yet been painted or on others that have been promised to a third party. He has hypothecated his house a couple of times, and as to his wife's inheritance, nothing less than the day of the Last Judgment will ever solve that puzzle.

"But here you are, my friend. Here is the report as I pieced it together from two dozen different sources. Sit down in that corner and read it while I cut myself a fresh pen. Why does it always rain in this damned country?"

I did as he told me. And here is that report.

For your exclusive information. The subject of this investigation is the son of very simple folk, but his parents were not without means and possessed one windmill, two small houses and a parcel of real estate in one of the poorer quarters of the town of Leiden. There were six children. Several seem to have died young. Those who are still alive have never done very well. It is said that their brother (the subject of this investigation) supports them and keeps them out of the poorhouse.

As for the subject, who hereafter will be designated as N.N., he was the brightest of the family and as such he was inscribed in the University of Leiden in the year 1620 at the age of fourteen. He left after one year, having decided to become a painter. In 1630 his father died. The brothers and sisters each received a small amount in cash. N.N. took his share, moved to Amsterdam and took a studio on the Bloemgracht, later moving to the Breestraat. At first he was a great success with our richest families; he was even commissioned to work for the Prince.

Meanwhile he had become engaged to a girl from Leeuwarden, the daughter of a former burgomaster and well-known political leader, called Rombertus van Uijlenburgh. The girl was an orphan and said to be wealthy. After the death of her parents she had moved to Amsterdam. N.N. met the girl through a cousin of hers, one Hendrick van Uijlenburgh, who at that time was a dealer in antiques and who also acted as entrepreneur for fashionable painters. N.N. married the girl in June of the year

1634 and went to live with her in his house on the Breestraat which he had already begun to convert into a museum of old paintings, bits of statuary and fine silks and brocades.

After his wedding he added pearls and diamonds and other bits of jewelry to his collection. He is still said to have those. During his first ten years in Amsterdam he seems to have received an average of about 500 guilders for his portraits. In addition, he had the right to sell the work of his pupils which must have netted him between 2000 and 2500 guilders a year. We were unable to find out how much profit he derived from his etchings during this period. But the sum total of his usual annual income probably exceeded 10,000 guilders.

But already in the year 1638 he seems to have been in financial difficulties. That was the year he bought himself a new and larger house in the Breestraat, the one he occupies at present. This house, the second one from the bridge, cost 13,000 guilders. One-fourth was to be paid a

Rembrandt painting Hendrickje

year after taking possession and the rest at regular intervals within six years. Why he bought a house so above his position in life is not clear except that at that period he is said to have tried hard to come up to the social standards of his wife's family, an attempt which also made itself evident in his art, for every time he painted either himself or his wife, he evidently tried to make the world believe that he was a member of the Medici family of Florence, rather than the son of a humble miller in the town of Leiden. Even then, when he was willing to spend any amount of money upon old pictures or pieces of silver, he was unable to pay the installments on his house. Of those 40,000 guilders which according to local rumor his wife had inherited from her parents, he never seems to have received a penny, for he had to wait until his mother died in 1640, when he received as his share in her inheritance a sum of 2,490 florins, before he was able to offer the former owner any money at all.

Eventually he was able to pay off one half of the 13,000 guilders he owed on the house. Thereafter he seems to have forgotten about that for he did not even attempt to keep up with the accumulated interest which has been growing larger every year, until today the debt is 8,470.06 guilders, which is entirely beyond his present financial means. In the meantime he appears to have contracted debts on all sides. As all of them have been made with private persons, it is impossible for us to discover the actual amount involved. We do know that from his friend Jan Six, the linen weaver, he borrowed a thousand guilders which My Lord Jan seems to consider such a risky investment that he has recently offered the IOU for sale and, according to rumor on the Exchange, he is willing to accept anything at all.

Finally there are countless unpaid food bills, doctor bills, and money he owes to frame makers and dealers in art supplies and manufacturers of copperplates and printer's ink, and also small amounts borrowed from those unfortunate tradespeople.

In the meantime N.N. has lost favor with the public. He ruined his reputation with a picture of the company of Captain Banning Cocq which he painted in 1642. The members of that company were so outraged with the arrangement of the figures that several refused to pay him.

If said N.N. owes you any money, I would, as your banker, advise you to get hold of it as soon as possible. You had better take a few of his valuable antiquities if he is willing, but don't count on ever getting a stiver in cash. His reputation of having married a rich wife will perhaps carry him a little longer. But sooner or later his credit will reach its end and then there will be quite a scandal, for N.N. has nothing and he owes everybody. The conclusion of our investigation is as follows:

Assets: Heavily mortgaged house full of objects of art on which, however, it will be very difficult to realize at the present moment owing to the unfavorable economic conditions which are the result of the present war with England; very little goodwill and no cash or securities.

Liabilities: The total amount is unknown but they must be well over 30,000 guilders.

Credit standing of the person under discussion—0.

378

I slowly folded the paper and made ready to put it in my pocket. "I suppose I can keep this?" I asked Lodewijk.

"You can keep it, my friend. But please don't let it fall into the wrong hands. It is bad enough as it is. That poor painter's goose is about cooked."

Then he dropped the pen with which he had been busy figuring all that time and rubbed his hand across his bald head.

"Too bad," he said, as if he were speaking to himself. "Too bad. Poor devil! I suppose he sees certain things we don't happen to see and so he fails to notice certain other things which we ordinary human beings must have before our eyes all the time."

HERE OF COURSE the question arises, why didn't I help Rembrandt at that critical moment in his life? I was supposed to be his most intimate friend and I had inherited wealth.

Why didn't I tell Lodewijk, my banker, to take care of that ghastly list of creditors and thus give Rembrandt a chance to begin all over again and this time with a slate that could be kept reasonably clean?

Well, the answer is very simple. When the crash came for Rembrandt, I was absolutely helpless.

Notice announcing auction of Rembrandt's drawings and etchings—"The trustees of the insolvent property of Rembrandt van Rijn . . . will sell . . . the hereafter mentioned paper art . . . together with good part of the drawings and sketches of the same Rembrandt van Rijn himself . . . Pass it on."

If I could have put my hands on the money my uncle had left me, Rembrandt would never have gone bankrupt. But my money was invested in my new hospital. All I could do was to gain enough by my practice to keep my own family alive and slyly give an occasional couple of guilders to Hendrickje for her household expenses. Temporarily, at least, the bulk of my fortune was not at my disposal.

CHAPTER 14

I HAD ALREADY NOTICED THAT Hendrickje was pregnant. Soon afterwards others noticed it too and then the trouble began. Not among Rembrandt's friends. They understood why he could not marry the girl. Even the exceedingly respectable family of My Lord Jan Six showed themselves rather more broad-minded than I had had reason to expect. Of course they had never met Hendrickje and had made no move which showed that they recognized her existence. But they continued to be on cordial terms with her husband (for as such she now invariably referred to Rembrandt) and that was more than could be said of most people.

They were shocked. They disapproved. If this sort of thing were tolerated once, where would the world end?

And since most people consider their own prejudices as part of the divinely inspired laws of a well-ordered universe, the scandal on the Breestraat became the most popular subject for family discussions and tea-party gossip. Nor could an event of such enormity as the prospective arrival of an illegitimate infant in the household of a painter be allowed to pass unnoticed by the reverend clergy who were supposed to be watching day and night over the morals of our New Zion on the Zuider Zee.

Thus the details of the case of Rembrandt van Rijn and his housekeeper were brought to the attention of a certain dominie by the name of Zebediah Hazewindus, and soon every self-respecting disciple of John Calvin was ransacking his Old Testament for suitable texts with which to bolster up the case of God *vs.* the painter. What then happened was something of which the people of our country may well be ashamed till the end of their days.

It is unnecessary for me to go into the details of the affair. They are only too well known.

On a summer day of the year '54 the members of the Amsterdam council of churches, gathered together in a plenary session, decided that "since a certain Henrickje had now for a considerable space of time been living in open concubinage with a painter at his home, she therefore was to be ordered to appear before the consistory within eight days of the issuance of this summons and explain what excuse she could offer for so scandalous a conduct."

This message was delivered at Rembrandt's house one evening when he and Hendrickje were sitting on the stoop enjoying a little respite from the day's work. It was brought by the sexton of the West Church, who was well known to the neighbors.

Etching of the Crucifixion

The message was not known to them, but they could guess at its nature. And soon all through the streets the news had spread: "The painter and his woman will have to appear before the dominies; it serves them right!"

But about one small detail these good neighbors were mistaken. The neatly folded piece of paper bearing the seal of Amsterdam's church council did not mention the name of Rembrandt. When I called later in the evening and was shown the document and asked why he had not been summoned, together with Hendrickje, he could at first not give me any reason. Then it dawned upon him.

"I am not a member of the church," he said. "Years ago, I forget just when, I withdrew or resigned or whatever one does when one bids farewell to the church. I let the ministers know that I would not attend divine service any longer and would refuse to pay my church taxes in the future and would they please take my name off their register, and they answered that I could not do this unless I could offer proof that I had joined some other denomination. I talked it over with old Anslo, the

Mennonite preacher, whom I had known for years, and I asked him whether there would be any objections if I joined his own church. I told him I was not a very regular churchgoer and perhaps not even a very good Christian. He said the Mennonites did not believe in bothering people about their beliefs, and they would be glad to have me.

"So I joined the Mennonites. I liked to hear Anslo preach. He never told me how wicked I was, but did his best to show me how good I might be if only I tried just a little harder. He was a good man. I am glad I went to him. I would be doubly glad if it were not for Hendrickje."

The girl, who had been studying the paper in her hand, now looked up at us. "Yes," she said, rather dryly, "I have no doubt of that. But meanwhile, what shall I do?"

Without a word Rembrandt took the summons out of her hand and tore it up into a thousand bits. "Do nothing," he answered. "Do nothing and forget about it. The dominies can make themselves very disagreeable to us, but that is about all. They can't send a company of town guards to come and fetch you to make a public confession. You are safe—perfectly safe."

But although Rembrandt was right, and the dominies could not drag Hendrickje to their solemn conclave, they soon proved that they had other means of spiritual torture at their disposal.

A great Parisian lady might have snapped her fingers at such clerical meddlesomeness, but Hendrickje was a simple Dutch peasant girl from a simple village with all of the peasant's traditional regard for those standards of respectability which she had learned as a child. To be publicly cited to appear before the consistory of the big town of Amsterdam, accused of the dreadful sins of lechery and adultery, was as terrible to her as if she had been condemned to undress in the municipal market-place. And I noticed the effects of this ordeal when a week later she was presented with a second summons which did not even reach her hands, as Rembrandt jerked it from the fingers of the sexton and threw it in the gutter without opening the seal.

"Get away from here!" he shouted at the poor fellow. "Get away and stay away and don't bother my wife anymore. And let me paint my pictures!"

All of which was beside the point. After all, the consistory had not told Rembrandt that he must not paint pictures. It had told his housekeeper that she must not live with him in sin. And poor Hendrickje, in great distress, saw no other course than to obey their solemn command and present herself that she might confess her guilt and ask their forgiveness.

Exactly when she made her decision to appear before the consistory, I never found out, for she kept the fact hidden from Rembrandt. Then one afternoon she slipped out and when she returned, it was all over. She went right up to her room and to bed. In the middle of the night, Rembrandt sent Titus to ask me to please come at once. Hendrickje seemed to have a fever. Her mind was wandering. She talked of hellfire and of Satan, who was chasing her with a torch. Then she called for her mother, saying that she would be a good girl and that she had done it because the man had been so good to her. "He is good to me," she kept on crying.

Burgomaster Jan Six

I gave her some hot milk and put a cold poultice on her forehead, and after a short while she calmed down. In the morning she was cheerful, as if nothing had happened.

Three days later I discovered that, as punishment for her sinful way of living, she had been forbidden to partake of the Lord's Holy Communion.

That may have been good church discipline. But it was not the best thing in the world for a woman who was eight months pregnant, as we were to find out soon afterwards.

IN SEPTEMBER OF THE YEAR '54 the blow fell.

During the first week of that month I lost two patients. They had died while I was administering the usual vapors and the thing had been a great surprise to me as the operations for which they had come to the hospital were not of a serious sort. But they passed out after a few whiffs of the fumes and all efforts made to bring them back to life were in vain. Both were middle-aged women who had borne many children and were not in good physical condition.

News of this disaster soon became known all over town and those who had always disapproved of my methods were de-lighted. They had always predicted that something like that would happen. The authorities ought to close my so-called hospital. As for me, I ought to be forced to resign from the Surgeons' Guild. I had defied the will of God and now see what had come of it!

Within less than twenty-four hours I received an official document bearing the signature of one of the burgomasters. Three physicians of good repute were delegated to perform an autopsy upon my unfortunate patients and report to Their Lordships. They reported unanimously that death had probably been due to natural causes as both women seemed to have suffered from inflammation of the valves of the heart and that the administration of a pain-relieving agency could not be held responsible for the unfortunate outcome. This was good news for me but unfortunately Their Lordships did not deem it necessary to communicate the findings of their committee to the public, and all over town the murmurs continued about the surgeon who was in the habit of poisoning his patients.

That was Trouble Number One.

Trouble Number Two happened immediately afterwards.

Now that I had come to know Hendrickje a little more intimately, she was no longer as shy with me as she had been in the beginning and so she told me of her worries in connection with her coming confinement.

She spoke of the baby she had had before. It had died im-mediately after its birth and she had had a most dreadful time. Even now, whenever she thought of the pain, she shuddered with the memory of so great an agony. She fully expected that this time the child would have to be taken by force, and if that were the case, would I perform the operation?

I examined her and realized that she might be right in her

fears. She had an unusually narrow pelvis and the child was already very large. I promised I would do as she asked and suggested that she come to my own place, where I had plenty of room and could work much better than in the stuffy, built-in beds of the ordinary household. At first she hesitated. Simple people seem to think that there is something sacrilegious about children that are born outside their own homes.

But Rembrandt was greatly in favor of this arrangement, and during the first week of October Hendrickje came to the hospital.

Five days later she had her first pains. Her labor lasted three whole days. In the end she suffered so terribly she asked that she be killed and even tried to throw herself out of the window. On the fourth day, when it looked as if I would have to perform the Caesarian cut, she told me she could stand it no longer and asked me to give her some quick-working poison. Instead, I administered my vapors. She was so exhausted that she was still unconscious long after the midwife had washed and cleaned the infant (a girl it was, and in the end no operation

Anslo, the Mennonite preacher, with his wife

had proved necessary). She recovered very rapidly and a fortnight later she was back in the house on the Breestraat, looking handsome and happy and quite like her old cheerful self.

The child was baptized in the Old Church in late October. The minister must have received a hint from the Town Hall that further censorious remarks were considered out of place, for little Cornelia was duly registered as the daughter of Rembrandt van Rijn and Hendrickje Stoeffels and no embarrassing questions were asked.

But for me it was only the beginning of my trouble.

Hendrickje had been deeply grateful. So grateful, indeed, that she told the nurse who took care of her how good I had been to her and how I had saved her from further pain when she thought that she could no longer stand the ordeal. The nurse, a competent and well-meaning woman, but like all members of her guild an uncurable chatterbox, had told the neighbors.

"You know," she said, "Doctor Jan gave her something at the last moment and then she never felt any pain at all. Isn't that wonderful? Though of course, it is not quite what we read in the Scriptures."

And then the fat was in the fire.

A week later, the Reverend Zebediah Hazewindus preached his famous sermon on "Childbearing without God's curse." For had not Jehovah in the first book of the Old Testament condemned Eve to bear children in pain? Now the whole town knew about the scandalous proceedings that went on in the hospital of "this libertine and Arminian who pretended to be wiser than God."

Within a month, feeling ran so high that Hazewindus led a delegation of outraged citizens to the town council to ask for my immediate arrest and to suggest that my place of business be closed for all time.

I would rather not write about what followed, for in a way it was a sincere tribute to the confidence which Their Lordships placed in me personally. They told the parson they would hang him from the highest gallows at the disposal of the city of Amsterdam if he ever bothered them again in this matter, and had the bailiff kick him bodily out of the council chamber.

I hoped that now I would be left in peace to continue my experiments. But two days later, during the middle of the night, a mob of several hundred men and women suddenly broke into the hospital, carried the eighteen patients they found there out into the street and then set fire to the premises, disappearing as quickly as they had arrived. The building burned until the next afternoon. Of my invested capital nothing remained but four charred walls and a pile of smoldering beams.

I petitioned the magistrates and insisted upon an indemnity, my property having been destroyed as the result of a riot which they had failed to repress. After deliberating this item for seven whole years, they finally voted me about one-third of the sum I had asked. After another four years, they paid me half of what they had promised.

And that is how I lost the money with which I might have helped poor Rembrandt during those dreadful years of his bankruptcy.

CHAPTER 15

THE FIRST FEW WEEKS after the disaster, I was too busy to pay attention to anything that did not have to do with the removal of the burned bricks and charred wooden beams, which were deemed by the city authorities a menace to public safety. Meanwhile I went back to general practice to make a living, and I soon was in very difficult straits.

I had gradually fallen into the unfortunate habit of not charging anything for my services beyond a nominal sum, which in most instances was never paid. Suddenly I found myself obliged to turn a "calling" into a "profession," and I discovered that those same patients who had been delighted to accept my services for nothing, while I was fairly well-off, deeply resented my charging them a small fee when, through circumstances beyond my own control, I was obliged to work for a living.

Those same tradespeople with whom I had dealt uninterruptedly for the last twenty years no longer bowed so low nor smiled so broadly when I entered. Nor did they hasten to the door when I left, although my bundles might be heavier than formerly (as I now often was forced to buy my household necessities in bulk for greater cheapness). And it came as a shock when I was reminded of the more direct sides of minor business transactions by such remarks as: "We hope you don't mind if we ask you to pay us now, but you see, the war and the unsettled conditions nowadays . . ."

But there was one man (outside my circle of loyal personal friends) who during this crisis in my affairs showed deep understanding of my problems and, quite unexpectedly, offered a solution. That was My Lord Jan de Witt, the distant relative of my former sponsors, the Bicker family, who now ruled the republic as if he were its undisputed sovereign instead of merely a paid official of the Estates General.

One day I received a note asking me to call on My Lord Jan the next time I was in the The Hague. I made the trip, and after some preliminary discussion he came to the point.

"Our war with England will soon come to an end," he said. "We are neither of us getting anywhere. We will both of course try and get some advantages out of the peace negotiations, but it will be a stalemate. Then we will prepare for the next war. It seems absurd but I don't see how it can be helped. As long as we human beings still have so much in common with dogs who fight for every bone, we shall probably continue to build warships and quarrel for islands in India and rivers in America.

"Meanwhile the medical care of our sailors and marine soldiers has been scandalously neglected. I want to reorganize that whole department. Will you do this for me?"

The question left me dumbfounded. "But, My Lord Jan," I answered, "you know what has just happened to me?"

"I do," he said.

"And you understand the opposition there would be to such an appointment if you were kind enough to suggest it to Their Lordships of the Admiralties?"

"I have taken that in consideration."

"You know that all the clergy would denounce you for having made an alliance with a man who has sold his soul to the devil?"

My Lord Jan was a very quiet man—a soft-spoken man of terrific power but a power held absolutely under control. It was the first time I saw him angry and his anger manifested itself only in a slight twitching of his lower lip.

"As long as I have any influence in our republic," he answered, "those clerical gentlemen will keep their place. This is a country in which every man ought to be allowed to think as he pleases, within certain limits laid down by the law. We have had the Inquisition here once and we do not want it again.

"I have heard what happened in Amsterdam. I shall do all I can to see that you get justice and get reimbursed for the loss you have suffered. In the meantime, as a public vindication of yourself and as an expression of my belief in your integrity and the usefulness of your aims, I offer you this post of fleet medical adviser. The Admiralties, I am sure, will follow my suggestion. Will you accept?"

The offer came so unexpectedly that I did not know what to say. I asked His Lordship for the time to talk over my problem with some of my friends. He assented. There was no hurry. Nothing could be done anyway until the end of the war. And so I bade him farewell and took the night boat back to Amsterdam.

THE NEXT FOUR WEEKS I spent almost entirely on board ship. Not on board one of those war vessels with which I had been asked to associate my future fate, but on board the little sailing craft of Jean-Louys, who had become the most enthusiastic of amateur sailors. His French mate and cook and body servant, François, proved indeed a jewel. He could handle a boat in any weather and could present us with a four-course meal half an hour after we had arrived in some village of the Zuider Zee.

During the first five days we enjoyed the companionship of Rembrandt. He had not wanted to come but we thought a little change would do him good after the harrowing experience of his wife (we invariably referred to Hendrickje as his wife and he seemed to like that). And we told him he could bring all the sketchbooks he wanted and sit on deck all day long and draw.

Jean-Louys had even persuaded him to take along a dozen copperplates for the purpose of doing drypoints of sea gulls and distant bits of shoreline. But almost from the first he complained that his plates would show spots—that his needles would rust, and that the sea air would ruin his pens, so that he could not work. And after two days he began to grow restless.

"This is not for me," he complained. "This sort of existence is too soft and too easy. Another week and I will jump overboard and swim home."

We argued that the lovely little cities along the Zuider Zee would provide him with an unlimited number of subjects for landscapes and seascapes. But he remained obstinate.

"I appreciate your hospitality," he told Jean-Louys. "But I can't work in this light. No more than I can work on really dry land, where there are forests and open sandy spaces covered with heather. I tried it once, but the light was too dry. Just as here the light is too wet. I need the sort of light that is neither too wet nor too dry. I would call it suspended light, but that expression can hardly tell you what I mean. And I don't quite know myself, except that we have got that particular light in Amsterdam. I suppose because the town is nothing but a stone pancake afloat on a sea of mud. Everything in my workshop is bathed in that light. It does something to the shadows, too. Here the shadows are too hazy. On land far away from the sea they were too abrupt, too severe, and that is no fun for me— any ordinary painter can paint that sort of shadows. But the shadows at home have a lucid quality, a little velvety as if they had been mixed with oil. They look as different from ordinary shadows as wet clay looks from sandy soil.

"I suppose I am talking nonsense, but as soon as we get to Monnikendam I hope you will set me ashore and let me peacefully walk home."

Jean-Louys did more than that. He returned to Amsterdam and landed Rembrandt almost within a stone's throw of his own house.

His homecoming was not very happy. Two sheriffs were waiting for him with an order for his arrest unless a bill which he had owed his frame maker for almost five years was immediately settled. Hendrickje had gone out and pawned one of Saskia's famous pearl earrings and the sheriffs had been satisfied and had gone their way.

But all this we did not learn until we returned to Amsterdam several weeks later. In the meantime we had gone as far north as Medemblik and as far east as Blokzijl and we had talked of everything under the sun, including the question: Should I accept My Lord de Witt's offer?

As soon as we returned I wrote His Lordship telling him that while I did not want to abandon my Amsterdam practice completely, I would be delighted to come to The Hague whenever he wanted me and act as his adviser in matters pertaining to the medical care of the fleet. His Lordship most kindly agreed to this arrangement.

MEANWHILE LITTLE TITUS, Rembrandt's son, had grown up to be a boy of almost fifteen and my own offspring was also approaching that age when a father asks himself: What in the name of high Heaven am I going to do with that boy?

Titus, I am sorry to say, was causing Rembrandt more worry than my own boy was causing me. The poor lad had inherited his father's face but his mother's delicacy of physique—her beautiful hands—her slender bones, but also her weak lungs and general lack of resistance. If only it had been the other way around! For his father had the strength of a cart horse, but the face of a good, honest blacksmith or carpenter, without the charm and vivaciousness that had belonged to his aristocratic wife.

The boy undoubtedly possessed a talent for painting but it was very slight. He gave the impression of being an amiable, rather tender boy with excellent manners (the work of Hendrickje, though where she had learned them herself I never was able to fathom) and the best of intentions, but lacking force or stamina. I asked his father what he intended to do with him and Rembrandt, in that vague way in which he dismissed all subjects that had not some direct bearing upon his work, answered: "Oh, well, I suppose he will become an artist."

But how was that innocent and rather incompetent child to survive in a world that had been turned completely upside down now that the war had ended, and ended in stalemate, just as My Lord de Witt had predicted. The Peace of Westminster had destroyed all the old values and most of the old fortunes of those merchants who had ruled our country for so long. Either their ships had been destroyed by the English or they had speculated in wood or gunpowder when they should have concentrated on hemp. Meanwhile younger, less conservative, and much less scrupulous firms had grabbed all the right profits at the right moment and had made millions. They were now buying up the town houses and country houses of those who had guessed wrong, and their taste in furniture and art and music was as bad as their manners.

How mild little Titus, with his mild little portraits (they were a very weak and therefore bad reflection of those of his father), would ever be able to sell one of his works to the bar-

barians of the new era I could not quite see. But the boy was still very young and might decide to do something different when he reached the age of discretion.

As for my own son, he never caused me any trouble. He seemed to have inherited absolutely nothing from his mother or me, or for that matter from his grandparents. Instead, he jumped right back to his great-grandfather, my own beloved grandfather, and I rejoiced to see all his independence and enthusiasm and efficiency return in my own flesh and blood.

He wanted to make things. And he wanted to make them not only with his brains but also with his hands, for he had fingers that were as strong as steel nippers and he liked to use them. From childhood on he had been busy with windmills and toy carriages and miniature dredges. And by this time he was beginning to revaluate his practical engineering experiments into abstract mathematical formulas—formulas which meant nothing at all to me but which he explained to me as representing wind velocities and the friction of wood upon wood and of stone upon stone. Where he had learned all this I was never able to find out.

Poor Rembrandt! I was sorry for him when on Sundays, as sometimes happened, we took our boys out for a walk. Titus was usually bored, would want to go back home and color his pictures or look at a book. After a time he would sit down and weep, for he really was not strong and got exhausted very easily.

Meanwhile my own young barbarian would occupy himself with some mechanical contrivance he had put together during the previous week—would try it out on the waters of the Amstel where the winds blew ever fresh, would talk of the day when mills would not only pump water and grind flour and saw wood but would also peel rice and make oil and perform Heaven knows what other miracles.

Then Titus would look at him and would say, "I hate mills. They are ugly."

And the answer would be: "But have you ever heard the regular *swish-swish* of a mill that is running full speed? Could anything be more wonderful or more beautiful than that? And besides, mills are useful. Useful things are never ugly."

As for Rembrandt, he would listen to this chatter, but it never seemed to penetrate to him. "They are young," he used to comment. "They will grow out of it, both of them."

But I had my doubts.

Does anyone ever really grow out of something that was put into him even before the day of his birth?

CHAPTER 16

FOR THE LAST EIGHT YEARS we had been building a new Town Hall. Jacob van Campen had been ordered to draw up plans for a civic center as soon as our independence had been recognized. The old Town Hall was considered too shabby for a city of such magnificence as ours. Besides, the building was now too small and no one felt sorry when it burned down during July of '52.

What had interested me most had been the plans for the interior decorating of our magistrates' new quarters. There were to be a great many pictures and who was better fitted for such a task than Rembrandt? He could handle the most complicated subjects superbly and size and shape of the canvas meant nothing to him provided he was interested in the subject. Accordingly I had made it a point to speak to everyone who might have some influence with the authorities. And many of those I approached had answered, "Yes, that is a good idea." And they had promised they would do their best to give my friend at least a few of the orders that were to be placed among the local painters.

But when I happened to meet them again, they were always full of excuses. They had mentioned his name, but the roof was not quite ready. It was impossible to judge of the light effects. It would be impossible to make a decision.

Meanwhile I learned that Bol and Flinck and Jan Lievens and several others were busy on portraits and allegorical works that were to find a place in the new edifice. I knew Flinck and Bol from the days they had been Rembrandt's pupils and I went to see them. They were quite loyal to their former teacher and wished they could be of help to him. But both agreed it would be suicidal for them to agitate on his behalf in any way that might be constructed as a personal interference with the plans of Their Lordships.

"Even now," Bol told me frankly, "we may be replaced by some Fleming who paints more in the Rubens manner than we do. Rubens is the great man now. He and Jacob Jordaens are our heroes. Rembrandt? Why, he is either too dark or too muddy or too something to please our public. Both Flinck and I and practically all the men that studied with our old master have been obliged to change our technique, to become a little more Flemish, more Rubenesque—if you understand me—to keep our customers. Otherwise we would now be starving to death. If you don't believe me, go to any of the art dealers and ask them whether they will take a chance on Rembrandt. Yes, here and there a man who sells

Old Town Hall after fire of 1652

to the Italian trade. Perhaps because there is so much sunshine in Italy that they can stand something a little dull better than we. But the others? They won't touch him. And if we suggested the name of Rembrandt to Their Lordships, they would show us the door and ask us to mind our own business."

I knew they were right, but refused to give up. During these years I was busy with my duties as fleet medical adviser (and some of the measures I had been permitted to suggest were being tried with considerable success on board our ships). In connection with this work, I often consulted with My Lord de Witt, and the next time I was in The Hague, I mentioned Rembrandt and the new Town Hall to His Lordship.

"I don't know much about such matters," he confessed, "and the Lord have mercy on my soul if ever I dared to make a suggestion concerning anything that had to do with the purely domestic affairs of that very independent city of Amsterdam. If it should be rumored that I was in favor of yellow curtains, Their Lordships would at once order every curtain in the whole place to be dyed a bright green. No, I dare not interfere in any way, but I will give you a letter to my uncle. He is a man of sense and a man of taste and not without influence in his own country."

This was expressing it mildly. Everyone knew that nothing could be accomplished in Amsterdam without the silent approbation of Cornelis de Graeff, the famous Lord of Polsbroek, who was known as the uncrowned king of Amsterdam and as one of the strongest men in the republic.

But in the matter of art, I found His Lordship was about as helpless as his nephew. "Ask me something else," he said, throwing his hands up in a gesture of despair. "Ask me something easy like declaring war upon the Emperor or making the East India Company publish a true account of their last year's budget. Ask to have the Amstel diverted into the North Sea instead of the Zuider Zee. But don't ask me to risk my position and my prestige in a matter of this sort."

I looked at him dumbfounded. Here was My Lord of Polsbroek, without whose permission (as the people used to say) it could not even rain in Amsterdam, confessing to me, a poor leech, that he could not order a few pictures for his new Town Hall from the greatest painter alive. I asked politely what political considerations could oblige him to give me such a disappointing answer.

"Politics be damned," he burst forth. "I will appoint any man to any place I please as long as it is a matter of politics, but this is not politics. This is a matter of religion—of theology—of the one thing I have vowed I would keep clear of."

"But surely," I answered, "Your Lordship need not ask Rembrandt to paint an allegorical picture that could possibly shock the pious. He is most excellent at portraits. You must need a great many portraits for the new Town Hall."

"My dear Doctor," he said, "you may think that we are almighty at the Town Hall, that we can do as we please. We can to a certain extent but we have to proceed very carefully. After all, there are windowpanes in our houses and it costs a lot to replace them. The clergy still has a hold upon the masses that we philosophers are a little too apt to overlook. And numbers count, especially in a city like this. What would the 'small people' say if I suggested giving a commission for an official portrait to a man who lives in open sin with his maidservant? The dominies would pound their pulpits and would start their usual fulminations against the new Sodom and would preach sermons about the whore of Babylon and it might end in bloodshed.

"And if it further became known that you, of all people, suggested this to me! You—a mere surgeon who tried to cheat Jehovah out of his allotted measure of pain—you, an iconoclast who tried to set woman free from one of her most disastrous burdens. Why, we would have to turn the whole city into an armed camp if I so much as suggested the name of this man van Rijn for a single piece of work. I would like to oblige you. I will give orders that the new Town Hall be burned down if that pleases you. But as for giving an order to van Rijn, no, that I can't do."

I saw his point, thanked him for his courtesy, and departed.

The new Town Hall was inaugurated with many ceremonies. I spent the day quietly at home and in the evening went to Rembrandt's house and helped him polish some plates, for he was in the midst of one of his attacks of etching when he was apt to work twenty hours a day.

But ere I finish this chapter, I must run ahead a few years and tell of something that happened much later.

IN FEBRUARY OF 1660 Govaert Flinck, who was still working on the decoration of the big gallery in the Town Hall, died. He had been sick for a long time and it was known that he would not be able to finish the work he had begun. Just then my old friend, Doctor Tulp, was treasurer of Amsterdam. He had achieved much greater honors in the world than I and was one of the most respected burghers of our town. But we had always remained on a pleasant and cordial footing and I knew that he admired Rembrandt, who had painted his picture twenty-odd years before.

Since then, Tulp had never again met Rembrandt, and the last time he had had his portrait painted he had had it done by a foreign artist. Nevertheless I decided to say a word for Rembrandt and, as the Town Hall was no longer a novelty and no one paid much attention to it except those who went there on business, and its decorations were no longer in the public and in the clerical eyes, the excellent Tulp complied with my wishes and Rembrandt was told to continue the work which his own pupil had been unable to finish.

It was to be an historical picture representing the great Batavian hero, Claudius Civilis, who for a short period of years had freed our country from Roman rule. This of course had happened a long time ago and no one knew exactly where or under what circumstances, but every well-behaved child could reel off the important dates: "100 B.C. the Romans arrived in our country and 50 B.C. Claudius Civilis set our country free from the Roman yoke."

Rembrandt showed less enthusiasm than I had expected. This order was what he called "mustard that comes after the meal," and true enough, it was not very flattering for him to be called in as a sort of stopgap.

But once he had started, his enthusiasm grew by leaps and bounds. He decided that, since this was to show a conspiracy against the conquerors, the scene must be laid at night and in the dark, when the Romans were supposed to have gone to bed. He chose an enormous canvas, almost sixty feet square, the largest he had ever handled, and he made the Batavian rebel the center of a festive meal, during which he explains his plans for the uprising to his followers.

The problem of having the entire scene bathed in the light of a few small oil lamps fascinated him. He spent months on it and produced something so weird and mysterious that it made me feel queer to look at it. The figure of the one-eyed Civilis dominated the scene. The sword in his hand glistened ominously.

THE BATAVIANS' OATH TO CLAUDIUS CIVILIS (1661–1662)

I expected great things of this work of art and eagerly awaited the day when it should be hung in its place.

Rembrandt was to get only a thousand florins for the whole picture (no more than Flinck would have received), but I was sure it would cause so much talk that he would be completely rehabilitated in the eyes of his neighbors and, what was even more important, in the eyes of the art dealers.

But the magistrates rejected it. They rejected it flatly and unceremoniously. Some said that Claudius Civilis looked too much like Hannibal. Although the Carthaginian hero also had lost one eye in battle, this complaint really had very little to do with the picture as a work of art. Others said it was too dark. Still others complained that no one ever had seen a lamp that threw such shadows.

The painting was never hung in the big gallery. It was removed to the attic to be stored away until some future date when Their Lordships should decide what else they could do with this monstrous canvas that was by far too large for any ordinary room and much too beautiful for ordinary people. I heard that it was cut into four pieces and sold to a junk dealer.

Just about a year ago I happened to have a patient who had been on a voyage to Sweden. He told me that in Stockholm he had seen a picture that looked very much like a sketch that was hanging on my wall. The sketch in question was a small pen-and-ink study for the Claudius Civilis which years before I had fished out of Rembrandt's fireplace (fortunately it was summer), into which he had thrown it in a moment of despair. I asked the young man how large the picture was and he answered, "About half of the wall of your room."

Then I begged him to describe it to me a little more in detail and I recognized the central part of the Civilis picture.

But it may have been merely a copy. Or the young man was mistaken. For although I wrote to Stockholm and for years afterwards interviewed everyone who returned from the Swedish capital, I never could discover another trace of this lost masterpiece.

The open space in the gallery left behind by the death of Flinck was filled in by some local talent whose name I have forgotten. And Rembrandt was obliged to split his fee with this young man, as it did not seem fair to Their Lordships that a man should be paid for work he had not really done.

CHAPTER 17

IT IS CURIOUS how one loses track of time when at sea. Besides, my inspection trips to our naval squadrons patrolling the Baltic to keep Dutch trade routes open took place so irregularly that I have no clear recollection of any of them. They have become one vast blur upon my memory—a blur composed of uncomfortable berths in uncomfortable cabins—of miserable hours of wetness and depression in some small boat that was being rowed to the flagship—of quarrels with obstinate ship's surgeons—of long, placid sails along the flat coasts of northern Germany and Denmark and of sick and wounded people who hated to die and whom one could not possibly save for lack of even the most elementary sanitary precautions.

Here and there in this blur is a short breathing space, a week or perhaps a fortnight on shore. During one of these periods, after a hard day's work preparing a report for My Lord de Witt, I decided to walk around the corner to Rembrandt's house.

As soon as I entered, I knew something was wrong. Two strange hats were lying on the table in the entrance and I heard unfamiliar voices coming from upstairs. I went into the living room where I found Hendrickje busy putting little Cornelia to bed. She asked me to wait for her in the little garden by the side of the house.

"We have had a terrible day," was the first thing she said when she joined me. "I am very tired. If you don't mind, I will sit down with you for a moment." For though we all liked her sincerely and treated her in every way as if she were really Rembrandt's wife, she could not get over a certain shyness in our company.

"What has happened?" I asked her.

"Oh, just the usual thing. People with bills. Grocers and bakers and the butcher. Then more people with bills. Paint dealers, moneylenders. I don't know them all by name but it was pretty awful."

Just then Rembrandt appeared in the doorway. "I got rid of those two," he said. "I wonder how many more there will be today? When they once begin to come, they go on the whole day. Is there any gin left? I shall have to work all night to make up for these interruptions."

Hendrickje got the gin. Rembrandt took two glasses.

"Such days are terrible," he said. "I have just started two new pictures and those fools come and talk to me about money! Well, I have not got any. That is simple enough, isn't it?"

There was a knock on the door.

"Don't open," Rembrandt told Hendrickje, who had got up. "Don't let them in. They will go away soon enough."

"But then they will be back early tomorrow morning."

"Meantime I shall have been able to do a whole night's work."

"What are you doing now?" I asked him.

"Mostly oil. I am doing one etching, a portrait of Jan Lutma, the goldsmith. His family ordered it. But there are not many portraits ordered these days. And so I paint Biblical pictures. When I do that my models can't talk back. If I want to put Joseph here and Potiphar there, they don't say, 'Ah, sir, but we would rather face the other way around.' They stay where I put them and when Jacob blesses the little children no one is going to tell me what color the counterpane of his bed should have. Meanwhile these people out there seem to have given up hope. At least, they have stopped knocking," and he poured himself another gin.

"A lovely day," I said, to say something.

But this merely angered him. "A lovely day indeed! Yes, the sun is shining, I believe, but if you had had my sort of a day—"

"What has happened?"

"Oh, the old story. It is about the inheritance."

And then I understood. It was the question which had been mentioned in Lodewijk's report. The uncles and aunts of young Titus had asked for an accounting and Rembrandt had put their letters aside and not even taken the trouble to answer them. Thereupon

A goldsmith working in his shop

they had insisted upon a public inspection of his books (as if the poor man had ever heard of such a thing as bookkeeping!) and now they had threatened him with court proceedings. They had hinted that they would ask the Board of Orphans to attach the house in the Breestraat and sell its contents at public auction that Titus might receive his legal share of his mother's inheritance.

I wish that I had been in town when that had happened, for he might have come to me and I could at least have sent him to a reliable advocate for advice. But Rembrandt, confused and panic-stricken, had asked the first person who happened to come to his studio to give him the name of a lawyer—"any lawyer will do"—and that person happened to be an art dealer of rather doubtful reputation who had called on him in the hope of selling him a spurious Michelangelo.

And he had sent Rembrandt to a shyster. This fellow probably knew that the situation was hopeless but, in order to keep his hands on at least part of his client's tangible assets, he suggested that Rembrandt have his house on the Breestraat transferred officially to Titus, as part of the boy's maternal inheritance.

The meaning of this move should have been clear to anyone not quite as inexperienced in such matters as Rembrandt. It was an attempt to placate the Uijlenburgh relatives by swindling the other creditors. But of course in order to make this transfer official, the deed of transfer had to be attested before the Board of Orphans, an institute known for its severity and its scrupulous honesty.

They had asked no questions, assuming that no one would dare appear before them and ask them blandly to register a house as "orphan's good" when said house actually belonged to a syndicate of creditors. But these worthy gentlemen were mistaken. Rembrandt, totally ignorant of business methods, had not even bothered to tell them

Jan Lutma, the goldsmith

that the house was heavily mortgaged. The transfer was made and next morning of course the creditors knew what had happened.

The two hats I had seen in the hall belonged to two of the main creditors. They had insisted upon being received. They had called Rembrandt a swindler, and had asked that the deed giving Titus his father's house as part of his mother's inheritance be revoked within twenty-four hours. Unless he gave them his written promise to this effect then and there, they would serve papers in bankruptcy on him before the end of the day.

Rembrandt had listened to them vaguely and then requested

to be excused for a moment. He had wanted to ask Hendrickje what he should do. But the door of the studio had been open and it was still light. Just when he passed that open door he noticed something he had for a long time wanted to change in the colored turban of Potiphar. He had picked up a brush to make this small correction. Then he had forgotten all about his visitors and continued to work until the loud slamming of the front door suddenly reminded him of the reason he had come upstairs.

At first he had felt rather ashamed of his rudeness, but by the time I saw him his annoyance had made place for merriment.

"Served them right," he said, "for disturbing me. And now they will probably leave me alone."

But at that moment there was another knock at the front door, a knock that sounded official and refused to be denied.

"I will open," Hendrickje said.

"You had better," I added.

"Oh, very well," was all that Rembrandt remarked.

A moment later Hendrickje returned. She was followed by a little man wearing a long brown cloak and looking for all the world like an undertaker's assistant.

"Have I the honor to address Mr. Rembrandt van Rijn?" he asked.

"Never mind the honor," Rembrandt answered roughly. "What do you want?"

"Nothing, except to give you this."

Rembrandt took the large yellow envelope which the undertaker's assistant handed him. "What is this?" he asked.

"An order in bankruptcy," the brown beadle answered.

"Oh," said Rembrandt. "Well, I suppose you can't help it."

"I can't, sir! It happens to be my business."

A moment later we heard him slam the door and all was quiet until the chimes of the South Church began to play the hour.

"What time is it?" Rembrandt asked. "It stays light so late these days."

"Ten o'clock," I answered, counting the strokes.

"Then I had better go back to my studio. I suppose I am in for a hard time. Well, I am young still. I painted myself into these difficulties. Now I will have to paint myself out of them."

But he never did. From that day on until the hour of his death, he remained an "undischarged bankrupt."

THE NEXT DAY HALF A DOZEN OF US, all good friends of Rembrandt, gathered at his house. We knew that all efforts to save this sinking ship would be useless. The question before us was how we could transfer the passengers of the doomed vessel to another one with as little delay as possible.

They could not remain in the house for they were not allowed to touch a thing and the officials of the Bankruptcy Court could come at any moment to make an inventory of the furniture and the paintings. After that they would not even be allowed to sleep in their own beds. I offered Hendrickje and little Cornelia the hospitality of my own house. They could have my room and Titus could share my son's room. The others agreed that this would be a good plan.

That left Rembrandt on our hands. We had to find quarters for him, for, left to his own devices, God only knew what he would do. He kept walking aimlessly through the house—picking up one piece of his collection after another—holding it in both hands and looking at it for a long time as if he were saying good-by to it. We had to take care of him as if he were a small boy, whereas Titus, to whom none of us had ever paid much attention, now stepped forward as if he were a full-grown man, sent for the baker, the grocer, and the vegetable man, explained the situation to them as briefly as possible, and made arrangements through which his father obtained at least a few days' further credit.

Then Abraham Francen, the art dealer, said: "There is a hotel called the Keyserskroon that is not too expensive. It is a large place. It used to be an orphan asylum. If all this has to be sold" (and he waved his hands around him) "the auction could be held right there, and meanwhile Rembrandt could live there."

I interrupted him. "Wouldn't it hurt him terribly to be present when all this is sold?"

But Francen was less sentimentally inclined than I. "Undoubtedly," he answered, "but just now it is not so much a question of how to save his feelings as how to save his family. If he is present, the dealers won't dare to offer as little as if they knew that he wasn't there."

We could all see the reasonableness of Francen's point. And I offered to tell Rembrandt what plans we had made.

I found him in his studio cleaning his palettes. "I don't suppose these belong to me anymore," he said. "But I can hardly let them go to ruin. They have been very faithful servants."

I assured him that no one, not even the most strict-minded notary, could object to his keeping his tools in order, and then I told him what we had decided for him and his family. He listened, carefully scraping the paint off his large round palette.

"When ought we to leave?" he asked.

"Oh, there is no hurry. Sometime within a week or ten days."

"Then why not today? It is hard to stay here."

"Very well," I replied. "I will ask Hendrickje."

I found her in Cornelia's room, packing. She was quiet and self-possessed. "It really does not mean so much to me," she explained. "I have always been poor and, to tell you the truth, all this luxury was just a little too much for me. But his heart is in these things. I hope it won't kill him."

I told her he came of a strong race and could stand a blow better than most people. Then I went back to the meeting and reported what we had decided. The others went home, but the poet Jeremias de Dekker and I remained. I sent Titus to ask a carpenter for the loan of one of his assistants and a cart and had the fellow take Hendrickje's belongings and Titus's small trunk and Cornelia's cradle to my house. I told de Dekker to go with them to see them safely there. Then I went upstairs and helped Rembrandt put a few clothes, shoes, shirts, sheets and blankets in a small leather portmanteau.

When this had been done, he returned to the studio. "I don't suppose I can take any of these things," he said.

I told him that I was afraid that could not be done.

He picked up a large surgeon's needle, which I had used for small operations until it had got too blunt, when I had given it to Rembrandt who was forever complaining that he could not get a piece of steel that was really fit for drypoint work. He held it out to me and asked: "You gave this to me, didn't you?"

"No," I replied. "I merely loaned it to you."

"Then it still belongs to you?"

"It most certainly does!"

"And you will let me borrow it a little longer?"

"With great pleasure."

He rummaged among leftovers of old tubes and old brushes on a small table in the corner until he produced an old cork. "I will just cheat the creditors out of the cork," he said, putting it on top of the steel needle, so as not to hurt the point, "and out of the copperplate. They won't notice the difference, and if they do, well, then, they can put me in jail for it. But I have to have something to make me pull through the next few weeks." And he slipped the needle and the copperplate into his pocket.

I picked up his satchel and carried it downstairs. There was a knock at the door. I opened. Two men in black capes, standing on the stoop, announced they were from the Bankruptcy Court, come to make an inventory.

"Isn't that rather soon?" I asked them.

"Yes," said one, "but some of the creditors are afraid that if we are not quick, part of these belongings might disappear."

Rembrandt was standing right behind me. It was impossible that he should not have heard that last remark. I saw him take the small copperplate out of his pocket.

"You were right," he said, "I was on the point of stealing this. You had better take it."

But the official shook his head. "I know how you feel, sir," he answered, with more consideration than I had expected. "But cheer up. You are a famous man. A few years from now you will come back here riding in your own coach and four."

And he saluted the master most politely while he took a piece of paper and pencil out of his pocket and with a short, "I am sure you will pardon me," began to jot down: "The entrance hall: one picture by—who is it?—one picture by Adriaen Brouwer representing . . ."

I quietly took Rembrandt's arm and pushed him toward the door. Rembrandt never entered his house again.

Two years later it was sold to a shoemaker who turned it into two small apartments. One of these he kept for himself and the other he rented to a butcher. For all I know, they are there yet. But I am not certain, for I have not set foot in the Breestraat for more than ten years. One should not spend too much time among dead memories. The living need us so much more.

CHAPTER 18

THE GREATER PART OF the year '57 I spent with the fleet in different parts of the North Sea and the Baltic. My son proved an erratic but trustful correspondent. His letters kept me informed of what was happening to my own family and to that of our friend.

Hendrickje was still living at the Houtgracht. I had been afraid that my own faithful Jantje might have felt jealous of her. But Hendrickje was so unassuming and Jantje, a good soul, became so devoted to the small bundle of clothes and smiles called Cornelia that the two women lived peacefully beneath the same roof.

As for the two boys, they were so absolutely different that it was easy for them to remain on friendly terms. Titus stuck to his paint box. And my own son stuck to his mills and his calculations and they met at meals and sometimes they took a walk together, but for the rest they left each other severely alone and caused very little trouble to their elders.

Rembrandt's position was more difficult. He had a good enough room in the Keyserskroon but he was lonely and complained that he could not work. He locked himself in his room for days at a time—drinking a great deal more than was good for him and alternately spending entire days in bed or working at his etchings with such uninterrupted violence that he was experiencing trouble with his eyesight.

Fortunately the next letter brought better news.

Rembrandt had left his hotel and would not return there until time for the sale of his furniture and his art treasures. He had accepted an offer I had made in a recent letter, to come and live in my study, and was painting again. As soon as he had once

more felt a brush in his hand, he had stopped drinking gin. But he complained that he was not feeling quite well and he was worried about the sale of his belongings. At least once a week he would send Titus or my son to the office of the Bankruptcy Court to ask when the sale would begin and invariably he got the answer: "Not yet. A few weeks more. Times are bad. We must wait until the war is a little further behind us and then we shall get better prices."

And he had to wait all this time in miserable uncertainty, for his only escape was by means of that sale. If it brought enough, he would be able to pay his creditors and would be discharged by the court. But if it did not produce enough, he would continue to be a bankrupt and every portrait he painted and every etching he made would belong to his creditors.

Finally, in the fall of '57, the commissioner appointed Thomas Jacobszoon Haringh to start the sale as soon as convenient. Rembrandt moved back to the Keyserskroon and waited. But the first bids showed that the public had not yet recovered from the ravages of the recent conflict, and after a week, Haringh, who was a friend of Rembrandt's, went to the commissioners and suggested that the bulk of the articles be reserved until next year when there would be a chance of them selling at double and triple the amount they brought now.

The commissioners acceded and the paintings, drawings and etchings which Rembrandt had collected with such great care went back to the storehouse. Meanwhile the creditors devised innumerable little tricks that should put them on the preferred list. And Rembrandt asked Jantje not to open the door unless she had first made certain that the caller was a personal friend and did not belong to the dunning guild.

In the spring of '58, I returned to Amsterdam and found my house occupied by a happy little family, Rembrandt painting and Hendrickje busy with Cornelia and my son working on a project for a sailing carriage that would be able to navigate against the wind, and Titus coloring pretty little pictures which unfortunately did not show a great deal of originality.

We let the boys sleep in the attic (a change which delighted them) and I took their room. Next day after dinner I had a long talk with Rembrandt and listened to his complaints. For that interminable year of enforced idleness and waiting had done him little good, and when he first opened his heart to me, it seemed as if he were suffering from every disease ever known to Galen or Hippocrates. His head ached. A million little ants were crawling up and down his arms. His fingers tingled as if they had been frozen. When he sat still for ten minutes, his feet would fall asleep. He had pains in his back and in his chest and was sure he was going to die of the same disease that had taken Saskia to her grave.

I soon realized that nothing was the matter with the poor patient except a too sedentary life—too much loneliness. I could only pray that his profound melancholic moods would not drive him to suicide. I watched him very carefully. I accompanied him whenever he went out for a walk or sent my son to go with him. In the beginning I also suggested that he join Jean-Louys when the latter went forth again upon one of his sailing expeditions, but I soon had to give this up as Rembrandt detested life on board ship as much as he always had.

Jean-Louys, on the other hand, declared that he had never quite understood why he had been born until he had been initiated into the secrets of navigation. As for me I divided my Sundays between walks along the Amstel and trips on the Zuider Zee and meanwhile I waited and Rembrandt waited and Hendrickje waited until finally in the fall of '58, exactly two years after he had been declared a bankrupt, the last chest and the last picture and the last etching press and the last chairs were auctioned off and were removed from the Keyserskroon by their new owners.

Then the bookkeepers of the Bankruptcy Court got busy and a few weeks later we were able to compare figures. According to Rembrandt (a most unreliable guide in matters pertaining to finance) he had spent between 30,000 and 35,000 guilders to buy all these treasures. According to the court officials (who as a rule are conservative in such matters) the sale ought to have produced approximately 13,000 guilders, which would have been enough to satisfy the most clamorous creditors and give Rembrandt a chance to begin again without obligations. And

according to the balance sheet that was produced after everything had been sacrificed, he had realized a trifle less than 5,000
guilders or about one-seventh of his original investment.

The house had fared a little better. The shoemaker who
bought it paid 11,000 guilders for it. And of these 11,000 guilders
Titus's relatives (after a terrific legal battle) salvaged 7,000
guilders for their young nephew, who now had a regular
guardian (a certain Jan Verbout, a very decent fellow, by
profession and inclination a clerk). And throughout all this,
Titus himself remained pathetically loyal to the man who
according to his mother's relatives was a spendthrift and good-
for-nothing paint slinger, but according to himself, the best and
kindest father that any boy had ever had.

THE SITUATION, instead of having been improved by this painful
sacrifice, had become considerably worse. The creditors still
besieged my house to see whether Rembrandt had perhaps
painted another picture which they could attach and claim as
their own. I knew two members of the Bankruptcy Court and
went to see them and I found that they understood and even
sympathized with our position but it was impossible for them
to suggest a way out.

Rembrandt, a man who could see things no other human
being had ever suspected, had been cast out. And he would
never (of that I felt convinced) be able to rehabilitate himself
in the eyes of respectable society.

The problem that faced us who loved him in spite of his
many failings (and perhaps a little on account of them) was this:
How could we make the rest of his days tolerably happy? And
then, when none of us seemed to know quite what to do, it
was the faithful Hendrickje who showed us the way out.

She was not at all well. Adversity had struck her a terrible
blow and she was failing fast. Rembrandt thought he was a very
sick man and on the point of dying; he was forever telling Hendrickje what she ought to do for Titus and little Cornelia when
he should be gone, but I knew that he would survive her for a
long time, while she, who never complained, had only a few
more years to live.

I think she realized this herself but she was a woman of incredible courage. She cooked for Rembrandt and Titus, refusing to let my own Jantje do this for her. She repaired their clothes, knitted their stockings, kept track of every cent that came into the house and somehow managed to hide these few poor pennies from the ever present creditors.

And then one evening she asked whether she could speak to me alone. As it was a pleasant night in June, I took her out into the garden and there she told me what she wanted to do.

"That poor man," she said, "is blind when it comes to money. His mind is on other things. It makes me uncomfortable to think how we are abusing your hospitality, but for the rest I have never been as happy as I am right now. I never really was happy in that big house. It was too grand and too rich for me. Only, I know that as soon as Rembrandt gets discharged by the court he will go right back to buying things. Not because he wants them—it is so hard to explain this. The things themselves mean nothing to him. But they seem to fill a gap somewhere—they are bits of upholstery for his mind—and when it comes to his work, he is in some ways the strangest man I ever knew and some ways the weakest.

"Now I have been thinking: Suppose Titus and I started a little art store of our own and hired Rembrandt to work for us—paid him just as a carpenter pays the assistants he hires. One of my brothers is a mason and hires two men to help him and one of those once had trouble with his wife who tried to attach his wages but the judge said she could not do it. That is how I happened to think of it.

"Of course, Titus is very young and I don't know anything about pictures, but you could help me or Francen or some other friends. I wish you would think of it and perhaps ask a lawyer about it. Then we could once more have a place of our own, for we have inconvenienced you quite long enough."

I took both her hands and assured her she could stay until the end of her days and at the same time I was deeply touched by the kindness of her heart, her loyalty and also, I might as well confess it, by the common sense of her suggestion.

The next day being Sunday, I asked Rembrandt to take a

walk with me. We sat by the side of a canal and I delivered myself of a short, carefully prepared speech. I knew Rembrandt had an almost physical aversion to any concrete discussion of his painful financial situation, but the thing had to be done. And upon this occasion too, as soon as he noticed what direction the conversation was taking, he took a small sketchbook out of his pocket and fished around for a piece of crayon. But I said, "Those sketches can wait. Suppose you listen for a moment to what I have to say. I just want to see whether we can't find some way to allow you to go back to work."

"You mean to say that I have abused your hospitality long enough?" he asked, stiffening up.

"Rembrandt, you are a full-grown man with a son who will soon need a razor. Don't behave like a child. As far as I am concerned, you can stay until you die, and you know it."

"Of course," he answered. "I am sorry, but I feel as if I were locked up. My head is full of ideas. Sometimes I find it difficult not to shriek when I have done a bit of work on a plate and want to try and find out what it looks like—just one proof would be sufficient—but all I can do is mess it up with a bit of black and then wait until some friend is kind enough to let me use his press for a few minutes. And I can't turn your house into a workshop. The smell of paint and of ink would be all over the place. Your patients would stay away. They would think you were busy cooking some evil poison. I don't know how I can ever thank you for all you—"

"You can thank me," I interrupted him, "by listening for about ten minutes and keeping your mind on what I am going to say."

"Very well," he said, "I will be good." And he closed the sketchbook and put it back again into his pocket.

"Well, then," I said, "I am not going to talk economy to you. It would not do any good. If you were the sort of person who could keep his accounts straight, you probably would be a bookkeeper at the West India House today instead of being—"

"Yes. Instead of being what?" he interrupted me.

"Instead of having painted a few pictures that the world will recognize—"

"Three hundred years after I am dead."

"Perhaps, and perhaps sooner. What your friends want to do is to get you back to a place of your own where you can work."

And then I explained what Hendrickje had suggested. "It seems an excellent idea to me," I finished.

Rembrandt sat silent for a while, picked up a few pebbles that were lying in the grass, and threw them into the water.

"Funny," he said at last. "And that is the woman whom they did not think fit to partake of Holy Communion." Then he got to his feet. "Of course I accept. Let us go home and tell her. And tomorrow I can begin working again."

CHAPTER 19

THAT EVENING FRANCEN CAME IN and he had still another plan.

"I thought of this," he told us, "the moment I left you yesterday. Rembrandt's creditors want their money. How they get it is all the same to them provided they get it soon. Of course Rembrandt can go back to painting portraits, but portraits are slow work and now that everybody is either bankrupt or afraid to spend a stiver portraits are hardly profitable. I know that I myself have not sold one for almost two years. But I *have* sold a lot of etchings. Even when people would no longer buy Rembrandt's paintings, they would always pay good prices for his etchings. Now what I would like to know is this: What has become of the plates?"

"I don't know," Rembrandt answered. "They were sold. Mostly to local art dealers."

"You can find out to which ones?"

"I think we could," Hendrickje said. "Titus kept a list."

"Well," Francen continued, "they won't be of much value to them. They can have others make prints off them, but that is never the same as when the artist does them himself. We ought to be able to get those plates back. We may have to pay something for them, but perhaps we can promise a small royalty for every print.

"A few days ago I heard where we can get a first-rate press for about sixty guilders. I will buy it and donate it as my contribution to the new venture. Tomorrow Rembrandt can go and look for a place to live that will have some sort of a room that can be fixed up as a studio. Hendrickje meanwhile can buy beds and sheets and a few pots and pans and Titus and I will make the rounds of the art shops and see if we can find the old plates."

"And I?" I asked. "What shall I do?"

"For the moment," Francen said, "you shall take it easy. You have done quite enough as it is. This begins to sound like one of those plays of Vondel's in which Virtue appears at the end of each act to offer bright consolation. And now, if the doctor will send out for a mug of beer, we will drink to the health of the new firm, van Rijn, van Rijn and Stoeffels."

I thought the occasion was worthy of something better than mere beer and went into the cellar myself to get one of my few remaining bottles of Papish wine. Going down the narrow staircase I bumped my head, as I had done these last twenty years, and I swore and stopped to rub the sore spot.

Standing there in the dark, I thought of what I had just seen: the greatest painter of his time being kept out of the poorhouse by the combined efforts of a sick girl who had nothing in this world beyond her beauty and her kind heart and a boy of sixteen or seventeen, who loved his father and who would probably die before very long. It struck me that the situation would have been more fit for the pen of gruesome Aeschylus than that of our own amiable Vondel.

THE FIRST THING FOR US to do was to get the permission of Titus's guardian, for his affairs were by now hopelessly interwoven with those of his father. Verbout, finding he was too busy to devote necessary time to the case, had been succeeded by a certain Louis Crayers, whom I had never met but who sent a courteous note saying he would be glad to see us the next Friday at eleven.

At the appointed hour Abraham Francen and I were ushered into Crayers's office. We found him an easy man with whom to transact business, for he went right to the point.

"Gentlemen," he said, "I hope you will understand my position. I have given my oath before the court that I would protect this boy's interests. Besides, I like him. All the same, I have rarely seen such a pleasant and affectionate relationship as exists between van Rijn Senior and his son. I never knew the father, but I sometimes buy a few etchings and I recognize his genius. Still, when it comes to business, may God have mercy upon me for the language I used when I first studied the documents in this case and saw the mess I had to straighten out!

"When the appraisers of the Bankruptcy Court went through that house, they collected three pailfuls of bills—old bills—new bills—paid bills—unpaid bills—protested bills. The house looked neat enough, so they told me, but in all the cupboards, behind the pictures and the mirrors, they found bills. And what was infinitely worse, they discovered almost as many notes and drafts and checks, all made out to Rembrandt and which he had never taken the trouble to turn into cash. They even found a dozen envelopes and a few small bags containing money which he had put somewhere and then forgotten about—just plain carelessness. Of course I tried to collect some of the notes, but in many instances, the people were dead or had moved away and could not be traced. The amount we lost that way must have run into several thousand guilders.

"You want to know what I think about your plans. Well, I am heartily in favor of them. I shall support you, gentlemen, in all you do for your friend. At the same time I shall use every means at my disposal to protect the interests of young Titus. Therefore whatever you do, I shall insist upon a contract."

We thanked Crayers for his patience and courtesy and asked whether he had any suggestions to make about the contract.

"No," he answered, "it had better be a regular partnership contract. I have a friend, Notary Listingh, who does that sort of work for me and who is a very reliable man."

We then agreed that the first thing to do was to find a place where our friends could live—some sort of place that could be used as a shop and where Rembrandt could work. When that had been done, we would return to Crayers and ask him to have Notary Listingh make out the necessary papers.

But house-hunting proved no easy task. During the war, very

little building had been done and as a result people were paying enormous prices for very inferior accommodations. When at last we found something, it was entirely through luck.

One day a new patient named Lingelbach came to me with a little open wound on his right hand that needed bandaging. By this time I had house-hunting on the brain and before the young man left I asked if he knew of any houses for rent. "Why, yes," he answered. "My father is the owner of the Labyrinth at the end of the Rozengracht. He had to break away several houses to make room for his place but right opposite us there are three houses left, and one of them is free, at least half of it."

"Is the rent very high?" I asked.

"I am going to have supper with the old man tonight," young Lingelbach answered, "and I will ask."

The next day he came back and told me, "It is the left half of the house that is for rent. It has one large room with a big window on the north that would make a wonderful studio. The other four rooms are much smaller and there is a kitchen. The rent is a hundred and fifty guilders a year, but you may be able to get it for less. The landlord is called van Leest, and he lives on the premises."

I took Rembrandt out to the Rozengracht late that same day. We saw the house and we saw van Leest and we signed a lease then and there at a rental of 125 guilders a year. A week later the van Rijn family moved into their new quarters.

When I arrived with Hendrickje and the children, we found everything in terrible disorder: beds, tables, washbasins and chairs all standing pell-mell in the front room and sheets and pillows and pots and pans filling the sleeping quarters in a most picturesque and disharmonious fashion. We had expected to meet Rembrandt on the doorstep, ready to welcome us, but we could not find him anywhere.

Then Hendrickje, inspecting her new domain, opened the door to the large room in the back of the house. Rembrandt was sitting in the center, right on the floor, in the most uncomfortable position imaginable, painting away for dear life at a large canvas that stood leaning against a barrel containing the family china.

"Oh," he said, without looking up. "Are you there? I hope you will pardon me, but the light was so good—I thought I had better begin."

"Yes, dear," said Hendrickje, "that is quite all right." And she came back to us and quietly started unpacking the small satchel containing Cornelia's clothes and toys.

THE FOLLOWING WEEK I was obliged to travel to Leiden. The town council of Amsterdam, still considering my claim for the indemnity they had promised when my little hospital was burned by the mob, had asked the medical faculty of the University of Leiden to report on the desirability of my methods for performing painless operations.

When I returned to Amsterdam, I heard that Hendrickje had been quite sick, that Titus was working hard, trying to convert the little front room into an art store, and that Rembrandt himself was busy with the sketches for that allegorical picture in the Town Hall which was to find a final resting-place in the rubbish corner of the aldermanic attic.

But of course at that moment we could not know all this and the mere fact that he was busy once more made him so happy that even Hendrickje was caught in an occasional smile and Titus had started to dream once more of becoming a famous painter.

They were delighted to see me, wanted to know what the Leiden professors had said (they had said nothing, so far) and they kept me for dinner and told me that the house was a great success. Of course, the creditors still came around, but the Rozengracht was far from the center of the town and not all of them would take the trouble to walk that long distance. And by the way, my friend Jean-Louys had come to visit them but he had looked very ill and had come in a coach, accompanied by his sailor, who had to support him when he climbed the stoop. He had made them promise that they would not write to me and tell me that he was sick. And Francen had been in and he had just returned from Haarlem where he had seen old Frans Hals and Hals had laughed merrily when Francen had told him he was a good friend of Rembrandt's.

"Tell him that now I can call him brother," Frans had said. "And tell him that he was a lucky devil. For when he went bankrupt, some of the grandest people in town were among his creditors while I was sold out at the behest of an ordinary, everyday baker, who was displeased with a picture I had painted of him blowing his horn to tell people fresh bread was ready. And when I went broke, all the sheriffs could find in my house were three mattresses, a table and a chest of drawers, and he, so I hear, had a house as full of things as the palace of the late King Solomon." And Francen said that Hals was painting again although he had done no work for almost twenty years (he could not sell anything anyway, so what was the use?) and he wanted Rembrandt to come see him, for he had made a wonderful discovery but he was eighty years old and could not make use of it himself.

"But tell Rembrandt," he had said, "that being poor is the best thing that can happen to any painter. For if you are poor, you can't afford to buy all those expensive colors. You have to get results with only two or three pots of paint and then you learn to suggest tints rather than put them down in the original red and yellow and green and blue—just hint at things—" And so on and so forth, for the old man was getting a little vague and repeated and contradicted himself continually, but then, he had been in the poorhouse for so long. When finally I went home, I was happier than I had been for a long time. For just ere I left, Hendrickje, her cheeks flushed by fever and her eyes wide with excitement, had drawn me aside and whispered: "He works all day long, and everything is all right."

Indeed, for the moment at least, the fates that had so doggedly followed this poor man's footsteps seemed to have wandered off in search of some fresh victim, for not only did the creditors gradually begin to leave him alone, but I was at last able to get him a commission that was exactly the sort of thing he liked to do best.

EXCEPT FOR MY SON, I had only one relative in Amsterdam. How we happened to be cousins, I did not know. My grandmother had explained it to me any number of times, but I was not greatly interested in the man and invariably I failed to listen. But we observed a certain cordiality towards each other, and made it a point to call upon each other every New Year's morning, though we had nothing in common except an accidental tie of blood.

This particular van Loon was a few years younger than myself and a cloth manufacturer in a small way. He had been several times elected into the board of managers of the clothworkers' guild and this year again he was one of the Syndics, as he told me when I met him by accident on the Rokin where he had his store.

I congratulated him and asked him, more as a matter of having something to say than through curiosity, whether he and his colleagues had made any plans yet to have their picture made. He said no, they hadn't thought about it yet. And then, through a sudden impulse, I found myself blurting out: "I have got just the man for you. He is a splendid painter and he won't charge you such a terrible sum either. When will you pose for him?"

But he asked me curtly, "Who may that be, Cousin?" and I answered, "A man by the name of Rembrandt, Cousin," and he again, "I have never heard of him, Cousin," and I, "That does not matter, Cousin. I will take you to see him and you can judge for yourself. I will call for you tomorrow at ten in the morning."

God only knows how I was able to persuade this dry-as-dust wool carder and his equally uninspired confreres that Rembrandt was the man for them, but it is a fact that they signed a contract for a picture and at a very fair price.

It was a long time since Rembrandt had painted anything of this sort and meantime he had been pulled through the mangle so repeatedly that nothing remained of his former self except his skin and his bones and his honest homely face. Twenty years before it had been all the same to him what size canvas he needed—what sort of color he used, nor had he given a fig for the opinion of those who would be asked to pay for the picture.

This time he had to think of the smallness of his studio, he must be careful not to waste any of the bright lakes and expensive ochers which Titus had bought for him on credit and, as he needed money badly, he must be very considerate of the feelings of his customers and give each of them equal chance.

I am not the best judge of paintings, but it struck me that Rembrandt had never come quite so near his ideal as this time. I was reminded of the somewhat incoherent message which Francen had brought back from Haarlem—that strange artistic message which exhorted the younger man to "suggest color" and "to hint at things" rather than expose them concretely.

Everything in this picture was a matter of suggestion and yet one felt the presence of those honest drapers as if one had been at one of their meetings—one sensed that they were secretly very proud of the high office which their fellow members had bestowed upon them and at the same moment one knew that in their hearts they were convinced that this much envied dignity had come to them entirely in recognition of their unimpeachable integrity. It was the strongest picture I had ever seen, and I am sure no one ever achieved such a brilliant effect with the help of such incredibly sober means.

I was delighted, and the day after the picture had been finished, I hastened to the house on the Rokin where I found my cousin, the honorable Syndic, eating his midday bowl of lentil soup. He looked at me with considerable surprise, for he was not accustomed to familiarities of this sort, and I said:

"Good morning, Cousin, have you seen your picture?"

And he answered, "Yes, Cousin, and none of us are particularly impressed by it, but we will pay the man all the same."

I turned on my heel and he called after me, "Don't you want to stay, Cousin, and share my meal with me?"

And I answered, "No, thank you, Cousin, some other time I shall be delighted."

Then I went home to talk with my son about a new sort of sawmill which he wanted to construct—a sawmill that should be able to take care of three trees at the same time.

The boy (he was taller than I but I could never think of him except in terms of a child—a sentiment which sometimes caused considerable difficulty between us)—the boy, who in his own way loved me very deeply, noticed at once that something was wrong.

THE SYNDICS OF THE DRAPERS' GUILD (1662)

"What has happened, Father?" he asked. "Uncle Rembrandt in trouble again?"

"No," I protested, but he knew that I lied.

"Too bad," he said quietly. "Uncle Rembrandt is a fine fellow and I like him tremendously, but he just has no sense. Who wants to go on painting pictures when the world needs mills?"

I suppose there was an answer to that question, but (for the moment, at least) I must confess I could not think of it.

I NOW COME TO THE YEARS between 1661 and 1668, when a great many things happened, but few, I am sorry to say, that contributed in any way to the happiness of myself or my friends.

For me, an incident that filled my heart with sorrow was the loss of my friend Jean-Louys. One day a letter from him was delivered to my house. Since good-bys were painful, Jean-Louys explained, he was writing to tell me he had already left in his sailboat for France—for home.

"I have been very ill," he wrote. "And now some strange and hitherto unsuspected instinct bids me go forth that I may die among my own people. My incomparable François tells me there is little danger connected with the voyage. I shall be home by the end of next month."

The letter ended with a postscript: "Present my humble duties to that poor old bear Rembrandt. All his life he has dwelled in a land of make-believe of such infinite beauty and integrity that the world has passed it by with a shrug of the shoulders. Now he is old and sick and growing stout and soon he will be an object of pity. When the end comes, they will take him away to an obscure grave. But was anyone ever richer than this poor wreck?"

Four weeks later a convoy of merchantmen returning from Batavia reported that just outside the British channel they had met a little vessel that flew the French flag but had hailed them in broken Dutch and declared that it came from Amsterdam and was bound for the south of France.

I never was able to find out whether Jean-Louys had finally reached the land of his birth or had sailed for another shore from which no one has yet returned.

Meanwhile there was Hendrickje's sickness. She had never quite been well since about a year after Cornelia's birth, when she had caught a cold and, refusing to stay in bed, had developed pulmonary trouble which made me fear that she was a candidate for an attack of phthisis. It seemed unbelievably cruel. Saskia had died of this dreadful disease and now Hendrickje was going the same way.

Rembrandt, singularly blind to symptoms of this sort, noticed nothing. He sometimes commented upon his wife's listlessness and lack of appetite, but as a rule he closed the sentence with a cursory, "Oh, well, she will be all right when spring comes."

When spring came she was much worse, however, and when summer came she was no better, and one day in the fall she asked me to send for the notary who had helped her and Titus draw up the agreement about their little art store, but to be careful that he did not call when Rembrandt was at home. She hoped to deceive him about her condition until the very last.

I knew that on the seventh of August Rembrandt was going to take Titus to see his friend Joris de Caulery, who was in Amsterdam to attend to some private business affairs. On the seventh, accordingly, I walked with Notary Listingh to the house on the Rozengracht and Hendrickje made her last will.

She had little enough to leave, poor dear, but all she possessed she bequeathed to her daughter Cornelia, or in case of her death, to her stepson Titus. Furthermore, she stipulated that Rembrandt should be the only guardian of her child and insisted upon including a paragraph which stated that if Titus should inherit her property, the revenue of her investments (such as they were) should be paid out to Rembrandt, who was to enjoy them until the day of his death. As she could not write, she merely made a cross at the end of the document.

When everything had been done according to the law, Hendrickje was so exhausted that she had to go and lie down.

For a few weeks it seemed that she was growing a little stronger, but in October she had to take to her bed and never got up again.

She lived almost a year longer. She never complained. Her love for Rembrandt and for her two children (Titus regarded her entirely as his own mother and she apparently knew no difference between her own child and Saskia's) never waned but seemed to grow stronger as she felt herself more and more slipping away from this world.

One morning Rembrandt found her unconscious on the floor. Apparently she had tried to get up to open a window to get some fresh air. She had often had attacks of choking that only fresh air could relieve. Titus ran as fast as his legs could carry him to fetch me, but when I reached the house on the Rozengracht, Hendrickje was dead.

That afternoon we discussed the funeral. Rembrandt wanted to bury her in the Old Church together with Saskia. But since the death of his first wife, he had moved to the other part of the city and the law provided that extra sums be paid the undertaker if dead people were not buried "in the church nearest to their most recent place of abode."

This was out of the question; it was too costly.

Early the next morning (it was the 27th of October, 1662) Rembrandt sold the grave containing the remains of Saskia to a certain Pieter van Geenen, who paid him cash. With that money he was able the next day to buy a grave in the South Church. And there Hendrickje was buried.

Strangely, Hendrickje's death did not seem to have made a very deep impression upon Rembrandt. There is apparently a saturation point for mental suffering as well as for physical pain, and during the last ten years Rembrandt had been dealt such terrible and incessant blows by fate that nothing now could make any impression upon him. After the very indifferent reception of his painting by the Syndics of the Cloth-workers' Guild he knew that, as far as his artistic career was concerned, there was to be no comeback for him. He was, in the parlance of that day, out of the running.

Painting of Christ

I tried to console him once by telling him of something I had found in one of the old Greek writers, how the Athenians were running a race in the Stadium and how the public, seeing a man a few feet behind the very last of all the others, began to chide him for his slowness until they discovered that the victim of their displeasure was so far ahead of all the others that he had already won the prize. But this neither amused nor interested him. He merely grunted and went back to his easel.

For he worked very hard those days—entirely too hard to please me when I looked at him with a professional eye. He rarely left the house. He was glad to see his few remaining friends and was polite to them and occasionally he even tried to be cordial. But all the time his mind was elsewhere and, when addressed, it took him some time before he realized that he had been spoken to and that one expected an answer.

Rembrandt came of a strong breed of men. His father and grandfathers and great-grandfathers had fought through the great rebellion and lived to tell the tale. They had been the sort of people that would never bend, but even the hardest iron will break if it is exposed to too severe a blow. Sometimes when I saw Rembrandt late at night, his short squat figure (much too stout around the hips on account of his lack of exercise) scratching away at some copperplate by the light of a single candle (the whole family sat and worked or read by the light of one single candle—they could not afford more), I wondered how long it would be before the crash came.

Rembrandt rarely spoke anymore of his work but everything he did was in a minor key. Gone were the days of the laughing cavalier and of Saskias and Hendrickjes dressed up like the ladies-in-waiting of those merry foreign queens. In his bare little house there was nothing left that could serve as a fitting background for such scenes of gaiety.

And as he had never read much, and considered the pursuit of literature a scandalous waste of time, his choice of subjects for his sketches was limited. He had to fall back upon memories of his childhood days and the biblical incidents of which his mother had told him when he was a small boy.

But the Christ he now painted was not the handsome young prophet of his Italian rivals, preaching the good tidings among the sunbaked boulders of some Palestine hill. No, it was invariably the man of sorrows—Christ being scourged—Christ bidding farewell to His followers—Christ standing in deep thought before the walls of the Temple! And the other problems that filled his mind until he had to rid himself of them by recounting them in the form of pictures—all had to do with that feeling of doom—that sense of futility, and that air of hopeless rebellion which had descended upon him the moment he had walked for the last time out of his house in the Breestraat.

Often I have sat in his studio and watched him painting. And every time I have been reminded of a picture he had painted years before when he was still quite young, of Samson threatening his father-in-law who had cheated him. The strong man who for reasons he has not been able to fathom has been struck what he considers an unfair blow, and who defies fate—who thumbs his nose at providence—shakes his fist at the Deity Himself, and with boylike bravado shouts: "All right! I will show you!"

For he was showing them, with a vengeance.

In that shabby room in a mean house on the Rozengracht, such miracles of color were now being performed that the world for ages to come will sit before them in stupefied silence and will say: "Beyond that point, no man could go without lifting himself to the rank of the gods."

Provided that any of these pictures survives long enough to allow mankind to catch up with their maker. For nothing Rembrandt finished during those days was ever sold. And where they are at present, only a year after his death, I could not possibly tell. A praying pilgrim he painted during that time I saw only a few months ago in a pawnshop in Leiden and it was hanging between a cheap fiddle and an old pair of sailor's trousers. What has happened to the others, I do not know. An intelligent art dealer with an eye to his grandsons' future would have hired himself a storehouse and filled it with the pictures Rembrandt finished during the period he lived on the Rozengracht, and which he was unable to sell for half a guilder or even less.

BY THE END OF '64 it became clear that Rembrandt could no longer afford the rent of the Rozengracht house and that he would have to look for cheaper quarters. Titus found a place just around the corner and the family once more pulled up stakes and went to live on the Lauriergracht. There they had only three rooms and in every one the light was bad. It was then that Titus thought of having his father do some book illustrations which would probably be more lucrative than painting pictures.

He went to a publisher but the publisher would not listen to the plan. "If only your father knew something about steel engraving, then I would have a job for him." And Titus, eager to get his father an order (any order at all), had answered, "But my father is one of the best steel engravers in town. Just give him a chance!"

The publisher agreed. Would Mr. van Rijn please engrave a picture of Jan Antonides van der Linden after a portrait that Abraham van den Tempel had painted half a dozen years before? Rembrandt said that he would. But he was an etcher and not an engraver and the experiment ended disastrously. And Rembrandt was once more at the mercy of his creditors.

Although I was no longer rich in those days, I would have been delighted to help him, but he would not hear of it. "You have trouble enough of your own," he invariably answered when I talked of taking over some of the burdens of his household, "and I am still strong enough to take care of my children myself."

He was immensely pleased when one day a young man named Aert de Gelder asked to become his pupil. De Gelder, who

Jan Antonides van der Linden

was then about twenty years old, hailed from Dordrecht and was a pupil of that Samuel van Hoogstraten who shortly after the English war had moved to England where it was said he had done very well and had become a rich man. As van Hoogstraten too had once worked in Rembrandt's studio, the old man felt touchingly grateful and de Gelder proved to be not only an apt student but a kind and loyal friend, which Rembrandt had not been able to say of all of his pupils.

But unfortunately I was not able to see much of Rembrandt during this period. For I was obliged to spend the greater part of the next three years at sea or in The Hague, so as to be at the beck and call of My Lord de Witt and the navy. The Peace of

Westminster had theoretically made an end to the hostilities between ourselves and England. But in practice there never had been a cessation of that warfare which is bound to spring up when two countries, almost equally matched, are contending for the monopoly of the world's trade.

To make matters worse, following the death of England's Lord Protector, Oliver Cromwell, in the year '58, a revolution had returned the House of Stuart to the throne of England in '60—and brought serious forebodings to our leaders. For King Charles of England considered it a personal insult that his nephew, Willem III, the Prince of Orange, had been excluded from the government of the United Netherlands.

So once again the two nations fought; and three years later, once again negotiations for peace were started. At their conclusion we had gained a number of colonies in South America, but lost the New Netherlands. For this I was sorry, remembering the happy years I had spent there, but few people shared my feelings.

"That part of the world is absolutely useless anyway," they used to reason. "What did we ever get out of it? Nothing but trouble, endless expense, and a few beaver skins. Now we have Surinam, where we can raise sugar. An excellent bargain."

And they were loud in their praises of the political sagacity which had given them the flourishing town of Paramaribo in return for the poverty-stricken village of Nieuw Amsterdam, which now was called New York by the English in honor of His Majesty's brother.

CHAPTER 20

MY LORD DE WITT had sent me a very flattering letter in which he expressed his gratitude for my services to the medical corps. And in August of 1667 I returned to Amsterdam. I hired a man to row me across the Ij and, finding it agreeable to take a little exercise after so many months of close confinement on board a war vessel, walked home through the twilight, happy to be once more among my own people.

My son was not at home. The excellent Jantje, who had kept

everything spick and span during my absence, explained that he had probably gone courting, and for the first time I realized how old I had grown. Jantje handed me a letter, adorned with a big seal which I recognized as the arms of Amsterdam and which, so she told me, had been delivered only that morning.

I opened it.

Their Lordships the Burgomasters informed me that in view of the "outrageous rebelliousness" which had caused the destruction of my property, they had voted to grant me the first part of my indemnity. Thirty thousand guilders in cash awaited my pleasure at the town treasury any time I cared to call.

Without bothering to get my hat I rushed out of the door and ran as fast as my old heart would permit me to the house on the Lauriergracht.

Titus was in the front room with Cornelia, hanging a number of etchings on strips that had been stretched across the windows, that they might dry during the night. They were delighted to see me and at once took me to the studio where Rembrandt was lying on a narrow cot.

"Look who is here," Titus shouted. But all Rembrandt answered was, "Please take away that candle. The light hurts my eyes." Then he recognized me and tried to get up. I bade him not exert himself and took possession of the only chair I could find. Titus and Cornelia sat down on the side of the cot. Soon I became accustomed to the darkness of the low-ceilinged room and I examined my old friend a little closer. His eyes looked bloodshot and he seemed to have trouble breathing. He was in a bad shape.

"Rembrandt," I said, "I have come with good news for you and for the children. I have got back part of my money. Now, what can I do for you?"

This was not very tactful, but in my enthusiasm, I had blurted out the first thing that came to my mind.

There was no immediate reply. Finally, a very tired voice said, "Nothing. It is too late." And then I realized how terribly he had altered during the three months I had not seen him. And I began again, and this time a little more carefully, to explain that soon I would be amply provided with funds and that I wanted Rembrandt to share in my good fortune. We sat there, the four of us, for a long time and finally Rembrandt was able to formulate a wish.

"If it would not be asking too much of you," he told me, "I would like very much to go back to the house on the Rozengracht. It had such excellent light and this place is so dark that I am afraid I shall go blind if I have to work another six months in such a cellar."

Then he excused himself. "If you don't mind, I would like to try and sleep now. I lie awake the greater part of every night and tomorrow I must be up early. I want to start work on my *Prodigal Son*. Titus thinks he has found someone who wants to buy it."

He reached out his hand which was covered with paint and a little shaky. "Please don't think I am not grateful," he said. "I am deeply grateful. But I am very tired and I have not seen anyone for so long that I am not much good at conversation nowadays." And he pulled his blankets over his head and turned his face towards the wall.

I remained talking to Titus and Cornelia for a few minutes before I went home.

"No," Titus said, "you must not think that things are as bad as he imagines them to be. I have got my money at last, I mean that share in my father's house. Crayers had to go to the Supreme Court to get it but the judges found for us, and it is quite a sum—almost five thousand guilders."

"Congratulations," and I shook the young man warmly by the hand. "And what do you mean to do with it?"

He looked at me a little sheepishly. "I think I will use it to get married," he answered.

"And who is the lucky girl?" I asked.

"Magdalena van Loo. She lives on the Singel with her mother. I will bring her around to see you tomorrow."

I turned to Cornelia. "And you, my darling," I said, "you too will soon say good-by to us to get married, won't you?"

She shook her head and solemnly answered, "No, Uncle Jan. I am always going to stay right here with Father."

And the poor girl meant it.

I AM REACHING THE END of my story.

Why dwell upon the misery of those last years?

Yes, Rembrandt returned to the house on the Rozengracht and financially was a great deal better off than before. Titus got his five thousand guilders which he administered carefully, almost penuriously, for he knew from experience what poverty meant and he now had a wife of his own to support.

As for the wife, the less said the better. She was of equal age with Titus—they both had celebrated their twenty-seventh birthdays just before they were married. And she too had inherited a few thousand guilders from her father and would get a few thousand more when her mother died. But she was a person without charm or color. She tolerated her father-in-law (who painted a magnificent likeness of her and Titus which she did not like as it made her look a little too old) and she was patronizing to her half-sister-in-law whom she called a bastard behind her back.

Was Titus in love with her? I never was able to discover. He seemed fond of her in a quiet sort of way, but I

The Return of the Prodigal Son

felt that he would have married almost anyone who set her cap at him. Being a very dutiful son and sincerely devoted to his father, he had suppressed all such longings as long as he was responsible for the welfare of his family.

Now that he was at last able to afford a wife of his own, the inevitable happened, and what that inevitable was, most people will know even if they have not been trained for the medical profession.

During that year I was busy with plans for a new infirmary. Late one evening in September of the year '68, Rebecca Willems, an old servant who took care of Rembrandt's household now that his son was married, came to me with a note

433

signed by Cornelia. She asked me to come at once to Titus's house on the Apple Market, as her brother had been taken ill and seemed in a bad way.

When I arrived, he was unconscious from loss of blood. He had suffered an internal hemorrhage and I knew he was doomed. He rallied a little towards morning, but died during the afternoon.

Rembrandt was present. He sat in a corner of the room. Cornelia and Rebecca took him back to the Rozengracht. He was sick for two weeks afterwards and could not attend the funeral of his son.

When Cornelia, trying to cheer him up, told him that Magdalena expected a baby, he shook his head.

"Merely someone else for me to lose," was his only comment.

He had reached the end of his strength and courage, and he knew it.

BUT AFTER A FEW MONTHS he seemed to rally. At least, he tried to paint again. But when he had sat in front of his easel for forty or fifty minutes, he would complain of pains in his back. He tried to do some etching while lying in bed, but his eyes had grown so weak that they no longer could stand the strain of that sort of work.

In the end he merely puttered around in his studio for a couple of hours every morning and then went back to his cot. He rarely undressed but slept in his old paint-covered smock, like a soldier who wanted to die in harness.

In the month of March of the next year, his first grandchild was born. It was a girl and it was called Titia after her father. We thought that it would do him good if he attended the baptism, and he finally allowed himself to be persuaded. But he could hardly stand on his feet during the short ceremony and his hands shook so severely when he tried to write his name that Frans van Bijlert, the other witness, had to help him.

I used to drop in every other day to tell him the latest news and cheer him up with little bits of local gossip. He was politely grateful, but answered little.

Once or twice he asked after Saskia, as if she had still been

435

alive, and occasionally he mentioned Hendrickje. "She was a good girl," he used to say. "Without her, I don't know what we would have done."

I sometimes asked him whether he wanted me to read to him, but he said no, he had so much to think about.

And then one evening in October of '69, when I was sitting by his bedside (he had not been able to get up for about a fortnight), he surprised me by asking that I get the family Bible for him. It was in Cornelia's room, and when I called to her, she brought it and put it on the table.

"I wish you would read me that story about Jacob," he said. "Do you know where to find it—the story of Jacob wrestling with the Lord?"

I did not know where to find it. Cornelia remembered that it was somewhere in Genesis. I turned the leaves until I found the name Jacob and then searched up and down the pages until I came to the passage which he seemed to have in mind. And I read:

"And Jacob was left alone; and there wrestled a man with him until the breaking of the day."

"Yes," Rembrandt nodded as I continued, "that is it."

"And he said, Let me go, for the day breaketh. And he said, I will not let thee go, except thou bless me.

"And he said unto him, What is thy name? And he said, Jacob.

"And he said, Thy name shall be called no more Jacob, but Israel: for as a prince hast thou power with God and with men, and hast prevailed."

When I had got that far, the sick man stirred and I stopped reading and looked at him. I saw him slowly lift his right hand and hold it close to his eyes and look at it as if it were something curious he had never observed before. And then his lips moved and very softly I heard him whisper:

"And Jacob was left alone. And there wrestled a man with him until the breaking of the day . . . but he did not give in and fought back—ah, yes, he fought back—for such is the will of the Lord—that we shall fight back . . . that we shall wrestle with him until the breaking of the day."

And then, with a sudden effort, he tried to raise himself from his pillow, but could not do it. His gnarled old fingers, still covered with the stains of ink and paint, fell back upon his breast. ". . . for as a prince hast thou had power with God and with men and hast prevailed—and hast prevailed unto the last . . . alone . . . but hast prevailed unto the last."

When Cornelia looked at me a moment later with questioning eyes and said, "Thank Heaven, for now he is asleep," I went up to her and took her by the arm and answered, "Thank Heaven, indeed, for now he is dead."

Epilogue by a distant descendant

If Doctor Jan had lived a few years longer, he would have seen the name of Rembrandt van Rijn completely disappear from the face of the earth.

Within less than a fortnight after Rembrandt's death, the body of Magdalena van Loo, the widow of Titus, was gently lowered into a grave in the West Church, not far away from that of his own.

As for Cornelia, on the third of May of the year 1670 she married one Cornelis Suythoff, a young painter who could not make a living at his art and who that same year sailed to Java on the good ship *Tulpenburg* and went to work for the East India Company.

Then on Saint Nicholas day of the year 1673, Cornelia gave birth to a son who was duly baptized and received the name of Rembrandt Suythof and who apparently died shortly afterwards. Five years later, another son was born to the couple, Hendric Suythof. What became of the parents, we do not know. A few years more and they disappeared from view as completely as if they had never existed.

Titia, the daughter of Titus and Magdalena van Loo, lived a little longer. When she was seventeen years old, she married the youngest son of her guardian, a certain Frans van Bijlert. They had a raft of children, whose funeral notices are duly recorded in the mortuary books of the West Church which soon became a sort of general receptacle for those who had a drop of Rembrandt blood in their veins.

But ere she herself died, in the year 1725, Titia could still have read the following estimate of her grandfather's work in a *History of Painting* that was considered the standard of good taste for all those who had genteel aspirations during the first quarter of the eighteenth century:

> In his effort to attain a mellow manner, Rembrandt van Rijn has merely succeeded in achieving an effect of rottenness. The vulgar and prosaic aspects of a subject were the only ones he was capable of noting, and with his so-called red and yellow tones, he set the fatal example of shadows so hot that they seem actually aglow and of colors that appear to lie like liquid mud on the canvas.

The man responsible for this piece of poetic prose was a now-forgotten painter who modestly confessed he himself had been tempted to try Rembrandt van Rijn's style of painting but soon had abjured "these errors and had abandoned a manner that was entirely based upon a delusion."

There it stands for everyone to read: "Rottenness of effect . . . the fatal example of shadows that were so hot as to appear to be aglow . . . vulgar and prosaic aspects of every subject . . . colors that appeared to lie like liquid mud on the canvas . . . a manner founded on a delusion."

A funeral in an unknown grave—a half-open coffin from which the bones had been removed and thrown on the rubbish pile . . . an undischarged bankrupt until this very day . . . as it was in the beginning . . . is now and probably ever will be . . . world without end. Amen.

Hendrik Willem van Loon.

LIFE
OF
CHRIST

A CONDENSATION OF

LIFE
OF
CHRIST

by
GIOVANNI
PAPINI

TRANSLATED FROM THE ITALIAN BY
DOROTHY CANFIELD FISHER

Although Giovanni Papini was one of the foremost Italian men of letters, the publication of this book in 1921 came as a stunning surprise. For Papini had been an atheist, a vocal enemy of the Church—a self-appointed debunker of any form of mysticism. A more unlikely source for a reverent portrait of Jesus could hardly be imagined.

What brought about his sudden conversion—so reminiscent of Saul's on the road to Damascus? Like many cynics Papini was a tormented soul, disgusted with a humanity that could accept the horrors of the first World War, unable to see hope for better things unless, somehow, the hearts of men could be changed.

During that war he took his family to live in a remote mountain village. There, living with the peasants, observing their devotions, something began to happen to him. Sometimes, in the evenings, he was asked to read aloud stories from the New Testament. This rediscovery of the Bible became a revelation to him, and soon he determined to write his own version of the life of Christ.

The result of that resolve is a book which, in the words of a distinguished critic, "will stand for many years as a rallying sign for thousands making their way painfully to a less inhuman, because a more Christlike, world."

FOR FIVE HUNDRED YEARS free spirits have been trying ond time—to kill Him in the

Jesus, some have said, was of Augustus and of Tiberius, reduced to a clumsy mosaic of those who call themselves desperately to kill Jesus a sec- hearts of men.

a myth developed in the time and all the Gospels can be prophetic texts. Others con- ceived of Jesus as a good, well-meaning man, but too high-flown and fantastic, who went to school to the Greeks, the Buddhists, and the Essenes and patched together His plagiarisms as best He could to support His claim to be the Messiah of Israel. Others made Him out to be an unbalanced humanitarian, precursor of Rousseau and of divine democracy; an excellent man for his time but who today would be put under the care of an alienist.

But who could have taken the place of the man they were trying to dispose of? The grave they dug was deeper every day, and still they could not bury Him from sight. On the walls of the churches and schools, on the tops of bell towers and moun- tains, in street shrines, at the heads of beds and over tombs, thou- sands of crosses recall the death of the Crucified One. Take away the frescoes from the churches, carry off the pictures from

443

the altars and from the houses, and the life of Christ fills museums and picture galleries. You find His name and His words in all the books of literature. Even oaths are an involuntary remembrance of His presence.

Christ is an abyss of divine mystery between two divisions of human history. Our civilization begins with the birth of Christ. What comes before Christ no longer moves our passions; it may be beautiful, but it is dead. Caesar was more talked about in his time than Jesus, and Plato taught more science than Christ; but who nowadays is hotly for Caesar or against him, and where now are the Platonists and the anti-Platonists?

Christ, on the contrary, is still living among us. There is a passion for the love of Christ and a passion for His destruction.

We live in the Christian era, and it is not yet finished. If we are to understand the world, our life, ourselves, we must refer to Christ. No life of Christ could be more beautiful and perfect than the Gospels. But who reads the Gospels nowadays?

Every generation has its preoccupations and its thoughts, and its own insanities. The old Gospels must be retranslated if Christ is to remain alive in the life of men.

The world is full of such bookish resuscitations of Christ, learned or literary. But which of them seeks, instead of learned discussions, to give food fit for the soul, for the needs of men of our time? The book we need is a living book to set Christ the Ever Living with loving vividness before the eyes of living men, to make us feel Him as actually and eternally present in our lives. The author of this book does not pretend to have written such a book; but at least he has tried to draw near to that ideal.

This book is not a "scientific history." It is based on the Gospels; on "the Logia and the Agrapha," which seemed to have the most evangelical flavor; on some apocryphal texts used with judgment; and finally, on nine or ten modern books. The author has approached Jesus with the simple-heartedness of longing and of love, just as during His lifetime He was approached by the fishermen of Capernaum.

THE BIRTH OF CHRIST

JESUS WAS BORN in a stable, a real stable, not the modern Christmas Eve "Holy Stable," made of plaster of paris, with little candylike statuettes, prettily painted, with a neat, tidy manger, an ecstatic ass, a contrite ox, and angels fluttering their wreaths on the roof.

A real stable is the prison of the animals who work for man. The poor, old stable of Christ's old, poor country is only four rough walls, a dirty pavement, a roof of beams and slate. It is dark, reeking. The only clean thing in it is the manger where the owner piles the hay and fodder.

Fresh in the clear morning, waving in the wind, sunny, lush, sweet-scented, the spring meadow was mown. The green grass, the long, slim blades were cut down by the scythe; and with the grass the beautiful flowers in full bloom—white, red, yellow, blue. They withered and dried and took on the one dull color of hay. Oxen dragged back to the barn the dead plunder of May and June. And now that grass has become dry hay and those flowers, still smelling sweet, are there in the manger. The animals take it slowly with their great black lips, and later the flowering fields, changed into moist dung, return to light on the litter which serves as bedding.

445

This is the real stable where Jesus was born. The Son of man had as His cradle the manger where the animals chewed the cud of the miraculous flowers of spring. There Jesus appeared one night, born of a stainless Virgin armed only with innocence.

First to worship Jesus were animals, not men. Among men He sought out the simplehearted; and among the simplehearted He sought out children. Simpler than children, and milder, the beasts of burden welcomed Him.

Up to that time the kings of the earth and the populace craving material things had bowed before oxen and asses. Christ's own people, the chosen people whom Jehovah had freed from Egyptian slavery, when their leader left them alone in the desert to go up and talk with the Eternal, did they not force Aaron to make them a golden calf to worship? In Greece the ass was sacred to Ares, to Dionysius, to Hyperborean Apollo.

But Jesus was to bring to an end the bowing down before beasts. In the meantime the beasts of Bethlehem warm Him with their breath.

After the animals came those who care for animals. Shepherds live almost always alone and far away. They are moved by whatever happens near to them. Even if the Angel had not announced the great birth, they would have gone to the stable to see the son of the stranger woman.

But as they were watching their flocks in the long winter night, they were shaken by the light and by the words of the Angel. "Fear not, for behold, I bring you good tidings of great joy. . . . Glory to God in the highest, and on earth peace to men of good will." In the dim light of the stable they saw a beautiful young woman gazing silently at her son. And they saw the baby with His eyes just open, His delicate rosy flesh, His mouth which had not yet eaten. For the shepherds forewarned, this newborn child was not just a baby, but He for whom their suffering race had been waiting for a thousand years.

The shepherds offered what little they had, that little which is so great when offered with love. They carried the white offerings of their craft, milk, cheese, wool, the lamb. Even today in our mountains, where one finds the last dying traces of hospitality and fraternal feeling, as soon as a wife is delivered of a

child, the sisters, wives and daughters of the shepherds come hurrying to her; and not one of them empty-handed. One has three or four eggs still warm from the nest, another a cup of freshly drawn milk, another a little cheese, another a pullet to make broth for the new mother.

Themselves poor, the old-time shepherds did not look down on the poor. Their first kings had been shepherds—Saul and David—shepherds of herds before being shepherds of tribes. These shepherds of Bethlehem knew that this boy, born of poor people in poverty, was to be the redeemer of the humble, of those men of good will, on whom the Angel had called down peace.

Some days after this, three wise men came and knelt before Jesus. They came perhaps from Chaldea, perhaps from the shores of the Caspian Sea. Mounted on their camels with their full-stuffed saddlebags, they had forded the Tigris and the Euphrates, crossed the great desert of the nomad tribes, followed along the Dead Sea. They were guided to Judea by a new star like the comet which appears every so often in the sky to announce the birth of a prophet or the death of a Caesar. They had come to adore a king.

The wise men found no king; they found a nursing baby, poorly swaddled, hidden within a stable, a tiny boy who could neither ask nor answer questions.

They were not kings, these wise men; but in Media and Persia the wise men directed the kings. They alone could communicate with Alma Mazda, the good God. They alone knew the future. Except from their hands God accepted no sacrifices. No king began a war without consulting them. In the midst of a people sunk in material things they represented the spirit.

After the animals which are nature, after the shepherds which are the common people, this third power which is knowledge knelt at the manger in Bethlehem. The old priestly caste of the Orient made its act of submission, the learned men knelt before Him who was to set above the learning of words and numbers the new wisdom of love.

Scarcely had the wise men gone when persecutions were begun by those who were to hate Him to the day of His death.

WHEN CHRIST APPEARED upon the earth, He was born subject to two sovereigns. One lucky adventurer after wholesale slaughter had seized the Roman empire, another had murdered his way to the throne of David and Solomon in Judea. They were, as a matter of fact, friends and accomplices.

Son of the usurer of Velletri, Octavius Augustus showed himself cowardly in war, vindictive in victory, false to his friends, cruel in reprisals. To a condemned man who begged only for burial he answered, "That is the business of the vultures." To the Perugians begging for mercy during the massacre he cried, *"Moriendum esse!"* [To die!] Now, possessed of the empire, with his enemies crushed and scattered, he put on a mask of mildness and of his youthful vices kept only his lust. He amused himself with the wives of his friends, and with posing as the restorer of morality.

This man, sovereign of the western world when Jesus was born, never knew that One had been born who would bring the dissolution of the empire he had founded. The philosophy of Horace was enough for him, "Today let us enjoy wine and love: hopeless death awaits us: there is not a day to be lost!"

But his vassal of Judea may have had a presentiment of the birth of Jesus, of the true King.

Herod was not a Jew, nor a Greek, nor a Roman. He was an Idumaean, a barbarian who prostrated himself before Rome and aped the Greeks, the better to secure his dominion over the Jews. Son of a traitor, he had usurped the kingdom of his sovereign from the last unfortunate Hasmonaeans. To legalize his treachery he married their niece. Afterwards, he had her killed. Her mother, her brothers (last of the conquered dynasty), even the sons he had had by her, were also put to death.

Voluptuous, impious, greedy of gold and of glory, Herod humiliated himself before Augustus to make him the accomplice of his infamies and, meanwhile, attempted to conciliate the Greeks and the Jews. In Athens they put up a statue to him, but to the Jews he was always the heathen and the usurper. It did him no good, in their eyes, to build up Samaria and restore the Temple of Jerusalem.

Apprehensive like all aging evildoers, and credulous of soothsayers, he readily believed the three wise men when they said that, led by a star, they had come from the interior of Chaldea, and when he knew from the wise men that a King of Judea was born, his uneasy barbarian's heart gave a great leap of fear. Seeing that the astrologers did not come back to tell him the place where the new nephew of David had appeared, he ordered that all the boy babies of Bethlehem should be killed.

Nobody ever knew how many children were sacrificed to the terror of Herod, but if we can believe Macrobius we know that among them was a little son of Herod who was at nurse in Bethlehem. For the old king, wife killer and son killer, who knows but that he suffered when they brought him news of the mistake? A short time after this, suffering from loathsome disease, burnt up with fevers, gasping, disgusting to himself, he tried to kill himself with a knife at table, and finally died.

A CHRISTIAN POET, an Italian, sang this lullaby to the newborn Jesus:

> "Sleep, baby, do not weep,
> Sleep, heavenly babe. . . .
> Over your head, the tempests shall not dare to rage!"

But how can the Son of Mary sleep when the shuffling steps of Herod's assassins draw near?

And Mary cannot sleep. In the evening as soon as the houses of Bethlehem disappear in the darkness and the first lamps are lighted, the mother steals away like a fugitive. She is snatching a life away from the king as she presses upon her breast her man-child, her hope, her sorrow.

She goes toward the west, she crosses the old land of Canaan and comes by easy stages—the days are short—to the Nile, to that country which had cost so many tears to her ancestors fourteen centuries before.

The people of Jesus left Chaldea with Abraham and came with Joseph into Egypt. When the Jews were under the whip of the Egyptian slaves, Moses, the Shepherd of Median, made himself the Shepherd of Israel, and led his people across the desert till they were in sight of the Jordan and of the miraculous vineyards. Jesus, who carried on the work of Moses and at the same time demolished the work of Moses, now in danger of his life, went back to the banks of that river where the first Saviour had been saved from the water and had saved his brothers.

Death was the obsession of Egypt. The rich, portly Egyptian, adorer of the sacred bull and the dogheaded god, would not accept death. He manufactured for his second life immense necropolises full of bandaged and perfumed mummies, of images of wood and marble, and raised up pyramids over his corpses, as if stone and mortar might save them from decay.

When Jesus could speak, He was to pronounce the verdict against Egypt with its kings, its sparrow hawks, its serpents, and its wealth which came from the rich snake-breeding mud that the Nile rolled out each year upon the desert. Christ was to condemn the wealth which comes from mud and returns to mud, and He was to conquer death by teaching that sin is greedier than worms and that spiritual purity is the only aromatic which preserves from decay.

BUT THE EXILE in Egypt was short. Jesus was brought back, held in His mother's arms, rocked throughout the long journey by the patient step of the ass, to His father Joseph's humble house and shop in Nazareth, where the hammer pounded and the rasp scraped until the setting of the sun.

The canonical gospels say nothing of these years: the Apocrypha give many details but are unworthy of belief. Luke, the wise doctor, is content to set down that the boy grew and was strong. He was healthy, a bearer of health, as was fitting in one who was to restore health to others by the touch of His hand.

Every year, says Luke, the parents of Jesus went to Jerusalem for the feast of unleavened bread in memory of the escape from Egypt. They went with a crowd of neighbors, friends, and acquaintances: for the Passover had become at Jerusalem a great feast day, when all the Jews scattered about the empire came together.

On the twelfth Passover after the birth of Jesus, as the group from Nazareth was returning from the holy city, Mary found that her son was not with them. All day long she sought for

Him, asking every acquaintance, but in vain. The next morning the mother turned back, retraced her steps over the road and went up and down the streets and open places of Jerusalem, fixing her dark eyes on every boy she met, asking the mothers standing in the open doors, begging her countrymen not yet gone, to help her find her lost son. A mother who has lost her son does not rest until she has found him; she thinks no more of herself, she does not feel weariness, effort, hunger. She does not shake the dust from her clothes nor arrange her hair. Her distracted eyes see nothing but the image of him who is no longer beside her.

Finally on the third day she came to the Temple, looked about in the courts, and saw at last in the shadow of a portico a group of old men talking. She came up timidly, for those men with long cloaks and long beards seemed people of importance, who would pay no attention to a plain woman from Galilee, and discovered in the center of the circle the shining eyes, the tanned face of her Jesus. Those old men were talking with her son of the Law and the Prophets. They were asking Him questions and He was answering; He put questions to them in His turn and they marveled at Him, astonished that a boy should know the words of the Lord so well. But His memory had retained every syllable of the books which He had heard read out in the little synagogue of Nazareth.

Mary remained for a few moments gazing at Him, hardly believing her eyes. But she could not restrain herself anymore and suddenly in a loud voice called Him by name. The old men took themselves off and the mother snatched her son to her breast and clasped Him to her, the tears which she had kept back till then raining down.

"Son, why hast thou thus dealt with us? behold, thy father and I have sought thee sorrowing."

"How is it that ye sought me? wist ye not that I must be about my Father's business?"

Weighty words when said by a twelve-year-old boy to a mother who had sought Him for three long days.

The Evangelist goes on, "And they understood not the saying which he spake unto them." But after so many centuries of

Christian experience we can understand those words, which seemed at first sight to be hard and proud.

"Who is this father of whom you speak to me? He is the human father. But my real Father is in heaven. If I am to do what He has commanded me, I must be busy about what is truly His. What is a temporal tie confronted with a mystic, spiritual and eternal bond?"

But the hour for really leaving His home had not come for Jesus. The voice of John the Baptist, last of the Prophets, had not yet been heard. With His father and mother Jesus once more went along the road to Nazareth and returned to Joseph's shop to help him in his trade.

Jesus did not go to school to the scribes nor to the Greeks. But He did not lack for teachers. He had three teachers greater than all the learned: work, nature and the Book.

It must never be forgotten that Jesus was born poor, among people who worked with their hands. The adopted son of a workingman, before He gave out His gospel, He earned His daily bread. Those hands which blessed the simplehearted, which cured the lepers, which gave light to the blind, which brought the dead to life, those hands which were pierced with nails upon the cross, were hands which had known the numbness of work, hands which were calloused with work, hands which had held tools, the hands of a workingman.

Jesus, descendant of kings, lived in a woodworker's shop: Son of God, He was born in a stable. He did not belong to the caste of the aristocracy of warriors, to the Sanhedrin of the priests. When He became no longer a manual worker, He went down lower yet in the eyes of respectable folk, and sought His friends in that miserable huddle which is even below the common people: the vagabonds, the beggars, the fugitives, the slaves, the criminals, the prostitutes.

Jesus' trade is one of the four oldest and most sacred of man's occupations. The peasant breaks the clod and takes from it the bread eaten by the saint in his grotto and the murderer in his prison; the mason squares the stone and builds up the house of the poor man, the house of the king, the house of God. The smith heats and fashions the iron to give a sword to the soldier, a plowshare to the peasant, a hammer to the carpenter. Jesus, the carpenter, made the table around which it is so sweet to sit in the evening with one's friends, the chest where the country wife keeps her handkerchiefs for festivals and the starched white shirts for great days. He made the kneading trough where the flour is put, and the leaven raises it until it is ready for the oven.

While the thin, light shavings curled up under His plane and the sawdust rained down on the ground, Jesus thought of the prophecies of old time, of what He was to create, not with boards and rules, but with spirit and truth. His trade taught Him that just as a child's crib or a wife's bed can be made out of a log of olive wood, gnarled, knotty and earthy, so the money changer and the prostitute can be transformed into true citizens of the Kingdom of Heaven.

IN NATURE, where wheat ripens and grows golden to give bread to Jew and heathen, where the stars shine on the shepherd's cabin and the murderer's prison; where grape clusters turn purple and swell to give wine to the wedding banquet; where the birds of the air freely singing find their food without fatigue, where thieving foxes have their refuge and the lilies of the field are clad in more splendor than kings, Jesus found the earthly confirmation of His eternal certainty that God is not a Master who punishes one day of enjoyment by a thousand years of reproach, nor a fierce warlike Jehovah who commands the extermination of enemies, nor a kind of grand sultan who delights in being served by satraps of high lineage.

As a Son, Christ knew that God is Father of all mankind and not only of the people of Abraham. This idea of God as Father, which is one of the great new ideas of the gospel of Christ, this profoundly renovating idea that God loves us as a father loves his children, and gives daily bread to all his children and has a loving welcome even for those who sin if only they return to lean their heads upon his breast: this idea Jesus found in nature. Sharing all human experience He was to use the most beautiful images of the natural world to transmit to men the first of His joyful messages.

Jesus, like all great souls, loved the country. His talk blossoms with colors, is perfumed by odors of field and of orchard, is peopled by the figures of familiar animals. He saw in His Galilee the figs swelling and ripening under the great, dark leaves: He saw the dry tendrils of the vine greened over with leaves: and from the trellises the white and purple clusters hanging down for the joy of the vintage; He saw from the invisible seed, the mustard raise itself up with its rich light branches, He heard in the night the mournful rustle of the reeds shaken by the wind along the ditches: He saw the seed of grain buried in the earth and its resurrection in the form of a full ear; when the air first began to be warm, He saw the beautiful red, yellow and purple lilies in the midst of the tender green of the wheat: He saw the fresh tufts of grass, luxuriant today and tomorrow dried and cast into the oven; He saw the peaceful animals and the harmful animals, the dove a little vain of its brilliant neck, cooing of love on the roof, the eagle swooping down with widespread wings upon its prey; the swallows of the air; the crows tearing flesh from carrion with their beaks; the loving mother hen calling the chickens under her wings when the sky darkens and thunders; the fox slinking back into its lair; and the dogs under the table of their masters begging for scraps that fall to the ground. He saw the serpent writhing through the grass and the viper hiding among the scattered stones of the tombs.

Born among the shepherds, He who was to become shepherd of men knew and loved the flocks; the ewes searching for the lost lamb, the lambs bleating weakly, and sucking, almost hidden under their mothers' woolly bodies, the flocks sweltering on the thin hot pastures of their hills; He loved with equal love the ancient fig tree, casting its shade over the poor man's house; the fish silvering the meshes of the nets to feed His faithful; and raising His eyes in the sultry evenings, He saw the lightning flashing out of the east and shattering the darkness of the night.

But Jesus did not read only in the many-colored book of the world. Jesus read the books where His ancestors had set down the story of His people, the will of the Lord, the vision of the Prophets. He knew that God spoke to men through angels, patriarchs and prophets, and His words, His laws, His victories are written in the Book.

Among all peoples the Jew was the most happy and the most unhappy. His story is a mystery which begins with the idyl in the Garden of Eden. His first parents were molded by the luminous hands of God, were made masters of Paradise, the country of eternal, fertile summer, set in the midst of rivers, where the rich Oriental fruits hung down ready to their hand, heavy with pulp in the shade of the new young leaves. The new-created sky watched over the first two with all its stars.

The first couple had as their duty to love God and to love each other. This was the First Covenant. Weariness unknown, grief unknown, unknown death and its terror! The first disobedience brought the first exile; the man was condemned to work, the woman to bring forth her young in pain. Work is painful, but it brings the reward of harvests; to give birth means suffering, but it brings the consolation of children. And yet even these inferior and imperfect felicities passed away. For the first time brother killed brother: human blood gave forth an exhalation of sin: from the daughters of men were born fierce hunters and slayers of men, who turned the world into a bloody hell.

Then God sent His second punishment: to purify the world He drowned in the waters of the flood all men and their crimes. One only, a righteous man, was saved and with him God signed the Second Covenant.

With Noah there began the happy days of antiquity, the epoch of the patriarchs, nomad shepherds, centenarians who wandered between Chaldea and Egypt searching for grazing lands, for wells, and for peace. They brought along in caravans, numerous as armies, their fruitful wives, their loving sons, their docile daughters-in-law, their innumerable descendants, obedient manservants and maidservants, goring, bellowing bulls, cows with hanging udders, playful calves, rams and strong-smelling he-goats, mild sheep laden with wool, great earth-colored camels, mares with round cruppers, she-goats holding their heads high and stamping impatiently; and hidden in the saddlebags, vases of gold and silver, domestic idols of stone and metal.

Arrived at their destination, they spread their tents near a cistern, and the patriarch sat out under the shade of the oaks and sycamores contemplating the great camp from which rose up the smoke of the fires, the bustling of the herdsmen, the moo-ings, the brayings, the bleating of the animals. And the patri-arch's heart was filled with content to see all this progeny issued from his seed, all these, his herds, the human increase and the animal increase multiplying year by year.

In the evening, he raised his eyes to greet the first punctual star which shone like white fire on the summit of the hill; and sometimes his curled white beard shone in the white light of the moon, which for more than a century he was wont to see in the sky at night.

Sometimes an angel of the Lord came to visit him, and before giving the message with which he was charged, ate at his table. Or, in the heat of the day, the Lord Himself, in the garb of a pilgrim, came and sat down with the old man in the shadow of the tent where they talked with each other, face-to-face, like two old friends who come together to discuss their affairs. And between Jehovah and Abraham was signed the Third Covenant, more solemn than the other two.

The son of a patriarch, sold by his brothers as a slave, rises to power in Egypt, and calls his race to him. The Jews think that they have found a fatherland and grow great in numbers and riches. But they allow themselves to be seduced by the gods of Egypt, and Jehovah prepares the third punishment. The envi-ous Egyptians reduce them to abject slavery. That the punish-ment may be longer, Jehovah hardens the heart of Pharaoh, but finally raises up the second Saviour, who leads them forth from their sufferings and from the mud of Egypt.

Their trials are not yet finished: for forty years they wander in the desert. A pillar of cloud guides them by day and a pillar of fire by night. God has assured them a Land of Promise, with rich grazing lands, well watered, shaded by grapevines and olives. But in the meantime they have neither water to drink nor bread to eat, and they yearn for the fleshpots of Egypt. God brings water gushing from a rock; and manna and quails fall from heaven; but tired and uneasy, the Jews betray their God, make a calf of gold and worship it.

Moses, saddened like all prophets, misunderstood like all saviours, followed unwillingly like all discoverers of new lands, falls back of the restive and rebellious crowd and begs God to let him lie down forever. But at any cost, Jehovah desires to sign the Fourth Covenant with His people. Moses goes down from the smoke-capped thundering mountain, with the two tables of stone whereon the very finger of God has written the Ten Commandments.

Moses is not to see the Promised Land, but the divine pledge is kept: Joshua and the other heroes cross the Jordan, enter into the land of Canaan, and conquer the people; the cities fall at the breath of their trumpets; Deborah can sing her song of triumph. The people carry with them the God of battles, hidden behind the tents, on a cart drawn by oxen. But the enemies are numerous and have no mind to give way to the newcomers. The Jews wander here and there, shepherds and brigands, victorious when they maintain the covenants of the Law, defeated when they forget them.

A giant with unshorn hair kills, single-handed, thousands of Philistines and Amalekites, but a woman betrays him; enemies blind him and set him to turn a mill. Heroes alone are not enough. Kings are needed. A young man of the tribe of Benjamin, tall and well-grown, while looking for his father's strayed asses, is met by a Prophet who anoints him with the sacred oil, and makes him king of all the people. Saul becomes a powerful warrior, overcomes the Ammonites and Amalekites and founds a military kingdom, dreaded by neighboring tribes. But the same Prophet who made him king, now aroused against him, raises up a rival. David, the boy shepherd, kills the king's giant foe, tempers with his harp the black rages of the king, is loved by the king's oldest son, marries the daughter of the king, is among the king's captains. But Saul, suspicious and unbalanced, wishes to kill him.

David hides himself in the caves of the mountains, becomes a robber chief. He goes into the service of the Philistines, and when they conquer and kill Saul on the hills of Gilboa, he becomes in his turn king of all Israel. The bold sheep-tender, great as poet and as king, founds his house in Jerusalem and subjugates the surrounding kingdoms. For the first time, the Jew is feared: for centuries after this he was to hope for a descendant of David to save him from his abject subjugation.

David is the king of the sword and of song. Solomon is the king of gold and of wisdom. Gold is brought to him as a tribute: he decks with gold the first sumptuous house of Jehovah. He sends ships to faraway Ophir in search of gold; the Queen of Sheba lays down sacks of gold at his feet. He takes strange women to wife and worships strange gods. The Lord pardons his old age, in memory of his youth, but at his death the kingdom is divided and the dark and shameful centuries of the decadence begin. Plots in the palace, murders of kings, revolts of chiefs, wretched civil wars, periods of idol worship, fill the period of the separation. Prophets appear and admonish, but the kings turn a deaf ear or drive them away.

The enemies of Israel grow more powerful. The Phoenicians, the Egyptians, the Assyrians, the Babylonians, one after another, invade the two kingdoms, extort tribute and finally, about six hundred years before the birth of Jesus, Jerusalem is destroyed, the Temple of Jehovah is demolished and the Jews are led as slaves to the rivers of Babylon. The same God who liberated them from the slavery of the Egyptians gives them over as slaves to the Babylonians.

This is the fourth punishment and the most terrible. From that time on, the Jews were always to be dispersed among strangers and subject to foreigners. Some of them were to return to reconstruct Jerusalem and its temple, but the country, invaded by the Scythians, tributary to the Persians, conquered by the Greeks, was after the last attempt of the Maccabeans finally given over to the hands of a dynasty of Arab barbarians, subject to the Romans. This race, which believed itself, under the protection of its God, the first people of the earth, was now dreadfully chastised, the Job among peoples.

FINALLY FROM THIS RACE was born He who had been awaited by all the Prophets.

India has its ascetics, who hide themselves in the wilderness to conquer the body and drown the soul in the infinite. China had its familiar sages, peaceful grandfathers who taught civic morality to working people and emperors. Greece had her philosophers, who in their shady porticos contrived harmonious systems and dialectic pitfalls. Rome had its lawgivers who recorded on bronze for the centuries the rules of the highest justice attainable to those who command and possess. The Jewish people had the Prophets.

The Jewish Prophet is not a priest, for he has never been anointed in the Temple. But he is a voice speaking in the name of God, or a hand writing at God's dictation, a voice speaking in the palace of the king or in the caves of the mountains, on the steps of the Temple. His mouth is full of bitterness, his arm is raised, pointing out punishment to come; because he loves his people, he vituperates them: and after massacres and flames, he teaches the resurrection and the life, the reign of the new David and the Covenant not to be broken.

The Prophet leads the idolater back to the true God, recalls charity to the oppressor, purity to the corrupt, mercy to the fierce, obedience to rebels, humbleness to the proud. He goes before the king and reproaches him, he greets priests with blame; and brings the rich to confusion. He announces consolation to the poor, health to the sick. A troublesome importunate voice, hated by the great, out of favor with the crowd, not always understood even by his disciples, the Prophet goes up and down the streets of Israel followed by suspicion and malediction, avoided like a leper, persecuted like an enemy.

Elijah is forced to flee before the wrath of Jezebel; Amos is banished beyond Israel by Amaziah, priest of Bethel; Isaiah is killed by the order of Manasseh; Uriah cut down by King Jehoiakim; Zacharias stoned between the temple and the altar; Jonah thrown into the sea; the sword is prepared for the neck of John; and the cross is ready from which Jesus will hang.

The Prophet is an announcer, but the deaf do not hear his promises. He is a saviour, but men refuse to be cured.

IN THE HOUSE at Nazareth Jesus recognizes in the fiery laments of the Prophets His destiny. When, at the beginning of His thirtieth year, He presents Himself to men as the Son of man, He knows what awaits Him. His life to come is already set down day by day in pages written before His earthly birth.

He knows that God promised Moses: "I will raise them up a Prophet from among their brethren, like unto thee, and will put my words in his mouth; and he shall speak unto them all that I shall command him." God will make a new covenant with His people. "Not according to the covenant that I made with their fathers . . . but I will put my law in their inward parts, and write it in their hearts. . . . I will forgive their iniquity, and I will remember their sin no more."

The Messiah will have a precursor to announce Him. "Behold, I will send my messenger, and he shall prepare the way before me."

"For unto us a child is born, unto us a son is given: and the government shall be upon his shoulder: and his name shall be called Wonderful, Counsellor, the mighty God, the everlasting Father, the Prince of Peace."

He will not come in proud triumph: "Rejoice greatly, O daughter of Zion; shout, O daughter of Jerusalem: behold, thy King cometh unto thee: he is just, and having salvation; lowly, and riding upon an ass, and upon a colt the foal of an ass."

He will bring justice and will lift up the unhappy: ". . . because the Lord hath anointed me to preach good tidings unto the meek; he hath sent me to bind up the brokenhearted, to proclaim liberty to the captives, and the opening of the prison to them that are bound; . . . to comfort all that mourn."

But He will be vilified and tortured by the very people He comes to save: "he hath no form nor comeliness; and when we shall see him, there is no beauty that we should desire him. He is . . . rejected of men; a man of sorrows, and acquainted with grief: and we hid as it were our faces from him; he was despised, and we esteemed him not."

Too late they will understand what they have done and will repent.

". . . and they shall look upon me whom they have pierced, and they shall mourn for him, as one mourneth for his only son, and shall be in bitterness for him, as one that is in bitterness for his firstborn."

"Yea, all kings shall bow down before him: all nations shall serve him."

These and other words are remembered by Jesus in the vigil before His departure. He knows that the Jews are not awaiting a poor, gentle, despised Messiah. They are dreaming of a terrestrial Messiah, a second David, a warrior who will rebuild more splendidly than ever the palace of Solomon and the Temple.

He knows He cannot give them what they seek, that His kingdom is not of this earth. But He knows that the seed of His word thrown into the earth among thistles and thorns, trampled underfoot, will start into life when spring comes. Little by little it will grow, until finally it becomes a tree stretching its branches up to the sky, covering the earth with the boughs. And all men can sit round about it, remembering the death of Him who planted it.

WHILE JESUS, in the poor little workshop at Nazareth, was handling the axe and the square, a voice was raised in the desert toward Jordan and the Dead Sea. Last of the Prophets, John the Baptist called the Jews to repent, announced the approach of the Kingdom of Heaven, predicted the coming of the Messiah, reproved the sinners who came to him, and plunged them into the water of the river, that this outer washing might be the beginning of an inner purification.

John's figure was one to conquer the imagination. A child sprung by a miracle from parents of great age, he was set apart from his birth to be *nazir*—pure. He had never cut his hair, had never tasted wine or cider, had never touched a woman nor

known any love except that for God. While he was still young, he had left his parents' home and buried himself in the desert. There he lived for many years alone, without a tent, wrapped in his camel's skin, his flanks girt by a leather belt, tall, bony, his chest hairy, his hair hanging long on his shoulders, his long beard almost covering his face. His piercing eyes flashed like lightning from under his bushy eyebrows when from his mouth hidden by his beard burst out the tremendous words of his maledictions.

This hypnotic wild man, solitary as a Yogi, despising pleasure like a stoic, seemed to those whom he baptized the last hope of a despairing people.

The desert sun burned John's body and he was a foreteller of fire who saw in the Messiah, soon to appear, the master of flame. He will gather His wheat into the garner, but He will burn up the chaff with unquenchable fire; and every tree which bringeth not forth good fruit will be hewn down and cast into the fire. He will be a baptizer who will baptize with fire.

Rigid, wrathful, harsh, shaggy, quick to insult, impatient and impetuous, John was not gentle with those who came to him. When Pharisees and Sadducees, notable men, learned in the Scriptures, esteemed by the crowd, of authority in the Temple, came to be baptized, he shamed them more than the others. "O generation of vipers, who hath warned you to flee from the wrath to come? Bring forth therefore fruits meet for repentance."

It is not enough to bathe in the Jordan. Change your life. "And the people asked him, saying, What shall we do then? He answereth and saith unto them, He that hath two coats, let him impart to him that hath none; and he that hath meat, let him do likewise.

"Then came also publicans to be baptized, and said unto him, Master, what shall we do? And he said unto them, Exact no more than that which is appointed you.

"And the soldiers likewise demanded of him, saying, And what shall we do? And he said unto them, Do violence to no man, neither accuse any falsely; and be content with your wages."

Almost superhuman when he announced the terrible separation of the good from the bad, John becomes commonplace when he descends to particulars. This is nothing more or less than the Mosaic Law. Long before him, Amos and Isaiah had gone further.

Perhaps the fierceness of John is justified by his consciousness of being an ambassador, a consciousness which leaves a tinge of sadness, even in his humility. They came from Jerusalem to ask him who he was, "What then? Art thou Elias?"

"No. I am not."

"Art thou the Christ?"

"No. . . . I am the voice of one crying in the wilderness. . . . He it is, who coming after me is preferred before me, whose shoe's latchet I am not worthy to unloose."

At Nazareth, meantime, an unknown workingman was lacing up His shoes with His own hands to go out to the wilderness. Jesus had heard the people talk of those "washed ones" who returned from Jordan and He understood that His day grew near. He was now in His thirtieth year, the destined age.

JESUS PRESENTED Himself to John to be baptized. Did He then acknowledge Himself a sinner? The prophet preached the baptism of repentance in remission of sins. He who goes to wash feels himself polluted.

The fact that we know nothing of the life of Jesus from His twelfth to His thirtieth year, exactly the years of fallible adolescence, of hot-blooded youth, has given rise to the idea that He held Himself to have been a sinner like other men. The three remaining years of His life are the most brightly lighted by the words of the four Gospels. Nothing of what we know of those three years gives any indication of this supposed existence of sin in Christ's life between the innocence of its beginning and the glory of its ending.

And yet Jesus came in the midst of a crowd of sinners to immerse Himself in the Jordan. The problem is not mysterious; He went to John that the prophecy of the precursor might be fulfilled. Jesus, about to begin His true life, did not go down to the Jordan to cleanse Himself, but to show that His second life was beginning.

AS SOON AS Jesus emerged from the water He went into the desert. He went up on the rocky mountains whence no springs arise, where the only living creatures are snakes.

For those rich in soul, solitude is a prize and not an expiation. The people who cannot endure solitude are afraid of their own emptiness. Jesus loved men. But in the years to come He often hid Himself, to be alone, far even from His disciples. To love your brothers, you need from time to time to depart from them: far from them, you draw near to them.

For Jesus these forty days of solitude are the last of His preparation. For forty years the Jewish people wandered in the desert before entering into the kingdom promised by God. For forty days Moses remained close to God to hear His laws; for forty days Elijah wandered, fleeing the vengeance of the wicked queen. So also the time allotted to the new liberator before announcing the promised kingdom, the Kingdom of Heaven which is in ourselves, was forty days of close communion with God to receive the supreme inspiration. About Him in His vigil will be animals and angels; beings all matter, beings all spirit.

Man is matter changing by slow transmutation into spirit. If the animal gets the upper hand, man descends below the level of the beasts because he puts the remnants of his intelligence at the service of bestiality: if the angel conquers, man partakes of divinity itself. But the fallen angel, Satan, condemned to wear the form of a beast, is the enemy of all men who wish to climb that height from which he was cast down. Satan seduced the innocence of the first two created beings, he suborned David the strong, corrupted Solomon the wise, accused Job the righteous before the throne of God. Satan tempts and always will tempt all those who love God.

Therefore at the end of the forty days, Satan came into the desert to tempt Jesus.

Whenever Jesus shared human lives, He consented to eat and drink, because it is right to give to the flesh that which belongs to the flesh. But our slavery to matter is branded on our lives by the daily need of our bodies for food, so His first act after His baptism had been a fast. After forty days He was hungry. Satan, tenacious and invisible, was waiting for this moment of material

467

need, and spoke: "If thou be the Son of God, command this stone that it be made bread."

The reproof was prompt: "It is written that man shall not live by bread alone, but by every word of God."

Satan, from the top of a mountain, showed Him all the kingdoms of the earth: "All this power will I give thee, and the glory of them: for that is delivered unto me; and to whomsoever I will I give it. If thou therefore wilt adore me, all shall be thine."

And Jesus answered, "Get thee behind me, Satan: for it is written thou shalt worship the Lord thy God, and him only shalt thou serve."

Then Satan took Him to Jerusalem and set Him on the pinnacle of the Temple: "If thou be the Son of God, cast thyself down from hence."

But Jesus answered quickly: "It is written; thou shalt not tempt the Lord thy God."

"And when the Devil had ended all the temptation," Luke goes on, "he departed from him for a season."

Satan asks material bread and a material miracle of Jesus and promises Him material power. Jesus refuses what is offered.

He is not the material Messiah. He did not come to bring food to bodies but food to souls—truth, that living food. Man does not live by bread alone, but by love, fervor, and truth. Jesus conquers Satan in Himself and now comes out of the desert to conquer him among men. He is ready to transform the kingdom of earth into the Kingdom of Heaven.

THE RETURN

As soon as Jesus came again among men, He learned that the tetrarch Antipas (son of Herod the Great and second husband of Herodias) had imprisoned John in the fortress of Machaerus. The voice crying in the wilderness was stilled and was now to give way to a more powerful voice. John waited in the blackness of the prison until his bloody head was carried on a golden platter to the banquet—almost the last dish served to Salome, that evil woman, betrayer of men.

Now Jesus understands that His day is at hand, and crossing Samaria He returns into Galilee to announce at once the coming of the Kingdom. There He is to find His first listeners, His first converts, His first disciples.

He does not wish to begin His message in Jerusalem. If He should go to that capital city of the great king now, He would be taken prisoner at once and would not be able to sow His word on less stony soil. At Jerusalem live the powerful of the world: the Romans, masters of the world and of Judea, with their soldiers in arms; the high priests, the old custodians of the Temple; the Pharisees, Sadducees, scribes, the Levites and their guards, the petrifiers of the Law.

He wishes to arrive at Jerusalem later with a following behind Him, when already the Kingdom of Heaven has begun slowly to lay siege to the city. The conquest of Jerusalem will be the last test, the supreme trial.

A man from the provinces, He goes back to His province. He arrives in Galilee, and begins to teach. He wishes to carry the tidings of good news to the poor and the humble because the tidings are especially for them, because they have long been waiting for them.

THE FIRST WORDS of Jesus are few and simple, very much like those of John, "The time is fulfilled, and the Kingdom of God is at hand: repent ye, and believe the Gospel."

Words incomprehensible to moderns by their very sobriety. To understand them and to understand the difference between the message of John and the message of Jesus, they need to be translated into our language, filled again with their eternally living meaning. John said that a King would come ready to found the new Kingdom, the Kingdom of Heaven. Now the King has come and announces that the doors of the Kingdom are open. He is the guide, the path, the hand.

When Jesus says "The time is fulfilled," he does not refer to the fact that it was the fifteenth year of the reign of Tiberius.

The time of Jesus is now and always is eternity. The Kingdom is not the worn-out fancy of a poor Jew nearly twenty centuries ago. The Kingdom is of today, tomorrow, of always. There is no chronology in eternity. Jesus threw the seed into the earth, but the seed has scarcely germinated in two thousand years passed like a stormy winter, in the space of sixty human generations. Begin at once: it is our work. The Kingdom of God will be founded among men. The spirit is the dominion of goodness.

Jesus added "repent," but the old word has been distorted from its true and magnificent meaning. *Metanoia*—a changing of the spirit—ought rather to be translated "conversion," that is, the renewing of the inner life of man.

As one of the conditions of the arrival of the Kingdom and at the same time as the very substance of the new order, Jesus demands complete conversion, a revolution of the common values of life, a transmutation of feelings, of intentions. Little by little He was to explain in what way this total transformation, this "second birth" of the ordinary human soul, is to be effected. But in the meantime, He contented Himself with adding one conclusion, "Believe in the Gospel."

By "Gospel" men nowadays mean usually the book where the quadruple story of Jesus is printed; but Jesus neither wrote books nor thought of volumes. By "Gospel" He meant, according to the plain and sweet meaning of the word, "good tidings." Jesus is a messenger (in Greek "angel") who brings good tidings: the cheerful message that the sick will be cured, that the blind will see, the poor will be enriched with imperishable riches, that the sad will rejoice, that sinners will be pardoned, the unclean purified, that the imperfect can become perfect.

With those few words Jesus began His teaching. He taught His Galileans on the thresholds of their shabby little white houses, on the small shady open places of their cities or the shore of the lake, leaning against a beached boat, His feet on the stones, toward evening when the sun sank red in the west.

Many listened to Him and followed Him because, says Luke: "His word was with authority." Here was a prophet living like a man among other men, friendly to the unfriended, searching out His brothers where they work in the houses, in the busy streets, eating their bread and drinking wine at their tables, lending a hand with the fisherman's nets, with a word for the sad, for the sick, for the beggar.

If He returned to Nazareth, He stayed there but a short time. He was to go back later, accompanied by the Twelve and preceded by the renown of His miracles, and they were to treat Him as all the cities of the world—even the most renowned for amenity, Athens and Florence—have treated those of their citizens who made them great above others. After ridiculing Him they tried to cast Him down from the precipice.

Jesus spent His time with them walking from one region to another. He was such a man as is called a vagabond. His life is an eternal journey. He is the true Wandering Jew. He was born on a journey. Still a baby at the breast, He was carried along the sun-parched road to Egypt; from Egypt He came back to the waters and greenness of Galilee. The voice of John called Him to the Jordan: an inner voice drove Him out into the desert; and after the forty days of hunger and the temptation, He began His restless vagabond life from city to city, from village to village, from mountain to mountain, across Palestine.

We find Him in Galilee, in Chorazin, in Cana, in Magdala, in Tiberias, but often He crosses Samaria to sit down near the well of Sychar. We find Him from time to time in the tetrarchy of Philip at Bethsaida, at Gadara, at Caesarea, also at Gerasa in the Perea of Herod Antipas. In Judah He often stops at Bethany, a few miles away from Jerusalem, or at Jericho, but He did not shrink from journeying outside the limits of the old kingdom and from going down among the Gentiles. We find Him in Phoenicia, in the regions of Tyre and Sidon, and in Syria. His bed is the furrow in a field, the bench of a boat, the shadow of an olive tree. Sometimes He sleeps in the houses of those who love Him, but only for short periods.

IN THE EARLY DAYS we find Him most often at Capernaum. His journeys began there and ended there. Matthew calls it "His city." Situated on the caravan route which from Damascus crosses Ituraea and goes toward the sea, Capernaum had become a commercial center of some importance. Artisans, bargainers,

brokers, and shopkeepers had come there to stay; publicans, excise men and other fiscal tools. The little settlement, half rustic, half a fishing village, had become a mixed and composite city where the society of the times—even to soldiers and prostitutes—was fully represented. And yet Capernaum, lying along the lake, freshened by the air from the nearby hills and by the breeze from the water, was not a prey to stagnation and decay like the Syrian cities and Jerusalem. There were still peasants who went out to their fields every day, and fishermen who every day went forth to their boats. Good, poor, simple, warm-hearted people who talked of other matters than money. Among them a man could draw his breath freely.

In Capernaum there is nothing to do on Sabbaths except go to the synagogue, where everybody has the right to enter, to read aloud, and to expound what has been read. The gardener who no longer turns his waterwheel to irrigate the green rows, and the country smith, whose face is scrubbed and rinsed in many waters like his hands, and whose beard is anointed with a cheap ointment (but still perfumed like a rich man's beard), come to the synagogue to hear the ancient word of the God of their fathers. Family, friends, neighbors—they find them all together.

The mason comes, he who has worked on this house and made it small because the Elders did not wish to spend too much. The mason still feels his arms a little numb and lame from his six days' labor. The fishermen have turned over their boats on the sand, have spread the nets on the roof and have come too, with faces tanned by the sun and with eyes half shut from the constant glare of sunlight reflected by the water. They are not used to being within walls and perhaps continue to hear a confused murmur of water lapping about the bow.

The peasants of the neighboring countryside are here, prosperous farmers who have put on a tunic as good as anybody's, who are satisfied with the harvest almost ready for the scythe. There are shepherds in town that morning, with the smell of their flocks still on them, shepherds who live all the week in the mountain pastures, alone with their quiet animals. The gentry of Capernaum all have come, the smaller property owners, the small-business men. They stand in the front row, their eyes cast down, the line of their well-clad backs bowed but broad and masterful—employers' backs, backs full of authority and of religion. There are also transient foreigners, merchants going toward Syria or returning to Tiberias.

At the back of the room (for the synagogue is only a long whitewashed room a little larger than a school) the poor of the countryside are huddled together like dogs near a door, like those who always stand in fear of being sent away: old widows, young orphans, humpbacked old men, those who are incurably sick, those whose wits no longer rightly serve them. Those who pick up what others throw away, the pieces of dry bread, fish heads, fruit cores and skins; those who suffer from the winter cold and every year wait for summer, paradise of the poor, for then there are fruits to be plucked along the roads. Every Sabbath the poverty-stricken throng at the back of the synagogue waits for somebody to read a chapter from Amos or from Isaiah because the Prophets take the part of the poor, and announce the punishment and the new world.

ON THAT SABBATH there was One who had come back from the desert to announce good tidings. He stood up, had someone give Him one of the scrolls of the Scriptures (more likely the Prophets than the Law) and recited in a tranquil voice two, three, four or more verses. Then He commenced to speak with a bold eloquence which put the Pharisees to confusion, touched sinners, won the poor, and enchanted women.

Suddenly the old text was transfigured, became transparent, belonged to their own times; the words, dried up by repetition, were fresh words coined at that moment, shining before their eyes like an unexpected revelation.

Nobody in Capernaum could remember having heard such a Rabbi. No one had ever spoken of the poor and the sick as He did, no one had shown so much love for them. Like the old Prophets, He had for them a special affection which offended more fortunate men, but which filled their hearts with comfort and hope.

When Jesus had finished speaking, the elders, lords, and Pharisees shook their heads forebodingly and got up, making wry faces among themselves, half contemptuous, half scandalized, and grumbling disapprobation. The merchants followed them, erect, already thinking of the next day.

There remained behind the shepherds, the peasants, the gardeners, the smiths, the fishermen, and the herd of beggars, the diseased, the maimed. When He came out from the synagogue all those stood waiting in the street. They followed Him timidly as if in a dream; then, grown more bold, they accosted Him and went along together beside the shores of the lake, and now one and now another (they were braver under the open sky) began asking questions. And Jesus paused and answered this obscure crowd with words never to be forgotten.

AMONG THE FISHERMEN of Capernaum, Jesus found His first disciples. Almost every day He was on the beach of the lake; sometimes the boats were going out, sometimes they were coming in, the sails swelling in the breeze; and from the barks the barefooted men climbed down, wading knee-deep in water, carrying the baskets filled with the wet silver of dead fish, and with the old dripping nets.

They put out sometimes at nightfall when there was a moon, and came back early in the morning just after the setting of the moon and before sunrise. Often Jesus was waiting for them on the strand. But sometimes they came back empty-handed, tired and depressed. Jesus greeted them with words which cheered them, and the disappointed men, although they had not slept, listened to Him willingly.

One morning two boats came back toward Capernaum while Jesus standing by the lake was talking to the people who had gathered around Him. The fishermen disembarked and began to arrange the nets; then Jesus entered into one of the boats and asked them to put it out a little from the land so that He might not be pressed upon by the crowd. Upright near the rudder He taught those who had remained on the land, and when He had left speaking He said to Simon, called Peter, "Launch out into the deep, and let down your nets for a draught."

Simon, son of Jona, owner of the boat, answered, "Master,

we have toiled all the night, and have taken nothing: nevertheless at thy word I will let down the net."

When they were only a short distance from the bank, Simon and Andrew, his brother, threw out into the water a large net. And when they drew it back it was so full of fish that the meshes were almost breaking. Then the two brothers called their partners in the other boat, that they should come to help them, and they threw out the net again and drew it up again full. Simon, Andrew and the others cried out "a miracle!" and thanked Jesus. Simon, impulsive by nature, threw himself at the knees of their guest crying, "Depart from me; for I am a sinful man, O Lord."

But Jesus, smiling, said, "Follow me, and I will make you fishers of men."

When they went back to the shore they pulled the boat up on the land, and leaving their nets, the two brothers followed Him. And a few days after this, Jesus saw the other two brothers, James and John, sons of Zebedee, who were partners of Simon and Andrew, and he called them, while they were mending the broken nets; and they too said farewell to their father, who was in the boat with the sailors, and leaving the broken nets half mended, followed Him.

Four poor men of the lake, men who did not know how to read, nor indeed how to speak correctly, were called by Jesus to found with Him a kingdom which was to occupy all the earth. Who among us today, among all those now living, would be capable of imitating those four poor men of Capernaum? "Give away all your goods, for you will acquire with me an inestimable treasure."

Not by chance did Jesus select His first companions from among fishermen. The fisherman who lives a great part of his days in the pure solitude of the water is the patient, unhurried man who lets down his nets and leaves the rest to God, who sends abundance and famine. He washes his hands in water and his spirit in solitude.

Jesus made saints whom even today remember and invoke. A great man creates great men.

When David appears he finds at once his *gibborim*—his bodyguard; an Agamemnon finds his heroes, an Arthur his knights, Charlemagne his paladins, Napoleon his marshals. Jesus found among the men of the people of Galilee His apostles. They were to speak in His name in places where He could not go, and in His name to carry on His work after His death.

THE MOUNT

THE SERMON ON THE MOUNT is the greatest proof of the right of men to exist in the infinite universe. It is the patent of our soul's worthiness, the pledge that we can lift ourselves above ourselves, the hope of our rising above the beast. And if men were called before a superhuman tribunal and had to give an account to the judges of all our inexplicable mistakes, our perfidy, our hardness of heart, the bloodshed between brothers, and the ancient infamies every day renewed, the one attenuation of all those accusations is the Sermon on the Mount. Who has read it and has not felt, at least in that brief moment while he read, a passion of love and remorse, a confused but urgent longing to act?

From the Mount on which Jesus sat the day of the sermon you could see only the plain, calm under the sunset light; on one side the silver-green oval of the lake, and on the other the long crest of Carmel where Elijah overcame the scullions of Baal. From this little rocky hill scarcely rising above the level earth, Jesus disclosed the song of the new man.

He sat in the midst of the first apostles and someone asked Him to whom would be allotted this Kingdom of Heaven, of which He so often spoke. Jesus answered with the nine Beatitudes.

The Beatitudes, so often spelled out even nowadays by people who have lost their meaning, are almost always misunderstood, mutilated, deformed, cheapened, distorted. And yet they epitomize the first day of Christ's teaching.

"Blessed are the poor in spirit: for theirs is the kingdom of heaven." Luke leaves out the words "in spirit," seeming to mean the "poor" and nothing else; and many people after him have understood him to mean the simpleminded. They see in the words only a choice between the bankrupt and the imbecile.

When He spoke, Jesus was not thinking either of the first or the second. For Him supreme intelligence consisted in realizing that the intelligence alone is not enough. Poor in spirit are those who are fully and painfully aware of their own spiritual poverty, of the smallness of the good that is in us all. The poor who realize that they are really poor suffer from their poverty, and try to escape from it. Those therefore who confess themselves poor and undergo suffering to acquire that veritable wealth named perfection, will become holy as God is holy, and theirs shall be the Kingdom of Heaven.

"Blessed are the meek: for they shall inherit the earth." The earth here promised is not monarchies with built-up cities. In the language of the Messiah, "to inherit the earth" means to partake of the New Kingdom. He who fights within himself for the conquest of the new earth and the new heaven does not break out into rage when things go badly. The meek are like water which seems to give way before other substances, but silently attacks, and calmly consumes, with the patience of the years, the hardest granites.

"Blessed are they that mourn: for they shall be comforted." Those who feel disgust for themselves; who weep over the wrong they have done and over the good they might have done and did not; hasten with their tears the day of grace, and it is right that they shall some day be comforted.

"Blessed are they that hunger and thirst after justice: for they shall be filled." The justice which Jesus means is not the justice of men, obedience to human law. The just man is he who lives according to the one simple Law which Jesus reduces to one commandment, "Love all men near and far, your fellow countrymen and foreigners, strangers and enemies." Those who hunger and thirst after this justice shall be filled in the Kingdom of Heaven.

"Blessed are the merciful: for they shall obtain mercy." We constantly commit sins against the spirit and those sins will be forgiven us only as we forgive those committed against us. Christ is in all men and what we do to others will be done to us. "Inasmuch as ye have done it unto one of the least of these my brethren, ye have done it unto me."

"Blessed are the pure in heart: for they shall see God." The pure of heart are those who have no other joy than victory over evil. He who has his heart crammed with furious desires, with the earthly ambitions which convulse this ant heap of the earth, can never see God face-to-face.

"Blessed are the peacemakers: for they shall be called the children of God." When Jesus said He had come to bring war and not peace, He meant, in short, war against war. The peacemakers are those who bring about concord. When every man loves his brothers more than himself, the peacemakers will have conquered the earth and they will be called the true children of God, and they will enter among the first into His Kingdom.

"Blessed are they who have been persecuted for justice' sake: for theirs is the kingdom of heaven." I send you out to found the Kingdom of Heaven, of that higher justice which is love. You will be tortured in body, crucified in soul, deprived of liberty and perhaps of life; but if you accept this suffering cheerfully to carry to others that justice which makes you suffer, this persecution will be for you an incontestable title to enter into the Kingdom which you have founded as far as was in your power.

"Blessed are ye, when men shall revile you, and persecute you, and say all manner of evil against you falsely, for my sake. Rejoice, and be exceeding glad: for great is your reward in heaven: for so persecuted they the prophets which were before you." The persecutors can take away your bread, and the clear light of the sun; they may break your bones. You must expect insult and calumny. But you must always rejoice because the mud thrown at you by evil men is the consecration of your own goodness. This is, as St. Francis says, "the perfect joy." All the prophets who have ever spoken upon the earth were insulted by men, and men will insult those who are to come. We can recognize prophets by this: that smeared with mud and covered with shame, they pass among men, bright-faced, speaking out what is in their hearts. Even if the obstinate prophet is killed, they cannot silence him. His voice multiplied by the echoes of his death will be heard in all languages and through all the centuries.

This promise brings the beatitudes to their end.

THE FIRST PROPHETS, the earliest legislators, the leaders of young nations, the saints, began the domination of the beast. The old law that is found with only a few variations in the Manava Dharmasastra, in the Pentateuch, in the Ta-Hio, in the Avesta, in the traditions of Solon and of Numa, in the sententious maxims of Hesiod and the Seven Wise Men, is the first attempt, rough and inadequate, to mold animality into a sketch of humanity.

This law reduced itself to a few elementary rules necessary for a common life, useful to all: not to steal, not to kill, not to perjure, not to fornicate, not to tyrannize over the weak, not to mistreat strangers and slaves any more than was necessary.

Men of ancient times, lusty, sanguine, ravishers, cattle stealers, warriors who, having dragged by the feet their slaughtered antagonists, refreshed themselves with haunches of oxen, emptying enormous cups of wine; such as we see them in the Mahabharata, and in the Iliad, in the poem of Izdubar, and in the book of wars of Jehovah; such men without the fear of punishment and of God would have been still more unrestrained and ferocious. In times when a head was asked for an eye, an arm for a finger, and a hundred lives for a life, a law of retaliation which asked only an eye for an eye and a life for a life was a notable victory of generosity, appalling though it seems after the teaching of Jesus.

They had come to this point when Jesus spoke on the Mount.

With Jesus therefore begins the new law: the old is abrogated and declared insufficient.

He begins at every example with the words: "Ye have heard it said . . ." and at once He substitutes for the old command, "But I say unto you . . ." With these "buts" a new phase of the human education begins.

"Ye have heard that it was said by them of old time, Thou shalt not kill; . . . But I say unto you, That whosoever is angry with his brother . . . shall be in danger of the judgment: and whosoever shall say to his brother, Raca [vain fellow], shall be in danger of the council: but whosoever shall say, Thou fool, shall be in danger of hell fire." A single moment of anger, a single abusive word, a single offensive phrase, are for Jesus the equivalent of assassination. Murder is only the final carrying out of a feeling.

Anger is like fire: it can be smothered only at the first spark. Jesus goes straight to the extreme and utters the profoundest truth when He decrees the same penalty for the first hot words as for murder.

"Ye have heard that it was said by them of old time, Thou shalt not commit adultery: But I say unto you, That whosoever looketh on a woman to lust after her hath committed adultery with her already in his heart."

Even here Jesus soars from the body to the soul, from flesh to will. What counts is the intention, the feeling; to imagine, to desire a betrayal is already a betrayal.

Jesus advises expressly to pluck out the eye and cast it away if evil comes from the eye, and to cut off the hand and throw it away if evil comes from the hand—advice which dismays the cowardly and even the strong. Yet even the most cowardly, when threatened by cancer, are ready to have their bodies cut open to save their lives. Men are concerned to save the body, but grudge any sacrifice to keep in health the soul.

"Let the dead bury their dead." In the old law there were hundreds of minute, tiresome, complicated precepts for the purification of the body, without any true earthly or heavenly foundation. The Pharisees made the best part of religion consist in their observance of these traditions because it is much less trouble to wash a cup than your own soul.

"Not that which goeth into the mouth defileth a man; but that which cometh out of the mouth, this defileth a man. . . . those things which proceed out of the mouth come forth from the heart; . . . out of the heart proceed evil thoughts, murders, adulteries, fornications, thefts, false witness, blasphemies: These are the things which defile a man: but to eat with unwashen hands defileth not a man."

Jesus does not believe in the perfection of the natural soul.

He believes in its future perfection, only to be reached by a complete overturning of its present nature.

Nothing is more common among men than the thirst for riches. But poverty is the first requisite for the citizenship of the Kingdom. He who wishes to come with me, said Jesus, must go and sell that which he has and give it to the poor and he shall have treasures in Heaven.

Men are always afraid lest there may not be enough bread to last to the next harvest. They fear that they will not have clothes to cover their bodies and the bodies of their children. But Jesus teaches us, "Take therefore no thought for the morrow: . . . Sufficient unto the day is the evil thereof."

The whole history of men is only the terror of standing second; but Jesus teaches us, "And whosoever of you will be the chiefest, shall be servant to all."

Vanity is another universal curse of men. Jesus commands us: "But when thou doest alms, let not thy left hand know what thy right hand doeth: . . . And when thou prayest, thou shalt not be as the hypocrites are: for they love to pray standing in the synagogues and in the corners of the streets, that they may be seen of men. . . . But thou, when thou prayest, enter into thy closet. . . ."

The instinct of self-preservation is the strongest of all those which dominate us. But Jesus tells us: "For whosoever will save his life shall lose it; but whosoever shall lose his life for my sake, . . . the same shall save it." Jesus says, "Judge not, that ye be not judged: condemn not, and ye shall not be condemned: forgive, and ye shall be forgiven."

The Pharisee avoids if possible the company of sinners, but Jesus tirelessly announces that He has come to seek for sinners, and sits down to dinner in the house of the publican, where a prostitute anoints his feet. The truly pure man does not feel that for fear of soiling his garments he needs must leave the corrupt to die in their own vileness.

The avarice of men is so great that everyone tries to take as much as he can from others and to give back as little; but Jesus affirms, "It is more blessed to give than to receive."

But Jesus had not yet arrived at the most stupefying of His

revolutionary teachings. "Ye have heard that it hath been said, An eye for an eye, and a tooth for a tooth: But I say unto you, That ye resist not evil: but whosoever shall smite thee on thy right cheek, turn to him the other also. And if any man will sue thee at the law, and take away thy coat, let him have thy cloak also. And whosoever shall compel thee to go a mile, go with him twain."

There could be no more definite repudiation of the old law of retaliation. "Not to resent offenses," says Aristotle, the disciple of Plato, to Nichomachus in the *Ethics*, "is the mark of a base and slavish man." For the greater part of those who call themselves Christians this principle of not resisting evil has been the unendurable scandal of Christianity.

Literally to follow this command of Jesus demands a mastery possessed by few, of the blood, of the nerves, and of all the instincts of the baser part of our being. But Jesus never said it would be possible to obey Him without harsh renunciations, without stern and continuous inner battles.

These are acts of heroic excellence, supine though they may appear. Only the saints can charm wolves to mildness. Only he who has transformed his own soul can transform the souls of his brothers, and transform the world into a less grievous place for all.

Love for ourselves is the origin of our hatred for others. He who conquers self-love is already entirely transformed. The greatest victory over the fierce, blind, brutal man of antiquity is this and nothing else.

"YE HAVE HEARD that it hath been said, Thou shalt love thy neighbour, and hate thine enemy. But I say unto you, Love your enemies, bless them that curse you, do good to them that hate you, and pray for them which despitefully use you and persecute you; That ye may be the children of your Father which is in heaven: for he maketh his sun to rise on the evil and on the good, and sendeth rain on the just and on the unjust. For if ye love them which love you, what reward have ye? do not even the publicans the same? And if ye salute your brethren only, what do ye more than others? do not even the publicans so?

Be ye therefore perfect, even as your Father which is in heaven is perfect."

People who refuse Christ have many easily understandable reasons: they are afraid of losing the dusty rubbish which seems magnificence to them. As an excuse for not following His teachings they claim that He said nothing new.

These experts in the genealogy of ideas do not look carefully to see whether there is a real identity of sense and of spirit between the ideas of Jesus and those other older ideas.

After the promulgation of the old Law there was amity between blood kin; and the citizens of the same city bore with each other; but for strangers there was only hatred and extermination. Centuries later voices were heard which asked for a little justice even for strangers, for enemies. These voices were not heeded.

Four centuries before Christ, a wise man of China, Mo Ti, wrote a whole book to say that men should love each other. "The wise man who wants to improve the world can improve it only if he knows with certainty the origin of disorders. Whence come disorders? They spring up because men do not love each other."

For Mo Ti, love is the mortar to hold citizens and the state more closely united, a social panacea.

"Answer insults with courtesy," suggests timidly the mysterious Lao-tse; but courtesy is prudence, not love. Confucius taught a doctrine which consisted in loving one's neighbor as oneself, but he did not dream of condemning hate. In the oldest Confucian text, the Ta-Hio, we find these words: "Only the just and human man is capable of justly loving and hating men."

His contemporary, Buddha, sees no other way to suppress suffering than to drown personal souls in Nirvana—in nothingness. The Buddhist loves his brother to avoid suffering, to approach absorption in the stream of life. His universal love is a form of indifference, stoical in grief as in joy.

In Egypt every dead body took with it into the tomb a copy of the book of the dead, an anticipatory apology of the soul before the tribunal of Osiris. The dead praises himself: "I have starved no one! I have made no one weep! I have not killed! I have not commanded treacherous murder! I have defrauded no one! I have given bread to the hungry, water to the thirsty, clothes to the naked, a boat to the traveler halted on his journey, sacrifices to the gods, funeral banquets to the dead." This is righteousness, but we find no love here.

Zarathustra also leaves a law for the Iranians. This law commands the faithful of Ahura Mazda to give clothes to the naked and they are not to refuse bread to the hungry workingman. There is no talk of love.

It is written in Exodus: "Also thou shalt not oppress a stranger: for ye know the heart of a stranger, seeing ye were strangers in the land of Egypt." This is a beginning; we have reached Love, but not for an enemy. The Psalms resound at every step with violent demands to the Lord to destroy enemies. "As for the head of those that compass me about, let the mischief of their own lips cover them. Let burning coals fall upon them: let them be cast into the fire; into deep pits, that they rise not up again. And my soul shall be joyful in the Lord!"

In such a world it is natural that Saul should be astounded that he was not killed by his enemy David, and that Job should boast of not having exulted in the misfortunes of an enemy. Only in the later proverbs does the anonymous moralist of the Old Testament come finally to charity, "If thine enemy be hungry, give him bread to eat; and if he be thirsty, give him water to drink."

This, too, is progress: but the marvels of love of the Sermon on the Mount cannot have sprung from these timid maxims hidden away in a corner of the Scriptures.

The world of antiquity did not know love. It knew passion for a woman, friendship for a friend, justice for the citizen, hospitality for the foreigner. Zeus protected pilgrims and strangers; he who knocked at the Grecian door was not denied meat, a cup of wine, and a bed. The poor were to be covered, the weak helped; but the men of antiquity did not know love that shares another's sorrow.

Jesus was the first to speak of such love in the Sermon on the Mount. Of all His teachings, this is the greatest and the most original of Jesus' conceptions; this is still his greatest innovation. Even to us it is new because it is not understood, not imitated, not obeyed; infinitely eternal like truth.

JESUS ON THE MOUNT taught for the first time the Paternoster, the only prayer which He ever taught. The apostles had asked Jesus for a prayer. It is one of the simplest prayers in the world, but it is not always understood.

"Our Father"—for we have sprung from Thee and love Thee as sons; from Thee we shall receive no wrong.

"Which art in heaven"—in that which is opposed to the earth, in the opposite sphere from matter, in spirit and in that small but eternal part of the spirit which is our soul.

"Hallowed be thy name." Let us not only adore Thee with words but be worthy of Thee, drawing nearer to Thee with greater love, because Thou art no longer the avenger, the Lord of Battles, but the Father who teaches the joyfulness of peace.

"Thy kingdom come"—the Kingdom of Heaven, of the spirit of love, that of the Gospel.

"Thy will be done, in earth as it is in heaven." May Thy law of goodness and perfection rule both spirit and matter, both the visible and invisible universe.

"Give us this day our daily bread." We do not ask of Thee riches, dangerous burden, but only that small amount which permits us to live, to become more worthy of the promised life.

"Forgive us our debts, as we forgive our debtors." Pardon us because we pardon others. It is more effort for us to forgive a single debt of our debtors than for Thee to sweep away the record of all we owe Thee.

"Lead us not into temptation." Help us that our struggling transformation may not be too difficult, and that our entry into the Kingdom may not be too long delayed.

"Deliver us from evil"— Thou who art spirit, who hast power over evil, over stubborn and hostile matter which surrounds us everywhere, and from which it is hard to free ourselves, Thou negation of matter, help us!

In the Lord's Prayer the only word of praise is the word "Father"; and that praise is a pledge, a testimony of love.

AFTER HE HAD given out the new law of the imitation of God, Jesus came down from the Mount. He knew that these exalted words would not be enough to spread the good news, His Gospel, to all.

But the rustic, coarse, humble people who followed Jesus were men who could not understand a spiritual truth without evidence stated in the terms of the everyday world. An illustrative fable can lead men to moral revelation, so Jesus spoke in parables. A prodigy is to them confirmation of a new truth, so Jesus had recourse to miracles.

For many moderns it is out of the question that Jesus can ever have raised the dead: therefore, the miracles recounted by the Evangelists are a compelling reason for turning away from His words.

The people who reason in this way give to miracles a weight and a meaning much greater than that which Jesus gave them. He does not feel that this divine power of His is of supreme importance. Often, as soon as the healing was complete, He asked the ones He had healed to keep it secret. "See thou tell no man; but go thy way."

Every time that He finds a fair reason for refusing, He refuses; if He yields, it is to reward the faith of the sorrowing man or woman who calls on Him; but the Gospels show that He performs no miracles at Nazareth when they wish to kill Him, none at Gethsemane when they come to arrest Him, nor on the cross when they challenge Him to save Himself.

Jesus never held that miracles were His exclusive privilege. This power was not denied to the Disciples. "Heal the sick, cleanse the lepers, raise the dead, cast out devils: freely ye have received, freely give."

But miracles are not enough to enter into the Kingdom. Even charlatanical wizards could perform prodigies which seemed

488

miracles. In His time a certain Simon was doing miracles in Samaria; even the disciples of the Pharisees performed miracles. And hardened hearts, locked shut against truth, are not converted even by the greatest miracles. "If they hear not Moses and the Prophets, neither will they be persuaded, though one rose from the dead."

Jesus heals the sick, but He is in no way like a wizard or an exorcist. His will is enough, and the faith of the petitioner. To them all He puts the question, "Dost thou believe I can do this?" and when the cure is accomplished, "Go, thy faith hath made thee whole."

For Jesus the miracle is the union of two wills for good, the living contact between the faith of the healer and the faith of the one healed. "Verily I say unto you, If ye have faith as a grain of mustard seed, ye shall say unto this mountain, Remove hence to yonder place; and it shall remove; and nothing shall be impossible unto you."

In the Gospels the miracles are called by three names: *dunameis*—forces; *terata*—marvels; *semeis*—signs. They are signs for those who remember the prophecies of the Messiah; they are marvels for those who look for proofs that Christ is the Messiah; but in Jesus there are only dunameis, victorious lightning flashes from a superhuman power. The healings of Jesus are healings not only of bodies but of souls.

Jesus cured the maimed, the fevered, a man with the dropsy, a woman with an issue of blood. He healed also a sword wound (Malchus' ear struck off by Peter on the night of Gethsemane); this only in order that His law—"do good to those who wrong you"—might be observed to the very last. But Jesus healed more often the paralytics, the lepers, the blind, the deaf-mutes, those possessed by devils.

The old name for mental diseases is possession by devils; even Aristotle believed in possession by devils. It was thought that lunatics, epileptics, hysterical patients, were invaded by malign spirits.

This learned and popular explanation lent itself admirably to that allegorical and figurative teaching of which Jesus was so fond. There is a likeness between the maniac and the epileptic, between the paralytic and the slothful, the vile and the leprous, the blind and he who cannot see the truth, the deaf and he who will not listen to the truth.

"THE DEAD shall arise!" The Evangelists know three resurrections, historical events narrated with a sober but explicit statement of the evidence. Jesus raised up three who were dead: a young lad, a little girl, and a friend.

He was entering Nain, "the beautiful," set on a little hill some miles from Nazareth, and met a funeral procession. They were carrying to the grave the young son of a widow. She had lost her husband a short time before. He saw the mother walking among the women, weeping with the amazed and smothered grief of mothers which is so profoundly moving.

Jesus had compassion on this mother; her grief was like an accusation. "Weep not," He said.

He went to the side of the cataleptic and touched him. The boy was lying there stretched out, wrapped in his shroud, but with his face uncovered, set in the stern paleness of the dead. The bearers halted; all were silent; even the mother, startled, was quiet.

"Young man, I say unto thee, Arise." And he that was dead sat up, and began to speak. And He delivered him to his mother.

Another day as he was returning from Gadara, a father fell at His feet. His only little daughter lay at the point of death. The man's name was Jairus, and although he was a leader at the synagogue he believed in Jesus. They went along together. When they were halfway, a servant met them, saying, "Thy daughter is dead; trouble not the Master." But when Jesus heard it, He answered him, saying, "Fear not: believe only, and she shall be made whole." When He came into the house, He suffered no man to go in, save Peter, and James, and John, and the father and the mother of the maiden. All wept, and bewailed her: but He said, "Weep not; she is not dead, but sleepeth." And they laughed, knowing that she was dead. He put them all out, and took her by the hand, and called, saying, "Maid, arise." And her spirit came again, and she arose straightway, a living body.

Lazarus and Jesus loved each other. More than once Jesus had eaten in his house at Bethany with him and his sisters. Now one day Lazarus fell ill, and sent word of it to Jesus. And Jesus answered, "This sickness is not unto death." Two days went by. But on the third day He said to His disciples, "Our friend Lazarus sleepeth; but I go, that I may awake him out of sleep." He was near to Bethany when Martha came to meet Him as if to reproach Him.

"Lord, if thou hadst been here, my brother had not died." And a little later Mary too said, "Lord, if thou hadst been here, my brother had not died." Their repeated reproach touched Jesus, not because He feared He had come too late, but because He was always saddened by the lack of faith even of those dearest to Him.

"And He said, Where have ye laid him? They said unto Him, Lord, come and see. . . . Jesus therefore again groaning in himself cometh to the grave. It was a cave, and a stone lay upon it. Jesus said, Take ye away the stone."

Martha, the housekeeper, the practical, concrete character, interrupted, "Lord, by this time he stinketh: for he hath been dead four days." But Jesus did not heed her, "Take away the stone." And the stone was rolled away. Jesus made a short prayer, His face lifted towards the sky, drew near to the hole and called His friend in a loud voice, "Lazarus, come forth."

And Lazarus came forth, stumbling, for his hands and feet were shrouded and his face covered with a napkin.

"Loose him, and let him go."

And all four, followed by the Twelve and by a throng of thunderstruck Jews, returned to the house. Lazarus's eyes grew used to the light again. He walked on his feet, although with pain, and used his hands. Martha, moving rapidly, got together the best dinner she could in the confusion after four days of demoralizing sorrow—and the man come back to life after death ate with his sister and his friends. Mary could scarcely swallow a mouthful of food, nor take her eyes from the conqueror of death, who, having wiped the tears from His eyes, broke His bread and drank His wine as if this day were like any other day.

These are the resurrections narrated by the Evangelists. In all

His life Jesus raised from the dead only three persons, and in all these three cases Jesus spoke to the dead person as if he were not dead but asleep. Death for Him was only a deeper sleep than the common sleep of everyday, a sleep to be broken by a superhuman love.

JESUS LIKED to go to weddings. In the old days, the workingman, the countryman, the Oriental who lived all the year round on barley bread, dried figs and a few fish and eggs, and only on great days killed a lamb or a kid, saw in weddings the truest and greatest festival of his life. The festivals of the people and those of the church were the same for everybody, and they are repeated every twelfth month; but a wedding was his very own and only came once for him in all the cycle of his years.

Marriage is the supreme effort of the youth of man to conquer Fate with love. All the delights and splendors of the world were centered around the bride and groom, to make the day unforgettable for them. Torches went at night to meet the groom with singers, dancers and musicians. The house was filled with all sorts of meats cooked in all sorts of ways; wineskins of wine leaning against the walls, vases of unguents for the friends; nothing was lacking for the gratification of the senses.

On that one day all the things which are the daily privilege of princes and rich men triumphed in the poor man's house.

Jesus was touched by the exultation of those simple souls, snatched for those few hours from the gloomy, niggardly poverty of their everyday life. It is not surprising therefore that He should have accepted the invitation to the wedding at Cana. Everyone knows the miracle He wrought that day. Six jars of water were changed by Jesus into wine, and into wine better than that which had been drunk. Old rationalists say that this was a present of wine kept hidden until then, a surprise from Jesus at the end of the meal, in honor of the bride and groom. And six hundred quarts of wine, they add, are a fine present, showing the liberality of the Master.

They have not noticed that only John, the man of allegories, tells of the marriage at Cana. It was not a sleight-of-hand trick, but a true transmutation, performed with the power of Spirit over matter, and at the same time it is one of those parables told by actual deeds.

ON ANOTHER OCCASION there was a multiplication of bread, similar in its spiritual meaning.

Thousands of poor people had followed Jesus into a place in the wilderness, far from any settlements. For three days they had not eaten, so hungry were they for the bread of life which is His word. But on the third day, Jesus took pity on them—there were women and children among them—and ordered His Disciples to feed the multitude. But they had only a little bread and a few fishes, and there were thousands of mouths. Then Jesus had them all sit down on the ground on the green grass, in circles of fifty to a hundred. He blessed the small amount of food they had; all were satisfied, and baskets of the broken pieces were left.

The less there is of the bread of truth, the more it satisfies. One Word alone will fill the soul; the multitudes will be satisfied and there will be enough to eat also for those who were not present on that day. A loaf of wheat bread is only enough for a very few, and when they have finished it, there is no more for anyone! But the bread of truth, spiritual bread, can never be finished.

The miracle of the loaves is the foundation of all the others. Every parable spoken in poetic words or expressed with visible prodigies was as bread prepared in different manners, so that His own followers should understand the one needful truth that the man who is nourished on the Spirit is master of the world. And yet the Twelve, the chosen, the blessed, the faithful, do not sufficiently believe.

In the boat, the night of the tempest, Jesus was obliged to reprove them. The Master had gone to sleep in the stern, His head on the pillow of one of the rowers. Suddenly the wind rose, a storm came down on the lake, the waves beat against the boat and it seemed from one moment to the next that they would be wrecked. The Disciples, alarmed, awakened Jesus, "Master, carest thou not that we perish?" And He arose, and rebuked the wind, and said unto the sea, "Peace, be still." And the wind ceased, and there was a great calm. And He said unto them, "Why are ye so fearful? how is it that ye have no faith?" And they feared exceedingly, and said one to another, "What manner of man is this, that even the wind and the sea obey him?" But there is one, Simon Peter, who has no fear. Great is his faith, great his love. Everyone can partake of this power.

A few years before Christ, a great captain in many wars was on a real sea, in a boat with a few rowers, in search of an army which had not come up in time to win the victory for him. The wind began to blow, the tempest bore down on the boat and the pilot wished to turn back to the harbor. But Caesar, taking the hand of the pilot, said to him, "Go forward, fear not, Caesar is with thee and his fortune sails with you." These words heartened the crew; every one, as if a little of Caesar's strength had entered into his soul, did his best to overcome the opposition of the sea. But notwithstanding the efforts of the seamen the ship was nearly sunk and was obliged to turn back.

Caesar's faith was only faith in himself: Christ's faith was love for the Father.

With this love He could walk to meet the boat of the Disciples tacking against a contrary wind, and could step upon the water as on the grass of a meadow. They thought in the darkness that it was a specter, and once again He was obliged to reassure them, "Be of good cheer; it is I; be not afraid." As soon as He was in the boat, the wind fell and in a few minutes they reached the shore. Once again they were astounded, says the honest Mark in a revealing comparison, "For they considered not the miracle of the loaves: for their heart was hardened."

CITY LADIES do not make their own bread, but old country-women and housewives know what leaven is. A handful of dough from the last baking, as big as a child's hand, wet with warm water and put into the new dough, raises even as much as three measures of flour.

The grain of wheat is not large, the farmer throws it into the ground and then goes on about his other affairs; he sleeps, he goes away from home and comes back. Days pass and nights pass, no thought is given to the seed, but underneath there in

the moist, plowed field the seed has germinated. There comes out a blade of green and at the top of this blade an ear, at first green and graceful, then becoming golden grain. Now the field is ready and the farmer can commence his harvesting.

Likewise with the Kingdom of Heaven and the first news of it. A word seems nothing. What is a word? And yet the word of the Kingdom is like yeast; it ferments and grows. It is like the seed of the fields, patient as the earth which hides it, which, when spring comes, grows green and strong and with the beginning of summer, lo, the harvest is ready!

The Gospel is made up of few words, "The Kingdom is at hand, change your souls!" Only a few men of those living about Christ believed in the Kingdom and prepared themselves for the great day. Only a few, insignificant men, scattered like tiny particles of yeast in the midst of the divided nations and the immense empires, but these few dozen insignificant men gathered together in the midst of a predestined people were to become, through the contagion of their example, thousands upon thousands, and only three hundred years after them, in the place of Tiberius, ruled a man who bowed the knee before the heirs of the Apostles.

THE PARABLES

WEDDINGS AND BANQUETS serve as subjects for many of Christ's parables.

The Kingdom is an eternal feast. There was a king who celebrated his son's wedding, and those whom he invited did not come. One had bought a piece of ground, another five yoke of oxen, a third had taken a wife that day. They were all deep in their affairs, and did not even trouble to send an excuse. Then the king sent his servants to pick up out of the streets the blind, the poor, the maimed and the halt, the lowest of the rabble.

The invitation to the banquet of the Kingdom is a promise of spiritual happiness, absolute, perpetual. And yet the men whom Jesus called first of all to the divine feast of the reborn did not respond. They made wry faces, complained, slipped away and continued their habitual actions. Then all the others were called in their place: beggars instead of the rich, sinners instead of Pharisees, women of the streets instead of fine ladies, the sick and sorrowing instead of the strong and happy.

Even the latest arrivals if they come in time will be admitted to the feast. The master of the vineyard saw in the marketplace certain laborers who were waiting for work and agreed on their wages. Later at noonday he sent others. They all worked, some at pruning and some at hoeing, and when the evening came the master gave the same pay to all. But those who had begun in the morning murmured, "Why do those who have worked less than we receive the same payment?" But the master answered one of them, "If it is my pleasure to give the same to the workingmen of the last hour, is that robbing you others?"

The apparent injustice of the master is only a more generous justice. He who arrived last but works with equal hope has the same right to enjoy that Kingdom for which he has labored.

The master has gone to the wedding and the servants do not know when he will come back. Fortunate are those whom he will find awake. The master himself will seat them at the table and will serve them. But if he finds in the house no lamp lighted, no water warmed, he will drive the servants out without pity.

Everyone should be ready because the Son of man is like a thief in the night who sends no word beforehand. Or like a bridegroom who has been detained by someone in the street.

In the house of the bride there are ten virgins who are to meet him with the light of the procession. Five wise virgins take oil for their lamps, and wait to hear the approaching voices. The foolish five do not think of the oil, and fall asleep. Suddenly there is the sound of the nuptial procession. The five wise virgins light their lamps and run joyfully to welcome the bridegroom. The other five wake up with a start and run from one house to another to get a little oil; but everybody is asleep, the shops are closed and the roaming dogs bark at their heels. They go back to the house of the wedding. The five wise virgins are already there and feasting with the bridegroom. The five foolish virgins knock and cry out, but no one comes to open for them. Through the cracks in the window casings they see the glowing lights of the supper. They hear the clatter of the dishes, the clinking of the cups, the songs of the young men, but they cannot enter; they stay there until morning, in the dark, and the wind.

"ASK, AND IT SHALL be given you; seek, and ye shall find; knock, and it shall be opened unto you." Even hard, slothful, obstinate men give way to persistent entreaty.

There was in a certain city a judge who cared for no one, a morose and scornful man who wanted to do everything as it suited him best. A widow went every day before him and asked for justice, and although her cause was just the judge would not do what she wished. But the widow patiently endured all his repulses and did not weary. And finally the judge, to get rid of this woman who wore him out with her supplications, pleadings, and prayers, gave the sentence and sent her in peace. If even men are not always insensible to pleadings, how much surer will be the response from a Father who loves us?

To listen to the word of the Kingdom is not enough. The only thing which counts is the actual doing. "Whosoever cometh to me, and heareth my sayings, and doeth them, I will show you to whom he is like: He is like a man which built an house, and digged deep, and laid the foundation on a rock: and when the flood arose, the stream beat vehemently upon that house, and could not shake it: for it was founded upon a rock. But he that heareth, and doeth not, is like a man that without a foundation built an house upon the earth; against which the stream did beat vehemently, and immediately it fell; and the ruin of that house was great."

The same teaching is in the parable of the sowing: "A sower went out to sow his seed: and as he sowed, some fell by the wayside; and it was trodden down, and the fowls of the air devoured it. And some fell upon a rock; and as soon as it was sprung up, it withered away, because it lacked moisture. And some fell among thorns; and the thorns sprang up with it, and choked it. And other fell on good ground, and sprang up, and bare fruit an hundredfold." This is the parable which the Twelve were incapable of understanding. Jesus was obliged to explain it Himself. The seed is the Word of God. But it is not enough to hear it merely, to understand it, to practice it. He who has received it should not keep it to himself. Who is the man who having a lamp hides it under the bed or covers it with a vessel?

A Lord traveling into a far country left to each of his servants ten talents with the understanding that they should use the money to good purpose. And when he came back he reckoned with them. And the first delivered to him twenty talents, because with the first ten he had earned ten other talents. And the Lord made him steward over all his goods. And the second delivered him fifteen talents, for he had not been able to earn more than five more. But the third presented himself timorously and showed him, wrapped up in a napkin, the ten talents which he had received. "Lord, I knew thee that thou art an hard man, reaping where thou hast not sown, and gathering where thou hast not strawed: And I was afraid, and went and hid thy talents in the earth." And the Lord answered, "Thou wicked and slothful servant, I will judge thee by thine own words. Take the talents and give them to him who has twenty. For unto every one that hath shall be given, and he shall have abundance: but from him that hath not shall be taken away even that which he hath." And the unprofitable servant was cast into outer darkness. He who has received the Word ought to double his wealth. Those who do not use the treasure of the Word are faithless husbandmen, to whom was entrusted the most fruitful field in all the universe.

A MAN HAD TWO SONS. His wife was dead. He loved his sons like his two eyes and his two hands, equally dear, and he saw to it that both lacked for nothing.

The older was a serious-minded young man, the head of a family. He respected his father as master, without any impulsive show of affection. He worked faithfully, but he was hard and captious with the servants; he went through all the religious forms, but did not let the poor come about him. He pretended to love his brother, but his heart was full of the poison of envy. For brothers rarely love each other. Jewish history, not to speak of any other, begins with Cain, goes on with Jacob's cheating Esau, with Joseph sold by his brothers, with Absalom, who killed Amnon, with Solomon who had Adonijah killed; a long bloody road of jealousy.

The second son splashed about and made merry in his youth as in a warm lake. He was fitful with his father. He was capable of not saying a word for weeks together and then suddenly throwing himself on his father's neck in the highest spirits. He refused no invitations to drink, stared at women and dressed better than other people.

But he was warmhearted; he gave money to the needy, was charitable without boasting of it. He was seldom seen at the synagogue, wanted to spend more than his father's resources allowed him, talked recklessly. He said it was better to look for adventure in rich countries, beyond the mountains and the sea, where the big, luxurious cities are, with marble buildings and the best wines and shops full of silk and silver, and women dressed in fine clothes like queens, fresh from aromatic baths, who lightly give themselves for a piece of gold.

His father, although he was rich, measured out the drachmas as if they were talents. His brother was vexed if he bought a new tunic or came home a little tipsy; in the family all they knew was the field, the furrow, the pasture, the stock; a life that was one long effort.

And one day (he had thought of it many times before, but had never had the courage to say it) he hardened his heart and his face and said to his father, "Father, give me the portion of goods that falleth to me, and I will ask nothing more of thee."

When the old man heard this, he was deeply hurt, and for a while neither of them spoke any more of this matter. But the son suffered, was sullen, and lost all his ardor and animation, even to the fresh color of his face. And the father, seeing his son suffer, suffered himself. Finally paternal love conquered self-love. The estimations and valuations of the property were made, and the father gave to both his sons their rightful part and kept the rest for himself.

The young man lost no time, he sold what he could not carry away, gathered together a goodly sum, and one evening, without saying anything to anyone, mounted his fine horse and went away. The older brother was rather pleased by his departure; now he was the only son, first in command.

But the father secretly wept. Every line of his old face was washed with tears, his aged cheeks were soaked with his grieving.

In the meantime the young man drew rapidly near to the rich city of revels where he meant to live. At every turning of the road he felt of the moneybags which hung at either side of his saddle. It seemed to him that those thousands of coins would last forever. He rented a fine house, bought five or six slaves, dressed like a prince, and soon had many friends who were guests at his table, and who drank his wine till their stomachs could hold no more.

He did not economize with women and chose the most beautiful the city contained, those who knew how to dance and sing and dress with magnificence, and undress with grace. The little provincial lord from the dull country, repressed in the most sensual period of his life, now vented his voluptuousness, his love of luxury, in this dangerous life.

But the moneybags of the prodigal son were not bottomless. There came a day when there were only empty bags of canvas and leather lying limp and flabby on the brick floor of his room. His friends disappeared, the women disappeared, slaves, beds and dining tables were sold. A famine came on the country and the prodigal son found himself hungering in the midst of a famine-stricken people.

The unfortunate man, destitute, left the city, traveling with a lord who was going to the country where he had a fine estate. The lord hired him as swineherd because he was young and strong and hardly anyone was willing to be a swineherd. For a Jew nothing could be a greater affliction than this. Even in Egypt, although animals were adored there, the only people forbidden to enter the temples were swineherds.

The prodigal son was given no pay and very little to eat, because there was only a little for anyone; but there was no famine for the hogs, because they could eat anything. There were plenty of carob beans and they gorged themselves. Their hungry attendant watched the pink and black animals rooting in the earth and longed to fill his stomach with the same stuff and wept, remembering the abundance of his own home. Sometimes, overcome with hunger, he took one of the black bean husks from under the grunting snouts of the pigs, tempering the bitterness of his suffering with that insipid and woody food.

His dress was a dirty slave's smock which smelled of manure, his footgear a pair of worn-out sandals scarcely held together with rushes; on his head a faded hood. His fair young face, tanned by the sun of the hills, was thin and long, and had taken a sickly color.

Who was wearing now the spotless homespun clothes, which he had left in his brother's chests? His father's hired servants were better dressed than he.

Returned to his senses, he said to himself, "How many servants of my father's have bread enough and to spare, and I perish with hunger!"

But how could he return without a garment, unshod, without a penny, without the ring—the sign of liberty—stinking and contaminated by this abominable trade, to show that his serious-minded brother was right, to bow himself at the knee of the old man whom he had left without a greeting!

No, there was something of his always in his home, his father! He was his creation, made of his flesh, issued from his seed in a moment of love. "I will arise and go to my father, and will say unto him, Father, I have sinned against heaven, and before thee, and am no more worthy to be called thy son: make me as one of thy hired servants."

And the young man gave back the hogs to his master, and went towards his own land. He begged a piece of bread from the countrypeople, and wept as he ate this bread of pity in the shadow of the sycamores. His sore and blistered feet could scarcely carry him, but his faith in forgiveness led him homeward step by step.

And finally one day at noon he arrived in sight of his father's house; but he did not dare to knock, nor to call anyone, nor to go in. He hung around outside to see if anyone would come out.

And behold, his father appeared on the threshold. His son was changed, but the eyes of a father even dimmed by weeping could not fail to recognize him. He ran towards him and caught him to his breast, and kissed him, and could not stop from pressing his pale, old lips on that ravaged face, on those eyes whose expression was altered but still beautiful, on that hair, dusty but still waving and soft, on that flesh that was his own.

The son, covered with confusion and deeply moved, did not know how to respond to these kisses, and as soon as he could free himself from his father's arms he threw himself on the ground and repeated tremulously the speech he had prepared. "Father, I have sinned against heaven, and before thee, And am no more worthy to be called thy son."

The old man never felt himself more father than at this moment; he seemed to become a father for a second time, and without even answering, with his eyes still clouded and soft, but with the ringing voice of his best days, he called to the servants:

"Bring forth the best robe, and put it on him; and put a ring on his hand, and shoes on his feet:

"And bring hither the fatted calf, and kill it; and let us eat, and be merry: For this my son was dead, and is alive again; he was lost, and is found."

The servants obeyed him and the calf was killed, skinned, cut up and put to cook. The oldest wine was taken from the wine cellar, and the finest room was prepared for the dinner in celebration of the return. Servants went to call his father's friends and others went to summon musicians, that there should be music.

The older son was in the field, working, and in the evening when he came back and was near to the house he heard shouts and stampings and clapping of hands, and the footsteps of dancers. And he could not understand. "Whatever can have happened? Perhaps a wedding procession has arrived unexpectedly at our house."

Disliking noise and new faces, he would not enter and see for himself what it was. But he called to a boy coming out of the house and asked him what all that clatter was.

"Thy brother is come; and thy father hath killed the fatted

calf, because he hath received him safe and sound." These words were like a thrust at his heart. He turned pale, not with pleasure, but with rage and jealousy. And he would not go into the house.

Then his father went out and entreated him: "Come, for your brother has come back and has asked after you, and will be glad to see you, and we will feast together."

But the serious-minded young man could not contain himself, and for the first time in his life ventured to reprove his father to his face.

"Lo, these many years do I serve thee, neither transgressed I at any time thy commandment: and yet thou never gavest me a kid, that I might make merry with my friends: But as soon as this thy son was come, which hath devoured thy living with harlots, thou hast killed for him the fatted calf."

With these few words he discloses all the ignominy of his soul hidden until then under the Pharisaical cloak of good behavior. "This thy son." He does not say "brother."

But his father pardoned this son, as he did the other son. "Son, thou art ever with me, and all that I have is thine. It was meet that we should make merry, and be glad: for this thy brother was dead, and is alive again; and was lost, and is found."

No story—after that of Joseph—that came from human lips ever touched more deeply the hearts of men. Interpreters are free to explain the story of the prodigal son, but Jesus Himself says expressly that the meaning is this: "More joy shall be in heaven over one sinner who repents than over all the righteous."

"What man of you, having an hundred sheep, if he lose one of them, doth not leave the ninety and nine in the wilderness, and go after that which is lost, until he find it? And when he hath found it, he layeth it on his shoulders, rejoicing. And when he cometh home, he calleth together his friends and neighbors, saying unto them, Rejoice with me; for I have found my sheep which was lost."

BUT FORGIVENESS CREATES an obligation for which there are no exceptions allowed. He who has received must give; it is better to give much, but it is essential to give a part at least.

A king one day wanted a reckoning with his servants and one by one he called them before him. Among the first was one who owed him ten thousand talents, but as he had not anything to pay this, the king commanded that he should be sold and his wife and his children and all that he had, in payment of a part of the debt.

The servant in despair threw himself at the feet of the king. He seemed a mere bundle of garments crying out sobs and promises. "Have patience with me, wait a little longer and I will pay you all, but do not have my wife and my children separated from me, sent away like cattle, no one knows where."

The king was moved with compassion—he also had little children—and he sent him away free and forgave him that great debt. The servant went out and he met one of his fellow servants who owed him a hundred pence, a small thing compared with ten thousand talents, and he sprang on him. "Pay me what thou owest and at once, or I will have thee bound by the guards." The unlucky man fell down at his feet and besought him and wept and swore that he would pay him in a few days and kissed the hem of his garment, and recalled to him their old comradeship and begged him to wait in the name of the children who were waiting for him in his home.

But the servant took his debtor by the arm and had him cast into prison. The news spread quickly to the ears of the king, who called that pitiless man and delivered him to the tormentors: "I forgave you that great debt, shouldst thou not have had compassion on thy brother, for his debt was so much smaller? I had pity on thee, oughtest thou not to have had pity on him?"

TWO MEN went up into the temple to pray; the one a Pharisee, and the other a publican. The Pharisee, with his phylacteries hanging upon his forehead and on his left arm, with the long, glittering fringes on his cloak, erect like a man who feels himself in his own house, prayed thus: "God, I thank thee, that I am not as other men are, extortioners, unjust, adulterers, or even as this publican. I fast twice in the week, I give tithes of all that I possess."

But the publican did not have the courage even to lift his

eyes and seemed ashamed to appear before his Lord. He sighed and smote on his breast and said only these words: "God be merciful to me, a sinner."

"I tell you, this man went down to his house justified rather than the other: for every one that exalteth himself shall be abased; and he that humbleth himself shall be exalted."

A LAWYER asked Jesus who is one's neighbor, and Jesus told this story: "A man, a Jew, went down from Jerusalem to Jericho through the mountain passes. Thieves fell upon him, and after they had wounded him and taken away his clothes, they left him upon the road half dead.

"A priest passed that way and saw the unfortunate man stretched out, but he passed by on the other side of the road. A little after came a Levite. He also knew every detail of all the holy ceremonies, and seemed more than a sacristan, seemed one of the masters of the Temple. He looked at the bloody body and went on his way.

"And finally came a Samaritan. To the Jews the Samaritans were only slightly less detestable than the Gentiles, because they would not sacrifice at Jerusalem and accept the reform of Nehemiah. The Samaritan, however, did not wait to see if the unfortunate man thrown among the stones of the street was circumcised or uncircumcised, was a Jew or a Samaritan. He was quickly moved to pity, took down his flasks from his saddle and poured upon the man's wounds a little oil, a little wine, bound them up as well as he could with a handkerchief, put the stranger across his ass and brought him to an inn, had him put to bed, tried to restore him, giving him something hot to drink, and did not leave him until he saw him come to himself and able to speak and eat.

"The next day he called the host apart and gave him two pence: 'Take care of him, do the best thou canst and whatsoever thou spendest more, when I come again, I will repay thee.'

"The neighbor, then, is he who suffers, he who needs help, whoever he is, of whatever nation or religion he may be. Even thine enemy, if he needs thee, even if he does not ask help, is the first of 'thy neighbors.' "

FATE KNOWS no better way to punish the great for their greatness than by sending them disciples. Every disciple, just because he is a disciple, cannot understand all that his master says, but at very best only half, and that according to the kind of mind he has. Thus without wishing to falsify the teaching of his master, he deforms it, vulgarizes it, belittles it, corrupts it.

Or else, sometimes, he twists and turns the master's thought to make it seem that he has a thought of his own, different and original, and teaches exactly the opposite of what he was taught.

And yet no one has been able to dispense with these pupils and followers, nor even to wish to. For the great man cannot teach without the illusion that someone understands his words, receives his ideas, transmits them to others far away before his death and after his death.

Christ accepted with the other trials of earthly life the burden of disciples. We know who His Apostles were. A Galilean, He chose them from among the Galileans. A poor man, He chose them from among the poor; a simple man, He called simple men.

He knew that these souls were rough but had integrity, were ignorant but ardent, and that He could in the end mold them like clay from the river, which is only mud, and yet when modeled and baked in the kiln, becomes eternal beauty.

But their imperfect nature had too often the upper hand. Our hearts ache if we look at them closely in the Gospels: those men who were so inestimably fortunate as to live with Christ, to walk, to eat with Him, to sleep in the same room, to look into His face, to touch His hand, to kiss Him, to hear His words from His very mouth; those twelve fortunate men, whom throughout the centuries millions of souls have secretly envied.

We see them, hard of head and of heart; not always capable of understanding, even after His death, who Jesus had been and what sort of a new Kingdom was proclaimed by Him; often lacking in faith, in love, in brotherly affection; envying each other; impatient for the revenge which would repay them for their long wait; intolerant of those who were not one with them; vindictive toward those who would not receive them, materialistic, avaricious, cowardly.

One of them denies Him three times; one of them delays giving Him due reverence until He is in the sepulcher; one does not believe in His mission because He comes from Nazareth; one is not willing to admit His resurrection; one sells Him to His enemies, and gives Him over with His last kiss to those who come to arrest Him. Others, when Christ's teachings were on a too lofty level, "went back, and walked no more with Him." Like the common people they constantly feel that Jesus should be the worldly Messiah, political, warlike, come to restore the temporal throne of David. Even when He is about to ascend into Heaven they continue to ask Him: "Lord, wilt thou at this time restore again the kingdom to Israel?"

PETER BEFORE THE RESURRECTION is like a body beside a spirit. He is the earth which believes in Heaven but remains earthy.

When Jesus pronounced the famous words: "It is easier for a camel to go through the eye of a needle, than for a rich man to enter into the kingdom of God," Peter thought this sweeping condemnation of wealth very harsh. "Then answered Peter and said unto him, Behold, we have forsaken all, and followed thee; what shall we have therefore?" Jesus promises him that everyone shall have a hundred times what he has given up.

Again Peter does not understand what Christ means when He asserts that only what comes from man himself can defile men. "Then answered Peter, and said unto him, Declare unto us this parable. And Jesus said, Are ye also yet without understanding? Do not ye yet understand?"

Peter was not an alert spirit. He fell asleep on the Mount of the Transfiguration. He fell asleep on the night at Gethsemane, after the Last Supper, where Jesus had uttered the saying which would have kept even a scribe everlastingly from sleep.

When Jesus that last evening announced that He was to suffer and die, Peter burst out: "Lord, I am ready to go with thee, both into prison, and to death. Although all shall be offended, yet will not I. If I should die with thee, I will not deny Thee in any wise."

Jesus answered him: "Verily I say unto thee, That this night, before the cock crow, thou shalt deny me thrice." Jesus knew him better than Peter knew himself.

Peter had, like all crude personalities, a tendency to see the material in spiritual manifestations. On the Mount of the Transfiguration, when he was awakened and saw Jesus refulgent with white light, speaking with two others, with two spirits, with two prophets, the first thought which came to him, instead of worshipping and keeping silence, was to build a tabernacle for these great personages.

"Master, it is good for us to be here: and let us make three tabernacles; one for thee, and one for Moses, and one for Elias." Luke, the wise man, adds to excuse him, "not knowing what he said."

When he saw Jesus walking in all security on the lake, the idea came to him to do the same thing. "And when Peter was come down out of the ship, he walked on the water, to go to Jesus. But when he saw the wind boisterous, he was afraid; and beginning to sink, he cried, saying, Lord, save me. And immediately Jesus stretched forth His hand, and caught him, and said unto him, O thou of little faith, wherefore didst thou doubt?"

His great love for Christ, which makes up for all his weakness, led him one day almost to rebuke Him. Jesus had told His disciples how He must suffer and be killed. "Then Peter took him, and began to rebuke him, saying, Be it far from thee, Lord: this shall not be unto thee. But he turned, and said unto Peter, Get thee behind me, Satan: thou art an offense unto me: for thou savorest not the things that be of God, but those that be of men."

Peter's mind was still occupied with the vulgar idea of the triumphant Messiah; he *thought as men do*. And yet he was the first to recognize Jesus as the Christ; and this primacy is so great that nothing has been able to cancel it.

THE TWO FISHERMEN, the brothers James and John, who had left their boat and their nets on the shore at Capernaum in order to go with Jesus, form together with Peter a sort of favorite triumvirate. They are the only ones who accompany Jesus into the house of Jairus, and on the Mount of the Transfiguration, and they are the ones whom He takes with Him on the night of Gethsemane. But in spite of their long intimacy with the Master, they never acquired sufficient humility. Jesus gave them the surname of "Boanerges—Sons of Thunder," an ironic surname, alluding perhaps to their fiery, irascible character.

When they all started together towards Jerusalem, they were crossing Samaria and were badly received in a village. "And they did not receive him, because his face was as though he would go to Jerusalem. And when his disciples James and John saw this, they said, Lord, wilt thou that we command fire to come down from heaven, and consume them? But he turned, and rebuked them." For them, Galileans, faithful to Jerusalem, the Samaritans were always enemies. In vain had they heard the Sermon on the Mount: "Do good to them that hate you, and pray for them which despitefully use you, and persecute you." Angry at an affront to Jesus, it seemed to them a work of righteous justice to reduce the inhospitable village to ashes. Yet far as they were from a loving rebirth of the soul, these men wanted to claim the first places on the day of triumph.

James and John, the sons of Zebedee, came unto him, saying: "Master, grant unto us that we may sit one on thy right hand and one on thy left hand in thy glory." But Jesus said unto them: "Ye know not what ye ask." And when the ten heard it they began to be much displeased with James and John. But Jesus called them to Him and saith unto them: "Whosoever will be great among you let him be your servant, for even the Son of man came not to be ministered unto but to minister."

This miraculous paradox is the proof of the fire of genius. He who cannot or will not serve shows that he has nothing to give. But the genius is no true genius if he does not exuberantly benefit his inferiors. There is nothing servile in serving.

James and John understood this stimulating saying of Jesus. We find one of them, John, among the nearest and most loving of the Disciples. At the Last Supper he leans his head on Jesus' breast; and from the height of the cross Jesus, crucified, confides the Virgin to him, that he should be a son to her.

THOMAS OWES his popularity to the quality which should be his shame. Thomas, the twin, is the guardian of modernity, as Thomas Aquinas is the oracle of medieval life. He is the true patron saint of Spinoza and of all the other deniers of the Resurrection, the man who is not satisfied even with the testimony of his eyes, but wishes that of his hands as well. And yet his love for Jesus makes him pardonable. When they came to the Master to say that Lazarus was dead, and the Disciples hesitated before going into Judea among their enemies, it was Thomas alone who said: "Let us also go, that we may die with him." The martyrdom which he did not find then came to him in India, after Christ's death.

Matthew is the dearest of all the Twelve. He was a tax gatherer, a sort of under-publican, and probably had more education than his companions. He followed Jesus as readily as the fishermen. "And after these things he went forth, and saw a publican, named Levi, sitting at the receipt of custom: and he said unto him, Follow me. And he left all, rose up, and followed him. And Levi made him a great feast in his own house." It was not a heap of torn nets which Matthew left, but a position, secure and increasing earnings. Of no other Disciple is it told that he could offer a great feast. Giving up riches is easy for a man who has almost nothing. Among the Twelve, Matthew was certainly the richest before his conversion.

Matthew and Judas were perhaps the only ones of the Disciples who knew how to write, and to Matthew we owe the first collection of Logia or memorable sayings of Jesus. In the Gospel which is called by his name, we find the most complete text of the Sermon on the Mount. Our debt to him is heavy; without him many words of Jesus, and the most beautiful, might have been lost.

Philip of Bethsaida also knew how to reckon. When the famished multitude pressed about Him, Jesus turned to him to ask what it would cost to buy bread for all those people. Philip answered Him: "Two hundred pennyworth of bread is not sufficient for them." It was to him that the Greeks of Jerusalem turned when they wished to speak to the new prophet, and he it was who announced to Nathanael the coming of Jesus.

Nathanael answered Philip's announcement with sarcasm: "Can there any good thing come out of Nazareth?" But Philip succeeded in bringing him to Jesus, who as soon as He saw him, exclaimed, "Behold an Israelite indeed, in whom is no guile! Nathanael saith unto him, Whence knowest thou me? Jesus answered and said unto him, Before that Philip called thee, when thou wast under the fig tree, I saw thee. Nathanael answered and saith unto him, Rabbi, thou art the Son of God; thou art the King of Israel. Jesus answered and said unto him, Because I said unto thee, I saw thee under the fig tree, believest thou? thou shalt see greater things than these."

Less enthusiastic and inflammable was Nicodemus, who, as a matter of fact, never wished to be known as a disciple of Jesus. Nicodemus was old, had been to school to the Rabbis, but the stories of the miracles had shaken him, and he went by night to Jesus to tell Him that he believed that He was sent by God. Jesus answered him, "Verily, verily, I say unto thee, Except a man be born again, he cannot see the kingdom of God." Nicodemus did not understand these words, or perhaps they startled him. He had come to see a miracle worker and had found a sibyl, and with the homely good sense of the man who wishes to avoid being taken in by a fraud he said, "How can a man be born when he is old? can he enter the second time into his mother's womb, and be born?"

Jesus answers with words of profound meaning, "Except a man be born of water and of the Spirit, he cannot enter into the kingdom of God." But Nicodemus still did not understand. "How can these things be?"

Nicodemus always respected the young Galilean, but his sympathy was as circumspect as his visit. Once when the leaders of the priests and the Pharisees were meditating how to capture Jesus, Nicodemus ventured a defense: "Doth our law judge any man, before it hear him, and know what he doeth?" A few words of reproof were enough to silence him. "They answered and said unto him, Art thou also of Galilee? Search, and look: for out of Galilee ariseth no prophet!" He belonged by right to the Sanhedrin, but there is no record that he raised his voice in favor of the accused when He was arrested. The trial was at night and probably to avoid his own remorse for the legal assassination, Nicodemus remained in his bed. When he awoke Jesus was dead, and then, forgetting his avarice, he bought a hundred pounds of myrrh and aloes to embalm the body.

Nicodemus is the eternal type of the lukewarm. He is the halfway soul.

But the Church to reward his posthumous piety has chosen him to become one of her saints. And there is an old tradition that he was baptized by Peter and put to death for having believed, too late, in Him whom he did not save from death.

THOSE WHOM Jesus sent out to the conquest of souls were rustic countrymen, but they could be mild as sheep, wary as serpents, simple as doves.

The Disciples destined to preach the beauty of poverty to both poor and rich were to set an example of happy poverty to every man in every house on every day. They were to carry nothing with them except the clothes on their backs and the sandals on their feet. They were to accept nothing; only the small piece of daily bread which they would find on the tables of their hosts. The wandering priests of the goddess Siria and of other Oriental divinities carried with them, along with the sacred images, the wallet for offerings, the bag for alms, because common people do not value things which cost them nothing. The Apostles of Jesus, on the contrary, were to refuse any gift or payment: "Freely ye have received, freely give."

They were to enter into the houses, open to all in a country where the locks and bolts of fear were not yet known, and which preserved some remembrance of nomad hospitality—they were to speak to the men and the women who lived there. Their duty was to announce that the Kingdom of Heaven was at hand, to explain in what way the kingdom of earth could become the Kingdom of Heaven, and to explain the one condition for this happy fulfilling of all the prophecies—repentance, conversion, transformation of the soul. Pilgrims without purses or bundles, they carried with them truth and life—peace.

"And when ye come into an house salute it," and this was the salutation, "Peace be with you."

OTHER TEACHINGS

JESUS IS THE POOR MAN, infinitely and rigorously poor. The prince of poverty. Richness is a curse. The rich man does not belong to himself, but to inanimate things. Outside of himself man can possess nothing. The absolute secret of owning other things is to renounce them. But he who wishes to grasp for himself alone a part of the world's goods loses both what he has acquired and everything else.

"For what shall it profit a man, if he shall gain the whole world, and lose his own soul?" This question of Christ's, simple like all revelations, expresses the exact meaning of the prophetic threat. The rich man not only loses eternity, but, pulled down by his wealth, loses his life here below, his present soul, the happiness of his present earthly life.

"Ye cannot serve God and mammon." He who desires gold puts an end to the spirit and renounces all the benefits of the spirit: peace, holiness, love, perfect joy. When the mystery of wealth is deeply probed, it is easy to see that the most precious thing is exchanged for the most worthless. For poverty, voluntarily accepted, joyfully desired, is the only poverty which gives spiritual wealth. Absolute poverty frees men for the conquest of the absolute. The Kingdom of Heaven does not promise poor people that they shall become rich, it promises rich people that they shall enter into it when they become freely poor.

"Sell whatsoever thou hast, and give to the poor, and thou shalt have treasure in heaven where neither moth nor rust doth corrupt and where thieves do not break through nor steal; for where your treasure is, there will your heart be also. Give to him that asketh thee, and from him that would borrow from thee, turn not thou away, for it is more blessed to give than to receive."

Jesus was not the first to find in poverty one of the steps to perfection. Buddha exhorted his disciples to a similar renunciation. The Cynics stripped themselves of all material goods to be independent of work and of men, and to be able to consecrate their freed souls to truth. Crates, the Theban nobleman, disciple of Diogenes, distributed his wealth to his fellow citizens and turned beggar. Plato wished the warriors in his Republic to have no possessions as a measure of political prudence. The first republics conquered and flourished as long as the citizens contented themselves, as in old Sparta and old Rome, with strict poverty, and they fell as soon as they valued gold more than sober and modest living.

But in Jesus the love of poverty is not an ascetic rule. In the Gospel, poverty of the body is a preliminary requisite, like humility of the spirit. The poor man who glories in his poverty instead of tormenting himself to convert it into wealth is nearer to moral perfection than the rich man. But the rich man who has despoiled himself in favor of the poor and has chosen to live side by side with his new brothers is still nearer perfection than the man who was born and reared in poverty. That he has been touched by a grace so rare and prodigious gives him the right to hope for the greatest blessedness.

EVERY TIME that the powerful have desired to sanctify violence and make Christ surety for Genghis Khan or for Bonaparte or even the outrider of Mohammed, you will see them quote the celebrated Gospel text, which everybody knows by heart and very few have ever understood.

"Think not that I am come to send peace on earth: I came not to send peace, but a sword." Some more learned add, "I am come to send fire on the earth." Others rush forward to present the decisive verse, "The kingdom of heaven suffereth violence, and the violent take it by force."

These hardened quoters do not look at the words which come

before and after; they pay no attention to the occasion on which they were spoken. They do not imagine for a moment that they can have another meaning from the common one.

When Jesus says that He has come to bring a sword—or as it is written in the parallel passage of Luke, "Discord," He is speaking to His Disciples who are on the point of departing to announce the coming of the Kingdom. And immediately after, He explains with familiar examples what He meant to say: "For I am come to set a man at variance against his father, and the daughter against her mother, and the daughter-in-law against her mother-in-law. And a man's foes shall be they of his own household. For from henceforth there shall be five in one house divided, three against two and two against three." The sword therefore is a figure of speech which signifies division; the preaching of the Gospel shall divide men of the same family; those who are slow and those who are quick, those who deny and those who believe. Until all are converted and "brothers in the Word," discord will reign on earth.

When Jesus proclaims that He comes to bring fire, only the literal-minded can think of destructive fire, auxiliary of human warfare. The fire desired by the Son of man is the fire of purification, of enthusiasm, the ardor of sacrifice, the flame of love, which Jesus came to kindle in our hearts.

Jesus can say, "The kingdom of heaven suffereth violence, and the violent take it by force." The word "violent" has as a matter of fact in the text the evident meaning of "strong," of men who know how to take doors by assault without hesitating or trembling. "Sword," "fire," "violence," are figurative words which we are forced to use to reach the imagination of the crowds. The sword is the symbol of the divisions between those first persuaded and those last to believe; fire is purifying love; violence is the strength necessary to make oneself over and to arrive on the threshold of the Kingdom.

Jesus is the Man of Peace. He has come to bring Peace. The Gospels are nothing but proclamations and instructions for Peace. The very night of His birth celestial voices sang in the sky: "Peace on Earth to men of good will." On the Mount one of the first promises is that directed to the peacemakers, "Blessed are the peacemakers: for they shall be called the children of God." To the disciples, to His friends, He counsels, "Have peace one with another." On that terrible night on the Mount of Olives, while the mercenaries armed with swords are binding Him, He pronounces the supreme condemnation of violence, "For all they that take the sword shall perish with the sword." He understands the evils of discord, "Every kingdom divided against itself is brought to desolation; and every city or house divided against itself shall not stand." And in His talk on the last things, in the grand apocalyptic prophecy, He announces among the terrible signs of the end together with famine, earthquakes and tribulation, also wars. "And ye shall hear of wars and rumors of wars. . . . For nation shall rise against nation, and kingdom against kingdom."

But when hate is abolished in every heart, then at last will arrive the day longed for by Isaiah when, "they shall beat their swords into plowshares, and their spears into pruning hooks: nation shall not lift up sword against nation, neither shall they learn war any more."

That day announced by Isaiah is the day on which the Sermon on the Mount shall become the only law recognized on earth.

In the Kingdom of Heaven men will not hate each other and will no longer desire riches; every reason and need for government will disappear immediately after these two great changes. The name of the path which conducts to perfect liberty is not Destruction but Holiness.

JESUS SANCTIONS the union of man and woman even in the flesh. In marriage Jesus sees first of all the joining of two bodies. On this point He ratifies the metaphor of the Old Law, "So then they are no more twain, but one flesh." Husband and wife are one body, inseparable.

This man shall never have another woman; this woman shall never know another man until death divides them. The mating has an almost mystic character which nothing can cancel. The two have been fused into one, their two souls become one soul, and from this communion will be born a new creature formed of the essence of both, which will be the visible form of their union. Love makes them like God, creators of a new and miraculous creation.

But this duality of the flesh and of the spirit—the most perfect among imperfect human relations—should never be disturbed or interrupted. Jesus always condemns adultery and divorce in the most absolute manner. His whole nature holds unfaithfulness in horror. There will come a day, he warns people, in speaking of heavenly life, in which men and women will not marry; but up to that day marriage should have at least all the perfections possible to its imperfection. In the new organization of salvation, spiritual affiliations will surpass the simple relationships of the flesh.

Jesus was speaking in a house, perhaps at Capernaum, and men and women, all hungering for life and justice, all needing comfort and consolation, had filled the house, had pressed close around Him.

There came a stir and voices were heard at the door. One of those present told Jesus, "Behold, thy mother and thy brethren without seek for thee." But Jesus did not stir. "Who is my mother, or my brethren?" And he looked round about on them which sat about him, and said, "Behold my mother and my brethren! For whosoever shall do the will of God, the same is my brother, and my sister, and mother."

He who wishes to serve the universe with a broad spirit must give up, and if that is not enough, deny the common affections. "If any man come to me, and hate not his father, and mother, and wife, and children, and brethren, and sisters, yea, and his own life also, he cannot be my disciple."

The family will disappear when men shall be better than men. "And call no man your father upon the earth: for one is your Father, which is in heaven." He who leaves his family shall be infinitely rewarded. "And he said unto them, Verily I say unto you, There is no man that hath left house, or parents, or brethren, or wife, or children, for the kingdom of God's sake, Who shall not receive manifold more in this present time, and in the world to come life everlasting."

According to Jesus, fathers have more duties towards their sons than sons towards their fathers. "Honor thy father and thy

mother," said Moses. But from Jesus' point of view, fathers are debtors. "Or what man is there of you, whom if his son ask bread, will he give him a stone? Or if he ask a fish, will he give him a serpent?"

JESUS, WHOM no one called Father, was drawn to children as to sinners. Lover of the absolute, He loved only extremes. Complete innocence and complete downfall were for Him pledges of salvation. Innocence because it does not need to be cleansed; abject degradation because it feels more keenly the need to be cleansed.

Mothers brought their children to Him to have Him touch them. The Disciples, with their habitual roughness, cried out on them—and Jesus once more was obliged to reprove them, "Suffer little children, and forbid them not, to come unto me: for of such is the kingdom of heaven."

The bearded men, proud of their authority as lieutenants of their future Lord, could not understand why their Master consented to waste time with children who could not yet speak plainly and could not understand the meaning of grown people's words. But Jesus set in their midst one of these children and said: "Verily I say unto you, Except ye be converted, and become as little children, ye shall not enter into the kingdom of heaven. Whosoever therefore shall humble himself as this little child, the same is greatest in the kingdom of heaven. And whoso shall receive one such little child in my name receiveth me. But whoso shall offend one of these little ones which believe in me, it were better for him that a millstone were hanged about his neck, and that he were drowned in the depth of the sea."

Here, too, Jesus reversed the Old Law. Perfection was supposed to lie in years of maturity, or, better yet, in old age. Jesus loves children as the actual mediums of truth. "I thank thee, O Father, Lord of heaven and earth, because thou hast hid these things from the wise and prudent, and hast revealed them unto babes."

Only the simple can understand simplicity; the innocent, innocence; the loving, love.

WOMEN LOVED JESUS. They stopped when they saw Him pass, they drew near to the house where He had gone in, they brought their children to Him, they blessed Him loudly, they touched His garment to be cured of their ills.

They would have liked to be His sisters, His servants, His slaves; to serve Him, to set bread before Him, to pour Him wine, to wash His garments, to anoint His tired feet and His flowing hair. Some of them were fortunate enough to be allowed to follow Him, and knew the still greater good fortune of helping Him with their money. ". . . and the twelve were with Him, And certain women, which had been healed of evil spirits and infirmities, Mary called Magdalene, out of whom went seven devils, And Joanna the wife of Chuza, Herod's steward, and Susanna, and many others, which ministered unto him of their substance."

Many followed Him to death. Salome, mother of James and John, the Sons of Thunder; Mary, mother of James the less; Martha and Mary of Bethany.

When He appears in the house of Lazarus, the man brought back from death, the two sisters seem distracted with joy. Martha rushes towards Him, leads Him to the couch that He may lie down, puts over Him a blanket lest He be cold, and runs with a pitcher to get fresh cool water. Then she sets to work to prepare for the Pilgrim a fine meal. With all haste she lights a great fire, goes to get fresh fish, new-laid eggs, figs and olives; she borrows from one neighbor a piece of new-killed lamb, from another a costly perfume, from another richer than she, a flowered dish. She pulls out from the linen chest the newest table-cloth, and brings up from the wine cellar the oldest wine. And while the wood snaps and sparkles in the fire and the water in the kettle begins to simmer, poor Martha, bustling, flushed, hurrying, sets the table, runs between the kneading trough and the fire, glances at the waiting Master, at the street to see if her brother is coming home, and at her sister, who is doing nothing at all.

For when Jesus passed the sill of their house, Mary fell into a sort of motionless ecstasy from which nothing could arouse her. She sees only Jesus, hears nothing but Jesus' voice. If He glances at her, she is happy to be looked at; if He speaks, His words drop one by one into her heart, there to remain to her death. And she is almost troubled by the bustling and stepping about of her sister. Why should Martha think that Jesus needs an elaborate dinner? Mary is seated at His feet and does not move even if Martha or Lazarus calls her. She is at the service of Jesus, but in another way. She is a contemplative soul, an adorer. She will take action only to cover the dead body of her God with perfumes.

Women loved Him and no woman who turned to Him was sent away disconsolate. The unknown woman which had a "spirit of infirmity" eighteen years, and was bowed together and could in no wise lift herself, was cured, although it was on the Sabbath day and the rulers of the synagogue cried, "Sacrilege!" In the first part of His wanderings He cured Peter's wife's mother of fever. He cured that unknown woman who had suffered for twelve years from a bloody flux.

"The words of the Law," says a rabbinical proverb of that time, "rather than teach them to a woman, burn them up!" Jesus on the other hand did not hesitate to speak to them of the highest mysteries. When He went alone to the well of Sichar, and the Samaritan woman who had had five husbands came there, He did not hesitate to proclaim His message to her, although she was a woman and an enemy of His people. "But the hour cometh, and now is, when the true worshippers shall worship the Father in spirit and in truth: for the Father seeketh such to worship him. God is a Spirit: and they that worship him must worship him in spirit and in truth." His Disciples came up, "And marveled that he talked with the woman." They did not yet know that the Church of Christ would make the Virgin Mother the link between the sons and the Son.

On another occasion, at Jerusalem, Jesus found Himself before a woman. A hooting crowd pushed her forward. The woman, hiding her face with her hands and with her hair, stood before Him, without speaking. Jesus detested adultery. But He detested still more the cowardice of talebearers, the hounding by the merciless. And He stooped down and with His finger wrote upon the ground. It is the first and last time that we see Jesus lower Himself to this trivial operation. No one has ever known what he wrote at that moment. He chose the sand on which to write expressly that the wind might carry away the words, which would perhaps frighten men if they could read them. But the persecutors insisted that the woman should be stoned. Then Jesus lifted Himself up, looked deep into their eyes, one by one: "He that is without sin among you, let him first cast a stone at her."

On this earth there are no innocents, and even if there were, their mercy would be stronger than justice itself.

Such thoughts had never occurred to those angry spies; Christ's words troubled them. Every one of them thought of his own secret sins of the flesh. The old men were the first to go. Then, little by little, all the others, avoiding each other's eyes, scattered and dispersed. Jesus had again stooped down to write upon the ground. The woman had heard the shuffling of the departing feet, and heard no longer any voice crying for her death, but she did not dare to raise her eyes. Jesus for the second time lifted Himself up and saw the open place was empty.

"Woman, where are those thine accusers? hath no man condemned thee?"

"No man, Lord."

"Neither do I condemn thee: go, and sin no more."

And for the first time the woman dared to look in His face. But Jesus had begun again to write on the ground of the court, His head lowered, and she saw only His finger moving slowly over the sunlit earth.

BUT NO WOMAN loved Him so much as the woman who anointed Him with nard and bathed Him with her tears in the house of Simon the Pharisee. Every one of us has seen that picture in imagination; and yet the true meaning of the episode is understood by very few, so greatly has it been disfigured by both the ordinary and the literary interpretations.

This woman who silently entered the house of Simon with her box of alabaster had heard the voice of Jesus; His voice had troubled her, His words had shaken her. When she came to the house of Simon the sinning woman wished to reward her Saviour with a token of her gratitude. She took one of the most costly things left to her, a sealed box full of nard. Hers was an act of public gratitude. The woman wished to thank Him who had brought her heart to life.

She went in silently with her little box of perfume, raising her eyes for only a moment to see at a glance where Jesus was reclining. She went up to the couch, her knees trembling under her, her hands shaking, because she felt all those men's eyes were fixed on her beautiful swaying body, wondering what she was about to do.

She broke the seal of the little alabaster flask, and poured half the oil on the head of Jesus. The whole room was filled with the fragrance; every eye was fixed on her with astonishment.

The woman, still silent, took up the opened box and knelt by the feet of the Peace-bringer. She poured the remaining oil into her hand and gently, gently rubbed the right foot and the left with loving care. Then she could restrain no longer the burst of tenderness which filled her heart, made her throat ache and brought tears to her eyes. She would have liked to speak, to say that this was her thanks for the great help she had received. But in such a moment, with all those men there, how could she find words worthy of the wonderful grace? And besides, her lips trembled so that she could not pronounce two words together. Her tears fell down one by one, swift and hot on the feet of Jesus, like so many silent thank offerings.

Yet it was not alone for her own sorrow and joy she wept. The tears that bathed His feet were also shed for Jesus. The unknown woman had anointed His head as the high priests had anointed the kings of Judea; she had anointed His feet as the lords and guests anointed themselves on festal days. But at the same time the weeping woman had prepared Him for death and burial. Jesus, about to enter Jerusalem, knew that those were the last days of His life in the flesh. He said to His disciples, "For in that she hath poured this ointment on my body, she did it for my burial."

Now the feet of the Saviour, the feet of the condemned one, are bathed with tears. The poor woman does not know how to dry those feet. She has no white cloth with her. Then she thinks of her long hair which has been so much admired for its fine silkiness. She loosens the braids. The blue-black tresses fall over her face, and taking these flowing curls in her hands, she dries the feet which have brought her King into that house.

Among the men who were present at this dinner there was no one except Jesus who understood the loving service of the nameless woman, but all respected obscurely the solemnity of the enigmatic ceremony, except two who wished to interpret the woman's action as an offense to the guest. These two were the Pharisee and Judas Iscariot. The first said nothing, but his expression spoke more clearly than words.

Simon the Pharisee thought to himself, "This man, if he were a prophet, would have known who and what manner of woman this is that toucheth Him: for she is a sinner."

There were still ringing in his ears the execrations of the Law against prostitutes. "Thou shalt not bring the hire of a whore, or the price of a dog, into the house of the Lord thy God for any vow: for even both these are abomination unto the Lord thy God." Jesus had read in the heart of Simon, and answered the Pharisee with the parable of the two debtors. "There was a certain creditor which had two debtors: the one owed five hundred pence, and the other fifty. And when they had nothing to pay, he frankly forgave them both. Tell me therefore, which of them will love him most? Simon answered and said, I suppose that he, to whom he forgave most. And he said unto him, Thou hast rightly judged.

"And he turned to the woman, and said unto Simon, Seest thou this woman? I entered into thine house, thou gavest me no water for my feet: but she hath washed my feet with tears, and wiped them with the hairs of her head.

"Thou gavest me no kiss: but this woman since the time I came in hath not ceased to kiss my feet.

"My head with oil thou didst not anoint: but this woman hath anointed my feet with ointment.

"Wherefore I say unto thee, Her sins, which are many, are forgiven; for she loved much: but to whom little is forgiven, the same loveth little.

"And he said unto her, Thy sins are forgiven. . . . Thy faith hath saved thee; go in peace."

Simon could think of no answer; but from the side of the Disciples a rough, angry voice was raised, well known to Jesus. It was the voice of Judas, who held the purse: "Why was this waste of the ointment made, why was not this ointment sold for three hundred pence and given to the poor?" And the other Disciples, so the Evangelists say, approved the words of Judas, and murmured against the woman.

But Jesus answered the words of Judas as He answered the silence of Simon. "Let her alone; why trouble ye her? she hath wrought a good work on me. For ye have the poor with you always, and whensoever ye will ye may do them good: but me ye have not always. She hath done what she could: she is come aforehand to anoint my body to the burying. Verily I say unto you, Wheresoever this gospel shall be preached throughout the whole world, this also that she hath done shall be spoken of for a memorial of her."

The woman listened. Then with her face hidden in her loosened hair, she went away as silently as she had come.

The Disciples were abashed. To hide his chagrin Simon filled the guest's cup with better wine, but in the yellow light of the lamps the silent table seemed a banquet of ghosts among whom had passed the shadow of death.

THOSE WORDS OF DEATH were not the first they had heard from Jesus' lips. They should have remembered that day, not long before, when on a solitary road near Caesarea, Jesus had asked His Disciples what people said of Him. "Who am I?"

"Some say that thou art John the Baptist: some, Elias; and others, Jeremias, or one of the prophets."

"But whom say ye that I am?" They should have remembered the impetuous outcry of belief from Peter's heart. "Thou art the Christ, the Son of the living God. Thou hast the words of eternal life. And we believe and are sure that thou art that Christ, the Son of the living God."

From Peter the Rock sprang forth this wellspring which from that day to this has quenched the thirst of sixty generations of men. Peter had been the first to follow Christ in the divine wanderings: it was for him to be the first to recognize in the wanderer the Messiah whom all men had been awaiting in the desert of the centuries, who had finally come and was there Himself, clothed in flesh, standing before their eyes, with His feet in the dust of the road.

"Blessed art thou, Simon Bar-jona: for flesh and blood hath not revealed it unto thee, but my Father which is in heaven.

"Thou art Peter, and upon this rock I will build my church; and the gates of hell shall not prevail against it. And I will give unto thee the keys of the kingdom of heaven: and whatsoever thou shalt bind on earth shall be bound in heaven: and whatsoever thou shalt loose on earth shall be loosed in heaven."

For these words many men suffered, many were tortured. To deny or uphold, to interpret or cancel these words, thousands of men have been killed in city squares and in battles; kingdoms have been divided, societies have been shaken and rent.

Their meaning in Christ's mouth is plain and simple. He means to say, "Thou, Peter, shalt be hard and staunch as a rock, and upon the staunchness of thy faith in me, which thou wast the first to profess, is founded the first Christian society, the humble seed of the Kingdom."

THE THREE-PEAKED MOUNTAIN of Hermon is covered with snow even in the hot season, the highest mountain of Palestine, higher than Mount Tabor. Jesus became incarnate light on this mountain.

Three Disciples alone were with Him: he who was called Peter, and the Sons of Thunder—the man with the rugged, mountainous character, and the stormy men—fitting company for the place and hour. He prayed alone, higher than all of them, perhaps kneeling in the snow. We have seen in winter how the snow on a mountain makes any other whiteness seem dull and drab. A pale face seems strangely dark, white linen seems dingy, paper looks like dry clay. The contrary of all this was seen on that day up in the gleaming, deserted height.

Jesus prayed by Himself apart from the others. Suddenly His face shone like the sun and His raiment became white "as no fuller on earth can white them." Over the whiteness of the snow a more brilliant whiteness, a splendor more powerful than all known splendors, outshone all earthly light.

The Transfiguration is the feast and the victory of light. Jesus' body, awaiting its liberation, became the most subtle, the lightest and most spiritual aspect of matter. His soul transfigured in prayer shone out through the flesh, pierced the screen of His body and His garments, like a flame consuming the walls and flashing through them.

But Jesus, all light, His face gleaming with quiet refulgence, was not alone. Two great figures, returned from death, gleaming like Him, stood by Him, and spoke with Him—the Prophets Moses and Elias. All those who have spoken with God remain radiant with light. The face of Moses when he came down from Mount Sinai had become so resplendent that he covered it with a veil, lest he dazzle the others. And Elias was caught up to Heaven in a chariot of fire drawn by fiery steeds. But on Hermon there was One whose face shone more than Moses' and whose ascension was to be more splendid than that of Elias. A luminous cloud hid the glorious three from the eyes of the obscure three, and from the cloud came out a voice: "This is my beloved Son: hear him."

The column of smoke which guided the fleeing Hebrews in the desert toward Jordan, the black cloud which hid the ark in the day of desolation and fear, had finally become a cloud of light so brilliant that it hid even the sunlike splendor of the face which was soon to be buffeted in the dark days, close at hand.

When the cloud disappeared, Jesus was once more alone. His face had taken on its natural color. His garments had their everyday aspect. Christ, once more a loving brother, turned back to His swooning companions. "Arise, and be not afraid. . . . Tell the vision to no man, until the Son of man be risen again from the dead."

MARANATHA
(OUR LORD, COME!)

JESUS HAD KNOWN that He must soon die a shameful death. The Disciples were troubled at this revelation and unwilling to believe. But Jesus, foreseeing those terrible last days of His life, could go on His way to Jerusalem in order that His words should be fulfilled. And yet for one day at least He was to be like that King awaited by the poor every morning on the thresholds of the holy city.

Passover draws near. It was the beginning of the last week which even now had not yet ended—since the new Sabbath has not yet dawned. But this time Jesus does not come to Jerusalem as in other years, an obscure wanderer mingled with the crowd of pilgrims, into the evil-smelling metropolis huddled with its houses, white as sepulchers, under the towering vainglory of the Temple destined to the flames. This time, which is the last time, Jesus does not come alone; He is accompanied by His faithful friends, by the women who were later to weep, by the Twelve who were to hide themselves, by His fellow Galileans, peasants who come in memory of an ancient miracle, but with the hope of seeing a new miracle. This time He does not come unknown; the cry of the Resurrection has preceded Him.

This time He does not come on foot into the city which was to be His tomb. When He had come to Bethpage, He sent two Disciples to look for an ass, "Go into the village over against you, and straightway ye shall find an ass tied, and a colt with her: loose them, and bring them unto me. And if any man say ought unto you, ye shall say, The Lord hath need of them."

Even up to our days it has been said that Jesus wished to ride on an ass as a sign of humble meekness, as if He wished to signify symbolically that He approached His people as the Prince of Peace. It has been forgotten that in the robust early periods of history the ass was a fiery and warlike animal; handsome and bold as a horse, fit to be sacrificed to divinities; rebellious to the end of time.

The ass's back is hard, and Christ's friends throw their cloaks over it. Stony is the slope which leads from the Mount of Olives and the triumphant crowds throw their mantles over the rough stones.

Then began the descent in the heat of the sun and of glory. It was at the beginning of breezy April and of spring. The golden hour of noon lay about the city with its green vineyards, fields and orchards. The sky, immense, deep blue, miraculously calm, clear and joyful, stretched away into the infinite. A warm breeze, still scented with the freshness of heaven, gently swayed the tender treetops and set the young, growing leaves aflutter.

Those who accompanied Christ in that descent were swept away by the rapture of the world and of the moment. Never before had they felt themselves so bursting with hope and adoration. The cry of Peter became the cry of the fervent little army winding its way down the slope towards the queen city. "Hosanna to the Son of David!" said the impetuous, exultant voices of the young men and of the women. Even the Disciples almost began to hope, although they had been warned that this would be the last sun, that they were accompanying a man about to die.

The procession approached the mysterious, hostile city with the roaring tumult of a torrent that has burst its banks. These countrymen, these people from the provinces, came forward flanked as by a moving forest, as if they had wished to carry a little country freshness into the noisome alleyways. The boldest had cut palm branches along the road, boughs of myrtle, clusters of olives, willow leaves, and they waved them on high, shouting out the impassioned words of the Psalmist.

Now the first Christian legion had arrived before the gates of Jerusalem and the voices did not still their homage: "Blessed be the King that cometh in the name of the Lord: peace in heaven, and glory in the highest!"

Their shouting reached the ears of the Pharisees, who arrived, haughty and severe. The seditious cries scandalized those learned ears and suspicious hearts; and some of them, well wrapped up in their doctoral cloaks, called from among the crowd to Jesus:

"Master, rebuke thy disciples."

And then He, without halting, "I tell you that, if these should hold their peace, the stones would immediately cry out!"

With this answer, Jesus had asserted His right to be called "the Christ." It was a declaration of war at the very moment of His entrance into His city.

HE WENT up to the Temple; there on the hilltop the sacred fortress sunned its new whiteness in the magnificence of the day. The old Ark of the nomads, drawn by oxen through sweltering deserts and over battlefields, had halted on that height, petrified as a defense for the royal city. The movable cart of the fugitives had become a pompous citadel of stone and marble, palaces and stairways, enclosed by walls, sheer above the valley. It was not only the precinct of the Holy of Holies, and the sacrificial altar, it was no longer only the Temple, the mystic sanctuary of the people. With its great towers, its guardrooms, its warehouses for offerings, its strongboxes for deposits, its open piazzas for trade and covered galleries for meetings and amusement, it was a stronghold in case of assault, a bank vault, a marketplace in time of pilgrimage and feast days, a bazaar on all days, a forum for the disputes of politicians, the wranglings of doctors and the gossip of idlers; a thoroughfare, a rendezvous, a business center. Built by a faithless king to win over the favor of a captious and seditious people, to satisfy the pride and avarice of the priestly caste, it must have seemed to the eyes of Jesus the natural focus for all the enemies of His truth.

Jesus goes up to the Temple to destroy the Temple. He will leave to the Romans of Titus the task of literally dismantling the walls, of stealing the bronze and gold, of reducing to a smoky and accursed ruin the great stronghold of Herod; but He will destroy the values which the proud Temple upheld with its piled-up blocks of ordered stone and its golden doors. Jesus goes up toward the Temple, among the songs of His fervent band.

Well does He know the street. How many times He had gone over it as a child led along by the hand in the crowd of Galilean pilgrims, longing to arrive at the summit, the sacred precincts!

But today everything is transformed. He is not led along. He leads along. He does not come to adore, but to punish.

He enters into the Court of the Gentiles, the most spacious and most densely crowded of all. From the great, sunny, well-paved terrace rises up an immense, roaring din. There are herdsmen with their oxen and their flocks of sheep; vendors of pigeons and turtledoves, standing by the long lines of their coops; bird sellers with cages of chirping sparrows; benches for money changers, a coin hung at their ears as a mark of their trade, with bowls overflowing with copper and silver. Merchants, their feet in the fresh-dropped dung, handle the flanks of the animals destined for sacrifice; or call with monotonous iteration women who have come there after childbirth, pilgrims who have come to offer a rich sacrifice, lepers who offer living birds for their cure. Wary provincials hold excited conferences before loosening their purse strings for a votive offering, and from time to time a restless ox drowns out with his deep bellow the thin bleating of the lambs, and shrill voices of the women, the clinking of drachma and shekels.

Christ was familiar with the spectacle. He knew that the house of God, instead of silently invoking the Spirit, had been turned into the house of Mammon. But this time He did not restrain His scorn and His repugnance.

He had in His hand a length of rope, which He knotted together like a whip, and with it He opened a passageway through the astonished people. The benches of the money changers crashed down at the first shock. The coins were scattered on the ground amid yells of astonishment and wrath; the seats of the bird sellers were overturned beside their scattered pigeons. The herdsmen began to urge towards the doors the oxen and the sheep. The sparrow sellers took their cages under their arms and disappeared. Cries rose to Heaven, some scandalized, some approving; from the other courtyards other people came running towards the disturbance. Jesus, surrounded by the boldest of His friends, was brandishing His whip on high, and driving the money changers towards the door. And He repeated in a loud voice, "My house shall be called the house of prayer; but ye have made it a den of thieves!"

With that violent action, Jesus antagonized all the commercial middle class of Jerusalem. The men He had driven away demanded that their patrons should punish Him, and they found ready hearing. Jesus in disturbing the business of the Temple had condemned and harmed the priests themselves. The most successful bazaars were the property of the sons of Annas, that is, close relations of the High Priest Caiaphas. And the money changers, who should not have been allowed to stay in the Temple, paid the great Sadducee families of the priestly aristocracy a goodly tithe on their profitable exchange of foreign money into Hebrew money. Had not the Temple itself perhaps become a national bank?

If Jesus had His way, He would ruin them all: the twenty thousand priests of Jerusalem and their associates, the merchants. The two threatened castes drew together to do away with the dangerous intruder. It was perhaps that very evening that they agreed on the purchase of a betrayer and a cross. The bourgeoisie were to give the small amount of money necessary; the clergy to find the religious pretext; the foreign government, naturally desiring to be on good terms with clergy and bourgeoisie, would lend its soldiers.

But Jesus, having left the Temple, went His way towards Bethany, passing by the Mount of Olives.

THE NEXT morning when He went back, the herdsmen and merchants had squatted down outside, near the doors, but the courts were humming with crowds of excited people.

The sentence pronounced and executed by Jesus had awakened the poor to joyous hope. Early in the morning, they had gone up there from the dark alleys, from the workshops and from the public squares, leaving their affairs, with the restless anxiety of those who hope for miracles, or revenge. The day laborers had come, the weavers, the dyers, the cobblers, the woodworkers, all those who detested the shearers of poverty. Among the first had come the lamentable vermin-ridden scum of the city, with leprous scabs, with their sores uncared for, with their bones showing beneath the skin to testify to their hunger. There had also come pilgrims from outside, those of Galilee, who had accompanied Jesus in His festal entrance; and with them Jews from the Syrian and Egyptian colonies.

But there came up also, in groups of four or five, the scribes and the Pharisees, the puritans of the Law. Nearly all the scribes were Pharisees, many Pharisees were scribes.

These men went up to the Temple proudly wrapped in their long cloaks, with their fringes fluttering, with sneering mouths and quivering nostrils, with a step which announced the indignation felt by them, God's privileged sheriffs.

Jesus, in the midst of all these eyes turned on Him, waited for them. It was not the first time that they had come about Him. How many discussions between Him and the provincial Pharisees had taken place in the country! They were Pharisees who had demanded a sign from Heaven that He was the Messiah—because the Pharisees, unlike the skeptical Sadducees, believed in the imminent arrival of the Saviour.

But the Pharisees expected to see this Saviour as a Jew, strictly observing all laws as they did. The Messiah, the son of David, would save only those who had avoided all contact with foreigners and with heathens, who had observed the smallest detail of legal purification, who had paid all the tithes of the Temple. In their eyes Jesus could not possibly be the Divine Redeemer. They had seen Him dining with publicans and sinners, and had heard with horror that His disciples did not always wash their hands before sitting down to the table. But the unendurable scandal had been that Jesus had not hesitated to cure the sick, even on the Sabbath, claiming blasphemously that the Sabbath was made for man, rather than man for the Sabbath.

As long as Jesus went about in the provinces drawing after Him a few dozen peasants, the Pharisees had let Him alone, sure that some day or other the last beggar, disillusioned, would leave Him. But, accompanied by a band of excitable countrymen, He had gone so far as to enter into the Temple as though it belonged to Him, and had seduced some unfortunates to call Him the Messiah. More than that, usurping the place of the priests, and almost giving Himself the airs of a king, He had roughly driven out the honest merchants, pious people who admired the Pharisees. The public challenge called for condemnation and punishment. The false Christ must be disposed of at once.

Jesus was waiting for just those men. He wanted to say to them publicly what He thought of them. The day before, with His whip, He had condemned the animal sellers and money changers. Now He was dealing with the merchants of the Word, the swindlers of Truth.

"Woe unto you, scribes and Pharisees, hypocrites!"

And so the indestructible race of Pharisees was created for all centuries, for all peoples. With every generation such men spring up again, innumerable, with new names. Everything in them is pretense: their dress and their talk, their teaching and their practice. What they say is contradicted by what they do. The Pharisees are those who wish to appear saints, and who hate the real saints. They are those who are not visibly sinners, but who are the incarnation of the ugliest of all sins, the betrayal of Truth. Whoever they are, wherever they are born, their faces are stamped forever by the condemnation of that day.

Jesus, while He spoke to them in the great open courtyard crowded with witnesses, knew that He spoke to His judges, and to those who would be, through intermediate persons, the real authors of His death. By speaking out on this day, He justified His later silence before Caiaphas and Pilate. For He had judged them first and had nothing more to add when they wished to judge Him.

THE THIRTEEN went down from the Temple to make their daily ascent to the Mount of Olives. One of the Disciples (who could it have been?—perhaps John, son of Salome, still rather childish and naively full of wonder at what he saw? Or Judas Iscariot, with his respect for wealth?) said to Jesus, "Master, see what manner of stones and what buildings are here!"

The Master turned to look at the high walls faced with marble which the ostentatious calculation of Herod had built up on the hill and said, "Seest thou these great buildings? there shall not be left one stone upon another, that shall not be thrown down."

The admiring exclamation suddenly died. Perplexed and surprised, each of them continued to turn over in his mind these words. He whom they loved had said in these last days many other hard words, hard to understand, hard to believe. But those ambitious provincials did not remember any other words so hard as these. They knew that He was the Christ and that He was to suffer and die, but they hoped that He would rise again at once in the glorious victory of the new David, to give abundance to all Israel and to award the greatest prizes and power to them, faithful to Him in the dangerous wanderings of His poor days. But if the world was to be commanded by Judea, Judea was to be commanded by Jerusalem, and the seats of command were to be in the Temple of the great King. Christ was to drive away the faithless Sadducees, the hypocritical Pharisees, the traitorous scribes, to give their places to His Apostles. How then could the Temple be destroyed, splendid memorial of the kingdom in the past; hoped-for rock of the new Kingdom?

They would not understand that those great massive stones, quarried out patiently from the mountains, drawn from afar by oxen, squared and prepared by chisels and mallets, put one upon another by masters of the art to make the most marvelous Temple of the universe; that these stones, warm and brilliant in the sun, should be pulverized into ruins.

They had scarcely arrived at the Mount of Olives, and Christ had only had time to sit down opposite to the Temple, when their curiosity burst out:

"Tell us, when shall these things be? and what shall be the sign when all these things shall be fulfilled?"

The answer was the discourse on the last things. This discourse, read all in one piece in the Gospels, is not, as is generally believed, the answer to one question only. The Disciples had put two questions, "When shall these things be?"—that is, the ruin of the Temple; and "What shall be the signs of Thy coming?"

Jesus first describes the events which will precede the destruction of Jerusalem, a prophecy that was fulfilled before the end of His generation.

His Disciples, He warns, cannot escape persecution: "Then shall they deliver you up to be afflicted, and shall kill you: and ye shall be hated of all nations for my name's sake. . . . take heed to yourselves: . . . in the synagogues ye shall be beaten: and ye shall be brought before rulers and kings for my sake, for a testimony against them. . . . Now the brother shall betray the brother to death, and the father the son; and children shall rise up against their parents, and shall cause them to be put to death. . . . And because iniquity shall abound, the love of many shall wax cold. But he that shall endure unto the end, the same shall be saved.

"And . . . ye shall hear of wars and rumors of wars. . . . For nation shall rise against nation, and kingdom against kingdom: and there shall be earthquakes in divers places, and there shall be famines and troubles. And when ye shall see Jerusalem compassed with armies, then know that the desolation thereof is nigh. . . . But when ye shall see the abomination of desolation, spoken of by Daniel the prophet . . . then let them that be in Judea flee to the mountains: And let him that is on the housetop not go down into the house, neither enter therein, to take any thing out of his house: And let him that is in the field not turn back again for to take up his garment. But woe to them that are with child, and to them that give suck in those days! And pray ye that your flight be not in the winter. . . . They shall fall by the edge of the sword, and shall be led away captive into all nations: and Jerusalem shall be trodden down of the Gentiles, until the times of the Gentiles be fulfilled."

This is the end of the first prophecy. Jerusalem shall be taken and destroyed and of the Temple there shall remain not one stone upon another.

But until now Jesus has not spoken of His Second Coming.

The Second Coming of Christ from Heaven, the Parousia, will be the end of this world and the beginning of the true world, the eternal Kingdom. This end will be preceded by signs divine and celestial. ". . . the sun shall be darkened, and the moon shall not give her light, And the stars of heaven shall fall. . . . and upon the earth distress of nations, with perplexity; the sea and the waves roaring; . . . And then shall appear the sign of the Son of man in heaven: and then shall all the tribes of the earth mourn, and they shall see the Son of man coming in the clouds of heaven with power and great glory."

It is the day of God's wrath described in their times by Eze-kiel, Jeremiah, Isaiah and Joel. But the day of the Son follows immediately after.

"When the Son of man shall come in his glory, and all the holy angels with him, then shall he sit upon the throne of his glory:

"And before him shall be gathered all nations: and he shall separate them one from another, as a shepherd divideth his sheep from the goats:

"And he shall set the sheep on his right hand, but the goats on the left.

"Then shall the King say unto them on his right hand, Come, ye blessed of my Father, inherit the kingdom prepared for you from the foundation of the world:

"For I was an hungered, and ye gave me meat: I was thirsty, and ye gave me drink: I was a stranger, and ye took me in:

"Naked, and ye clothed me: I was sick, and ye visited me: I was in prison, and ye came unto me.

"Then shall the righteous answer him, saying, Lord, when saw we thee an hungered, and fed thee? or thirsty, and gave thee drink?

"When saw we thee a stranger, and took thee in? or naked, and clothed thee?

"Or when saw we thee sick, or in prison, and came unto thee?

"And the King shall answer and say unto them, Verily I say unto you, Inasmuch as ye have done it unto one of the least of these my brethren, ye have done it unto me.

"Then shall he say also unto them on the left hand, Depart from me, ye cursed, into everlasting fire, prepared for the devil and his angels:

"For I was an hungered, and ye gave me no meat: I was thirsty, and ye gave me no drink;

"I was a stranger, and ye took me not in: naked, and ye clothed me not: sick, and in prison, and ye visited me not.

"Then shall they also answer him, saying, Lord, when saw we thee an hungered, or athirst, or a stranger, or naked, or sick, or in prison, and did not minister unto thee?

"Then shall he answer them, saying, Verily I say unto you,

Inasmuch as ye did it not to one of the least of these, ye did it not to me.

"And these shall go away into everlasting punishment: but the righteous into life eternal."

On that great day of final judgment, the code of this dividing of good from evil men will be based on one idea only: compassion—charity. During all the time which lies between His first and second coming He has gone on living under the appearance of the poor and the pilgrims, of the sick and persecuted, of wanderers and slaves. And on the last day He pays His debts. Only those who did not receive Him when He appeared in the innumerable bodies of the poverty-stricken will be condemned to eternal punishment, because when they drove away the unfortunate they drove away God.

BUT WHEN shall these things come to pass? The first prophecy of Jesus announces the destruction of the Temple as close at hand. It was fulfilled to the letter, detail by detail, about forty years after the Crucifixion.

A few years after Jesus' death the signs of the first prophecy began to be seen. The persecutions arrived promptly. The Disciples had scarcely begun to preach the Gospel in Jerusalem when Peter and John were thrown into prison; freed, they were captured again, and beaten and commanded to speak no more in the name of Jesus. Stephen, one of the most ardent of the neophytes, was taken by the priests outside the city and stoned.

Then the war against Christian converts began in the capital of the empire. In 64 the burning of Rome, desired and executed by Nero, was the pretext for the first great persecution. An innumerable multitude of Christians obtained their martyrdom in Rome and in the provinces. Many were crucified; others wrapped in the *tunica molesta* lighted up the nocturnal amusement of the Caesar: others wrapped in animal skins were given as food to dogs: many, enforced actors in cruel comedies, made a spectacle for amphitheaters and were devoured by lions. Peter died on the cross, nailed head downward. Paul ended under the axe a life which since his conversion had been one long torment.

Most of the other Disciples met with similar fates. Thomas

met a martyr's death in India, Andrew was crucified at Patras, Bartholomew was crucified in Armenia. Simon the Zealot and Matthew, like their Master, ended their lives on the cross.

Nor were there lacking wars and rumors of wars. When Jesus was killed, the "peace" of Augustus still existed, but very soon nations rise against nations and kingdoms against kingdoms. Under Nero the Britons rebel and massacre the Romans, the Parthians revolt and force the legions to pass under the yoke; Armenia and Syria murmur against foreign government; Gaul rises with Julius Vindex.

In 69, insurrection breaks out in the north, with the Batavians led by Claudius Civilus; and in Palestine the insurrection of the Jews is fomented by the Zealots, who claim that the Romans and all the heathen should be driven out in order that God might return to triumph with His own people. In less than two years Italy is invaded twice, Rome taken twice, two emperors kill themselves; two are killed.

The other afflictions announced by Jesus accompany these upheavals. In the time of Claudius a series of poor crops brought famine even to Rome. Under Nero pestilence was added to the famine. In 61 and 62 earthquakes shook Asia, Achaia and Macedonia. In 63 it was Italy's turn: at Naples, Nocera and Pompeii the earth shook. All the signs were fulfilled: now had come the fullness of time for the punishment of Judea.

For forty years the country had had no peace, not even the peace of defeat and slavery. Under the Roman procurators the disorders knew no truce; the flames of the revolt flared ever more boldly. The holy place, during the great rebellion, had become a refuge for assassins; and the Zealots took possession of the Temple.

Then Vespasian, going to Rome to become emperor, gave the command to his son Titus, who on Easter Day in the year 70 came up before Jerusalem and laid siege to it. Horrible days began. The Zealots, carried away by wild frenzy, quarreled among themselves and split up into factions, who fought for the control of the city and cut the throats of those whom the Romans had not yet killed. To the horror of fratricidal massacre and of the siege was added that of hunger. The famine was so great that mothers were seen, so says Josephus, to kill their children and eat them.

On the tenth of August the Temple was taken by Titus and burned; the Zealots succeeded in shutting themselves up into the upper city, but conquered by hunger they were obliged to surrender on the seventh of September.

The prophecies of Jesus had been fulfilled: by Titus' order the city was laid waste: and of the Temple, already swept by fire, there remained not one stone upon another. The Jews who had survived hunger and sword were massacred by the victorious soldiery. Those who still remained were deported into Egypt to work in mines, and many were killed for the amusement of the crowd in the amphitheaters of Caesarea and Berytus.

"Verily I say unto you, This generation shall not pass, till all these things be fulfilled." It was the seventieth year of the Christian era and His generation had not yet gone down into the tomb when these things happened. One at least of those who heard Him on the Mount of Olives, John, was witness of the destruction of Jerusalem and of the ruin of the Temple.

Now nothing remains of the Temple, three times built and three times destroyed, but a piece of a wall, barely enough so that a line of mourners may lean their heads against it to hide their tears.

THE SECOND COMING, the triumphal Parousia, is still awaited by those who believe what Jesus said that day on the Mount of Olives: "Heaven and earth shall pass away, but my words shall not pass away."

If the words of the second prophecy are true, as the words of the first prophecy were shown to be true, the Second Coming cannot be far distant. Once again in these years nations have risen against nations, the earth has quaked, destroying many lives, and pestilences, famines and seditions have decimated nations.

For more than a century the words of Christ have been translated and preached in all languages. And still men do not think of Jesus and His promise.

They live as if the world were always going to continue as it has been, and they work only for their earthly interests. They hurry about without rest, occupied by possessions. They never look up to Heaven—they fear only their brothers. No one thinks of the Divine Thief who will come suddenly in the night, no one waits for the Real Master, who will return unexpectedly.

THE HIGH PRIEST AND JUDAS ISCARIOT

WHILE JESUS was condemning the Temple and Jerusalem, those maintained by the Temple and the lords of Jerusalem were preparing His condemnation. They believed that they would save themselves by putting Him to death. To have an idea of the hatred which the upper classes of Jerusalem felt towards Jesus, priestly hatred, scholastic hatred and commercial hatred, we must remember that the Holy City apparently lived by faith, but in reality on the faithful. Only in the capital could valid and acceptable offerings be made to the old God, and therefore every year, especially on great feast days, streams of Israelites poured in from all the provinces. Josephus says that at Jerusalem on special occasions there were gathered together as many as three million pilgrims.

The priestly caste, which numbered in Christ's lifetime twenty thousand descendants of Aaron, got their living from the taxes of the Temple, from the payments for the firstborn—five shekels a head!—and got their food from the flesh of the sacrificial animals, of which only the fat was burned. They were the ones who had the pick of herds and crops; even their bread was given them by the people, for the head of every Jewish family was obliged to hand over to the priests the twenty-fourth part of the bread which was baked in his house. It is not impossible that some of them were really bankers, because people readily deposited their savings in the strongboxes of the Temple.

Religion was thus the greatest and perhaps the only business in Jerusalem, and the Gospel of Jesus threatened directly the positions and fees of the prosperous. If all the prescriptions of the

Law were to be reduced to the practice of love, there would be no place for the scribes and doctors of the Law who made their living out of their teachings. If God did not wish animal sacrifices and asked only for purity of soul and secret prayer, those who did business in oxen and calves and sheep and lambs and kids and doves and sparrows would have seen their business slacken and perhaps disappear. If to be loved by God you needed to transform your life, if it were not enough to wash your drinking cups and punctually pay your tithes, the doctrine and the authority of the Pharisees would be reduced to nothing.

Thus, as a matter of course, Jesus, who preferred fishermen, if they were pure and loving, to members of the Sanhedrin; who took the part of the poor against the rich, who valued ignorant children more than scribes, drew down on His head the hatred of the priests, the merchants and the doctors.

When He came back to Jerusalem, the attack with the whips on the animal sellers and money changers, the loud invectives against the scribes and Pharisees, the allusion to the ruin of the Temple, made the cup run over. The high priests, the Pharisees and the scribes, uneasy and embittered, set on His track spies, destined to become false witnesses in a few days. If we are to believe John, the order was given to certain guards to capture Him, but they were afraid to lay their hands upon Him. Time pressed; Jerusalem was full of foreigners and many were listening to Him. An uprising of the provincial crowds who were less attached to the privileges and interests of the metropolis might easily spring up. A meeting of the Sanhedrin to reconcile law with assassination was arranged.

THE SANHEDRIN was the supreme council of the aristocracy which ruled the capital. It was composed of the priests jealous of the clientele of the Temple which gave them their power and their stipends; of the scribes responsible for preserving the purity of the law and of tradition; of the elders who represented the interests of the moderate, moneyed middle class.

They were all in accord that it was essential to take Jesus on false pretenses and to have Him killed as a blasphemer against the Sabbath and the Lord. Only Nicodemus attempted a defense, but they were able quickly to silence him. "What do we? for this man doeth many miracles. If we let him thus alone, all men will believe on him: and the Romans shall come and take away both our place and nation."

Caiaphas, who that year was high priest, settled their doubts with the maxim which has always justified in the eyes of the world the immolation of the innocent. "Ye know nothing at all, Nor consider that it is expedient for us, that one man should die for the people, and that the whole nation perish not." This maxim, transposed into a higher meaning and transferred into the Absolute, changing nation into humanity, was a principle which Jesus Himself had accepted and which has become under another form the crucial mystery of Christianity. Caiaphas did not know—he who had to enter alone into the Holy of Holies to offer up to Jehovah the sins of the people—how much his words, cynical in sentiment as they were, were in accord with his victim's thought. Caiaphas who, together with the crown of thorns and the sponge of vinegar, was to be one of the instruments of the Passion, did not imagine in that moment that he was bearing witness solemnly, though involuntarily, to the divine tragedy about to begin.

And yet the principle that the innocent can pay for the guilty, that the death of one man can be salvation for all, was not foreign to the consciousness of ancient peoples. The heroic myths of the pagans recognize and celebrate voluntary sacrifices of the innocent. They record the example of Pylades, who offered himself to be punished in place of the guilty Orestes; Macaria of the blood of Hercules, who saved her brother's life with her own; Alcestis, who died that she might avert from her Admetus the vengeance of Artemis; and Iphigenia, who offered her throat to the knife that Agamemnon's fleet might sail safely towards Troy.

But such sacrifices were for the salvation of one being alone, or of a restricted group of men. No man had yet taken upon his head all the sins of men, a God who would imprison Himself in the wretchedness of flesh to save all the human race.

The perfect man, who takes upon himself all imperfections, the pure man who burdens himself with all infamies, the righteous man who shoulders the unrighteousness of all men, had now appeared under the aspect of a poor Galilean workingman. He who was to die for all was disquieting the rich and the priests of Jerusalem, was there on the Mount of Olives only a short distance from the Sanhedrin.

The Seventy, who knew not what they did, who did not know that they were obeying the will of the very man they were persecuting, decided to have Him captured before the Passover; but one thing restrained them, the fear of the people who loved Jesus. They consulted that they might take Jesus by subtlety and kill Him. But they said, "Not on the feast day, lest there be an uproar among the people." To solve their difficulty, by good fortune, there came to them the day after one of the Twelve, he who held the purse, Judas Iscariot.

ONLY TWO CREATURES in the world knew the secret of Judas: Christ and the traitor.

Sixty generations of Christians have racked their brains over it, but the man of Iscariot remains stubbornly incomprehensible. His is the only human mystery that we encounter in the Gospels. We can understand without difficulty the depravity of Herod Antipas, the rancor of the Pharisees, the revengeful anger of Annas and Caiaphas, the cowardly laxity of Pilate. But the four Gospels tell us too little of Judas and of the reasons which induced him to sell his King.

"Then entered Satan into Judas." But these words are only the definition of his crime. Evil took possession of his heart, therefore it came suddenly. Before that day Judas was not in the power of the Adversary. But why did Satan enter into him and not into one of the others?

Thirty pieces of silver are a very small sum, especially for an avaricious man. In modern coinage it would amount to about twenty dollars, and, granting that, as the economists say, its buying power was in those days ten times greater, two hundred dollars seems hardly a sufficient price to induce even a man whom his companions describe as grasping to commit the basest perfidy recorded by history. It has been said that thirty pieces of silver was the price of a slave, but the text of Exodus states that thirty shekels was the compensation to be paid by the owner of an ox which had injured a slave. The cases are too far apart for the doctors of the Sanhedrin to have had this early precedent in mind.

The most significant indication is the office which Judas held among the Twelve. Among them was Matthew, a former tax collector, and it would have seemed almost his right to handle the small amount of money necessary for the expenses of the brotherhood. In place of Matthew, we see the man of Iscariot as the depository of the offerings. Money is insidious and saturated with danger.

John said of Judas the thief, that he, "having the bag, took away what was put therein." If he had needed those miserable thirty pieces of silver, could he not have procured them by running away with the purse, without needing to propose the betrayal of Jesus to the high priests?

These common-sense reflections about a crime so extraordinary have induced many to seek other motives for the infamous transaction.

A sect of heretics, the Cainites, had a legend that Judas sorrowfully accepted eternal infamy, knowing that Jesus through His will and the will of the Father was to be betrayed to His death. A necessary and voluntary instrument of the Redemption, Judas was according to them a hero and a martyr to be revered and not reviled.

According to others, Iscariot, loving his people and hoping for their deliverance, perhaps sharing the sentiments of the Zealots, had joined with Jesus, hoping that He was the Messiah such as the common people then imagined Him: the King of the revenge and restoration of Israel. When little by little it dawned on him from the words of Jesus that he had fallen in with a Messiah of quite another kind, he delivered Him over to His enemies to make up for the bitterness of his disappointment.

Others have said that Judas, mingling with the people to find out the temper of the day, had perhaps heard a rumor as to the decisions of the meeting of the elders and feared that the Sanhedrin would not be satisfied with one victim alone, but would condemn all those who had long followed Jesus. Overcome by fear, he thought he could ward off the danger and save his life by treachery.

Others give revenge as the reason. Why did Judas hate Jesus? They remember the dinner in the house of Simon and the nard of the weeping woman. The reproof for his stinginess and hypocrisy must have exasperated the Disciple who perhaps had been reproved for these faults on other occasions. And as soon as he could revenge himself without danger, he went to the palace of Caiaphas.

But did he really think that his denunciation would bring Jesus to His death or did he rather suppose that they would content themselves with flogging Him and forbidding Him to speak to the people? The rest of the story seems to show that the condemnation of Jesus unnerved him as a terrible and unexpected result of his kiss. Matthew describes his despair in a way to show that he was horrified by what had happened through his fault. The money which he had pocketed became like fire to him: and when the priests refused to take it back he threw it down in the Temple. Even after this restitution he had no peace and hastened to kill himself. He died on the same day as his victim.

In spite of all the unraveling of unsatisfied minds, mysteries are still tangled about the mystery of Judas. But we have not yet invoked the testimony of Him who knew better than all men, even better than Judas, the true secret of the betrayal. Jesus alone could give us the key to the mystery; Jesus who saw into the heart of Judas as into the hearts of all men, and who knew what Judas was to do before he had done it.

Jesus chose Judas to be one of the Twelve and to carry the Gospel to the world along with the others. Would He have chosen him, kept him with Him, beside Him, at His table, for so long a time if He had believed him to be an incurable criminal?

Up to the last days, up to that last evening, Jesus treated Judas exactly like the others. To him He gave His body, symbolized by bread, His soul, symbolized by wine. He washed and wiped, with His own hands, the feet of Judas, those feet which had carried him to the house of Caiaphas—with those hands which, through Judas' fault, were to be nailed to the cross on the following day. And when, in the red light of the flickering lanterns and the flashing of swords, Judas, under the dark shadow of the olive trees, came and kissed that face still wet with bloody sweat, Jesus did not repel him, but said, "Friend, wherefore art thou come?"

Friend! It was the last time that Jesus spoke to Judas, and even in that moment He would use none other than that word. Jesus had said at the Last Supper, "Woe unto that man by whom the Son of man is betrayed! it had been good for that man if he had not been born." These words might have been, rather than a condemnation, an exclamation of pity at the thought of a fate which could not be escaped. He knew that Judas must needs do what he did and He did not curse him, as He did not curse the people who wished His death, or the hammer which drove the nails into the cross. One prayer alone broke from him, to beg Judas to shorten the dreadful agony, "That thou doest, do quickly."

Thus the testimony of Him who was betrayed increases our bewilderment instead of raising the veil of the dreadful secret. The mystery of Judas is doubly tied to the mystery of the Redemption and we lesser ones shall never solve it.

THE BARGAIN was struck, the price paid, the buyers were impatient to finish the transaction. They had said "not on the feast day." The great feast day of the Passover fell on a Saturday and this was Thursday.

Jesus had but one more day of freedom, the last day.

Before leaving His friends, those who were to abandon Him that night, He wished once more to dip His bread in the same platter with them. This last evening before His death was to be like an anticipation of the banquet of the Kingdom.

On the evening of Thursday, the Disciples asked Him, "Where wilt thou that we go and prepare that thou mayest eat the passover?"

The Son of man, poorer than the foxes, had no home of His own. He had left His home in Nazareth forever. The home of Simon of Capernaum, which had been in the early days like His own, was far away; and the home of Mary and Martha in Bethany, where He was almost Master, was far outside the city.

548

He had only enemies in Jerusalem or shamefaced friends: Joseph of Arimathea was to receive Him as his guest only the next evening, in the dark cave, the banquet hall of worms.

But a condemned man on his last day has a right to any favor he might ask. The Father would give Him the house best suited to shelter His last joy. He sent two Disciples with this mysterious command, "Go ye into the city, and there shall meet you a man bearing a pitcher of water: follow him. And wheresoever he shall go in, say ye to the goodman of the house, The Master saith, My time is at hand; where is the guestchamber, where I shall eat the passover with my disciples? And he will shew you a large upper room furnished and prepared: there make ready for us."

The Disciples set out, found the man with the pitcher, entered the house, talked with his master, prepared there what was necessary for the supper: lamb cooked on the spit, round loaves without leaven, bitter herbs, red sauce, the wine of thanksgiving, and warm water. They set the couches and pillows about the table and spread over it the white cloth. On the cloth they set the few dishes, the candelabra, the pitcher full of wine, and one cup—one cup only to which all were to set their lips. Both were experienced in this preparation. From childhood up, in their home beside the lake, they had watched, wide-eyed, the preparations for the most heartwarming feast of the year. And it was not the first time since they had been with Him whom they loved, that they had thus eaten all together of the feast of the Passover.

But for this last supper—and perhaps their dull minds had finally understood the dreadful truth that it was really the last —which all the thirteen were to have together, the Disciples performed those humble menial tasks with a new tenderness, with that pensive joy that almost brings tears.

With the setting of the sun, the other ten came with Jesus and placed themselves around the table, now in readiness. All were silent, as if heavyhearted with a presentiment which they were afraid to see reflected in their companions' eyes. They remembered the repeated warnings of ignominy and of the end; the signs of hatred increasing about them, and the indications, now very plain, of the conspiracy, which with all its torches was about to come out from the darkness.

Judas had finished his bargain, he had the thirty pieces of silver on his person wrapped tightly so that they would not clink. But he knew no peace. To see Him still at liberty in the company of those who loved Him—and yet the affair was arranged for that very night—those bargainers who had paid the price were only waiting for Judas to act.

All these thoughts darkened his somber face, more and more blackly, and he looked furtively at the eyes of Jesus. Jesus broke the silence:

"With desire I have desired to eat this passover with you before I suffer: For I say unto you, I will not any more eat thereof, until it be fulfilled in the kingdom of God."

Such great love had not up to that moment been expressed by any words of Christ to His friends: such a longing for the day of perfect union. He had eaten with them thousands of other times, seated in boats, in their friends' houses, in strangers' houses, in rich men's houses, or seated beside the road, in mountain pastures, in the shadow of bushes on the shore. The blue skies of happy Galilee, the soft winds of the spring just passed, the sun of the last Passover, the waving branches of His triumphant entry, did He think of them now? Now He saw only His first friends and His last friends, the little group destined to be diminished by treachery and dispersed by cowardice. For a time they were still there about Him in the same room, and at the same table.

Now that He was on the point of being snatched from those whom He loved, He wished to give them a supreme proof of this love.

For raw, untrained minds, action has more meaning than words. Jesus prepared Himself to repeat, with the symbolic aspect of a humiliating service, one of His most important instructions.

John tells us, "He riseth from supper, and laid aside his garments; and took a towel, and girded himself. After that he poureth water into a basin, and began to wash the disciples' feet, and to wipe them with the towel wherewith he was girded."

Only a mother or a slave would have done what Jesus did that evening. And yet He was willing to wash and wipe those twenty-four calloused and sweaty feet.

After He had finished and taken His garments, He sat down again and said unto them, "Know ye what I have done to you? Ye call me Master and Lord: and ye say well; for so I am. If I then, your Lord and Master, have washed your feet; ye also ought to wash one another's feet. For I have given you an example, that ye should do as I have done to you. Verily, verily, I say unto you, The servant is not greater than his lord; neither he that is sent greater than he that sent him. If ye know these things, happy are ye if ye do them."

Jesus had not only given them a memory of complete humility, but an example of perfect love. "A new commandment I give unto you, That ye love one another; as I have loved you, that ye also love one another. Greater love hath no man than this, that a man lay down his life for his friends."

THESE THIRTEEN men seemed to be thirteen devout men of the people, come together to perform the old social rite in memory of the liberation of their people from Egyptian slavery. In reality it was a vigil of leave-taking and separation. Two of these thirteen, He into whom God had entered and he into whom Satan had entered, were to die terrible deaths before the next nightfall. The very next day the others were to be dispersed, like reapers at the first downfall of hail.

But this supper which was an ending, was also a wonderful beginning. In the midst of these thirteen Jews the observance of the Passover was about to be transfigured into something more universal, into something unequaled; into the great Christian mystery. The simple eating of bread was to become actual communion with God.

For the Jews, Passover commemorates their victorious flight from Egypt, accompanied by so many prodigies, so manifestly under God's protection. Exodus prescribed an annual festivity which took the name of the Passover; Pasch, the paschal feast. It was intended to bring to mind the hastily prepared food of the fugitives.

A lamb or a goat should be roasted over the fire, that is, cooked in the simplest and quickest way; bread without leaven, because there was no time to let yeast rise. And they were to eat of it with their loins girded, their staves in their hands, eating in haste, like people about to set out upon a journey. The bitter herbs were the poor wild grasses snatched up by the fugitives as they went along, to dull the hunger of their interminable wanderings. The red sauce, where the bread was dipped, was in memory of the bricks which the Jewish slaves were obliged to bake for the Pharaohs. The wine was something added: the joy of escape, the hope of the land of promise, the exaltation of thanksgiving to the Eternal.

Jesus changed nothing in the order of this ancient feast. After the prayer He had them pass from hand to hand the cup of wine, calling on God's name. Then He gave the bitter herbs to each one and filled a second time the cup which was to be passed around the table for each to sip.

Jesus in that deep silence pronounced those words of longing and hope: Take this and divide it among yourselves, "But I say unto you, I will not drink henceforth of this fruit of the vine, until that day when I drink it new with you in my Father's kingdom."

A sad farewell; but comforted by the certainty of an early and glorious reunion, they chanted together, as the custom was, the Psalm of the first Thanksgiving.

Then Jesus, who saw how insufficiently they understood, took the loaves, blessed them, broke them and, as He gave them each a piece, set the dreadful truth before their eyes. "Take, eat; This is my body which is given for you: this do in remembrance of me."

So He was not to return as quickly as they thought! After His brief stay during the Resurrection, His Second Coming was to be delayed, so long that it might be possible to forget Him and His death.

"This do in remembrance of me." Eat this unleavened bread, these loaves which have felt the heat of the oven and which my hands, not yet cold in death, have divided amongst you—and which my love has changed into my flesh so that it may be your everlasting food. You know how many efforts, how much anxiety, are contained in a piece of bread; how the great oxen cultivated the earth, how the countrymen threw great handfuls of the grain into the fallow land in winter, how the first blade softly penetrated the damp darkness of the earth, how the reapers all day long cut down the ripened stalks, and then the sheaves were bound, and carried to the threshing floor and beaten so that the ears let fall the grain. The workers must wait for a little wind, neither too gentle nor too violent, to winnow out the good grain from the chaff. Then they grind it, sift out the bran from it, make a dough with warm water, heat the oven with dry grass or twigs.

All this must be done with love and patience before the father may break a piece with his children, the friend with his friends, the host with strangers; before the golden wheat can be transformed into well-baked golden bread for our table.

Remember the prayer which I taught you: "Give us this day our daily bread—" For today and for always your bread is this bread, my Body.

AS SOON as they had eaten the lamb with the bread and the bitter herb, Jesus filled the common cup for the third time and gave it to the Apostle nearest Him, "Drink ye all of it; For this is my blood of the new testament, which is shed for many."

If bread is the body, blood is in a certain sense the soul. When Moses had received the Law, he had sacrificed oxen, took half of the blood and put it in basins, and half of the blood he sprinkled on the altar:

"And Moses took the blood, and sprinkled it on the people, and said, Behold the blood of the covenant, which the Lord hath made with you concerning all these words."

The blood of oxen, the impure blood of earthly animals, involuntary and inferior victims, is no longer sufficient. The New Covenant was established that night with the words of Christ. "This cup is the new testament in my blood, which is shed for you."

The bread given by Christ does not strengthen the flesh, but the soul, and His wine gives that divine intoxication which is

553

Love, that Love which the Apostle was to call in his Epistle to the Corinthians, "the foolishness of God."

Judas also ate that bread and swallowed that wine, partook of that body, in which he had trafficked, drank that blood which he was to help shed, but he had not the courage to confess his infamy, to throw himself at the feet of Him who would have wept with him. Then the only friend remaining to Judas warned him, "Verily I say unto you, that one of you shall betray me."

The eleven were capable of leaving Him alone in the midst of Caiaphas' guards, but they never could have brought themselves to sell Him for money, and at this they shuddered. Everyone looked in his neighbor's face, almost dreading to see in his companion the look of guilt, and all, one after the other, said, "Lord, is it I?"

Even Judas was able to force his voice to say, "Lord, is it I?" But Jesus, who the next day would not defend Himself, would not even bring an accusation and only repeated the sad prophecy in more definite words, "He that dippeth his hand with me in the dish, the same shall betray me." And while they all still gazed at Him in painful doubt, for the third time He insisted ". . . the hand of him that betrayeth me is with me on the table." He added no more, but to follow the old customs up to the last, He filled the cup for the fourth time and gave it to them to drink. And once more the thirteen voices rang out in the old hymn, the "great Hallel" which ended the liturgy of the Passover. Jesus repeated the vigorous words of the Psalmist which were like a prophetic funeral oration for Him, pronounced before His death.

"The Lord is on my side; I will not fear: what can man do unto me? . . . They compassed me about like bees; they are quenched as the fire of thorns: . . . I shall not die, but live. . . . The Lord hath chastened me sore: but he hath not given me over unto death."

When the hymn was ended they left the room and the house, at once. As soon as they had emerged from the house Judas disappeared into the night. The remaining eleven silently followed Jesus, who, as was His wont, made His way to the Mount of Olives.

On the Mount there was a garden, and a place where olives were crushed, which gave it its name, Gethsemane. Jesus and His friends had been spending the nights there, either to avoid the odors and noise of the great city, distasteful to them, country-bred as they were, or because they were afraid of being treacherously captured in the midst of their enemies' houses.

And when He was at the place, He said to His Disciples, "Sit ye here, while I go and pray yonder."

But He was so heavyhearted that He dreaded being alone. He took with Him the three whom He loved the best, Simon Peter, James and John. And when they had gone a little way from the others, He began to be sorrowful and very heavy. "My soul is exceeding sorrowful, even unto death: tarry ye here, and watch with me."

He withdrew Himself from them. He was alone now in the night, before God, and He could show His weakness without shame. He fell on the ground on His face and prayed, saying, "Abba, Father, all things are possible unto thee; O my Father, if it be possible, let this cup pass from me."

This was the second temptation. Jesus knew that He had to confirm by His death that greater life which He announced. The Cross is the rigorously necessary consequence of the Sermon on the Mount. He who brings love is given over to hatred, and He can conquer hatred only by accepting condemnation. The greatest good, which is love, must be paid for by the greatest evil in men's power, assassination.

But if the torture and the end of His body had really terrified Him, was there not yet time to save Himself? Even on that night there were ways of escaping. He would have been safe if, either alone or with His most faithful friends, He had taken the road back to the Jordan, and thence by hidden paths have passed across Perea into the tetrarchy of Philip, where He had already taken

refuge to escape the ill will of Herod Antipas. The Jewish police were so few and primitive that they could scarcely have found Him.

The fact that He did not flee shows that He did not try to escape death and the horrors that were to accompany it. From the point of view of our coarse human logic His death was a suicide—not unlike that of the heroes of antiquity who fell upon the sword of a slave. But what sort of a life would He have had after such a flight? To grow old obscurely, the timorous master of a hidden sect, to die at the last, worn out, like any other man! Better, infinitely better to finish the sowing of the Gospel on the Cross.

If the cup that Jesus wished to pass from Him was not fear of death, what else could it have been? Had He in the darkness of this last vigil glimpsed the fate which would befall His children later on, the bewilderment of the first saints, the martyrdoms, the massacres? Was He asking from His Father not His own safety from death, but safety from the evils which were to overwhelm those who believed in Him?

No one will ever know the true meaning of the words cried out by the Son to the Father, in the black loneliness of the Olives. A great French Christian called the story of this night the "Mystery of Jesus." The mystery of Judas is the only human mystery in the Gospels; the prayer of Gethsemane is the inscrutable, divine mystery of the story of Christ.

AND WHEN He had prayed, He turned back to find the Disciples, who were to wait for Him to return. But crouching on the ground, wrapped as best they could in their cloaks, Peter, James and John, the faithful, the specially chosen, had allowed themselves to be overcome with sleep. The voice of the Master called them: "What, could ye not watch with me one hour? . . . the spirit indeed is willing, but the flesh is weak." Did they hear these words in their sleep? Did they answer, shamefaced, putting their hands to their confused eyes?

Jesus went away again, more heavyhearted than ever. He was once more alone, utterly alone as men are alone who raise themselves above other men. Every hero is always the only one awake in a world of sleepers, like the pilot watching over his ship in the solitude of the ocean and of the night.

Of all these eternally solitary souls, Jesus was the most solitary. Everything slept about Him. The city slept, its white, shadow-checkered mass sprawling beyond the Kidron; and in all the houses the blind race of ephemeral men were sleeping. The only ones awake at that hour were His enemies and their guards. Caiaphas was not asleep and the only Disciple awake was Judas.

Until the arrival of Judas, He was alone, and that He might feel less alone He began to pray to His Father; once more those imploring words rushed to His lips. The effort to keep them back, the conflict which convulsed Him, the tension of the terrible struggle did such violence that the sweat stood out on Him, not merely the natural sweat which runs down the face of the man working in the fields. Great drops of blood mixed with sweat fell on the earth as a first offering of His conquered flesh. It was the beginning of liberation, almost a relief to that humanity which was the greatest burden of His expiation.

Then from His lips arose a new prayer: "O my Father, if this cup may not pass away from me, except I drink it, thy will be done . . . not my will, but thine, be done."

From that moment His victory over death is assured, because he who gives himself wholly to the Eternal cannot die. "For whosoever will save his life shall lose it: and whosoever will lose his life for my sake shall find it."

He stood up calmed, and turned back toward His Disciples. His sad reproof had been vain; worn out and exhausted, the three were again sleeping. But this time Jesus did not call them.

Now He can listen almost longingly for the footsteps of Judas.

For a time He hears only the beating of His own heart, so much calmer than at first, now that the horror is nearer. But after some moments, He hears approaching the sound of cautious shuffling, and there among the bushes which border the road, red flickerings of light appear and disappear in the darkness. They are the servants of the assassins who are following Iscariot along the path.

Jesus turns to the Disciples, still asleep, "Behold, the hour is come; Rise up, let us go; lo, he that betrayeth me is at hand."

The eight other Disciples, sleeping farther away, are already aroused by the noise, but have no time to answer the Master because while He is still speaking the crowd comes up and stops.

IT WAS THE RABBLE who swarmed around the Temple, bunglingly made over for the time being into warriors; sweepers and doorkeepers who had taken up swords; a great multitude, so the Evangelists say, although they knew they were going out against only twelve men, who had only two swords. It is not credible that there were Roman soldiers among them. Caiaphas wished to make Christ a prisoner before he presented Him to the procurator, and the few forces at his disposition (the last vestiges of David's army) with the addition of some clients and relatives were enough to carry out the far-from-dangerous capture.

This haphazard mob had come with torches and lanterns almost as if out for an evening celebration. The face of Judas seemed to waver in the torchlight. Christ offered His face, more luminous than the lights, to Judas' kiss. "Betrayest thou the Son of man with a kiss?" He knew what Judas came to do, and He knew that this kiss was the first of His tortures and the most unendurable. This kiss was the signal for the guards who did not know the delinquent by sight. "Whomsoever I shall kiss, that same is He; take Him, and lead Him away safely," Judas had told the rough crowd who followed him as they came along the road.

As soon as the sign was given the boldest came up to their enemy.

"Whom seek ye?"

"Jesus of Nazareth."

"I am he." Even at such a moment Jesus took thought of His friends. "I have told you that I am he: if therefore ye seek me, let these go their way."

At the moment, profiting by the confusion of the guards, Peter, coming suddenly to himself from his sleep and from his panic, laid his hand to a sword and cut off the ear of Malchus, a servant of Caiaphas. Peter on that night was full of contradictory impulses; after the supper he had sworn that no matter what happened he would never leave Jesus; then in the garden he could not keep himself awake; after that, tardily he set himself up as a militant defender; and a little later he was to deny that he had ever known his Master. Peter's untimely and futile action was at once repudiated by Christ: "Put up thy sword into the sheath: for all they that take the sword shall perish with the sword. . . . the cup which my Father hath given me, shall I not drink it?" And He offered His hands to be tied with the rope which they had brought.

While they were busy tying Him, the prisoner accused them of cowardice. "Are ye come out, as against a thief, with swords and with staves to take me? When I was daily with you in the temple, ye stretched forth no hands against me: but this is your hour, and the power of darkness."

The guards, eager to return triumphantly and to receive their fees, did not trouble to answer; they dragged Him by the rope towards the road to Jerusalem. Then, confesses Matthew, ". . . all the disciples forsook him, and fled." Only two followed the procession, and they from a safe distance. We shall see them later in the courtyard of Caiaphas' house.

All this bustle awakened a young man who had been sleeping in the house in the grove of olives. Inquisitive like all young men, he did not take the time to dress, but wrapping a sheet about him, stepped out to see what was happening. The guards thought him a disciple who had not had time to escape, and laid hands on him, but the young man, casting off the sheet, left it in their hands and fled from them naked.

No one has ever known the identity of this mysterious man who appeared suddenly in the night, and as suddenly disappeared. Perhaps he was the youthful Mark, the only one of the Evangelists who tells this story. If it were Mark, it is possible that on that night the involuntary witness of the beginning of the Passion conceived the impulse to become, as Mark did, its first historian.

IN A SHORT TIME the criminal was taken to the house which Annas shared with his son-in-law, the high priest Caiaphas. Although the night was now well advanced, and although the assembly had been warned the day before that Caiaphas hoped to capture the blasphemer early in the morning, many of the Sanhedrin were still in bed and the prosecution could not begin at once. In order that the common people might not have time to rise in rebellion, nor Pilate to take thought, Annas was in haste to finish the affair that very morning. Some of the guards who returned from the Mount of Olives were sent to awake the more important scribes and elders, and in the meantime old Annas, who had not slept all that night, set himself on his own account to question this false prophet.

Annas had been for seven years high priest, and though deposed in the year 14 under Tiberius, he was still the real primate of the Jewish church. A Sadducee, head of one of the most aggressive and wealthy families of the ecclesiastical patriarchate, he was still, through his son-in-law, leader of his caste. Five of his sons were afterwards high priests, and one of them, also called Annas, later caused James, the brother of the Lord, to be stoned to death.

Jesus was led before him. It was the first time that the woodworker of Nazareth found Himself face-to-face with the religious head of His people. Up till then He had met only the subalterns in the Temple, the common soldiers, the scribes and Pharisees; now He was before the head, and He was no longer the accuser but the accused. This was the first questioning of that day. In the space of a few hours, four authorities examined Him: two rulers from the Temple, Annas and Caiaphas; and two temporal rulers, Antipas and Pilate.

The first question Annas put to Jesus was to ask Him who His disciples were. The old political priest wished to know who were the followers of the new prophet, and from what rank of society He had picked them up. But Jesus looked at him without answering.

Then Annas asked about His doctrine. Jesus answered that it was not for Him to explain: "I spake openly to the world; . . . in secret have I said nothing. Why askest thou me? ask them which heard me, what I have said unto them: behold, they know what I said."

Annas must have made a wry face at an answer which presupposed an honest trial, for one of the officers standing by struck Jesus with the palm of his hand, saying, "Answerest thou the high priest so?"

This blow was the beginning of the insults which were henceforth rained upon Christ up to the cross. But He who had been struck, with His cheek reddened by the boor, turned towards the man who had struck Him. "If I have spoken evil, bear witness of the evil: but if well, why smitest thou me?"

Annas, seeing that he was not succeeding in extracting anything from Him, sent Him bound to Caiaphas, the high priest, so that the fiction of a legal prosecution might begin at once.

ONLY TWO of the fleeing Disciples repented of their cowardice, and trembling in the shadow of the walls, followed from afar the swaying lanterns which accompanied Christ: Simon Peter, son of Jonas, and John, son of Zebedee.

John, who was known in the household of Caiaphas, went into the courtyard of the building with Jesus; then after a few moments, not seeing his companion, and wishing to have him at hand for sympathy or defense, went out and persuaded the suspicious doorkeeper to let Peter also come in. But as Peter stepped through the door, the woman recognized him: "Art not thou also one of his disciples?"

But Peter took on an offended air. "I know not, neither understand I what thou sayest. I know him not."

And he sat down with John near the brazier which the servants had kindled in the courtyard because, although it was in April, the night was cold. But the woman would not give up her idea, and coming to the fire and looking at him earnestly, said, "Thou also wast with Jesus of Nazareth," and he denied again with curses, "Woman, I know him not!"

The gatekeeper, shaking her head, turned back to her gate, but the men aroused by these heated denials looked at him more closely and said, "Surely thou art one of them: for thou art a Galilean, and thy speech agreeth thereto."

Then Peter began to curse and to swear, but another, a kinsman of Malchus whose ear Peter had cut off, broke into his testimony: "Did I not see thee in the garden with him?"

But Peter, now hopelessly involved in lies, began again to protest that they had mistaken him for another and that he was not one of the friends of the Man.

At this very moment Jesus, bound among the guards, crossed the courtyard after His colloquy with Annas, passing to the other part of the palace, where Caiaphas lived: and He heard the words of Simon Peter and looked at Him, with eyes whose gentleness was more unendurable than any contempt. And this look pierced the pitiable, distracted heart of the fisherman. To the day of his death he could never forget those sad, mild eyes fixed on him in that terrible night; those eyes which in one flash expressed more and moved him more than a thousand words.

Under the weight of his look, Simon hung his head and his heart beat furiously in his breast. Torn by an unbearable tumult of passion and of remorse, he was scarcely able to drag himself to his feet and to stumble to the door. As he went out into the street in the silent, solitary darkness a distant cock crew. This gay, bold note was for Peter like the cry which awakens a sleeper from his nightmare. Then in the dim light of dawn the last stars saw a man staggering along like a drunkard, his head hidden in his cloak, his shoulders shaken by the sobs of a despairing lament.

CAIAPHAS' REAL NAME was Joseph. Caiaphas is a surname and is the same word as Cephas, Simon's surname, that is to say, Rock. On that Friday morning's dawn, between the denial of Simon Peter and the hatred of Joseph, between those two rocks Jesus was like wheat between the millstones.

The Sanhedrin had already come together and was awaiting Him. Together with Annas and Caiaphas who presided, the Sanhedrin was composed of twenty-three priests, twenty-three scribes, twenty-three elders, and two presidents, in all, seventy-one. But on this occasion some were absent, those who had more fear of an uprising of the people than hatred for the blasphemer, and those few who would not lift a finger to condemn Him, but would not defend Him openly: among these last was certainly Nicodemus, the nocturnal disciple, and Joseph of Arimathea, who was devoutly to lay Jesus in His tomb.

The great room of the council was already full of people. The new day showed itself hesitatingly: the orange-colored tongues of the torches were scarcely visible in the dim light of dawn. In this sinister half shadow the Sanhedrin waited: aged, portly, harsh, wrapped in their white cloaks, their heads covered, seated in a half circle. The rest of the hall was occupied by the clients of the seated assembly, by guards with staves in their hands, by the domestic servants of the house. The air was heavy and dense.

Jesus, His wrists still tied with ropes, was thrust into their midst. Annas had gathered in all haste from among the rabble some false witnesses to make an end of any discussion or defense. The pretense of a trial began with calling these perjurers. Two of them came forward and swore that they had heard these words: "I will destroy this temple that is made with hands, and within three days I will build another made without hands."

At the time and for those hearers this accusation was a very grave one, meaning nothing less than sacrilege and blasphemy. For in the minds of its upholders the Temple of Jerusalem was the one intangible home of the Lord. And to threaten the Temple was to threaten the Master of all the Jews. But Jesus had never said these words or at least not in this form, nor with this meaning. It is true that He had announced that of the Temple not one stone would remain upon another, but not through any action of His. And the reference to the Temple not made with hands, built up in three days, was part of another discourse in which He had spoken figuratively of His resurrection.

The false witnesses could not even agree about these words, confusedly and maliciously repeated, and one statement from Jesus would have been enough to confound them utterly. But Jesus held His peace.

The high priest could not endure this silence, and standing up, cried out, "Answerest thou nothing? what is it which these witness against thee?"

Jesus answered nothing, but looked about Him with His great calm eyes, at the troubled faces of His judges.

These silences of Jesus were weighty with magnetic eloquence, and enraged his judges. Caiaphas, exasperated by this disrespectful taciturnity, finally hit on a way to make him speak. "I adjure thee by the living God, that thou tell us whether thou be the Christ, the Son of God."

The priest's invocation of the living God was irresistible. Jesus could not deny Himself to the living God, to the God who will live eternally, and who lives in all of us. And yet He hesitated a moment with the splendor of His formidable secret.

"If I tell you, ye will not believe: And if I also ask you, ye will not answer me."

Now Caiaphas was not alone in putting the question; all of them, excited, sprang to their feet and cried out, "Art thou then the Son of God?"

Jesus could not, like Peter, deny the irrefutable certainty which was the reason for His life and for His death. But, as at Caesarea, He wished others to be the ones to pronounce His real name, and when they had said it He did not refuse it, even though death were the penalty. "Ye say that I am. I say unto you, Hereafter shall ye see the Son of man sitting on the right hand of power, and coming in the clouds of heaven."

He had condemned Himself out of His own mouth. He had proclaimed what He had secretly admitted to His most loving friends. Although they might betray Him, He had not betrayed Himself or His Father. Now He was ready for the last degradation.

Caiaphas was triumphant. Pretending a shocked horror which he did not feel—because like all the Sadducees he had no faith whatever in the apocalyptic writers and cared about nothing but the fees and honors of the Temple—he rent his priestly garments, crying out, "He hath spoken blasphemy; what further need have we of witnesses? behold, now ye have heard his blasphemy. What think ye?" And without any further examination they condemned Him to death as a blasphemer and false prophet.

The comedy of legal pretense was played to an end.

WHILE THE high officials went apart to take counsel on the manner of securing the ratification from the procurator and executing the death sentence with all speed, Jesus was thrown to the rabble in the palace.

The captors of Christ had been awake all night long, and the night had been cold; they had made the march up to the Mount of Olives, fearing resistance, a well-grounded fear, since one of them had had his ear stricken off. It was a very tiring business especially on those festal days when the city and the Temple were full of foreigners. They felt that they really deserved some amusement.

But they did not know how to begin. He was tied and his friends had disappeared. This man, bound, exhausted, condemned to death by the highest and holiest tribunal of the Jewish people, this human rubbish destined to the cross of slaves and thieves, this man who did not speak nor complain nor weep, but who looked on them as if He had compassion on them, inspired a mysterious reverence.

But one of the scribes or the elders gave the example, and spat at Jesus as he passed by Him. Then the guards who were nearest Him struck Him in the face; those who could not strike His face rained down blows and threats. Then one of the mob, more quick-witted than the others, had an idea: he took a dirty cloth and with it covered the bleeding, buffeted face, tying the corners behind. And he said: "Let us play blind-man's buff. This man boasts of being a prophet; let us see if he can guess which of us is striking him."

Was that look of suffering love really unendurable to them? With childish cruelty, they arranged themselves in a circle about Him and first one and then another twitched a fold of His garment, gave Him a blow on the shoulder, struck Him with a staff over the head: "Prophesy, who it it that smote thee?"

Luke adds, "And many other things blasphemously spake they against him."

But Caiaphas and the others were in haste. The false king must be taken to Pilate that his sentence be confirmed: the Sanhedrin could pronounce judgment, but since Judea was under Roman rule, it had no longer, unfortunately, the *Jus Gladii* [the right of the sword]. And the high priests, scribes and elders, set out for the palace of the procurator, followed by the guards leading Jesus with ropes, and by the yelling horde which grew larger as they went.

SINCE A. D. 26, Pontius Pilate had been procurator in the name of Tiberius Caesar.
Historians know nothing of him before his
arrival in Judea. If the name comes from
Pileatus it may be supposed that he was a
freedman or descendant of freedmen, since
the *pileus*, or skull cap, was the headgear of
freed slaves. He had been in Judea only a few
years, but long enough to draw upon himself the bitterest hate
of those over whom he ruled. It is true that all our information
about him comes from Jews and Christians, who were, of course,
his declared enemies.

In the first place the hatred of the Jews came from the profound scorn which he showed from the start for this stiff-necked,
indocile people, who must have seemed to him, brought up in
Roman ideas, a low crowd. To have an idea of Pilate's personality, make a mental picture of an English viceroy of India, a
subscriber to the *Times*, a reader of John Stuart Mill and Shaw—
with Byron and Swinburne on his bookshelves—destined to
administer the government over a ragged, captious, hungry and
turbulent people, wrangling among themselves over a confusion
of castes and mythologies for which their ruler feels in his heart
the deepest aversion. Pilate was one of those skeptics of the
Roman decadence, a devotee of Epicurus, an encyclopedist of
Hellenism without any belief in the gods of his country, nor
any belief that any real God existed at all.

The idea certainly can never have occurred to Pilate that the
true God could be found in this superstitious mob, in the midst
of this factious and jealous clergy, in this religion which must
have seemed to him like a barbarous mixture of Syrian and
Chaldean oracles. The only faith remaining to him, or which he
needed to pretend to hold because of his office, was the new Roman religion, civic and political, concentrated on the cult of the
emperor. The first conflict with the Jews arose in fact from this

religion. When he had changed the guard of Jerusalem, he ordered the soldiers to enter the city by night, without taking off from their ensigns the silver images of Caesar. In the morning, as soon as the Jews were aware of this, great was the horror. It was the first time that the Romans had lacked in external respect for the religion of their subjects in Palestine. These figures of the deified Caesar planted near the Temple were for them an idolatrous provocation. All the country was in an uproar. A deputation was sent to Caesarea to have Pilate take them away. Pilate refused; for five days and nights they stormed about him. Finally the procurator convoked them in the amphitheater and treacherously had them surrounded with soldiers with naked swords, assuring them that no one would escape if they did not make an end of their clamor. But the Jews, instead of asking for mercy, offered their throats to the swords, and Pilate, conquered by this heroic stubbornness, ordered that the insignia be carried back to Caesarea.

A little while after this, he introduced into Herod Antipas' palace, where he lived when he stayed at Jerusalem, votive tablets dedicated to the emperor. But the priests heard of it and once more the people were aroused to outraged anger. He was asked to take away the idolatrous objects at once. Pilate this time also did not yield. The Jews then appealed to Tiberius, who decreed that the tablets should be sent back to Caesarea.

Twice Pilate had had the worst of a dispute. But the third time he was triumphant. Coming from the city of public baths and aqueducts, he noticed that Jerusalem lacked water and he planned to have a fine large reservoir constructed and an aqueduct several miles long. But the undertaking was expensive and to pay for it he used a goodly sum taken from the treasury of the Temple. The priests cried out on the sacrilege, and the people incited by them made such a commotion that when Pilate came for the Feast of the Passover to Jerusalem, thousands of men gathered in a tumultuous crowd in front of his palace. But this time he sent among the multitude a large number of disguised soldiers who at a given signal began to lay about them so vigorously that they all fled, and Pilate could enjoy in peace the water of the reservoir paid for with the Jews' money.

Only a short time had passed since this last encounter and now these very priests who three times had risen against his authority were forced to have recourse to him. Only hard necessity drove them to it, because death sentences could not be carried out if they were not confirmed by Caesar's representative.

That Friday, at dawn, Pontius Pilate, wrapped in his toga, still sleepy and yawning, was waiting for them in Herod's palace, very ill-disposed towards those tiresome troublemakers.

THE CROWD of the accusers and of the rough populace finally came before Herod's palace, but they stopped outside, because if they went into a house where there was leaven and bread baked with leaven, they would be contaminated all day long and could not eat the Passover.

Pilate, warned of their coming, went out on the doorsill and asked abruptly: "What accusation bring ye against this man?"

Instinctively Pilate took the part of their enemy.

Caiaphas answered at once as if offended: "If he were not a malefactor, we would not have delivered him up unto thee."

Then Pilate, who wished to lose no time with ecclesiastical squabbles and did not think that there was any question of a capital crime, answered dryly: "Take ye him, and judge him according to your law."

Already in these words appears his wish to save the man without being forced to take sides openly, because the Sanhedrin could inflict only light sentences. They answered: "It is not lawful for us to put any man to death."

Pilate suddenly understood what sentence they wished passed on the wretched man who stood before him, and he wished to find out what crime He had committed.

The foxes of the Temple had thought of this difficulty before taking action. They were prepared to lie. They knew very well that Pilate would not be satisfied if they told him that Jesus was a false Messiah. Pilate would smile. But if they said that He was trying to rouse the common people against Rome, Pilate could not do less than put Him to death.

"We found this fellow perverting the nation, and forbidding to give tribute to Caesar, saying that he himself is Christ, a

King. . . . He stirreth up all the people, teaching throughout all Jewry, beginning from Galilee to this place."

Every word was a lie. Jesus had commanded men to render unto Caesar that which was Caesar's. He said that He was Christ but not in the political meaning of a King of the Jews. These accusations increased Pilate's suspicions of the priests. Was it probable that they, whose one dream was to sweep away the governing pagans, should suddenly be kindled with so much zeal to denounce a rebel of their own nation?

Pilate wished to find out for himself, by questioning the accused man in private. He went back into the palace and commanded that Jesus be brought to him. Disregarding the less important accusations, he went at once to the essential: "Art thou the King of the Jews?"

But Jesus did not answer. How could He ever make this Roman understand! This Roman whose only religion was the artificial cult of a living man—and of what a man—the Emperor Tiberius!—how could He ever explain to this pupil of the lawyers and rhetoricians of decadent Rome that He was the King of a spiritual Kingdom which would abolish all human kingdoms?

Jesus made no answer, as He had kept silent at first before Annas and before Caiaphas.

The procurator could not understand this silence on the part of a man over whom hung the threat of death. "Hearest thou not how many things they witness against thee?"

Pilate, who wished to triumph over those who hated him as much as they hated this man, insisted, hoping to extract a denial which would permit him to set Him at liberty: "Art thou the King of the Jews?"

Jesus had said to His disciples and to the Jews that He was Christ. The better to sound the Roman's mind He answered him, as was his wont, with another question: "Sayest thou this thing of thyself, or did others tell it thee of me?"

Pilate answered, as if offended, "Am I a Jew? Thine own nation and the chief priests have delivered thee unto me. Art thou the King of the Jews?"

Jesus determined to try to shed more light on this pagan. "My kingdom is not of this world: if my kingdom were of this world, then would my servants fight, that I should not be delivered to the Jews: but now is my kingdom not from hence."

The difference between "of this world" and "my kingdom is not from hence" was obscure to Pilate. And once more he asked: "Art thou a king then?"

"Thou sayest that I am a king. To this end was I born, and for this cause came I into the world, that I should bear witness unto the truth. Every one that is of the truth heareth my voice."

Then Pilate, annoyed by what seemed to him truculent mystification, answered with the celebrated question: "What is truth?"

And without waiting for an answer, he rose to go out.

JUST AS Pilate was preparing to go out and give his answer to the Jews, who were muttering restlessly and impatiently before the door, a servant sent by his wife came up to him, giving him this message:

"Have thou nothing to do with that just man: for I have suffered many things this day in a dream because of him."

No one in the four Gospels tells us what impression was made on the procurator by this unexpected intercession. We know nothing of his wife except her name. According to the Apocryphal Gospel of Nicodemus her name was Claudia Procula, and if this name was really hers she may have belonged to the *gens* Claudia, distinguished and powerful at Rome. We may thus suppose that she was by birth and connections of a higher social rank than her husband, and that Pilate, a mere freedman, may have owed to her influence in Rome his post in Judea.

If all this was true, certainly the request of Claudia Procula must have made some impression on Pilate, especially if he loved her; and that he loved her seems proved by the fact that he had asked to take her with him into Asia. The *Lex Oppia* usually forbade the proconsuls to take their wives with them, and Pontius Pilate had a special permit from Tiberius allowing Claudia Procula to accompany him.

The motives for this intercession, so briefly stated, are mysterious. The words of Matthew refer to a dream in which she had suffered because of Jesus: it is probable that she had heard people talking for some time of the new Prophet; perhaps she had seen Him, and Jesus' words had been pleasing to the imagination of a fanciful Roman woman. She did not understand the language spoken in Jerusalem, but some interpreter of the law courts might have accompanied her.

In those days the Romans, especially Roman women, were beginning to feel the attraction of Oriental cults, which gave more satisfaction to the longing for personal immortality than the old Latin religion, a cold, legal, businesslike exchange of sacrifices to obtain utilitarian ends. Patrician women had been initiated into the mysteries of Mithra and Osiris, and of Isis, the Great Mother, and in that very reign of Tiberius many Jews living in Rome were exiled from the capital because, according to Josephus, some of them had converted to Judaism a matron, Fulvia; and Fulvia, as we see from a reference of Suetonius, was not the only one.

Together with the centurion of Capernaum and with the Canaanite woman, Claudia Procula is the first pagan who believed in Christ, and the Greek Church has good reason to revere her as a saint.

This message from his wife strengthened Pilate's reluctance. Claudia Procula had not said, "Save Him"—but: "Have thou nothing to do with that just man." This was Pilate's idea, also. A way to evade the responsibility occurred to him. He went back to Jesus and asked whether He were a Galilean.

The procurator had found a legitimate subterfuge. Jesus did not belong to his jurisdiction, but to that of Herod Antipas. By good luck Antipas was there at Jerusalem, come for the Passover. Losing no time, he ordered the soldiers to take Jesus before Antipas.

THE THIRD JUDGE before whom Jesus was led was a son of that bloody-minded Herod the Great, by one of his five wives. Antipas was the true son of his father because he wronged his brothers as his father had wronged his sons. When his half brother, Archelaus, was accused by his subjects, he managed to have him exiled. At seventeen years of age he began to reign as tetrarch over Galilee and over Berea.

To ingratiate himself with Tiberius, he offered himself as a secret talebearer of the sayings and doings of his brothers and of the Roman officials in Judea. On a voyage to Rome he fell in love with Herodias, who was both his niece and his sister-in-law, since she was the daughter of his brother Aristobulus, and wife of his brother Herod, and not shrinking from the double incest, he persuaded her to follow him, together with Salome, her daughter. His first wife, daughter of Aretas, king of the Nabatei, went back to her father, who declared war on Antipas and defeated him.

This happened while John the Baptist was beginning to be talked about among the people. That Prophet let slip some words of condemnation against these two adulterers, and this was enough for Herodias to persuade her new husband to have him taken and shut up in the fortress of Machaerus. Everyone knows how the tetrarch, inflamed by cruel Salome and perhaps meditating a new incest, was forced to offer her the bearded head of the Prophet of Fire on a golden platter.

But even after his decapitation John's shade disturbed Herod Antipas, and when he began to hear talk of Jesus and of His miracles he said to his courtiers, "This is John the Baptist; he is risen from the dead."

Deciding that he would have no more to do with prophets, he saw that the best way was to force Jesus to leave his tetrarchy. One day some Pharisees, very probably acting on Herod Antipas' instructions, went to say to Jesus: "Get thee out, and depart hence: for Herod will kill thee."

"And he said unto them, Go ye, and tell that fox . . . I must walk today, and tomorrow, and the day following: for it cannot be that a prophet perish out of Jerusalem."

And now at Jerusalem near His death, He appeared before that fox. Jesus had named him well: he was more fox than tiger, and he shrank from being a substitute for Pilate.

Antipas began to put many questions, to which Jesus made no answer. But the high priests and the scribes had followed their victim there, and their furious accusations as well as the silence of the accused man deepened the hidden rancor of Antipas. He threw over Jesus' shoulders a gorgeous mantle, shining with whiteness, which was, so Josephus says, the garment of the Jewish kings, and sent Him again to Pilate.

Antipas wished to ridicule the pretensions of Jesus by ironically making him a present of the regal robe; but when he covered Him with that whiteness, which is the symbol of innocence and of sovereignty, he sent to Pilate a symbolical message which involuntarily confirmed the message of Claudia Procula, the accusation of Caiaphas, and what Christ Himself had said.

PILATE SAW Jesus wrapped in that regal white garment and understood that he must get the matter settled. He had decided to save Jesus.

Perhaps while Jesus was with the tetrarch, Pilate had learned from one of His followers more about the pretended King. Jesus taught love for enemies, and in Judea the Romans were considered enemies; He called the poor blessed, hence He exhorted them to resignation and not to revolt; He advised men to render unto Caesar that which was Caesar's, that is, to pay tribute to the emperor; He was opposed to the Pharisaical formalism which made the relations of the Romans with their subjects so difficult; He did not respect the Sabbath; He ate with publicans and with Gentiles. If Pilate knew these things, he must have said to himself that it would be good for Rome if many Jews followed Jesus, rather than fomented rebellion in the councils of the Zealots.

Therefore, causing Jesus to be led out, Pilate went to the door and said to the high priests and the others who crowded about, their faces thrust forward to hear the sentence given at last, "Ye have brought this man unto me, as one that perverteth the people: and, behold, I, having examined him before you, have found no fault in this man touching those things whereof ye accuse him: No, nor yet Herod: for I sent you to him; and, lo, nothing worthy of death is done unto him. I will therefore chastise him, and release him."

This was not the answer awaited by the horde yelling in the square before the procurator's house. A bestial cry burst out, "Kill Him!"

As soon as this uproar was a little quieted, Pilate asked, "What will ye then that I shall do unto him whom ye call King of the Jews?"

And they all answered, "Crucify him!"

But the procurator resisted. "Why, what evil hath he done?"

And they cried out the more exceedingly, "Crucify him!"

Jesus, pale and calm in the whiteness of the mocking, regal cloak, looked quietly at the crowd, which desired to give Him what in His heart He had been seeking.

But obstinate Pilate at any cost wanted to win his point. He had not succeeded in transferring to Antipas the disagreeable responsibility of a death sentence; he had not succeeded in persuading the people of the innocence of their wretched king. The mob wanted to see a little blood; on these festival days they wanted to enjoy the spectacle of a crucifixion. He would satisfy them with a bargain, giving them the carcass of a murderer in exchange for the body of an innocent man.

"I find in him no fault at all. But ye have a custom, that I should release unto you one at the passover. Whom will ye that I release unto you? Barabbas, or Jesus which is called Christ?" Taken by surprise, the people did not know what to answer. Until then there had been but one name, one victim, one punishment asked for; everything was as clear as the sky on that mid-April morning.

But the elders, scribes and priests were still there and they had no intention of letting Jesus escape. When Pilate asked them a second time which of the two they wished him to free, they answered with one voice, "Away with this man, and release unto us Barabbas!"

The common tradition has preserved Barabbas' memory as a street ruffian, a criminal by profession. Mark and Luke say expressly that he was accused of having committed murder during a sedition, hence a political assassin. Barabbas, a student in the school of the scribes, lamenting the loss of the Jewish kingdom, hating Judea's pagan masters, was probably a Zealot and had been captured in one of the unsuccessful revolts, so common at that time. Was it likely that such an absurd bargain would satisfy the Sadducee and Pharisee assembly which shared the sentiments of the Zealots, even if for reasons of state they hid them?

Barabbas, precisely because he was an assassin, was a patriot, a martyr, persecuted by the foreigners. On the other hand, Jesus, although He had never killed anyone, had wished to overturn the law of Moses, and to ruin the Temple. "Free Barabbas! Let this man die!"

Once more Pontius Pilate had failed to save Christ or himself.

Pontius Pilate was cowardly. He was afraid of displeasing his wife; he was afraid of giving satisfaction to his enemies; but at the same time he was afraid to have his soldiers disperse that sullen, arrogant crowd. A Roman of the true Roman stock would not have wasted a moment in defending an obscure visionary; or would at once have decreed that this man was innocent and was under the august protection of the empire. The fact that Pilate had not decided the question with a yes or no had increased the insolence of the high priests and the excitement of the people.

Now there were only two alternatives: either to give in shamefully after resisting so long, or to risk starting a tumult which in those days, when Jerusalem included almost a third of the population of Judea, might become a perilous uprising.

Undone by his own wavering, deafened by the yells, the only thing that came into his mind was to ask once more the advice of men to whom he should have issued orders.

"What shall I do then with Jesus which is called Christ?"

"Crucify him, let him be crucified!"

"Why, what evil hath he done?"

"Crucify him! Crucify him!"

"Take ye him and crucify him," cried Pilate, "for I find no fault in him."

"We have a law, and by our law he ought to die, because he made himself the Son of God."

But Pontius Pilate still would not yield the point. He would restore Barabbas to his accomplices, but he would not give up Jesus. The crowd was still shrieking, "Let him be crucified!" But Pilate gave Jesus over to the Roman soldiers to be flogged. Perhaps when the people saw the bruises and the blood dripping from His back they would be satisfied with that punishment.

THE MERCENARIES, WHO (in the provinces) were the majority in the Roman legions, were to have their turn at amusing themselves. All the company was ordered into the courtyard of the palace, and the white cloak given by Antipas was taken from Jesus' back—the first spoils of the enterprise—together with part of His other clothes. The lictors chose the rods, and the strongest among the soldiers snatched at them.

Jesus, half of His body bared, tied to a pillar that He might not lessen the force of the blows by bending forward, silently prayed. "Love those who hate you, do good to those who persecute you, offer the left cheek to him who has struck the right." They knew not whom they were flogging with such innocent heartiness. They themselves had been flogged sometimes for small breaches of discipline.

Finally, the number of blows prescribed had been duly administered, but the legionaries wished to have some further entertainment. This man pretended to be a king. Let us give Him His wish.

A soldier took off his scarlet cloak, the chlamys of the legionaries, and threw it over those red, torn shoulders; another took up a handful of dry thorns, kindling for the brazier of the night watch, twisted a couple of them together like a crown and put it on His head; a third had a slave give Him a reed and forced it into the fingers of His right hand; then, roaring with laughter, they pushed Him upon a seat. One by one, passing before Him, they bent their knees awkwardly, crying: "Hail, King of the Jews!"

But some were not satisfied with this burlesque homage, and one of them, snatching the reed out of His hand, gave Him a blow on the head, so that the thorns of His crown pierced the skin and made about His forehead a border of red drops.

The procurator appeared and smiled. He ordered them to lead the scourged King outside. This fitted in well with Pilate's sarcastic intention. Taking Jesus by the hand, he presented Him to the crowd.

"Behold the man!"

And he turned Christ's shoulders so that they might see the welts left by the rods, oozing blood. It was as if he said: Was it

His blood you desired? It is shed as a favor to you—to satisfy you. And now be off from here, for you have troubled me long enough!

But the crowd was not quieted by that spectacle. Pilate thought that he could make mock of them, but he would realize that this was no time for feeble jokes. They had had the best of him twice already and they would again. And their hoarse voices shouted all together, "Let him be crucified! Let him be crucified!"

Too late Pilate realized that they had driven him into a tangle from which he could not disengage himself.

By a flash of inspiration he had pronounced the great words, "Behold the man!" But he himself did not understand that he had found the truth he was seeking. Jesus is the Man of Sorrows announced by Isaiah, the man without form or comeliness, despised and rejected of men, who was to be killed for all men; He is God's only Son who had taken on man's flesh. But to the eyes of Pilate, He was wretched, insignificant flesh for rods.

And yet, standing beside that silent man, the Roman felt his heart heavy with an oppression he had never known before. Who could this man be whom all the people wished to kill, and whom he could neither save nor sacrifice? He turned once more to Jesus. "Whence art thou?"

But Jesus gave him no answer.

"Speakest thou not unto me? knowest thou not that I have power to crucify thee, and have power to release thee?"

Then the insulted King raised His head. "Thou couldest have no power at all against me, except it were given thee from above: therefore he that delivered me unto thee hath the greater sin."

The procurator in his perplexity found no new expedient to free himself from the net about him, and returned to his fixed idea. "Behold your King!"

The Jews, infuriated by this repeated insult, burst out, enraged, "If thou let this man go, thou art not Caesar's friend: whosoever maketh himself a king speaketh against Caesar."

At last they had hit on the right words to bring pressure on weak, cowardly Pilate. Every Roman magistrate depended on Caesar's favor.

Pilate surrendered. All his maneuvers had failed, and he certainly did not wish the whole province to rise on account of that unfortunate prophet; and even less was he willing that on His account they should accuse him before Tiberius and have him deposed.

In order that they might all have a visible representation which they would not forget, Pilate had a basin of water brought to him and washed his hands there before them all, saying, "I am innocent of the blood of this just person: see ye to it.

"Then answered all the people, and said, His blood be on us, and on our children.

"Then released he Barabbas unto them: and when he had scourged Jesus, he delivered him to be crucified."

Little did his shift avail him; for the fate he now sought to avert by giving Jesus over into the hands of his adversaries fell upon him a few years later. The Jews and the Samaritans accused him; the governor of Syria deposed him in A.D. 36, sending him to Rome to justify himself before the emperor. And Caligula banished him to Gaul. But he was followed by the shade of that great, silent man; exiled into Gaul, he killed himself.

FORGIVE THEM

THE SUN rose higher in the clear April sky and now it was near noon. The contest had wasted most of the morning, and there was no time to lose. According to Mosaic law, the bodies of executed criminals could not remain after sunset on the place of punishment. Moreover, Caiaphas remembered how, a few days before, Jesus had entered the city surrounded with waving branches and joyful hymns. Those Galileans who had followed Him until now, who loved Him, might make some effort at resistance and put off, even if they did not actually prevent, the real votive offering of that day.

Pilate, too, was in haste. He hoped to forget his own corroding uneasiness, so painfully like remorse. To vent his uneasiness on those who really caused it, he dictated the wording of the *titulus*, or superscription, which the condemned man was to wear about His neck until it was fastened above His head at the top of the cross, as follows: "Jesus of Nazareth the King of the Jews." The scribe wrote these words three times in three languages— Latin, Greek and Hebrew—in clear, red letters on the white wood.

The leaders of the Jews, who had remained there to hasten the preparations, read this sarcastic inscription and protested. They said to Pilate, "Write not, The King of the Jews; but that he said, I am King of the Jews."

But the procurator cut them short with a dry brevity: "What I have written I have written."

In the meantime the soldiers had put back on the King His poor-man's garments and had tied the notice about His neck. Others had brought out three massive crosses of pine, the nails, the hammer and the pincers. Pilate pronounced the usual formula: *"Io lictor, expedi crucem"* [Ho, Lictor, make ready the cross]— And the sinister procession moved forward.

The centurion rode at the head, he whom Tacitus calls with terrible brevity, *exactor mortis* [collector of the dead]. Immediately after him came, in the midst of the armed legionaries, Jesus and the two thieves who were to be crucified with Him. Each of them carried a cross on his shoulders, according to the Roman rule. And behind them, the uproar of the excited crowd, increased at every step by idle sightseers.

It was Parasceve, the day of preparations, the last night before the Passover. Thousands of lambs' skins were stretched out on the sunlit roofs; and from every house rose a column of smoke, delicate as a flower bud, which opened out in the air and then was lost in the clear, festal sky. Old women emerged from the dark alleyways; bearded men carried on their shoulders a kid or a cask of wine; children stared at the foreigners. In every home the housemother was busy, preparing everything needful for the next day, because with the setting of the sun everyone was exempt for twenty-four hours from the curse of Adam.

The lambs, skinned and quartered, were all ready for the fire; the loaves of unleavened bread were piled up fresh from the oven; men were decanting the wine, and the children to lend a hand somewhere were cleaning the bitter herbs.

Everywhere there was that good-natured tumult, that joyous bustle which goes before a great, popular feast day. And the great eastern sun sent down a flood of light upon the four hills.

SLOW as a funeral procession, the column of the bearers of the cross made its way. About them everything spoke of life, and they were going to burning thirst and to death; cold in death, they would be thrown into the cold earth.

At the sound of the centurion's horse, people stepped to one side and stopped to look at the wretched men toiling under their dreadful burden. The two thieves seemed more sturdy, but the first seemed scarcely able to take another step. Worn out by the endless night, by His four questionings, by the buffetings, by the flogging; disfigured with blood, sweat, saliva, and by the terrible effort of this last task set Him, He did not seem like the fearless young man who a few days before had scourged the money changers out of the Temple. His face was drawn and contracted by the convulsions of pain; His eyes, red with suppressed tears, were sunken in their sockets; His clothes clung to the wounds on His shoulders, His legs bent under His weight and under that of the cross.

Some women, their heads wrapped in their cloaks, came behind all the rest, weeping, but trying to hide this seditious grief.

They were almost to the Gate of Gardens when Jesus fell to the ground and lay there stretched under His cross. The reddened eyelids were dropped over His eyes; He would have seemed dead if it had not been for the painful breath coming and going through His half-open mouth.

They all stopped, and a dense circle of jeering men stretched out their faces and hands towards the fallen man.

"He is only pretending," they cried. "He ought to carry the cross to the last! That is the law! Give Him a kick, and let Him get along!"

But the centurion saw clearly that the unfortunate Jesus

would never be able to drag the cross all the way to Golgotha. He cast his eyes about to find someone to carry that weight. Just at that moment a Cyrenian called Simon had stepped into the crowd and was looking with an astonished and pitying expression at the body prostrate under the two beams. He was strongly built, and the centurion called to him, saying, "Take this cross and come after us."

Without a word the Cyrenian obeyed.

We know nothing more of the merciful-hearted man who lent his broad countryman's shoulders to lighten Jesus' load, but we know that his sons, Alexander and Rufus, were Christians. It is probable that they were converted by their father's telling them of the death of which he was an enforced witness.

Two soldiers helped the fallen man up on His feet, and urged Him forward. The procession took up its way again under the noonday sun.

THE CENTURION halted outside the old walled city, in the midst of the young green of the suburban gardens. The city of Caiaphas did not allow capital punishment within its walls.

They had stopped on the summit of a mound of limestone resembling a skull. This resemblance might seem to be the reason for choosing this place for executions, but the reason was rather because the two great roads from Jaffa and Damascus crossed each other close at hand, and it was well that the cross should show its terrible warning to the traveling multitude.

The sun, the high noonday sun, shone on the white mound and on the mattocks ringing sonorously in the rock. In the nearby gardens singing birds filled the sky with the silver arrows of their warblings; doves flew about in pairs in the warm, pastoral peace. It would be sweet to live there in some well-watered garden, in the perfume of the earth awakening and clothing itself, awaiting the harvest moon, in company with loving friends! Days of Galilee, days of sunshine among the vineyards, beside the lake, days of wandering with friends who listened understandingly, days drawing to a close with the well-earned cheerfulness of supper, days which seemed eternal, although they were so short!

Now Thou hast no one with Thee, Jesus, called the Christ. These soldiers preparing that appalling bed are only shadows, cast by the great shadow of God. God's human face is wet with cold sweat. The blows of the mattocks ring in His head; His whole body aches with weariness, trembles in a yearning for rest. At the same time it seems to Him that He loves with a more intimate tenderness those whom He is leaving, even those who are working for His death.

From the depths of His soul, like a song of victory over the torn flesh, rise up the words, never to be forgotten: "Father, forgive them; for they know not what they do."

It is not the prayer of a man, but of a God to a God.

Wrongs consciously wrought cannot be absolved without assurance of repentance. But the ignorance of men is so appallingly great that only a few really know what they do. The Pharisees, fearful of losing their preeminence; the doctors, fearful of losing their privileges; the rich, fearful of losing their money; Pilate, fearful of losing his office; and most ignorant of all were the people, misled by their leaders, and the soldiers obedient to orders; none of them knew who Christ was and what He came to do.

Now, at the point of death, He had confirmed His most difficult and divine teaching, "Love for enemies."

The crosses had been raised; they were piling stones about them to steady them under the weight, and were filling the holes with earth, stamping it down with their feet.

ON THE TOP of the Hill of the Skull the three crosses, tall, dark, with outspread beams like giants with outstretched arms, stood against the great sweep of the sweet spring sky, outlined by brilliant reflections from the sun. The beauty of the world on that day in that hour was so great that tortures were unthinkable; could they not, those wooden branches, blossom out with field flowers, and be wreathed with garlands of tender green, hiding the scaffold with verdure, in the shade of which reconciled and friendly brothers might sit down?

But the priests, the scribes, the Pharisees were stamping with impatience, and hastening on the Romans.

The centurion gave an order. Two soldiers approached Jesus and with rough gestures removed all His clothes. The criminal condemned to crucifixion must be entirely naked.

They passed two ropes under His armpits, and hoisted Him on the cross. Halfway up on the upright was a rough wooden peg like a seat where the body was to find a precarious and painful support. Another soldier leaned the ladder against one of the arms of the cross, climbed up on it, hammer in hand, seized the hand which had cured lepers, spread it out on the wood and drove a nail into the middle of the palm. The nails were long, and with a wide head so that they could be easily hammered. The soldier struck a vigorous blow, which pierced the flesh at once, and then another and a third so that the nail would hold firmly and so that only the head would remain outside. Then the diligent workman came down the ladder; and did the same to the other hand.

All the spectators had fallen silent, hoping to hear screams from the condemned man. But Jesus made no sound.

Now they turned their attention to the feet. This was work which could be done standing on the ground, for the Roman crosses were set low.

The soldier who was nailing Christ on the cross now lifted up His knees so that the soles of His feet should be flat against the wood, and taking the measure so that the iron nail should be long enough to go through the instep, he pierced the first foot, and drove the nail home. He did the same to the other foot, and at the end glanced up, still with his hammer in his hand, to see if anything was lacking. He remembered the scroll which they had taken from Jesus' neck and flung to the ground. He picked it up, climbed again on the ladder, and with two nails fastened it on the upright of the cross, above the thorn-crowned head.

Then he came down for the last time, threw away his hammer, and looked to see if his companions had finished their work. The thieves, too, were now in place. The four soldiers could divide the garments. These came to them by law. This left Jesus' tunic, which was without seam, woven all in one piece. It would be a sin to cut it; one of them took out his dice, threw them, and the tunic was awarded by luck.

All was done: the drops of blood fell slowly from His hands on the ground and the blood from His feet reddened the cross.

The throne of the King was a hard wooden peg; the Master with so many disciples now had as companions only two thieves.

Some of the priests, shaking their heads, said: "Thou that destroyest the temple, and buildest it in three days, save thyself. If thou be the Son of God, come down from the cross." Now their consciences were perfectly at rest. If any miracle were possible, He would no longer be crucified there to agonize; but the sky was empty and the sun, God's light, shone clearly that all men might see the contractions of His face and the painful heaving of His chest.

THE THIEVES who had been crucified with Jesus had begun to be hostile to Him in the street when He was liberated from the weight of His cross. No one seemed to think of them; it was for Him that the women were weeping and that even the centurion was moved to pity.

But one of them, when he heard the great words, "Forgive them; for they know not what they do," suddenly fell silent. This prayer of Jesus' found an unexpected echo in his own thought, which now seemed to him luminous in the darkness of his fate. Had he really known what he was doing? If he had had a little more bread and love, a friendly word when suddenly temptations laid siege to his lonely and dissatisfied soul, would he have committed the actions which had brought him to Golgotha?

These thoughts went through his distracted heart while he waited to be fastened to the cross.

When they were all on the cross, the other thief, suffering terribly from his pierced hands and feet, began to insult Jesus. "If thou be Christ, save thyself and us."

But the good thief, listening to the voices shrieking down below, now turned to his companion. "Dost not thou fear God, seeing thou art in the same condemnation? And we indeed justly; for we receive the due reward of our deeds: but this man hath done nothing amiss." And he cried out these words, "Lord, remember me when thou comest into thy kingdom."

Jesus, who had answered no man, turned His head as well as
He could toward the pitying thief and answered, "Verily I say
unto thee, Today shalt thou be with me in paradise."

The good thief was Jesus' last convert, the last disciple. We
know nothing more of him; only his name preserved in an apocryphal manuscript. The Church has received him among her
saints because of this promise of Christ, with the name of Dismas.

AS ANCIENT WRITERS admitted, crucifixion was the cruelest of
punishments. It gave the greatest torture for the longest time.
If tetanus set in, a merciful torpor hastened death; but there were
men who held out until the second day after crucifixion, and
even longer. The thirst of their fever, the congestion of their
hearts, the rigidity of their veins, their cramped muscles, the
dizziness and terrible pains in the head, the ever greater agony
—all these were not enough to make an end of them. But most
men died at the end of twelve hours.

The blood from the four wounds of Jesus had clotted about
the nailheads. His head drooped on His neck; His eyes, those
mortal eyes from which God had looked out upon the earth,
were glazing over in the death stupor.

A king of barbarians pronounced the most vigorous words
ever spoken by Christian lips about that agony. They were reading to Clovis the story of the Passion, and the fierce king was
sighing and weeping when suddenly, no longer able to contain
himself, clapping his hand to the hilt of his sword, he cried out,
"Oh, that I had been there with my Franks!" Words of a soldier
and of a violent man, but words beautiful with all the naïve
beauty of a candid and virile love.

Now Nature itself seemed to wish to hide the horror of that
sight: a thick cloud rose above the hills and little by little spread
to every corner of the horizon. Black clouds gathered about the
sweet, clear April sun, encircled it, laid siege to it ... "and
there was a darkness over all the earth until the ninth hour."

Many, alarmed by the falling of that mysterious darkness,
fled away from the Hill of the Skull, and went home, silenced.
But not all; the air was calm; no rain fell as yet, and in the obscurity, the three pallid bodies shone out whitely.

The women had not deserted Him. On one side at some distance from the cross, through fear of the howling men, Mary, His mother, Mary Magdalene, Mary of Cleophas, Salome, mother of James and John—and perhaps also Joanna of Cusa, and Martha—were present, terrified witnesses. He still had the strength to confide to John's care the Virgin of Sorrows. But after this, through the veil of His suffering, He saw no one and believed Himself alone. Even the Father seemed remote, inexplicably absent. And then there was heard in the silence of the darkness, these words, *"Eli, Eli, lama sabachthani?"* that is to say, "My God, my God, why hast thou forsaken me?"

This was the first verse of a psalm which He had repeated to Himself many times because He had found there so many presages of His life and His death; but He no longer had the strength to cry it all aloud as He had in the desert.

"My God, my God, why hast thou forsaken me? why art thou so far from helping me? . . . Our fathers trusted in thee: they trusted, and thou didst deliver them. They cried unto thee, and were delivered: . . . But I am a worm, and no man; a reproach of men, and despised of the people. All they that see me laugh me to scorn: . . . they shake the head, saying, He trusted on the Lord that he would deliver him: let him deliver him, seeing he delighted in him. . . . Be not far from me; for trouble is near; for there is none to help. . . . I am poured out like water, and all my bones are out of joint: my heart is like wax; it is melted in the midst of my bowels. . . . my tongue cleaveth to my jaws; and thou hast brought me into the dust of death. . . . the assembly of the wicked have inclosed me: they pierced my hands and my feet. . . . they look and stare upon me. They part my garments among them, and cast lots upon my vesture. But be not thou far from me, O Lord: O my strength, haste thee to help me."

The supplications of this prophetic psalm rose as the last expression of His dying humanity.

One of the soldiers now took a sponge, soaked it in vinegar, put it on a reed and held it to the lips of Christ. But certain of the Jews nearest to the cross thought that He was calling Elias, the Prophet, who in the popular imagination was to appear with

Christ, and said, "Let alone; let us see whether Elias will come to take him down."

The legionary, not wishing to make trouble, laid down the reed. But after a little Christ's voice came down as if from a great distance, "I thirst."

The soldier took up the sponge again, dipped it once more in the vessel full of the mixture of water and vinegar and once more held it to the parched mouth. And Jesus when He had taken the vinegar said, "It is finished."

With His last strength He cried with a loud voice in the darkness: "Father, into thy hands I commend my spirit!"

And Jesus bowed His head and gave up the spirit. That cry, so powerful that it freed the soul from the flesh, rang out of the darkness and lost itself in the furthermost ends of the earth.

More than nineteen hundred years have passed and men have intensified the tumult of their lives that they may drown out that cry. But in the fog and smoke of our cities, in the darkness ever more profound where men light the fires of their wretchedness, that prodigious cry of joy and of liberation still summons every one of us.

WATER AND BLOOD

CHRIST WAS DEAD. Some people, says Luke, went away smiting their breasts. Some did not speak, they hurried home to their supper—perhaps it was terror which they were feeling. But a foreigner, the centurion, Petronius, who had been the silent witness of the execution, was moved, and from his pagan mouth came the words of Claudia Procula, "Certainly this was a righteous man."

The leaders of His people had no thought of recantations. Evening was close at hand and with the setting of the sun the great Sabbath began. The Passover would be spoiled if the bloody corpses were not carried away at once. Therefore they sent word to Pilate to have the condemned men's legs broken at once and to have them buried. The breaking of the legs was to shorten the sufferings of crucified men. The soldiers, when they had received the order, came up to the bad thief, who, more robust than his companions, was still alive, and they broke his legs with a club.

They had seen Jesus die, but John says that one of them, to make quite sure, pierced His side with a spear, and saw with astonishment that water and blood came out from the wound. The name of this soldier according to an old tradition was Longinus, and it is said that some drops of that blood fell upon his eyes which had been infected, and immediately cured them. The history of martyrs tells of him that Longinus believed in Christ from that day on, and was a monk for twenty-eight years at Caesarea until he was murdered because of his faith.

Now that He was a silent, harmless, quiet corpse, His friends of the twenty-fifth hour, the tepid followers, the secret disciples, the anonymous admirers, came out from the houses where they had shut themselves in. To His sorrow in life Christ had many friends of this sort. Two of them stepped forward in that Good Friday twilight. They were notables of Jerusalem, rich lords; in short, two members of the Sanhedrin—Joseph of Arimathea and Nicodemus—who had hidden themselves in their houses. But in the evening when they ran no risk of offending their colleagues, when the elders had left Golgotha, the two nocturnal disciples thought that they would diminish their remorse by providing for the burial of the executed man.

The bolder of the two, Joseph, ". . . went in . . . unto Pilate" (Mark noted the fact as remarkable) and asked for the body of Jesus. Pilate was astonished that He should already be dead, since crucified men often lived for two days; he called in Petronius, who had been charged with the execution.

After Pilate had heard his report, he "gave" the body to Joseph. The procurator was generous on that day because as a rule the Roman officers forced the families of condemned men to pay for the corpses.

When Joseph had received permission he took a fine white winding-sheet and linen bands, and went toward the Hill of the

Skull. On the way there he met Nicodemus, who may have been his friend, and who had come with the same thought. Nicodemus also had not spared expense, and had brought with him on the shoulders of a servant a hundred pounds of a mixture of myrrh and aloes.

And when they came to the crosses, while the soldiers were taking down the two thieves to throw them into the common grave of condemned men, they prepared themselves to take down the body of Jesus.

NIGHT WAS shutting down on the world which had lost the only Being which could give it light. Against the scarcely visible whiteness of the Hill of the Skull, the naked corpses glimmered dimly. The soldiers were obliged to work by the light of torches, flaming without smoke in that windless air.

Joseph, aided by Nicodemus and by a third helper, was scarcely able to draw out the deep-driven nails which held the feet. The ladder was still there. One of them, climbing up on it, took out the nails from the hands, supporting the loosened body with his shoulder. The others helped him to lower the corpse, and the body was placed on the knees of the Virgin of Sorrows who had borne Him. Then they all made their way towards a garden nearby belonging to the rich Joseph, who had had a sepulcher hewn out of the stone for himself and his family. In those days every well-to-do Jew had a family sepulcher.

As soon as they had arrived at the garden, the two bearers of the dead had water brought from the well, and washed the body. Now the women, the three Marys—the Virgin Mary, the contemplative Mary, the liberated Mary—more skillful than men, began to help in order that this burial, performed thus at night and in haste, would not be unworthy of Him. They lifted from His head the crown of Pilate's legionaries, and plucked out the thorns which had penetrated the skin. Many loving tears fell upon that face where in the calm paleness of death the old sweetness shone once more.

When the washing was finished, the corpse was sprinkled abundantly with Nicodemus' spices. Then, when the hundred pounds had covered Jesus with a fragrant pall, the winding-sheet was tied about the body with long linen bands, the head was wrapped in a napkin and another white cloth was spread over the face, after they had all kissed Him on the forehead.

Recently made, the open sepulcher had never been used. According to the ritual the two members of the Sanhedrin recited aloud the mortuary psalm, and finally, after they had placed the white-wrapped body in the cave, they closed the opening with a great stone and went away silently.

But the women did not follow them. They could not bring themselves to leave that rock which separated them forever from Him whom they loved. They whispered prayers, and recalled to each other memories of Him. Sometimes they called Him by name as they leaned against the rock, and spoke to Him.

Then, chilled and terrified by the night's blackness, they too went away, stumbling amid the bushes and the stones, promising one another to return there as soon as the feast day had passed.

THE SUN had not yet risen on the day which for us is Sunday, when four women once more drew near to the garden; but over the eastern hills a white hope rose slowly in the midst of the throbbing constellations. The clear air seemed stirred as by a recent stir of angels' wings.

In the half-light, the women advanced, lost in their sadness, under the spell of an emotion they could not have explained. Were they returning to weep upon the rock? Or to see Him once more, He who had captured their hearts without laying them waste? And speaking among themselves, they said, "Who shall roll us away the stone from the door of the sepulcher?"

There were four of them; Joanna of Cusa and Salome had joined Mary of Magdala and Mary of Cleophas.

But when they came to the rock they stood astounded. The opening into the sepulcher showed black against the darkness. Not believing her eyes, the boldest of them touched the sill with her trembling hands. In the daylight, brightening now with every moment, they saw the stone there beside them, leaning against the rocks.

The women, struck into silence by their fright, turned around as if expecting someone to come tell them what had happened in those two nights which had passed. Mary of Magdala feared at once that the body had been stolen by those unwilling to have the honorable Jewish sepulcher used by a heretic; perhaps they had thrown Him into the shameful common grave for men stoned and crucified.

But perhaps Jesus was still lying inside in His perfumed wrappings. As the sun, climbing at last above the summit of the hills, shone into the opening of the sepulcher, they took courage and entered.

At first they saw nothing, but they were shaken by a new fear. At their right, seated, was a young man clothed in a long white garment, showing in that darkness like snow. He seemed to be awaiting them.

"Be not affrighted: he is not here: for he is risen. Why seek ye the living among the dead? Remember how he spake unto you when he was yet in Galilee, saying, the Son of man must be delivered into the hands of sinful men, and be crucified, and the third day rise again."

The women listened, terrified, not able to answer, but the youth went on, "Go quickly, and tell his disciples that he is risen from the dead; and, behold, he goeth before you into Galilee; there shall ye see him."

All four of them, quivering with terror and joy, left the grotto. But after a few steps, when they were almost outside the garden, Mary of Magdala stopped, and the others went along the road towards the city without waiting for her. She herself did not know why she had remained behind. Perhaps she remembered that they had not even made sure that the sepulcher was really empty; perhaps the youth in white was an accomplice of the priests who wished to deceive them?

Suddenly she turned and saw a man near her, outlined against the green of the garden; but she did not recognize Him even when He spoke. "Woman, why weepest thou? whom seekest thou?"

Mary thought that it might be Joseph's gardener come early to his work. "Because they have taken away my Lord, and I know not where they have laid him. Sir, if thou have borne him hence, tell me where thou hast laid him, and I will take him away."

The unknown man, touched by this impassioned childlike simplicity, answered only one word, her name: "Mary!"

At this, as if awakened with a start, the despairing woman found her lost Master: "*Rabboni*, Master!" And she fell at His feet in the grass and clasped in her hands those bare feet still showing the two red marks of the nails.

But Jesus said to her, "Touch me not; for I am not yet ascended to my Father: but go to my brethren, and say unto them, I ascend unto my Father, and your Father; and to my God, and your God."

And at once, He withdrew from the kneeling woman, and moved away. Mary lifted herself up from the grass, her face convulsed, wild, blind with joy, and ran after her companions.

They had but just come to the house where the Disciples were in hiding and they had told breathlessly the incredible news: the sepulcher opened, the youth clad in white, the things which he had said, the Master risen, the message to His brothers.

But the men, still stunned by the catastrophe, were not willing to believe this wildly improbable news. Hallucinations, hysterical women's dreams, they said. How could He be risen from the dead after only two days?

They believed in the resurrection of the Master, but not before the day when all the dead would rise again, and He would come in glory to rule His kingdom.

But in the meantime, Mary of Magdala rushed in, all haste. She herself had seen Him with her own eyes, and He had spoken to her: she had touched His feet with her hands, had seen the wounds on His feet; and He had told her to go to His brethren, so that they should know that He had risen from the dead as He had promised.

Simon, called Peter, and John, finally aroused, rushed out of the house and began to run towards Joseph's garden. John, who was younger, outran Peter and came first to the sepulcher. He looked through the door but did not go in. Peter came up panting and rushed into the grotto. The linen cloths were lying on the ground, but the napkin which had been about the head of the corpse was folded together in a place by itself. John also went in, saw, and believed.

And without another word they returned towards the house, still running, as if they expected to find the Risen One in the midst of the others whom they had left.

But Jesus, after He had left Mary, withdrew from Jerusalem.

EMMAUS

AFTER THE solemn interval of the Passover, plain everyday life began again for all men. Two friends of Jesus, among those who were in the house with the Disciples, were to go that morning on an errand to Emmaus, a hamlet about two hours' journey from Jerusalem. They left as soon as Simon and John had returned from the sepulcher. All these amazing tales had shaken them, but had not really convinced them.

Cleopas and his companion were good Jews, men burdened with many material cares who left a place for the ideal in their minds. Like almost all the Disciples, they had expected the coming of a Messiah who should be the son of David, a warrior on horseback, a Liberator who would liberate Israel first of all. The words of Christ had almost given them a glimpse of higher truths, but the Crucifixion disheartened them. His death—what a death, on a scaffold of murderers and parricides!—looked to their narrow, practical minds sadly like a failure.

They were reasoning together of all these things as they went along under the warm noonday sun. Then suddenly they caught a glimpse of a shadow on the ground near them. They turned around. The shadow was that of a man who was following as if he wished to hear what they were saying. They stopped, as was the custom, to greet him, and the traveler joined them. His did not seem an unknown face to the two men, but they could not think who it was. The newcomer asked them, "What manner of communications are these that ye have one to another, as ye walk?"

Cleopas, who must have been the older, answered with a wondering gesture, "Art thou only a stranger in Jerusalem, and hast not known the things which are come to pass there in these days?"

"What things?" asked the unknown man.

"Concerning Jesus of Nazareth, which was a prophet mighty in deed and word before God and all the people: And how the chief priests and our rulers delivered him to be condemned to death, and have crucified him. But we trusted that it had been he which should have redeemed Israel: and beside all this, today is the third day since these things were done. Yea, and certain women also of our company made us astonished, which were early at the sepulcher; And when they found not his body, they came, saying, that they had also seen a vision of angels, which said that he was alive. And certain of them which were with us went to the sepulcher and found it even so as the women had said: but him they saw not."

"O fools, and slow of heart to believe all that the prophets have spoken," exclaimed the stranger. "Ought not Christ to have suffered these things, and to enter into his glory?" And almost indignantly He recited the old words and the prophecies of Ezekiel and Daniel, recalled the description of the Man of Sorrows given by Isaiah. The two listened, docile and attentive, without answering, because the newcomer spoke with so much heat, and the old admonitions in His mouth took on a meaning so clear that it seemed almost impossible that they had not understood them before.

In the meantime they had arrived at the entrance of Emmaus, and the sun was going down. Now the two friends were not willing to part with their mysterious companion, and they begged Him to stay with them.

"Abide with us," they said, "for it is towards evening, and the day is far spent." And they took Him by the hand and made Him come into the house.

When they were at table, the guest who sat between them took bread, and broke it and gave a little to one of His friends.

At this action, the eyes of Cleopas and the other man were opened. They had recognized His blessed and wounded hands, and they found themselves face-to-face with the splendor of Christ risen from the dead. Both of them sprang to their feet, pale, amazed.

But they had no time even to run to kiss Him, for Jesus vanished out of their sight.

Tired and fasting as they were, they went back over the road which they had come, and after nightfall arrived at Jerusalem.

The Disciples were still awake. Without drawing breath the newcomers told of their encounter and how they had recognized Him only at the moment when He broke the bread. And in answer to this new confirmation, three or four voices cried out together, "The Lord is risen indeed!"

In the excitement of the day no one had eaten. The women had prepared supper, and now all sat down to the table. Simon, called Peter, remembered the Last Thursday: "This do in remembrance of me."

And tears dimmed his eyes while he broke the bread and gave it to his friends.

THEY HAD scarcely eaten the last mouthfuls when Jesus appeared in the doorway, tall and pale. He looked at them, and in His melodious voice greeted them: "Peace be unto you."

No one answered. Their astonishment overcame their joy, even for those who had already seen Him since His death. On their faces He read the doubt which He knew they all felt. "Art Thou really Thyself a living man, or a spirit which comes from the caverns of the dead to tempt us?"

"Why are ye troubled? and why do thoughts arise in your hearts? Behold my hands and my feet, that it is I myself: handle me, and see; for a spirit hath not flesh and bones, as ye see me have."

And He stretched out His hands towards them, showed them the marks still bloody left by the nails, opened His garment over His breast so that they could see the mark of the lance in His side. Some of them, rising from their couches, knelt down and saw on His bare feet the two deep wounds, each with its livid ring around it. But they could not bring themselves to touch Him.

To make an end of their last doubts, Jesus asked, "Have ye here any meat?"

A piece of broiled fish was left in a dish. Simon put it before the Master, who sat down at the table and ate the fish with a piece of bread while they all stared at Him.

And when He had finished, He raised His eyes towards them. "When I was with you, did I not tell you that all things which were written and which I announced must be fulfilled; that it behooved Christ to suffer and to rise from the dead on the third day, and that repentance and remission of sins should be preached in His name among all nations, beginning at Jerusalem? . . . Go ye into all the world, and preach the gospel to every creature. All power is given unto me in heaven and in earth, and as the Father sent me, I send you. He that believeth and is baptized shall be saved; but he that believeth not shall be damned. I am with you alway, even unto the end of the world."

Little by little as He spoke, His Disciples' faces lighted up with a forgotten hope, and their eyes shone with exaltation. Their enemies, apparently victorious, were conquered; the visible truth bore out all the prophecies. If the Master was risen from the dead, they themselves could not die; if He could leave the sepulcher, His promises were the promises of a God and He would fulfill them to the uttermost.

THOMAS, CALLED DIDYMUS, was not present when Jesus appeared, but the day after, his friends ran to seek him, still agitated by what Jesus had told them. "We have seen the Lord!" they said. "It was really He. He talked with us. He ate with us like a living man."

Thomas was one of those who had been profoundly shaken by the shame of Golgotha. He had said once that he was ready to die with his Master, but he had fled away with the others when the lanterns of the guard had appeared on the Mount of Olives. He hoped for the Kingdom—not a spiritual Kingdom but a kingdom where living, warm-blooded men might govern with new laws a fairer earth assigned to them by God.

After the scandal of the Crucifixion, Thomas was not at all disposed to believe a hearsay report of the Resurrection. He answered to those who joyfully brought him the news, "Except I shall see in his hands the print of the nails, and put my finger into the print of the nails, and thrust my hand into his side, I will not believe."

This answer of Thomas has made him one of the most famous men in the world: for it is Christ's eternal characteristic to immortalize even those men who affronted Him.

A week later, the Disciples were in the same house as on the first occasion and Thomas was with them. Suddenly Jesus entered at the door, his eyes seeking out Thomas, and He called him by name and came up to him so that he could see Him clearly, face-to-face. "Reach hither thy finger, and behold my hands; and reach hither thy hand, and thrust it into my side: and be not faithless, but believing."

But Thomas did not obey Him. He dared not put his finger in the nail print nor his hand in the wound. He only said to him: "My Lord and my God."

Then Jesus, who could not forget Thomas' doubt, answered, "Thomas, because thou hast seen me, thou hast believed: blessed are they that have not seen, and yet have believed."

This is the last of the Beatitudes and the greatest.

Thomas is one of the saints and yet he was not one of those blessed by that Beatitude.

CHRIST'S FIRST COMPANIONS were at last convinced that His second and eternal life had begun. But how long it took them to admit the reality of His return!

And yet the enemies of Christ have accused those very astonished, perplexed Disciples with having willingly or unwillingly invented the myth of the Resurrection. The Disciples, they say, hoped so vividly to see Jesus rise from the dead as He had promised, and the Resurrection was so urgently needed to counteract the disgrace of the Crucifixion, that in that atmosphere of superstitious suspense, the visions of hysterical women, the delusions of unbalanced men sufficed to spread the news of the appearance of Christ about the little circle of desolate survivors.

But those who try to undermine the certainty of the first Christian generation forget the testimony of Paul.

Saul the Pharisee had been to school in Gamaliel, and might have been present, even though at a distance and as an enemy, at Christ's death, and certainly knew all the theories of his early teachers, the Jews, about the pretended Resurrection. But Paul, who received the first Gospel from the lips of James, called the brother of the Lord, and from Simon, Paul famous in all the churches of the Jews and the Gentiles, wrote thus in his first letter to the Corinthians: "Christ died for our sins according to the scriptures; And that he was buried, and that he rose again the third day according to the scriptures: And that he was seen of Cephas, then of the twelve: After that, he was seen of above five hundred brethren at once; of whom the greater part remain unto this present. . . ." The first letter to the Corinthians is generally recognized as authentic. It cannot have been written later than the spring of the year 58, and hence it is older than the oldest Gospel. Many of those who had known the living Christ were still living at that time. If Paul could have thought a valid confutation possible, he never would have dared write those words.

It is extremely probable that the appearance of Christ to the five hundred happened in Galilee on the mountain spoken of by Matthew, and that the Apostle had known one of those who had been present at that memorable meeting.

WHEN THE TRAGEDY of the Crufixion had drawn to a close with its greatest sorrow, its greatest joy, everyone turned again to his own destination, the Son to the Father, the King to His Kingdom, the high priest to his basins of blood, the fishermen to their nets.

These water-soaked nets, with broken meshes, torn by the unaccustomed weight of the great draughts, so many times knotted together again, which had been left by the first fishers of men without one backward look, on the shores of Capernaum, had been laid on one side, by someone with the prudence of the stay-at-home who knows that dreams are soon over and hunger lasts for all one's lifetime. The wife of Simon, the father of James and John, the brother of Thomas, had saved their casting nets and their dragnets as tools which might be useful, in memory of the exiles.

And for a time the wisdom of the stay-at-homes, taken root in their native countryside like moss on a stone, was vindicated. The fishers of men appeared again in Galilee and once more took the old nets into their hands. Christ on His return had said, "We will meet again in Galilee." And they had gone away away from ill-omened Judea and they had trod once more the road back to their sweet, calm fatherland.

The old houses had a mellow beauty, with the white banners of newly washed linen, and the young grass greening along the old walls, and the tables cleaned by humble old hands, and the oven, which every week spat out sparks from its flaming mouth. And the quiet fishing town had beauty, too; with its tanned, naked boys, the sun high over the level marketplace, the bags and baskets in the shadow of the inns, and the smell of fish which at dawn was wafted over it, with the morning breeze. But more beautiful than all was the lake: a gray-blue and slate-colored expanse on cloudy afternoons; a milky basin of opal with lines and patches of jacinth on warm evenings; a dark shadow flecked with white on starry nights; a silvery heaving shadow in the moonlight.

On this lake which seemed the very spirit of the quiet, happy countryside, the boat with its slanting sails, its worn seats, the high red rudder, had from their childhood been dearer to them than that other home which awaited them, stationary, whitened, foursquare on the bank. Those infinitely long hours of tedium and of hope as they gazed at the brilliant water, the swaying of the nets, the darkening of the sky, had filled the greater part of their poor and homely lives.

Before beginning the work which He had commanded, they were waiting to see Him whom they loved in the place which He had loved. They were different men from the men who had gone away, more restless, sadder, almost estranged. But the nets were there, hung up on the walls, and the boats at anchor rode up and down. Once more the fishers of men, perhaps out of material need, began to be lake fishermen.

SEVEN DISCIPLES of Christ were together one evening in the harbor of Capernaum, Simon called Peter, Thomas called Didymus, Nathaniel of Cana, James, John and two others. Simon said, "I go afishing."

His friends answered, "We also go with thee."

They went into the boat and put off, but all that night they caught nothing. When day broke, a little depressed because of the wasted night, they came back towards the shore. And when they were near they saw in the faint light of the dawn a man standing on the shore, who seemed to be waiting for them. "But the disciples knew not that it was Jesus."

"Children, have ye any meat?" called the unknown man.

And they answered, "No."

"Cast the net on the right side of the ship, and ye shall find."

They obeyed and in a moment the net was so full that they were scarcely able to draw it in. And they all began to tremble because they had guessed who it was awaiting them.

"It is the Lord," said John to Simon.

Peter answered nothing, but hastily drew on his fisher's coat (for he was naked), and cast himself into the sea that he might be first on shore. The boat was scarcely two hundred cubits from the land and in a few moments the seven Disciples were about their Lord. And no one asked Him, "Who art thou?"

On the shore there was bread and a lighted brazier with fishes broiling on it, and Jesus said, "Bring of the fish which ye have now caught."

And for the last time He broke the bread and gave to them and the fish likewise. After they had finished eating Jesus turned to Simon and under His look the unhappy man, silent till then, turned pale: "Simon, son of Jona, lovest thou me more than these?"

The man who had denied Him, when he heard this question full of tenderness, but for him so cruel, felt himself carried back to another place beside another brazier with other questions put to him, and he remembered the answer he had made then, and the look from Christ about to die and his own great lamentation in the night. "Yes" in his mouth would have been shamelessness: "No" would have been a lie.

"Yea, Lord; thou knowest that I love thee."

He had not the courage to add "more than these" in the presence of the others, who knew what he had done.

Christ said to him, "Feed my lambs."

And for the second time He asked him: "Simon, son of Jona, lovest thou me?"

And Peter in his trouble found no other answer than, "Yea, Lord; thou knowest that I love thee."

Then Jesus said, "Feed my sheep."

And for the third time He insisted, "Simon, son of Jona, lovest thou me?"

He was drawing from Peter three affirmations, three new promises to cancel his three denials at Jerusalem. But Peter could not endure this repeated suffering. Almost weeping, he cried out, "Lord, thou knowest all things; thou knowest that I love thee!"

The terrible ordeal was over, and Jesus went on, "Feed my sheep. Verily, verily, I say unto thee, When thou wast young, thou girdest thyself, and walkedst whither thou wouldest: but when thou shalt be old, thou shalt stretch forth thy hands, and another shall gird thee, and carry thee whither thou wouldest not."

You must answer for all the lambs which I leave in your care and as reward at the end of your labors you will have two crossed beams, and four nails as I had, and life eternal. Choose: it is the last time that you can choose and it is a choice for all time—irrevocable.

"Follow me!"

Peter obeyed, but turning about saw John coming after him and said, "Lord, and what shall this man do?"

Jesus said to him, "If I will that he tarry till I come, what is that to thee? follow thou me!"

For Simon the primacy and martyrdom. John, who bore the same name as the precursor of Christ's first coming, was to prophesy His second coming. The historian of the end was to be persecuted, a solitary prisoner, but he was to live longer than all the others and to see with his own eyes the crumbling of the stones, not one left upon another, of the ill-omened hill of Jerusalem. Peter followed Christ, was crucified for Christ and left behind him the eternal dynasty of the Vicars of Christ: but John was not permitted to find rest in death: he waits with us, the contemporary of every generation, eternal as hope.

THE CLOUD

ONCE MORE they returned to Jerusalem, leaving their nets, this time forever, travelers setting out upon a journey, the stages of which were to be marked by blood. In the same place where He had gone down to the city glorified by men, He was to rise again after the interval of His dishonor and His Resurrection, in the glory of Heaven. He remained in the midst of men, for forty days after the Resurrection, for as long a time as He had remained in the desert after His baptism—His symbolic death by water. He did not, as before, lead a life in common with the Disciples, because He was separated now from the life of living men; but he reappeared to them more than once to confirm His great promises.

The last time they saw Him was on the Mount of Olives, where before His death He had prophesied the ruin of the Temple and of the city and the signs of His return.

It was one of the last evenings of May and the clouds in that golden hour, like celestial islands in the gold of the setting sun, seemed to rise from the warm earth towards nearby heaven. In the fields of grain, the birds began to call back the fledglings to the nests, and the cool breeze lightly shook the branches and their drooping, unripened fruit. From the distant city, still intact, from the pinnacles, the towers and the white squares of the Temple rose a smoky cloud of dust.

And once more the Disciples asked Jesus the question they had put to Him on the evening of the two prophecies. "Lord, wilt thou at this time restore again the kingdom to Israel?"

603

They may have meant the Kingdom of God, which in their minds, as in the minds of the Prophets, was one with the Kingdom of Israel, since the divine restoration of the earth was to begin with Judea.

Christ answered: "It is not for you to know the times or the seasons, which the Father hath put in his own power. But ye shall receive power, after that the Holy Ghost is come upon you: and ye shall be witnesses unto me both in Jerusalem, and in all Judea, and in Samaria, and unto the uttermost part of the earth."

And having said this, He lifted up His hands and blessed them. And while they beheld, He was taken up from the earth and suddenly a shining cloud as on the morning of the Transfiguration wrapped Him about and hid Him from their sight. But they could not look away from the sky and continued to gaze steadfastly up in their astonishment, when two men in white apparel spoke to them: "Ye men of Galilee, why stand ye gazing up into heaven? this same Jesus, which is taken up from you into heaven, shall so come in like manner as ye have seen him go into heaven."

Then having prayed in silence, they entered Jerusalem, but heaven was no longer merely the barren dome where swift, tumultuous storm clouds appear and disappear; where the stars shine out silently.

He is still with us, the Son of man, who was light made manifest. He is still present in the world which He meant to free. He is still attentive to our words and to our tears, if they truly come from the depths of our hearts. He is with us, an invisible, benignant guest, never more to leave us, because by His wish our earthly life is an anticipation of the Kingdom of Heaven, and is a part of Heaven from this day on.

ACKNOWLEDGMENTS

The condensations in this volume have been created by The Reader's Digest
Association, Inc., and are used by permission of and special arrangement with
the publishers and the holders of the respective copyrights.
QUEEN VICTORIA, copyright © 1921 by Harcourt, Brace & World, Inc., renewed © 1949
by James Strachey, is reprinted by permission of Harcourt Brace Jovanovich Inc.
YANKEE FROM OLYMPUS: JUSTICE HOLMES AND HIS FAMILY, copyright
© 1943, 1944 by Catherine Drinker Bowen, renewed © 1970, 1971 by Catherine Drinker
Bowen, is reprinted by permission of Harold Ober Associates Inc.
R.V.R. THE LIFE & TIMES OF REMBRANDT VAN RIJN, copyright © 1930 by
Horace Liveright, Inc., renewed © 1959 by Helen C. van Loon, is reprinted by permission of
Liveright Publishing Corporation.
LIFE OF CHRIST, copyright © 1923 by Harcourt, Brace & World, Inc., renewed © 1951 by
Dorothy Canfield Fisher, is reprinted by permission of Harcourt Brace Jovanovich Inc. and
Arnoldo Mondadori Editore.

ILLUSTRATION CREDITS

COVER AND INSERT: portrait of Oliver Wendell Holmes by Howard Sanden; portraits of Queen
Victoria by Arthur Barbosa; portrait of Christ, Basilica of S. Apollinare in Classe, Ravenna, Italy/The
Granger Collection, New York. COVER: Rembrandt, *Self-portrait*, private collection. INSERT:
Rembrandt Leaning Forward, Bibliothèque Nationale, Paris.
RVR: THE LIFE AND TIMES OF REMBRANDT VAN RIJN: (All except *pages 263, 275, 379* by
Rembrandt van Rijn.) *Pages 250–251: View over the Amstel from the Rampart* (detail), National
Gallery of Art, Washington, Rosenwald Collection. *259: Self-portrait* (1656–58), © Kunsthistorisches
Museum, Vienna. *264: Rembrandt in Studio Attire* (c. 1655), Museum "Het Rembrandthuis,"